Development
of Mental Representation

Theories and Applications

Development of Mental Representation

Theories and Applications

Edited by

IRVING E. SIGEL
Educational Testing Service, Princeton, New Jersey

LEA LAWRENCE ERLBAUM ASSOCIATES, PUBLISHERS
1999 Mahwah, New Jersey   London

Lawrence Erlbaum Associates, Inc., Publishers
10 Industrial Avenue
Mahwah, NJ 07430

Cover design by Kathryn Houghtaling Lacey

Library of Congress Cataloging-in-Publication Data

Development of Mental Representation : Theories and Applications
/ edited by Irving E. Sigel.
    p. cm.
    Includes bibliographical references and indexes.
ISBN 0-8058-2228-3 (alk. Paper) 1. Mental representation in
children. 2. Connectionism. 3. Knowledge, Theory of. I.
Sigel, Irving E.
BF723.M43T47 1999
153.2—dc21   98-30736
                                                    CIP

Books published by Lawrence Erlbaum Associates are printed on
acid-free paper, and their bindings are chosen for strength and durability.

Printed in the United States of America
10 9 8 7 6 5 4 3 2 1

Contents

Introduction   vii
From *Terra Incognita* to *Terra Cognita*: The Science
of Representation
    Rodney R. Cocking

1   Theories of Representation   1

1   Approaches to Representation as a Psychological Construct: 3
A Treatise in Diversity
    Irving E. Sigel

2   Cognitive Representations: Distinctions, Implications,   13
and Elaborations
    Michael E. Martinez

3   Representation: Picture or Process?   33
    April A. Benasich and Heather L. Read

4   Early Symbolic Representation   61
    Judy S. DeLoache and Catherine M. Smith

5   What's in a Concept? Context, Variability,   87
and Psychological Essentialism
    Susan A. Gelman and Gil Diesendruck

6   Representing Logic   113
    Ellin Kofsky Scholnick

7   Constructivism, Communication, and Cooperation: 129
Implications of Michael Chapman's "Epistemic Triangle"
    Jeremy I. M. Carpendale

8   The Properties of Representations Used in Higher   147
Cognitive Processes: Developmental Implications
    Graeme S. Halford

9   A Dialectical Constructivist View of Representation: 169
Role of Mental Attention, Executives, and Symbols
    Juan Pascual-Leone and Janice Johnson

10 Representation Once Removed: Children's Developing   201
    Conceptions of Representational Life
    Michael J. Chandler and Bryan W. Sokol

11 The Development of Representation as the Coordination   231
    of Component Systems of Action
    Michael F. Mascolo and Kurt W. Fischer

12 A Bakhtinian View of Egocentric Speech   257
    Bruce Dorval

13 The Nature and Development of Representation: 273
    Forging a Synthesis of Competing Approaches
    James P. Byrnes

II Application of Representation in Practice   295

14 Developing an Understanding of External Spatial   297
    Representations
    Lynn S. Liben

15 The Development of Representational Abilities in Middle   323
    School Mathematics
    Richard Lesh

16 Representational Issues in Assessment Design   351
    Drew H. Gitomer and Linda S. Steinberg

17 Representational Competence   371
    Uri Shafrir

18 Representational Thought in Ego Identity, Psychotherapy,   391
    and Psychosocial Developmental Theory
    James E. Marcia

19 The Use of Cultural Tools: Mastery and Appropriation   415
    Leslie Rupert Herrenkohl and James V. Wertsch

20 A Representational System for Peer Crowds   437
    Jeffrey McLellan and James E. Youniss

III Visual Representation as Pictorial   451

21 The Form of Thought   453
    Sandra L. Calvert

    Author Index   471

    Subject Index   483

Introduction

From *Terra Incognita* to *Terra Cognita*: The Science of Representation

RODNEY R. COCKING
National Academy of Sciences

The cognitive (Gardner, 1985) and neuroscience revolutions (Gazzaniga, 1997) of the last decade have advanced the efforts of identifying and localizing cognitive processes. One of the enduring problems in cognitive-developmental psychology has been that of cognitive representation—in its many forms that include the entity called *representations*, the activities of representing, the uses of representations in learning, memory, and thinking, and the mechanisms that control the formation of representations. Developmental theory has been a fruitful source for generating hypotheses to guide research studies in this area and as a result, a vast database has been built around theoretical conceptions of representational processes (Cocking & Renninger, 1993).

Now, a third revolution in technology is expanding cognitive and neuroscience research in new directions and the databases are once again growing. Imaging technologies are enabling researchers to test theoretical conceptions of cognitive representation more precisely. At the same time, new learning technologies, especially computer and interactive technologies, are expanding the scope of developmental theory by adding new issues of representation, such as visual cognition. This volume is about the new growth, new directions, and new insights that are emerging around representation and representational thinking as a result of these three scientific revolutions.

Some of the research questions are familiar ones and some are new. The familiar ones have taken on new meaning as research and theory have converged to explain the processes of representation. At the same time, the familiar questions have shifted directions and new understandings are emerging. Indeed, because of new evidence and new methodologies, the long-standing research topic of representational thinking has moved from speculation to science. In this evolution, the science of representation has played an important role as a unifying concept across many research disciplines.

The move from *terra incognita* to *terra cognita* in any discipline involves a number of issues; and the ways in which these issues are framed determine the kinds of research studies that are conducted. The shift from theoretical conceptions to emergent ideas from cognitive science and neuroscience have propelled research in (at least) three directions: Based on theoretical formulations, new methods have established an evidentiary base for the concept of representation. Second, the territory of representation has been charted to move it into the realm of an explanatory construct by specifying its structural and functional properties. Third, studies now focus on a systems concept of representation, which has moved the research from a prior focus on single systems to current views of representation as multiple systems that have overlapping functions and yet also maintain certain individual unique functions and properties.

Short-term memory, for example, is a subtopic of memory research that has drawn upon psychological and neurological research aspects of representation. The result has been a convergence of research that has propelled scientific growth in both domains. The research has indicated that people are limited by the amount of information that they can hold in short-term memory for executing tasks so that information processing is facilitated by chunking information in meaningful ways. This conceptualization of memory functions sparked new research in both memory and cognition on categorical thinking, information chunking, and the mechanisms by which memory is enhanced through representation. In these studies, the topic of representation is seen as a *tool* of short-term memory.

Three large branches of study now characterize the field of representation research. Those that ask: What is representation?; what are the acquisition and developmental issues of representation formation?; and what are the uses of representation? A number of different issues guide the research within each of these three branches.

NEW DISCOVERIES AND NEW UNDERSTANDINGS
IN REPRESENTATION RESEARCH

Asking what *it* is has led to studies that ask if the *it* is different in some individuals (e.g., studies of aging), if *it* changes over time, if *it* has different functions, and how *it* is structured and structurally altered by injury and disease.

Are representations for working memory different from stored representations? This question is intended to address the functional roles of representation and the governing mechanisms. In this case, the question is whether representation is a storage and retrieval mechanism of memory or a tool of thinking for "on line" processing. It is now clearer how both kinds of roles are filled by representations.

How are updating mechanisms of short-term memory related to representational thinking? This kind of question has led to several types of studies that converge on the role of representation in the regulation of behavior. Smith (1998) asked if the 7-digit template of the representation of a phone number is in working memory? Asking what the role of representation is in the construction of mental maps has similarly led to new discoveries and new understandings about mental processes and the role played by representation.

Systems and Functions of Representation

Many of the imaging studies imply components of representation—spatial, verbal, affective, etcetera—by localizing brain sites for these functions. Impairments in one type of representation do not always implicate other systems. Older research addressed the separateness of representational systems, since they clearly had individual functions. Findings that impairments in one do not affect others led to the conclusion that they are separate entities. One of the biggest barriers to understanding representation had been characterizing it as a single entity, and imaging studies confirmed the separate and distinctive aspects of the systems. The studies in this volume, together, attest to the new thinking of representation as more than singular and separate.

Imaging studies indicate that while there are separate neural representations and separate brain loci, the *psychological* aspects of representation often unify the separate systems. Again, memory studies and cognitive inferencing studies illustrate psychological processes of representation. Schacter (1997) discussed the relationship between inferential thinking and memory and illustrated the active mind at work using psychological processes. Given word lists to remember, subjects report previous exposure to words that were not in the original list if the real and falsely reported words are categorically related. That is, *sweet* will be reported as having been in a list of words containing other words like: *cake, candy, horse, turnip,* and *cookie.* Clearly, the phenomenon is psychological, not neural, although imaging studies indicate that the same area of the brain "lights up" as if both words were encoded in memory. Cognitive economy is gained by using categories of information—representations.

Information processing (IP) theorists, however, have long held that the representation storage is fragmentary. Byrnes (1996) said that for IP theorists "information such as the name of an object (how it sounds, how to spell it) and what the object looks like, the kind of thing it is, and so on are all held in separate places in long-term memory" (p. 28). Studies within domains such as memory, are contrasting the structural and functional differences of representations in short-term and long-term memory systems.

The issue of systems and functions of representations has also led to some interesting comparative analyses between younger and older people. Smith

(1998) reports that imaging studies indicate that younger subjects show more brain lateralization of spatial and verbal functions while older subjects carry out the same functions in a more bilateral fashion. That is, spatial and verbal tasks *become* more bilateral with aging and this finding is especially true of verbal tasks. Similarly, there are longer latencies in older subjects. What does this mean? The question of whether representational systems are separate and distinct takes on a different meaning when considered from the perspective of neural representation. Newer work that builds upon categorical thinking, undoubtedly, will fill the gap between neural and psychological processes to tell us how declines in brain efficiency are compensated for by distributed processing and the ability to use categories of information to facilitate fluent processing, although perhaps accompanied by longer latencies over time.

Systems and Functions of the Feeling Thinker

Memory studies have generated a number of questions about the role of representation in aspects of human behavior other than reasoning and thinking, especially when considered from the perspective of emotions. Does emotion involve a separate representational system or does affect piggyback onto other systems? A particular class of memory studies had its beginnings in the early 1960s when psychologists noticed the alarming accuracy (or what is now thought to be a *perceived* accuracy) and florid details with which individuals could report what they were doing at the moment they heard about the death of John F. Kennedy. The term "flashbulb memory" was coined to illustrate the instantaneous and vivid brightness of events that were encoded in memory. But when Roger Brown discovered that his African-American bank teller had equally vivid stories to tell about her and her friends' vivid memories of the shooting of Martin Luther King, he began to study the problem in a different way. Brown and his colleagues eventually came to the conclusion that individuals' flashbulb memories are created by highly personal events that are important to them. Asking how these memories are formed and how they function is no different from asking about symbol formation and the construction of representations, with the exception that the question, as phrased by Brown and colleagues, now asks how the emotional system is involved. The concept of *representation* has served as a unifying theme to link domains of behavior. Research, doubtless, will eventually integrate the individual's systems of behavior and it appears as if the concept of representation will play an important theoretical and conceptual role in making that happen.

The Organization of Representation

One answer to the "why" or "for what purpose" question of representation is the economy it affords cognitive processing, both in terms of fluency and reduction on memory load to the individual. As the functional questions emerged, such as whether the concept functioned as a tool of thinking or in the service of memory, structural questions also gained prominence. Learning theorists, for example, asked if there is a structure to representation that is generic and promotes generalization, such as the move from generic skills to targeted skill development. Other studies have addressed specific issues of transfer of learning as building upon the structural organization of representations.

ISSUES OF STABILITY AND CHANGE

Nativist–Constructivist issues have also re-emerged as new evidence about human cognitive functioning has come from cognitive neuroscience. The concept of representation has been evoked in these debates, as well. The developmental question is how so-called privileged classes of behavior, such as children's early awareness of number, physical causality, and language, which are clearly modes of representation, are templates that guide perceptual learning and how these functions are integrated with other representational learning. Language studies, such as those by Kuhl (1993) addressed this interaction as it relates to how the infant learns to represent the linguistic sounds of its community (e.g., Japanese vs. Inuit or English). Other studies (e.g., Neville, 1995) look at the modifiability of representations at the neural level and how one system can take over the representational functions of another in the case of injury or neural compromise, such as the neural representational pathways showing how manual sign languages are learned by deaf individuals.

USING REPRESENTATIONS

An important set of research findings from learning research is how scientists think and reason and how young people can be taught these scientific skills and habits of mind. One fundamental aspect of scientific reasoning is the use of representational systems. Scientists use visual imagery and they reason from models. Scientists typically develop hypotheses and reach theoretical insights by reasoning by analogy as a means of rethinking concepts and making intuitive leaps. They reason together in groups, termed distributed reasoning, and several people contribute to the development and interpretation of the same information. They organize information, measure, graph, and reflect on the course of events. These skills all rely upon taking perceptual information to a conceptual and often abstract level; in other words, to various levels of representation.

Another perspective on how representations are used comes from studies of the meanings of cultural symbols and how they guide daily behavior. Greenfield and Suzuki (1998), for example, report how cultural representations of daily events, viewed differently from individualistic and collectivistic cultural perspectives, can cause culture clash. For example, mothers who bring all of their children to a school's breakfast program that is intended for one of the children in the family are behaving consistently with a representation of mealtime as a collective, family event. Teachers and parents from individualistic cultural backgrounds interpreted these mothers' behaviors as opportunistic—feeding all of the family's children at the expense of the school. Clearly, cultural practices are representations of how groups organize life's activities differently.

REPRESENTATION:
A UNIFYING CONCEPT IN SCIENCE

In summary, views of representation and representational thinking have changed and the reasons for these changes are due to the convergence of information from many sources. Brain lateralization studies, understanding the distributed properties of representations, and localization of brain functions and the corresponding neural representations are some of the newer studies that draw upon the theories that gave symbolic functioning a prominent role. All of these studies have directly and indirectly addressed the issues of whether representations entail single and separate entities and functions.

With the objective of developing a set of principles of representation, we now know that representation is not unitary, that it has structure, it has domain specificity, is different from metacognition, that individuals actively participate in the formation of representations, that there is a role played by privileged classes of information, that culture plays an important role, and that there are systems of representation. These generalized principles are becoming clarified through a new generation of studies represented by the diverse approaches taken in the present volume. Studies such as these attest to the important role representation has taken as a unifying concept in behavioral and neural sciences.

REFERENCES

Byrnes, J. P. (1996) *Cognitive development and learning in instructional contexts*. Boston: Allyn and Bacon.

Cocking, R. R., & Renninger, K. A. (1993). *The development and meaning of psychological distance*. Hillsdale, NJ: Lawrence Erlbaum Associates.

Gazzaniga, M. S. (1997). *Conversations in the cognitive neurosciences.* Cambridge, MA: Bradford Books.

Gardner, H. (1985). *The mind's new science: A history of the cognitive revolution.* New York: Basic Books.

Greenfield, P. M., & Suzuki, L. K. (1998). Culture and human development: Implications for parenting, education, pediatrics, and mental health. In W. Damon (Editor-in-Chief) & I. E. Sigel & K. A. Renninger, (Vol. Eds.) *Handbook of Child Psychology: Vol. 4. Child psychology in practice* (5th ed., pp. 1059–1109). New York: Wiley.

Kuhl, P. K. (1993). Innate predispositions and the effects of experience on speech perception: The native language magnet theory. In B. deBoysson-Bardies, S. deSchonen, P. Juscyzyk, P. M. McNeilage, & J. Morton (Eds.) *Developmental neurocognition: Speech and face processing in the first year of life.* Dordrecht, the Netherlands: Kluwer Academic.

Neville, H. J. (1995). Effects of experience on the development of the visual systems of the brain on the language systems of the brain. [Videotape in the series, *Brain mechanisms underlying school subjects, Part 3*]. Eugene, OR: University of Oregon.

Schacter, D. L. (1997, April). Neuroimaging of memory and consciousness. Symposium of the National Academy of Sciences, Washington, DC.

Smith, E. E. (1998, August). What neuroimaging can tell us about aging and working memory. Presentation to the Federation of Behavioral, Psychological, and Cognitive Sciences, Washington, DC.

PART I

Theories of Representation

Approaches to Representation as a Psychological Construct: A Treatise in Diversity

Irving E. Sigel
Educational Testing Service

How knowledge is acquired, organized, and made available for use is the basic theme of this volume. The processes involved in such a profound activity require the individual to transform everyday perceptual and sensory experiences into some form of mental representation. This mental activity is a necessary requirement for adapting and functioning effectively in complex and diverse environments.

The challenge for social and behavioral scientists is to understand the nature of this process in a developmental context from the moment of birth, continuing throughout the life span.

The investigators devoted to the problem have to construct a theoretical model and appropriate methodology to zero in on the complex issues inherent in this type of research. A variety of theoretical models ranging from connectionism to constructivism and beyond to radical constructivism is extent (Damon, Kuhn, & Siegler, 1998). At first blush this diversity in concept and method, as well as in the populations studied, is disheartening and disquieting. The fragmentation, the lack of dialogue, and the stringent commitment to a point of view that at times borders on the polemic, would seem to preclude scientific progress. If, however, we are willing to view the field in evolutionary terms, we can expect some points of view to wither on the vine while others prosper. The reasons are too complex to discuss here, but reviews of the history of developmental science by Cairns (1998) and Valsiner (1998) provide perspectives that are more encouraging than despairing.

In this volume, the focus is on diversity and applicability of the psychological

3

construct of mental representation, a central construct generally accepted as basic to knowledge acquisition, organization, and application. (See Damon, Kuhn, & Siegler, 1998, for a review of the various developmental theories that employ the mental representation construct.)

Essentially, the term *representation* refers to an instance that is equivalent to its referent; for example, the word *landscape* is equivalent to the three-dimensional natural landscape. Simply put, the word *landscape* has a meaning similar to not only the natural landscape, but also to a painting or a photograph of a landscape. In fact, each of these three instances (the word, the painting, and the photograph) are equivalent, but not identical. What makes the three instances equivalent is the common meaning attributed to them.

In sum, a *representation* refers to instances that are equivalent in meaning and in class membership, but different in mode of expression.

Although there is general agreement among most behavioral scientists, philosophers, and educators as to the basic definition, there is disagreement as to the universality, the origins, the developmental course, and the practical use of the term *representation*. The reasons for such diversity may be due to the aspects of representation that are being studied.

Thus in spite of agreement as to the importance of the representation construct, not only for cognitive functioning, but also for general functioning in the social and physical world, there is still considerable difference among those interested in mental representation, who differ with regard not only to definitions of mental representations but also to developmental course.

Bever (1986) summarized the issues where he wrote:

> There are two fundamental processes that occur when we perceive and represent the world. We automatically form representations of what we perceive. We integrate conflicts in those representations by accessing perceptual and conceptual knowledge of a variety of kinds. The integration of such representational conflicts is itself accompanied by a release of emotional energy. These processes are functional in everyday perception, conceptual development, and problem solving. (pp. 325–326)

When this paragraph is read more closely and analyzed for clarification of the meaning for each of the terms (such as *automatization* or *integration* or *representation*), we discover the need to define each of the processes involved to reduce the potential ambiguities in the statement. A reflective analytic process will lead to divergences of opinion because some will argue, for example, about the form images take (or even whether there are images), whereas others might contend that images are representations "housed" in semantic or neural networks. What does integration of conflicts imply? Is there some resolution process involved? If automatic, does it mean we are not in control of these developing representational issues? The meanings of representation and of integration are probably the most contentious because of differences in the basic assumption of how to focus and describe these mental activities. (See Keil, 1997, for a discussion of some of the issues.) As it is written, the devil is in the details.

In addition, there are differences as to how *representation* is construed. Mandler (1998) describes the current representation landscape most clearly where she writes, "The diversity of approaches to representation breeds debate as to whether more than one kind of representation is necessary to describe the mind" (p. 256). The debate among developmental psychologists has moved from a conception of representation as the mental manipulation of symbolic forms to a host of other conceptions such as those exemplified within diverse theoretical orientations such as connectionism, symbol systems, and constructivism.

The intrinsic changes in the conception of representation has been the redefinition of the specific topics elected for study, for example, analogical representation and acquisition of declarative and procedural representational systems. Of even greater significance is the study of representation among infants. With this shift, the debates have moved beyond the singular notion of representation in the context of knowledge acquisition and symbolic transformations to the basic questions of "foundations of mind and how to characterize the nature of knowledge in infancy" (Mandler, 1998, p. 256). In spite of the diversity and debate, however (Thelen & Smith, 1994), there is general agreement that representation is central to human cognitive function and further the understanding of its nature will contribute to our unraveling of some of the mysteries of organismic development. The consequence of this interest is a burgeoning literature in the fields of cognitive science, neuropsychology, developmental psychology, education, visual media, and even psychotherapy and social cognition. However, there is no single place where such discussion of these various fields can be found. This volume is especially intended to help developmental psychologists to become acquainted with an array of literature. In this way I see this set of chapters as a sample contributing in three ways: (a) providing new knowledge, (b) encouraging dialogue and helping to move the field forward, and (c) demonstrating the general usefulness of mental representation in practical settings. Thus in the long run such increased awareness of what has been done and what is being done should yield a richer corpus of integrated knowledge (Sigel, 1993).

A BRIEF HISTORY

During the past 100 years, increasing efforts have been made to come to understand the *how* and *why* of mental functioning, such as thought and language. Interest in these problems has waxed and waned because of continual changes in epistemologies influencing psychological theory and methods of research. The major shifts were from mentalistic models with introspection to behavioristic strategies eschewing mentalisms while focusing only on actions and behavior.

Currently there is acceptance of mental models with an emphasis on mental processes incorporating language and thought (Valsiner, 1998).

The increased interest and proliferation of research in the cognitive genre, however, did lead to an exponential increase in the creation of diverse approaches to the study of the development of representational thought and language. The problems of interest were framed using different epistemologies, theories, and methods. For example, Piaget and his colleagues at the Institute of Genetic Epistemology in Geneva developed a unique and original approach to the studying the development of representational thought with children from infancy to adolescence (Piaget, 1962). Perhaps it is coincidental, but soon after Piaget's work became known in the United States, especially after the publication of Flavell's major summary of his work in 1963, behavioral scientists began working on developing a new interdiscpinary science of cognition, which they called *cognitive science.* A framework was developed by which to examine issues such as intelligence, knowledge acquisition, and the utilization and development of language in appropriate ecological settings. Cognitive science evolved into an interdisciplinary science when it became evident that no one field could encompass the complexity of the functioning human mind. So, the field was defined as comprised of "elements of psychology, computer science, linguistics, philosophy and education" (Bobrow & Collins, 1975, p. ix). Central to this science was the development of the *theory of representation.* (See Bobrow & Collins, 1975, for a review of this early development.)

As the work of Piaget became better known among developmental psychologists, interest turned to cognitive development. Concomitant research activity in the cognitive science field led to considerable research productivity. Add to this the creation of additional mental models of cognitive development in the fields of language, computer science, brain function, and the ecological setting in which all of these cognitive functions evolve, a proliferation of theories and models for research emerged. (See Keil, 1998, for a thorough exposition of the field of cognitive science, including development.) Within each of these, the development of representation has remained of central importance.

That debates in the cognitive development arena still prevail speaks to its vitality. These discussions are exegeses of different theories and methods, all directed at the same set of processes and functions inherent in Bever's (1986) aforementioned quotation. What makes the debates so complex is that each investigator unpacks the concept of representation by differentionally targeting representational systems, for example, words, pictures, music, or mathematics. The particular choice an investigator makes leads to findings relative to that particular system only, so that representation as a singular overall process is elaborated or explained. Thus there is the question as to whether the findings from a particular study (e.g., representational understanding of media) allow for universal generalization to other systems such as words or musical notations or are they particular to that system. Or, to frame the question in developmental terms, does understanding the course of development of picture comprehension inform us about the course of the development of verbal language? Similarly, are generalizations obtained in the study of children's comprehension of language comprehension applicable to children's developing representational competence in general (Sigel, 1993)?

Ernst von Glasersfeld (1987) addressed the basic question of representational generalizations. The essential meaning that undergirds the various uses of representation from an essential perspective, irrespective of context or content, is that a representation stands for something other than itself. As von Glasersfeld has indicated, its identity is relative to its referent. It is not an independent entity. As a painting is a representation of a landscape, that landscape, even if material, is a representative of landscapes. In this case it is an instance of a population of landscapes. So, in a sense, every instance is a representative of its class. We never see the whole. If it is the case that representation or representativeness (or the synonym replica) is beset with so many definitional concerns, then is representation a useful scientific concept because it fails to meet the criterion of specificity and particularity? From a positivistic view, a definition requires these criteria so an operation can instantiate the definition. In effect, the definition becomes an operation of the concept in question. However, such definitions do not necessarily disambiguate the term because operational definitions are intrinsically verbal and/or actions that cannot avoid ambiguity.

Von Glasersfeld (1987) went further when he developed definitional problems where he wrote about conceptualizing representation: "The situation is particularly complicated because the word 'representation' is fraught with ambiguity that, for the most part, remains hidden and thus creates untold conceptual confusion. As so often, however, ambiguities surface and become quite obvious when we translate into another language" (p. 216). Later on, von Glasersfeld (1995) continued his analysis of problems of representation, where he argued that there is no a device to decide what meaning is to be conveyed. For meaning to be shared it is necessary for the writer to specify the referents if mutual understanding is to occur.

Definitions of the word representation usually assume a common referent so that the meaning of the concept is shared. Yet, in the psychological literature, the term representation is often used without providing any context. Thus in psychological parlance, invoking the term representation alone does not provide a common referent, thereby leading to misunderstanding and miscommunication. It seems to be the case that the meaning is dependent on the epistemological orientation of the user. If the reader of the text employing the term does not share the epistemological base or the referents for the term, it then results in misunderstanding. For example, for Piaget (1951), representation is used in two ways: (a) as the common meaning of something standing for something else, such as a picture of a flower standing for the three-dimensional living flower, and (b) as referring to general intelligence. In the latter case, the referents are ambiguous and not specified, so the reader is left to his or her own interpretive differences. For now, each one is dedicated to the search for understanding how knowledge is organized, represented, and utilized within his or her conceptual system with little interest in mutual engagement. .

Representation as described previously implies a one-way process; that is, the child assimilates an experience that forms an internal image or a verbal representation. However, the process does not stop there. When the child uses this internal representation in the service of solving a problem, uttering a statement, or drawing a picture, he or she is re-presenting that experience. The form in which the experience is re-presented may be in a form other than its original. For example, the child reads a story and then creates a narrative. The words that were read silently are now transformed into oral language. This interactive process is how representation usually functions in our daily lives. In fact, Hillary Putnam (1988) stated it so well when he wrote:

> What makes it plausible that the mind (or brain) thinks (or "computes") using representations is that all the thinking we know about uses representations. But none of the methods of representation that we know about—speech, writing, painting, carving in stone, etc.—has the magical property that there *cannot be* different representations with the same meaning. None of the methods of representation that we know about has the property that representations *intrinsically* refer to whatever it is that they are used to refer to. All of the representations we know about have an association with their referent which is contingent, and capable of changing as the culture changes or as the world changes. This by itself should be enough to make one highly suspicious of theories that postulate a realm of "representations." . . . (pp. 21–22)

These representations are all mental, but it is important to realize that the same representation may have a common referent but a different meaning. The meaning is in the head of the speaker and a different meaning may be in the head of the listener.

The concerns voiced by Putnam (1988) and von Glazersfeld (1987) about the complexity of the issues involved in conceptualization and methods of study of mental representation have not seemed to influence the main stream of research. A variety of models currently being employed in the study of representation vary from how the term is used to how it is embedded in a complex cognitive system as describing mental functional properties of thought, such as how categories are formed. For others, assumptions are made that the referent and the word are fixed in the natural language, whereas still others will take the relative position indicated by Putnam. Add to this the differences in opinion as to whether the concept needs to be considered within a context and a function or could it be dealt with as an isolated unit of analysis that moves the debate to whether the theoretical grounding is holistic or isolated and unidimensional. Still other views are expressed in terms of symbolic constructivism derived from Piaget, with considerable revisions as evidenced in the chapter by Pascual-Leone and Johnson (chap. 9, this volume) to those derived from cognitive science or computer models (chap. 8, Halford, this volume). Still others are derived from language models (Gelman & Diesenbruck, chap. 5, this volume).

Other investigators have devised unique paradigms using more sophisticated experimental designs, technical equipment, and sophisticated analytic procedures (e.g., structural modeling), as well as new theories (see Mandler, 1997). Not only have dramatic changes in models of the mind come about, but also interest in the origins of cognition has been extended to human infants as young as 2 days of age (e.g., Benasich & Read, chap. 3, this volume; Gopnik & Meltzoff, 1997). These new models of cognitive development emerged concomitantly with an upsurge in the search to identify the neurological substrate of mental functioning, for example, increased interest in the brain-behavior connection (Posner & Rothbart, 1994). These multiple voices do not sing in harmony, but rather, as isolated soloists with good choruses. Although there are differences in how to conceptualize the issues and devise methods, there is agreement on the question—to wit—What is knowledge, what is the course of its development, and how is it organized and used?

The fact of the matter is that because theories of representational thought are derived from particular epistemological positions, and because epistemological perspectives are embedded in scientists' and philosophers' work from their worldviews, and not always conscious at that, there is every reason to assume that diversity in conceptualization is a natural state of affairs (Pepper, 1942/1970).

ORGANIZATION OF THE VOLUME

My first decision in developing this volume was to think through the statement by Bever (1986) and the subsequent questions implied in his summation. Thus, the order of chapters is consistent with Bever's (1986) sequencing of the development of representation from automatic acquisition of representation to theory and research dealing with processes of acquisition and use. I conclude with how the representation construct is used in practical settings. The volume's organization unfolds accordingly, as becomes evident by perusing the table of contents. Each chapter is an exemplar of a unique voice in the field.

Because representation involves perceptual processing, it requires neural mechanisms to enable it to emerge and function. Answers require attention to the brain and its development. But, the brain is developing in a social and physical world which, for many theories, is a requirement for both brain and intellectual development. Now we come to the social world, which is another area of complexity. The sights, sounds, objects, and people—in fact, all social objects—are the stuff of perceptual experience and require cognitive integration to serve the individual well.

This now brings us to the development of social knowledge in the form of acquisition of verbal concepts and skills in their use for thinking and reasoning of physical and social problem-solving concepts and in the service of problem solving. As I saw the task before me unfolding, it became clear that how concepts, skills, and reasoning are studied depends on the epistemological views of the investigator. So the chapters addressing each of these topics represent different theoretical perspectives with a singular orientation, such as semantic, lexical, sociocultural, or idiosyncratic models developed by individual investigators. Thus, we see the variation in points of view as embedded in a particular topic area.

I grouped the chapters into three parts. The first part deals with theoretical and experimental models. The second part deals with the representation construct in education, for example, spatial relations and understanding of maps (maps as representations), and assessment of academic achievement. In addition, representations provide a fundamental basis for conceptualization for the acquisition of social knowledge and understanding of peer relations. The third part focuses on a special case of television viewing.

REFLECTIONS

How do we come to terms with this state of confusion, fragmentation, and separation? Obviously, representation is such a ubiquitous term, with ambiguous referents, that it is difficult to slot it coherently into any system.

Each of the authors has voiced different conceptual models in the course of studying representation. Each acknowledges the multidimensional view of the construct. Some of the individuation among the authors is due to the different facets of representation selected for study emerging from their epistemological orientation and interests. Some of authors reflect the connectionist orientation, others constructivist, whereas others evolve a distinct model reflecting a unique set of concepts. Of course, it is the case that I selected these authors to represent their unique perspectives so the chapters would be diverse by design. However, each reflects a constituency actually representing major streams of thinking in the field.

On first reading one would think that all I did was to present a volume to confuse, to tease, and to force the reader to pick one position and stay there. It would be, on first blush, easier than attempting to unravel each one of them to search out sufficient commonality or sharpen differences. One might ask, "Why should this be the case?" The challenge is that each of the authors presents data supporting his or her theory. Mascolo and Fischer, for example, report convincing evidence for their model. Yet, if they had employed the experimental techniques of Carpendale, would their theory have held up? However, because most psychological research methods are intimately derived from the epistemological orientation of the experimenter, it follows that the findings are destined to follow the pattern expected by the researcher. In a sense, this argument seems to be as if the science of developmental psychology is one of self-fulfilling prophesies.

Considerable concern has been voiced regarding the fractionation of developmental psychology because of its diverse, noncoherent, theoretical, and methodological epistemologies. This description of psychology at the end of the 20th century seems to square with the facts. The diversity of theories, the substantive problems addressed, and the methods of investigation bear witness to these assertions.

What are some of the values of this diversity? Diversity in the genetics of species is an important requisite for survival. The argument for diversity is the reality of scientific development, a necessary requirement for social, biological, and intellectual change. The analogue is morphologic evolution. The species arise and descend through evolutionary changes which, in the long run, enable them to survive, but not as individuals. Specie survival is the analogue to theory survival. This is not necessarily a Hegelian dialectic, although resemblances are there in that some theoretical models may become synthesized whereas others may form new organisms or new systems theories. My contention is that this evolutionary perspective is applicable to the current state of developmental theory of representation.

The perspectives reflected in this volume can contribute to conceptual change by presenting diversity or viewpoints collected in one place. In this way the greater the opportunitythere is for cross-fertilization and syntheses, and the more likely those perspectives which have seen their time go by will also fly away.

The integration of this volume was left to the interested reader who hopefully will struggle with the conceptual and practical issues that have been discussed. This is the reader's challenge and professional responsibility. Had I created such an integration I would have presented my construction. Critics of edited volumes argue that the essays should be conceptually joined. This volume is joined in its basic theme. I leave the final word on the uncovering of the fundamental meaning of the development of mental representation to the readers of this volume and to future generations of students of human development.

ACKNOWLEDGMENT

I would like to thank Linda Kozelski for her invaluable help in preparing this set of materials for publication. Without her careful editorial help, this volume would not be as well organized and integrated as it is.

REFERENCES

Bobrow, D. G., & Collins, A. (Eds.). (1975). *Representation and understanding.* New York: Academic Press.

Bever, T. G. (1986). The aesthetic basis for cognitive structures. In M. Brand & R. M. Harnish (Eds.), *The representation of knowledge and belief* (pp. 314–356). Tucson: University of Arizona Press.

Cairns, R. B. (1998). The making of developmental psychology. In W. Damon (Editor-in-Chief) & R. M. Lerner (Vol. Ed.), *Handbook of child psychology: Vol. 1. Theoretical models of human development* (5th ed., pp. 25–105). New York: Wiley.

Damon, W. (Editor-in-Chief), & Kuhn, D., & Siegler, R. (Vol. Eds.). (1988). *Handbook of child psychology: Vol. 2. Cognition, perception, and language* (5th ed.). New York: Wiley.

Flavell, J. H. (1963). *The devleopmental psychology of Jean Paiget.* New York: Van Nostrand.

Gopnik, A., & Meltzoff, A. N. (1997). *Words, thoughts, and theories.* Cambridge, MA: MIT Press.

Keil, F. C. (1998). Cognitive science and the origins of thought and knowledge. In W. Damon (Series Ed.) & R. M. Lerner (Vol. Ed.), *Handbook of child psychology: Vol. 1. Theoretical models of human development* (5th ed., pp. 341–414). New York: Wiley.

Mandler, J. (1998). Representation. In W. Damon (Editor-in-Chief) & D. Kuhn & R. Siegler (Vol. Ed.), *Handbook of child psychology: Vol. 2. Cognition, perception, and language* (5th ed., pp. 255–308). New York: Wiley.

Pepper, S. C. (1970). *World hypotheses: A study in evidence.* Berkeley: University of California Press. (Original work published 1942)

Piaget, J. (1951). *Play, dreams and imitation in childhood.* New York: Norton.

Posner, M. I., & Rothbart, M. K. (1994). Attentional regulation: From mechanism to culture. In P. Bertelson, P. Elen, & G. D'Ydewalle (Eds.), *International perspectives on psychological science* (Vol. 1, pp. 41–55). Hillsdale, NJ: Lawrence Erlbaum Associates.

Putnam, H. (1988). *Representation and reality.* Cambridge, MA: MIT Press.

Sigel, I. E. (1993). The centrality of a distancing model for the development of representational competence. In R. R. Cocking & K. A. Renninger (Eds.), *The development and meaning of psychological distance* (pp. 141–158). Hillsdale, NJ: Lawrence Erlbaum Associates.

Thelen, E., & Smith, L.B. (1994). *A dynamic systems approach to the development of cognition and action.* Cambridge: MIT Press.

Valsiner, J. (1998). The development of the concept of development: Historical and epistemological perspectives. In W. Damon (Editor-in-Chief) & R. M. Lerner (Vol. Ed.), *Handbook of child psychology: Vol. 1. Theoretical models of human development* (5th ed., pp. 189–232). New York: Wiley.

von Glasersfeld, E. (1987). Preliminaries to any theory of representation. In C. Janview (Ed.), *Problems of representation in the teaching and learning of mathematics* (pp. 215–225). Hillsdale, NJ: Lawrence Erlbaum Associates.

von Glasersfeld, E. (1995). *Radical constructivism: A way of knowing and learning.* London: The Falmer Press.

CHAPTER 2

Cognitive Representations: Distinctions, Implications, and Elaborations

MICHAEL E. MARTINEZ
University of California, Irvine

The processed and stylized worlds we create and manipulate in our minds are composed of mental representations, knowledge simplified and abstracted as symbols, and structured in such a way as to facilitate the pursuit of goals and plans in a complex and dynamic environment. Representations are the means by which we think and behave intelligently, and so are fundamental to our understanding of the way the mind works (McNamara, 1994; Thagard, 1996). Expressing this principle cogently, Dalenoort (1990) observed that, "The nature of representations is of fundamental importance for the way we view and understand the world. It may be expressed more strongly: our representations *are* our view of the world" (p. 233). Johnson-Laird (1983) affirmed the precept: "Human beings, of course, do not apprehend the world directly; they possess only an internal representation of it, because perception is the construction of a model of the world. They are unable to compare this perceptual representation directly with the world—it *is* their world" (p. 156).

WHAT IS A REPRESENTATION?

The term *representation* has a diversity of meanings, a fact that has led to considerable confusion and perhaps some doubt that the construct serves a useful function in the science of mind. It is worthwhile to look for order in this semantic chaos for, as Denis (1994) argued, such "effort . . . reaps benefits, since it can either lead to theoretical advances in circumscribing a federating concept of cognitive psychology, or eliminating a concept that is too fuzzy to be really useful" (p. 1). Consistent with this principle, Denis has proposed fundamental distinctions in the meanings of representation, and these serve as a starting point here (Fig. 2.1). First, he distinguished between representation as process and representation as product—the term refers to something that people do as well as a consequent or concomitant of that action. Second, a representation can be a physical object (such as a painting) or a strictly cognitive entity. Denis drew yet finer distinctions among representations as cognitive entities, separating those that are actively used from those that are merely available for use (apparently a difference corresponding to the working memory/long-term memory distinction), and those that are used consciously versus those that are used automatically.

Mandler (1983) drew quite different distinctions, arguing that *representation* is used in two ways. One meaning is knowledge and its organization, that is, how knowledge is structured in the mind. The other sense is representation as symbolism, as a word is symbolic of its referent. It is the former sense on which I focus—representation as structured knowledge. In Denis' (1994) typology, I refer primarily to representations as cognitive entities, whether stored in long-

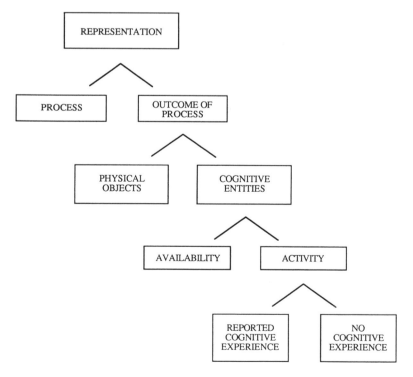

FIG. 2.1.   Meanings for *representation*, from Denis (1994). Copyright © 1994 by Presses Universitaires de France. Reprinted by permission.

term memory or actively processed. Representations, then, are provisionally defined to be more-or-less coherent structures that are cognitive (rather than physical) and that stand for, or represent, some real or imagined situation.

Further elaboration of the meaning of *representation* can be gained from studying how the term is used in the research literature. Quite commonly the term refers to alternative means of constructing the essence and operation of some reality. For example, in traveling through a city from one point to another, one person might employ a maplike or "bird's eye" view (sometimes called survey knowledge), whereas another might visualize the path from the perspective of what a traveler would see and do along the way—as a series of left and right turns cued by landmarks (route knowledge) (Millis & Cohen, 1994). Thus, the term representation can refer to different, but possibly interchangeable, ways of understanding a situation.

Different representations of the same phenomenon are unlikely to be strictly equivalent in a functional sense. Performance in problem solving is known to depend on the problem solver's representation of the problem at hand (Larkin & Simon, 1987). Each representation is likely to capture certain features of the problem and miss others, and the success or efficiency of problem solving will likely depend on the representation chosen.

Representations, therefore, have the following features:

1. They are knowledge structures that symbolize some state of affairs.
2. Each is likely to be one of a set of alternative structures.
3. They may differ in their ability to facilitate solving particular problems.

Certain questions follow: Is it possible to identify recurrent categories of representations? And how does the term representation differ from similar terms such as schema and mental model? Clearly, a good deal more analysis is needed before anything like a clear model of representations can be advanced.

DISTINCTIONS

Representational Forms

Although theorists have advanced differing typologies of representational forms, there may be sufficient commonality among them to propose a model that distinguishes between types. Limiting the discussion to representations as cognitive entities (i.e., knowledge structures), discussions of representations often involve a fundamental distinction between mental imagery and verbal accounts of phenomena. Ford (1994), for example, posed the question, "How do people represent and solve syllogistic problems?" To answer, she provided evidence that subjects tended to adopt one of two strategies. One group solved syllogisms by constructing diagrams and the other used primarily verbal representations to support their reasoning. Ford concluded that "there are two very different ways in which people reason about the syllogisms—there are those that reason verbally . . . and those who reason primarily spatially . . ." (p. 11). Other research on representations is consistent with this dichotomy. For example, in dealing with the subject of mental imagery, Denis (1994) distinguished between semantic representation and imaginal (or image-based) representation. Kosslyn (1980) drew similar (description/depiction) distinctions. Refinements to the conceptualization of working memory (Baddeley, 1986) also consist of corresponding "slave" systems known as the visuospatial scratchpad and the (verbal) articulatory loop. Other researchers have suggested similar dichotomies (e.g., McNamara, 1994; Paivio, 1970), and the distinction is perhaps best formulated in what is known as dual-code theory (Bower, 1972; Paivio, 1971).

One home-grown illustration of the image/symbol distinction is the explanation by my daughter Amy (then 8 years old) of the way she remembers phone numbers. On the left side of Fig. 2.2 is her drawing of the sequence of buttons she pushes to reach a certain phone number. Most of us would represent this number exactly as a series of digits. The right panel is her way of showing that, for this particular number, she does not remember it as a series of digits, but as a spatial pattern. In principle, an entire phone book could be organized so that phone numbers are not represented as numbers at all, but as choreographed finger movements played out on the stage of the phone keypad.

Generalizing from the image/verbal dichotomy, representations can be thought of as differing along a continuum whose poles are propositional knowledge (e.g., involving such symbol systems as are found in language) and analogical knowledge (e.g., involving imagery). Both propositions and imagery are to be regarded as symbolic, because both stand for, but do not represent exactly, something outside the mind. Propositional knowledge is not limited to verbal representations but can take several forms, such as mathematical formulas and

FIG. 2.2.   Amy's spatial representation of a phone number.

musical notation. Analogical knowledge, although perhaps experienced primarily as imagery akin to vision, can also take several forms corresponding to other sensory experience, such as sound, smell, and taste (McNamara, 1994).

What is known about the development of propositional and analogical reasoning? Thinking can occur through the use of symbols or images independently (both "imageless thought" and "thoughtless images" are possible), or through the combination of the two. Research findings imply that there is no developmental precedence of one form over the other. Mandler (1983) noted that many developmental psychologists, including Piaget, have proposed that image-based symbols ontogenetically precede propositional symbols, and that image-based concepts themselves appear only after a transition from sensorimotor to preoperational thought. There is, however, little evidence for the idea that different representations develop sequentially as a function of maturation. Rather, they appear to differentiate and elaborate mainly as a function of experience.

It is possible that representations of all forms are subtended by a lower level "machine language" of the mind (so-called amodal representations). According to this hypothesis, all representations are coded in an elemental symbolic form that is, presumably, not directly accessible (Denis, 1994). In some sense, this assertion must be true if it is acknowledged that, ultimately, mental processes are reducible to electrochemical processes in the brain. A basic symbolic code may in fact underlie imagery, a possibility that has led some theorists to suggest that personal experiences of mental imagery are epiphenomenal. Whether imagery is in fact epiphenomenal has been hotly disputed and may in fact be unresolvable (Kosslyn, 1980; Pylyshyn, 1973). At *functional* and *experiential* levels, however, both verbal knowledge and imagery are important to cognition and are essential to any discussion of mental representation. Functionally, propositional representations and images are not strictly interchangeable because they are unequally facilitative in the solution of problems (Larkin & Simon, 1987). Experientially, each is important because, whether or not they are subtended by a cognitive machine language, both propositions and images are part of the mental life and awareness of nearly every person.

Mental Models and Schemas

In piecing together a model of cognitive representations, it may be helpful to compare usage of the term representation with the ways other terms are used to describe the structure of knowledge. These terms include *mental models, schemas, frames, scripts, semantic networks, neural networks,* and *production systems.* I focus on mental models and schemas, two terms that are used most widely and are perhaps also closest to representations in meaning.

Mental Models. According to Johnson-Laird (1983), mental models consist of knowledge that "plays a direct representational role since it is analogous to the structure of the corresponding state of affairs in the world—as we perceive or conceive it" (p. 156). Johnson-Laird argued that analogical representations have specific relations to propositional knowledge and to mental images, and can be separated conceptually from these. Propositional knowledge, which can be expressed as verbal propositions, has truth value and that truth value is computed with respect to mental models (see also Kosslyn, 1980). If I have a mental model of a certain state of affairs, I can answer "true" or "false" to assertions about the world reflected in that model. Imagery, on the other hand, is more akin to mental models by virtue of its analogical character and reference to observable objects and events, and it seems to "correspond to *views* of models" (Johnson-Laird, 1983, p. 157). Although Johnson-Laird did distinguish between imagery and mental models, he acknowledged that both are analogical in nature. He apparently regarded a mental model not as a particular image, but as a composite of images or, more likely, a dynamic and "runnable" image system that can be used to depict a range of possible conditions and states, and therefore to make predictions. This is consistent with Ford's (1994) interpretation of Johnson-Laird's model, in which Ford viewed mental models as a subset of imagery.

The dynamic image interpretation is consistent with the use of the term *mental model* by Gentner and Gentner (1983), according to whom explanations of electricity might draw upon "teeming crowd" or "flowing waters" mental models. In the teeming crowd model, "electric current is seen as masses of objects racing through passage ways" (p. 111). In the flowing water model, by contrast, "the base domain is a plumbing system . . . and flowing water is mapped onto electric currents" (p. 108). Gentner and Gentner found these two mental models to be unequal in their computational properties. Each led to its own accurate predictions and flawed inferences. Again, like representations generally, different mental models of the same phenomenon cannot be assumed to have the same computational or generative properties.

A brief look at the use of the term mental model seems to support its definition as a dynamic, runnable, analogical system experienced as imagery (Glaser, Lesgold, & Lajoie, 1987). Its function is to simulate, rather than merely describe, events (Greeno, Collins, & Resnick, 1996). I therefore take mental models to be a subset of all possible representations, a form of knowledge that is a dynamic composite of analogical representations. Accordingly, it belongs to the analogical end of the propositional-analogical continuum.

Schemas.   As the term has been used historically and is used currently, schema refers to a broad array of cognitive phenomena. Ancient Greek philosophers used the term schema to refer to both propositional and analogical forms of knowledge. Plato's use of the term, for example, conforms to what we refer to as imagery—form, shape, figure, color, sound. But Plato also used schema to refer to abstract concepts, as in "the schema of the law" (Marshall, 1995, p. 4).

In *Metaphysics*, Aristotle made a similar distinction between schemas as "geometrical figure and physical shape" and "fundamental categories" (Marshall, 1995, p. 6). Thus, the ancient Greeks' use of the term schema embraces both analogical and propositional mental phenomena.

Marshall (1995) acknowledged that schema can be either very broad or highly specific. Although the term may refer to a constrained knowledge system (such as might be processed in working memory as a system, e.g., a mental model) it is commonly used to refer to larger entities of organized knowledge stored in long-term memory. For example, in attempting to define the nature of a schema, Reed (1993) explained that "a schema for the American Psychological Association annual meetings would contain the standard properties of a scientific conference such as its location, date, attenders, session types, and the length of presentations" (p. 42).

Reed's (1993) example of schema is variegated in composition, includes considerable detail as well as overarching categories, and seems to embrace perhaps dozens of representations, as that term is used here. Yet schemas have certain unifying features. One is that schemas are often hierarchically organized (Thorndyke, 1984). Another is that, despite their typical breadth, schemas tend to be sufficiently constrained in scope that they can be processed in working memory as a system and so are functionally adapted to conscious mental processing. Drawing upon Miller's (1956) magical number seven and terminology from computer science, we might say that representations are "byte-sized" and therefore adapted to the constraints of working memory. Besides being conceptually broad, schemas also tend to be fairly abstract, built through exposure to multiple experiences (Marshall, 1995). Finally, representations are not isomorphic with the external world, a fact elaborated in the next section of this chapter.

By example and by definition, therefore, more is meant by the term schema than either representation or mental model. It follows that a schema for any domain would likely consist of multiple representations or mental models. Whereas an individual might be said to have "teeming crowd" or "flowing water" mental models, another representation altogether (in this case propositional) might be the equation: Voltage = Current × Resistance. A schema for electricity, however, would almost certainly be larger still, consisting not only of the mental model and the equation, but also of many other representations including, say, images of wires, batteries, light bulbs, and switches; knowledge of Benjamin Franklin's experiments; perhaps even the sense memory of electrical shock, as well as many more ideas in many different forms, all of which enlarge upon, define, and help exemplify electricity.

Integrating the distinctions made in the foregoing paragraphs, Fig. 2.3 illustrates that the terms mental model, representation, and schema can be nested, with mental model being the most narrow construct and schema the most general. The middling level of generality of the term representation gives it special importance. The term conveys a range of ways in which knowledge can be held,

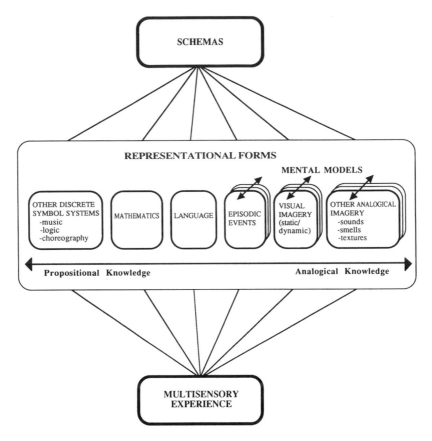

FIG. 2.3.   A spectrum of representational forms.

but it is also narrow enough that it can be used readily to refer to different means of understanding and reasoning about the same phenomenon.

The central band depicts the main propositional-analogical continuum, and along that continuum several major forms of representation are distinguished. Discrete representational forms include language and mathematics, each of which features symbol systems with essentially arbitrary associations between symbol and referent. Each, also, has its own syntax or rule set for combining, analyzing, and transforming symbols. The extreme category, other discrete symbol systems, is a catch-all for remaining notational systems (e.g., choreographic). The three boxes at the right end of the continuum depict representations that are analogical. Primary among these is visual imagery. The right-most box represents imagery derived from forms of sensory perception other than visual.

The representation types indicated correspond to some degree with findings from diverse research traditions. Three categories of representation types—

mathematics, language, and visual imagery—correspond quite well to psychometric factors of human abilities (Cattell, 1987; Guilford, 1967; Thurstone, 1938), to neurological studies of modules of cognition (Gardner, 1983), and to typologies of symbol systems (Gross, 1974). Representation of episodic events seems to be a special category that is somewhat eclectic in drawing from multiple forms of imagery as well as language. It is, of course, linked to the category of human memory known as episodic memory—memory that is essentially autobiographical (Tulving, 1972). It is also distinguished from the other representational forms by being organized primarily by *time.*

The arrows and staggered boxes shown in the analogical types of representations indicate that these forms can be integrated to run as mental models. If, as Johnson-Laird (1983) indicated, an image is a particular view of a model, then a model would seem to be a composite of images, articulated and integrated in such a way as to be "runnable" as a system. This flexible, dynamic quality permits propagation of effects and therefore prediction.

The model corresponds to some extent with Mandler's (1983) typology. She distinguished, for example, representations defined according to imagery, space, events, and categories. In the model shown in Fig. 2.2, representation of space can be considered to be a three-dimensional form of imagery. Representations of events correspond to episodic representations. Categorical representations are apparently more complex than the others, involving mixtures of propositional and imaginal knowledge. Categories contain knowledge of classes and relations that are themselves apparently propositional, but may look to perceptual cues for distinctions. All forms of representation cited by Mandler appear to consist of various organizations of propositional and image-based thought and therefore can be fitted to a propositional-analogical continuum.

The forms shown in Fig. 2.3 are not meant to be exhaustive—indeed, it is impossible to be exhaustive of all representational forms, because propositional representations involve arbitrary associations of symbols with referents. The invention of notation for a particular sport or a new computer-programming language would constitute a new representational form at the propositional end of the continuum.

IMPLICATIONS

The human mind is not a video camera. We do not process and store countless sensory bits; rather, we construct our inner and outer worlds according to the organizing principle of meaning. The fact that knowledge can be represented in different ways implies that knowledge is not a sensory transcription of the external world into the inner world of the mind. Since Piaget and the Gestaltists at least, psychologists have known that the mind's representations are not facsimiles of experience, doubles of the world "out there." According to Mandler (1983),

"Piaget wishes to combat the old associationist view of the image as a copy of perception, replacing this ancient idea with the more modern view that images reflect what we know rather than what we see (or hear or feel). To the extent that images are more than copies or extensions of perception and, hence, have a constructed, 'non-primitive' character, they tend to 'acquire the status of a symbol' (Piaget & Inhelder, 1971)" (p. 434).

In his classic studies of memory, Bartlett (1932) demonstrated vividly that experience can be severely distorted to fit expectations embodied in prior knowledge and referent culture. Bartlett's British subjects were asked to read traditional Native American stories. When asked to recount these stories later, these subjects consistently distorted the stories so as to increase their conformity to Western prototypes of character and plot. It is notable that these distortions escaped the notice of those who made them.

Philosophers have long maintained that the "world" of the mind does not mirror the external world. Kant, for example, argued that the mind links percepts of the external world to a priori pure categories that have an existence independent from experience (Marshall, 1995). In a contemporary account, Goodman noted in *Ways of Worldmaking* (1978) that one (mental) world will differ from another in the weighting of some elements in comparison with others, a truth exemplified by variations of portrayals of similar subjects among different artists. In the process of worldmaking, there is considerable deletion and supplementation—"weeding out" and "filling in," a gentle distortion reminiscent of the perceptual "sharpening" and "leveling" processes noted by Gestalt psychologists. Goodman observed that "our capacity for overlooking is virtually unlimited, and what we do take in usually consists of significant fragments and clues that need massive supplementation" (p. 14).

Gell-Mann (1994) noted that "the schema is not a complete description of the data stream, but only the identified regularities abstracted from the available data" (p. 55). But in using the word *schema*, Gell-Mann referred not only to the cognitive structures of human beings, but also to the compression of complex sensory experience employed by all complex adaptive systems, including immune systems, economies, and ecosystems. The ideational patterns we call representations link the human mind to all forms of complex adaptive systems.

Perhaps it is necessary that the flexibility allowed by representations (or mental models or worlds) would permit errors and distortions to creep in, greatly complexifying the problem of how to educate. So widespread and serious are distortions in formal educational settings that Perkins (1992) has argued the existence of a coherent set of "symptoms," which include missing knowledge, inert knowledge, naive knowledge, and ritualized knowledge, and that he referred to collectively as the "fragile knowledge syndrome." According to Perkins, fundamental conceptual errors can persist despite ostensible success by students in school performances. The fact that bogus understanding can pass for the real thing makes it doubly problematic.

The prevalence and seriousness of naive theories and misconceptions have been amply demonstrated. In a seminal study, Clement (1982) found that college students who had completed coursework in physics were unable to answer questions about simple mechanics. For example, in a problem that called for the application of Newton's first law of motion, students were told to consider a rocket in space drifting sideways. They were told that the rocket's forward thrusters were turned on briefly, then turned off again. The task was to draw the rocket's path before, during, and after the forward thruster was turned on. In a correct response, the rocket's velocity becomes diagonal as it begins to acquire a forward component to its velocity, and its path continues to be diagonal even after the thruster is turned off. Students were likely, however, to indicate the path as changing abruptly to diagonal when the thruster is turned on, and then instantly reverting to horizontal movement once the thruster was turned off. The reversion to a horizontal direction was as if the rocket somehow retained a memory of its initial direction.

In a more recent and vivid demonstration of misconceptions in science, the film *A Private Universe* depicts interviews with Harvard students and professors at commencement (Schneps, 1989). A large percentage of those interviewed offered nonscientific explanations for the phases of the moon and seasons. When students were asked about the cause of the seasons, for example, these responses were typical:

- Student 1: I think the seasons happen because as the earth travels around the sun it gets nearer to the sun, which produces warmer weather, and gets farther away, which produces colder weather, and hence the seasons.
- Student 2: How hot it is or how cold it is any given time of the year has to do with the closeness of the earth to the sun during the seasonal periods.
- Student 3: The earth goes around the sun, and it gets hotter when we get closer to the sun, and it gets colder when we get further away from the sun.

In all, 21 of 23 randomly selected students, faculty, and alumni of Harvard University revealed misconceptions when asked to explain either the cause of the seasons or the phases of the moon. The sum of this body of research points to the principle that what learners actually learn and what they *should* understand as a consequence of instruction are often far apart. Moreover, it is often difficult to discern faulty or incomplete knowledge on the basis of performance on conventional tests. Students and teachers are both likely to be unaware of the discrepancy between ostensibly successful academic performance and deep underlying misconceptions.

For cognitive psychologists concerned with education, the possibility and existence of errorful knowledge is not a mere theoretical curiosity, but a major practical concern. So serious is the depth and extent of errorful knowledge that in *The Unschooled Mind* Gardner (1991) portrayed the ubiquitous phenomenon of misconceptions, rote performances, and naive theories as *the* central problem of formal education and therefore a monumental testimony to the inadequacies of conventional schooling. To Gardner, the syndrome demonstrates a failure of schools to inculcate what developing minds need most, namely, understanding.

The widespread phenomenon of "fragile knowledge" (or, to say it another way, the failure of schooling to engender understanding) is germane to the present topic, representations, on two counts. First, representations must be understood to be more than mere simplifications of complex reality (they are that, but they are more). Second, the construction of knowledge as representations invites distortions (a fact appreciated by the Gestaltists). It is just such distortions that Piaget took as evidence that knowledge is constructed—built by the learner rather than imported full-form in some kind of pure state. Not only can representations be fundamentally flawed, but these flaws are often persistent. Thus, the existence of *fragile* representations is descriptive of the mind, of thinking, and of the present topic, representations. Distortion occurs even at the basic information-processing stages of storage and retrieval of information from long-term memory. Memory for events is notoriously unreliable (Loftus, 1975) and human reasoning is consistently biased in ways that lead to irrational beliefs and decisions (Baron, 1985).

Is it adaptive that the human mind uses representations as a substrate for thought? Wouldn't it be better to use high-fidelity recordings, if that were possible? If we borrow a heuristic from David Perkins (1992) and view "knowledge as design," what are the design features afforded by representations? Representations are functional in that they must encode not only understanding in the world, but also rules, procedures, and strategies for acting in that world. The mind's machinery is a design for the reciprocal functions of knowing and doing —accurate knowledge is not enough.

Representations fulfill the requirement that the human mind excel as an adaptive structure in the service of goals in a sometimes uncertain environment. Representations must permit pattern matching, but because no pattern is ever observed identically twice, flexibility is essential. In meeting the need of flexibility, one property of representations is crucial—their generativity. Here I refer to the ability of the mind to generate new information that aids the solution of the problem at hand. Patterns must be identified in complex experience, and on the basis of identified meaning, other relevant knowledge and procedures must be assembled so that adaptive action can ensue. Rapid access to potentially relevant information is enabled by a long-term memory that is organized not by sensation but by meaning, and retrieval is facilitated by a look-up system that is, in Herbert Simon's (1981) words, "liberally cross-referenced [associational links], and with an elaborate index [recognition capability] that gives direct access through multiple entries to the topics" (p. 104). Think about a subject, and instantly all manner of related ideas are available. This kind of flexibility is exceedingly facilitative and is likely to be a major point of distinction between human- and machine-based information processing.

To summarize, the inherent flexibility of representations invites distortions that some writers characterize as a plague on attempts to educate. But the same quality that admits distortions—flexible knowledge organized by meaning— also permits robust and facilitative understanding. The conditions that lead to true understanding are considered in the conclusion of this chapter.

ELABORATIONS

Certain aspects or dimensions of representations often go unnoticed or are given short shrift in theoretical accounts. Representations are, for example, often depicted as cool, rather static entities. But their role in the regulation of thought and action requires that they be dynamic entities, undergoing constant transformation and modification. Representations can support exploration of the unknown and best guesses about how to proceed. It is possible for represen tations to have a strong affective element: Representations can induce excite- ment, fear, discomfort, exhilaration, and an assortment of other emotions and motivations. These features, which are some of the neglected dimensions of representations, are more clearly identified and elaborated next.

Representations Have Conative and Affective Elements

Although psychologists acknowledge that thought is laced with personal signifi- cance and affect, representations are often portrayed as valueless, cool records of information and experience. This portrayal is misleading because represented knowledge very often does have emotional and motivational value; representa- tions are words, images, goals, and plans charged with meaning, valence, emo- tion, and energy. Representations not only inform; they motivate and channel action. High levels of motivation and interest are, in fact, associated with expert knowledge and the development of expertise (Meichenbaum & Biemiller, 1992). Csikszentmihalyi's (1975) account of flow a state of intense yet effort less concentration—also suggests a tight coupling of expert performance and enthusiastic, even obsessive, engagement in an activity. Conceptions of repre- sentations that fail to acknowledge the "hot" nature of representations in use are incomplete. Representations are therefore explicitly recognized here to pos- sess affective and motivational characteristics.

Representations Facilitate the Pursuit of Goals Through Plans

Representations have meaning in the context of pursuing goals in problem situ- ations and therefore have certain ad hoc qualities. In conventional accounts, representations are depicted as ready-made and preformed, extractable from long-term memory to meet the demands of the moment. However, specific components of any representation—what is included and what is left out—depend vitally on the problem to be solved. In other words, representations are problem- and context-sensitive, constructed in the present to meet present demands, including chosen goals and possible actions to take in pursuit of those goals. In the language used by some cognitivists, representations are often situated (Brown, Collins, & Duguid, 1989). Any representation is likely to include old elements, drawn from memory, as well as new elements, introduced as features of the problem at hand.

To give a brief example involving some introspection on my part, my representation of "computer" changes depending on the situation I am facing. If everything is proceeding as expected, my model of the computer is one thing. But if something goes wrong a new set of features comes to the fore and my representation of the computer changes accordingly. In a crisis I may be concerned about insufficient memory, when I last saved the current document, whether there is a bug in the application program, and so on. These features of my representation of *computer* are unimportant and not really part of my working model of *computer* as long as everything is going as expected. Once the problem changes, however, the representation changes along with it.

The utility of representations in the pursuit of goals through plans was recognized by Kenneth Craik as early as 1943. He noted: "If the organism carries a 'small scale model' of external reality and of its own possible actions within its head, it is able to try out various alternatives, conclude which is the best of them, react to future situations before they arise, utilize the knowledge of past events in dealing with the present and future, and in every way to react in a much fuller, safer and more competent manner to the emergencies which face it" (p. 61). In discussing the features of schemas, Marshall (1995) likewise recognized that one function is planning. She noted that a "schema can be used to make plans, create expectations, and set up goals and subgoals" (p. 41).

Representations Involve Uncertainty

Representations are by nature incomplete, and often the elements and relations composing representations are uncertain. Active representations are "under construction" as new knowledge is added, often through the consideration of possibilities and evidence bearing on their validity and implications (Baron, 1985). When considering *what to believe* or *what to do,* rationality requires considering possible assertions or courses of action and the evidence supporting these. Ideally, evidence is weighed and a rational decision is made. There is, however, a persistent human bias to be overconfident in one's construal of a situation. This kind of bias—which indicates a lack of appreciation for the uncertainty of one's own beliefs—is a major point of foundering in rational thinking (Nickerson, 1986).

Uncertainty is relevant to the understanding of representations in two ways. First, existing knowledge is virtually always held without complete certainty. This is uncertainty operating inward on representations we already have. Second, uncertainty is characteristic of knowledge drawn from the outside, which is in the process of being incorporated into our existing representations. The "necessary uncertainty" of representations is rarely addressed by cognitive scientists. This omission reflects, in part, a tendency by cognitive scientists to attend to human *performance* at the expense of *learning*. If the subject of research is assumed to have a stable knowledge structure, then it is easy to regard that knowledge as either existing or not existing—as an all-or-none phenomenon. However, a person who is learning or trying to apply knowledge rationally to decision making is perpetually in a state of needing to weigh evidence to support beliefs and possible actions. An orientation to cognition that recognizes learning makes it clearer that knowledge is often held in graded states of certainty or uncertainty.

Representations Require Executive Control

Another important but often neglected aspect of representations is that they are subject to executive control. The importance of executive control as an aspect of metacognition has been amply described and demonstrated (Flavell, 1979). The relevance of executive control to representation is obvious when the functions and features of representations are appreciated, especially the importance of planning and goal setting, and the uncertainty of knowledge. Because representations are by nature collections of constructed knowledge, one *functionally* important aspect of any representation is knowing which knowledge is dependable, which is suspect, and where there are gaps. If a representation consists of a plan, one important aspect of that representation is the varying degrees of confidence in possible routes or strategies toward attainment of the goal.

Although the executive qualities and functions of representations are often not recognized, one exception is Sigel's (1993) proposal of representational competence—a kind of meta-knowledge that permits recognition of equivalence across representational types. Sigel's research has shown that this basic principle of interchangeability can be a major point of foundering for learners at all levels. This gap in metacognitive knowledge can have serious consequences because the making of meaning so often depends on the linking of multiple representational forms, such as spoken and written words, nonlinguistic symbols, images, and artifacts. Marshall (1995) also acknowledged executive control, including in her definition of schemas the capacity to "draw inferences, make estimates, create goals, and develop plans using the framework [of the schema]" (p. 39). It is reasonable, therefore, to include in our understanding of representations the executive knowledge needed to build, modify, and use representations effectively.

CONCLUSION

The study of representations and their cognates, mental models and schemas, has contributed profoundly to our understanding of the nature and use of knowledge in the human cognitive system. What has emerged is an understanding of representations as consisting in propositional and image-based knowledge of the world. Mental models can be regarded as a type of representation, one that is analogical in nature. Schemas, on the other hand, form a broader category and represent *compositions* of representations in a domain.

Cognitive theorists have tended to neglect certain aspects of representations. For example, there has been little emphasis on their functional nature. There has also been a tendency to ignore or downplay the complex, dynamic, fuzzy, and emotionally charged aspects of representations, and the construction and use of representations in problem-solving activities supported by metalanguage. To the degree that these aspects of representations are understood and appreciated, we can construct a theory that is not only more complete regarding cognition, but also more useful in encouraging the development of minds.

The very idea of representations recognizes the constructed nature of knowledge—that the picture inside is not some sort of retinal photocopy of the sensory field. The constant construal of meaning from our environment affords us knowledge structures (i.e., representations) that have utility in perceiving features of our environment that are functionally important. In this sense, representations are as unlike textbook diagrams as they are unlike photographs. Their selective, multimodal, functional, and fuzzy nature affords them tremendous flexibility as tools for problem solving. But these same characteristics make them also vulnerable to distortion.

Under what conditions are representations likely to be robust (rather than fragile, in Perkins' sense) and effective, that is, serviceable in the pursuit of goals and the solution of problems en route? According to Gardner (1991), genuine understanding is most likely to emerge, and be apparent to others, if learners possess a number of ways of representing knowledge of a concept or skill and can move readily back and forth among these forms of knowing. Gardner asserted that "An important symptom of an emerging understanding is the capacity to represent a problem in a number of different ways and to approach its solution from varied vantage points; a single, rigid representation is unlikely to suffice" (p. 18). One link between representations and the pedagogical goal of understanding is that understanding is much more likely to occur when multiple representations can be formed and integrated for the same phenomenon. Put another way, if an idea or concept is represented *in one way only,* it is unlikely that the knowledge so represented can be used to communicate understanding. For example, a learner who is able to balance a chemical equation (symbolic external representation) but who cannot explain it in words (linguistic representation) probably does not understand what the equation means. It is the lack of ability to translate across equivalent representational forms that led Sigel (1993) to characterize some children as lacking representational competence.

Making much the same point, but using different language, Goodman (1978) described one aspect of cognitively synthesized "worlds" as composition and decomposition, a kind of analysis and synthesis, a splitting and lumping that allows one to see in this world (mental model, representation) the whole and its parts. This kind of mental reversibility is akin to Piagetian notions of operations and conservation. It seems likely that the achievement of this kind of conservancy with a domain is yet another indicator of understanding.

Flexible, connected analogical representations compose what we have referred to as mental models. Johnson-Laird (1983) asserted that the connection between models and understanding is direct: "The psychological core of understanding, I shall assume, consists in having a 'working model' of the phenomenon in your mind" (p. 2). It would seem that mental models, in this view, consist of the composition and integration of a variety of image-based "views." For all their generative power, mental models are incomplete and, as we have seen, may contain serious flaws. Representations more generally, in their varied and sometimes vexing instantiations, are notoriously vulnerable to distortion and error. They are also, however, the key to robust understanding, to seeking, striving, and discovery, and to all the possibilities implicit.

ACKNOWLEDGMENTS

The author wishes to thank Eamonn Kelly and Mike Scaife for their helpful comments on a previous version of this chapter.

REFERENCES

Baddeley, A. (1986). *Working memory.* Oxford, England: Clarendon.
Baron, J. (1985). *Rationality and intelligence.* New York: Cambridge University Press.
Bartlett, F. C. (1932). *Remembering: A study in experimental and social psychology.* Cambridge, England: Cambridge University Press.
Bower, G. H. (1972). Mental imagery and associative learning. In L. Gregg (Ed.), *Cognition in learning and memory* (pp. 51–88). New York: Wiley.
Brown, J. S., Collins, A., & Duguid, P. (1989). Situated cognition and the culture of learning. *Educational Researcher, 18,* 32–42.
Cattell, R. B. (1987). *Intelligence: Its structure, growth, and action.* New York: North-Holland.
Clement, J. (1982). Students' preconceptions in introductory mechanics. *American Journal of Physics, 51*(1), 66–71.
Craik, K. (1943). *The nature of explanation.* Cambridge, England: Cambridge University Press.
Csikszentmihalyi, M. (1975). *Beyond boredom and anxiety.* San Francisco: Jossey-Bass.
Dalenoort, G. J. (1990). Toward a general theory of representation. *Psychological Research, 52,* 229–237.
Denis, M. (1994). *Image and cognition* (2nd ed.). Paris: Presses Universitaires de France.
Flavell, J. H. (1979). Metacognition and cognitive monitoring. *American Psychologist, 10,* 906–911.
Ford, M. (1994). Two modes of mental representation and problem solution in syllogistic reasoning. *Cognition, 54,* 1–71.
Gardner, H. (1983). *Frames of mind: The theory of multiple intelligences.* New York: Basic Books.
Gardner, H. (1991). *The unschooled mind: How children think and how schools should teach.* New York: Basic Books.

Gell-Mann, M. (1994). *The quark and the jaguar.* New York: Freeman.

Gentner, D., & Gentner, D. R. (1983). Flowing waters or teeming crowds: Mental models of electricity. In D. Gentner & A. L. Stevens (Eds.), *Mental models* (pp. 99–129). Hillsdale, NJ: Lawrence Erlbaum Associates.

Glaser, R., Lesgold, A., & Lajoie, S. (1987). Toward a cognitive theory for the measurement of achievement. In R. Ronning, J. A. Glover, J. C. Conoley, & J. C. Witt (Eds.), *The influence of cognitive psychology on testing* (pp. 41–85). Hillsdale, NJ: Lawrence Erlbaum Associates.

Goodman, N. (1978). *Ways of worldmaking.* Indianapolis: Hackett Publishing Company, Inc.

Greeno, J. G., Collins, A. M., & Resnick, L. B. (1996). Cognition and learning. In D. C. Berliner & R. C. Calfee (Eds.), *Handbook of educational psychology* (pp. 15–62). New York: Simon & Schuster Macmillan.

Gross, L. (1974). Modes of communication and the acquisition of symbolic competence. In D. R. Olson (Ed.), *Media and symbols: The forms of expression, communication, and education* (73rd Yearbook of the National Society for the Study of Education) (pp. 56–80). Chicago: University of Chicago Press.

Guilford, J. P. (1967). *The nature of human intelligence.* New York: McGraw-Hill.

Johnson-Laird, P. N. (1983). *Mental models: Towards a cognitive science of language, inference, and consciousness.* Cambridge, MA: Harvard University Press.

Kosslyn, S. (1980). *Image and mind.* Cambridge, MA: Harvard University Press.

Larkin, J. H., & Simon, H. A. (1987). Why a diagram is (sometimes) worth ten thousand words. *Cognitive Science, 11,* 65–99.

Loftus, E. F. (1975). Leading questions and the eyewitness report. *Cognitive Psychology, 7,* 560–572.

Mandler, J. (1983). Representation. In P. H. Mussen (Series Ed.) & J. H. Flavell & E. M. Markman (Vol. Eds.), *Handbook of child psychology: Vol. 3. Cognitive development* (4th ed., pp. 420–494). New York: Wiley.

Marshall, S. P. (1995). *Schemas in problem solving.* New York: Cambridge University Press.

McNamara, T. P. (1994). Knowledge representation. In R. J. Sternberg (Ed.), *Thinking and problem solving* (pp. 83–117). San Diego: Academic Press.

Meichenbaum, D., & Biemiller, A. (1992). In search of student expertise in the classroom: A metacognitive analysis. In M. Pressley, K. Harris, & J. T. Guthrie (Eds.), *Promoting academic competence and literacy skills in schools* (pp. 3–56). San Diego: Academic Press.

Miller, G. A. (1956). The magical number seven, plus or minus two. *Psychological Review, 63,* 81–97.

Millis, K. K., & Cohen, R. (1994). Spatial representations and updating situation models. *Reading Research Quarterly, 29,* 369–380.

Nickerson, R. S. (1986). *Reflections on reasoning.* Hillsdale, NJ: Lawrence Erlbaum Associates.

Paivio, A. (1970). On the functional significance of imagery. *Psychological Bulletin, 73,* 385–392.

Paivio, A. (1971). *Imagery and verbal processes.* New York: Holt, Rinehart & Winston.

Perkins, D. (1992). *Smart schools: Better thinking and learning for every child.* New York: The Free Press.

Piaget, J., & Inhelder, B. (1971). *Mental imagery in the child: A study of the development of imaginal representation.* London: Routledge & Kegan-Paul.

Pylyshyn, Z. W. (1973). What the mind's eye tells the mind's brain: A critique of mental imagery. *Psychological Bulletin, 80,* 1–24.

Reed, S. K. (1993). A schema-based theory of transfer. In D. K. Detterman & R. J. Sternberg (Eds.), *Transfer on trial: Intelligence, cognition, and instruction* (pp. 39–67). Norwood, NJ: Ablex.

Schneps, M. H. (1989) (Project Star, Harvard University). *A private universe* [Video]. (Available from Pyramid Film & Video, 2801 Colorado Avenue, Santa Monica, CA 90404).

Sigel, I. E. (1993). The centrality of a distancing model for the development of representational competence. In R. R. Cocking & K. A Renninger (Eds.), *The development and meaning of psychological distance* (pp. 141–158). Hillsdale, NJ: Lawrence Erlbaum Associates.

Simon, H. A. (1981). *The science of the artificial.* Cambridge, MA: MIT Press.

Thagard, P. (1996). *Mind*. Cambridge, MA: MIT Press.

Thorndyke, P. W. (1984). Applications of schema theory in cognitive research. In J. R. Anderson & S. M. Kosslyn (Eds.), *Tutorials in learning and memory* (pp. 167–191). San Francisco: Freeman.

Thurstone, L. L. (1938). Primary mental abilities. *Psychometric Monographs, 1*.

Tulving, E. (1972). Episodic and semantic memory. In E. Tulving & W. Donaldson (Eds.), *Organization and memory* (pp. 382–403). New York: Academic Press.

CHAPTER 3

Representation: Picture or Process?

APRIL A. BENASICH
Center for Molecular and Behavioral Neuroscience,
Rutgers University, Newark

HEATHER L. READ
Keck Center, University of California at San Francisco

> *Behold! Human beings living in an underground den . . . like ourselves . . .*
> *they only see their own shadows or the shadows of another, which the fire*
> *throws on the opposite wall of their cave. To them the truth (reality)*
> *would be literally nothing but the shadows of images.*
> —Plato, *The Republic*, Book VII

How might information be represented in the brain? To attempt to answer such a question, one must consider what the brain actually "does," not at the level of the individual neuron but rather at the level of what ensembles of neurons accomplish, and how this is accomplished in a *real* brain rather than in a theoretical model of information processing (with lots of "black boxes") or in a simplified neural net. The neural contribution to a cognitive process can be explored by observing how the process changes with lesions of a given brain structure. In adults this approach is quite difficult because: (a) there are multiple neural structures supporting any given cognitive process, and (b) lesions are rarely specific or complete (clinically or experimentally). However, a unique opportunity for study presents itself in the developing infant. In infancy, different brain structures mature at different rates. Patterns of connectivity change over time as a function of increasing mylenization, exuberant connectivity, and neuronal pruning. Thus, the period of infancy provides an unparalleled perspective for observing how perceptions of the external world change as a function of neural substrate. For example, cortex is slow to mature making it necessary for other neural structures to support cognitive processes such as sensory representation in the infant. Although the study of developing neural substrates in humans is still largely unexplored, a number of studies indicate a developmental shift from a subcortical to a cortical level of functioning during the first 2 years of life (Chugani & Phelps, 1986; Chugani, Phelps, & Mazziotta, 1987; Goldman-Rakic, 1987b). Moreover, nonhuman primate studies suggest that successive cortical maps are built up over time, superimposing sensory input upon motor function thus allowing more complex linked systems to develop (Jay & Sparks, 1987; Meredith & Stein, 1996; Wang, Merzenich, Beitel, & Schreiner, 1995; Withington-Wray, Binns, & Keating, 1990; Wurtz, Goldberg, & Robinson, 1992).

The question of how information could be represented in the brain becomes particularly germane when studying the neural bases of normal cognitive and language development. There is a multiplicity of meanings for the term *representation*. In the cognitive realm, it refers to the perceptual information held in the mind (both the actual information as well as how it is structured). When operating in the realm of neuroscience, however, representation refers to a set of physical events, specifically the projections of sensory inputs onto defined cortical areas. In our laboratory, we are at the intersection of these two interpretations, attempting to take account of both.

We have adopted two strategies for studying representational processes. First, a number of behavioral tasks designed to assess sensory information processing in the *normally developing infant* are used. Sensory processing abilities are assessed in infancy and early childhood using habituation, recognition memory, and cross-modal tasks. In addition, several measures of auditory temporal processing are employed. We have found that our measures of sensory information processing are predictive of later neurocognitive and linguistic outcomes (Benasich & Spitz, 1996; Benasich, Spitz, Flax, & Tallal, 1997). This area of developmental study has recently been transformed by a flurry of studies supporting the predictive strength of early perceptual-cognitive abilities as indexed by paradigms (i.e., habituation, visual recognition memory, and cross-modal matching) thought to tap infant information processing and concept formation (see McCall & Carriger, 1993, for a review). Conversely, studies which use global neurocognitive exams and standard infant tests (such as the Bayley Scales) are poor predictors of later cognitive and language outcomes.

A second research strategy we have used to explore the representational process is the study of *altered sensory processing* manifested in children with specific language impairment (LI). LI or developmental dysphasia is a form of developmental speech or language disorder that can not be traced to a known cause such as hearing impairment, mental retardation, childhood schizophrenia, infantile autism, or frank neurological causes such as seizures or motor paralysis. Some 5% to 10% of preschool children are estimated to have such disorders (Robinson, 1987; Tallal, 1988). Across laboratories, research investigating sensory processing in LI individuals suggests that impairment of low-level auditory temporal processing (ATP) hinders the development of normal language and reading abilities (Godfrey, Syrdal-Lasky, Millay, & Knox, 1981; Reed, 1989; Snowling, Goulandris, Bowlby, & Howell, 1986; Tallal & Piercy, 1973a, 1973b; Werker & Tees, 1987). Such temporal processing deficits directly interfere with adequate perception of those speech sounds which are characterized by very rapid acoustic changes. Significant links between developmental disorders in speech perception and auditory temporal processing deficits have been shown in children above the age of four (Tallal & Piercy, 1973a, 1973b, 1974, 1975). Moreover, performance on temporal perception and production tasks enable correct identification of 98% of LI from normal children (Tallal, Stark, & Mellits, 1985a). Given that temporal processing deficits can be used in older children (and adults) as a behavioral "marker" of language impairment, we predicted that measures of temporal processing would be useful in early (infant) screening for language delays. Indeed, we have found that differences in auditory temporal processing thresholds in infancy are related to later language development even in normal control infants (Benasich & Spitz, 1998, 1996; Benasich, Spitz, & Tallal, 1995).

HOW WE WILL PROCEED

In presenting our working construct of the development of representation we first give you an overview of some key concepts, research issues and our own methodology. Second, we address the question of how normal development as well as altered developmental trajectories might be reflected in emerging representational processes. Third, we discuss the candidates for an organic instantiation of mental representation and the cortical mechanisms that might be called into service. Fourth, we present our evolving model of representation in infants and posit a construct that might capture the differing levels of neuronally-mediated representation. Finally, we discuss what further predictions, hence future studies, such a model might dictate.

OVERVIEW: KEY CONCEPTS NEEDED FOR DESIGNING STUDIES OF INFANT INFORMATION PROCESSING

Several bodies of research suggest that it should be possible to identify temporal processing deficits in infants. First, the acoustic abilities infants need to effectively process the phonetic units of speech are in place from a very early age, even before expressive language emerges. One- to 2-month-old infants can discriminate between-category differences for most phonetic contrasts, even those not used in their native language (Aslin, Pisoni, & Jusczyk, 1983; Best, 1984; Kuhl, Williams, Lacerda, Stevens, & Lindblom, 1992). Young infants can also perceive brief, rapidly changing temporal cues that are not language based

(Aslin, 1989; Eilers, Morse, Gavin, & Oller, 1981; Jusczyk, Smith, & Murphy, 1981). Second, it has been shown that there is a significantly higher incidence of language disabilities in families of LI children—they are more likely to have an impaired parent and/or sibling—than well-matched control families (Bishop, North, & Donlan, 1995; R. J. Robinson, 1987; Spitz, Tallal, Flax, & Benasich, 1997; Tallal, Ross, & Curtiss, 1989; Tallal, Townsend, Curtiss, & Wulfeck, 1991). Infants born into such families are therefore at increased risk to develop the disorder. Finally, results of neuropathological as well as brain imaging (MRI; PET) studies suggest that neuropathology that appears to be implicated in LI occurs very early in life, thus the processing deficits seen in children with specific language impairments should also be detectable well before a reading or language disorder is noted (Galaburda & Livingstone, 1993; Hagman et al., 1992; Jernigan, Hesselink, Sowell, & Tallal, 1991; Livingstone, Rosen, Drislane, & Galaburda, 1991; Tallal et al., 1990).

Given that it is likely that temporal processing deficits will be present in some infants and should be predictive of linguistic outcome, what sorts of temporal windows are important to consider? Much of the sensory processing necessary for language comprehension and production occurs within a brief window of time. In order to process speech it is necessary to hear and respond to auditory cues that signal what words are being produced. This information is carried by the elements of the speech sound that are called "formants" which represent sound waveforms across time. The rapid transitional cues that facilitate decoding of language are contained within the consonants, in particular, stop consonants such as p, t, k, b, d, and g. These transitional cues are only about 40 ms. in length (a millisecond is 1/1000 of a second). These critical cues must be processed if speech is to be perceived accurately. Vowels, on the other hand, are at steady state across the waveform, and thus depend less on temporal processing abilities in the millisecond domain. Thus, the first time window to consider in assessing temporal processing limits in infants is on the order of tens of milliseconds.

Evidence suggesting that the sensory processing in the time window of tens of milliseconds is relevant to language comprehension derives from studies of auditory temporal processing (ATP) in children and adults (see Farmer & Klein, 1995, for a review). Children (and adults) with ATP deficits and an associated language impairment hear normally and can sequence sounds, however, they need orders of magnitude more processing time than unimpaired children. While most 5- to 10-year-olds only need tens of milliseconds to process incoming signals, these children need hundreds of milliseconds to process the same stimuli. These difficulties occur whether the incoming signals are language, for example consonant-vowel syllables such as /da/ or /pa/, or nonlanguage signals such as tone pairs. A classic study by Tallal and colleagues (Tallal, Stark, & Mellits, 1985a) revealed marked differences between children with specific language impairment (LI) and control children on an auditory temporal processing task using two tones with varying interstimulus interval (ISI) between the tones. Performance was shown to be identical for LI and control children for stimuli with ISIs of 500 ms. but the curves sharply diverged at about 300 ms.; LI children fell rapidly to chance performance levels while well-matched control children continued to perform at high levels down to 8 ms. ISI. Recently, Wright and colleagues (Wright et al., 1997) provided further evidence that LI children are severely impaired in their ability to separate successive rapid brief sounds of similar frequencies and also demonstrated excessive amounts of interference (auditory backward masking) when two auditory stimuli are presented in rapid succession.

A wider time window, on the order of hundreds of seconds, must be investigated if one is interested in more complex representations including representational memory. As we will describe below, measures of representational memory and habituation tap into this wider time window. For example, habituation occurs over the time window of hundreds of seconds (given multiple presentations across time). We have found that measures of longer temporal intervals contribute to prediction of language delays and, in particular, to general cognitive outcomes.

MEASURING INFANT INFORMATION PROCESSING

We use three experimental paradigms for assessment of sensory information processing abilities in infants: habituation, recognition memory, and visually-reinforced conditioned head-turning. These paradigms tap processing speed as well as memory and discrimination. In addition, habituation and recognition memory tap abstraction and categorization skills. All of these abilities are critical for linguistic development as well as for more general cognitive abilities. It has been found that decrement in habituation, and measures of recognition memory in infants predict language outcome as well as general cognitive outcomes (Bornstein & Sigman, 1986; Rose, Feldman, Wallace, & Cohen, 1991; Sigman, Cohen, & Beckwith, 1997; Tamis-LeMonda & Bornstein, 1989; Thompson, Fagan, & Fulker, 1991). A recent meta-analysis of infant habituation and recognition memory as predictors of later IQ concluded that independent of laboratory or response measure, in both risk and nonrisk samples, habituation and recognition memory reliably and substantially predict to childhood IQ (McCall & Carriger, 1993).

Paradigms for assessing both recognition memory and habituation are based on the well-known tendency of infants to differentially fixate novel as compared to previously-seen visual stimuli. Habituation refers to the progressive decrement in attending to one or more stimuli when they are presented repeatedly or are available continuously. This response decrement to redundant stimulation appears to involve both perception and memory, specifically recognition mem-

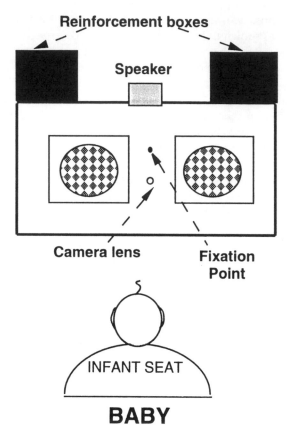

FIG. 3.1. Diagram of the testing apparatus used for habituation, recognition memory and the two-alternative forced-
choice head-turn tasks. The reinforcement boxes contained
two different animated toys that could be illuminated and set
in motion. The infant's head direction and visual fixations were
videotaped via a camera lens located directly below the fixation point.

ory of the familiarized stimulus. Typically, introduction of a novel stimulus
produces a recovery of attention, ruling out decline due to sensory or subject
fatigue. Recognition memory or novelty preference is tested by presenting the
infant with one, or two identical, stimuli (visual or auditory–visual) to study for
a preset looking time and then pairing the now familiar stimulus with a new or
novel stimulus. When the two stimuli are presented to either side of a central
fixation point (see Fig. 3.1) then the total looking time at either stimulus can be
determined by head orientation and eye fixations. A *novelty preference* score is
computed for each test item by dividing the time spent looking at the novel

stimulus during the test trial by the total amount of looking at both stimuli during that time. These fairly simple paradigms allow us to assess the development of infant cognitive and memory processes without relying on linguistic measures.

The habituation and recognition memory paradigms are primarily used to evaluate the infant's learning acquisition curve, speed of encoding, and recognition memory (see Benasich & Bejar, 1992; Bornstein, 1985). In our laboratory, each infant receives at least one standard infant-control habituation and recognition memory test using face stimuli (see Bornstein & Benasich, 1986).[1] We also administer habituation tasks that evaluate each infant's ability to discriminate consonant-vowel (CV) pairings (i.e., /ba/ vs. /da/ with normal 40 ms. transitions) in order to provide a measure of auditory temporal discrimination without the memory load of learning a contingency (see ATP paradigms below). The infant is habituated to an abstract visual pattern paired with one speech stimulus. Following this familiarization procedure, the infant receives four test trials; two test trials involving the now familiar auditory-visual pairing and two trials involving a novel auditory-visual pairing. The novel pairing is a second speech stimulus paired with the *same* visual stimulus. Because nothing changes in the test but the auditory stimulus, the infant's looking time (our dependent measure) should only increase if the CV change is discriminated.

MEASURING INFANT AUDITORY TEMPORAL PROCESSING

We use an infant operant conditioning paradigm designed to have the same parameters as the Tallal Repetition Test (Tallal & Piercy, 1973a), a highly reliable test of ATP designed for individuals from age 4 years through adulthood. This infant methodology (also referred to as visually-reinforced conditioned head-turning) allows us to obtain individual auditory temporal processing thresholds. (See Morrongiello, 1990, for a review.) Two different operant conditioning paradigms were used to investigate infant auditory temporal processing abilities: a Two-Alternative Forced-Choice Head-Turn (2-AFC) task and a Go/No Go Operant (G/N-G) Head-Turn procedure.

During the 2-AFC task, infants must learn to discriminate between two auditory tone sequences and associate each auditory stimulus with a visual reward. They must anticipate which of two toy reinforcers will be illuminated and set in motion by looking at the correct place. Infants are first trained to turn their

---

[1]The mean duration of the infant's first two looks constitutes a baseline and are automatically set at 100%. The same stimuli are presented until the infant reaches a habituation criterion of two consecutive looks each less than or equal to 50% of the baseline. Immediately following habituation, the infant is tested with the habituation stimulus and a novel stimulus in a preferential-looking design. Each stimuli pair is presented twice for 10 s each with right–left positions reversed for the second 10-s presentation.

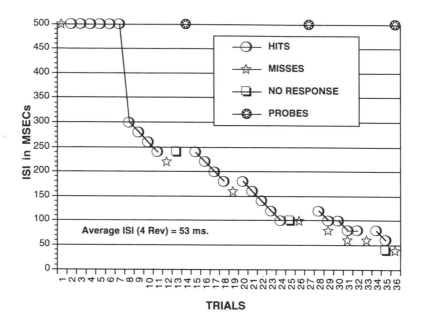

FIG. 3.2.   Trial-by-trial recording from a 26-week-old infant completing the test phase of the Auditory Temporal Processing (ATP) Threshold Task. Infants were required to score 6 of 7 correct responses at 500 ms ISI before proceeding to the test phase. (See text and Footnote 2). The ATP threshold is 53 ms.

heads to the right for one tone sequence and to the left for a second tone sequence. The stimuli are two 75 ms. duration complex tones combined into two different sequences with an interposed ISI (i.e., 100 Hz; 200 Hz and 100 Hz; 100 Hz). By training the infant with a large ISI of 500 ms. between tones within a tone sequence, dropping that ISI to 300 ms. when the contingency is acquired, and then gradually decreasing the interval between the tones using an up-down adaptive procedure, we can identify the point at which the infant can no longer discriminate between the two tone sequences (the infant's auditory temporal processing threshold).[2] (See Benasich & Tallal, 1996, for further procedural de-

[2]During the training phase reinforcement is not contingent on response. Two seconds after presentation of the tone sequence, the appropriate toy is automatically lit and activated whatever the infant's response; the reward segment (toy activation) lasts approximately 4 s. After 15 trials, the infant's knowledge of the contingency is assessed using the two tone pairs randomly presented with ISIs of 500 ms. Reinforcement is contingent on a correct head turn. When a criterion of six correct responses out of seven consecutive trials was reached, the infant entered the test phase. The same contingent procedure outlined previously was followed for the variable ISI test phase. The two tone pairs are randomly presented with ISIs varying from 300 ms to 8 ms, using a 1-up, 1-down adaptive procedure (Levitt, 1971) with a step size of 20 ms, until the infant attains six reversals. A reversal is a move from a correct response (Hit) to an incorrect response (Miss) or from a Miss to Hit. A Probe stimulus (500 ms ISI) is presented after two Misses or two No Response trials or any combination of

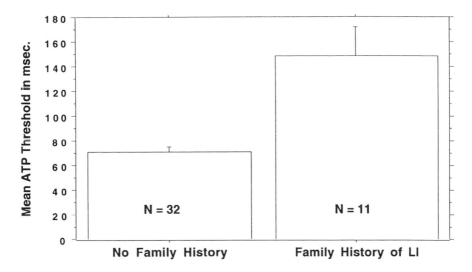

Unpaired two-tailed t (41) = -5.04, p < .0001

FIG. 3.3.   Comparison of mean ATP thresholds (across four reversals) for infants (mean age = 7.6 mths) with and without a family history of language-based learning disabilities. (Copyright 1996 by Ablex Publishing Corporation. Reprinted by permission.

tails). Fig. 3.2 illustrates an infant's trial-by-trial performance on the Variable ISI Test Phase of this task.

Using the 2-AFC task, we have found that ATP thresholds vary among normal healthy control infants and that these differences in rapid processing are related to later language development. ATP thresholds at 6 to 9 months strongly and significantly predict language comprehension at 12 months and language comprehension and production at 16 months (Benasich et al., 1995). Furthermore, mean ATP thresholds (group scores) are elevated for infants from families with a history of language-based learning impairments as compared to control infants with no family history of LI (see Fig. 3.3).

Moreover, the pattern of performance on the 2-AFC task differs in infants with a family history of LI. Fig. 3.4 illustrates the trial-by-trial performance of an infant with a positive family history of LI on the same Variable ISI Test Phase. Note how performance rapidly drops to chance when the ISI drops below 250 ms. About 45% of infants with a family history of LI show this type of pattern. The remaining 55% show trial-by-trial performance (and thresholds) similar to control infants (e.g. Fig. 3.2).

---

these two. After a correct response to a Probe, the program resumes stimulus presentation at the last correct step in the adaptive procedure. Probe ISIs are not included in threshold or reversal computations. The mean of the last four reversal points is calculated for each infant in order to estimate ATP thresholds.

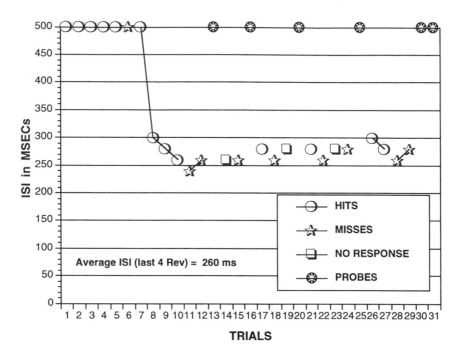

FIG. 3.4.   Trial-by-trial recording for the test phase of the ATP threshold task from a 26-week-old infant with a family history of language-based learning disability. At 500 ms ISI this infant had no difficulty discriminating one tone sequence from another, but once the ISI dropped below 250 ms discrimination dropped to chance levels. The ATP threshold is 260 ms.

The G/N-G Procedure is a shorter, less demanding variant of the above technique. Here, infants are operantly conditioned to make a 60° head-turn to the left in response to a target tone sequence imbedded within a standard repeating sequence, e.g. high–low, high–low, *low–high*, high–low. The training stimuli are paired 75 ms. duration complex tones (100 Hz and 200 Hz; 200 Hz and 100 Hz) separated by a 500 ms. ISI. The training criterion is four consecutive correct anticipatory head-turns orienting to the reward location for the target tone sequence. During the Test phase, twenty trials for each of four blocked ISIs are presented: 300, 180, 70, and 10 ms. for both standard and target sequences. (See Benasich et al., 1995, for further procedural details). We were able to replicate our previous findings of differences in individual ATP abilities among infants using the G/N-G technique, as well as the predictive relations with later language. For example, Fig. 3.5 shows the relations between infants' ATP thresholds at 9 months of age and their standardized scores of language comprehension and production at 16 months of age. Thus, we can identify a subset of infants who are particularly poor at processing rapidly changing auditory temporal cues, whether these are speech or nonspeech sounds, and these differences in ATP

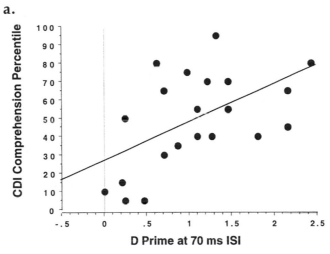

a.

CDI COMP = 26.641 + 20.675 * DP ISI 70; R^2 = .295

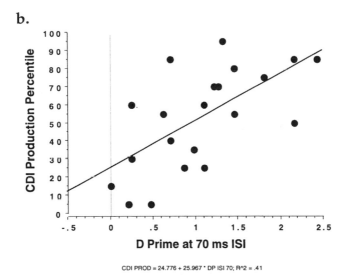

b.

CDI PROD = 24.776 + 25.967 * DP ISI 70; R^2 = .41

FIG. 3.5. ATP thresholds of normal control infants (as measured by D prime) at 9 months and the relationship with performance on the Mac-Arthur Communicative Developmental Inventory (CDI) at 16 months as measured by the standardized percentile scores for comprehension (a) and production (b).

thresholds in infancy are related to later language (Benasich & Spitz, 1996; Benasich et al., 1995). Moreover, we have found that infants with difficulty processing differences in rapid tones also have difficulty discriminating between /ba/ and /da/ (Benasich et al., 1997).

We have shown that measures of habituation, recognition memory and temporal processing all make independent contributions to prediction of later language abilities in infants with a family history of language impairments as well as in healthy control infants (Benasich & Spitz, 1996; Benasich & Tallal, 1996). Specifically, infants who are better temporal processors (i.e., those with lower auditory temporal processing thresholds) also habituate more efficiently (i.e., they require fewer trials to criterion and exhibit steeper habituation slopes). These infants also discriminate better (i.e., they have higher visual recognition memory scores) and score higher in language tests at 12, 16, and 24 months of age. Conversely, poor temporal processors habituate more slowly, discriminate more poorly and have poorer language skills than matched controls (Benasich & Tallal, 1996; Spitz et al., 1997). In sum, these data lend strong support to the notion that the ability to perform fine acoustic discriminations in early infancy are critically important to later language development. This appears to be the case even when specific predictors such as a positive family history for LI or prematurity are not present. In addition, these findings suggest that the early processes that support perceptual-cognitive abilities in infancy are also important for language acquisition and cognitive development in early childhood.

TIME AND MODALITY DEPENDENCE
OF INFANT INFORMATION PROCESSING

We are still exploring the links between time-dependent information processing in the rapid time domain (tens of milliseconds) as compared to the global time domain (seconds) and associations with intermodal or multimodal processing in infancy. Given that sensory systems develop at different rates, the relations among systems (intersensory and intrasensory competition and intersensory linking) at different points in development could markedly influence brain organization. Turkewitz and Kenny (1982) suggest that the effect that a change in the "nature of functioning" in a particular modality will have, critically depends on both the corresponding developmental level of the other modalities and on the timing of the alteration of function. Evidence continues to accumulate that suggests that slowed temporal processing thresholds may extend across modalities. Moreover, many children with LI go on to develop reading problems similar to those seen in dyslexics (American Psychiatric Association, 1987; Tallal, 1988). As noted, Tallal found that a combination of measures of processing speed in the auditory, visual, somatosensory, and oral-motor domains identified 98% of LI from control children (Tallal et al., 1985a). Eden and colleagues report differences in adult dyslexics as compared to controls using fMRI (functional MRI) during a task designed to test perception of rapidly-moving visual stimuli (dots) (Eden, VanMeter, Maisog, Rumsey, & Zeffiro, 1995). Control subjects show activation in area V5 (specialized for processing of visual motion) whereas very little activation was seen in the same area in the dyslexic group. Although Eden et al. have not shown specific relationships between this abnormality and poor reading skills, it suggests that the neurons specialized for processing rapid transient stimuli (magnocellular neurons) in both visual and auditory thalamic regions may be implicated in the temporal processing deficits seen in language-impaired and dyslexic subjects (Galaburda, Menard, & Rosen, 1994; Livingston et al., 1991). It has been shown that dyslexic humans have smaller and fewer magnocellular neurons in the visual thalamus (Galaburda & Livingstone, 1993; Galaburda et al., 1994; Livingstone et al., 1991). Although a similar deficit has not been described for auditory magnocellular neurons in dyslexic humans, it has been suggested as a plausible explanation for poor discrimination of rapidly presented auditory stimuli observed in animal models of dyslexia (Fitch, Tallal, Brown, Galaburda, & Rosen, 1994; Herman, Fitch, Galaburda, & Rosen, 1995).

The most common interpretation of these data is that as a function of these abnormalities in the magnocellular system, these neurons may be slower to fire to very brief stimuli (in the tens of milliseconds) thus impeding encoding for these rapid on/off stimuli. From that a cascade of processing problems can be hypothesized. Difficulties in clearly defining phonemes may induce an over inclusive categorical response to acoustic stimuli preventing "good" phonological representation of CV syllables. Differences in processing speed within one modality (perhaps the auditory modality) could also alter characteristics of connectivity both within and across modalities (Merzenich, Schreiner, Jenkins, & Wang, 1993). It has been suggested that the slowest sensory system sets the pace for all others in order to facilitate linking of multimodal perceptions (Llinás, 1993).

AN ORGANIC INSTANTIATION
OF MENTAL REPRESENTATION?

Several models have been suggested over the years for how sensory information may be cortically represented. Hebb (1949) was the first to propose a mechanism that could link cognitive and neural functioning. He offered the concept of "cell assemblies" that would continue to fire after environmental stimulation ended—essentially the first neural net model. However, the neurological model most frequently invoked in the infancy field is that of Sokolov (1963), who theorized that as organisms initially orient to a new stimulus in the environment, a cortical representation is gradually constructed, facilitated by continued availability of the stimulus or by stimulus repetition. The neuronal model increases in level and amount of detail preserving information about the stimulus such as intensity, duration, and critical features. Successive presentations prompt re-orienting and continuing comparison of the stimulus with the neuronal model developing in memory. The degree of discrepancy between the current stimulation and the developing cortical representation determines the behavioral outcome. Continued discrepancy or novel input will recruit further orienting and attention; high levels of matching will depress or inhibit the orienting response.

Over the last 25 years, a number of infant researchers, including McCall and Kagan (1970), Lewis, Goldberg, and Campbell (1969), and Cohen (1973) have proposed Sokolov-like models for habituation of visual attention in human infants (See Colombo & Mitchell, 1990 for a review). The comparator model, (described above), adapted from Sokolov's original formulation is the most widely accepted theory, however, none of the currently proposed models provides a perfect fit for the observed infant behavioral responses (Colombo & Mitchell, 1990). Moreover, many infant researchers make no attempt to map such processes onto actual cortical function (but see Diamond, 1990a; Goldman-Rakic, 1987b; Johnson, 1990). This is evident in the neurologically implausible models sometimes proposed. In fact, the neuronal model that Sokolov originally described could not strictly copy external stimulation, because that would rule out conceptual habituation to classes of stimuli (prototypes) (e.g., Caron, Caron & Meyers, 1982; Strauss, 1979). The fact that infants categorize and can match across modalities also casts doubt on any simple match–mismatch theory. Furthermore, such a model does not incorporate features such as each infant's enduring preference for the mother's face and voice or the effects of context (e.g., Butler & Rovee-Collier, 1989) seen very early on in infancy.

NEURAL SUBSTRATES AND STRATEGIES FOR SENSORY REPRESENTATION

At this point it seems appropriate to briefly discuss the current theories and key principles of neuronal representations of sensory information. A general process that occurs in all sensory systems (at many levels of the nervous system) is the spatial or topographic representation of a sensory stimulus in neuronal ensembles. The retinotopic map observed in the primary visual cortex is an elegant example of such topographic representation (Tootell, Silverman, Switkes, & De Valois, 1982). As can be so clearly seen in Fig. 3.6, in primary visual cortex there is a point-for-point mapping of visual space onto neurons across the surface of the visual cortex. Hence, activation of neurons on the two-dimensional surface of the cortex generates the same image shown on the retina. A retinotopic topography can also be visualized with fMRI and MEG (magnetoencephalography) in human cortex as subjects perform simple visual perception tasks, although there is a significant drop in temporal and spatial resolution with such

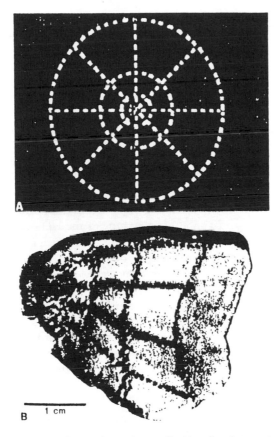

FIG. 3.6.   The visual stimulus used by Tootell et al. (A) and
the pattern of brain activation produced by this stimulus as
revealed by an autoradiograph of area V1 in the macaque
monkey (B). These results illustrate the representation of a
retinotopic map (a point-for-point mapping of visual space)
onto primary visual cortex. From Tootell et al. (1982).
(Copyright © 1982, by the AAAS. Reprinted by permission.

techniques (Fox, Miezin, Allman, Van Essen, & Raichle, 1987; Sereno et al.,
1995; Tootell et al., 1995). Nevertheless, it is clear that there is an organic instantiation or "virtual image" generated in the brain when we see. Similar "sensory
maps" are generated in primary somatic and auditory sensory cortices. Indeed,
these cortical sensory maps are all reminiscent of the motor homunculus or
motor map observed in primary motor cortex.

What is particularly interesting with respect to the cognitive level of sensory
representation is how these sensory maps are generated developmentally and
how they interact. There are two principle means for different sensory modali-

ties to interact in the central nervous system. First, at the cortical level there appears to be a hierarchical processing stream for building progressively more complex sensory maps or representations (Colby & Duhamel, 1991; Goodale & Milner, 1992; Van Essen & Maunsell, 1983). At the apex of these sensory processing streams are the associative cortical areas, where the sensory maps are considerably more complex, so that fewer and fewer neurons represent large portions of the sensory parameter space (e.g., small clusters of neurons can be activated by rather large regions of sensory space such as the entire visual field). Furthermore, the representations become categorical in a psychological sense. Whereas simple sensory organ topography (i.e., retinotopic position, a point-to-point map of what is on the retina) was a principal feature of cortical representation at the primary cortical level, the associative cortex is sensitive to distinct sensory qualities (movement direction, object shape, and color). At this level of sensory processing there is an interesting type of modality convergence. Auditory, somatic, and visual modalities are largely segregated, in that separate neural populations are primarily driven by one modality (Andersen, Asanuma, Essick, & Siegel, 1990; Goldman-Rakic, 1987a; Motter & Mountcastle, 1981). However, a given sensory subregion of associative cortex receives convergent input either from a second modality or from the motor system.

The driving organizing principle for convergence at this level appears to be how we (mammals, primates) interact (e.g., orient toward, track, reach for objects) within the sensory environment (Baizer, Ungerleider, & Desimone, 1991; Goodale & Milner, 1992). Thus in the posterior parietal association cortex one group of visual neurons has a crude retinotopic map as well as an oculomotor map (Andersen, Essick, & Siegel, 1985; Read & Siegel, 1997). The "alignment" or multiplicative interaction of these two maps is computationally sufficient to uniquely identify any location in space (Pouget & Sejenowski, 1996; Salinas & Abbott, 1995; Zipser & Andersen, 1988). A similar phenomenon exists for parietal and premotor cortical neurons which are somatosensory driven (Graziano & Gross, 1994; Graziano, Yap, & Gross, 1994). For instance, these neurons "represent" locations in space via combined sensitivity to direction of movements of the body (limb or head) and directions of visualized movement (Graziano et al., 1994). These representations are dynamic in that as the animal "acts" on the environment (grasps, wave its hand, moves its head) the retinotopic map shifts—operationally this means that the retinotopic and oculomotor or motor maps are updated and realigned constantly (e.g., Duhamel, Colby, & Goldberg, 1992; Graziano et al., 1994). Clearly, this is a level of neural processing at which the cumulative effects of "slowed" speed of encoding could be manifested in infants.

A sizable body of research suggests that the associative cortical centers are not fully developed in human and non-human primates until sometime after the first year of life (for review, see Goldman-Rakic, 1987b). The superior colliculus, however, matures very early and the deep layers (IV–VII) are comprised of largely mutimodal cells that respond to input from two or more sensory modalities. Thus, a given multimodal neuron in this region responds to auditory and visual stimuli which are located within a restricted and common region of space (see Stein & Meredith, 1993). The interactions between and alignments of converging sensory maps on clusters of neurons in the mature deep colliculi are not unlike those observed in the association cortices. In fact, the deep colliculi derive much of their sensory sensitivity from the cortices in the adult animal (Kao, McHaffie, Meredith, & Stein, 1994; Schiller, Stryker, Cynader, & Berman, 1974). In the first year of life, however, the superior colliculi are very likely responsible for integrating much of the incoming intramodality information (Diamond, 1990b; Johnson, 1990; Kao et al., 1994). Furthermore, the mode of sensory integration is quite different at the neuron level in colleculi of the immature animal (Meredith & Stein, 1996).

An interesting developmental consequence of such sensory map alignment is the need for coincident neural activity to establish the proper weighting or relative influence that the converging sensory modalities have on multimodal sensory neurons (Salinas & Abbott, 1995; Stein & Meredith, 1993). Animal studies suggest that normal intermodal sensory map alignment requires coincident experience of the divergent modalities in space and time (Graziano & Gross, 1984; Meredith & Stein, 1996). For example, if the ears are experimentally occluded during early life and subsequently cleared, there is a faulty orienting response to multimodal stimuli, presumably due to inappropriate alignment of auditory and visual sensory maps (Knudsen, 1983). Young human infants apparently rely on a similar intermodal learning principle to develop complex motor pattern representations; hence they bring their hand into their visual field to "practice" movements and conversely, they are less likely to move their hand when it falls outside their field of view (van der Meer, van der Weel, & Lee, 1995). We would like to suggest that the infant techniques we are using provide a means of pinpointing poor intermodal sensory map alignment at this early stage of development.

REPRESENTATIONAL MEMORY

Neural Substrates

Though many neural substrates are involved in the construction of multisensory representations, it appears that the maintenance of sensory images for an extended window of time critically depends upon the function and proper development of prefrontal associative cortex. Goldman-Rakic (1987a, 1987b) hypothesized that the prefrontal cortex is a crucial site for construction and maintenance of multimodal sensory representations for processing time windows of up to 15 seconds. Goldman-Rakic and colleagues have shown, in infant monkeys, that developmentally the ability to perform the Piagetian A not B object permanence task[3] (see Diamond, 1990a, for a review) closely parallels the maturation of the associative cortices, including prefrontal cortex. The neural connections that underlie successful performance on the A not B task are present in the immature form 2 months before birth in the monkey. Thus, it appears that the rudiments of frontal lobe function emerge much earlier than has been generally thought. In contrast, avoidance of the A not B error awaits the period of generation of connections between neurons (synaptogenesis) in the cerebral cortex, an event that occurs postnatally. These changes seem to relate to the emergence of a *mature representational memory*. This discrete window for cortical synaptogenesis is a global phenomenon and it coincides with the 7–12 month developmental shift in human infants during which major progress in function occurs in many areas (Chugani & Phelps, 1986; Johnson, 1990).

Possible Model For Representational Memory In Infants

We would like to suggest that construction of representational memory may also be affected by low level sensory processing deficits (such as an impairment in ATP) via a cumulative processing error leading to inadequate intersensory map alignment. Although prefrontal cortex would be greatly affected by such a processing constraint we would not expect any *selective* impairment of prefrontal cortex over other areas of associative cortex. The observed relations between discrimination of rapidly changing auditory temporal cues and language delays in infants would suggest that the auditory modality is an important contributor to non-linguistic representational memory in infants. Unfortunately, little evidence exist for how simple auditory stimuli let alone complex CV transitions (e.g., /ba/ and /da/) map onto the multimodal sensory regions such as the associative cortices and the superior colliculus (deep nuclei). A tonotopic map exists in the primary auditory cortex in most mammals studied to date including non-human primates (for review see Merzenich & Schreiner, 1991) and there is also considerable evidence for the convergence of auditory perceptual input onto multimodal neurons in the superior colliculus (Stein & Meredith, 1993).

Unfortunately, there has been little work on auditory sensory mapping in associative cortices (however, see Stricanne et al., 1993). Recently, the Schreiner laboratory has been characterizing the topographic layout in primary auditory

---

[3]This is a task of Piagetian object permanence that involves the infant finding an object hidden at one of two locations while they watch. By 7½ to 9 months of age infants are able to find the hidden object in one place (A) if there is no delay between the hiding and retrieval. However, if the object is then hidden at another place (B), infants of this age will often search again at A, even though they have watched it hidden at B. Thus, A not B error. The standard test used in both monkey and human infants uses two covered wells for hiding small toys or treats. Once the infant succeeds on the task, an incremented delay is interposed between hiding of the object and retrieval. Infants will continue to make the A not B error up to about 12 months at the longest delays. See Diamond (1990a) for a review.

cortex for selective responses to simple linguistic elements, including CV transitions such as /ba/ and /da/ (Schreiner, Wong, & Bonham, 1996). It is quite possible that such representations would be laid out (i.e., mapped) onto the appropriate associative cortices according to categorical properties not unlike those for object shape or faces. If this is indeed the case, a problem discriminating one stop consonant from another could be associated with a degraded categorical representation at the cortical level of processing. Kuhl suggests that infants are developing "phonetic bins" in the first year of life, that is, grouping similar sounds together; formation of "prototypes" or best exemplars of acoustic events would allow the infant to partition auditory stimuli into phonetic categories (Kuhl, 1993). Individuals with ATP disorders may generate an aberrant representation, a flawed prototype that is not like those of normal individuals. Presumably, in the normal case, a separate neural population is activated upon hearing the syllable /ba/ versus /da/ (Eggermont, 1995; Schreiner et al., 1998; Steinschneider, Arezzo, & Vaughan, 1990) in the same way that separate cortical columns in the associative cortices are activated when the retinal image is a star versus a circle (Tanaka, 1992). If the critical temporal information regarding the formant transition never reaches the associative cortex then the representation for syllables such as /ba/ and /da/ would be assumed by a common set of neurons. Thus, phonetic partitions might be made based on a different subset of sounds causing difficulties with emerging language and later with reading. In addition, it is critically important to be able to discriminate *within* categories. For example, if infants treat /ba/, /da/, and /pa/ as equivalent, their ability to group sounds into words and sentences as they later develop language will be impaired. In cases of ATP deficits, linguistic performance might be based or depend more heavily on a different set of cues (e.g., context and repetition).

Sensory Representation Versus Representational Memory: Picture or Process?

Over the past 20 years, there has been much debate over the nature of mental representations. One view is that mental representations are held in the mind as veridical images, that they are *depictive* (e.g., Kosslyn, 1994). Others have suggested that mental imges are the result of a series of processes, that they are *propositional* in nature (e.g., Pylyshyn, 1973). We would like to suggest that both are true in a psychological framework and that there are likely neural mechanisms to support both types of mental representations. In the simplest of schemes, one might suggest that a "depictive mental representation" is a "sensory representation" and is carried out primarily by the recombination of sensory cues such as that described above. Conversely, propositional representations may involve a series of neural processing events which culminate in the associative cortices participating in representational memory (e.g., prefrontal cortex). To a degree both cortical levels of processing will be involved in any given sensory experience. One might suggest that the two forms of "mental" and "neural" imagery or representation have characteristically distinct time constants as we have suggested is the case for sensory representation versus representation memory. However, this need not always be the case as both systems are necessarily involved in brief sensory encounters for the normal adult. Indeed the neural cortical substrates for sensory representation and representation memory are to a large degree activated in parallel (though delayed output from cortices such as prefrontal certainly occurs). We would like to suggest that the "depictive versus propositional" or "picture vs. process" debate may be suitably addressed in developmental models such as ours.

An Evolving Model of Neuronally Mediated Representation

How could representation evolve over infancy? And, how might a "flawed" representation affect behavioral outcome? In order to examine such issues in infancy we use a combination of tasks that allow us to examine information processing for rapid temporal transitions (in the tens of ms time frame) as well as steady state processing. We believe that the techniques we use facilitate development of a progressive knowledge of the stimuli; all paradigms repeatedly present the same stimuli over time. (However, we don't know if all infants actually process in this progressive manner. For example, only about 50% of infants habituate in the exponential fashion that such a model would predict [Bornstein & Benasich, 1986]). Nevertheless, our working hypothesis is that a multiply-specified mental representation is gradually built up over the habituation procedure or learned in our ATP tasks. Our testing paradigms as well as more naturalistic experiences permit the infant to make successive approximations of the representation and incorporate multisensory as well as context information. Such a gradually evolving representation would simultaneously facilitate construction of the necessary multimodal sensory maps.

Problems processing temporally-bounded stimuli might be seen as an impairment of the ability to form a comprehensive multimodal representation. The representation is formed over time but development (or moment by moment construction) of such a representation is slowed and constrained by the difficulty in encoding temporal cues. The infant must then use other cues, perhaps repetition and context cues, rather then more direct perceptual information. However, such representations may be flawed (inadequately specified or overly general) slowing down on-line processing even more. This might be expressed as an aberrant prototype of a phonological category (Kuhl, 1993) or by the representation of a series of different phonemes, including the critical CV transition, as the same. Thus, the representation would lack critical features that allow it to be used efficiently for immediate discrimination (short-term recognition) and as a long-term model for language comprehension and production.

If infants with slowed temporal processing are generating impoverished, poorly specified, or misaligned intermodal sensory maps, carefully designed experiments will demonstrate this. A recent study reporting on the effects of subependymal and mild interventricular lesions on visual attention and memory in premature infants found habituation decrement and average number of trials to habituation to be a more sensitive index of subcortical damage than Bayley Scales or an object permanence task (Ross, Tesman, Auld, & Nass, 1992). To test the hypothesis that subcortical insult might specifically impair temporal processing abilities, we are following several clinical populations prospectively, including very low birth weight preterm infants with and without intraventricular hemorrhages (IVH) and infants with focal brain lesions, in order to track the emergence of temporal and multimodal processing abilities. IVH can substantially impact the subcortical regions implicated in rapid temporal processing (e.g., the caudate nucleus, amygdala, and thalamus), and could partially account for the high incidence of language-based learning disorders in VLBW infants with IVH.

CONCLUSIONS AND IMPLICATIONS FOR INTERVENTION

The research discussed here suggests that ATP deficits are present *before* phonological processing deficits, although causality has not yet been established. The data we have collected so far suggests that even in normal, full-term infants a relationship exists between temporal processing efficiency and language in the second year. Studies in our laboratory also suggest that ATP thresholds differ in infants with a family history of LI (Benasich & Tallal, 1996; Spitz et al., 1997). We have found that "speed of processing" or "encoding", is much poorer in infants who are later found to be language delayed. Processing speed is slower in the rapid auditory temporal domain (i.e., tens of milliseconds) as well as for overall acquisition of information (i.e., time in seconds needed for habituation). Thus we have identified infants who are going to be delayed prior to the onset of language.

Preliminary analyses also suggest that poor ATP thresholds in infancy (in the millisecond domain) predicts selectively to language delays whereas slower speed of encoding across all time windows may be associated with more global cognitive and linguistic deficits in childhood. Research (electrophysiological, physiological, and anatomical) tying behaviorally observed deficits in perceiving rapidly presented speech and nonspeech stimuli to neural processes (in adults) suggests that such deficits are likely due to lower level processing deficits that subserve both linguistic and nonlinguistic processes (Galaburda & Livingstone, 1993; Jernigan et al., 1991; Tallal, Jernigan, & Trauner, 1994). In the case of temporal processing within the time window with which we are primarily concerned in our studies (tens of ms), deficits in this very basic level of processing could further constrain "speed of encoding" and construction of detailed, multiply specified representations, as well as formation of linked sensory maps.

Our hypotheses about how our recent research findings could actually map onto brain substrates have been modified over the last several years to reflect the emerging view of the brain as much more plastic and dynamic than previously thought. In particular, the work of Merzenich and colleagues (Merzenich et al., 1993; Recanzone, Schreiner, & Merzenich, 1993) suggests that even in adult (nonhuman) primates cortical maps can be radically altered via environmental/perceptual inputs. Two recent papers directly test this dynamic view of the brain and suggest some exciting implications of the infant research discussed in this chapter (Merzenich et al., 1996; Tallal et al., 1996). These studies were based on the same model of the neurobiology of speech that is outlined here. Basically, that the primary deficit in LI is the inability to discriminate rapid temporal changes in two or more stimuli arriving in the time frame of tens of ms and that this deficit could occur as a result of a defective representation of speech phonetics (Merzenich et al., 1996). Previous studies in animals had shown that neuronal reorganization underlies practice-based improvements in temporal segmentation and discrimination (Merzenich et al., 1993; Recanzone et al., 1993). The Tallal and Merezenich groups constructed an intervention for LI children (5 to 10 years old) based on previous research showing that stretching of the critical CV transitions resulted in an increase in the number of LI children who could then discriminate the phonemes (Tallal & Piercy, 1975). A training program was developed using acoustically modified speech (a computer algorithm stretched out and amplified the CV transitions) paired with adaptive acoustic training (a shaping paradigm) designed to force temporal processing thresholds lower (i.e., faster). Significant improvements in speech discrimination and language outcomes were shown in two independent groups of LI children over a period of just 4 weeks of intensive training (Merzenich et al., 1996; Tallal et al., 1996). The implications of these results for our research are fairly obvious.

We have shown that we can identify those infants who are poor at processing rapid temporal cues. Such infants may greatly benefit from new interventions modeled on those reported above. During early infancy the critical foundations of phonemic perception and later language are being laid down. If the characteristics of the mental representation or "prototype" being formed could be manipulated, infants may be induced to reassemble complete and useful representations, whether they be picture, process or a chimeric hybrid of both. Our notions about how sensory input could be represented and our understanding of the consequences of "flawed" representations on developmental trajectories will continue to evolve as we learn more about how representations can be altered via environmental/perceptual inputs and about the underlying neuronal processes.

ACKNOWLEDGMENTS

The research summarized in this chapter was supported by grant RO1-HD29419 from the National Institute of Child Health and Development to A.A.B. with additional support from the Charles A. Dana Foundation. H.L.R.'s research was supported by grants N00014-93-1-0334 (Office of Naval Research) and NEI 5 R01 9223 (NIH) to R. M. Siegel. We thank Mary Gibbons, Wiveca Ramel, Suganda Khanna, and Romy Spitz for assistance with data collection, data analysis, and manuscript preparation. Thoughtful and constructive feedback on an earlier draft was provided by Gary Byma, James Chrobak, and James Melcher.

REFERENCES

Andersen, R. A., Asanuma, A C., Essick, G K , & Siegel, R. M. (1990). Cortico-cortical connections of anatomically and physiologically defined subdivisions within inferior parietal lobule. *Journal of Comparative Neurology, 296,* 1, 65–113.

Andersen, R. A., Essick, G. K., & Siegel, R. M. (1985). The encoding of spatial location by posterior parietal neurons. *Science, 230,* 456–458.

American Psychiatric Association. (1987). Diagnostic and Statistical Manual of Mental Disorders. 3rd ed. revised. American Psychiatric Association, Washington, DC.

Aslin, R. N. (1989). Discrimination of frequency transitions by human infants. *Journal of the Acoustical Society of America, 86,* (2), 582–590.

Aslin, R. N., Pisoni, D. B., & Jusczyk, P. W. (1983). Auditory development and speech perception in infancy. In M. M. Haith & J. J. Campos (Eds.), P. H. Mussen (Series Ed.), *Handbook of child psychology: Vol. 2. Infancy and developmental psychobiology* (4th ed., pp. 573–688). New York: Wiley.

Baizer, J. S., Ungerleider, L. G., & Desimone, R. (1991). Organization of visual inputs to the inferior temporal and posterior parietal cortex in macaques. *Journal of Neuroscience, 11,* 168–190.

Benasich, A. A., & Bejar, I. I. (1992). The Fagan Test of Infant Intelligence: A critical review. *Journal of Applied Developmental Psychology, 13,* 153–171.

Benasich, A. A., & Spitz, R. V. (1998). Insights from infants: Temporal processing abilities and genetics contribute to language development. In G. Willems & K. Whitmore (Eds.), *Specific Learning Disorders: Neurodevelopmental Approach* (pp. 191–210). London: Mac Keith Press.

Benasich, A. A., & Spitz, R. V. (1996, March). *Relationships among early auditory temporal processing abilities and later language and nonlinguistic correlates of early language.* Paper presented at the Annual Meeting of the Cognitive Neuroscience Society, San Francisco.

Benasich, A. A., Spitz, R. V., Flax, J., & Tallal, P. (1997). *Early auditory temporal processing abilities and later language among children with a family history of language impairment.* Paper presented at the Annual Meeting of the Cognitive Neuroscience Society, Boston.

Benasich, A. A., Spitz, R. V., & Tallal, P. (1995). *Relationships among infant auditory temporal processing, perceptual-cognitive abilities and early language development.* Paper presented at the Annual Meeting of the Cognitive Neuroscience Society, San Francisco, CA.

Benasich, A. A., & Tallal, P. (1996). Auditory temporal processing thresholds, habituation, and recognition memory over the first year. *Infant Behavior and Development, 19,* 339–357.

Best, C. T. (1984). Discovering the messages in the medium: Speech and the prelinguistic infant. In H. E. Fitzgerald, B. Lester, & M. Yogman (Eds.), *Advances in pediatric psychology, Vol. 2,* (pp. 97–145). New York: Plenum.

Bishop, D. V. M., North, T., & Donlan C. (1995). Genetic basis of specific language impairment: Evidence from a twin study. *Developmental Medicine & Child Neurology, 37,* 56–71.

Bornstein, M. H. (1985). Habituation of attention as a measure of visual information processing in human infants: Summary, systematization, and synthesis. In G. Gottlieb & N. A. Krasnegor (Eds.), *Measurement of audition and vision in the first year of postnatal life: A methodological overview* (pp. 253–301). Norwood, NJ: Ablex.

Bornstein, M. H., & Benasich, A. A. (1986). Infant habituation: Assessments of individual differences and short-term reliability at 5 months. *Child Development, 57,* 87–99.

Bornstein, M. H., & Sigman, M. D. (1986). Continuity in mental development from infancy. *Child Development, 57,* 251–274.

Butler, J., & Rovee-Collier, C. (1989). Contextual gating of memory retrieval. *Developmental Psychobiology, 22,* 533–552.

Caron, A. J., Caron, R. F., & Meyers, R. S. (1982). Abstraction of invariant face expressions in infancy. *Child Development, 53,* 1008–1015.

Chugani, H. T., & Phelps, M. E. (1986). Maturational changes in cerebral function in infants determined by ^{18}FDG Positron Emission Tomography. *Science, 231,* 840–843.

Chugani, H. T., Phelps, M. E., & Mazziotta, J. C. (1987). Positron emission tomography study of human brain functional development. *Annals of Neurology, 22,* 487–843.

Cohen, L. B. (1973). A two-process model of infant visual attention. *Merrill-Palmer Quarterly, 19,* 157–180.

Colby, C. L., & Duhamel, J. R. (1991) Heterogeneity of extrastriate visual areas and multiple parietal areas in the macaque monkey. *Neuropsychologia, 29,* 517–537.

Colombo, J., & Mitchell, D. W. (1990). Individual differences in early visual attention: Fixation time and information processing. (pp. 193–227). In J. Colombo & J. Fagen (Eds.), *Individual differences in infancy: Reliability, stability, prediction.* Hillsdale, NJ: Lawrence Erlbaum Inc.

Diamond, A. (1990a). The development and neural bases of memory functions, as indexed by the AB and delayed response tasks, in human infants and infant monkeys. In A. Diamond (Ed.), *The development and neural bases of higher cognitive function, Annals of the New York Academy of Sciences,* (Vol. 608, pp. 267–317). New York: The New York Academy of Sciences.

Diamond, A. (1990b). Development time course in human infants and infant monkeys, and the neural bases, of inhibitory control of reaching. *Annals of the New York Academy of Sciences, 608,* 637–676.

Duhamel, J., Colby, C. L., & Goldberg, M. E. (1992) The updating of the representation of visual space in parietal cortex by intended eye movements. *Science, 255,* 90–92.

Eden, G. F., VanMeter, J. W., Maisog, J. M., Rumsey, J., & Zeffiro, T. A. (1995). Abnormal visual motion processing in dyslexic subjects demonstrated with functional magnetic resonance imaging. *Society for Neuroscience Abstract, 21,* 662.

Eggermont, J. J. (1995). Representation of a voice onset time continuum in primary auditory cortex of the cat. *Journal of the Acoustical Society of America, 98,* 911–920.

Eilers, R. E., Morse, P. A., Gavin, W. J., & Oller, D. K. (1981). Discrimination of voice onset time in infancy. *Journal of the Acoustical Society of America, 70,* 955–965.

Farmer, M. E., & Klein, R. (1995). The evidence for a temporal processing deficit linked to dyslexia: A review. *Psychonomic Bulletin Review, 2,* (4), 460–493.

Fitch, R. H., Tallal, P., Brown, C. P., Galaburda, A. M., & Rosen, G. D. (1994). Induced microgyria and auditory temporal processing in rats: A model for language impairment?, *Cerebral Cortex, 4,* 260–270.

Fox, P. T., Miezin, F. M., Allman, J. M., Van Essen, D. C., & Raichle, M. E. (1987). Retinotopic organization of human visual cortex mapped with positron-emission tomography. *Journal of Neuroscience, 7,* 913–922.

Galaburda, A. M., & Livingstone, M. (1993). Evidence for a magnocellular defect in developmental dyslexia. In P. Tallal, A. M. Galaburda, R. R. Llinás, and C. von Euler (Eds.), *Temporal information* processing in the nervous system: Special reference to dyslexia and dysphasia. *Annals of the New York Academy of Sciences,* Vol. *682* (pp. 70–82). New York: The New York Academy of Sciences.

Galaburda, A. M., Menard, M. T., & Rosen, G. D. (1994). Evidence for aberrant auditory anatomy in developmental dyslexia. *Proceedings of the National Academy of Sciences, USA, 91,* 8010–8013.

Godfrey, J. J., Syrdal-Lasky, A. K., Millay, K. K., & Knox, C. M. (1981). Performance of dyslexic children on speech perception tests. *Journal of Experimental Child Psychology, 32,* 401–424.

Goldman-Rakic, P. S. (1987a). Circuitry of primate prefrontal cortex and regulation of behavior by representational memory. In V. B. Mountcastle, F. Plum, & S. R. Geiger (Eds.), *The Nervous System, Higher Functions of the Brain, Vol. 5, Handbook of Physiology* (pp. 373–417). Washington DC: American Physiological Society.

Goldman-Rakic, P. S. (1987b). Development of cortical circuitry & cognitive function, *Child Development, 58,* 601–622.

Goodale, M. A., & Milner, A. D. (1992). Separate visual pathways for perception and action. *Trends In Neuroscience, 15,* 20–25.

Graziano, M. S. A., & Gross, C. G. (1994). Mapping space with neurons. *Current Directions in Psychological Science, 4,* 164–167.

Graziano, M. S. A., Yap, G. S., & Gross, C. G. (1994) Coding of visual space by premotor neurons. *Science, 266*(5187), 1054–1057.

Hagman, J., Wood, F., Buchsbaum, M., Flowers, L., Katz, W, & Tallal, P. (1992). Cerebral brain metabolism in adult dyslexics assessed with positron emission tomography during performance of an auditory task. *Archives of Neurology, 49,* 734–739.

Hebb, D. O. (1949). The organization of behavior: A neuropsychological theory. New York: Wiley.

Herman A., Fitch, R. H., Galaburda, A. M., & Rosen, G. D. (1995). Induced microgyria and its effects on cell size, cell number, and cell packing density in the medial geniculate nucleus. *Society for Neuroscience Abstracts, 21,* 1711.

Humphreys, P., Kaufmann, W. E., & Galaburda, A. M., (1990). Developmental dyslexia in women: neuropathological findings in three cases. *Annals of Neuroscience, 28,* 727–738.

Jay, M. F., & Sparks, D. L. (1987) Sensorimotor integration in the primate superior colliculus. II. Co-ordinates of auditory signals. *Journal of Neurophysiology, 57,* 35–55.

Jernigan, T., Hesselink, J. R., Sowell, E., & Tallal, P. (1991). Cerebral structure on magnetic resonance imaging in language- and learning-impaired children. *Archives of Neurology, 48,* 539–545.

Johnson, M. H. (1990). Cortical maturation and the development of visual attention in early infancy. *Journal of Cognitive Neuroscience, 2,* 81–95.

Jusczyk, P. W., Smith, L. B., & Murphy, C. (1981). The perceptual classification of speech. *Perception & Psychophysics, 30,* 1, 10–23.

Kao, C. Q., McHaffie, J. G., Meredith, M. A., & Stein, B. E. (1994). Ontogeny of the visual map in the superior colliculus of the cat. *Journal of Neurophysiology, 72,* 266–272.

Knudsen, E. I. (1983) Early auditory experience aligns the auditory map of space in the optic tectum of the barn owl. *Science, 222,* 939–942.

Kosslyn, S. M. (1994). *Image and brain: The resolution of the imagery debate.* Cambridge, MA: MIT Press.

Kuhl, P. K. (1993). Developmental speech perception: Implications for models of language impairment. In P. Tallal, A. M. Galaburda, R. R. Llinás, & C. von Euler (Eds.), *Temporal information processing in the nervous system: Special reference to dyslexia and dysphasia. Annals of the New York Academy of Sciences,* Vol. *682* (pp. 248–263). New York: The New York Academy of Sciences.

Kuhl, P. K., Williams, K. A., Lacerda, F., Stevens, K. N., & Lindblom, B., (1992). Linguistic experience alters phonetic perception in infants by 6 months of age. *Science, 255,* 606–608.

Levitt, H. (1971). Transformed up–down methods in psychoacoustics. *Journal of the Acoustical Society of America, 40,* 467–477.

Lewis, M., Goldberg, S., & Campbell, H. (1969). A developmental study of learning within the first three years: Response decrement to a redundant signal. *Monographs of the Society for Research in Child Development, 34* (9, Serial No. 133).

Livingstone, M. S., Rosen, G. D., Drislane, F. W., & Galaburda, A. M. (1991). Physiological and anatomical evidence for a magnocellular defect in developmental dyslexia. *Proceedings of the National Academy of Sciences, USA, 88*, 7943–7947.

Llinás, R. (1993). Is dyslexia a dyschronia? In P. Tallal, A. M. Galaburda, R. R. Llinás, & C. von Euler (Eds.), *Temporal information processing in the nervous system: Special reference to dyslexia and dysphasia* Annals of the New York Academy of Sciences, Vol. *682* (pp. 48–56). New York: The New York Academy of Sciences.

McCall, R. B., & Kagan, J. (1970). Individual differences in the infant's distribution of attention to stimulus discrepancy. *Developmental Psychology, 2*, 159–170.

McCall, R. B., & Carriger, M. S. (1993). A meta-analysis of infant habituation and recognition memory performance as predictors of later IQ. *Child Development, 64*, 57–79.

Meredith, M. A., & Stein, B. E. (1996). Spatial determinants of multisensory integration in cat superior colliculus neurons. *Journal of Neurophysiology, 75*, 1843–1857.

Merzenich, M. M., Jenkins, W. M., Johnston, P., Schreiner, C., Miller, S. L., & Tallal, P. (1996). Temporal processing deficits of language-learning impaired children ameliorated by training. *Science, 271*, 77–81.

Merzenich, M. M., & Schreiner, C. E. (1991). Mammalian auditory cortex—some comparative observations. In D. B. Webster, R. R. Fay, & A. N. Popper (Eds.), *The Evolutionary Biology of Hearing* (pp. 673–689). New York: Springer-Verlag.

Merzenich, M. M., Schreiner, C. E., Jenkins, W. M., & Wang, X. (1993). Neural mechanisms underlying temporal integration, segmentation, and input sequence representation: Some implications for the origin of learning disabilities. (pp.1–22). In P. Tallal, A. M. Galaburda, R. R. Llinás, & C. von Euler (Eds.), *Temporal information processing in the nervous system: Special reference to Dyslexia and Dysphasia. Annals of the New York Academy of Sciences*, Vol. 682 (pp. 1–22). New York: The New York Academy of Sciences.

Morrongiello, B. A. (1990). The study of individual differences in infants: Auditory processing measures. In J. Colombo & J. Fagen (Eds.), *Individual differences in infancy: Reliability, stability, prediction* (pp. 271–320). Hillsdale, NJ: Lawrence Erlbaum Associates.

Motter, B. C., & Mountcastle, V. B. (1981). The functional properties of the light-sensitive neurons of the posterior parietal cortex. *Journal of Neuroscience, 1*, 3–26.

Pouget, A., & Sejnowski, T. J. (1994). A neural model of the cortical representation of egocentric distance. *Cerebral Cortex, 4*, 314–329.

Pylyshyn, Z. W. (1973). What the mind's eye tells the mind's brain: A critique of mental imagery. *Psychological Bulletin, 80*, 1–24.

Read, H. L., & Siegel, R. M. (1997). Modulation of resposes to optic flow in area 7a by retinotopic and oculomotor cues in monkey. *Cerebral Cortex, 7*, 647–661.

Recanzone, G. H., Schreiner, C. E., & Merzenich, M. M. (1993). Plasticity in the frequency representation of primary auditory cortex following discrimination training in adult owl monkeys. *Journal of Neuroscience, 13*, 87–104.

Reed, M. A. (1989). Speech perception and the discrimination of brief auditory cues in reading disabled children. *Journal of Experimental Child Psychology, 48*, 270–292.

Robinson, R. J. (1987). Introduction and overview. In *Proceedings of the First International Symposium on Specific Speech and Language Disorders in Children* (pp. 1–19). London: AFASIC.

Rose, S. A., Feldman, J. F., Wallace, I. F., & Cohen, P. (1991a). Language: A partial link between infant attention and later intelligence. *Developmental Psychology, 27*, 798–805.

Rose, S. A., Feldman, J. F., Wallace, I. F., & McCarton, C. (1991). Information processing at 1 year: Relation to birth status and developmental outcome during the first 5 years. *Developmental Psychology, 27, 5*, 723–737.

Ross, G., Tesman, J., Auld, P. A., & Nass, R. (1992). Effects of subependymal and mild intraventricular lesions on visual attention and memory in premature infants. *Developmental Psychology, 28, 6*, 1067–1074.

Salinas, E., & Abbott, L. F. (1995). Transfer of coded information from sensory to motor networks. *Journal of Neuroscience, 15* (10), 6461–6474.

Schiller, P. H., Stryker, M., Cynader, M., & Berman, N. (1974). Response characteristics of single cells in the monkey colliculus following ablation or cooling of visual cortex. *Journal of Neurophysiology, 37*, 181–194.

Schreiner, C. E., Wong, S., & Bonham, B. H. (1996). Spatial-temporal representation of syllables in cat primary auditory cortex. In A. R. Palmer, A. Rees, A. Q. Summerfield, & R. Meddis (Eds.), *Psychophysical and physiological advances in hearing* (pp. 529–535). London: Whurr Publishers.

Sereno, M. I., Dale, A. M., Reppas, J. B., Kwong, K. K., Belliveau, J. W., Brady, T. J., Rosen, B. R., & Tootell, R. B. H. (1995). Borders of multiple visual areas in humans revealed by functional magnetic resonance imaging. *Science, 268*, 889–893.

Sigman, M., Cohen, S. E., & Beckwith, L. (1997). Why does infant attention predict adolescent intelligence. *Infant Behavior and Development, 20*, 133–140.

Snowling, M., Goulandris, N., Bowlby, M., & Howell, P. (1986). Segmentation and speech perception in relation to reading skill: A developmental analysis. *Journal of Experimental Child Psychology, 41*, 489–507.

Sokolov, E. N. (1963). Perception and the conditioned reflex. New York: Macmillan.

Spitz, R. V., Tallal, P., Flax, J., & Benasich, A. A. (1997). Look who's talking: A prospective study of familial transmission of language impairments. *Journal of Speech and Language Research, 40*, 990–1001.

Stein, B. E., & Meredith, M. A. (1993). *Merging of the Senses.* Cambridge, MA: MIT Press.

Steinschneider, M., Arezzo, J. C., & Vaughan, H. G. (1990). Tonotopic features of speech-evoked activity in primate auditory cortex. *Brain Research, 519*, 158–168.

Strauss, M. S. (1979). The abstraction of prototypical information by adults and 10-month infants. *Journal of Experimental Psychology: Human Learning and Memory, 5*, 618–635.

Stricanne, B., Mazzoni, P., & Andersen, R. A. (1993). Modulation by the eye position of auditory responses of macaque area LIP in an auditory memory saccade task. *Society of Neuroscience Abstracts, 19*, 26.

Tallal, P. (1988). Developmental language disorders. In J. Kavanagh & T. T. Tarkton (Eds.), *Proceedings of the National Conference on Learning Disabilities* (pp. 181–272). Parkton, MD: York Press.

Tallal, P., Jernigan, T., & Trauner, D. (1994). Developmental bilateral damage to the head of the caudate nuclei: Implications for speech-language pathology. *Journal of Medical Speech Language Pathology, 2*, 23–28.

Tallal, P., Miller, S., Bedi, G., Byma, G., Wang, X., Nagarajan, S. S., Schreiner, C., Jenkins, W. M., & Merzenich, M. M. (1996). Language comprehension in language-learning impaired children improved with acoustically modified speech. *Science, 271*, 81–84.

Tallal, P., & Piercy, M. (1973a). Defects of non-verbal auditory perception in children with developmental aphasia. *Nature, 241*, 468–469.

Tallal, P., & Piercy, M. (1973b). Developmental aphasia: Impaired rate of nonverbal processing as a function of sensory modality. *Neuropsychologia , 11*, 389–398.

Tallal, P., & Piercy, M. (1974). Developmental aphasia: Rate of auditory processing and selective impairment of consonant perception. *Neuropsychologia, 12*, 83–93.

Tallal, P., & Piercy, M. (1975). Developmental aphasia: The perception of brief vowels and extended stop consonants. *Neuropsychologia, 13*, 69–74.

Tallal, Ross, R., & Curtiss, S. (1989). Familial aggregation in specific language impairment, *Journal of Speech and Hearing Disorders, 54*, 167–173.

Tallal, P., Stark, R., & Mellits, D. (1985a). Identification of language impaired children on the basis of rapid perception and production skills. *Brain and Language, 25*, 314–322.

Tallal, P., Stark, R., Mellits, D. (1985b). Relationship between auditory temporal analysis and receptive language development: Evidence from studies of developmental language disorders. *Neuropsychologia, 23* 527–536.

Tallal, P., Townsend, J., Curtiss, J. & Wulfeck, B. (1991). Phenotypic profiles of language impaired children based on genetic/family history, *Brain and Language, 41,* 81–95.

Tallal, P., Wood, F., Buchsbaum, M., Flowers, L., Brown, I., & Katz, W. (1990). Decoupling of PET measured left caudate and cortical metabolism in adult dyslexics. *Society for Neuroscience Abstracts, 16* (2), 1241.

Tamis-LeMonda, C. S., & Bornstein, M. H. (1989). Habituation and maternal encouragement of attention in infancy as predictors of toddler language, play, and representational competence. *Child Development, 60,* 738–751.

Tanaka, A. K. (1992). Inferotemporal cortex and higher visual functions. *Journal of Current Opinions in Neurobiology, 2* (4), 502–505.

Thompson, L. A., Fagan, J. F., & Fulker, D. W. (1991). Longitudinal prediction of specific cognitive abilities from infant novelty preference. *Child Development, 62,* 530–538.

Tootell, R. B. H., Reppas, J. B., Dale, A. M., Look, R. B., Sereno, M. I., Brady, T. J., & Rosen, B. R. (1995). Functional MRI evidence for a visual motion after effect in human cortical area MT/V5. *Nature, 375,* 139–141.

Tootell, R. B. H., Silverman, M. S., Switkes, E., & De Valois, R. L. (1982). Deoxyglucose analysis of retinotopic organization in primate striate cortex. *Science, 218,* 902–904.

Turkewitz, G., & Kenny, P. A. (1982). The role of developmental limitations of sensory input on sensory/perceptual organization. *Journal of Developmental and Behavioral Pediatrics, 6,* 302–306.

van der Meer, A. L. H., van der Weel, F. R., & Lee, D. N. (1995). The functional significance of arm movements in neonates. *Science, 267* (3), 693–695.

Van Essen, D. C., & Maunsell, J. H. R. (1983). Hierarchical organization and functional streams in the visual cortex. *Trends in Neuroscience, 6,* 370–375.

Wang, X., Merzenich, M. M., Beitel, R., & Schreiner, C. E. (1995). Representation of the species-specific vocalization in the primary auditory cortex of the common marmoset: Temporal and spectral characteristics. *Journal of Neurophysiology, 74,* 2685–2706.

Werker, J. F., & Tees, R. C. (1987). Speech perception in severely disabled and average reading children. *Canadian Journal of Psychology, 41,* 48–61.

Withington-Wray, D. J., Binns, K. E., & Keating, M. J. (1990). The maturation of the superior collicular map of auditory space in the guinea pig is disrupted by developmental visual deprivation. *European Journal of Neuroscience, 2,* 682–703.

Wright, B. A., Lombardino, L. J., King, W. M., Puranik, C. S., Leonard, C. M., & Merzenich, M. M. (1997). Deficits in auditory temporal and spectral resolution in language-impaired children. *Nature, 387,* 176–178.

Wurtz, R. H., Goldberg, M. E., & Robinson, M. E. (1992). Behavior modulation of visual responses in the monkey: Stimulus selection for attention and movement. In S. M. Kosselyn & R. A. Andersen (Eds.), *Frontiers in cognitive neuroscience* (pp. 346–365). Cambridge, MA: MIT Press.

Zipser, D., & Andersen R. A. (1988). A back-propagation programmed network that simulates response properties of a subset of posterior parietal neurons. *Nature, 331,* 679–684.

CHAPTER 4

Early Symbolic Representation

JUDY S. DeLOACHE
CATHERINE M. SMITH
University of Illinois

As the introduction and other chapters in this volume make clear, representation has many guises. We focus on one in particular—symbolic representation—and its role in reasoning. The invention of symbols played a vital role in the evolutionary development of mankind, and symbols play a vital role in the ontogenetic development of children. Every human culture has a variety of symbols and symbol systems that support cognition and communication. Children must master a set of culturally important symbols to participate fully in their society. They begin to do so very early, and our interest is in the advent and early course of this crucial domain of development.

As Vygotsky (1978) emphasized, many symbols serve as cognitive tools: They lighten the burden of memory, record events and transactions, facilitate planning, and so forth. Symbols support reasoning and problem solving; the existence of a symbol-referent relation implies that some (but not all) of the characteristics of a symbol will also be true of its referent (and vice versa). Thus, the relation can serve as the basis for drawing inferences. For example, if you see that the town of Mattoon appears on the highway map between St. Louis and Chicago, you can infer that you will encounter it when traveling between the two cities. If a child knows that the number five stands for a larger quantity than the number three, he or she can figure out that an offer of "five candies" is a better deal than an offer of "three candies." We focus on young children's ability to exploit symbols to gain information and solve problems.

Like *representation,* the term *symbol* has been used in many different ways. Thus, it is important at the outset of this chapter to define what we mean by symbols and to delineate what kinds of symbols we discuss. *Symbol* is commonly used to refer to all mental representations, that is, to anything encoded in the mind. The term is also regularly used to refer to a variety of nonmental representations, ranging from language and gestures to symbolic artifacts, such as maps, models, and money. The common element in the various usages is the representation of one entity by a qualitatively different kind of entity. However, there are so many differences among these disparate types of symbols that it is probably counterproductive to lump them all together: Failure to distinguish between, for example, purely mental representations and symbolic artifacts may obscure our understanding of either one (DeLoache, 1995a).

Our concern is with objects and artifacts designed or appropriated for a symbolic function. Our working definition of this type of symbol is *some entity that someone intends to stand for something other than itself* (DeLoache, 1995a). By this definition, virtually anything can be either a symbol or a referent. The heart of a symbol-referent relation is inherently abstract; the necessary and sufficient factor is that some person has stipulated that something is *in some way* to take the place of something else. Note that the stands-for relation does not preclude the existence of other relations among the same entities. They may, for example, also be related by similarity. Highly iconic symbols resemble their referents; the degree of iconicity can vary from that of a lifelike statue or color photograph to that of a simple line drawing or a map. Other symbols are totally noniconic; in no way does a printed word resemble either its referent or the sound of the spoken word.

SYMBOLS AS A SOURCE OF INFORMATION

Many symbols carry information from which inferences can be drawn about their referents. To illustrate the processes involved in using such a symbol, we rely on Fig. 4.1, described by Tufte (1983) as possibly "the best statistical graphic ever drawn" (p. 40). If you are not already familiar with this item, you can easily figure out several things about it. You probably identify it immediately as some kind of map, albeit a fairly unusual kind. This identification draws on your substantial experience with maps, your knowledge about how some landscape features such as rivers are typically represented on maps, and perhaps also your knowledge that Minsk and Moscou are cities. (From your recognition of Minsk, you infer that "Moscou" must be "Moscow.") Looking further, you either can read the caption in French or can figure out that the bottom part of the figure is a representation of temperature. The lines going from the temperature graph into the body of the figure seem to indicate a correspondence between the temperatures shown on the bottom with places represented on the map. You can also read the numbers printed on the body of the map.

At this point, however, you may be stuck. You don't know what the numbers refer to. Without knowing the point of the figure (and without the title normally printed at the top), you are unlikely to be able to figure out what the black and gray bands of varying width stand for, how they are related to temperature, what any of this has to do with Russia, and so on.

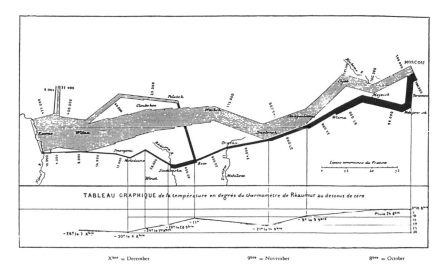

X^bre = December   9bre = November   8bre = October

FIG. 4.1. Example of the difficulty of interpreting a novel symbol-referent relation. From *La Méthode Graphique* (p.73), by E. J. Marey, 1885, Paris.

In fact, this extraordinary graph, drawn by Charles Joseph Minard in 1861, represents Napoleon's ill-fated Russian campaign of 1812. Multiple variables are plotted, including number, space, time, temperature, direction of movement, and geographical features:

> Beginning at the left on the Polish-Russian border near the Niemen River, the thick band shows the size of the army (422,000 men) as it invaded Russia in June 1812. The width of the band indicates the size of the army at each place on the map. In September, the army reached Moscow, which was by then sacked and deserted. The path of Napoleon's retreat from Moscow is depicted by the darker, lower band, which is linked to a temperature scale and dates at the bottom of the chart. It was a bitterly cold winter, and many froze on the march out of Russia. As the graphic shows, the crossing of the Berezine River was a disaster, and the army finally struggled back into Poland with only 10,000 men remaining. Also shown are the movements of auxiliary troops, as they sought to protect the rear and the flank of the advancing army. (Tufte, 1983, p. 40)

We presented this figure to illustrate how difficult it can be to figure out the relation between a novel symbol and its referent. Young children are often in this situation, albeit with less complex representations. Nevertheless, our exercise illustrates the importance of experience and knowledge in symbol-based reasoning. To begin with, you did not, even for a moment, entertain the possibility that Fig. 4.1 could be anything but a representation of something else. Its two-dimensionality alerted you immediately to its symbolic character. For the discoverers of the Rosetta Stone, the problem was figuring out exactly *what* the incisions on its surface meant, not figuring out *that* they meant something.

This immediate apprehension of two-dimensional patterns as representational is learned. Infants do not share it. Nine-month-old infants who are presented with color photographs of objects manually explore them; they pat and rub the images and even attempt to grasp and pick them up (DeLoache, Pierroutsakos, Uttal, Rosengren, & Gottlieb, 1998). After further experience with pictures, infants come to realize exactly how depicted objects differ from real objects. They learn that the function of pictures is to stimulate thought, not action.

To use a symbol, one must know not only that it represents something, but what its referent is. If you don't know what a symbol stands for, you cannot learn anything from it. Another component of symbol use is mapping between symbol and referent. With Fig. 4.1, for example, one must match the elements in the graphic with the places (cities, rivers in Russia), events (battles, river crossings), and so forth, to which they correspond. Finally, using a symbol often involves drawing inferences from it, acquiring new information. Thus, studying Fig. 4.1 can expand one's knowledge about Napoleon's fateful exploits in Russia and the role of weather in his defeat. Symbols make possible the acquisition of knowledge through indirect experience, thus vastly expanding opportunities for learning.

VERY YOUNG CHILDREN'S UNDERSTANDING
AND USE OF SYMBOLS

Our research is concerned with the origins of symbolic functioning. How do very young children decipher the Rosetta Stones of their existence; that is, how do they come to interpret a novel entity in terms of something other than itself? What helps them achieve insight into symbol-referent relations, and what makes it difficult for them to detect such relations?

Investigations with a variety of symbolic media have provided some answers to these questions. At the most general level, our research has revealed that the process of understanding and using even apparently simple symbols is very complex and is influenced by many factors (DeLoache, 1995a, 1995b). As we see later, symbol-referent relations that are transparent to adults and older children are often opaque to young children.

To study the origins of symbol understanding and use, we and our colleagues have designed tasks in which the information to solve a problem must be obtained from a symbol (e.g., a picture, model, map). The prototypical, and most studied, task in this program of research involves a scale model that stands for a room (DeLoache, 1987). In our standard task, the model is highly iconic, that is, similar in appearance to the room except for size (e.g., all the corresponding small and large items of furniture are the same color and texture, and some are even covered with the same fabric). A child watches as a miniature toy is hidden somewhere in the model, and the experimenter says that a similar but larger toy will be hidden in the corresponding place in the room. Thus, on a given trial, the child might observe the experimenter put a small plastic dog (referred to as "Little Snoopy") behind the miniature couch in the model. The child would then be asked to find "Big Snoopy" in the room. Only by understanding something about the model-room (symbol-referent) relation can the child figure out where to search in the room. If he or she realizes that the model and room are related and maps the toy-hiding place relation from one to the other, then it is easy to find the large toy even though the child did not see it being hidden. Finally, on each trial, the child returns to the model to retrieve the toy he or she observed being hidden. Children are always successful on this memory-based retrieval, with performance averaging between 75% and 95% correct.

Two aspects of this task have contributed to the success we have had using it with children as young as 2.5 years of age. First, it requires a minimum of verbal skill on the part of the child: Relatively few instructions are necessary, and the child's response is completely nonverbal and unambiguous. Second, object retrieval games are inherently interesting and highly motivating for very young children, so even toddlers are quite cooperative subjects.

Successful performance in the model task is based on the mental representation of multiple relations. First, the child must have an accessible memory representation of the relation between the miniature toy and its hiding place on each trial. Without representing this concrete spatial relation, it would be impossible to succeed. Second, the relation between model and room must be represented in some form. On the basis of this second relation, the child constructs a third— that between the large toy and its hiding place in the room.

It is the abstract stands-for relation between model and room that stipulates that the observed hiding event in the model has significance for the unseen hiding event in the room. This higher level relation is thus the basis for drawing an inference, for reaching a conclusion about an existing state of affairs based on knowledge of a different situation. What our task asks the young child to do, then, is to construct a mental representation of a reality the child has not experienced; the child must interpret the hiding event in the model to mean that a corresponding situation exists in the room.

Note that it is not necessary to represent all the internal relations among the elements within the spaces. Reasoning from Little Snoopy-in-miniature basket in the model to Big Snoopy-in-large basket in the room does not necessitate knowing the relative spatial positions of all the items of furniture within both spaces. Representing the higher level relation between model and room is not tantamount to representing everything about them.

In numerous studies employing this basic task, a dramatic developmental difference has repeatedly occurred in young children's performance (DeLoache, 1987, 1991; DeLoache, Kolstad, & Anderson, 1991; Dow & Pick, 1992; Marzolf

& DeLoache, 1994). Three-year-olds readily use their knowledge of the hiding place of the miniature toy in the model to infer where to find the larger toy in the room. The rate of errorless retrievals typically ranges between 75% and 90%. Children just 6 months younger give little evidence of appreciating the model-room relation; their typical performance of around 20% correct is at chance. The younger children's failure is not due to an inadequate or inaccessible memory representation; they can retrieve the miniature toy in the model. However, they do not use their memory representation of the hiding event in the model as the basis for constructing a representation of the location of the larger toy in the room.

It is important to note that the younger children understand everything about the task except the crucial model-room relation. They know there is a toy hidden for them to try to find, and they readily search for it. They search relatively systematically, in that, on a given trial, they most often look in the location where the toy had been hidden on the previous trial. Thus, they are motivated, they are paying attention, and they are keeping track of information (just not the right information).

Many questions arise regarding the often replicated difference in performance between 2.5- and 3-year-old children. We focus initially on the older children, considering first the representational underpinnings for their success in the standard task, followed by a discussion of some exceptions to their generally successful performance. We then shift our focus to the 2.5-year-olds, describing two of the most important factors that contribute to their typical failure in the standard model task, as well as some situations in which they succeed. Our consideration of the two age groups separately highlights the complexity of young children's early symbolic functioning.

Older Children's Success

We believe that success in this task is based on a mental representation of the model-room relation and that this representation serves as the basis for drawing an inference from one space to the other. This interpretation is not a logical necessity; it is conceivable, as some have argued (Blades & Spencer, 1994; Lillard, 1993; Perner, 1991), that successful performance in the standard model task could be based on simply detecting the correspondence between the individual objects in the two spaces. By this view, each successful trial involves the mapping of a single relation in one space onto another single relation in the second space. On the first trial, for example, the child maps the Little Snoopy-miniature chair relation in the model onto the Big Snoopy-large chair relation in the room. On the second trial, the child *independently* maps Little Snoopy-tiny pillow onto Big Snoopy-real pillow, and so on.

We see several problems with this account. For one thing, it seems implausible that children would perform a series of local mappings on successive trials, without ever noticing any common relation between them. We do not, however, have to rely solely on plausibility for our argument.

One relevant set of empirical results comes from a study in which 2½-year-olds identified the corresponding items of furniture in the model and room, but nevertheless failed the model task (DeLoache, Troseth, Smith, & Burch, 1995). On each trial, the child was shown an item of "Little Snoopy's" furniture from the model and asked to "find the one in Big Snoopy's room that's just like it." The children readily did so, selecting the correct item 79% of the time. The same children were then administered the standard model task, which they failed (only 21% errorless retrievals). If, as has been claimed, all that is required for success in our model task is the detection of simple correspondences, children who can detect simple correspondences ought to solve the task. They do not; however, awareness of the lower level object correspondences is not enough for mapping from one space to the other.

Another reason to reject the simple correspondence view is that it can account for only a small fraction of the results of the many model studies we have conducted. It could be considered adequate for the original study and a few others; however, it is silent with respect to most of the rest of the experiments that are described later in this chapter (especially those on transfer and dual representation). An account that can deal with only a portion of a large, consistent, and highly replicable set of studies is not an acceptable alternative to an account that explains a diverse set of data and generates novel hypotheses confirmed by empirical tests. Although the simple correspondence view has the appearance of parsimony, it has inadequate explanatory power and hence is ultimately *less* parsimonious.

Representational Basis for Older Children's Success.   We have argued that the higher level model-room relation must be represented in some way for success in our task. Good performance could be based on an explicit representation of the relation that is accessible to conscious reflection, such as an adult would have, or on some inexpressible, implicit sense of relatedness (Zelazo & Frye, 1996). What level of representation supports the successful performance of 3-year-old children in our standard task?

We have conducted three studies trying to answer this question (DeLoache et al., 1995). In the first, we employed a "surprise" procedure that we hoped would elicit revealing verbalizations. A group of 3-year-old children participated in the standard model task, and were, as expected, very successful (88% errorless retrievals). However, on the fourth and sixth of seven trials, the toy was not hidden appropriately in the room; that is, it was not in the place corresponding to where the child had seen the miniature toy being hidden in the model. We were interested in what the children would say when they failed to find the toy where it should have been, specifically, whether their verbalizations would reveal conscious knowledge of the relation between the hiding events in the two spaces.

Three of the eight children said something more or less explicit in response to probes from the experimenter. The following dialogue ensued after Kate failed to find Big Snoopy behind the couch in the room:

E: Is he where he was supposed to be?
S: *No!*
E: Where was he supposed to be?
S: [points to couch]
E: How come?
S: I don't know.
E: Why should he be back there?
S: 'Cause Little Snoopy was there. Let's try it again.

Similarly, in response to the experimenter's question regarding why she thought the toy should have been behind the chair, Caitlin said, "Because the Little Snoopy was behind his chair." Responding to the same question, Katie said, "Because it's the same thing as Little Snoopy." On the last trial, in which the toy was hidden properly, she announced happily, "He was where he was supposed to be!"

The responses of the other five children were not so clear. To the question of where Big Snoopy was supposed to be, Stephanie said, "Back here," pointing to the shelves. When asked why, she shrugged her shoulders, saying, "I don't know." Molly seemed to have the right idea, but had difficulty making it more explicit:

E: How come you knew to look there?
S: Because there's two of 'em.
E: 'Cause why?
S: Because there's two of 'em.

What this study reveals is that successful performance in the standard model task can be based on representations of the model-room relation that are more or less explicit. None of our subjects gave us the sort of verbal response that one would want to call metarepresentation in the usual sense of the term (Perner, 1991). Some of them did say something relatively inarticulate but nevertheless indicative of an explicit awareness of the model-room relation, others made comments suggesting a vague sense of the relation, and a few never verbally expressed any basis for their successful performance. Thus, 3-year-old children represent the model-room relation, and their representation of that relation guides their behavior, but they are very poor at reflecting upon and talking about their knowledge.

In a second study, we reasoned that if children's representation of the model-room relation were relatively explicit, they should recognize how the model and room correspond. As a result, they should be able to identify which of two models corresponds to a room. Three-year-old children were first given experience with the standard model task, and they performed successfully (78%). They returned a day later and were shown a tentlike portable room, introduced as Big Snoopy's room. They were told that "Little Snoopy wants his room to be just like Big Snoopy's." On a series of trials, the children were asked which of two scale models would be better for Little Snoopy. The models varied on two dimensions independently—object similarity and spatial relations (i.e., whether the corresponding items of furniture were in the same relative positions in the two spaces).

The results were clear: The children did not choose systematically; they selected the best model (high similarity, same spatial arrangement) exactly 54% of the time. Thus, 3-year-old children who can exploit the relation between a room and model are not able to select the model that corresponds more closely to a larger space. Because other results suggest that 3-year-old children have some awareness of how model and room are related, it seemed possible that having to compare two whole models, each containing many items within it, was simply too complex. Accordingly, we performed a follow-up study in which we reduced the information load.

Instead of choosing between two full models, another group of 3-year-olds (who had first participated in the standard task) was asked to choose which items of furniture should go in a single model. The child was presented with a model containing only a few elements (pictures on the walls, plastic plant, table, etc.). On each trial, the child was shown two items of furniture from the same category (two chairs, two couches, etc.), but differing in surface appearance. For example, the stimuli for one trial were two miniature couches, one covered with the same fabric as the real couch in the room and the other covered with a different fabric. The child was asked which one would "make Little Snoopy's room just like Big Snoopy's room." In this greatly simplified task, the 3-year-olds were successful; they selected the more similar object 81% of the time. Thus, these children were aware that the objects in the model should resemble those in the room in physical appearance.

These studies suggest that, although 3-year-olds' representation of the model-room relation is functional, it is still somewhat tenuous. Their representation enables them to map from one space to the other, and to make simple judgments about the relation between the spaces, but they have at best limited conscious access to that representation. As Zelazo and Frye (1996) might say, 3-year-olds know the model-room relation, but they do not know that they know it.

Limitations on Older Children's Success. Although the high level of success achieved by 3-year-old children in our standard task has been replicated many times, it is nevertheless relatively fragile. For one thing, it is limited to the standard task in which complete instructions are provided regarding the model-room relation. If the experimenter does not explicitly call attention to the individual object correspondences (miniature couch-large couch, etc.), then 3-year-olds fail to draw an inference from model to room (DeLoache, 1989). In addition, their success depends on a high level of physical similarity between the model and room. When the corresponding objects are dissimilar in surface appearance, 3-year-olds again fail to use the model as a basis for drawing an inference about the room (DeLoache et al., 1991). Children of 3.5 years perform successfully with a low level of object similarity, but it is not until 4 years of age that children exploit the model-room relation without explicit instructions.

Another limitation on 3-year-olds' performance concerns the number of relations they must represent. In the standard task, as we described earlier, the child has to mentally represent two relations (miniature toy-hiding place in model and model-room) and construct a third (large toy-hiding place in room). Marzolf (1994) examined children's ability to carry out a more complex mapping, one in which they had to represent three relations and construct two more. He designed a modified model task in which the toys were always hidden in one of a set of identical hiding places. There were four tiny white boxes in the model and four larger boxes in the room. To know where the toy was hidden on a given trial, the child had to encode the relation between the target box and one or more landmarks. For example, the child might encode that the miniature toy was hidden in "the box sitting on the chair." Thus, to retrieve the larger toy in the room, the child had to represent three relations (toy-box, box-landmark, and model-room) and construct two more (toy-box and box-landmark).

In a series of studies using this multiple-relations task, 3-year-olds performed relatively poorly (ca. 41%). This was in spite of evidence that they had separately encoded all three of the relations. They always searched for the toy in a box, indicating that the toy-box relation was represented. They remembered which box contained the toy in the model (they could retrieve it when asked to do so), showing that they had represented the target box-landmark relation. The children also knew the higher level model-room relation, in that they had previously succeeded in the standard model task (without boxes). The results of these studies thus reveal a limit on the number of relations that 3-year-olds can use in mapping from a symbol to its referent.

Younger Children's Failure

We now turn to the younger subjects in this program of research—the 2.5-year-old children who have repeatedly been unsuccessful in the standard model task. Most children of this age give no evidence of appreciating the model-room relation, and they have proven resistant to a variety of manipulations designed to improve their performance.

Clearly, 2.5-year-old children's failure in our model task does not indicate an absence of symbolic capacity. Not only do they talk and use symbolic gestures (Acredolo & Goodwyn, 1988), but they also engage in meaningful symbolic play. Indeed, most children of this age perform a variety of symbolic substitutions in their play, drafting one object to stand for something other than itself (Leslie, 1987; Lillard, 1993). The child's mental representation of a pencil as an airplane or a block of wood as a boat takes precedence over the real, known identity of those objects. Most important for this discussion, 2.5-year-olds are able to use pictures (DeLoache, 1987; DeLoache & Burns, 1994) and videos (Troseth & DeLoache, 1996) as a source of information in tasks very similar to the model task.

The failure of 2.5-year-olds in model tasks does *not* mean that they are *incapable* of understanding and using scale models. These children can use a model if the level of physical similarity between the two spaces is increased even more than in our standard model task. When the model and the larger space it represents are similar in scale (i.e., the "room" is only twice as big as the model), 2.5-year-olds are quite successful (around 70% errorless retrievals) (DeLoache et al., 1991; Marzolf & DeLoache, 1994). Thus, the frequently replicated failure of 2.5-year-olds in scale model tasks does not reveal an absolute inability to use a model as a source of information; rather, it indicates that representing the relation between a scale model and its referent is challenging for this age group and they manage to do so only under very facilitative conditions.

Why is it so difficult for 2.5-year-olds to succeed in the standard task? We discuss two factors that our research has revealed to be very important.

Dual Representation. An important source of difficulty for very young children in our model task—and in understanding and using symbols in general—is *dual representation* (DeLoache, 1986, 1991, 1995a, 1995b). Symbolic objects and artifacts have a "dual reality" (Gibson, 1979; Gregory, 1970; Potter, 1979; Sigel, 1978). To understand and use a symbol, one must achieve dual representation; that is, one must mentally represent both aspects of its dual reality—its concrete characteristics and its abstract function. For example, one perceives the physical features of a picture, but one also "sees through" the picture to its referent.

It may be particularly difficult for young, inexperienced symbol users to "see through" a scale model, such as those used in our research. To succeed in our task, the child must represent the model both as an object (or set of objects) and at the same time as a symbol for something other than itself. Our models are three-dimensional, complex, interesting, and attractive in their own right, and very young children are inclined to respond to a model in terms of its physical reality, ignoring its symbolic import. The younger the child, the more difficult it is to think about both the concrete model and the abstract stands-for relation between it and the room. They see the symbol itself, but fail to "see through" it to its referent.

The dual representation hypothesis has generated several counterintuitive predictions, all of which have been confirmed. The logic underlying the first two of these studies is that changing the salience of the model as a concrete object should change the difficulty of using it as a symbol. Accordingly, in one study, we tried to *increase* the salience of the model as an object, expecting this to make it more difficult to achieve dual representation. Three-year-old children (the age group that is typically highly successful in the standard model task) were simply given 5 to 10 minutes' experience playing with the model before participating in the standard task. Our reasoning was that interacting with the model in a nonsymbolic mode would make it more difficult to appreciate its symbolic function. As predicted, the performance of the children who had extra experience with the model was poorer (only 44%) than the typical level (around 80%) for 3-year-olds.

In another study, we did the opposite: We tried to *decrease* the salience of the model as an object, a manipulation hypothesized to make dual representation easier. Although this prediction reasonably follows both from our concept of dual representation and Sigel's (1970) concept of distancing, it is otherwise counterintuitive. The subjects this time were 2.5-year-olds, the age group that typically fails the standard model task. To effect this reduction in the model's salience as an object, we placed it behind a window in a puppet theater. Neither the child nor the experimenter ever touched the model or its contents; the experimenter simply pointed to the appropriate place in the model, saying, "This is where Snoopy's hiding in his room." As predicted, distancing the model from the child led to improved performance: The 50% errorless retrievals of the 2.5-year-olds in the window condition was better than the 20% typically achieved by children of the same age in the standard model task.

As these two studies show, increased physical access to the model makes children less able to represent its relation to something other than itself, whereas physically separating children from the model makes them more able to do so. Physical distance from the model apparently helps young children achieve psychological distance (Sigel, 1970) from it, enabling them to detect its symbolic role.

According to the logic followed here, it should be easier for young children to achieve dual representation with a symbol that is naturally less salient as an object than a model. Pictures are not very interesting or salient as objects, so a series of studies was performed using pictures instead of a scale model to communicate the location of a hidden object (DeLoache, 1987, 1991; DeLoache & Burns, 1994; Marzolf & DeLoache, 1994). In all of them, the experimenter pointed to the relevant picture or part of a picture and said, "This is where Snoopy's hiding in the room." The prediction of better performance with pictures is counterintuitive in that pictures generally provide less effective support than three-dimensional objects for learning, memory, categorization, and other cognitive activities (e.g., Daehler, Lonardo, & Bukatko, 1979; DeLoache, 1986; Sigel, Anderson, & Shapiro, 1966).

Figure 4.2 shows the results of four studies in which the performance of 2.5-year-olds was compared in the standard scale model task versus various picture

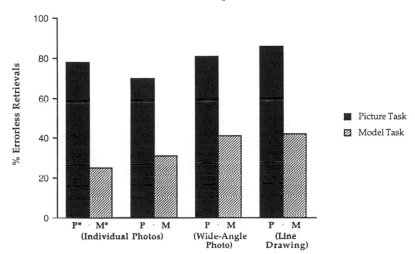

FIG. 4.2. The picture-superiority effect: 2.5-year-old children are more successful in tasks in which information about the location of a hidden object is provided by pictures than by a scale model.

tasks. As the figure shows, the children always performed better with pictures (70% to 85%) than they did with a scale model (15% to 25%). Thus, very young children who fail to use a three-dimensional scale model as a source of information successfully get the same information from pictures.

The dual representation hypothesis has therefore received very strong support from a series of predicted, but counterintuitive, results: Young children who had no experience with the experimental materials were more successful than children who had manipulated them, greater psychological distance (Sigel, 1970) between two entities helped young children detect the relation between them, and two-dimensional stimuli produced better performance than did three-dimensional stimuli.

The most stringent test of dual representation involved an even more counterintuitive prediction: If 2.5-year-old children could be convinced that a shrinking machine had shrunk a room (into the scale model), then they should be able to transfer what they know about the room to the model (DeLoache, Miller, & Rosengren, 1997). Our reasoning was that if children believe that the model *is* the room, then there is no symbolic relation between them. Hence, dual representation is not required, and retrieving the miniature toy from the model involves only remembering the location of the large toy in the room.

Each 2.5-year-old in this study was first shown "Terry the Troll" and "Terry's room" (the portable room), and then the powers of the "shrinking machine" were demonstrated. The troll was placed in front of the shrinking machine (which looks suspiciously like an oscilloscope to naive adults). The machine was "turned on," and the child and experimenter retired to an adjoining area, where they heard what was described as the "sounds the shrinking machine makes while it's working." When the child returned to the lab, a miniature troll sat in front of the machine. Figure 4.3 shows the troll before and after the shrinking event. As can be seen, the shrinking machine had a dramatic effect.

The child was then shown that the machine could also make the troll "get big again." A demonstration of the power of the machine to shrink and enlarge Terry's room followed. The sight of the small model sitting in the middle of the large space previously occupied by the portable room was very striking.

All the children but one were judged by the experimenters and parents alike to have completely accepted the shrinking room scenario. Of course, all of them probably also believe in the tooth fairy!

The child then watched as the experimenter hid the larger troll somewhere in the portable room. After waiting for the machine to shrink the room, the child was asked to "find Terry." (The miniature troll was, of course, hidden in the same place in the model as the larger troll had been in the room.) Thus, just as in the standard model task, the child had to use his or her memory representation of where the toy was hidden in one space to guide searching in the other.

Figure 4.4 shows the performance of the 2.5-year-olds in the nonsymbolic, shrinking room task and that of another group in a control task with the usual

FIG. 4.3.   Terry the Troll in front of the shrinking machine, before and after the shrinking event.

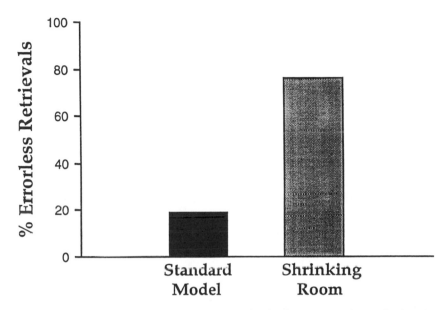

FIG. 4.4.   Retrieval performance of 2.5-year-olds in the shrinking room and control tasks. The children successfully retrieved the toy when they thought the model and room were the same thing, but not when the model was a symbol for the room.

symbolic relation between the model and room. As predicted, performance was significantly better in the nonsymbolic (76%) than in the symbolic task (19%).

Note that the superior score in the shrinking room task occurred even though the delay between the hiding event and the child's retrieval was much longer than in the standard model task. Indeed, the 2½-year-olds' performance was better than that of older children, in that a long delay between the hiding event in the model and the opportunity to search in the room has a pronounced detrimental effect on 3-year-old children's level of success in the standard, symbolic model task (Uttal, Schreiber, & DeLoache, 1996). The children in the shrinking room task behaved like children of the same age and younger in memory studies, in which long delays between a hiding event and the opportunity to search have little negative impact on memory-based retrievals (e.g., DeLoache & Brown, 1983).

The shrinking room study demonstrates that it is the nature of their mental representation of the relation between two entities that determines young children's ability to reason between them. Young children readily represent a nonsymbolic, identity relation, for which dual representation is unnecessary, and draw an inference from one entity to the other. They fail to represent a symbolic relation between the same entities, for which dual representation is required, and hence they fail to apply what they know about one to the other. This study thus provides very strong support for the dual representation hypothesis.

A Matter of Experience.   A second factor that contributes to the poor performance of 2.5-year-olds in the standard task is their relative lack of symbolic experience. The younger a child is, the less experience he or she has had with symbols. We think that through experience with a variety of symbolic representations (including the symbol-referent relations that they themselves create in play), young children develop a general symbolic sensitivity, a readiness to consider a novel entity as a representation of something other than itself. During the second and third year of life, many very young children in our society have a great deal of experience with pictorial stimuli in picture books, as well as television and movies. They are also exposed to the medium of print; they gradually realize that the marks on the pages of books mean something, and then start learning to identify and to recite letters of the alphabet, although initially without understanding what they stand for (Treiman, Tincoff, & Richmond-Welty, 1996). Young children also begin to learn number words and to count (Gelman & Gallistel, 1978). Our view is that this cumulative experience with entities that are to be interpreted in terms of what they stand for leads to a general inclination to consider the possibility that some new entity may also have symbolic status.

Direct evidence for this view comes from a series of transfer studies within our general paradigm. Several such studies have been successfully conducted (Marzolf & DeLoache, 1994), but we discuss only our most recent one here (Marzolf, Pacha, & DeLoache, 1996). This study was designed to see if 2.5-year-old children who had successful experience in a relatively easy symbolic task would subsequently succeed on a more difficult task that they would otherwise fail. Our reasoning was that prior experience using one model as a symbol would make children more likely to realize that a different model should be interpreted in the same way. In this study, we explored whether such transfer could occur in the absence of any contextual support.

A group of 2.5-year-old children was tested in the relatively easy similar-scale model task (DeLoache et al., 1991; Marzolf & DeLoache, 1994); as expected, they were reasonably successful (63%). A week later, the same children were again tested, this time in our standard model task. To see if transfer could occur with no supportive context, everything but the basic elements of the task differed from the children's first visit to the second. Thus, not only were different model-room arrangements used, but on the two occasions the children were tested in two different buildings by different experimenters using two different pairs of toys (Snoopys and trolls). The only thing that was common across the 2 days was the need to use their memory for a hiding event in a model to know where to search for a toy in a larger space. A control group received the more difficult, standard model task both days; for them, all the contextual factors (labs, experimenters, toys) were the same both times.

Figure 4.5 shows the results of this study. As is clear from the figure, substantial evidence of transfer was found. The transfer group, which was successful on the easy task on the first day, also performed well on the more difficult transfer

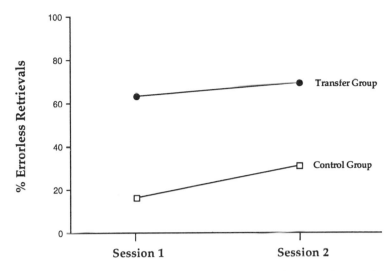

FIG. 4.5.   Retrieval performance of 2.5-year-olds in a transfer study. The Transfer group participated in the similar-scale model task in one context in the first session and in the standard (different-scale) model task in the second session a week later. The Control group participated in the standard task in the same context in both sessions separated by only 1 day.

task (that their age group normally fails) on the second day. The control group performed poorly on both days.

This study, along with several other transfer studies (summarized in De-Loache, 1995a), establishes that experience with a symbol-referent relation they understand helps children detect and exploit a less obvious symbolic relation they would otherwise not appreciate. The study described here makes it clear that this transfer occurs at a relatively high level: Prior symbolic experience helps young children perform in a model task when the only thing in common between the training and transfer tasks is the fact that a scale model is to be interpreted as a source of information about another larger space. The series of transfer studies supports the suggestion that cumulative experience with a variety of different symbols makes children increasingly sensitive to symbol-referent relations (Marzolf & DeLoache, 1994). Like the discoverers of the Rosetta Stone who drew on their lifetime of symbolic experience to identify its symbolic nature, our subjects drew on their prior experience in our lab to detect the representational nature of a novel entity.

IMPLICATIONS FOR THE USE OF SYMBOLIC OBJECTS WITH YOUNG CHILDREN

The research described previously, and especially the concept of dual representation, has clear implications for a variety of situations in which young children are required to use symbols. It is relevant, for example, to the common educational practice of using three-dimensional materials, *manipulatives,* to teach mathematical concepts to young children in school. The assumption is too often made that the relation between the object symbols (e.g., blocks of varying sizes) and the concepts they are intended to represent (e.g., different numerical quantities) will be obvious or easily understood (Uttal, Scudder, & DeLoache, 1997). Not surprisingly, there is evidence that the point of such manipulatives often eludes children (e.g., Friedman, 1978; Sowell, 1989).

Another domain for which our research has important implications is the common practice of using dolls to interview young children in investigations of suspected sexual abuse. The research described earlier suggests that it would be worthwhile to examine the conceptual and empirical basis for this widespread practice in which children are essentially asked to use dolls to represent themselves.

Dolls as Self-Representations

Investigating allegations of child sexual abuse is a difficult task. Often, critical information must be obtained from a child who may have trouble talking about his or her experience for a variety of reasons. Anatomically detailed dolls are consistently recommended as tools to help suspected abuse victims express themselves (Everson & Boat, 1994). They are especially recommended for use with very young children, that is, children below the age of 3 or 4 years, in an attempt to circumvent their limited vocabulary and verbal skills (Kendall-Tackett & Watson, 1992; Yates & Terr, 1988). Surveys of professionals, such as mental health workers and law enforcement officers, have found that a large proportion of them do use dolls in this type of investigation, frequently asking children to use dolls to "show what happened" to them (Boat & Everson, 1988; Conte, Sorenson, Fogarty, & Rosa, 1991: Kendall-Tackett & Watson, 1992).

Underlying this practice is the assumption that using dolls to reenact personal experience is easy for young children. This assumption is presumably based on the fact that by 2 years of age children engage in meaningful and recognizable pretend play with dolls (Belsky & Most, 1981; Corrigan, 1987; Fenson & Ramsay, 1980; Watson & Fischer, 1977).

However, in forensic or clinical doll interviews, children are generally asked to use dolls in a very specific way—as representations for themselves. They must be able to interpret a doll as standing for themselves, and they must also be able to map particular parts of their own bodies onto the corresponding parts of the doll (e.g., their own genitalia and those of the anatomically detailed doll). These requirements are much like those faced by children in the research described earlier on children's use of scale models. In each case, in order to successfully use the symbol, children must take one thing as a representation of another (i.e., dolls for themselves, or a scale model for a room) and must map between them. Given previous demonstrations of very young children's difficulty with symbols that seem transparent to adults and older children, it is possible that they might have similar difficulty using dolls to represent themselves.

Studies of the effectiveness of dolls in interviews of young children have suggested that they may not be of benefit to 3-year-old (or younger) children (Ceci & Bruck, 1993; DeLoache & Marzolf, 1995; Goodman & Aman, 1990; Gordon, Ornstein, Nida, Follmer, Crenshaw, & Albert, 1993; but see Leventhal, Hamilton, Rekedal, Tebano-Micci, & Eyster, 1989). In an attempt to have a good analog of actual abuse interviews, some researchers have interviewed children about pediatric exams, which sometimes involve fear, pain, and genital touching (Ceci & Bruck, 1993; Gordon et al., 1993). For example, Gordon et al. interviewed 3- and 5-year-old children about a routine physical examination by their pediatrician that included elements such as measuring height and weight, checking ears, listening to the chest, obtaining a blood sample, and checking the child's genitalia. One group of children was asked to "show what happened" to them with a doll; another group was interviewed in a verbal condition with no dolls present. The 5-year-olds who were interviewed with dolls recalled more than those interviewed without dolls. However, the 3-year-olds interviewed with dolls did not report more than their agemates in the verbal-only condition. These results are consistent with those reported in other studies of young children (Ceci & Bruck, 1993; DeLoache & Marzolf, 1995; Goodman & Aman, 1990): Children 3 years and younger do *not* provide more information when interviewed with dolls than when dolls are not used.

In a recent study in our lab, designed as a different sort of analog to a typical abuse situation, 3- to 5-year-old children were interviewed about instances in which someone had done something to them at their preschool that had upset them. For example, one child was interviewed about being hit on the head with a block, another about getting a bloody nose after being punched. Written descriptions of the events were provided by the children's teachers. One or 2 days after each incident, a female experimenter interviewed the child involved. Half the children of each gender were encouraged to use dolls to act out the event. In each case, the dolls used were matched to the gender and race of the participants in the altercation. The other half of the children were simply questioned about the event with no dolls present. The results of this study mirrored those found in previous research. The amount of information provided by children in the doll condition was no different from that provided by children interviewed without dolls. Thus, the presence of dolls did not facilitate the children's memory reports of an emotionally upsetting experience in their everyday lives.

Why don't dolls help very young children? Smith (1995) hypothesized that the fundamental requirement of a doll-based interview—the ability to use a doll to specifically represent oneself—may not be within children's capabilities at 2.5 or 3 years of age. To isolate the issue of representational competence, a task was designed that required children to map from themselves to a doll, as is the case in an interview, but that minimized all other factors, such as memory demands and emotional strain. Children between the ages of 2.5 and 3.5 years were introduced to a clothed anatomically detailed doll that matched their race and gender. The experimenter described the doll as "like you in a lot of ways," and to emphasize this similarity, she named four locations (e.g., nose, foot, hair, shoulder) one at a time and asked the child to point to each location on him- or herself and on the doll. Children were highly successful at identifying the named body parts on both themselves and the doll (96% correct).

A book was then introduced that contained four pairs of matching large and small stickers. The experimenter explained that she would place a sticker on the child, and that the child should then place a sticker on the doll in "just the same place as the big sticker is on you." For example, after placing the bear sticker on the child, the experimenter said, "The big teddy bear is right here on you (pointing to the sticker). Your job is to put the little bear on the doll in just the same place as the big bear is on you right now." The children were thus asked to use the (unnamed) location of a large sticker on themselves to guide their placement of a similar but smaller sticker in the corresponding location on a doll. The stickers, presented one pair at a time, were placed in innocuous locations (foot, knee, stomach, upper arm) and were removed from both child and doll after each trial. Coding was liberal and ignored left–right reversals.

Performance was surprisingly poor given the extreme simplicity of the task and the relative sophistication of children this age with dolls in pretend play. In fact, these 2.5- to 3.5-year-olds made only 62% correct placements on the doll. This suggests that children between the ages of 2.5 and 3.5 years have some difficulty mapping between themselves and a doll.

Although statistically above chance, 62% correct performance on this simple task is disconcerting given the outcomes often based, at least in part, on children's behaviors with dolls in clinical or forensic settings (e.g., removal of the child from his or her home, criminal charges against the suspected abuser). Children's difficulty with this task suggests one should not place too much confidence in any individual behavior with a doll in an actual interview of a child in this age range, especially in light of the additional memory demands and emotional strain involved in forensic situations.

This should not be taken to suggest, however, that dolls could never be useful in interviews of young children. In the work reviewed earlier (Ceci & Bruck, 1993; Goodman & Aman, 1990; Gordon et al., 1993), dolls were found to improve 5-year-olds' memory reports. In our work, 4-year-olds who were asked to perform the sticker-placement task were highly successful mapping between themselves and a doll, with 97% correct sticker placements. This suggests that children do soon develop the representational competence with dolls that is one component of a successful doll interview.

Why do very young children have difficulty using a doll to represent themselves? One possibility is that they have trouble reasoning about dolls. However, when 2.5- to 3.5-year-old children were asked to perform the corresponding-sticker task from one doll to another doll, their performance was excellent (94%). This was true whether the children were asked to work with two similarly sized dolls or two that differed in size. Whether the experimenter placed the large sticker on a standard-size or a child size doll, children were highly successful at placing a small sticker in the corresponding location on a standard-size doll. Thus, the children's poor performance in the original study is not due to problems with dolls per se.

Another possible explanation for children's poor performance in using a doll as a representation for themselves is some specific difficulty reasoning about themselves. However, when the experimenter placed the large sticker on herself and 2.5- to 3.5-year-old children were asked to place the small sticker on themselves, their performance was quite good (86% correct placements).

Thus, children have difficulty mapping between themselves and a doll, but they are successful at reasoning between one doll and another or another person and themselves. One way to classify the difference between cases where 2.5- to 3 5-year-old children were successful and cases where they were not is whether or not different categories were involved. Children were successful reasoning between two instances from the same category, whether dolls or people. However, when asked to reason between two different categories—a doll and a person—they found the task much more difficult.

Two further studies have produced the same pattern. In one study, we asked children to place a sticker on a doll corresponding to the location of a large sticker on *another* child. Thus, the task was the same as that in the original experiment (child to doll), except that the children were not asked to reason about themselves. Performance on this task averaged 56% correct. In another study, children were asked to place a sticker on a picture (a color drawing of the doll) in the location that corresponded to that of a sticker placed on them by the experimenter. Children's performance in this child-to-picture task was again poor (55% correct placements).

Figure 4.6 summarizes the results of this series of studies. In three cases where children were asked to reason between two entities of different kinds (self-to-doll, other child-to-doll, and self-to-picture), they had marked difficulty. In contrast, in cases where children were reasoning between two entities of the same kind, either two people (86% correct) or two dolls (94% correct), their performance was much better. Thus children's difficulty in the original self-to-doll task may well have been a result of being asked to map between two different *kinds* of things.

Very young children's difficulty in placing a sticker on a doll to correspond to the location of a sticker on themselves has clear implications for the use of dolls in directed forensic or clinical interviews. Before the age of 4, children have difficulty with an extremely simple task that makes the same representational demands but minimizes all other requirements. In a forensic interview not only

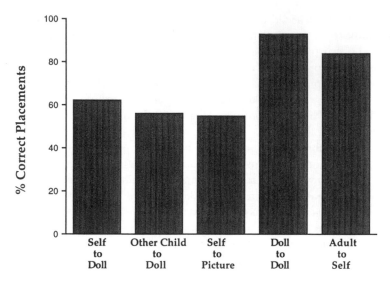

FIG. 4.6.   The performance of 2.5-year-old children in a series of studies of their use of self-representations.

are children faced with this representational demand, but also with remember-ing their experience and dealing with emotional strain on themselves and oth-ers. Thus, the use of dolls for very young children to "show what happened" to them should be viewed with caution.

CONCLUSION

The representational ability that most distinguishes humans from other species is our capacity for creating, understanding, and using symbols. Symbolic repre-sentation contributes to or underlies many of the other forms of representation discussed in this volume.

Because adults are so well practiced and facile with a multitude of symbols, the magnitude of the developmental task facing young children in this domain often goes unappreciated. When adults encounter novel symbols, as in the two examples we used here (the Rosetta Stone and Minard's remarkably informative graph of Napoleon's campaign), they bring to bear a wealth of experience and knowledge. They can immediately identify *that* some novel entity is a symbol, even if they do not know *what* it represents or *how* it represents it. As the re-search summarized here shows, young children can have difficulty with any of these components—the *that, what,* or *how*—of symbol use. We have emphasized the representational demands of symbol use. To fully exploit any symbol, even a highly iconic one, one must mentally represent the higher order relation between symbol and referent. Representing that relation involves some cognitive load; as a result, detecting and using a given symbol-referent relation may exceed the cognitive capacity of a given age group of children in a given situation.

The development of early symbol understanding and use involves several factors. First, a certain level of cognitive capacity is required. For example, for dual representation, the child must be able to have two mental representations active at the same time and draw inferences based on the relation between them. Children's functional capacity expands in part as a result of symbolic experience. Second, symbol use (and dual representation) requires cognitive flexibility in that a given entity must be thought about in two different ways. Third, as a function of their symbolic experience, young children acquire conceptual knowledge about symbols. They come to understand that there are many entities whose importance derives from what they stand for, not what they themselves are. The more experience children have with entities of this type, the more readily they identify novel instances of the same class. Finally, the development of symbolization involves increasingly conscious control over children's representational functioning. Eventually, children have explicit, accessible representations of symbol-referent relations, and they can reflect upon these representations. Our emphasis on cognitive flexibility and conscious representation is consistent with Zelazo and Frye's (1996) cognitive complexity and control theory.

In closing, we return to the practical implications of the research reviewed in this chapter. As our review makes clear, materials for use with young children should not be designed or implemented on the assumption that symbol-referent relations that are transparent to adults will be equally obvious to young children. As we have shown, assumptions of this sort are often misplaced. Such materials should instead be designed taking into account the nature of the symbol itself, the cognitive capacities of the potential symbol user, and the context in which it is to be used.

ACKNOWLEDGMENTS

Preparation of this manuscript was supported in part by Grant HD-25271 from the National Institute for Child Health and Human Development. The chapter was completed while the first author was a Fellow at the Center for Advanced Study in the Behavioral Sciences with financial support from the John D. and Catherine T. MacArthur Foundation Grant 95-32005-0. The authors thank Hallie Sturdyvin for her invaluable assistance with some of the research described here, and Kathy Anderson, Sophia Pierroutsakos, and Georgene Troseth for helpful comments on the chapter.

REFERENCES

Acredolo, L., & Goodwyn, S. (1988). Symbolic gesturing in normal infants. *Child Development, 28,* 40–49.

Belsky, J., & Most, R. K. (1981). From exploration to play: A cross-sectional study of infant free play behavior. *Developmental Psychology, 17*(5), 630–639.

Blades, M., & Spencer, C. (1994). The development of children's ability to use spatial representations. In H. W. Reese (Ed.), *Advances in child development and behavior* (pp. 157–199). San Diego: Academic Press.

Boat, B. W., & Everson, M. D. (1988). Use of anatomical dolls among professionals in sexual abuse evaluations. *Child Abuse & Neglect, 12,* 171–179.

Ceci, S. J., & Bruck, M. (1993). Child witnesses: Translating research into policy. *Social Policy Report: Society for Research in Child Development, 7*(3), 1–30.

Conte, J. R., Sorenson, E., Fogarty, L., & Rosa, J. (1991). Evaluating children's reports of sexual abuse: Results from a survey of professionals. *American Journal of Orthopsychiatry, 61*(3), 428–437.

Corrigan, R. (1987). A developmental sequence of actor-object pretend play in young children. *Merrill–Palmer Quarterly, 33*(1), 87–106.

Daehler, M., Lonardo, R., & Bukatko, D. (1979). Matching and equivalence judgments in very young children. *Child Development, 50*(1), 170–179.

DeLoache, J. S. (1986). Memory in very young children: Exploitation of cues to the location of a hidden object. *Cognitive Development, 1,* 123–137.

DeLoache, J. S. (1987). Rapid change in the symbolic functioning of very young children. *Science, 238,* 1556–1557.

DeLoache, J. S. (1989). Young children's understanding of the correspondence between a scale model and a larger space. *Cognitive Development, 4,* 121–139.

DeLoache, J. S. (1991). Symbolic functioning in very young children: Understanding of pictures and models. *Child Development, 62,* 736–752.

DeLoache, J. S. (1995a). Early symbolic understanding and use. In D. Medin (Ed.), *The psychology of learning and motivation* (Vol. 33, pp. 65–114). New York: Academic Press.

DeLoache, J. S. (1995b). Early understanding and use of symbols. *Current Directions in Psychological Science, 4,* 109–113.

DeLoache, J. S., & Brown, A. L. (1983). Very young children's memory for the location of objects in a large scale environment. *Child Development, 54,* 888–897.

DeLoache, J. S., & Burns, N. M. (1994). Early understanding of the representational function of pictures. *Cognition, 52,* 83–110.

DeLoache, J. S., Kolstad, D. V., & Anderson, K. N. (1991). Physical similarity and young children's understanding of scale models. *Child Development, 62,* 111–126.

DeLoache, J. S., & Marzolf, D. P. (1995). The use of dolls to interview young children: Issues of symbolic representation. *Journal of Experimental Child Psychology, 65*(1), 155–173.

DeLoache, J. S., Miller, K. F., & Rosengren, K. (1997). The credible shrinking room: Very young children's performance in symbolic and non-symbolic tasks. *Psychological Science, 8,* 308–313.

DeLoache, J. S., Pierroutsakos, S., Uttal, D. H., Rosengren, K., & Gottlieb, A. (1998). Grasping the nature of pictures. *Psychological Science, 9,* 205–210.

DeLoache, J. S., Troseth, G. L., Smith, C. M., & Burch, S. (1995). [Young children's awareness of model-room relations]. Unpublished raw data.

Dow, G. A., & Pick, H. L. (1992). Young children's use of models and photographs as spatial representations. *Cognitive Development, 7,* 351–363.

Everson, M. D., & Boat, B. W. (1994). Putting the anatomical doll controversy in perspective: An examination of the major uses and criticisms of the dolls in child sexual abuse evaluations. *Child Abuse & Neglect, 18*(2), 113–129.

Fenson, L., & Ramsay, D. S. (1980). Decentration and integration of the child's play in the second year. *Child Development, 51*, 171–178.

Friedman, M. (1978). The manipulative materials strategy: The latest pied piper? *Journal for Research in Mathematics Education, 9*, 78–80.

Gelman, R., & Gallistel, C. R. (1978). *The child's understanding of number.* Cambridge, MA: Harvard University Press.

Gibson, J. J. (1979). *The ecological approach to visual perception.* Boston: Houghton Mifflin.

Goodman, G. S., & Aman, C. (1990). Children's use of anatomically detailed dolls to recount an event. *Child Development, 61*, 1859–1871.

Gordon, B. N., Ornstein, P. A., Nida, R. E., Follmer, A., Crenshaw, M. C., & Albert, G. (1993). Does the use of dolls facilitate children's memory of visits to the doctor? *Applied Cognitive Psychology, 7*, 459–474.

Gregory, R. L. (1970). *The intelligent eye.* New York: McGraw-Hill.

Kendall-Tackett, K. A., & Watson, M. W. (1992). Use of anatomical dolls by Boston-area professionals. *Child Abuse & Neglect, 16*, 423–428.

Leslie, A. M. (1987). Pretense and representation: The origins of "theory of mind." *Psychological Review, 94*(4), 412–426.

Leventhal, J. M., Hamilton, J., Rekedal, S., Tebano-Micci, A., & Eyster, C. (1989). Anatomically correct dolls used in interviews of young children suspected of having been sexually abused. *Pediatrics, 84*(5), 900–906.

Lillard, A. S. (1993). Pretend play skills and the child's theory of mind. *Child Development, 64*, 348–371.

Marey, E. J. (1885). *La méthode graphique.* Paris.

Marzolf, D. P. (1994, June). *Remembering and mapping relations in a symbolic task.* Poster presented at the International Conference for Infant Studies, Paris.

Marzolf, D. P., & DeLoache, J. S. (1994). Transfer in young children's understanding of spatial representations. *Child Development, 64*, 1–15.

Marzolf, D. P., Pacha, P., & DeLoache, J. S. (1996, April). *Transfer of a symbolic relation by young children.* Poster presented at the biennial meeting of the International Conference on Infant Studies, Providence, RI.

Perner, J. (1991). *Understanding the representational mind.* Cambridge, MA: Bradford Books/MIT Press.

Potter, M. C. (1979). Mundane symbolism: The relations among objects, names, and ideas. In N. R. Smith & M. B. Franklin (Eds.), *Symbolic functioning in childhood* (pp. 41–65). Hillsdale, NJ: Lawrence Erlbaum Associates.

Sigel, I. E. (1970). The distancing hypothesis: A causal hypothesis for the acquisition of representational thought. In M. R. Jones (Ed.), *Miami symposium on the prediction of behavior, 1968: Effect of early experiences* (pp. 99–118). Coral Gables, FL: University of Miami Press.

Sigel, I. E. (1978). The development of pictorial comprehension. In B. S. Randhawa & W. E. Coffman (Eds.), *Visual learning, thinking and communication* (pp. 93–111). New York: Academic Press.

Sigel, I. E., Anderson, L. M., & Shapiro, H. (1966). Categorization behavior of lower and middle class Negro preschool children: Differences in dealing with representation of familiar objects. *Journal of Negro Education, 35*, 218–229.

Smith, C. M. (1995, March). *Young children's use of dolls as self symbols.* Poster presented at the biennial meeting of the Society for Research in Child Development, Indianapolis.

Sowell, E. J. (1989). Effects of manipulative materials in mathematics instruction. *Journal for Research in Mathematics Education, 20*(5), 498–505.

Treiman, R., Tincoff, R., & Richmond-Welty, E. D. (1996). Letter names help children to connect print and speech. *Developmental Psychology, 32*(3), 505–514.

Troseth, G. L., & DeLoache, J. S. (1996, April). *The medium can obscure the message: Understanding the relation between video and reality.* Poster presented at the biennial meeting of the International Conference on Infant Studies, Providence, RI.

Tufte, E. R. (1983). *The visual display of quantitative information*. Cheshire, CT: Graphics Press.

Uttal, D. H., Schreiber, J. C., & DeLoache, J. S. (1996). Waiting to use a symbol: The effects of delay on children's use of models. *Child Development, 66*, 1875–1891.

Uttal, D. H., Scudder, K. V., & DeLoache, J. S. (1997). Manipulatives as symbols: A new perspective on the use of concrete objects to teach mathematics. *Journal of Applied Developmental Psychology, 18*, 37–54.

Vygotsky, L. S. (1978). *Mind in society*. (M. Cole, V. John-Steiner, S. Scribner, & E. Souberman, Eds.). Cambridge, MA: Harvard University Press.

Watson, M. W., & Fischer, K. W. (1977). A developmental sequence of agent use in late infancy. *Child Development, 48*, 828–836.

Yates, A., & Terr, L. (1988). Anatomically correct dolls—Should they be used as the basis for expert testimony? *Journal of the American Academy of Child and Adolescent Psychiatry, 27*(2), 254–257.

Zelazo, P. D., & Frye, D. (1996). Cognitive complexity and control: A theory of the development of deliberate reasoning and intentional action. In M. Stamenov (Ed.), *Language structure, discourse, and the access to consciousness* (pp. 113–153). Philadelphia: John Benjamins.

CHAPTER 5

What's in a Concept?
Context, Variability, and
Psychological Essentialism

Susan A. Gelman
Gil Diesendruck
University of Michigan, Ann Arbor

In this chapter we focus on the representation of concepts. We begin with what seems to be a paradox: How can nonobvious features be essential or core to a concept at the same time that concepts are context sensitive and ever changing? On the one hand, a growing literature argues that theories determine the structure and function of categories, at times even overriding salient perceptual information, and that even children treat concepts as having essences (S. A. Gelman, Coley, & Gottfried, 1994; Medin, 1989). On the other hand, concepts are highly flexible, sensitive to context, variable depending on the task, and influenced by perceptually immediate (online) properties (Barsalou, 1993a; Jones & L. B. Smith, 1993). Thus, there would seem to be a contradiction here: One proposal is that essences are at the core of concepts; the other proposal is that perceptual features are core or, in the extreme, that concepts have no core. Accordingly, a number of scholars suggest that essentialism is incompatible with context sensitivity (Braisby, Franks, & Hampton, 1996; Malt, 1994; L. B. Smith & Heise, 1992).

In contrast, we argue that the contradiction is only apparent: psychological essentialism is compatible with the context sensitivity noted in recent years by cognitive scientists. The organization of the chapter is as follows. First, we briefly summarize the arguments for essences and for contextually driven variability. In the next section we provide a resolution that can account for both the importance of essences and the variability in performance. To do so, we clarify what is meant by essentialism, demonstrate the limits of relying on perception as providing a conceptual core, and examine some of the consequences of claiming that concepts have no core. In the final section, we return to the theme of the book: representations. We attempt to characterize what is represented in a concept, and what implications this has for representations more generally.

BACKGROUND

Essences and Theories

In the past 25 years, theorizing about how people represent concepts and word meanings has undergone two major shifts (Medin, 1989). The "traditional" view, assumed in psychological, linguistic, and anthropological analyses of concepts, was that concepts can be represented by lists of features that are singly necessary and jointly sufficient for picking out all and only those instances of the concept (E. E. Smith & Medin, 1981). Just as *bachelor* can be characterized as "unmarried, marriageable male," so too can concepts such as *dog* and *vehicle* be decomposed into atomic units. *The first shift* moved away from the traditional view to propose that membership in a category is probabilistically determined. Three implicit assumptions of the traditional view were challenged:

1. Concepts encoded in natural language are not arbitrary, but reflect real-world feature correlations (Rosch, 1978).
2. Relatedly, all concepts are not alike. The use of arbitrary concepts invented in the laboratory often obscured the structure of concepts in natural language.
3. Category boundaries are not clear-cut; rather, probabilistic models (such as prototypes) determine category membership.

The second shift moved to incorporate commonsense theories into models of categorization. The major limitation seen with the prototype view was its reliance on similarity as an explanatory mechanism. There are epistemological problems with defining similarity in a theory-neutral way (Goodman, 1972). Moreover, much of categorization behavior requires appeal to more knowledge-rich, explanatory models. Especially within certain domains (e.g., living kinds), categorization shows evidence of rich inductive potential, use of nonobvious information, and openness to revision—properties associated with theories. The theory view retains some of the insights of the probabilistic view: Concepts are not arbitrary inventions, not all concepts are alike, and identifying category boundaries is not the most important task of categorization. The theory view does not *replace* prototype theory; instead, it argues for its insufficiency. That is, prototypes are accurate descriptions of the information people use to identify instances on many tasks (a point to which we return later).

There is now growing evidence that for adults, concepts are influenced by theoretical belief systems and cannot be characterized by statistical information alone (Heit & Rubinstein, 1994; Keil, 1989; Murphy & Medin, 1985; Quine, 1977; Rips, 1989; see Murphy, 1993, for review). How subjects incorporate different features varies, depending on their theories about the domain (Wisniewski & Medin, 1994). The probability of incorporating novel instances is also dependent on theoretical beliefs rather than statistical correlations (Medin & Shoben, 1988). Thus, in some cases a property equally true of two different concepts is more central to one than the other (e.g., "curved" is more central to boomerangs than to bananas). The extent to which features are weighted in classification judgments is influenced by causal understandings: properties that are causes are viewed as more central to a concept than properties that are effects (Ahn & Lassaline, 1996), again demonstrating that correlations alone cannot account for the centrality and significance of features in a concept (see also Ahn, Kalish, Medin, & S. A. Gelman, 1995; Keil, 1989; White, 1995).

The theory-based model of concepts is argued to be a *contributor to* concept development rather than the *outcome of* concept development (see Wellman & S. A. Gelman, 1992). Indeed, without theoretical commitments of some sort, it may be difficult for children to acquire concepts at all. Murphy (1993) noted that theories help concept learners in three respects: (a) Theories help identify those features that are relevant to a concept, (b) theories constrain how (e.g., along which dimensions) similarity should be computed, and (c) theories can influence how concepts are stored in memory. The implication here is that concept acquisition may proceed more smoothly with the help of theories, even though the theories themselves are changing developmentally.

Children appear to use theoretical knowledge in their classifications by preschool age. In a by-now classic series of studies, Keil (1989) asked children to consider animals and objects that had undergone transformations leading them to appear to be something else—for example, a raccoon that underwent an operation so that it looked and acted like a skunk. Second-graders realized that animal identity was unaffected by superficial transformations (e.g., the animal was judged to be a raccoon despite its skunklike properties). Even younger children demonstrated a similar understanding when considering items that were transformed to resemble something from a different ontological category (e.g., preschoolers reported that a porcupine that was transformed to look like a cactus was still a porcupine), or that were transformed by means of a costume. S. A. Gelman and Wellman (1991) similarly found that preschool children appreciated that for some objects, insides are more important than outsides for judgments of identity and functioning (e.g., a dog without its insides cannot bark and is not a dog, whereas a dog without its outsides can bark and is a dog).

Similarly, Barrett, Abdi, Murphy, and Gallagher (1993) demonstrated that children's intuitive theories help determine which properties and which feature correlations children attend to in their classifications. For example, in a task that required children to categorize novel birds into one of two novel categories, first- and fourth-grade children noticed the association between brain size and memory capacity and used that correlation to categorize new members. Specifically, exemplars that preserved the correlation were more often judged to be category members, and to be more typical of the category. The children did not make use of features that correlated equally well but were unsupported by a theory (e.g., the correlation between structure of heart and shape of beak).

Barrett et al. (1993) extended these findings in a second experiment. Third-grade children were presented with stimuli that were described as either animals or tools, and then learned five properties about each category. When the category was described as an animal, children selectively focused on a subset of the properties that are relevant to animals: habitat (e.g., is found in the mountains) and physical adaptation (e.g., has thick wool). In contrast, when the category was described as a tool, children selectively focused on a different subset of properties that are relevant to artifacts, namely those involving function (e.g., can crush rocks, catches snakes).

The aforementioned studies demonstrate that similarity is insufficient to account for human categorization. The conclusion is further bolstered by research suggesting that classifications may at times privilege information that is nonobvious or even runs counter to observable features. Several years ago, S. A. Gelman and Markman (1986, 1987) demonstrated that categories have an *inductive* function even for preschool children; that is, they have the potential to generate novel inferences. For example, on one item children learned a new property of a brontosaurus ("a dinosaur") and a rhinoceros (that they had cold blood and warm blood, respectively), and were asked which property was true of a triceratops ("a dinosaur"). Children reported that the triceratops had cold blood like the brontosaurus, even though it more closely resembled the rhinoceros. The results of this and other related experiments showed that by 2.5 years of age, children base inferences on category membership, even in the strong case when outward appearances conflict (S. A. Gelman & Coley, 1990). Thus, children do not assume that labels are mere conveniences—ways of efficiently referring to perceptually encountered information. Instead, children expect certain labels to capture properties well beyond those they have already encountered. A variety of control studies showed that these effects were not simply a response bias due to hearing the same word for the two category members. For example, children do not base inferences consistently on novel labels (Davidson & S. A. Gelman, 1990), nor do they generalize accidental properties, such as an animal's age, on the basis of category membership (S. A. Gelman & Markman, 1986).

In addition to basing inductive inferences on category labels, children use essential properties as an index to naming. Diesendruck, S. A. Gelman, and Lebowitz (1998) conducted a study that capitalized on a well-known word-learning error studied by Markman and others (Markman, 1989; Merriman & Bowman, 1989). Children have a powerful tendency to assume that each object has only one label, the "mutual exclusivity" assumption. For example, if a child knows that a poodle is a "dog," she will typically deny that it is a "poodle" or an "animal." Diesendruck et al. predicted that children would overcome this mutual exclusivity tendency if they learned that dogs and poodles (for instance) share nonobvious properties. Three- to 5-year-olds learned new words for a series of animals, then were tested on their interpretations of the new words. For example, children saw two distinct kinds of squirrels (a standard squirrel and a flying squirrel) and heard: "This one [the flying squirrel] is a squirrel; it's a mef. This one [the standard squirrel] is a squirrel; it's not a mef." Before teaching the new word, the experimenter described how the two instances were alike. In the "insides" condition, internal, hidden properties were described (e.g., "has the same stuff inside . . . the same kind of bones, blood, muscles, and brain"). In the control condition, superficial similarities were described (e.g., "is the same size . . . it lives in the same zoo in the same kind of cage").

The labeling phase alone provided all the information children needed to construct the hierarchy accurately. However, we know from past work (e.g., S. A. Gelman, Wilcox, & Clark, 1989) that children tend to collapse such a hierarchy into two mutually exclusive sets. The question, then, is whether the brief description of internal similarities is sufficient to alter subjects' patterns of word learning. Indeed, the results demonstrated a clear-cut condition effect. When the similarities were superficial, children showed their usual pattern of treating the two labels (e.g., *squirrel* and *mef*) as mutually exclusive. In contrast, describing internal similarities helped children overcome the error. Diesendruck (1996) has replicated this finding in Brazil, with Portuguese-speaking children of widely varying socioeconomic backgrounds. Again, there was the same weakening of mutual exclusivity in the insides condition.

These data converge to provide a picture of preschool children as attending to theory-relevant properties even when they are subtle and relatively nonobvious. Medin (1989) invoked the notion of "psychological essentialism" to account for findings such as these. Philosophers have long proposed that the categories we use are supported by underlying "essences"—an underlying reality or true nature that one cannot observe directly but that gives an object its identity (Locke, 1894/1959; Schwartz, 1977). In contrast to this metaphysical claim about the structure of reality, the psychological claim is that ordinary people *believe* (probably incorrectly; Dupré, 1993; Mayr, 1991; Sober, 1994) that the categories of ordinary language are of this sort. In other words, psychological essentialism is the proposal that people (children and adults) maintain a dual assumption: (a) that the world has a natural order that is not imposed by the observer; (b) that the symbolic system humans use to represent the world (namely, concepts and words) maps onto this natural order. Psychological essentialism posits that people believe categories are *real,* in several senses: They are discovered (vs. invented), they are natural (vs. artificial), they predict other properties, and they carve up nature at its joints.

Essentialist concepts and theory-laden concepts are related but distinct notions. The set of theory-laden concepts is broader than (and superordinate to) the set of essentialized concepts. Thus, there are theory-laden concepts that are not essentialized. For example, Murphy and Medin (1985) convincingly made the case that we use theories to classify items such as trash cans, but we do not need to appeal to essentialism in such cases. On the other hand, people may appeal to essences without having detailed theoretical belief systems (Atran, 1990). Thus, psychological essentialism does not imply full-fledged explanatory theories, but rather theoretical commitments in the sense of adherance to nonobvious (theorized) entities to account for observable structure. Evidence for essentialism versus other theory-laden concepts is indirect (see later section "What Is Psychological Essentialism: A Clarification"), but is marked by appeal to invisible causal mechanisms, assumption of innate dispositions or potential, maintenance of identity over superficial transformations, and rich inductive potential of categories (S. A. Gelman et al., 1994).

Variability and Context Sensitivity

There are at least two major challenges to the claim that children hold essentialist beliefs about the core of concepts. One fundamental objection argues against the very notion that concepts have mentally stable represented cores. A more specific variation on this objection asserts that whereas concepts may have more or less determining components, perceptual features are just as important as (or more important than) nonperceptual ones.

The claim that concepts are not stably represented takes the form that concepts are constructions in working memory, shifting and unstable as the surrounding context. Barsalou (1993a) suggested that people hold conceptual cores in long-term memory, but because such cores do not affect behavior, the term *concept* should be saved for the dynamic temporary representations in working memory that do control behavior (though see Barsalou et al., 1993, for an alternative usage). Such representations allow for the widely noted flexibility and linguistic vagary of concepts (Barsalou, 1993b). We review some of these phenomena in the remainder of this section.

For example, the features that are most salient vary with linguistic context (e.g., weight vs. sound of a piano; McCloskey & Glucksberg, 1978). When asked to define concepts, subjects generate variable responses from one occasion to the next (Barsalou, 1993b). The prototypes subjects generate can be manipulated consistently by contextual cues (e.g., telling subjects to rate typicality of birds from the point of view of the average American citizen vs. from the point of view of the average Chinese citizen; Barsalou, 1991). Hierarchies are not fully transitive (Hampton, 1982), suggesting inconsistency across uses. And finally, the dimensions along which adjectives are used are contextually sensitive (Bierwisch & Lang, 1989; Coley & S. A. Gelman, 1989; Maloney & S. A. Gelman, 1987).

Similarly, L. B. Smith and Jones (1993; see also Jones & L. B. Smith, 1993) argued that categorization and labeling are best predicted by online, context-specific considerations. That is, cognitive acts are a result of dynamic processes, and not of structural representations. In their view, "concepts are not represented entities that exist as a unit . . . there is no set intension (definition in the head) or extension (category in the world). Both are transient and emergent in the task at hand" (Jones & L. B. Smith, 1993, p. 136).

According to Barsalou (1993a), one reason concepts have been presumed to be stable representations is that most tasks focus on "taxonomization" as the primary function of categories. That is, the traditional account regards people as intuitive taxonomists engaged in the categorization of the world based on the discovery of essential features of different classes. Once discovered, such features serve to identify and make inferences about other exemplars of the same category. Yet clearly concepts are used for a variety of functions aside from taxonomization (see also S. A. Gelman & Medin, 1993). Concepts are also used for effective communication, for goal-oriented classifications, and for building world models. In these tasks, concepts do not necessarily capture the taxonomic essence of categories, but instead help establish and describe referents.

In communication, for instance, when a waitress refers to a customer as "the ham sandwich at the corner table," the term "ham sandwich" does not refer to the essence of the category ham sandwich but rather establishes as a referent the customer who ordered the sandwich and his or her location (Barsalou, 1993b). Similarly, people commonly violate ontological distinctions, such as that between animate and inanimate entities, in their object naming (Jones & L. B. Smith, 1993; Landau, Jones, & L. B. Smith, 1992). For example, we use the label *bear* to refer to both real and toy bears, even though we do not mean to say that a toy bear is truly a bear.

In goal-oriented classification, objects or events are grouped into categories according to the specific goals of the person categorizing. Thus, in contrast to taxonomic categories, goal-oriented categories may include objects of widely varying ontological kinds (e.g., "things to take out of a burning house" includes pets, photographs, and VCRs). Finally, in the construction of world models, concepts do not necessarily capture the taxonomic essence of categories. Instead, concepts are derived so as to reflect a person's belief about the current state of the world (Barsalou et al., 1993). World models (e.g., of one's office) are representations of individuals, their state, and their locations, in diverse situations. Because these individual models are situation specific, a concept does not represent properties that are universally true of all its individuals, but instead represents properties that are true of only certain individuals in particular situations.

The suggestion that concepts are contextually based is closely related to the claim that perceptual features are crucial determinants of children's representations. Barsalou (1993a, 1993b) proposed that perceptual symbols constitute the core of concepts. Through processes involving selective attention, introspection, and compositional analyses, perceptual symbols get combined to give rise to abstract concepts. Moreover, perceptual symbols serve as the basis for linguistic ones, and the flexibility of concepts arises from interactions among such symbols (Barsalou, 1993b). In a study by Olseth and Barsalou (1995), adults were asked to judge whether a property was a physical part of an object (e.g., whether a claw is a part of a chair). Subjects were given numerous pairs of property and object, some true and some false, and their verification time was measured. The authors found that perceptual properties of the pairs (e.g., distance between the center of the object and the part) significantly accounted for the variance in correct verification time, even when the experimenter did not explicitly instruct subjects to create an image of the property-object pair. Olseth and Barsalou concluded that conceptual representations have perceptual content that is spontaneously used by adults.

In a similar vein, Eimas (1994) claimed that "nonperceptual knowledge . . . finds its origins and basis in the same processes of perception and categorization that make possible the initial perceptually driven categorical representations; thus it too is perceptually based" (p. 86). Likewise, L. B. Smith and Jones (1993; see also Jones & L. B. Smith, 1993; L. B. Smith, Jones, & Landau, 1996) argued that children's performance on cognitive tasks is determined by their weighting of perceptual dimensions, attention to physical regularities, and consideration of context-specific contingencies. These processes function online, focusing children's attention on the dynamic similarity space, and thus not resorting to some kind of deeper conceptual knowledge. Perceptual categories derived from these processes, though, can represent conceptually relevant abstract knowledge (e.g., surface gradient differences between natural and manufactured kinds; L. B. Smith & Heise, 1992; see also L. B. Smith, 1993).

One of the most commonly cited sources of evidence for the primacy of perceptual properties in children's concepts is that of children's lexical extensions. In one standard procedure, children are introduced to a target object labeled with a novel word, and then presented with a set of test objects, similar to the target on some property but different from it on others. Children are asked to identify a referent of the novel word among the test objects. Various studies report that when provided with items that are either taxonomically, thematically, or perceptually similar (e.g., same shape) to the target object, children most commonly choose the object similar in shape to the target object as the referent of the novel word (Baldwin, 1992; Gentner & Imai, 1994; Imai, Gentner, & Uchida, 1994). Landau, L. B. Smith, and Jones (1988) concluded that children's preference is quite specific to shape. In their studies, 2- and 3-year-olds saw a standard novel object (e.g., a U-shaped piece of plywood) and three alternatives differing from the standard either in size (e.g., 2 inches vs. 2 feet), texture (wood vs. wire), or shape. Children extended a novel noun most often to objects of the same shape as the standard, even when they differed considerably in texture and size.

Summary. To summarize, the evidence sketched out in this section demonstrates that concepts are highly variable and context sensitive. Jones and L. B. Smith (1993) proposed that this demonstration argues against the role of essences/theories in two major ways: concepts have no stable core (i.e., no essence), and perceptual features (vs. nonobvious features) are most central.

A RESOLUTION OF THE PARADOX

In the following four sections, we argue for a resolution of the apparent contradiction between early essentialism and early context sensitivity. The resolution rests on four main points:

1. First, we clarify what is meant by psychological essentialism, and what this theoretical construct does *not* entail. Contrary to common depictions, essentialism is a skeletal, guiding heuristic rather than a detailed set of scientific beliefs.
2. Next, we outline a sample of the major distinctions among concepts, arguing that different kinds of concepts require different theories to account for their structure.
3. Third, we cast a critical eye on the role of perceptual features, in particular shape, as prime determinants of conceptual structure. We argue that the power of perceptual features often derives from their status as markers of theory-relevant information.
4. Finally, we examine what is stable in the variability and context sensitivity of concepts. We suggest that the variability in the information people use is patterned, predictable, and consistent with the notion of a theory-based "core."

What Is Psychological Essentialism: A Clarification

Resolving the paradox between the "essences-are-core" and the "concepts-have-no-core" positions first requires a clarification of what is meant by psychological essentialism. To quote Medin (1989), psychological essentialism entails the following: "People act as if things (e.g., objects) have essences or underlying natures that make them the thing that they are. Furthermore, the essence constrains or generates properties that may vary in their centrality. One of the things that theories do is to embody or provide causal linkages from deeper properties to more superficial or surface properties" (p. 1476).

At first blush, essentialism may sound like a return to the defining-features view of categories outlined earlier. It is not, and to see why, one must clarify what essentialism does *not* entail. Essentialism does not entail that people know (consciously or unconsciously) what the essence is. Medin and Ortony (1989) referred to this unknown-yet-believed-in entity as an "essence placeholder." People may implicitly assume, for example, that there is some quality that bears have in common that confers category identity and causes identifiable surface features, and use this belief to guide inductive inferences and explanations—without being able to identify any feature or trait as the bear essence. This belief can be considered an unarticulated heuristic rather than a detailed theory.

Furthermore, an essence is rarely consulted to determine category membership, for the simple reason that people often do not know (or cannot readily access) the relevant information. In such instances, people use other features instead. Gender provides a useful example: Although we typically assess someone's gender based on outward (clothed) appearance and voice, even young children acknowledge that genital information is more diagnostic (Bem, 1989), and in our technological society we even use chromosomal information in certain contexts (e.g., amniocentesis, Olympic committees). Thus, evidence that people use salient observable cues for categorization cannot be taken as evidence against essentialism.

A related point is that the folk essence may include notions that have no scientific counterpart (e.g., "soul" in Western philosophy, "kunam" among the Tamil; Daniel, 1985). Indeed, Atran (1990) argued that essences are presumed to exist even among those living in cultures with no scientific tradition. Moreover, some argue that essentialism and current biological theory are incompatible (Hirschfeld, 1996; Mayr, 1991; Sober, 1994).

These initial points of clarification imply that essentialism is difficult (perhaps impossible) to study *directly*. Psychological essentialism posits that people believe in the existence of essences, not that people have detailed knowledge regarding the content of essences, nor that the world is organized in accord with essences. Studies demonstrating that people classify instances based on nonessential features, or that people cannot specify an essence, or that people's representation of a concept does not match that of science (e.g., Dupré, 1993) are not evidence against psychological essentialism. They are valuable for examining what kinds of information are used on certain tasks, but do not constitute tests of psychological essentialism as a theory of concepts.

In sum, contrary to common depictions, essentialism is a skeletal principle (Medin, 1989; see also R. Gelman, 1990, for a discussion of skeletal principles) rather than a detailed set of beliefs, scientific or otherwise. It is a guiding assumption in the mind of the cognizer (a "stance," "construal," or "heuristic"; Keil, 1995), rather than a fixed set of features contained within the concept. In this sense, we are sympathetic to the portrayal of essentialism as a metaconceptual belief about conceptual structure (Barsalou, 1993a; Malt, 1990). However, metaconceptual does not mean epiphenomenal or divorced from conceptual structure; essentialism is a metaconceptual construal with extended conceptual implications. Although essentialism does not *specify* particular conceptual content, it constrains and generates such properties (to use Medin's, 1989, terminology), and guides further knowledge acquisition. As Atran, Estin, Coley, and Medin (1996) explained:

> [People] believe that visible morpho-typical patterns of each readily identifiable generic species, as well as non-obvious aspects of biological functioning, are causally produced by an underlying essence. The nature of this essence is initially unknown, but presumed. The learner (e.g., a child) then attempts to discover how essences govern the heritable teleological relations between visible parts, how they link initially ill-perceived internal parts to morpho-typical parts through canonical patterns of irreversible growth, and how they determine the stable and complex functioning of visible and non-obvious parts. (p. 33)

This excerpt reveals two additional points that are worth highlighting. First, important consequences follow from the skeletal nature of essentialism. When the essence is unknown, it may serve as a motivator and source for conceptual change (see Waxman & Braig, 1996). We suggest that, armed with a heuristic notion that a category has a causal essence, people will search for evidence of the essence, and for consequences of the essence, and for the essence itself. Because it is the (unknown) essence and not any particular set of features that is regarded as necessary, essentialized categories can incorporate anomalies and thus better account for conceptual change than models of concepts that presume the existence of fixed features. Because essentialism is a placeholder notion, it provides stability in the face of conceptual change and context sensitivity: What is stored is not *what* the essence is, but *that* it exists.

The second point is that perceptual features are closely linked to the essence; thus, essentialism is also not a claim that perceptual features are unimportant. Essences are often correlated with and predictive of perceptual features. According to a somewhat oversimplified folk portrayal, XY chromosomes *cause* the observable properties of a male. Given that typically we do not have direct access to the essence, the correlated observable properties become crucial to many tasks (see Keil, 1989). This linkage between observable properties and assumption of underlying causal (essential) properties can provide an account of why perceptual prototypes, though insufficient for characterizing many categorization decisions (see Keil, 1989; Rips & Collins, 1993), are so prevalent in on-line processing of concepts.

Domain Specificity and Conceptual Variation

Sensitivity to distinctions among categories promises to bring order to the inconsistency that appears when one tries to characterize "conceptual structure" in a way that encompasses the full variety of all forms of human categorization. For example, does the concept "things to take from a burning house" differ from the concept "dogs," or are they indistinguishable in structure? Common sense tells us that, at the very least, they differ in the perceptual similarity among instances, richness of stored knowledge, inferences that can be made, stability over time, position in a hierarchy, and so on. Moreover, we suggest that the concept of "dogs," but not the concept of "things to take from a burning house," is treated as having an essence. Although Medin (1989) allowed for the possibility that all natural language concepts (including, e.g., wastebasket) are essentialized (see also Carey, 1995), we suspect instead that different categories have fundamentally different kinds of structure, for children and adults.

At least three factors are relevant: category domain, category level, and linguistic expression. *Domain differences* have consequences for a variety of tasks that tap essentialist reasoning. Radical transformations result in judgments of category change for artifacts, but stability for animals (Keil, 1989), thus implying that animals—but not artifacts—retain some essential qualities that persist despite external appearance changes. Information about internal parts is used when extending novel labels for animals but not for artifacts (Diesendruck et al., 1998), thus suggesting that the relevance of nonobvious internal parts (a close stand-in for essences) is domain specific. Inductive inferences are more powerful for animal categories than for artifact categories (S. A. Gelman, 1988). Children are also more likely to attribute immanent (inherent) causes for animals than for artifacts (S. A. Gelman & Gottfried, 1996). In categorization, adults also distinguish between the two domains. They believe membership in animal categories is more "absolute" than membership in artifact categories (Kalish, 1995), and that animal categories have defining features to a larger extent than artifact categories do (Malt, 1990). In general, these findings support the notion that children and adults hold essentialist beliefs about living kinds but not about artifacts. Explanations for the domain differences vary: They may reflect an innate domain-specific module for reasoning about living kinds (Atran, 1995), a teleological/essentialist construal that finds a better match with particular domains in the world (Keil, 1995), or an assumption that entities without external similarities (i.e., natural kinds) must have internal essential causal properties (S. A. Gelman et al., 1994).

At this point, very little is known regarding how *category level* intersects with judgments of essentialism, though some evidence is suggestive. The distinction between basic-level categories (e.g., dog) and superordinate-level categories (e.g., animal) may be particularly relevant. Relatedly, Atran et al. (1996) found that the "generic-species" level (e.g., oak, robin) is favored for drawing inductive inferences, for both people raised in Michigan and the Itzaj Maya people of Guatemala. Similarly, although there appears to be no endorsement of H_2O as the essence of "water" when the word is used at a superordinate level (including pond water, polluted water, etc.), H_2O may be the essence of "water" when the word is used at a more subordinate level ("pure water") (Malt, 1994; although her interpretation differs).

Linguistic expression is also predictive of category structure: Essentializing may be more likely to occur when a concept is encoded in language than when it is not. Certainly hearing a familiar name can foster essentializing (S. A. Gelman & Markman, 1986), though not every word carries with it essentialist assumptions (Davidson & S. A. Gelman, 1990). The reasons for the importance of lexicalization are not entirely clear—it may be that concepts so important as to be essentialized are prime candidates for lexicalization because of their salience, frequency, and stability. Or it may be that having a name helps fix the concept in people's minds, transmit it to new generations, and so reify its existence. Linguistic form class also appears to be important, though to date this is an underexplored direction. Markman (1989) suggested that nouns are more likely than adjectives to capture essentialized kinds (see also Waxman & Markow, 1995).

Altogether, then, it appears that essentialism is most likely to appear for basic-level living kinds that are referred to by common nouns, at least among adults. A major source of confusion in the literature is that the dimensions of domain, level, and linguistic expression have generally been ignored in discussions of the validity of psychological essentialism. The scope of essentialism can be exaggerated when derived from a database focused on natural kind categories, especially basic-level animal categories with familiar common nouns as names. Conversely, the role of perception can be misleading when focused on nonlexicalized categories for which essences or theories are barely possible. For example, Landau et al. (1988) found that children had a strong tendency to extend labels on the basis of perceptual features such as shape—a finding that is not surprising, given that the stimuli in that study were simple novel objects (e.g., U-shaped piece of plywood), for which children had little prior knowledge. Similarly, Mervis, Johnson, and Scott (1993) reported a study in which subjects sort on the basis of shape—yet the task was a silhouette identification task, in which shape and size are the only dimensions available. If the only information children receive concerns shape, texture, and size, then frequent use of shape is unsurprising. In contrast, when children are reasoning about real-world living kinds, issues of ontology, essence, and kind become important.

Role of Shape

In this section we reexamine the question of the centrality of shape to children's early concepts. The notion that words capture theory-based categories or essences is called into question by recent studies (reviewed earlier) suggesting that shape is a crucial component of children's semantic representations, even overriding ontological distinctions. On this view, children have a general shape bias in their interpretations of novel count nouns, such that a new word (e.g., "a dax") is assumed to refer to a set of objects that share a common shape (Imai et al., 1994; Landau et al., 1988, 1992). One interpretation of the bias is that ontological status is irrelevant, at least in naming and perhaps in conceptualization (e.g., toy bears and real bears are both "bears" because they have a common shape; Jones & L. B. Smith, 1993). In favor of this position, many studies indicate that shape is a salient feature for children, particularly in word-learning contexts (Baldwin, 1989, 1992).

However, children may attend to shape not because it is the basis on which words are extended, but rather because it is an indirect indicator of category membership; it correlates with and "is often . . . a good source of information about" what kind of thing an object is (Soja, Carey, & Spelke, 1992, p. 102). More generally, the power of perceptual features often derives from their status as markers of theory-relevant information. If this interpretation is correct, then when children receive information about theoretical kind directly, this should influence which features are used.

A particularly relevant study here is one by Jones, L. B. Smith, and Landau (1991), who found that adding eyes to a set of U-shaped objects substantially affected 3-year-old children's sorting of those objects, specifically leading to a decrease in the use of shape and an increase in the use of texture cues (e.g., a reluctance to extend a word from an object made of sponge to one made of wood). Jones et al. (1991; see also L. B. Smith & Heise, 1992) interpreted these data as evidence for children's use of perceptual (not conceptual) features— namely, that children have learned an abstract association between the presence of eyes and object texture. However, much conceptual information may have been conveyed along with the perceptual information. Specifically, eyes provide information regarding the ontological status of these objects, that they are (representations of) animals rather than inanimate pieces of wood, sponge, and so forth. At this point, the data can be interpreted either as demonstrating that eyes are important perceptual cues, or that eyes index ontological kind. Further studies will be necessary to dissociate the perceptual-features interpretation from the ontological interpretation (e.g., by providing the objects with eyes but telling children that the object is a tool, not an animal, and that the "eyes" are really buttons for making the tool work). Preliminary support for the conceptual reading comes from Keil's (1995) studies demonstrating that verbal cues alone can shift the weighting of subjects' features. When the very same object is described as a "frog" versus a "rock," subjects use different perceptual features to extend the word (shape and surface markings in the case of the frog; color and surface markings in the case of the rock).

There is ample evidence showing that shape cannot be the central determinant of children's nonlinguistic classifications. There are striking counterexamples to the use of shape, even when perceptually rich stimuli (e.g., realistic color photographs or actual objects) are provided. In these examples, fundamental conceptual distinctions—often ontological—are more predictive than shape. Infants form categories that cross-cut overall shape: By 9 months of age, they sort together different basic-level animal categories (e.g., dogs and fish) and separate birds-with-outspread-wings from airplanes (Mandler & McDonough, 1993). Ten-month-olds classify together containers differing in shape and distinguish between same-shaped objects that differ in their capacity to contain (Kolstad & Baillargeon, 1996). By age 2 years, children weight substance more heavily than shape on a match-to-sample task on which the items are nonsolid masses (Soja, Carey, & Spelke, 1991). By 3 and 4 years of age, children treat plants and animals as belonging to a single category (living things), despite the extreme differences in shape between, say, a cow and a tree (Backscheider, Shatz, & S. A. Gelman, 1993; Hickling & S. A. Gelman, 1995). Conversely, children treat humans and apes as belonging to distinctly different categories, despite their greater similarity. Thus, when given triads consisting of a human, a non-human primate, and a nonprimate animal, elementary-school children are more likely than adults to group together the primate and the animal, isolating the human (Johnson, Mervis, & Boster, 1992). This pattern is also found among preschoolers, even when the primate and animal differ radically in shape (e.g., chimpanzee and centipede) (Coley, 1993). Preschool children also overlook similarity in shape when making predictions about how statues versus live animals will move (Massey & R. Gelman, 1988).

Shape and Overextensions.   Particularly crucial for the shape-bias hypothesis are its implications for language. Yet one of the more puzzling aspects of the shape-bias theory is that it runs counter to much of children's natural language use. By 2.5 years of age, children appropriately provide the same label for objects of different shapes (e.g., round cookie, windmill cookie), and appropriately provide different labels for objects of the same shape (e.g., round plate, round cookie). This discrepancy between the experimental evidence (with shape-based responses persisting throughout the preschool years and beyond) and the natural language evidence (with clear counterexamples to shape-based naming) suggests that the experimental tasks may not be tapping natural word-learning processes. Thus, it would seem important to examine children's use of words learned in natural settings. Indeed, *below* age 2.5, children make many overex-tension errors (e.g., calling a round ball "moon"), and these errors are often described as being shape based (Clark, 1973). However, previous analyses rarely attempted to tease apart shape from taxonomic relatedness as the basis of children's overextensions.

S. A. Gelman, Croft, Fu, Clausner, and Gottfried (1998) examined the basis of children's overextensions—specifically, the relative role of taxonomic related-ness and shape—using two tasks, productive labeling and comprehension. Subjects were 2, 2.5, and 4 years of age. For the production task, subjects were simply asked to name a series of photographs. For the comprehension task, subjects received a series of experimental trials testing two words that are commonly overextended (*apple* and *dog*). The experimental trials included photographs of actual instances (e.g., a typical and an atypical apple), distractors of the same shape and same superordinate category (orange and pomegranate), distractors of the same shape but different superordinate category (baseball and round can-dle), and distractors of the same superordinate category but different shape (ba-nana and starfruit).

The results argue against a shape bias in overextensions in three ways. First, children were typically correct in comprehension. Even when presented with objects of the same shape *and* same taxonomic kind, most children refrained from extending a word erroneously. Second, in both comprehension and production, children typically overextended to items that matched the target word in both shape *and* taxonomic relatedness. Third, in comprehension children were as likely to overextend based on taxonomic relatedness alone as on shape alone. For example, when asked for an "apple," children picked a banana as often as they picked a baseball. All of these findings suggest that shape has no special priority in young children's semantic representations. Both superordinate-level taxonomic relatedness and shape are salient in children's early word meanings.

Shape and Representations.   If, as we suggest, shape is not central to children's naming, then why are ontological distinctions commonly ignored in ordinary language use? Soja et al. (1992) suggested that it is not shape per se that children are naming; rather, children are attempting to name that which the shape represents. A toy bear is called a "bear" because it represents a bear, not because it is shaped like a bear. Indirect support for this argument comes from the observation that objects not designed to represent another kind of thing are rarely mislabeled (e.g., footballs are rarely called "eggs"). Gelman and Ebeling (1998) have conducted a pilot study designed to test this hypothesis more directly. Subjects were 47 preschool children (2;5 to 3;11). They saw line drawings roughly shaped like various nameable objects, such as a bear. For half the subjects, we described each line drawing as depicting a shape that was created *intentionally*— for example, someone painted the picture. For the remaining subjects, we described the same drawing as depicting a shape that was created *accidentally*—for example, someone spilled the paint. For each item, subjects first heard the brief story, then were shown the corresponding line drawing and asked, "What is this?" Children's open-ended responses were coded as naming the shape (e.g., "a bear"), naming the actual materials (e.g., "paint"), or other (e.g., "this looks like a bear," "I don't know").

We hypothesized that subjects' use of shape as the basis of naming would be influenced by the representational status of the pictures: When the drawings were intended, subjects should name the shapes; when the drawings were unintended, subjects should not name the shapes (e.g., describing the literal materials instead). In other words, the hypothesis is that when children name in accordance with shape, it is not because shape is paramount, but rather because shape is a representation. When the shape does not stand for a kind—as with accidental paint spills—then shape is no longer relevant. The findings fit the predictions: 2- and 3-year-olds named on the basis of shape (e.g., referring to the bear-shaped drawing as a "bear") significantly more often when the shape was intended (85%) than when it was not (54%).

Shape and Taxonomic Level.   Most prior studies examining the shape bias have pitted shape against superordinate category membership (e.g., food). For example, given a target picture of a round cake, subjects were permitted to choose among a hat (shape match), a pie (superordinate-level taxonomic match), or a gift (thematic match) (Imai et al., 1994). The taxonomic match was not from the same basic-level category as the target (e.g., a heart-shaped cake). However, it is well known that children's earliest words typically name basic-level object categories, and that children have relative difficulty reasoning with superordinate-level categories (Markman & Callanan, 1984). Thus, pitting shape against superordinate-level categories provides a particularly stringent test of whether shape "wins out" over taxonomic kind in children's word learning. Moreover, if children are searching for a basic-level match but cannot find one (because there is no basic-level match in the experimental array), they may rely on shape because it typically is a strong predictor of basic-level category membership.

A more sensitive test would involve pitting shape against basic-level category membership. Golinkoff, Shuff-Bailey, Olguin, and Ruan (1995) have conducted a set of experiments examining children's extensions of novel words, in which the taxonomic choices were of the same basic-level category as the targets (e.g., if the target was a high-heeled shoe, the taxonomic match was a boot). The other choices matched in perceptual similarity or thematic relatedness. Corresponding to our predictions, 2-year-olds in their studies generalized novel nouns to members of the same basic-level category, overriding perceptual similarity. However, that work pitted taxonomic kind against overall perceptual similarity rather than specifically against shape. Thus, the results do not speak directly to the issue of whether children have a preference for extending words based on taxonomic relatedness versus shape.

Gelman and Kirzhner (1995) conducted a study in which shape and basic-level category membership were placed into direct conflict. Subjects were 37 Russian-speaking children (ages 3–5 years) living in the United States, but tested in Russian. They saw nine sets of photographs, in which a target item was presented along with three choices: taxonomic, shape, and thematic. A sample set was a round cookie (target) presented with a gingerbread-man cookie (taxonomic match), a round coin (shape match), and a glass of milk (thematic match). Children in the word condition learned a new word for the target and were asked which of the choices the word also applied to. Children in the goes with condition saw the target and were asked which of the choices went with it. Taxonomic choices were higher than shape choices, in both the word (63% vs. 33%) and goes with (28% vs. 19%) conditions. Use of the word drew children's attention away from thematic choices (5% in the word condition; 53% in the goes with condition).

To summarize, shape is not the sole or even primary factor in children's naming and classification. On tasks that provide information only about perceptual dimensions (e.g., sorting of simple, novel artifacts that vary only in shape, texture, and color), shape is an especially salient dimension. However, its salience derives largely from its value as an index or predictor of other information (Medin, 1989; Soja et al., 1992; Waxman & Braig, 1996). When ontological knowledge and theoretical beliefs are available, and when they conflict with shape, children often sort and name on the basis of these other factors.

Stability in Conceptual Representation

What is stable in the representation of concepts? Barsalou (1993a) has argued that stability is in the long-term knowledge, rather than in the concepts that draw on such knowledge. Jones and L. B. Smith (1993) proposed an even more extreme position, that nothing is stable: "Concepts have no constant structure, but are instead continually created. There is, in brief, a dynamic conceptual space of which the dynamic similarity space is part" (p. 130). There are at least two problems, however, with arguing that concepts are not stable. First, at the very least there is stability in what gets linked to a word. Phonetic representations are stored in long-term memory, and we treat some meanings linked to these representations as importantly the "same" (e.g., brown flying bat and gray flying bat), but others as mere homophones (e.g., brown flying bat and baseball bat). Important to note, children as young as 2 years of age share these intuitions (Backscheider & S. A. Gelman, 1995).

Second, there appear to be constraints on which kinds of information get stored with a word or concept (Markman, 1989). Presumably even the dynamic conceptual space referred to by Jones and L. B. Smith (1993) obeys certain constraints. For example, their use of a spatial metaphor ("conceptual space") suggests a finite, contiguous region. It seems unlikely that all such constraints could be provided by the perceptual system. How would, say, mutual exclusivity be perceptually represented? Similarly, Jackendoff (1996) pointed out that conceptualizing an object as a category member (what he called a concept of *type*) is an abstraction: Unlike a concept of an individual (i.e., a concept of *token*), it cannot be represented in a concrete image or fully embodied in any set of real-world individuals. Moreover, constraints are not universally constant (as might be predicted on a perceptual analysis) but instead are sensitive to linguistic input (Choi & Bowerman, 1991; Choi & Gopnik, 1995; Tardif, 1996).

At this point, the no-core view, though important for reminding us of the variability in concepts, seems particularly ill-suited to provide a portrait of stability, because it denies its very existence. Although we do not propose to solve the problem of stability, a couple of points are worth noting. First, the nature of conceptual stability may be quite abstract, at the level of ontological commitments ("X is an animal") rather than particular features. Ontological status appears to be remarkably stable and unchanging across uses of a word or variations of a concept (Keil, 1989). Ontologies are implicitly built into our grammar (e.g., with classifier systems; see Silverstein, 1986). Even when concepts are variable, ontological commitments tend not to change. For example, although prototypes change with context (Barsalou, 1991), such changes typically leave ontological kind unaffected (e.g., although typicality ratings of birds vary depending on whether one adopts an "American" vs. "Chinese" point of view, across both contexts birds are presumed to be animate, egg-laying creatures). Psychological essentialism may be one kind of ontological commitment.

The other point is that there is more stability when task is kept constant than when averaging across tasks. Task effects are clearly systematic. Similarity judgments, categorization, and inductive inferences all yield different patterns of responses (Carey, 1985; Deák & Bauer, 1995; S. A. Gelman, Collman, & Maccoby, 1986; Rips, 1989; Taylor & S. A. Gelman, 1993). Subjects who are expert in a domain classify differently from novices (Chi, Hutchinson, & Robin, 1989). Under time pressure, subjects are more likely to use global similarity than dimensional similarity (Ward, 1983), and more likely to use perceptual salience than formal category structure (Lamberts, 1995). And, as noted earlier, use of language has implications for classification (Markman & Hutchinson, 1984; Waxman, 1991). There is a general pattern here that tasks reflecting the accumulation of expertise and deeper analysis are the tasks for which subjects more consistently use information that can be characterized as nonobvious. Roughly, there seems to be a distinction between rough-and-ready information, used when we need to be quick, versus more time-consuming, less obvious information, used when we need to be accurate. The "quick" information is what we find salient; the "accurate" information is what we believe the world is like. Although the two are highly correlated, nonobvious properties are privileged on tasks requiring expertise and lexicalization.

It is important to note, however, that this does not mean that perceptual information is developmentally prior to theoretical information (Bruner, 1973). There is no perceptual-to-conceptual shift in ontogenesis (S. A. Gelman, 1996; Jones & L. B. Smith, 1993; Simons & Keil, 1995). Young children are sensitive to the task effects described earlier. Thus, given the appropriate task (e.g., induction), even 2-year-olds give essentialist responses (S. A. Gelman & Coley, 1990). Moreover, even on "quick" identification tasks, detection and use of subtle ontological information may be quite immediate, allowing children to identify an instance as a real animal versus a statue, for example (Massey & S. A. Gelman, 1988). Similarly, 2-year-olds attend to eyes, 3-year-olds attend more to tiny self-initiated movements than to large other-initiated movements, when explaining animal movement (S. A. Gelman & Gottfried, 1996), and 4-year-olds attend to subtle details of a drawing to detect the category membership of an item (e.g., the antennae on a leaf insect; S. A. Gelman & Markman, 1987). L. B. Smith and Heise (1992) have suggested that these sorts of subtle perceptual cues are what make perception smart, and argued against the need to posit theories or essentialism; we suggest instead that these provide evidence that perception is constrained by and imbued with theories.

WHAT'S IN A CONCEPT?
THE QUESTION OF REPRESENTATION

Our review points out that concepts pose a puzzle for the study of representations: They are context sensitive, leading some to question what (if anything) is stable in their representation. The skeptic might insist that nothing is stable and so nothing is represented. We have been arguing that much is represented, but it is of skeletal form and varies depending on the kind of concept and kind of conceptual task under consideration. The argument for skeletal structures is akin to R. Gelman's (1990) suggestion regarding skeletal principles underlying children's acquisition of fundamental concepts such as number and animacy. It differs, however, in that R. Gelman's skeletal principles are domain-specific, contentful proto-theories that are extended in domain-specific ways, whereas our notion of essentialized concept may span across domains (Carey, 1995; Hirschfeld, 1996; Wellman & S. A. Gelman, in press). Here we sketch out what might be represented in a basic-level natural kind concept.

Three components seem to be central: (a) an ontology, (b) a notion of "essence" or "kind", and (c) a perceptually based prototype. The evidence for early representation of ontology is too vast to review here, but is supported by developmental evidence (Mandler, 1993) and neuropsychological evidence (e.g., Caramazza, Hillis, Leek, & Miozzo, 1994). Once again, we stress that the notion of essence or kind is skeletal: What is stored is not *what* the essence is, but *that* it is there. We suggest either essence or kind as two related versions, the former stronger than the latter (S. A. Gelman, 1995). The notion of kind suggests that the category is real and entails rich commonalities; the notion of essence includes the notion of kind plus the additional element that there is some entity or force that is causally responsible. Finally, the linking of the first two components with a perceptually based prototype would account for how reasoners (naturally) link theories with evidence, and would account for the information used during rapid identification of instances.

We conclude with the observation that essentialism does not make the problem of representation easier, and may even complicate it considerably. Because the essence itself typically is not represented in full, it does not solve the problem of what specifically is stored in memory. Moreover, knowledge—especially causal knowledge, or what we have been calling "theories"—becomes an important part of the concept. This conclusion should not be surprising, however, when we consider that one of the primary functions of concepts is to work with our theory-rich understandings of the world.

ACKNOWLEDGMENTS

This research was supported by National Science Foundation grant BNS-9100348 to Gelman and a University of Michigan Rackham Graduate Fellowship to Diesendruck. We thank Marilyn Shatz, Michelle Hollander, and Irv Sigel for helpful comments on an earlier draft. We have also benefited from discussions with Marilyn Shatz and Ellen Markman.

REFERENCES

Ahn, W.-K., Kalish, C. W., Medin, D. L., & Gelman, S. A. (1995). The role of covariation versus mechanism information in causal attribution. *Cognition, 54,* 299–352.

Ahn, W.-K., & Lassaline, M. E. (1996). *Causal structure in categorization.* Unpublished manuscript.

Atran, S. (1990). *Cognitive foundations of natural history.* New York: Cambridge University Press.

Atran, S. (1995). Causal constraints on categories and categorical constraints on biological reasoning across cultures. In D. Sperber, D. Premack, & A. Premack (Eds.), *Causal cognition: A multidisciplinary debate* (pp. 205–233). Oxford, England: Oxford University Press.

Atran, S., Estin, P., Coley, J., & Medin, D. (1996). *Generic species and basic levels: Essence and appearance in folk biology.* Manuscript submitted for publication.

Backscheider, A. B., & Gelman, S. A. (1995). Children's understanding of homonyms. *Journal of Child Language, 22,* 107–127.

Backscheider, A. B., Shatz, M., & Gelman, S. A. (1993). Preschoolers' ability to distinguish living kinds as a function of regrowth. *Child Development, 64,* 1242–1257.

Baldwin, D. A. (1989). Priorities in children's expectations about object label reference: Form over color. *Child Development, 60,* 1289–1306.

Baldwin, D. A. (1992). Clarifying the role of shape in children's taxonomic assumption. *Journal of Experimental Child Psychology, 54,* 392–416.

Barrett, S. E., Abdi, H., Murphy, G. L., & Gallagher, J. M. (1993). Theory-based correlations and their role in children's concepts. *Child Development, 64,* 1595–1616.

Barsalou, L. W. (1991). Deriving categories to achieve goals. In G. H. Bower (Ed.), *The psychology of learning and motivation* (pp. 1–64). New York: Academic Press.

Barsalou, L. W. (1993a). Challenging assumptions about concepts. *Cognitive Development, 8,* 169–180.

Barsalou, L. W. (1993b). Flexibility, structure, and linguistic vagary in concepts: Manifestations of a compositional system of perceptual symbols. In A. F. Collins, S. E. Gathercole, M. A. Conway, & P. E. Morris (Eds.), *Theories of memory* (pp. 29–101). Hillsdale, NJ: Lawrence Erlbaum Associates.

Barsalou, L. W., Yeh, W., Luka, B. J., Olseth, K. L., Mix, K. S., & Wu, L.-L. (1993). Concepts and meaning. In K. Beals, G. Cooke, D. Kathman, S. Kita, K. E. McCullough, & D. Testen (Eds.), *What we think, what we mean, and how we say it: Papers from the parasession on the correspondence of conceptual, semantic and grammatical representations* (pp. 23–61). Chicago: Chicago Linguistic Society.

Bem, S. (1989). Genital knowledge and gender constancy in preschool children. *Child Development, 60,* 649–662.

Bierwisch, M., & Lang, E. (Eds.). (1989). *Dimensional adjectives: Grammatical structure and conceptual interpretation.* New York: Springer-Verlag.

Braisby, N., Franks, B., & Hampton, J. (1996). Essentialism, word use, and concepts. *Cognition, 59,* 247–274.

Bruner, J. S. (1973). *Beyond the information given*. New York: Norton.

Caramazza, A., Hillis, A., Leek, E. C., & Miozzo, M. (1994). The organization of lexical knowledge in the brain: Evidence from category- and modality-specific deficits. In L. A. Hirschfeld & S. A. Gelman (Eds.), *Mapping the mind: Domain specificity in cognition and culture* (pp. 68–84). Cambridge, England: Cambridge University Press.

Carey, S. (1985). *Conceptual change in childhood*. Cambridge, MA: MIT Press.

Carey, S. (1995). On the origins of causal understanding. In D. Sperber, D. Premack, & A. Premack (Eds.), *Causal cognition: A multidisciplinary debate* (pp. 268–302). Oxford, England: Oxford University Press.

Chi, M., Hutchinson, J., & Robin, A. (1989). How inferences about novel domain-related concepts can be constrained by structured knowledge. *Merrill–Palmer Quarterly, 35*, 27–62.

Choi, S., & Bowerman, M. (1991). Learning to express motion events in English and Korean: The influence of language-specific lexicalization patterns. *Cognition, 41*, 83–121.

Choi, S., & Gopnik, A. (1995). Early acquisition of verbs in Korean: A cross-linguistic study. *Journal of Child Language, 22*, 497–529.

Clark, E. V. (1973). What's in a word? On the child's acquisition of semantics in his first language. In T. E. Moore (Ed.), *Cognitive development and the acquisition of language* (pp. 65–110). New York: Academic Press.

Coley, J. D. (1993). *Emerging differentiation of folkbiology and folkpsychology: Similarity judgments and property attributions*. Unpublished doctoral dissertation, University of Michigan, Ann Arbor.

Coley, J. D., & Gelman, S. A. (1989). The effects of object orientation and object type on children's interpretation of the word "big." *Child Development, 60*, 372–380.

Daniel, V. (1985). *Fluid signs*. Los Angeles: University of California Press.

Davidson, N. S., & Gelman, S. A. (1990). Inductions from novel categories: The role of language and conceptual structure. *Cognitive Development, 5*, 151–176.

Deák, G., & Bauer, P. J. (1995). The effects of task comprehension on preschoolers' and adults' categorization choices. *Journal of Experimental Child Psychology, 60*, 393–427.

Diesendruck, G. (1996). *Essentialism and word learning: A cross-cultural investigation*. Manuscript submitted for publication.

Diesendruck, G., Gelman, S. A., & Lebowitz, K. (1998). Conceptual and linguistic biases in children's word learning. *Developmental Psychology, 34*, 823–839.

Dupré, J. (1993). *The disorder of things: Metaphysical foundations of the disunity of science*. Cambridge, MA: Harvard University Press.

Eimas, P. D. (1994). Categorization in early infancy and the continuity of development. *Cognition, 50*, 83–93.

Gelman, R. (1990). First principles organize attention to and learning about relevant data: Number and the animate-inanimate distinction as examples. *Cognitive Science, 14*, 79–106.

Gelman, S. A. (1988). The development of induction within natural kind and artifact categories. *Cognitive Psychology, 20*, 65–95.

Gelman, S. A. (1995, November). *The development of a concept of "kind"* (Workshop on permanence and change in conceptual knowledge). Kazimierz, Poland.

Gelman, S. A. (1996). Concepts and theories. In R. Gelman & T. K. Au (Eds.), *Perceptual and cognitive development* (pp. 117–150). New York: Academic Press.

Gelman, S. A., & Coley, J. D. (1990). The importance of knowing a dodo is a bird: Categories and inferences in two-year-olds. *Developmental Psychology, 26*, 796–804.

Gelman, S. A., Coley, J. D., & Gottfried, G. M. (1994). Essentialist beliefs in children: The acquisition of concepts and theories. In L. A. Hirschfeld & S. A. Gelman (Eds.), *Mapping the mind: Domain specificity in cognition and culture* (pp. 341–365). Cambridge, England: Cambridge University Press.

Gelman, S. A., Collman, P., & Maccoby, E. E. (1986). Inferring properties from categories versus inferring categories from properties: The case of gender. *Child Development, 57*, 396–404.

Gelman, S. A., Croft, W., Fu, P., Clausner, T., & Gottfried, G. (1998). Why is a pomegranate an "apple"? The role of shape, taxonomic relatedness, and prior knowledge in children's overextensions. *Journal of Child Language.*

Gelman, S. A., & Ebeling, K. S. (1998). Shape and representational status in children's early naming. *Cognition, 66,* B35–B47.

Gelman, S. A., & Gottfried, G. M. (1996). Children's causal explanations of animate and inanimate motion. *Child Development, 67,* 1970–1987.

Gelman, S. A., & Kirzhner, M. (1995). [Taxonomic, shape, and thematic classification of photographs by preschool children.] Unpublished raw data.

Gelman, S. A., & Markman, E. M. (1986). Categories and induction in young children. *Cognition, 23,* 183–209.

Gelman, S. A., & Markman, E. M. (1987). Young children's inductions from natural kinds: The role of categories and appearances. *Child Development, 8,* 157–167.

Gelman, S. A., & Medin, D. L. (1993). What's so essential about essentialism? A different perspective on the interaction of perception, language, and conceptual knowledge. *Cognitive Development, 8,* 157–167.

Gelman, S. A., & Wellman, H. M. (1991). Insides and essences: Early understandings of the nonobvious. *Cognition, 38,* 213–244.

Gelman, S. A., Wilcox, S. A., & Clark, E. V. (1989). Conceptual and lexical hierarchies in young children. *Cognitive Development, 4,* 309–326.

Gentner, D., & Imai, M. (1994). A further examination of the shape bias in early word learning. In *Proceedings of the Child Language Research Forum* (pp. 167–176). Stanford, CA: Center for the Study of Language and Information.

Golinkoff, R. M., Shuff-Bailey, M., Olguin, R., & Ruan, W. (1995). Young children extend novel words at the basic-level: Evidence for the principle of categorical scope. *Developmental Psychology, 31,* 494–507.

Goodman, N. (1972). Seven strictures on similarity. In N. Goodman (Ed.), *Problems and projects* (pp. 437–447). Indianapolis: Bobbs-Merrill.

Hampton, J. A. (1982). A demonstration of intransitivity in natural categories. *Cognition, 12,* 151–164.

Heit, E., & Rubinstein, J. (1994). Similarity and property effects in inductive reasoning. *Journal of Experimental Psychology: Learning, Memory, and Cognition, 20,* 411–422.

Hickling, A. K., & Gelman, S. A. (1995). How does your garden grow? Early conceptualization of seeds and their place in the plant growth cycle. *Child Development, 66,* 856–876.

Hirschfeld, L. A. (1996). *Race in the making.* Cambridge, MA: MIT Press.

Imai, M., Gentner, D., & Uchida, N. (1994). Children's theories of word meaning: The role of shape similarity in early acquisition. *Cognitive Development, 9,* 45–75.

Jackendoff, R. (1996). Semantics and cognition. In S. Lappin (Ed.), *The handbook of contemporary semantic theory* (pp. 539–559). Cambridge, MA: Blackwell.

Johnson, K., Mervis, C., & Boster, J. (1992). Developmental changes within the structure of the mammal domain. *Developmental Psychology, 28,* 74–83.

Johnson-Laird, P. N., & Wason, P. C. (1977). *Thinking: Readings in cognitive science.* Cambridge, England: Cambridge University Press.

Jones, S. S., & Smith, L. B. (1993). The place of perception in children's concepts. *Cognitive Development, 8,* 113–139.

Jones, S. S., Smith, L. B., & Landau, B. (1991). Object properties and knowledge in early lexical learning. *Child Development, 62,* 499–516.

Kalish, C. (1995). Essentialism and graded membership in animal and artifact categories. *Memory and Cognition, 23,* 335–353.

Keil, F. C. (1989). *Concepts, kinds, and cognitive development.* Cambridge, MA: MIT Press.

Keil, F. C. (1995). *The growth of causal understandings of natural kinds.* In D. Sperber, D. Premack, &

A. Premack (Eds.), *Causal cognition: A multidisciplinary debate* (pp. 234–262). Oxford, England: Oxford University Press.

Kolstad, V., & Baillargeon, R. (1996). *Appearance- and knowledge-based responses of 10.5-month-old infants to containers.* Manuscript under revision.

Lamberts, K. (1995). Categorization under time pressure. *Journal of Experimental Psychology: General, 124,* 161–180.

Landau, B., Jones, S. S., & Smith, L. B. (1992). Perception, ontology, and naming in young children: Commentary on Soja, Carey, and Spelke. *Cognition, 43,* 85–91.

Landau, B., Smith, L. B., & Jones, S. S. (1988). The importance of shape in early lexical learning. *Cognitive Development, 3,* 299–321.

Locke, J. (1959). *An essay concerning human understanding* (Vol. 2). New York: Dover. (Original work published 1894)

Maloney, L. T., & Gelman, S. A. (1987). Measuring the influence of context: The interpretation of dimensional objectives. *Language and Cognitive Processes, 2,* 205–215.

Malt, B. C. (1990). Features and beliefs in the mental representation of categories. *Journal of Memory and Language, 29,* 289–315.

Malt, B. C. (1994). Water is not H_2O. *Cognitive Psychology, 27,* 41–70.

Mandler, J. M. (1993). On concepts. *Cognitive Development, 8,* 141–148.

Mandler, J. M., & McDonough, L. (1993). Concept formation in infancy. *Cognitive Development, 8,* 291–318.

Markman, E. M. (1989). *Categorization and naming in children: Problems of induction.* Cambridge, MA: MIT Press.

Markman, E. M., & Callanan, M. A. (1984). An analysis of hierarchical classification. In R. J. Sternberg (Ed.), *Advances in the psychology of human intelligence* (Vol. 2, pp. 325–365). Hillsdale, NJ: Lawrence Erlbaum Associates.

Markman, E. M., & Hutchinson, J. E. (1984). Children's sensitivity to constraints on word meaning: Taxonomic versus thematic relations. *Cognitive Psychology, 16,* 1–27.

Massey, C., & Gelman, R. (1988). Preschoolers' ability to decide whether a photographed unfamiliar object can move itself. *Developmental Psychology, 24,* 307–317.

Mayr, E. (1991). *One long argument: Charles Darwin and the genesis of modern evolutionary thought.* Cambridge, MA: Harvard University Press.

McCloskey, M. E., & Glucksberg, S. (1978). Natural categories: Well defined or fuzzy sets? *Memory and Cognition, 6,* 462–472.

Medin, D. L. (1989). Concepts and conceptual structure. *American Psychologist, 44,* 1469–1481.

Medin, D. L., & Ortony, A. (1989). Psychological essentialism. In S. Vosniadou & A. Ortony (Eds.), *Similarity and analogical reasoning* (pp. 179–195). Cambridge, England: Cambridge University Press.

Medin, D. L., & Shoben, E. J. (1988). Context and structure in conceptual combination. *Cognitive Psychology, 20,* 158–190.

Merriman, W. E., & Bowman, L. L. (1989). The mutual exclusivity bias in children's word learning. *Monographs of the Society for Research in Child Development, 54* (Serial No. 3–4).

Mervis, C. B., Johnson, K. E., & Scott, P. (1993). Perceptual knowledge, conceptual knowledge, and expertise: Comment on Jones and Smith. *Cognitive Development, 8,* 149–155.

Murphy, G. L. (1993). Theories and concept formation. In I. Van Mechelen (Ed.), *Categories and concepts: Theoretical views and inductive data analysis* (pp. 173–200). New York: Academic Press.

Murphy, G. L., & Medin, D. L. (1985). The role of theories in conceptual coherence. *Psychological Review, 92,* 289–316.

Olseth, K. L., & Barsalou, L. W. (1995). The spontaneous use of perceptual representations during conceptual processing. In *Proceedings of the seventeenth annual meeting of the Cognitive Science Society* (pp. 310–315). Hillsdale, NJ: Lawrence Erlbaum Associates.

Quine, W. V. O. (1977). Natural kinds. In S. P. Schwartz (Ed.), *Naming, necessity, and natural kinds* (pp. 155–175). Ithaca, NY: Cornell University Press.

Rips, L. J. (1989). Similarity, typicality, and categorization. In S. Vosniadou & A. Ortony (Eds.), *Similarity and analogical reasoning* (pp. 21–59). New York: Cambridge University Press.

Rips, L. J., & Collins, A. (1993). Categories and resemblance. *Journal of Experimental Psychology: General, 122*, 468–486.

Rosch, E. (1978). Principles of categorization. In E. Rosch & B. B. Lloyd (Eds.), *Cognition and categorization* (pp. 27–48). Hillsdale, NJ: Lawrence Erlbaum Associates.

Schwartz, S. P. (Ed.). (1977). *Naming, necessity, and natural kinds.* Ithaca, NY: Cornell University Press.

Silverstein, M. (1986). Cognitive implications of a referential hierarchy. In M. Hickmann (Ed.), *Social and functional approaches to language and thought* (pp. 125–164). New York: Academic Press.

Simons, D. J., & Keil, F. C. (1995). An abstract to concrete shift in the development of biological thought: The insides story. *Cognition, 56*, 129–163.

Smith, E. E., & Medin, D. L. (1981). *Categories and concepts.* Cambridge, MA: Harvard University Press.

Smith, L. B. (1993). The concept of same. In H. Reese (Ed.), *Advances in child development and behavior* (pp. 216–253). New York: Academic Press.

Smith, L. B., & Heise, D. (1992). Perceptual similarity and conceptual structure. In B. Burns (Ed.), *Percepts, concepts and categories* (pp. 233–272). Amsterdam: North-Holland.

Smith, L. B., & Jones, S. S. (1993). Cognition without concepts. *Cognitive Development, 8*, 181–188.

Smith, L. B., Jones, S. S., & Landau, B. (1996). Naming in young children: A dumb attentional mechanism? *Cognition, 60*, 143–171.

Sober, E. (1994). *From a biological point of view.* Cambridge, England: Cambridge University Press.

Soja, N. N., Carey, S., & Spelke, E. S. (1991). Ontological categories guide young children's inductions of word meaning: Object terms and substance terms. *Cognition, 38*, 179–211.

Soja, N. N., Carey, S., & Spelke, E. S. (1992). Perception, ontology, and word meaning. *Cognition, 45*, 101–107.

Tardif, T. (1996). Nouns are not always learned before verbs: Evidence from Mandarin speakers' early vocabularies. *Developmental Psychology, 32*, 492–504.

Taylor, M. G., & Gelman, S. A. (1993). Children's gender- and age-based categorization in similarity judgments and induction tasks. *Social Development, 2*, 104–121.

Ward, T. B. (1983). Response tempo and separable-integral responding: Evidence for an integral-to-separable processing sequence in visual perception. *Journal of Experimental Psychology: Human Perception and Performance, 9*, 103–112.

Waxman, S. R. (1991). Convergences between semantic and conceptual organization in the preschool years. In S. A. Gelman & J. P. Byrnes (Eds.), *Perspectives on language and thought* (pp. 107–145). Cambridge, England: Cambridge University Press.

Waxman, S. R., & Braig, B. (1996, April). *Stars and starfish: How far can shape take us?* Paper presented at the Tenth Biennial International Conference on Infant Studies, Providence, RI.

Waxman, S. R., & Markow, D. B. (1995, April). *Object properties and object kind: 21-month-old infants' extension of novel adjectives.* Poster presented at the Biennial Meeting of the Society for Research in Child Development, Indianapolis.

Wellman, H. M., & Gelman, S. A. (1992). Cognitive development: Foundational theories of core domains. *Annual Review of Psychology, 43*, 337–375.

Wellman, H. M., & Gelman, S. A. (1997). Knowledge acquisition. In D. Kuhn & R. Siegler (Eds.), *Handbook of child psychology, 5th ed., Cognitive development* (pp. 523–573). New York: Wiley.

White, P. A. (1995). *The understanding of causation and the production of action: From infancy to adulthood.* Hove, England: Lawrence Erlbaum Associates.

Wisniewski, E. J., & Medin, D. L. (1994). On the interaction of theory and data in concept learning. *Cognitive Science, 18*, 221–281.

CHAPTER 6

Representing Logic

ELLIN KOFSKY SCHOLNICK
University of Maryland

Representation is the way the mind encodes the world. Different theories of the mind lead to different definitions of representation, and conversely, different definitions of representation shape diverse views of cognition and its development. Just as the problem solver's definition of the initial state of a problem constrains the goals to be reached and the ways to achieve them, so the theorist's definition of the way external information is taken in and transformed into the mind's vocabulary shapes our theories of cognition and its development. This chapter focuses on the interplay between definition and development in approaches to two kinds of representation, categorical and conditional connections. Because representation is a rich and complicated term, the first section briefly situates discussion of selected aspects of representation within a broader context. The second section reviews a set of parallel paradigm shifts in explaining categorical and conditional relations. The third section examines the implications of these paradigm shifts for understanding conceptual development.

THE RICHNESS OF REPRESENTATION

Terms like representation are multidimensional. Take the simplest instance of registering an event. A theory of representation must account for the modality in which the event is encoded, its format, content, and connections with other representations, the mechanisms producing the representations, the consequences of the representations for the cognitive system, and the psychological/ physical nature of the representation. Cognitive science is rife with debates about these issues (Fodor, 1985; Stich, 1994). Resolution of these disagreements is difficult, not merely because the conflicts stem from radically different theoretical perspectives, but also because representations are multifaceted and the material to be represented is incredibly diverse. Consequently in this chapter, I narrow the discussion to the content and form in which two types of relations, categories and conditionals, are represented.

Categories are the means by which we summarize diverse instances under one representation. We identify instances by representing them as members of a group, such as turtles. Categorical relations are also used to connect representations in a hierarchy, as in the sentence, "All turtles are reptiles." Category linkages also allow extension of knowledge about the entire group to specific members of the class. If all reptiles lay eggs, then cobras and turtles may bear young in the same way. Theories of categorization privilege different means of grouping members into a class and different functions of categorization.

The language of conditional relations is different. It is approximated by, "If it snows, then schools close" where the proposition in the if-clause is the sufficient but not necessary condition for the other proposition. Schools close for other reasons. Like categories, conditionals support reasoning. When we see snow, we know the school schedule. Just as category content varies enormously, so do conditional relations. "If-then" statements refer to causes, enablements, social rules, signals, and definitions. Consequently, as with categorical relations, explanations of conditional reasoning vary in whether they emphasize semantic content or the syntactic form (Scholnick, 1990).

PARADIGM SHIFTS

Categories and conditionals are central to scientific thought, because they are, respectively, the basis for taxonomies and hypothesis testing. They are also logically interconnected. Class inclusion can be described as a conditional, as in "If it is a turtle, then it is a reptile." All turtles are part of the class of reptiles. Comprehension of each relation may draw upon the nature of the instances (semantics) and the nature of the relational rule (syntax). Moreover, there have been parallel shifts in descriptions of conditional and categorical relations. In each case, initially the relation was characterized in terms of logical rules. Arguments that people either could not or did not represent the relation in logical terms led to the contention that general mechanisms of semantic interpretation more validly expressed people's interpretations of categories and conditional sequences. This view was succeeded by discussions of domain-specific categorical and conditional reasoning. The theoretical shifts included changes in the description of children and their developmental course.

Categorical Thinking

The Syntactic Approach.   Medin (1989) has characterized a succession of three paradigms for understanding categorization. A key issue in categorization is the definition of the criteria for class membership. In the "classical" approach to categories and concepts, a category was defined by necessary and sufficient features. Categories were formed by using an "all and only" rule. *All* members of the category necessarily shared some common criterial property. Satisfying the criterion was sufficient for category membership. This criterion also made the category unique. *Only* members of the category had that property. All even numbers and only even numbers are divisible by two. Categories are related through class inclusion. Members of a superordinate class share a few common attributes. Subclasses are created by adding additional criteria. Therefore superordinate classes are more inclusive and the properties defining the superordinate class must be shared by members of the subordinate class.

Equivalence pervades classical descriptions of categorization. Category members are equivalent because each obeys the rule; all categories have the same equivalence structure; and expert categorizers are general problem solvers able to apply the rule with equal facility to any content. Notice that classical categories are also sharply defined. Something is either in the category or it is not by virtue of a set of qualitative criteria. The categorical label either applies (is true) or it does not (is false). By extension, the categorizer either knows the rule or does not.

Classical categories are created using a syntactic rule to make qualitative contrasts. The approach to cognition and its development had the same properties. Development is the acquisition of logical rules. The stages of development are general (as logical rules are general) and they consist of qualitative transformations. For Piaget (Inhelder & Piaget, 1964), the development of this logic rested on the initial emergence of the capacity to code representations symbolically followed by the growth of the capacity to integrate representations into a taxonomic hierarchy based on a system of rules.

Piaget's (1980, 1985, 1991) general description of equilibration is analogous to his specific account of the formation of categories and taxonomies. For example, when young children try to predict which letters will be reversed when reflected in a mirror, they eventually observe that all and only the asymmetrical letters are reversed. They form two mutually exclusive classes. A search for a reason why the same mirror has different effects on symmetrical and asymmetrical letters leads them to correlate the properties of mirrors and the definition of symmetry. Mirrors rotate letters around a vertical axis, and the definition of symmetry is equivalence on rotation. Cognitive development progresses through analysis of problem states into distinctive subclasses and subsequent synthesis into a higher order law. Conscious awareness of this mechanism marks the transition from concrete to formal operations. Thus categorical representation is the product of and producer of development.

General Semantics. Piaget's theory of categorization is syntactic or generalized. A stage theory incorporating categorical competence is also generalized.

But categorical skill is not. Children's performance varies depending on the nature of the materials, the level of the category in the hierarchy, and the language by which the task is framed (Scholnick, 1983; Winer, 1980).

Rosch (Mervis & Rosch, 1981; Rosch & Mervis, 1975; Rosch, Mervis, Gray, Johnson, & Boyes-Braem, 1976) drew attention to a more fundamental problem that shifted the emphasis in category theory from syntax to semantics. People's category labels do not refer to sharply defined groups of instances and their cognitive representation of those groups usually does not conform to equivalence categories. Instead their categories are graded and probabilistic. Categories are defined by bundles of features. Some members have more of those features than others, and some features are possessed by more class members than other features. Contrast the prototypical small, flying, singing robin with the large, flightless, songless emu. Both are birds, but less representative members are often difficult to classify because they lack many of the definitional features. The sharp definition of classes was also questioned. A whale and a platypus are both mammals. The whale swims like a fish but bears live young. The platypus is terrestrial but lays eggs.

Rosch suggested that the structure of categories mirrored the natural order, which also consisted of peaks and valleys (much like probability curves). In each group some members possessed many diagnostic indices, but these diagnostic signs tapered off to category members with very few characteristic features. Usually the diagnostic features, such as shape, were perceptually or culturally salient. Thus the natural landscape yielded affordances to enable the categorizer to detect category membership and the prime exemplars of the category. Whereas the syntactic theory attributed the structure of categories to the observer's imposition of rule applicable to all contents, Rosch's theory attributed the structure to a universal property of the external environment. Mervis and Rosch (1981) also claimed that there was a basic level at which we formed classes that provided an optimal balance between commonality of the category members and distinctiveness from other groups. Socializers introduced categories to children at this level and labeled first the most diagnostic instances within categories.

Thus categorizers merely need to observe nature closely and make frequency counts of associations between clusters of features. Even infants can form categories because they are capable of detecting features and retaining information about frequencies of co-occurrence (Cohen & Younger, 1983). They simply need the opportunity to discover categories and encode them in representations that mirror the natural world.

Categorical competence emerges early and is dependent on the instances provided the child. Development is graded and probabilistic. More atypical instances are categorized later than typical ones, and abstract superordinate categories are acquired later because there are fewer features shared by their members than in the more cohesive basic categories. Whereas Piaget claimed categorization depended on prior advances in symbolization and in constructing the rules for combining symbols, Rosch presupposed direct perception of categories. There was, however, debate about whether a class was formed by tabulating feature correlations or by noting similarities to core exemplars (Smith & Medin, 1981).

Rosch's perspective provides a fine-grained view of category structure. But it does not permit easy generalization of properties from a superordinate to a subordinate class because there is no guarantee that any particular property is found at every level of the hierarchy.

Domain Specificity. Family resemblance classes are semantic, shaped by their members. But each class has the same structure and is formed by the same cognitive mechanisms of detection and association. The approach foundered because the categorical cuts and learning mechanisms postulated by Rosch were too vague and general (Medin, 1989). The theory could not explain why the designation of the prototype or central example shifts across cultures and task contexts. Therefore, appeals to a natural determination of category boundaries seemed insufficient. Without any guide for deciding which features are central to defining a category, the task of category construction seems intractable. The categorizer would have to sort through an infinite number of features before discovering the right ones. Thus the approach was considered incomplete because it described categorization unmediated by the interpretations of the observer based on specific knowledge of the domain. Debates also arose about definitions of a feature, and the ways features were linked. This led to a different characterization of category knowledge (Gelman & Coley, 1991; Gelman, Coley, & Gottfried, 1994; Keil, 1991, 1994; Medin, 1989).

We began with the claim that a theory of representation is a theory of the mind and its development. From this third perspective, categorical representations are, themselves, theories. The concept of turtle is a theory about how its features reflect a design solution to a problem facing all life forms, how to survive and reproduce in a particular ecological niche. Like equivalence concepts, all the members of the theory-based class share a common property (an essence). The theory produces a *causal* (not a logical) network that translates the essence into a set of obvious features (shell) and not so obvious features (leucocyte) of category members. Each feature is linked to the essential design form and to one another because the features are expressions of some basic ground plan defining the category. However, the causal mechanisms and "inner essentials" may differ for biological kinds, artifacts, or mental life (Keil, 1991). So theories are based on domain-specific knowledge. Because essence is substituted for the content-free necessary and sufficient features that underlie classical categories, both conceptual frameworks support inferences and generalizations about category properties. But the inferences of interest in the theory-based approach are inductive—from one subordinate class to another based on inferred similar essences.

Like family resemblance categories, theory-based categories are structured by the properties of their instances. But the surface features are not linked together associatively but by their causal connections to the inner essences that define life forms or artifacts. However the links vary in strength as they do in Rosch's theory. Understanding is graded with easier induction within basic categories and among typical instances (Osherson, Smith, Wilkie, Lopez, & Shafir, 1990).

Construction of a category requires principled selection of features and causes. Persons must understand intuitively what a theory is (as opposed to an associative network or rule). They must also know what qualifies as a constituent of each specific theory (look for organs on animals) and what qualifies as an acceptable causal-explanatory link (organs serve some life function). Theory-theorists take different stances on the origin and development of this knowledge. The predominant view incorporates domain-specific innate constraints on the contents and procedures for theory construction (Carey & Spelke, 1994; Gelman & Coley, 1991; Keil, 1991). The structure and initial principles that guide a domain are set tentatively and then elaborated and reorganized. This starting state for theory construction presumes considerable representational competence. Initially theory construction is intuitive, but the emergence of language and accumulating knowledge may enable more refined, conscious, and explicit understanding (Karmiloff-Smith, 1992).

Conditional Thinking

Logical Rules.   Category theory has shifted from logic to reference. So have analyses of conditional thinking. As in his treatment of categories, Piaget (Inhelder & Piaget, 1958) grounded conditional thinking in grasp of logic. Whereas classical categories require finding the necessary and sufficient conditions for membership, conditional reasoning is based on multiple, sufficient conditions. The conditional statement, "If it snows, schools close," implies that snow is sufficient to close schools, but there are other occasions for holidays. Let us call the content of the if-clause p, the content of the main clause q, and their complements, not-p ($\sim$p) and not-q ($\sim$q). The logical interpretation of "if p, then q" covers three situations: p only occurs with q (p.q), and $\sim$p can co-occur with either q or $\sim$q ($\sim$p.q or $\sim$p.$\sim$q). In snow, schools close; at other times, the school schedule is unpredictable. Logic enables solving this problem:

If it snowed (p), schools were closed (q).

My school was open ($\sim$q).

Did it snow?

No, it did not. $\sim$Q can only appear with $\sim$p. This understanding applies to precipitation and school schedules, abstract p's and q's, and even impossible or contrary to fact events such as congressional harmony producing balanced budgets. Semantic content is irrelevant.

Piaget (Inhelder & Piaget, 1958) embedded conditional thinking in a larger system of logic, the INRC group, which was the foundation for formal operations. The INRC group provided structure and coherence for several logical, mathematical, and physical representations. Additionally formal operations, which worked on a high level of abstraction, enabled individuals to represent explicitly and consciously the workings of their own minds. The logic of formal operations evolved from concrete operations, the stage where classification and quantification skills emerged, and was considered a means to consolidate and integrate qualitative and quantitative thought under one rubric.

Piaget's analysis of conditional thought raised the same problems as his analysis of categories. Although the same logic should apply to diverse tasks, participants perform unevenly on them. Accuracy in conditional reasoning varies across contents. Even with the same content, some conditional deductions are harder than others. Even mature reasoners or students majoring in philosophy do not behave as if they were using conditional logic. They cannot select the instances that falsify a conditional rule (p should never appear with ~q) and cannot grasp the nature of multiple sufficient contingencies: The consequent, q can appear with both p and ~p because p is only one possible precondition for q (Braine & Rumain, 1983; Johnson-Laird, 1983).

General Semantics. One response to these anomalies was to modify the syntax, and link it to a set of innate processing programs that differed in required cognitive resources (Braine & Rumain, 1983). Johnson-Laird (Johnson-Laird, 1983; Johnson-Laird & Byrne, 1991; Johnson-Laird, Byrne, & Schaeken, 1992) abandoned syntactic rules and suggested that individuals rely on their representation of the semantic content of events and on specific interpretive processes to draw conclusions. Reasoning is based on two representational skills, the ability to use the meaning of connectives to construct a format into which events can be slotted, and the ability to map the events in a clause into the anticipated format. *If* means [p] q where the brackets signify *implicitly* that p only appears with q, but the unbracketed, unconstrained q can appear with p or ~p. When new information arrives about the status of p or q, reasoners represent the new data as a model and then use a set of semantic procedures to combine the new and old models into a parsimonious set. Next they draw a conclusion about the integrated representations and test the conclusion to see if no alternative models of the premises could refute it.

It would seem as if Johnson-Laird simply substituted the meaning of the connective for a logical rule. But reasoning also depends on how information is combined from each premise. Premises may give rise to a single or to multiple models. For the conditional premise [p] q, when the next premise and its associated model is p, then it is easy to integrate the initial and additional model because they overlap. But when the second premise describes ~q, the individual must flesh out the [p] q to produce the three implicit models of the initial premise p.q, ~p. q and ~p.~q. Only the third model contains ~q and therefore leads to the conclusion ~p. Failures in fleshing out the premise or production of models in excess of one's processing capacity produce errors in integrating models and searching for counterexamples.

Johnson-Laird assumed that model-building capacity unfolds under the guidance of innate constraints. Presumably their representational skills enable children to acquire two knowledge bases. First, perception and discourse with others enable construction of representations of various situations (Johnson-Laird & Byrne, 1991). Growing linguistic competence also contributes to a second knowledge base, which provides interpretation of connectives. When given a deductive task, children use these two bases to generate a model of the initial premise. Then they incorporate information from additional premises to find a conclusion. It is assumed the principles guiding integration across models and premises are unlearned, but developmental limitations in the size of working memory constrain the number of models children can generate, and the extent to which implicit information can be made explicit. Finally, reasoning hinges on a metarepresentational skill, enabling the reasoner to reflect on performance and prompting the search for alternative explanations and counterexamples (Johnson-Laird & Byrne, 1991). Perhaps there are developmental limitations here, too.

Domain-Specific Theories.   Johnson-Laird used a general model that accounted for reasoning with conditionals and other rules under the same rubric. Differences among rules were explained by quantitative considerations, like the number of steps in the reasoning program or the number of models to be generated. But the analysis failed to account for a pervasive finding in the literature: Premise content affects performance (Evans, 1993). Instead content differences were often attributed to familiarity or invited inferences. There were no principled explanations of content variations.

However, some recent proposals suggest that some conditional reasoning is based on domain-specific knowledge of various social conventions, such as permission, obligation, and social exchange (Cheng & Holyoak, 1985; Cosmides, 1989). The structure of these situations happens to mirror the structure of conditionals. Within these contexts, people appear to use conditional logic, but they are actually invoking a familiar schema for each situation. For permissions, if someone takes an action, the person must satisfy some precondition. American teenagers know when alcohol consumption is permitted. If you order drinks in a bar, you must be 21. A particular age limit licenses drinking. It is easy to work out the implications of the rule. Drinkers must be 21, but the age of teetotallers is irrelevant. Twenty-one-year-olds can decide whether or not they want to drink in public, but younger persons must not drink in bars. Even if we were to invent a new permission rule, as governmental institutions often do, people would understand the implications. An abstract formula such as "if you want to do A, you must have satisfied precondition B" suffices to produce a high level of performance on *"if-then"* problems (Cheng, Holyoak, Nisbett, & Oliver, 1986). Even young children solve conditional tasks couched in deontic content (Girotto, Light, & Colbourn, 1988). And the performance is content specific because adept reasoners will falter if another schema is used (Cheng et al., 1986).

The underlying representation is called a pragmatic schema. The schema conjoins four social goal-oriented situations describing what happens when a precondition is satisfied or it is not, or the action has been taken or it has not. So when premises are presented, people use semantic knowledge to identify the appropriate social schema, and then select the part of the schema that applies. Cheng and Holyoak (1985) claimed the schema is derived from repeated experiences in early childhood with permission situations, whereas Cosmides (1989) argued that the importance of quick and accurate reading of social exchanges necessitates innate interpretive biases in this domain.

DIFFERENT PARADIGMS, DIFFERENT LEVELS, OR DIFFERENT STRATEGIES?

Historical Shifts

I have presented a historical progression of paradigms of representation of categorical and conditional understanding that presuppose different abilities and different developmental paths. The story of reliance on generally applicable logical rules acquired late in development ceded to accounts of general perceptual and linguistic representations acquired early in development. Recently, domain-specific semantic theories are thought to provide the representations permitting reasoning. Their emergence depends on both innate constraints and life experiences.

Are we at the end of the progression? What problems remain to be solved? There is a need for a more precise delimitation of domains (Keil, 1994), a more specific description of the theories that comprise them (e.g., Wellman, 1990), and a better specification of the processes that permit application of conceptual knowledge to particular tasks (Keil, 1994). Because contemporary work on categories and conditionals uses domain-specific analyses, it may be profitable to explore linkages. What is implicit in each area is explicit in the other. The theory-based approach to categorization takes causal and contingent reasoning for granted whereas a schema-based approach to conditional thought assumes formation of semantic schemas is straightforward. What is the interplay between the formation of causal and contingent connections within a domain and the formation of the semantic concepts linked by the connections?

Integration of the two approaches raises fundamental questions about the nature of conceptual representation because differences exist between the two approaches. Intuitive theories of biology or psychology are more general than deontic schemas. Do the schemas and theories provide equivalent supportive context for reasoning? Do children reason as well when conditionals describe biological connections as they do with deontic content? Do people postulate the underlying rationale for permission rules and make inductive generalizations based on the rationale?

Deontic schemas also have a looser structure than intuitive theories (Cheng & Holyoak, 1985). Folk theories contain causal networks, but schemas are simply packages of rules. However, Manktelow and Over (1990, 1991) have proposed that some deontic schemas may rest on a conceptual analysis of costs and benefits. Are there intuitive theories of deontic schemas?

The stories of origin differ. Most accounts of the theory-based approach stress innate constraints (Gelman & Coley, 1991), whereas pragmatic schemas are thought to be gained from experience. However, Cosmides (1989) offered a nativist account of the origins of pragmatic schemas.

Stages

Maybe the different accounts of conditional and category representation are not merely paradigms succeeding one another, but snapshots of different steps in development. Each "paradigm" provides a different way of viewing a conceptual connection that privileges different aspects of the relation: the perceptual features of category members, the interconnectedness of the features in a causal network, or the abstract nature of groups. Similarly, theories of conditional reasoning emphasize the nature of domain-specific contingencies, the reasoning programs by which conclusions are derived from a set of premises, or the general structure of conditional relations. The pragmatic approach stays close to experiential data, the mental models approach focuses on integration of information across premises, and the logical approach examines the abstract structure of conditional relations.

Children's early representations and reasoning may be based on detecting empirical regularities (perhaps guided by innate attentional biases). The data are then organized into narrow theories, which make the material more cohesive and memorable. Then children derive a broader theory based on analogies and generalizations across data sets. Multiple influences may produce this developmental progression: the child's own efforts and construction, the advent of language that draws attention to connections, and informal and formal instruction.

Many researchers have postulated a shift from perceptually given to conceptually driven categories based on either domain-specific theories or syntactic rules. Keil (1989) once described the characteristic to defining shift (from family resemblance to classical concepts) and currently he notes that within a domain the child may start with a bundle of associated features along with some simple causal links that eventually multiply to form causal theories (Keil 1991, 1994). Carey (1985) suggested that children progress from a biology in which humans are used as a prototype for explanation to a theory-based view in which design for survival governs a wide range of biological organisms. Neimark (1983) argued that the earlier primitive prototype-based categories give way to classical categories because the classical categories are more abstract. Gentner and Ratterman (1991) noted that children begin by detecting low-level perceptual similarities among objects but they eventually construct analogies across domains and therefore produce more abstract rules and relations.

There are similar developmental stories of conditional logic. Piaget and Garcia (1991) observed that infants engage in content-specific actions that mimic logical relations, such as nesting cups (class inclusion) or discovering sequential contingencies. The early logic is fragmented and lacks consistency, coherence, and symbolic coding. These semantic and pragmatic procedures coalesce later and become syntactic and explicit as the child constructs symbolic representations and gains the capacity for abstraction and reflection.

Falmagne (1990) proposed that abstract logic develops through a process of semantic (and syntactic) bootstrapping. Knowledge of specific contingencies give rise to pragmatic schemas and then, with the advent of language, schemas become consciously represented rules of increasingly broader scope. Even before the advent of language, children are constrained by social rules. If they want dessert, they must first eat their lima beans. These repeated event schemas teach the child that certain acts must be preceded by satisfying particular preconditions, but that when the precondition is met, taking the action is optional. Initially, this knowledge is tied to a given event. The child's understanding of particular contingencies provides the context that enables the child to interpret the meaning of specific *if*-sentences and supports deduction from *if*. Language also provides a tool for coalescing representations so that the common structure (pragmatic schema) of all permission situations expressed in adverbial-clause *if*-sentences are placed under the same rubric.

There are further commonalities among adverbial clause *if*-sentences. In some, the *if*-clause describes the antecedent event and the main clause relates the consequent. If it rains, then the ground becomes wet. If it snows, schools close. When children recognize the co-occurrence of syntactic frame and temporal sequence, then whenever the *if*-sentence describes a sensible temporal sequence in which the antecedent is a sufficient but not necessary precondition for the consequent, the child generates a similar pattern of deductions. Disparate event schemas may feed into a more general model of antecedent *if*-clause and consequent then-relations. Although most people never derive a full-blown abstract conditional rule generalizable across radically different event relations and temporal sequences (e.g., Johnson-Laird, 1983), certainly highly trained individuals such as logicians do. It would be hard to verify scientific hypotheses without recourse to conditional logic. Thus there may be a route from domain-specific, associative contingencies to domain-specific patterns of contingencies or schemas that by dint of language become represented more generally and abstractly. Induction becomes deduction.

Different Strategies

The preceding account assumes that one mode of representation is supplanted by another and that all modes of representation serve the diverse functions of categorization or contingency reasoning equally well. Neither assumption is valid. Instead we have multiple, overlapping means of representation. They privilege different kinds of information varying in accessibility and different procedures varying in their processing demands. They may be better adapted to particular tasks or stimulus materials. Some of these representations may be available by the second year of life, although abstract representations may be the artifices acquired through schooling.

Not all domains are structured as intuitive theories (Gelman & Coley, 1991; Keil, 1991). Artifacts are less likely to be organized around a central core, though there are some broad design features. Some categories such as numbers begin as equivalence classes.

Some tasks are easier to perform with particular representations than others. Deduction, particularly predicate logic, is based on classical categories. An inference is valid or it is not. It would wreak havoc on building mental models for deduction if the model had to represent the graded internal structure of each of the common nouns in propositions (Smith & Medin, 1981). Theory-based categorization facilitates identification of the commonalities among diverse instances, construction of an explanation of the clustering of properties in a class, and inductive generalizations. Drawing boundaries among classes is helped by appreciation of the graded structure of categories.

Pragmatic schemas may be ideally suited for detecting violations of deontic rules. Mental models may be more useful for encoding other meaningful propositions and for evaluating the truth of rules and validity of conclusions (Manktelow & Over, 1990). Logical rules may be called upon with unfamiliar and abstract material.

Because children acquire their representations of categories and connections in diverse settings and apply their understanding in different contexts, they may acquire multiple ways of representing the same event or instance. The child may have a set of pragmatic schemas representing permissions, promises, and warnings, but can also represent the connection as a contingent or a conditional relation. One way of representing events may supplement or scaffold another or serve as a fallback when another representational strategy fails. Thus children may acquire overlapping models of concepts and connections that provide a rich context for cognitive processing.

There are also processing costs for each representational strategy. Abstract categories and symbols are difficult to use, whereas meaningful material facilitates reasoning (Evans, 1993). The degree of facilitation depends on the coherence of the child's own conceptual structure and the obviousness of the mapping between the structure and the reasoning task.

Reasoners, who can operate with different representational strategies, may learn to choose which one applies in different situations. Thus the development of representation involves both acquisition of a representational strategy and of intuitive knowledge about its deployment. Performance on reasoning and categorization tasks may resemble models of strategy choice (Siegler & Schrager, 1984). Choice is dependent on effort and appropriateness of the strategy.

There is ample evidence of multiple representations. The strategy choice literature is rife with multiple solutions to the same task that draw upon different representations. Siegler and Schrager (1984) have demonstrated a child can represent numbers both as tokens to be counted and as members of an addition equation with a retrievable sum. During paired associate learning, the same child shows a mixture of strategies. Children connect items by supplying a meaningful connection but when none is forthcoming, they simply rehearse the duo together (Beuhring & Kee, 1987). Adults can supply typicality ratings for members of classical categories (Armstrong, Gleitman, & Gleitman, 1983). The same 2-year-old will use category membership as the basis for inferences about dissimilar instances when given a noun label but use perceptual similarity as the basis for inferences when the label is absent (Gelman & Coley, 1990). And when the category consists of very dissimilar members, even labeling them by the same novel noun does not permit the young child to make theory-based inferences about their common essential properties (Davidson & Gelman, 1990).

Young children also represent a variety of conditional relations. Scholnick and Wing (1992, 1995) have analyzed the spontaneous conditional inferences made during parent–child conversation by children as young as 2 years of age. The pragmatic perspective on reasoning would predict that young children would make their first inferences in social rule contexts. Parents commonly state threats, bribes, warnings, and directives as conditional statements, for example, "If you don't eat food, you're going to die," or "If I spill it, you can sweep it up." In the period in which children comprehended but did not yet produce *ifs*, 78% of their inferences were made in response to parental statements of social control; but when they produced their own *ifs*, they responded as often to parental predictions and descriptions of natural phenomena or non-rule-governed social interactions as to social rules. They used a wide variety of contingencies as the basis for inference.

We also examined what children tried to accomplish by their inferences. Manktelow and Over (1990, 1991) claimed that adults evaluate deontic rules by detecting violators who fail to satisfy the precondition, or defaulters who bar people from actions even though the people have fulfilled the precondition. Because adult–child conversation is replete with threats, bribes, and warnings, we examined whether children's reasoning was devoted to evaluating whether parents would follow through or to preventing the precondition in the threat (or warning) from occurring. An example is the threat, "If you say that, then I'll be mad," and the response that prevents the precondition is, "Don't get mad at me. I won't say it." This strategy accounted for about 20% to 25% of the inferences regardless of age.

But children also used other inferential strategies. One, consistent with the mental models view, evaluated whether the *if*-statement was true. About half the children's inferences arose when the child refuted the connection between the antecedent and consequent clause or noted that the *if* was counterfactual. The father of a 4-year-old commented, "*If* you're ice, you better get outside or you'll melt." The child replied, "Ice will melt but I'm not ice. I'm as cold as ice," and then justified staying inside. Reasoners also changed the scope of the initial premises as in this discussion of biological categories. The father generalized, "*If* you have blood, you'll die." His 4-year-old then asked, "Do dinosaurs have blood?" In response to the father's affirmation, the child made a *modus ponens* inference, "Some blood, then they'll die." Six months earlier the child, while constructing a Star Wars scenario, remarked, "*If* I fight [and] fall in the sarlacs and then I'll die. All of the guys that almost falled in the sarlacs almost died." The changes in the scope of the argument appear in about 30% of the inferences made by 3- and 4-year-olds taking to their parents. The different levels of abstraction within an inference may underlie building different levels of abstraction of inferential rules. It is also possible to train second- and third-graders on one pragmatic schema and get generalization to others (Robison & Scholnick, 1995). This is additional evidence for flexibility in representation.

An Embarrassment of Riches

It would be parsimonious if mental representation were a monolithic medium acquired by a single route and mapped in a single fashion. An eclectic model seems unconstrained and redundant. It places a heavy burden on selection mechanisms. But eclecticism is advantageous because it enables people to match the interpretation to the task and to employ either fall-back strategies or strategies that check one another. Far from being unconstrained, representation may be guided by the purposes for which information is acquired and deployed. A more eclectic model also shifts developmental analysis, which has been confined to a chronology of acquisitions, to include a terrain populated by sites of deployment of representational strategies.

REFERENCES

Armstrong, S. L., Gleitman, L. R., & Gleitman, H. (1983). What some concepts might not be. *Cognition, 13*, 263–308.

Beuhring, R., & Kee, D. W. (1987). Developmental relationships among metamemory, elaborative strategy use, and associative memory. *Journal of Experimental Child Psychology, 44,* 377–400.

Braine, M. D. S., & Rumain, B. (1983). Logical reasoning. In J. H. Flavell & E. M. Markman (Eds.), *Handbook of child psychology: Vol 3. Cognitive development* (4th ed., pp. 263–340). New York: Wiley.

Carey, S. (1985). *Conceptual change in childhood.* Cambridge, MA: MIT Press.

Carey, S., & Spelke, E. (1994). Domain-specific knowledge and conceptual change. In S. A. Gelman & J. P. Byrnes (Eds.), *Perspectives on language and thought: Interrelations in development* (pp. 169–233). New York: Cambridge University Press.

Cheng, P. W., & Holyoak, K. J. (1985). Pragmatic reasoning schemas. *Cognitive Psychology, 17,* 391–416.

Cheng, P. W., Holyoak, K. J., Nisbett, R. E., & Oliver, L. M. (1986). Pragmatic versus syntactic approaches to training deductive reasoning. *Cognitive Psychology, 18,* 293–328.

Cohen, L. B., & Younger, B. A. (1983). Perceptual categorization in the infant. In E. K. Scholnick (Ed.), *New trends in conceptual representation: Challenges to Piaget's theory?* (pp. 197–220). Hillsdale, NJ: Lawrence Erlbaum Associates.

Cosmides, L. (1989). The logic of social exchange: Has natural selection shaped how people reason? Studies with the Wason selection task. *Cognition, 31,* 187–276.

Davidson, N. S., & Gelman, S. A. (1990). Inductions from novel categories: The role of language and conceptual structure. *Cognitive Development, 5,* 151–176.

Evans, J. St. B. T. (1993). The cognitive psychology of reasoning: An introduction. *The Quarterly Journal of Experimental Psychology, 46A,* 561–567.

Falmagne, R. J. (1990). Language and the acquisition of logical knowledge. In W. F. Overton (Ed.), *Reasoning, necessity, and logic: Developmental perspectives* (pp. 111–131). Hillsdale, NJ: Lawrence Erlbaum Associates.

Fodor, J. (1985). Fodor's guide to mental representation: The intelligent auntie's vade mecum. *Mind, 94,* 76–100.

Gelman, S. A., & Coley, J. D. (1990). The importance of knowing a dodo is a bird: Categories and inferences in two-year-olds. *Developmental Psychology, 26,* 796–804.

Gelman, S. A., & Coley, J. D. (1991). Language and categorization: The acquisition of natural kind terms. In S. A. Gelman & J. P. Byrnes (Eds.), *Perspectives on language and thought: Interrelations in development* (pp. 146–196). New York: Cambridge University Press.

Gelman, S. A., Coley, J. D., & Gottfried, G. M. (1994). Essential beliefs in children: The acquisition of concepts and theories. In L. A. Hirschfeld & S. A. Gelman (Eds.), *Mapping the mind: Domain specificity in cognition and culture* (pp. 346–365). New York: Cambridge University Press.

Gentner, D., & Ratterman, M. J. (1991). Language and the career of similarity. In S. A. Gelman & J. P. Byrnes (Eds.), *Perspectives on language and thought: Interrelations in development* (pp. 225–277). New York: Cambridge University Press.

Girotto, V., Light, P., & Colbourn, C. J. (1988). Pragmatic schemas and conditional reasoning in children. *Quarterly Journal of Experimental of Psychology: Human Experimental Psychology, 40,* 469–482.

Inhelder, B., & Piaget, J. (1958). *The growth of logical thinking from childhood to adolescence.* London: Routledge & Kegan Paul.

Inhelder, B., & Piaget, J. (1964). *The early growth of logic in the child: Classification and seriation.* New York: Harper & Row.

Johnson-Laird, P. N. (1983). *Mental models: Toward a cognitive science of language, inference. and consciousness.* Cambridge, England: Cambridge University Press.

Johnson-Laird, P. N., & Byrne, R. M. J. (1991). *Deduction.* Hove, England: Lawrence Erlbaum Associates.

Johnson-Laird, P. N., Byrne, R. M. J., & Schaeken, W. (1992). Propositional reasoning by model. *Psychological Review, 99,* 418–439.

Karmiloff-Smith, A. (1992). *Beyond modularity: A developmental perspective on cognitive science.* Cambridge, MA: MIT Press.

Keil, F. C. (1989). *Concepts, kinds, and cognitive development.* Cambridge, MA: MIT Press.

Keil, F. C. (1991). Theories, concepts, and the acquisition of word meaning. In S. A. Gelman & J. P. Byrnes (Eds.), *Perspectives on language and thought: Interrelations in development* (pp. 197–221). New York: Cambridge University Press.

Keil, F. C. (1994). The birth and nurturance of concepts by domains: The origins of concepts of living things. In S. A. Gelman & J. P. Byrnes (Eds.), *Perspectives on language and thought: Interrelations in development* (pp. 234–254). New York: Cambridge University Press.

Manktelow, K. I., & Over, D. (1990). Deontic thought and the selection task. In K. J. Gilhooly, M. Y. G. Keane, & G. Erdos (Eds.), *Lines of thinking* (Vol. 1, pp. 153–164). London: Wiley.

Manktelow, K. I., & Over, D. (1991). Social roles and utilities in reasoning with deontic conditionals. *Cognition, 39,* 85–105.

Medin, D. L. (1989). Concepts and conceptual structure. *American Psychologist, 44,* 1469–1481.

Mervis, C. B., & Rosch, E. (1981). Categorization of natural objects. *Annual Review of Psychology, 32,* 89–115.

Neimark, E. D. (1983). There is one classification system with a long developmental history. In E. K. Scholnick (Ed.), *New trends in conceptual representation: Challenges to Piaget's theory?* (pp. 111–127). Hillsdale, NJ: Lawrence Erlbaum Associates.

Osherson, D., Smith, E. E., Wilkie, O., Lopez, A., & Shafir, E. (1990). Category-based induction. *Psychological Review, 97,* 185–200.

Piaget, J. (1980). *Experiments in contradiction.* Chicago: University of Chicago Press.

Piaget, J. (1985). *The equilibration of cognitive structures: The central problem of intellectual development.* Chicago: Chicago University Press.

Piaget, J. (1991). *Morphisms and categories.* Hillsdale, NJ: Lawrence Erlbaum Associates.

Piaget, J., & Garcia, R. (1991). *Toward a logic of meaning.* Hillsdale, NJ: Lawrence Erlbaum Associates.

Robison, G., & Scholnick, E. K. (1995, June). *The effects of pragmatic reasoning training on conditional reasoning in children and adults.* Paper delivered at the Jean Piaget Society Symposium, Berkeley, CA.

Rosch, E., & Mervis, C. B. (1975). Family resemblances: Studies in the internal structure of categories. *Cognitive Psychology, 7,* 573–605.

Rosch, E., Mervis, C. B., Gray, W. D., Johnson, D. M., & Boyes-Braem, P. (1976). Basic objects in natural categories. *Cognitive Psychology, 8,* 382–439.

Scholnick, E. K. (1983). Why are new trends in conceptual representation a challenge to Piaget's theory? In E. K. Scholnick (Ed.), *New trends in conceptual representation: Challenges to Piaget's theory?* (pp. 41–70). Hillsdale, NJ: Lawrence Erlbaum Associates.

Scholnick, E. K. (1990). The three faces of if. In W. F. Overton (Ed.), *Reasoning, necessity, and logic: Developmental perspectives* (pp. 159–181). Hillsdale, NJ: Lawrence Erlbaum Associates.

Scholnick, E. K., & Wing, C. S. (1992). Speaking deductively: Using conversation to trace the origins of conditional thought in children. *Merrill–Palmer Quarterly, 38,* 1–20.

Scholnick, E. K., & Wing, C. S. (1995). Logic in conversation: Comparative studies of deduction in children and adults. *Cognitive Development, 10,* 319–345.

Siegler, R. S., & Schrager, J. (1984). Strategy choices in addition and subtraction: How do children know what to do? In C. Sophian (Ed.), *Origins of cognitive skills* (pp. 229–293). Hillsdale, NJ: Lawrence Erlbaum Associates.

Smith, E. E., & Medin, D. L. (1981). *Three views of concepts.* Cambridge, MA: Harvard University Press.

Stich, S. P. (1994). What is a theory of mental representation? In S. P. Stich & T. A. Warfield (Eds.), *Mental representation: A reader* (pp. 347–364). Cambridge, MA: Blackwell.

Wellman, H. M. (1990). *The child's theory of mind.* Cambridge, MA: MIT Press.

Winer, G. A. (1980). Class-inclusion reasoning in children: A review of the empirical literature. *Child Development, 39,* 449–465.

CHAPTER 7

Constructivism, Communication, and Cooperation: Implications of Michael Chapman's "Epistemic Triangle"

JEREMY I. M. CARPENDALE
Simon Fraser University

The problem of the relations between the mind and the world is a fundamental philosophical issue that permeates psychology because the assumptions we make about how we acquire knowledge of the world entail views of the mind and representation. In a paper entitled "Constructivism and the Problem of Reality," Michael Chapman (in press) described the general epistemological problem concerning how it is that we come to acquire knowledge of reality and considered a solution to this problem in the form of constructivism. Chapman extended the constructivism known from Piaget's theory, according to which we develop knowledge through acting on the world, by more explicitly incorporating a social component in the development of knowledge. Recognizing the role of communicative interaction in the process of knowledge acquisition results in a triangle consisting of subject–object relations as well as communicative interaction with other people (Chapman, 1991, in press). Chapman referred to this triadic interaction as the "epistemic triangle," and he applied this way of thinking about development to his research on children's reasoning.

In this chapter I outline Chapman's "operational semantic" theory of reasoning. I then present a study illustrating the direction in research suggested by Chapman (in press), concerning the role of language in the process of internalization (interiorization in Piaget's terminology). The general conception of knowledge reflected in the metaphor of an epistemic triangle can be applied to areas of development beyond the specific example of children's reasoning. In the final section I sketch an initial application of this way of thinking to research on the development of children's understanding of mental life.

EPISTEMOLOGY AND DEVELOPMENTAL PSYCHOLOGY

As a step in introducing a constructivist approach to the development of knowledge, Chapman described the epistemological problem concerning how it is that we come to know reality. This "problem of reality" has been debated for years but its relevance for theories of development is rarely recognized. Piaget (e.g., 1970) and others (e.g., Bickhard, 1992b; Davidson, 1992; Glasersfeld, 1979, 1995) have argued that theorietical accounts of how reasoning develops are necessarily based on theories concerning how people come to acquire knowledge of the world. These epistemological assumptions about the relation between the mind and the world entail views about the nature of the mind and mental representation, and have empirical implications.

Differing views of mental representation follow from different assumptions regarding the relations between the mind and the world. A general meaning of mental representation that is fairly widely accepted is that it refers to our knowledge of the world. What is controversial, however, is how representations re-represent; that is, how we explain our knowledge of the world. One common view is that "knowledge consists in having a mental representation that corresponds to reality *as it really is*" (Chapman, in press, p. 1). A classical problem with this commonsense understanding of knowledge is that it presupposes knowledge when that is exactly what it is meant to explain. In this view, knowledge must be presupposed because otherwise there would be no way to check the accuracy of our mental representations of the world except against other mental representations of equally unestablished accuracy (e.g., Davidson, 1992). To illustrate this skeptical argument with an analogy adapted from Wittgenstein (1953/1968), this would be like buying two copies of the morning newspaper to check the accuracy of the facts reported. This skepticism is the classical critique of the traditional view of knowledge and serves as a way of illustrating some of the problems with the traditional view of knowledge and cognition (Bickhard, 1992b). There are also additional problems with the traditional view of knowledge, and the debate over views of knowledge and the mind continues in a number of different fields (e.g., Bickhard, 1992b; Müller, Sokol, & Overton, 1998; Overton, 1994; Putnam, 1988, 1990; Taylor, 1995).

An alternative to the correspondence theory of knowledge is constructivism, according to which we construct knowledge of reality as a result of our interactions with the world. Rather than somehow forming mental representations that reproduce or "match" a pregiven reality as it really is independent of our experience, according to constructivism, we construct knowledge of reality that "fits" our experience as the result of our interactions with the world (e.g., Carpendale, 1997; Glasersfeld, 1984, 1995). In contrast to the empiricist view of mental representations as passive reproductions caused by the effects of the world on the mind like a camera or a fossil (Gillett, 1992), according to constructivism, representation is the re-presentation of aspects of experience or variations and combinations of experience.

If certain, objective knowledge of reality is questioned, relativism and solipsism due to being isolated in one's own mind might seem the inevitable result. The rejection of the possibility of stepping outside our own experience to obtain a "God's eye view" (Putnam, 1988) of an experiencer-independent reality only implies solipsism, however, if we continue to accept the traditional picture of the problem of knowledge in terms of a division between the subject and object (Overton, 1994). Constructivism transforms this picture by focusing on the triadic interaction between subjects and objects and other subjects. In this view of development we continue to develop progressively more complete and coherent knowledge of the world through coordinating our experience of the world with other people's experience (Chapman, 1988b).

The best known constructivist theorist in psychology is, of course, Piaget. But a number of scholars who do not mention Piaget, such as Putnam (1988, 1990) in philosophy, Lakoff (1987) in linguistics, and Varela, Thompson, and Rosch (1991) in cognitive science, have all advanced views that are consistent with constructivism (Overton, 1994).

The constructivist view of knowledge on which Piaget's theory is based is not always fully recognized (Glasersfeld, 1982, 1995), resulting in a variety of common misunderstandings of Piaget's theory. During his career Chapman (e.g., 1986, 1988a, 1992) rebutted many criticisms of Piaget (see also Lourenço & Machado, 1996), but he wrote that clearing up such common misunderstandings does not mean that there are no further problems with Piagetian theory. In fact, the remaining problems are often considerably more interesting. For example, it is commonly assumed that Piaget neglected the role of social factors in development. Chapman and others (e.g., Smith, 1995) corrected this misconception and pointed out that, in fact, Piaget was well aware of the influence of social factors on development. In his early work (e.g., 1923/1955, 1924/1928) Piaget believed that reasoning develops through the internalization of argumentation. But when Piaget developed his theory of concrete operations in the 1940s he wrote that he had overemphasized the role of language in the development of thought (Piaget, 1954/1973). Although Piaget emphasized that language is not sufficient for the development of thought, he continued to claim that language is necessary for the completion of certain cognitive structures. Piaget recognized the need to consider the relations between language and operations but he focused on operations because of his personal interests. Consequently, he did not successfully clarify the relations between language and operations (Chapman, 1991).

This apparent gap in Piaget's theory can be seen as an area in which constructivism needs further extension or clarification, rather than as a fatal flaw in the theory. In contrast to Piaget's emphasis on subject–object interaction, Vygotsky (e.g., 1934/1986), like the early Piaget, is usually interpreted as being primarily concerned with the internalization of social interaction. Chapman (1991) coordinated these two views of the nature of development with his proposal that "human knowing involves an irreducible *epistemic triangle,* consisting of an active subject, the object of knowledge, and a (real or implicit) interlocutor, together with their mutual relations" (p. 211). According to this approach, knowledge is constructed through coordinating one's own operative action on the world with other people's experience of the world by means of communicative interaction. The implications of this view of knowledge for theories of reasoning are evident in Chapman's theory of children's reasoning.

THE OPERATIONAL SEMANTIC THEORY OF REASONING

Chapman's "operational semantic" theory of reasoning is an extension and reinterpretation of Piaget's theory of operations (Carpendale, McBride, & Chapman, 1996). This way of thinking involves a synthesis of Piaget's theory and Wittgenstein's philosophy because Chapman described the relationship between words and actions in terms of Wittgenstein's concept of criteria (Chapman, 1987). According to Wittgenstein, there are certain publicly observable criteria for any word that determine whether that word is being used correctly. Criteria are the things that we can see and point to in order to teach someone the correct use of a word. In the case of a relational concept such as "longer than," the criteria for the correct use of the words involve *operations.* In teaching a child what "longer than" means, we could align two sticks with their bases even and check the other ends to see which stick is protruding farther. This is what "longer than" comes to mean. Chapman's idea is that children understand certain relational concepts, such as "longer than" or "more than," in terms of the operations associated with the correct use of these words. When children are asked to solve a reasoning task, they generate an answer by implicitly performing the operations that correspond to the concepts contained in the test question (e.g., "longer than" or "more than") and combining these operations (Chapman & Lindenberger, 1992).

According to operational semantic theory, concrete operational reasoning does not involve the application of a general logical principle, or rule—as assumed in the "mental logic" view of reasoning (Braine, 1990)—rather, a particular instance of the principle is generated out of the set of operations and their composition. From this perspective, rather than thinking of Piaget's operatory logic as a system of logical rules that are applied to problems, it can be interpreted as a structural description of the system of operations involved in comprehending and solving a problem (Carpendale et al., 1996; Chapman & Lindenberger, 1992).

Another prominent theory of reasoning is the theory of mental models (Johnson-Laird, 1983), according to which reasoning involves the manipulation of mental representations that correspond to the problem situation. Chapman (in press) criticized this view of reasoning as being based on untenable epistemological assumptions, and argued that if mental representation is thought of in visual-spatial terms, as in mental models theory, then an account of reasoning based on the manipulation of such mental representations cannot provide an adequate explanation of reasoning. Although visual-spatial mental representation may play a role in reasoning, the manipulation of visual-spatial representations cannot explain reasoning because such representations, whether they are mentally or physically present, still require interpretation (Chapman, in press; Russell, 1987, 1996). Instead of reasoning consisting of the mental manipulation of visual-spatial mental representations that reproduce or stand in for aspects of the world, according to operational semantic theory, reasoning involves a combination of the potential operations that are criterial for the use of certain relational terms.

Because the set of operations is assumed to develop as the result of the internalization of action, this constructivist approach accounts for the dependence of reasoning on the content of the problem for the reason that action is tied to the particular content and context. For example, the operations involved in solving a transitivity of length problem are specifically adapted to the physical dimension of length because these operations are assumed to develop from the internalization of physical action involving length. Thus, a child who could solve transitivity problems based on length would not necessarily be able to solve transitivity of weight tasks. From a constructivist interpretation of Piaget's theory, this evidence of "horizontal decalage" is not an embarrassment; rather, it should be expected because thought is assumed to develop through the internalization of action, which is content specific (e.g., dealing with length or with weight) (Chapman, 1988a).

To take another example, Chapman applied his operational semantic theory to the class inclusion problem. Here it is assumed that children's understanding of a class of objects develops through internalizing the operations of grouping the members of a class together. When this action has been mastered, the children no longer need to actually perform the operation; they can understand that certain objects belong to a class because these objects could potentially be collected together based on some criteria. From this perspective, the logical rule on which the class inclusion task is based (i.e., the major and minor subclasses added together equals the supraordinate class) captures a single moment in this process of performing implicit operations (of grouping the objects into the classes) and combining these operations (Carpendale et al., 1996).

According to operational semantic theory, operations develop through the internalization of action, and once internalized these potential actions can be performed implicitly, without external action. From this assumption we would expect that the performance of young children, who are in the process of internalizing these actions, might be improved by having just physically performed the operations in question. This expectation was supported in a study on class inclusion. We found that young children (5 to 6 years of age) did better on the task when they had just performed the operations of collecting the objects into the supraordinate class, but not when they grouped the objects into the subclasses. As expected from operational semantic theory, this grouping helped when the children did the grouping, but not when they simply watched the experimenter group the objects (Carpendale et al., 1996).

Just as the process of internalization is important in the theories of Piaget and Vygotsky, it is also central in Chapman's reinterpretation of Piagetian theory. The concept of internalization from constructivism is not a simple copying of the external to the internal (see Furth, 1969).[1] Instead of knowledge simply being transmitted, it must be reconstructed by the child. The metaphor of the epistemic triangle highlights the fact that we should pay particular attention to the relation between language and action in the process of internalization because in this view knowledge develops as the result of coordinating one's own experience with other people's experience. Thus, the nature of communication and social interaction should influence development. The direction in research proposed by Chapman (in press) was a renewed attempt to study the relation between interpersonal interaction and children's subject–object interaction in process of internalization. In order to study this internalization process, it is necessary to make repeated observations of the same children as they come to master a task. In the next section I summarize a study illustrating this approach that reveals the promise, as well as the problems, of this type of research.

LANGUAGE AND THE INTERNALIZATION OF ACTION: A STUDY OF DEVELOPMENT PROCESS

Although internalization plays a central role in theories such as Piaget's and Vygotsky's, this process is rarely explicitly studied. The problem we addressed in the study reported here is the relationship between language and thought in the context of children's reasoning, and the role of language in the process of internalization. In this study, we explored the hypothesized influence of communication, especially the role of justification, in the development of children's reasoning. Most of the research on the relations between language and thought has

---

[1]The process of internalization has recently received some theoretical attention in the sociocultural literature (e.g., Lawrence & Valsiner, 1993). In this approach the emphasis has been on social interaction, but there is movement toward including the role of children's practical activity by appealing to Gal'perin's theory (Arievitch & van der Veer, 1995).

been done in a Vygotskian framework and is usually cross-sectional in nature (e.g., Diaz & Berk, 1992). Such studies also tend to focus on developmental *outcomes* rather than the *processes* that are thought to underlie these outcomes. Chapman argued, however, that we should more directly study the hypothesized processes by repeatedly observing the same children as they work on a specific task. This type of methodology has been termed process studies or the microgenetic method (Siegler & Crowley, 1991).

In a rare longitudinal process study, Schmid-Schönbein (1990) observed the process of children slowly mastering a set of tasks over a number of sessions. Although Schmid-Schönbein was not expecting the children to talk while they worked on the tasks, she observed that over a number of sessions certain forms of children's spontaneous speech seemed to facilitate the development of their understanding of the tasks. Schmid-Schönbein suggested that this "action accompanying speech" serves the function of externalizing aspects of the child's ongoing action, and that it can be used to organize these externalized aspects. She argued that speech concerning the child's action was helpful, but speech about only the results of the child's action was not helpful. This was a small sample of children and the results were correlational, but in reviewing these videotapes Schmid-Schönbein claimed that in her interactions with the children she occasionally unintentionally encouraged or discouraged this spontaneous speech, suggesting that it might be possible to experimentally manipulate the form of speech employed by children.

We hypothesized that the process of *justifying* or explaining one's actions should facilitate the development of children's understanding of a problem, whereas just making *judgments* about the results of their actions should not help subjects in the process of mastering a task. We studied this process by videotaping 22 4- and 5-year-old children as they repeatedly returned to work on the same task over a series of six sessions. This process focused methodology allowed us to observe the possible differential effects of two language conditions. We attempted to influence the children's speech by the use of different questions from an experimenter. We expected the form of speech used by the children (justification or judgment) to influence how they developed an understanding of the principles on which the experimental task was based.

In a process study such as this, it is important to select a task that is at an appropriate level of difficulty for the age group being studied, but that also takes into consideration that the children must work on the same task over a series of sessions. This means that subjects must experience some partial success with the task even in the first session to provide motivation, but there must also be other aspects of the task that they can learn about over the course of the succeeding sessions. In this study, children were videotaped as they worked on a circular puzzle, one of the tasks used by Schmid-Schönbein (1990), over a series of six sessions. The puzzle consisted of four concentric rings that were cut into equally sized pieces, grouped around a middle circle, and surrounded by a solid frame. All the puzzle pieces were white and looked similar, but the puzzle involved a classification principle because the pieces could be classified according to ring by their curvature. Thus, the puzzle could be solved either by fitting single pieces to their places in a trial-and-error fashion, or by classifying the pieces by their curvature into the rings to which they belonged. We expected that over the course of the sessions the children would develop an understanding of the classification principle on which the puzzle is based and manifest this understanding by moving from an initial simple trial-and-error strategy to a more efficient strategy based on classifying the pieces according their curvature, which would then allow the children to visually select the pieces based on curvature.

For half of the children an experimenter asked questions that were designed to encourage them to justify or explain their actions while they made the puzzle (justification group). These children were asked questions such as, "What are you doing now?" and "How do you do that?" The other half of the children were asked questions such as "Does that piece fit?" which required only that the children make judgments about the outcome of their actions (judgment group). The strategies the children used for the selection of pieces, fitting, and correction were scored for each trial. The pieces either could be selected randomly, or the child could attempt to select correct pieces by looking at them. In order to visually select pieces the children must become aware of the criteria (i.e., the curvature) for the four types of pieces that made up the puzzle. The strategies employed by the children revealed their understanding of the classification principle on which the puzzle is based.

As expected, children in the justification group developed more competence with the puzzle than the children in the judgment group. They developed the strategy of visually selecting pieces rather than randomly picking up pieces from the pile. The use of this strategy revealed their understanding that there is a way to classify the pieces. This result held only for the young age group because the older children were already employing this strategy.

How did justifying or explaining their action help the young children in the justification group? An analysis of the videotapes revealed that the young children in both groups began the first session by randomly choosing pieces and trying them in the puzzle. The children in the judgment group tended to continue with this strategy, but the young children in the justification group began to talk about the process of fitting the pieces in the puzzle because the experimenter was asking them questions requiring them to justify or explain what they were doing. Because of this questioning, children began to verbalize the criteria for fitting the pieces and they began to understand that, although all the pieces are white, there were four classes or categories of pieces based on their curvature (i.e., all the pieces in one ring were exactly the same). With this realization the children began to look at the pile of pieces and attempt to choose one that would fit the ring they were currently working on, rather than randomly selecting a piece from the pile.

If this visual selection of pieces based on the appropriate criteria is a useful strategy, it should have resulted in increased accuracy in selecting correct pieces. To address this question we examined the percentage of pieces that were correctly placed and found that this strategy did help the young children—that is, the young children in the justification group were more accurate in their selection of pieces than the young children in the judgment group. But, unexpectedly, the older children in the *judgment* group developed more competence with the puzzle than the older children in the *justification* group.

To explore this unexpected finding, we analyzed the mistakes that children made in their corrections and found that the older children in the justification group made more mistakes in their corrections. That is, they made more irrelevant corrections (i.e., moving pieces that were already correct) than did the older children in the judgment group. The older children already had a partial understanding of how to complete the puzzle and the justification condition actually seemed to impede their development of competence with the puzzle. This unexpected result may have been because the older children were confused by the experimenter's questions, as indicated by their use of irrelevant corrections. The older children may have been more aware of conversational norms (Grice, 1975) than the young children, and when an adult continued to ask them questions they may have believed that the experimenter was implying that they had made a mistake, and, therefore, they sometimes moved or exchanged the puzzle piece.

Although this early research effort cannot provide conclusive support for the role of language in the internalization of action, these results are consistent with the hypothesis that justification can influence the development of children's understanding of problems. In this research, language seems to facilitate the development of understanding, but only during certain phases in the development of children's knowledge of a particular task. Justifying their action helped the young children discover that, although all the pieces were white, they could be classified according to curvature, and therefore, could be visually selected based on this criteria. The fact that the justification condition seemed to impede the older children's mastering of the puzzle illustrates the problems with studying communication and the potential for misinterpretation. But this study also reveals the promise of this type of experimentation. Furthermore, if, as Chapman argued, the development of knowledge involves a communicative component, then this essential aspect of development cannot be avoided in research. Although the process of internalization is important in the theories of Piaget and Vygotsky, it is not often studied, perhaps because this type of research is time consuming and expensive. In this investigation we have shown that the methodology of process studies, in which the same children are observed as they return to work on the same task, allows us to study the child coming to understand the solutions of tasks.

The research just summarized, in which an attempt was made to experimentally manipulate one aspect of the communicative component—the role of justification—within a series of experimental sessions, represents a fairly specific application of the idea that development includes a communicative component as well as an operative component. The series of experimental sessions was a very small window on children's development, and the idea of the epistemic triangle has far wider implications. The explicit inclusion of a communicative component in the development of knowledge directs our attention to the influence of the communicative interaction children experience in their relationships with parents and peers on their social and cognitive development. I now consider the implications of this perspective for the development of children's understanding of their own and other people's minds.

CONSTRUCTING AN UNDERSTANDING OF MIND

Chapman illustrated his general approach to the development of knowledge with research on children's reasoning, but his idea of the epistemic triangle can alsc be applied to other areas, such as the development of children's understanding of mental life. The recent literature on what has been termed children's developing "theories of mind" is primarily concerned with the development of children's understanding of the nature of belief (e.g., Hala & Carpendale, 1997; Lewis & Mitchell, 1994). This insight is most often assessed with what is known as a "false belief" test (Wimmer & Perner, 1983), because in order to confidently attribute an understanding of the nature of belief to young children it is necessary to demonstrate that they realize that beliefs about the world can be mistaken. Older children pass various false belief tests by demonstrating their understanding that a puppet character unfortunate enough to be out of the room when one of his or her possessions is moved to a new location will lack key information, and thus hold an outdated, and now false, belief about the object's location. Younger children, by contrast, apparently have no idea that beliefs about the world can be different from the way the world actually is, and they mistakenly claim that the puppet protagonist will somehow know the new location of his or her prized possession.

This counterintuitive and robust finding has generated a huge amount of research and the dominant theoretical explanation is that children understand the nature of beliefs by developing a "theory" that accounts for their observations of both themselves and other people (e.g., Gopnik & Wellman, 1994; Perner, 1991). This "theory theory" has been criticized as not being constructivist (Bickhard, 1992a). It would be possible to formulate a more explicitly constructivist approach to this area of development by employing the notion of the epistemic triangle. In this model, children construct knowledge of reality by coordinating their actions involving objects with other people's experience as the result of communicative interaction. Because this model includes fundamentally social as well as operative characteristics, it follows that at the same time that children are constructing knowledge of the world they are also constructing knowledge of other people. That is, children construct a model of how they and other people acquire knowledge of the world—a so-called "theory of mind."

Several steps could be described in the progressive construction of increasingly complex understandings of mind. Initially, young children may assume that other people have the same knowledge of the world that they possess. At this point children would not think that someone else could possibly hold a belief that the child knows to be false, and therefore, these young children would fail false belief tests. However, this implicit model of how knowledge is acquired will not prove adequate for long. In order to maintain the assumption of an independent external world, in the face of evidence of other people's differing beliefs about the world and their own changing beliefs based on different information, children must modify their model of the relations between their own and others' beliefs about the world to include the notion that one's beliefs about the world depend on the information to which one is exposed. With this model of how beliefs are acquired, children realize the people exposed to different information will hold different beliefs (Chandler & Boyes, 1982). This understanding is sufficient for passing a false belief test.

Even this model of the nature of beliefs and mind is not, however, equivalent to a mature adult understanding of mind. A mere false belief understanding will not allow children to make sense of situations in which people with exactly the same information still arrive at different, but equally legitimate, interpretations of this selfsame information. To accommodate to this experience of interpretive diversity, while still maintaining the assumption of an independently existing external world, children must again modify their model of the process of knowledge acquisition to achieve an early insight into the interpretive nature of knowledge. In other words, when children encounter situations in which different beliefs are apparently based on the very same information, they must revise their earlier understanding that beliefs depend on the information one is exposed to (i.e., false beliefs understanding) and achieve an "interpretive theory of mind" (Carpendale & Chandler, 1996).

The idea of the epistemic triangle is useful in this context because it is only through becoming aware of other people's beliefs about the world and coordinating these often differing perspectives with one's own beliefs that children develop an understanding of mind and the process of knowledge acquisition. The importance of communication in this development directs our attention to the nature of this communication within different relationships. There is accumulating evidence from recent research indicating that social interaction plays an important role in the development of social understanding. For example, in one study examining the influence of the child's socialization history on their understanding of mind, Perner, Ruffman, and Leekam (1994) reported evidence that the more siblings a child has the earlier he or she will develop false belief understanding. Jenkins and Astington (1996) replicated this "sibling effect," but also found that the effect of family size was greater for preschoolers who were less linguistically competent. In another study exploring the influence of children's socialization history on their subsequent understanding of mind, Lewis, Freeman, Kyriakidou, Maridaki-Kassotaki, and Berridge (1996) found that interacting with older, and thus more socially experienced, partners such as older siblings and adults was more consistently related to children's false belief understanding than interactions with younger siblings.

From the constructivist perspective outlined here, it would be expected that beyond the sheer amount of social interaction, the quality of this interaction should be important. If, as Chapman argued, knowledge of the world develops through coordinating other people's perspectives with our own, then aspects of relationships and communication that facilitate our understanding of other people's perspectives should have a positive effect on development. One aspect of relationships that was important in Piaget's (1932/1965, 1965/1995) work on moral judgment is the degree of constraint versus cooperation present in relationships. This aspect of Piaget's approach to moral development was not taken up by Kohlberg in his theory of moral development, but more recently it has been discussed by Davidson and Youniss (1995) and Youniss and Damon (1992). In his work on moral judgment, Piaget argued that children initially encounter morality within relationships of constraint with their parents in which moral rules tend to be imposed on children by parents. Young children's general immaturity of thought as well as the structure of the relationships of constraint both contribute to difficulties in parents and children reaching an understanding of each other's perspective. Because of the inequality in the relationship, parents may not feel obliged to justify their positions, or listen to and consider their children's positions.

Piaget (1932/1965) contrasted parent–child relationships of constraint with children's experience of cooperative relationships among peers. Ideally, among peers power differential is less extreme and, unlike relationships of constraint, equals have an obligation to justify their positions, as well as listen to what others have to say. Cooperative relationships, then, have the potential of approaching Habermas' (1983/1990) conception of the ideal conditions of unrestrained communication, allowing all participants to fully understand each other's positions and arrive at solutions to conflicts that everyone can agree with. Of course, actual peer relationships depart in varying degrees from this ideal. The relationships of constraint between parents and children and cooperation among peers was introduced by Piaget as a dichotomy, but he clearly acknowledged that there is a continuum of different relationships. That is, every relationship involves both cooperation and constraint. Even in relationships of constraint some cooperation is may be present, and relationships of cooperation can involve some degree of constraint; thus, most relationships involve some mixture of constraint and cooperation.

It would follow from a constructivist perspective outlined earlier, that cooperative relationships allowing free communication between parents and children should facilitate the development of an understanding of mind. Parents differ in how much they feel obliged to justify their positions and listen to their children's perspective, and thus, in how much cooperation they allow or encourage in their relationships with their children. Relationships among parents and peers that are more cooperative than constraining should facilitate children's understanding of other people's points of view. In support of this expectation, Dunn and her colleagues (e.g., Dunn, 1994; Dunn, Brown, Slomkowski, Tesla, & Youngblade, 1991) found in a longitudinal study of family interaction in the home that young children who had more conversations with their mothers about feelings and beliefs demonstrated greater understanding of false beliefs 7 months later. This interpretation is consistent with research showing that parental styles (Baumrind, 1991) differing in the extent to which parents reason with their children differentially affect development.

Another prediction following from a constructivist view of the development of knowledge is that if knowledge develops in interaction we should expect to first observe early forms of this knowledge in interaction. This prediction is consistent with research on children's social understanding (Selman, Schorin, Stone, & Phelps, 1983), as well as with research on theories of mind demonstrating improved performance with 3-year-olds when false belief tests are modified to give the child subject a role as an active participant in the interaction (Chandler & Hala, 1994; Hala & Chandler, 1996) or when subjects actually act out the answer by demonstrating with a doll (Freeman, Lewis, & Doherty, 1991). In addition, young children tended to have more success in demonstrating some "implicit" form of understanding false belief in action, through eye movements than on standard test questions (Clements & Perner, 1994).

CONCLUSION AND FURTHER IMPLICATIONS

In discussing Piaget's theory of equilibration, Chapman (1992) suggested that the significance of a theory can be measured in terms of the problems it addresses rather than just its completeness. With this criterion for success, Chapman's work should be judged to be significant because he reminded us of the importance of our underlying epistemology for our theories of development and views of the mind and representation. The constructivist view advanced by Chapman assumes that knowledge is constructed through our interaction with the world. This interaction is not restricted to just subject–object interaction or just social interaction, but both of these inseparable components of knowledge at the same time (Chapman, 1991, in press).

Beyond the examples of children's reasoning and their understanding of mind discussed previously, this general approach to the development of knowledge involving both subject–object and communicative components has important implications for theories of development in all areas. An implication of Chapman's notion of an epistemic triangle consisting of interaction involving oneself, the world, and other people is that all aspects of this triangle become internalized. Chapman (1991) wrote that the coordination of views may involve "a real (or implicit) interlocutor." That is, the interlocutor or interlocutors become internalized. According to Chapman (1991), "exchange between the subject and the interiorized interlocutor is the origin of reflective awareness" (p. 219). This idea leads to Chapman's argument that forms of reasoning develop as internalized argumentation (Chapman, 1993; Chapman & McBride, 1992). This position is consistent with Piaget's (1923/1955, 1924/1928) early work, Vygotsky (e.g., 1934/1986), and the view of moral reasoning as internalized moral dialogue (Carpendale & Krebs, 1995). Although there are many issues to work out, there is the potential to relate this approach to theories in the sociocultural tradition such as Bakhtin's view of the dialogical nature of consciousness (e.g., Taylor, 1991; Wertsch, 1991).

Although the metaphor of the epistemic triangle offers the potential to integrate some of the work in the sociocultural approach with constructivism, there is an important caveat to be aware of. The implications one draws from introducing a social dimension to constructivism depends on one's epistemological assumptions. One response to the argument that knowledge is constructed through interaction involving a social dimension is that knowledge must therefore be an arbitrary, cultural-specific, social invention. An implication of this postmodern interpretation is that it makes no sense to search for universal aspects of development, and it would appear to follow that we can study development only within specific situations. There are several reasons to question this relativistic position (for further discussion see Chandler, 1997). Chapman's position is that knowledge of reality is constructed by coordinating our own experience with other people's experience. In this view, knowledge is not an arbitrary invention and constructivism does not lead to relativism. Knowledge is constructed from something, and there is progress toward more complete and coherent knowledge of reality (Chapman, 1988b). The social or communicative leg of the epistemic triangle is not independent of action involving the world. Language is not independent of the world, and theorists such as Grice (1975), Habermas (1983/1990), and Piaget (1932/1965) have worked to describe universal aspects of communicative interaction.

ACKNOWLEDGMENTS

The preparation of this chapter was supported by a Social Sciences and Humanities Research Council of Canada Post Doctoral Fellowship. The research reported in this chapter was conducted with Peter Valentin. I would like to thank

Michael Chandler, Charlie Lewis, Irv Sigel, and Bryan Sokol for their helpful comments on earlier drafts of this chapter.

REFERENCES

Arievitch, I., & van der Veer, R. (1995). Furthering the internalization debate: Gal'perin's contribution. *Human Development, 38,* 113–126.

Baumrind, D. (1991). Parenting styles and adolescent development. In R. M. Lerner, A. C. Petersen, & J. Brooks-Gunn (Eds.), *Encyclopedia of adolescence* (Vol. 2, pp. 746–758). New York: Garland.

Braine, M. D. S. (1990). The "natural logic" approach to reasoning. In W. F. Overton (Ed.), *Reasoning, necessity, and logic* (pp. 133–157). Hillsdale, NJ: Lawrence Erlbaum Associates

Bickhard, M. H. (1992a). Commentary. *Human Development, 35,* 182–192.

Bickhard, M. H. (1992b). How does the environment affect the person? In L. T. Winegar & J. Valsiner (Eds.), *Children's development within social contexts: Vol. 1. Metatheory and theory* (pp. 63–92). Hillsdale, NJ: Lawrence Erlbaum Associates.

Carpendale, J. I. M. (1997). An explication of Piaget's constructivism: Implications for social cognitive development. In S. Hala (Ed.), *The development of social cognition (pp. 35–64).* London: University College London Press.

Carpendale, J. I. M., & Chandler, M. J. (1996). On the distinction between false belief understanding and subscribing to an interpretive theory of mind. *Child Development, 67,* 1686–1706.

Carpendale, J. I. M., & Krebs, D. L. (1995). Variations in level of moral judgment as a function of type of dilemma and moral choice. *Journal of Personality, 63,* 289–313.

Carpendale, J. I., McBride, M., & Chapman, M. (1996). Language and operations in children's class inclusion reasoning: The operational semantic theory of reasoning. *Developmental Review, 16,* 391–415.

Chandler, M. J. (1997). Stumping for progress in a post-modern world. In E. Amsel & K. A. Renninger (Eds.), *Change and development: Issues of theory, method, and application (pp. 1–26).* Mahwah, NJ: Lawrence Erlbaum Associates.

Chandler, M. J., & Boyes, M. (1982). Social cognitive development. In B. B. Wolman (Ed.), *Handbook of developmental psychology* (pp. 387–402). Englewood Cliffs, NJ: Prentice-Hall.

Chandler, M. J., & Hala, S. (1994). The role of interpersonal involvement in the assessment of early false-belief skills. In C. Lewis & P. Mitchell (Eds.), *Children's early understanding of mind: Origins and development* (pp. 403–425). Hove, England: Lawrence Erlbaum Associates

Chapman, M. (1986). The structure of exchange: Piaget's sociological theory. *Human Development, 29,* 181–194.

Chapman, M. (1987). Inner processes and outward criteria: Wittgenstein's importance for psychology. In M. Chapman & R. A. Dixon (Eds.), *Meaning and the growth of understanding: Wittgenstein's significance for developmental psychology* (pp. 103–127). Berlin: Springer-Verlag.

Chapman, M. (1988a). *Constructive evolution: Origins and development of Piaget's thought.* New York: Cambridge University Press.

Chapman, M. (1988b). Contextuality and directionality of cognitive development. *Human Development, 31,* 92–106.

Chapman, M. (1991). The epistemic triangle: Operative and communicative components of cognitive competence. In M. Chandler & M. Chapman (Eds.), *Criteria for competence: Controversies in the conceptualization and assessment of children's abilities* (pp. 209–228). Hillsdale, NJ: Lawrence Erlbaum Associates.

Chapman, M. (1992). Equilibration and the dialectics of organization. In H. Beilin & P. B. Pufall (Eds.) *Piaget's theory: Prospects and possibilities* (pp. 39–59). Hillsdale, NJ: Lawrence Erlbaum Associates.

Chapman, M. (1993). Everyday reasoning and the revision of belief. In J. Puckett & H. W. Reese (Eds.), *Mechanisms of everyday cognition* (pp. 95–113). Hillsdale, NJ: Lawrence Erlbaum Associates.

Chapman, M. (in press). Constructivism and the problem of reality. *Journal of Applied Developmental Psychology.*

Chapman, M., & Lindenberger, U. (1992). Transitivity judgments, memory for premises, and models of children's reasoning. *Developmental Review, 12,* 124–163.

Chapman, M., & McBride, M. (1992). The education of reason: Cognitive conflict and its role in intellectual development. In C. U. Shantz & W. W. Hartup (Eds.), *Conflict in child and adolescent development* (pp. 36–69). Cambridge, England: Cambridge University Press.

Clements, W. A., & Perner, J. (1994). Implicit understanding of belief. *Cognitive Development, 9,* 377–395.

Davidson, P. M. (1992). The role of social interaction in cognitive development: A propaedeutic. In L. T. Winegar & J. Valsiner (Eds.), *Children's development within social contexts: Vol. 1. Metatheory and theory* (pp. 19–37). Hillsdale, NJ: Lawrence Erlbaum Associates.

Davidson, P., & Youniss, J. (1995). Moral development and social construction. In W. M. Kurtines & J. L. Gewirtz (Eds.), *Moral development: An introduction* (pp. 289–310). Boston: Allyn & Bacon.

Diaz, R. M., & Berk, L. E. (Eds.). (1992). *Private speech: From social interaction to self-regulation.* Hillsdale, NJ: Lawrence Erlbaum Associates.

Dunn, J. (1994). Changing minds and changing relationships. In C. Lewis & P. Mitchell (Eds.), *Children's early understanding of mind: Origins and development* (pp. 297–310). Hove, England: Lawrence Erlbaum Associates.

Dunn, J., Brown, J., Slomkowski, C., Tesla, C., & Youngblade, L. (1991). Young children's understanding of other people's feelings and beliefs: Individual differences and their antecedents. *Child Development, 62,* 1352–1366.

Freeman, N. H., Lewis, C., & Doherty, M. J. (1991). Preschoolers' grasp of a desire for knowledge in false-belief prediction: Practical intelligence and verbal report. *British Journal of Developmental Psychology, 9,* 139–157.

Furth, H. G. (1969). *Piaget and knowledge: Theoretical foundations.* Englewood Cliffs, NJ: Prentice-Hall.

Gillett, G. (1992). *Representation, meaning, and thought.* Oxford, England: Clarendon.

Gopnik, A., & Wellman, H. M. (1994). The theory theory. In L. A. Hirschfeld & S. A. Gelman (Eds.), *Mapping the mind: Domain specificity in cognition and culture* (pp. 257–293). New York: Cambridge University Press.

Grice, H. P. (1975). Logic and conversation. In P. Cole & J. L. Morgan (Eds.), *Syntax and semantics: Vol. 3. Speech acts* (pp. 41–58). New York: Academic Press.

Habermas, J. (1990). *Moral consciousness and communicative action.* Cambridge, MA: MIT Press. (Original work published 1983)

Hala, S., & Carpendale, J. I. M. (1997). All in the mind: Children's understanding of mental life. In S. Hala (Ed.), *The development of social cognition* (pp. 189–239). London: University College London Press.

Hala, S., & Chandler, M. J. (1996). The role of strategic planning in accessing false-belief understanding. *Child Development, 67,* 2948–2966.

Jenkins, J. M., & Astington, J. W. (1996). Cognitive factors and family structure associated with theory of mind development in young children. *Developmental Psychology, 32,* 70–78.

Johnson-Laird, P. N. (1983). *Mental models.* Cambridge, MA: Harvard University Press.

Lakoff, G. (1987). *Women, fire, and dangerous things: What categories reveal about the mind.* Chicago: University of Chicago Press.

Lawrence, J. A., & Valsiner, J. (1993). Conceptual roots of internalization: From transmission to transformation. *Human Development, 36,* 150–167.

Lewis, C., Freeman, N. H., Kyriakidou, C., Maridaki-Kassotaki, K., & Berridge, D. (1996). Social influences on false belief access: Specific sibling influence or general apprenticeship? *Child Development, 67,* 2930–2947.

Lewis, C., & Mitchell, P. (Eds.). (1994). *Children's early understanding of mind: Origins and development.* Hove, England: Lawrence Erlbaum Associates.

Lourenço, O., & Machado, A. (1996). In defense of Piaget's theory: A reply to 10 common criticisms. *Psychological Review, 103,* 143–164.

Müller, U., Sokol, B., & Overton, W. F. (1998). Reframing a constructivist model of the development of mental representations: The role of higher-order operations. *Developmental Review, 18,* 155–201.

Overton, W. F. (1994). The arrow of time and cycles of time: Concepts of change, cognition, and embodiment. *Psychological Inquiry, 5,* 215–237.

Perner, J. (1991). *Understanding the representational mind.* Cambridge, MA: MIT Press.

Perner, J., Ruffman, T., & Leekam, S. R. (1994). Theory of mind is contagious: You catch it from your sibs. *Child Development, 65,* 1228–1238.

Piaget, J. (1928). *Judgment and reasoning in the child.* London: Kegan. (Original work published 1924)

Piaget, J. (1955). *The language and thought of the child.* New York: Meridian Books. (Original work published 1923)

Piaget, J. (1965). *The moral judgment of the child.* New York: The Free Press. (Original work published 1932)

Piaget, J. (1970). Piaget's theory. In P. Mussen (Ed.), *Carmichael's manual of child psychology* (3rd ed., pp. 703–732). New York: Plenum.

Piaget, J. (1973). *The child and reality.* New York: Grossman. (Original work published 1954)

Piaget, J. (1995). *Sociological studies.* New York: Routledge. (Original work published 1965)

Putnam, H. (1988). *Representation and reality.* Cambridge, MA: MIT Press.

Putnam, H. (1990). *Realism with a human face.* Cambridge, MA: Harvard University Press.

Russell, J. (1987). Rule following, mental models, and the developmental view. In M. Chapman & R. A. Dixon (Eds.), *Meaning and the growth of understanding: Wittgenstein's significance for developmental psychology* (pp. 23–48). Berlin: Springer-Verlag.

Russell, J. (1996). *Agency: Its role in mental development.* Hove, England: Lawrence Erlbaum Associates.

Schmid-Schönbein, C. (1990, June). *Explicating some aspects of the process of reflective reconstruction.* Paper presented at the meeting of the Jean Piaget Society, Philadelphia.

Selman, R. L., Schorin, M. Z., Stone, C. R., & Phelps, E. (1983). A naturalistic study of children's social understanding. *Developmental Psychology, 19,* 82–102.

Siegler, R. S., & Crowley, K. (1991). The microgenetic method: A direct means for studying cognitive development. *American Psychologist, 46,* 606–620.

Smith, L. (1995). Introduction to Piaget's sociological studies. In J. Piaget, *Sociological studies* (pp. 1–22). London: Routledge.

Taylor, C. (1991). The dialogical self. In D. R. Hiley, J. F. Bohman, & R. Shusterman (Eds.), *The interpretive turn: Philosophy, science, culture* (pp. 304–314). Ithaca, NY: Cornell University Press.

Taylor, C. (1995). *Philosophical arguments.* Cambridge, MA: Harvard University Press.

Varela, F. J., Thompson, E., & Rosch, E. (1991). *The embodied mind: Cognitive science and human experience.* Cambridge, MA: MIT Press.

von Glasersfeld, E. (1979). Radical constructivism and Piaget's concept of knowledge. In F. B. Murray (Ed.), *The impact of Piagetian theory: On education, philosophy, psychiatry, and psychology* (pp. 109–122). Baltimore: University Park Press.

von Glasersfeld, E. (1982). An interpretation of Piaget's constructivism. *Revue Internationale de Philosophie, 142–143,* 612–635.

von Glasersfeld, E. (1984). An introduction to radical constructivism. In P. Watzlawick (Ed.), *The invented reality* (pp. 17–40). New York: Norton.

von Glasersfeld, E. (1995). *Radical constructivism: A way of knowing and learning.* London: The Flamer Press.

Vygotsky, L. (1986). *Thought and Language.* Cambridge, MA: MIT Press. (Original work published 1934)

Wertsch, J. V. (1991). *Voices of the mind: A sociocultural approach to mediated action.* Cambridge, MA: Harvard University Press.

Wimmer, H., & Perner, J. (1983). Beliefs about beliefs: Representation and constraining function of wrong beliefs in young children's understanding of deception. *Cognition, 13,* 103–128.

Wittgenstein, L. (1968). *Philosophical investigations* (3rd ed.). Oxford, England: Basil Blackwell. (Original work published 1953)

Youniss, J., & Damon, W. (1992). Social construction in Piaget's theory. In H. Beilin & P. B. Pufall (Eds.) *Piaget's theory: Prospects and possibilities* (pp. 267–286). Hillsdale, NJ: Lawrence Erlbaum Associates.

CHAPTER 8

The Properties of Representations Used in Higher Cognitive Processes: Developmental Implications

Graeme S. Halford
University of Queensland

As children develop, their thought undergoes many changes, but some that I would like to consider here are that it becomes more explicit, more independent of content, and more flexible with age. Many cognitive developmental scholars have drawn attention to these properties before. Among them, Karmiloff-Smith (Clark & Karmiloff-Smith, 1993; Karmiloff-Smith, 1990) has shown how cognitive development within any domain is characterized by a transformation from implicit to explicit. Implicit knowledge is sufficient for tasks to be performed, but cannot be modified strategically, and is not accessible to other cognitive processes. The content-independence of thought has been addressed by Sigel (1984) under the title of *distancing strategies,* which help to separate the child mentally from the here and now. Flexibility has been addressed in many contexts but two of the most notable include Siegler and Shipley (1995), who has shown that children's strategies vary according to the circumstances, and Piaget (1950) who has long insisted on the increasing mobility and reversibility of thought as the child develops.

Cognitive theories have grown greatly in flexibility and power in the last three decades. Prior to the cognitive revolution in the 1960s, the dominant theories were behaviorist, and were founded on the idea of a link between a stimulus and a response. By contrast, work in cognitive psychology and cognitive science in the last three decades has given us theories that come much closer to accounting for the power and flexibility of human thought. Perhaps more importantly, we are starting to understand control processes and meta-domain knowledge. This means we can start to understand how humans devise strategies for performing tasks, and modify the strategies to adapt to changing conditions of performance. These theories entail recognition that human cognition is fundamentally autonomous. By contrast with most forms of artificial intelligence, humans are self-programming. We devise our own procedures and strategies for performing cognitive tasks. There is still only a minority of cognitive development models that recognize this explicitly, but these have an important influence on our conceptions of cognitive development.

There has also been important progress in our understanding of the processes that underlie human cognition. Work on natural categories beginning with Rosch (1978), on decision mechanisms originating with Kahneman and Tversky (1973), and work on mental models by Johnson-Laird (1983) and others have enabled us to see the uniquely human nature of cognitive processes. Then work by Anderson (1990) and others has demonstrated the subtlety and complexity of the way human cognition adapts to the environment. This in turn has provided an alternative definition of rationality to one based on logic. Humans are not natural logicians so much as we are adaptive organisms. This is reminiscent of Piaget's (1947/1950) contention that thought is an extension of biological adaptation, but this insight has now been carried much further. The present generation of neural net models has penetrated deeper into the way information is represented and processed than had earlier models, the many questions that are still to be answered notwithstanding. The result is that we are now much better able to explain transitions to more explicit, content-independent, and flexible cognitive function that occurs as children develop.

The main purpose of this chapter is to apply the insights we now have into cognitive processes to the understanding of cognitive development. We want to know what kinds of representations, and what kinds of processes operating on them, would produce the kinds of developments that we have observed. One proposal that has arisen from the work in our laboratory in recent years is that processing relations is the core of higher cognitive processes (Halford, Wilson, & McDonald, 1995; Phillips, Halford, & Wilson, in press). The properties of higher cognitive processes are essentially the properties of relations. We will consider how relations are important in cognitive development.

RELATIONAL CONCEPTS IN COGNITIVE DEVELOPMENT

Some concepts that have been important to cognitive development manifestly entail reasoning about relations. Transitive inference has been a central, if controversial concept in cognitive development. It entails reasoning that if *aRb* and *bRc,* and if *R* is transitive, then *aRc* (e.g., if a>b and b>c, then a>c). Some well-validated models (Riley & Trabasso, 1974; Sternberg, 1980) have shown that it is performed by integrating the premises into an ordered set. Thus a>b and b>c can be integrated into a>b>c. This means the binary relations >(a,b) and >(b,c) are integrated into the ternary relation monotonically greater(a,b,c). The processing load imposed by this integration is a significant factor in the difficulty of transitive inference for both children (Halford, 1993; Halford, Maybery, & Bain, 1986) and adults (Maybery, Bain, & Halford, 1986).

A slightly less obvious case of reasoning with relations is class inclusion, which is concerned with relations between superordinate and subordinate classes. It is a truism that mathematics is about relations. Elementary knowledge of number includes knowing about binary relations like larger and smaller (e.g., 5>3, 4<8), whereas arithmetic operations addition and multiplication are equivalent to ternary relations. We can think of addition as the set of ordered triples $+\{. ., (2,3,5), . ., (5,4,9), . .\}$ such that the first two arguments sum to the third (2+3=5 etc.). Similarly, multiplication is the set of ordered triples $\{. ., (2,3,6), . . (5,4,20), . .\}$. Proportion is the quaternary relation $a/b = c/d$. Quantification entails relations between quantities, so an ordinal scale has entities arranged in monotonic order of quantity, whereas an interval scale has an addition operation and a ratio scale has both addition and multiplication operations. Counting entails incrementing numbers in correspondence with the succession relation between entities counted.

Physical concepts are concerned about relations between entities such as mass, force, electromagnetic attraction, and so forth. Perhaps the best known instance in cognitive development research is the balance scale, which entails relations between balance state, and weight and distance on left and right. And of course it is another truism that relations are the essence of social psychology.

Clearly the relations are the building blocks of our knowledge about the world. In fact, relations are central to the mathematical definition of a representation (Halford & Wilson, 1980; Suppes & Zinnes, 1963). The essence of representations is the *correspondence principle*. That is, relations in a cognitive representation correspond to relations in the situation of phenomenon represented. This topic has been treated in a more formal way elsewhere (Halford, 1993; Holland, Holyoak, Nisbett, & Thagard, 1986; Palmer, 1978).

Despite the central role of relations in higher cognitive processes, relational knowledge as such has received comparatively little explicit attention in psychology, by contrast with other disciplines such as computer science, which have developed extensive theory of relational databases. This prompted Smith (1989) to observe that "despite all the empirical work, and the importance of relational concepts, there is no unified framework for thinking about their structure and about how they develop" (p. 147). Our work has suggested that many fundamental properties of higher cognitive processes can be defined in terms of the properties of relations. What then are the properties of relational knowledge? We examine that question and contrast relational knowledge with more primitive processes.

ASSOCIATIVE AND RELATIONAL KNOWLEDGE

Though higher cognitive processes undoubtedly entail processing relations, they have not played a prominent role in traditional explanations of psychological processes, particularly within the British empiricist tradition. Associationism on the other hand has always played a prominent role, at least since Aristotle. There has been debate between proponents of various associationist viewpoints and Gestaltists, structuralists, and others (Humphrey, 1951). I do not wish to enter into, or even review, this debate here, but I want to make two proposals. The first is a set of criteria by which associations and relations may be distinguished objectively, and in a way that can be incorporated into cognitive models. The second is that associations can be seen as the more basic process, one that is shared by virtually all animals with neurons, whereas relational processing appears to be restricted to higher animals, and indeed may occur only in primates. When we consider neural net models, I argue that associative processes require representations that are simpler in important respects than those required for relations, and impose lower processing loads. First, however, I want to define the properties of relational knowledge.

A representation of a relation has three components: a relation symbol or predicate, the argument(s) of the predicate, and the binding between the two.[1] For example, the binary relation BIGGER-THAN(horse, dog) is a binding between the predicate BIGGER-THAN and the arguments "horse" and "dog." Representation of "horse" and "dog" alone is insufficient, because it fails to specify the relation. It is necessary to have a specific symbol or predicate, indicating that the relation is "larger-than." However this also is insufficient because it fails to specify whether the horse is bigger than the dog or vice versa. A binding is necessary to integrate the components and indicate which entity fills which role. The fact that "horse" fills the role of the larger entity, and "dog" the role of the smaller entity, must be represented.

Some properties of relational knowledge, and its role in higher cognitive processes, have been specified by Halford, Wilson, and Phillips (1998). The main properties are as follows:

1. *Predication,* or use of an explicit label, is one property that distinguishes relations from associations. The link between the arguments of a relation is explicitly symbolized by the predicate; in our example, the link between "horse" and "dog" is explicitly symbolized by the predicate LARGER-THAN. The property of using labeled links is shared by propositional networks, but is not characteristic of the associationist tradition, in which all links are of the same kind, and are unlabeled (Humphrey, 1951). The use of an explicit label helps make a relation accessible to other cognitive processes.

---

[1] An N-ary relation $R(a_1, a_2, \ldots, a_n)$ is a subset of the cartesian product $S_1 \times S_2 \times \ldots \times S_n$.

2. *Higher order relations* have relations as arguments, whereas first-order relations have objects as arguments. For example: BECAUSE(LARGER-THAN (horse,dog), AVOIDS(dog,horse)). BECAUSE is a higher order relation, the arguments of which are LARGER-THAN(horse,dog) and AVOIDS(dog,horse). This property means that certain relations can imply other relations, which is the property of *relational systematicity*. For example $>(a,b) \rightarrow <(b,a)$, whereas sells(seller,buyer,object) $\rightarrow$ buys(buyer,seller,object). The first instance can be written as the higher order relation IMPLIES($>(a,b)$, $<(b,a)$).

Higher order relations also distinguish relations from associations, because they mean that a relational instance can be an argument to another relation, as in the previous examples. However, an associative link per se cannot be an argument in another association, so associations cannot be recursive. When associations are chained, so that $E_1 \rightarrow E_2 \rightarrow E_3 \ldots \ldots \rightarrow E_n$, the output of one link is the input of the next. An example is the stimulus-response chains in learning theory, where the response to one stimulus produces further stimulation, which is then associated with a further response, and so on. In this case the output of one association is a component of another association, but the associative link is *not* a component of another association.

3. *Omni-directional access* means that, given all but one of the components of a relation, we can access (i.e., retrieve) the remaining component. For example, the relational schema $R(a,b)$, and given any two components as input, the third component can be retrieved. That is, any of the following can be performed:

$$R(a,-) \rightarrow b$$
$$R(-,b) \rightarrow a$$
$$-(a,b) \rightarrow R$$

This can be illustrated with the balance scale. The balance state, that is whether the beam balances, or the right or left side goes down, is a function of four variables, weight and distance on the left and weight and distance on the right. Given any subset of $N-1$ variables as input, the Nth variable can be generated as output. A common test is to present a child with a balance scale with weights on both sides and ask her to predict the balance state (e.g., Siegler, 1976, 1981). This has proved to be a successful way of investigating children's cognitive development, but it does not exhaustively test a child's understanding. A child who really understands the balance scale should also be able to determine a missing weight or missing distance. For example, given weight and distance on the left, distance on the right, and the fact that the beam is balanced, it can decide what weight must be on the right. An appropriate test item would be: If we place three weights on peg 2 on the left, how many weights must be placed on peg 3 on the right to make the beam balance (two)? Similarly, we could ask on which peg on the right two weights should be placed to achieve balance. Thus understanding of the balance scale really entails being able to start with all the variables specified except one and then determine that one, at least in an approximate fashion. This has been required in many tests of the balance scale (e.g., Surber & Gzesh, 1984). We would be unwilling to attribute understanding to a child who could compute only one type of output (such as whether the beam would balance), but could say nothing about, for example, which weights and distances were required to produce a given state of balance or imbalance. Understanding of the balance scale entails the kind of flexibility that corresponds to the omni-directional access property.

4. *Argumentation* means that relational knowledge entails representation of argument roles or slots, independent of specific instances. Thus BIGGER-THAN(-,-) entails representation of slots for a larger and a smaller entity.

5. *Dimensionality of relations* means that each argument of R can be instantiated in more than one way, and therefore represents a source of variation, or dimension. An N-ary relation may be thought of as a set of points in N-dimensional space. The number of arguments, N, corresponds to the number of dimensions in the space defined by the relation.[2] This is the basis for the complexity metric proposed by Halford et al. (1998).

The basic idea here is that processing capacity is limited, not by the number of items, but by the number of entities that have to be related. It is important to distinguish between two different concepts of working memory. It has been common for working memory to refer to information that is stored for later processing. For example, in adding 276 to 397, we might add 7 and 6 in the right column and store the tens digit for adding into the middle column later. Storage for later processing is a legitimate use of the term working memory, but it is distinct from information that is currently being processed. For example, while we are adding 6 and 7 we are not simply storing the addends. They are being actively processed, and they constrain our decision.

The processing-storage distinction is supported by working memory research (Baddeley, 1986; Halford, 1993; Halford, Maybery, O'Hare, & Grant, 1994). When tasks have been performed while concurrently storing a short-term memory load, storage has not typically interfered with processing, suggesting that the two systems are to some extent distinct. The implication is that different metrics are required for storage and processing limitations. It has been common to use short-term memory span (e.g., digit span), but these are mainly measures of storage. Another approach has been to use tasks that blend storage and processing, such as the sentence span task (Daneman & Carpenter, 1980), but this clouds the storage-processing issue, and does not lead to a complexity metric.

The number of entities that have to be related provides the most effective metric for conceptual complexity (Halford, Wilson, et al., 1994, 1998). The basic idea here is that each argument in a relation constitutes a source of variation,

---

[2]In terms of sets; a unary relation R on a set S is a subset of S. It is the set of objects $\{x \in S \mid R(x)$ is true$\}$. Similarly, a binary relation on a set S is a subset of the cartesian product $S \times S$ of elements S, a ternary relation is a subset of $S \times S \times S$ of elements of S, and so on. Each set contributes a dimension of the cartesian product.

and can function as a variable. Thus the number of arguments corresponds to the number of variables that have to be related. There is a higher processing load in computing relations between (say) three variables than two.

The contrast between integers and fractions illustrates the way processing load varies as a function of number of variables. If asked to compare ½ and ¼, young children sometimes say ¼ is more because they focus on the "4." Our innate tendency to focus on whole numbers may be a factor, as proposed by Gelman (1991). However, comparison of integers entails two dimensions, one for each integer, whereas comparison of fractions entails four dimensions, corresponding to numerator and denominator in each number. Thus comparison of fractions is inherently more complex than comparison of numbers. This can be quickly seen when we consider the variations that can occur, as English and Halford (1995) pointed out. Consider the following:

$$\frac{2}{3} > \frac{2}{4}$$
$$\frac{2}{3} < \frac{1}{3}$$
$$\frac{2}{3} = \frac{4}{6}$$
$$\frac{3}{3} > \frac{4}{3}$$

The point is that variation in any of the four dimensions, numerator or denominator, on either left or right, can affect the comparison. When comparing integers only two sources of variation must be considered. The tendency to focus on the largest number is probably a default reaction for children who cannot process all dimensions. That is, when unable to integrate all the relevant information, people focus on the most salient information. Therefore the tendency to say that focusing on the largest number is the cause of failure is an example of the common fallacy of misinterpreting defaults as causes.

6. *Decomposability* means that some relations can be composed of simpler relations. For example, the ternary relation MONOTONICALLY-LARGER(a,b,c) can be decomposed into $>(a,b)$ and $>(b,c)$ and $>(a,c)$. This permits inferences to be made, for example; MONOTONICALLY-LARGER(a,b,c) → $>(a,c)$, which forms part of the process of transitive inference.

7. *Operations on relations* include select, project, join, add, delete, union, intersect, and difference (Codd, 1990; Phillips et al., 1995). These operations permit information stored in relational knowledge structures to be accessed and manipulated in flexible and powerful ways. The structures that have been important in modeling higher cognitive processes, such as lists and trees, can all be expressed as relations.

8. *Planning and analogy*. Relational representations are essential to planning, or the organization of a sequence of actions to achieve a goal, and to analogy. Analogy has become a major topic of research in cognitive psychology, and a number of process models have been developed (Falkenhainer, Forbus, & Gentner, 1989; Halford, Wilson, et al., 1994; Holyoak & Thagard, 1989). Although its importance was recognized early this century (e.g. Piaget, 1947/

1950; Spearman, 1923), it received comparatively little attention until the present revival of interest. It is now recognized that analogy is central to most higher cognitive processes, including reasoning, language comprehension, and creativity (Halford, 1992, 1995; Holyoak & Thagard, 1995). The essence of analogy is a map from one cognitive representation, the base or source, to another, the target (Gentner, 1983). The map must be such that relations in the base correspond consistently to those in the target. There is thus a lot of similarity between analogy and cognitive representation. The main difference is that a cognitive representation is a map between a cognitive structure and a structure in the world, whereas analogy is a map from one cognitive representation to another (Holland et al., 1986). The important point for our present purposes is that analogy depends on representation and processing of relations.

Planning, which has been explicitly modeled by VanLehn and Brown (1980), Greeno, Riley, and Gelman (1984), and Halford, Smith, et al. (1995), entails representing relations between components of a task. Planning is essential to the acquisition and modeling of cognitive strategies. It corresponds to the self-programming capability of humans that is so vital to their reasoning and creativity.

These properties mean that relational schemas have considerable generality and content independence. Because of the predication and argumentation properties relational representations are independent of specific contents (e.g., the relation larger-than remains the same irrespective of what arguments are bound to the predicate), whereas analogy enables relational schemas to be transferred across domains.

REPRESENTATIONAL RANKS

I now consider a number of distinct levels of cognitive functioning that are arranged along a scale of structural complexity. This scale is defined by representational rank, that is, the number of distinct components that are linked within a representation. To constitute a rank a component must retain its identity within the binding, and not be fused into another representation from which it is indistinguishable. Representational ranks 0–6, and the type of neural nets to which they are linked are shown in Fig. 8.1. The two lowest ranks correspond to associative processes, whereas the remainder are relational processes.

Rank 0: Elemental Association, Without Representation. Rank 0 corresponds to elemental association, which is a link between two entities, without intervening representation (other than input and output). This is the most primitive level of functioning, and presumably occurs in all animals with multiple neurons. It comprises links between pairs of entities:

$$\text{entity}_1 \rightarrow \text{entity}_2.$$

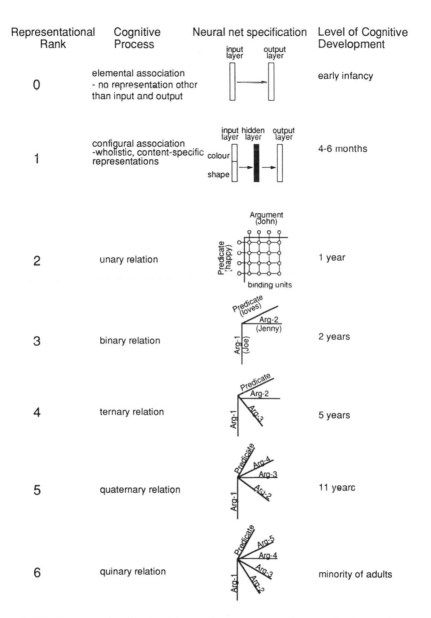

Representational Rank	Cognitive Process	Neural net specification	Level of Cognitive Development
0	elemental association - no representation other than input and output	input layer / output layer	early infancy
1	configural association -wholistic, content-specific representations	input layer / hidden layer / output layer (colour, shape)	4-6 months
2	unary relation	Argument (John) / Predicate (happy) / binding units	1 year
3	binary relation	Predicate (loves), Arg-1 (Joe), Arg-2 (Jenny)	2 years
4	ternary relation	Predicate, Arg-1, Arg-2, Arg-3	5 years
5	quaternary relation	Predicate, Arg-1, Arg-2, Arg-3, Arg-4	11 years
6	quinary relation	Predicate, Arg-1, Arg-2, Arg-3, Arg-4, Arg-5	minority of adults

FIG. 8.1. Representational rank, with cognitive process, neural net specification, and approximate level of cognitive development.

The concept of association has been interpreted in many ways (Humphrey, 1951), but stimulus → response (without mediation) is one interpretation that has had wide currency in associationist explanations this century.

Rank 1: Wholistic and Configural Representations. This level corresponds to *configural associations,* which entail links in which one cue is modified by another. They have the form:

$$E_1, E_2 \rightarrow E_3.$$

Conditional discrimination, in which choice of stimuli is dependent on background, is a well-known instance of configural learning (Lashley, 1938 ; Rudy, 1991). For example, if the stimuli were triangle and square, on black or white backgrounds, conditional discriminations might have the form:

Configuration triangle/black → *R+*
Configuration square/black → *R−*
Configuration triangle/white → *R−*
Configuration square/white → *R+*

Configural learning tasks such as conditional discrimination cannot be acquired through elemental association, because of associative interference (each element, and each background stimulus, is equally associated with each outcome). Configural associations are links between fused or "chunked" elements, which avoids associative interference because elements lose their identify (e.g., "triangle" is not the same entity in "triangle/black" as in "triangle/white," because if it were associative interference would still occur). The problem then is that structure cannot be represented, and transfer between isomorphs is impossible.

Associations can be chained, so that the output of one association is the input to another, as mentioned earlier. Associations may also converge, so that E_1 and E_2 elicit E_3, or diverge, so that E_1 elicits E_2 and E_3. Chained, converging, and diverging associations can all be reduced to sets of pairs, because the links do not modify each other; for example, E_3 does not modify the link $E_1 \rightarrow E_2$. In configural learning, however, the associative link between E_1 and E_3 is modified by E_2, and vice versa, so configural associations are not reducible to sets of ordered pairs, whereas elemental associations are.

At Rank 1 many features can be represented, but no relations with semantic interpretations are defined between components of the representation. Another example of this level of performance would be the representation of objects in space in the manner that has been observed in 5-month-old infants by Baillargeon (1987). Infants represent features of objects, such as height, and their distance from other objects, but there is no evidence that they can relate such representations to other representations. They can represent perceptible features, but presumably have no explicit representations of relations.

Rank 2: Unary Relations.   At this level, representation has two components that can be linked to one another, but retain their identity. This is the lowest level at which explicit relations can be represented. Unary relations, $R(x)$, have two components, predicate and argument, that are bound together.

Propositions can be treated as relational instances. Propositions representing attributes, for example, BIG(horse); states, for example, HAPPY(Joe); class membership, for example, HORSE(Hercules); and variable-constant bindings, for example, HEIGHT(1 meter), can be expressed as unary relations.

Rank 3: Binary Relations.   Structures of this rank have three linked, but distinct, components, representing predicate and two arguments. Binary relations, $R(a,b)$, for example, BIGGER(dog, mouse), can be represented. Univariate functions, $f(a) = b$, and unary operators, $\{(x, -x)\}$ can also be represented at this level.

At Rank 2 more complex variations between components can be represented. The binary relation $R(x,y)$ represents the way x varies as a function of y, and vice versa, neither of which is possible with Rank 2 representations. More complex propositions can be processed, for example, LOVES(Joe, Jenny).

Rank 4: Ternary Relations.   With four linked, distinct components, ternary relations $R(a,b,c)$ can be represented. Concepts based on ternary relations include the "love triangle," in which two persons, x and y, both love a third person, z. Concepts such as transitivity and class inclusion entail core representations that are ternary relations.

The number of possible relations between elements increases again with ternary relations: $R(x,y,z)$ represents three binary relations, $R_1(x,y)$, $R_2(y,z)$, and $R_3(x,z)$, as well as the three-way relation, $R(x,y,z)$, which is not defined in a binary relation. This means that with a ternary relation, but not with unary or binary relations, it is possible to compare x with yz, or y with xz, or z with xy. It thus becomes possible to compute the effects on x of variations in yz, and so on. More complex interactions can be represented than at the lower levels, which increases the flexibility and power of thought.

Bivariate functions and binary operations may also be represented at this level. A binary operation is a special case of a bivariate function. A binary operation on a set S is a function from the set $S \times S$ of ordered pairs of elements of S into S; that is, $S \times S \rightarrow S$. For example, the binary operation of arithmetic addition consists of the set of ordered three-tuples $+\{\ldots (3,2,5), \ldots (5,3,8), \ldots\}$.

Rank 5: Representations With Five Components.   At this level quaternary relations, $R(w,x,y,z)$ may be represented. An example would be proportion; $a/b = c/d$ expresses a relation between the four variables a, b, c, and d. It is possible to compute how any element will vary as a function of one or more of the others. With a quaternary relation all the comparisons that are possible with ternary relations can be made, as well as four-way comparisons: the effect on w of variations in x,y,z, the effects on x of variations in w,y,z, and so on.

Quaternary relations can also be interpreted as functions or as operations. A trivariate function is a special case of a quaternary relation. It is a set of ordered four-tuples (a,b,c,d) such that for each (a,b,c) there is precisely one d such that $(a,b,c,d \in f)$. Quaternary relations may be interpreted as a composition of binary operations. For example $(a + b) \times c = d$ is a quaternary relation. As with Rank 4 there do not appear to be any concepts using associative representations.

Rank 6: Representations With Six Components. At this level there would be a predicate and five arguments. The psychological existence of this level is speculative, and if it exists, it is probably available only for a minority of adults, which makes evidence about it difficult to obtain. It would permit processing of quinary relations, which would enable people to reason about relations between systems, each of which is composed of compositions of binary operations. If we assume that theories are composed of mathematical expressions each of which integrates a set of binary operations, then representation of the relation between theories amounts to representing the relation between structures defined by a composition of binary operations. This means that the ability to work within a theory would require Rank 5 reasoning, whereas ability to deal with relations between theories would require Rank 6.

NEURAL NET REPRESENTATION OF RELATIONS

The properties of neural nets in general are covered in many general texts on cognitive psychology (e.g., Best, 1995). In this section we want to contrast some of the more commonly used nets, such as the two- and three-layered nets, which have been employed very successfully to model basic processes, with nets that have been used to model relational knowledge. We are providing a quick overview of a complex topic, and there is no pretense to offer an exhaustive taxonomy. Rather we want to sketch the main kinds of nets that are typically employed and consider their properties in respect of the psychological processes discussed earlier.

Rank 0 can be captured by two-layered nets, as shown in Fig. 8.1. A two-layered net consists of two layers, one representing input and one representing output, each corresponding to a vector of activation values. We refer to sets of units within a layer or rank as a vector. The formation of an association entails adjusting the weights of connections between input and output layers according to a learning algorithm.

Rank 1 can be captured by three-layered nets, comprising input, output, and hidden layers, as shown in Fig. 8.1. Configural learning tasks such as conditional discrimination can be performed by using units in the hidden layer that represent conjunctions of features such as "circle&white" (Schmajuk & DiCarlo, 1992), just as hidden units can be used to represent conjunctions in the exclusive-OR task. In spatial tasks, hidden units could represent various features of objects such as height and distance from other objects.

Representation of relations is the subject of much current research, and we do not try to review the many complex issues here. We have no commitment to specific formalisms, but we are committed to the following points:

1. The representation must conform to the properties of relational knowledge outlined earlier, that is predication, higher order relations, relational systematicity, omni-directional access, argumentation, dimensionality, decomposability, and operations (such as select, project, etc.).

2. The components, predicate and arguments, must be represented independently of each other, and retain their identity when linked (bound) to other components.

3. Predicate-argument bindings are necessary, so that all functions linking predicates and arguments can be computed. For example, in arithmetic addition, given +(3,2,5), and with input +(3,2,-) we can retrieve "5" (addition), or with input +(3,-,5) we can retrieve "2" (subtracting 3 from 5). Again, knowing (3,2,5) we can determine that the operation is addition, rather than multiplication.

In our work so far (Halford, Wilson, et al., 1994), we have found that the most convenient representation uses a vector representing the predicate and each argument, and the tensor product of the vectors represents the predicate-argument binding. The representation of a binary relation, such as LARGER-THAN is shown in Fig. 8.2.

In order to represent (say) the fact that a horse is larger than a dog, we need to represent four things. These are: (a) the relation symbol, or predicate, LARGER-THAN, (b) the first argument, horse, (c) the second argument, dog, and (d) the binding of the predicate to the arguments.

In our representation, a vector is used to represent the predicate, LARGER-THAN, and another vector is used to represent each argument. In this example, there is a vector representing arguments *horse* and *dog*. The predicate-argument binding, that is, the fact that horse is larger than a dog, is represented by the tensor product of the three vectors, as shown in Fig. 8.2. Actually, each of the units in the vectors representing "larger than," "horse," and "dog" is connected to one of the tensor product units in the interior of the figure, but the connections are not shown because they would make the figure too cluttered. The activations on these units effectively code the relation between the vectors.

This representation implements the omni-directional access property. Given the predicate and an argument we find possible cases of the second argument. For example, given the predicate "larger-than" and "horse," the representation permits retrieval of things (such as dogs) that are smaller than horses. This is

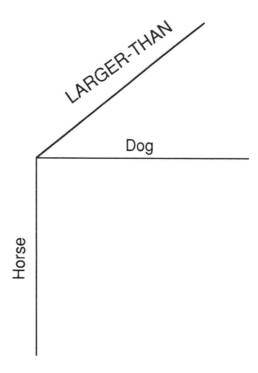

FIG. 8.2. Schematic tensor product representation of binary relation.

equivalent to asking, "What is smaller than a horse?" The retrieval is achieved by activation spreading from the units representing the predicate (larger-than) and the argument (horse), through the binding units, to the units representing the second argument (dogs, etc.). The activation is multiplied by the activations in the binding units, which effectively code the relation. Alternatively, given the arguments, the predicate can be found, equivalent to asking what is the relation between horse and dog. Again, this is achieved by activation spreading from the units representing the arguments, through the binding units, to the units representing the predicate.

Because LARGER-THAN is a binary relation, with two arguments, it is represented by a Rank 3 tensor product, that is, one with three vectors. However, more complex concepts are represented by structures with more vectors. Neural net representations of relations from unary to quinary are shown schematically in the rightmost column of Fig. 8.1. The input and output layers are omitted for the sake of simplicity. Thus the nets from Ranks 2–6 show only representation vectors.

Unary relations are represented by Rank 2 tensor products, binary relations by Rank 3 tensor products, and so on. The rank of the representation is one more than the number of arguments of the relation. It is also one more than the dimensionality of the relation. Though tensor products may not be the only or ultimately, even the best, way of representing bindings, any formalism that meets our criteria will have to provide for bindings between a predicate and each argument, all represented as independent entities.

The essential point is that representation of relations in neural nets is computationally costly, and the cost increases with the dimensionality (number of arguments) of the relation. In tensor product models, representation of a relation of rank r with m units in each vector, requires m^r bindings units. Other formalisms will yield different functions linking rank to computational cost, but it appears inevitable that computational cost will be a monotonically increasing function of rank. This in turn provides at least a potential explanation for empirical observations that cognitive processing load increases with relational complexity (Halford et al., 1998).

PROCESSING LOAD AND CAPACITY LIMITATIONS

There is no mathematical limit to the number of arguments that a relation can have, but computational cost increases with representational rank, and there may be psychological limits to the complexity of relations that can be computed in parallel. There is evidence that normal human cognition entails representations only up to Rank 5 (Halford, 1993; Halford, Wiles, Humphreys, & Wilson, 1993; Halford et al., 1998). This means that adult humans would be limited to processing one quaternary relation in parallel.

Concepts more complex than Rank 5 are handled by *segmentation* and *conceptual chunking* (Halford et al., 1998). Segmentation means that complex tasks can be decomposed into smaller segments that can be processed serially. The development of serial processing strategies permits complex tasks to be performed without exceeding limits on the amount of information that can be processed in parallel. Conceptual chunking means that representations of high dimensionality, represented by tensor products of high rank, are recoded into fewer dimensions, with tensor products of lower rank. An example would be velocity, defined as $v = st^{-1}$ (velocity = distance / time). This is three-dimensional, but it can be recoded into one dimension (as occurs when we think of speed as the position of a pointer on a dial). However, this does not mean that all processing loads can ultimately be reduced to that for a one-dimensional concept, because conceptual chunking results in loss of representation of some relationships. For example, when velocity is chunked as one dimension, the three-way relation between v, s, and t is no longer represented, so changes in v as a function of s and/or t cannot be computed without returning to the threee-dimensional representation, which entails the higher processing load.

In our tensor product model conceptual chunking is handled by convolving vectors into a single vector. For example, if the relation $R(a,b,c)$ was chunked to $R(a,b/c)$ by chunking b and c into one argument, then vectors representing b and c

would be convolved into a single vector and the new tensor product computed on three vectors instead of four. Conceptual chunking reduces the rank of a representation, which reduces computational cost and processing load. The cost, however, is that relations between chunked entities become inaccessible.

One implication of this approach is we cannot assess processing loads of tasks unless we know how the task is performed. Many tasks can be performed in more than one way, and different strategies can impose very different processing loads. Therefore it makes no sense to assess processing loads unless we have validated models of the processes entailed in performing the task. Sometimes tasks can be performed either by associative or by relational processes. Some variants of transitive tasks can be performed by associative processes (Wynne, von Fersen, & Staddon, 1992). The distinction is very important here because if the task is performed in an associative mode it can be performed in principle by children of any age, and by animals other than humans. If it is performed in a way that entails integrating binary into ternary relations, as mentioned earlier, there is evidence that it is not performed successfully until a median age of 5 years (Andrews & Halford, 1998).

THOUGHT AND RANK OF REPRESENTATION

Rank of representation is a measure of the power and flexibility of thought. Higher rank representations permit higher levels of relations to be represented, and permit more of the structure of a concept or situation to be processed in thought. Rank is analogous to the number of facets of a situation that can be viewed simultaneously. It is also analogous to the number of factors in an experimental design. An experimental design can be thought of as a set of relations between independent and dependent variables. A one-way experimental design is equivalent to a binary relation between one independent and one dependent variable. A two-way experimental design is equivalent to a ternary relation, between two independent and one dependent variables. Experimental designs with more factors permit more complex interactions, but at the cost of more observations (participants) being required. This is analogous to the processing load imposed by problems of high relational complexity.

Rank of representation has been associated with phylogenetic and ontogenetic development. We briefly review evidence of the type of representation that is within the capacity of each level in the evolutionary scale, and at each age range in human development.

EXPLICATION

The transition from associative to relational knowledge corresponds in principle to the transition from implicit to explicit knowledge. Associative processes are essentially implicit because an association cannot be an argument to another association, and associative processes cannot be recursive. This means that associative processes cannot be brought under the strategic control of other cognitive processes. They can be changed only through experience, not by cognitive manipulation.

REPRESENTATIONAL RANK OF ANIMALS AND CHILDREN

Levels of representation equivalent to those defined here have been related to species differences by Halford and Wilson (1993), Halford et al. (in press), and Holyoak and Thagard (1995). Rank 0, equivalent to simple associations, appears to be possible for all species of animals, albeit with varying degrees of efficiency. Mammals appear capable of Rank 1, as indicated by the fact that rats are capable of configural learning (Rudy, 1991). Rank 2 appears to be possible for monkeys, because they can represent the binding between attributes and objects. For example, they can learn to choose which of two objects is like a sample. If they are shown, say, an apple as the sample object, and are required to choose between an apple and (say) a hammer, they can learn to choose the apple. This could be done, of course, by elemental associative learning, which is Rank 0. However they can transfer to a new task in which (say) the sample is a hammer, and the choices are a banana and a hammer. Transfer of the principle implies they can represent a binding between an attribute (hammerlike) and a specific object. This can be represented by a Rank 2 tensor product. They can represent a dynamic binding between an attribute and an object.

Chimpanzees appear capable of representing a relation between objects, which implies Rank 3 representations, although this ability has been demonstrated only for language-trained chimpanzees (Premack, 1983). For example, they can learn that if the sample is XX, they should choose AA rather than BC. If the sample is XY, they should choose BC rather than AA. They learn to choose a pair of objects that has the same relation as the sample. This implies they can represent binary relations, a Rank 3 representation. As Holyoak and Thagard (1995) have shown, such performances are really a form of analogical reasoning, which requires representation of relations. It appears then that ability to represent relations and to change the representation dynamically is a factor that differentiates species at different points in the phylogenetic scale.

Children's abilities to process relations have been reviewed elsewhere (Halford, 1993). Neonates and fetuses in utero are capable of Rank 0 associative learning, but there is evidence that Rank 1 representations are possible at 5 months. This is indicated by infants' awareness of properties of recently vanished objects (Baillargeon, 1987), which suggests that content-specific representations, about attributes such as size, location and shape, are available at this age. Rank 2 representations are possible at approximately 1 year, when infants become capable of treating hiding place of an object as a variable, and recognize category memberships explicitly, which in turn leads to their understanding referents of words; for example, "doggy gone" can be represented as GONE (doggy), which is a predicate with one argument.

Rank 3 representations appear to be possible at age 2, because children of this age can make discriminations based on explicit representation of binary relations. One consequence is that they can perform proportional analogies of the form $A:B::C:D$, provided the content is familiar to them.

Rank 4 representations become possible at approximately age 5, and they open up a wide range of new performances, including transitive inference, hierarchical classification and inclusion, certain kinds of hypothesis testing, and many others. Transitivity entails a ternary relation, because premises $R(a,b)$ and $R(b,c)$ are integrated into the ordered triple, monotonic-$R(a,b,c)$. Class inclusion and the part–whole hierarchy are essentially ternary relations. A class inclusion hierarchy has three components, a superordinate class, a subclass, and a complementary class—for example, fruit, divided into apples and nonapples. Part–whole hierarchies are similar, and comprise a whole divided into a part and a complementary part. Though the age of attainment of these concepts has been controversial, it appears that children have difficulty processing tasks that entail ternary relations until approximately 5 years. This issue has been discussed in greater detail elsewhere (Halford, 1992, 1993).

Representations of Rank 5 are typically understood at about age 11, as evidenced by understanding of proportion and a number of other concepts, including understanding of the balance scale. This entails representing the interaction of four factors, weight and distance on the left and weight and distance on the right.

COGNITIVE TRANSITIONS

Cognitive development does not depend solely on progression to representations of higher rank, but is also dependent on acquisition and organization of knowledge, both procedural and declarative. I have considered learning mechanisms that serve this function elsewhere (Halford, 1993, 1995; Halford et al., 1995). However, I would like to address the specific process of how representations of higher rank emerge from lower ranks.

The basic process is by *differentiation* of the neural net representation. Referring to the schematic neural net representations in Fig. 8.1, notice that a Rank 2 representation can be formed from a Rank 1 representation by dividing the representation layer (hidden unit layer) in two and forming interconnections corresponding to the binding units for the Rank 2 representation. Thus a single vector is differentiated into two components, which are then reconnected through binding units. This process could be continued by dividing one vector in the

Rank 2 representation and reconnecting through binding units, forming a Rank 3 representation.

This process is analogous to taking an experimental design with one independent variable, then dividing the scores into categories representing another variable, thereby creating a two-way design. Suppose, for example, that we had a one-way design with eight levels of the dependent variable *A*. Now we decide to reallocate the sample according to a second dependent variable *B* with two levels, so that now we have four levels of *A* crossed with two levels of *B*. We still have eight cells, but the design has become more powerful in the sense that we can examine not only two main effects, but also an interaction. We could continue this process so that we had factors *A*, *B*, and *C*, each with two levels, and then we could analyze both one-way and two-way interactions. This is analogous to being able to represent relations of higher dimensionality. Notice that this process would not necessarily entail representation of more information. We could use the same set of scores, and the same number of cells, in all three analyses. But the restructuring of the sample, consisting of differentiation into more independent variables, means that more complex data structures can be represented. Analogously, the differentiation of relational representations can conceivably lead to representations of higher rank.

I certainly would not want to gloss over the technical complexities of this proposal. It is important to note that, to the best of my knowledge, no algorithm currently exists that would yield this differentiation, though there are algorithms that can restructure neural nets in a more limited way, such as cascade correlation (Schultz, Schmidt, Buckingham, & Mareschal, 1995). The main import of this proposal is that it gives a new direction in which to look for the sources of cognitive growth. It may depend on differentiation of representations thereby yielding capacity to process more complex relations. This would not necessarily increase overall information-processing capacity, any more than dividing an experimental design into more factors increases the amount of data available for analysis. However, just as higher levels of interaction emerge as the number of factors in a design increases, ability to represent more complex relations could emerge through differentiation of representations. This is consistent with proposals by developmental psychologists such as Werner (1948), who held that differentiation is the basic process of development, but it proposes a much more specific mechanism.

CONCLUDING COMMENTS

I do not want to gloss over the many and complex technical questions that are entailed in developing this approach. For example, even finding the best way to implement relations in neural nets is currently a major issue in research. Not that this approach is based on sketchy ideas, because it is in fact supported by a great deal of careful and detailed model building. However, my main purpose here has been to suggest that there is some value in providing an overall framework that puts some questions into perspective, integrates concepts and data that formerly seemed unrelated, and opens new ways of investigating basic issues. An example of this is the way the vexed question of capacity change was reformulated as mentioned earlier. That is, the question now is not whether capacity increases or remains constant over age, but whether the complexity of relations that are represented in parallel increases with age. This formulation implies that overall capacity does not necessarily increase, even though ability to represent relations evidently does. Therefore it has potential to reconcile data indicating increased ability to process complex relational concepts, such as transitivity, with data indicating that overall capacity remains constant.

I have tried to show, in broad terms, how the transition from elemental association to configural association, then through unary to quinary relations corresponds to the acquisition of cognitive processes that are more flexible, explicit, and content independent. One advantage of the approach is that the levels correspond, at least in broad outline, to neural net structures that are tractable to theoretical and experimental investigation. This opens the way to investigation of the processes that deeply underlie the transitions in cognitive development.

ACKNOWLEDGMENTS

This work was supported by grants from the Australian Research Council.

REFERENCES

Anderson, J. R. (1990). *The adaptive character of thought* (Vol. 1). Hillsdale, NJ: Lawrence Erlbaum Associates.

Andrews, G., & Halford, G. S. (1998). Children's ability to make transitive inferences: The importance of analogical mapping and structural complexity. *Cognitive Development, 13*(4), 479–513.

Baddeley, A. D. (1986). *Working memory.* Oxford, England: Clarendon.

Baillargeon, R. (1987). Young infants' reasoning about the physical and spatial properties of a hidden object. *Cognitive Development, 2,* 179–200.

Best, J. B. (1995). *Cognitive psychology* (4th ed.). St. Paul, MN: West.

Clark, A., & Karmiloff-Smith, A. (1993). The cognizer's innards: A psychological and philosophical perspective on the development of thought. *Mind and Language, 8*(4), 487–519.

Codd, E. F. (1990). *The relational model for database management: Version 2.* Reading, MA: Addison-Wesley.

Daneman, N., & Carpenter, P. (1980). Individual differences in working memory and reading. *Journal of Verbal Learning and Verbal Behavior, 19,* 405–438.

English, L. D., & Halford, G. S. (1995). *Mathematics education: Models and processes.* Hillsdale, NJ: Lawrence Erlbaum Associates.

Falkenhainer, B., Forbus, K. D., & Gentner, D. (1989). The structure-mapping engine: Algorithm and examples. *Artificial Intelligence, 41,* 1–63.

Gelman, R. (1991). Epigenetic foundations of knowledge structures: Initial and transcendant constructions. In S. Carey & R. Gelman (Eds.), *The epigenesis of mind* (pp. 293–322). Hillsdale, NJ: Lawrence Erlbaum Associates.

Gentner, D. (1983). Structure-mapping: A theoretical framework for analogy. *Cognitive Science, 7,* 155–170.

Greeno, J. G., Riley, M. S., & Gelman, R. (1984). Conceptual competence and children's counting. *Cognitive Psychology, 16,* 94–143.

Halford, G. S. (1992). Analogical reasoning and conceptual complexity in cognitive development. *Human Development, 35,* 193–217.

Halford, G. S. (1993). *Children's understanding: The development of mental models.* Hillsdale, NJ: Lawrence Erlbaum Associates.

Halford, G. S. (1995). Commentary on Moshman (1995). *Human Development, 38,* 65–70.

Halford, G. S., Maybery, M. T., & Bain, J. D. (1986). Capacity limitations in children's reasoning: A dual task approach. *Child Development, 57,* 616–627.

Halford, G. S., Maybery, M. T., O'Hare, A. W., & Grant, P. (1994). The development of memory and processing capacity. *Child Development, 65,* 1338–1351.

Halford, G. S., Smith, S. B., Dickson, J. C., Maybery, M. T., Kelly, M. E., Bain, J. D., & Stewart, J. E. M. (1995). Modelling the development of reasoning strategies: The roles of analogy, knowledge, and capacity. In T. Simon & G. S. Halford (Eds.), *Developing cognitive competence: New approaches to cognitive modelling* (pp. 77–156). Hillsdale, NJ: Lawrence Erlbaum Associates.

Halford, G. S., Wiles, J., Humphreys, M. S., & Wilson, W. H. (Eds.). (1993). *Parallel distributed processing approaches to creative reasoning: Tensor models of memory and analogy.* Menlo Park, CA: AAAI Press.

Halford, G. S., & Wilson, W. H. (1980). A category theory approach to cognitive development. *Cognitive Psychology, 12,* 356–411.

Halford, G. S., & Wilson, W. H. (1993). Creativity and capacity for representation: Why are humans so creative? *AISB Quarterly*(85), 32–41.

Halford, G. S., Wilson, W. H., Guo, J., Gayler, R. W., Wiles, J., & Stewart, J. E. M. (1994). Connectionist implications for processing capacity limitations in analogies. In K. J. Holyoak & J. Barnden (Eds.), *Advances in connnectionist and neural computation theory: Vol. 2. Analogical connections* (pp. 363–415). Norwood, NJ: Ablex.

Halford, G. S., Wilson, W. H., & McDonald, M. (1995, July). *Complexity of structure mapping in human analogical reasoning: A PDP model.* Paper presented at the Seventeenth Annual Conference of the Cognitive Science Society, Pittsburgh.

Halford, G. S., Wilson, W. H., & Phillips, S. (1998). Processing capacity defined by relational complexity. Implications for comparative, developmental, and cognitive psychology. *Behavioral and Brain Sciences, 21.*

Holland, J. H., Holyoak, K. J., Nisbett, R. E., & Thagard, P. R. (1986). *Induction: Processes of inference, learning and discovery.* Cambridge, MA: Bradford Books/MIT Press.

Holyoak, K. J., & Thagard, P. (1989). Analogical mapping by constraint satisfaction. *Cognitive Science, 13*(3), 295–355.

Holyoak, K. J., & Thagard, P. (1995). *Mental leaps.* Cambridge, MA: MIT Press.

Humphrey, G. (1951). *Thinking: An introduction to its experimental psychology.* London: Methuen.

Johnson-Laird, P. N. (1983). *Mental models.* Cambridge, England: Cambridge University Press.

Kahneman, D., & Tversky, A. (1973). On the psychology of prediction. *Psychological Review, 80*(4), 237–251.

Karmiloff-Smith, A. (1990). Constraints on representational change: Evidence from children's drawing. *Cognition, 34*(1), 57–83.

Lashley, K. S. (1938). Conditional reactions in the rat. *Journal of Psychology, 6,* 311–324.

Maybery, M. T., Bain, J. D., & Halford, G. S. (1986). Information processing demands of transitive inference. *Journal of Experimental Psychology: Learning, Memory and Cognition, 12,* 600–613.

Palmer, S. E. (1978). *Fundamental aspects of cognitive representation*. Hillsdale, NJ: Lawrence Erlbaum Associates.

Phillips, S., Halford, G. S., & Wilson, W. H. (Eds.). (1995). *The processing of associations versus the processing of relations and symbols: A systematic comparison*. Mahwah, NJ: Lawrence Erlbaum Associates.

Piaget, J. (1950). *The psychology of intelligence* (M. Piercy & D. E. Berlyne, Trans.). London: Routledge & Kegan Paul. (Original work published 1947)

Premack, D. (1983). The codes of man and beasts. *The Behavioral and Brain Sciences, 6*, 125–167.

Riley, C. A., & Trabasso, T. (1974). Comparatives, logical structures and encoding in a transitive inference task. *Journal of Experimental Child Psychology, 17*, 187–203.

Rosch, E. (1978). *Principles of categorization*. Hillsdale, NJ: Lawrence Erlbaum Associates.

Rudy, J. W. (1991). Elemental and configural associations, the hippocampus and development. *Developmental Psychobiology, 24*(4), 221–236.

Schmajuk, N. A., & DiCarlo, J. J. (1992). Stimulus configuration, classical conditioning, and hippocampal function. *Psychological Review, 99*, 268–305.

Schultz, T. R., Schmidt, W. C., Buckingham, D., & Mareschal, D. (1995). Modeling cognitive development with a generative connectionist algorithm. In T. J. Simon & G. S. Halford (Eds.), *Developing cognitive competence: New approaches to process modeling* (pp. 205–261). Hillsdale, NJ: Lawrence Erlbaum Associates.

Siegler, R. S. (1976). Three aspects of cognitive development. *Cognitive Psychology, 8*, 481–520.

Siegler, R. S. (1981). Developmental sequences within and between concepts. *Monographs of the Society for Research in Child Development, 46*, 1–84.

Siegler, R. S., & Shipley, C. (1995). Variation, selection, and cognitive change. In T. Simon & G. S. Halford (Eds.), *Developing cognitive competence: New approaches to process modeling* (pp. 31–76). Hillsdale, NJ: Lawrence Erlbaum Associates.

Sigel, I. E. (1984). Distancing theory: Its implications for the development of representational thought. In W. E. Fthenakis (Ed.), *Trends in early childhood education* . Dusseldorf: Schwann.

Smith, L. B. (1989). From global similarities to kinds of similarities: The construction of dimensions in development. In S. Vosniadou & A. Ortony (Eds.), *Similarity and analogical reasoning* (pp. 146–178). Cambridge, MA: Cambridge University Press.

Spearman, C. E. (1923). *The nature of intelligence and the principles of cognition*. London: Macmillan.

Sternberg, R. J. (1980). The development of linear syllogistic reasoning. *Journal of Experimental Child Psychology, 29*, 340–356.

Suppes, P., & Zinnes, J. L. (1963). *Basic measurement theory*. New York: Wiley.

Surber, C. F., & Gzesh, S. M. (1984). Reversible operations in the balance scale task. *Journal of Experimental Child Psychology, 38*, 254–274.

VanLehn, K., & Brown, J. S. (1980). Planning nets: A representation for formalizing analogies and semantic models of procedural skills. In R. E. Snow, P. A. Federico, & W. E. Montague (Eds.), *Aptitude learning and instruction: Vol. 2. Cognitive process analyses of learning and problem solving* (pp. 95–137). Hillsdale, NJ: Lawrence Erlbaum Associates.

Werner, H. (1948). *Comparative psychology of mental development*. Chicago: Follet.

Wynne, C. D. L., von Fersen, L., & Staddon, J. E. R. (1992). Pigeon transitive inferences are the outcome of elementary conditioning principles: A response. *Journal of Experimental Psychology: Animal Behavior Processes, 18*, 313–315.

CHAPTER 9

A Dialectical Constructivist View of Representation: Role of Mental Attention, Executives, and Symbols

JUAN PASCUAL-LEONE
JANICE JOHNSON
York University

> *Representation certainly implies the constitution of a symbolic function, i.e., of a differentiation of signifiers from significates, for it consists of evoking non-present significates and it cannot evoke them without using differentiated signifiers.*
>
> —Piaget (1975, p. 170, translated by JPL)

> *I have proposed that . . . conceptual representation begins early and develops in parallel with the sensorimotor system. In my view neither system is derivable from the other . . . except insofar as one must perceive stable perceptual displays in order to analyze them. . . . Perceptual analysis uses attentive processing*
>
> —Mandler (1998, p. 273)

> *If I understand a new mechanical contrivance, it is a concept for me, even if I do not give it a name. The functional relation, transferable to an indeterminate manifold, is the concept*
>
> —Burkamp (quoted in Cassirer, 1929/1957, p. 328)

Plato was the first thinker to formulate the dialectical view that humans partake of two distinct worlds of conscious existence (two modes of knowing/processing), "the world of ideas and that of the senses, the world of being and that of becoming, the noetic (intelligible) world and the world of appearance" (Jaspers, 1957/1962, p. 30). The world of ideas, or of being, categorizes the world of the senses, or becoming, making possible human knowledge. Implicit in this description are problems that Plato did not solve and that cognitive science currently is facing. One of these problems is how to differentiate two irreducible modes of cognitive processing, the *conceptual* (logological, logico-mathematical, or generic knowledge—high cognitive functions) versus the *experiential* (mereological, perceptual-motor/spatiotemporal, infralogical, or knowledge of particulars—low cognitive functions); and at the same time explain the emergence of both modes of processing from the *same origin:* as resulting from interactions among innateness (maturation) and experience (learning, whether culturally mediated or direct). A second problem is that of *continuous representation:* How can direct-perceptual or conceptual-processual forms (codes, schemes) adapt to the evolving constraints of hard reality (the world of the senses and of learned experience) so as to embody these constraints, even in truly novel situations where subjects lack proper representational forms? We refer to these as *Plato's problems,* because Plato's formulation, having created an absolute dichotomy between "conceptual" and "experiential," caused the problems' emergence.

Central to Plato's problems is the issue of how "representation" develops: the ability of humans and high mammals to generate and store in memory (i.e., learn) stand-by "models," real or imagined, of cognitive states of affairs, whether external or mental. There is no consensus in the psychological literature about how to explain the emergence and growth of representation, and there is little awareness that the problems of representation are in fact the same as the problems of Plato (Pascual-Leone, 1996). Here we sketch a dialectical constructivist model that can unify various current alternative views on representation and help to solve the problems of representation.

The epigraphs of this chapter highlight the key controversial issues we address. The quotation from Piaget states explicitly his classic view on representation: The organism requires symbols (defined as Piaget did in this quote) to produce representations. We deny this claim and correct it as follows: No complex executive-driven (i.e., operational) representation is possible without the symbolic function. We believe, however, that simpler representations are possible before the symbolic function has appeared, and these representations are not reducible to coordinations among sensorimotor schemes (i.e., information-bearing processes). This may be Mandler's meaning in the second epigraph. Here she seems to equate "concept" with "representation"; this is a broad interpretation of concepts, which other developmentalists currently share (e.g., Baillargeon, Kotovsky, & Needham, 1995; Case & Okamoto, 1996; Halford, 1993; Houdé, 1992). The quotation from Cassirer shows that this broad interpretation of concepts has early distinguished precursors. Cassirer intimated here what his books explain: Whether verbally abstracted or not, a functional relation abstracted as a type (i.e., generically) is a concept, because it is then transferable to any experience (or "manifold") that is a token of it. Thus a concept broadly defined is, like any representation, characterized by what we call *reductive abstraction:* the extracting from a manifold of experiences the common functional or perceptual characteristics, so as to constitute a cognitive "invariant" that can stand for them all (Pascual-Leone, 1987, 1995; Pascual-Leone & Irwin, 1994; Pascual-Leone & Johnson, 1991; Pascual-Leone & Morra, 1991). We have long claimed that reductive abstraction requires mental attention, both to boost with activation the relevant schemes to be highlighted from the manifold and to actively inhibit or interrupt from the experiential manifold other irrelevant schemes. Mandler (1998; see second epigraph), neo-Piagetians (e.g., Case, 1992; Demetriou, Efklides, & Platsidou, 1993; Halford, 1993; Houdé, 1992), developmental neuropsychologists (e.g., Bell, 1989; Diamond, 1988), and many other researchers today might agree with our model of mental attention, because it explicates intuitions they all share.

As Mandler (1998) has emphasized, current theories of representation must be contrasted with that of Piaget, whose work synthesizes the classic view. Thus, we begin by summarizing in a number of "P" points Piaget's theory of representation. In a parallel series of "DC" points, we then summarize our dialectical constructivist correction to Piaget's theory. Against this background, we next present a summary of our theory (theory of constructive operators), and finally, illustrate the application of this theory by task analyzing four representational tasks studied by other researchers.

A DIALECTICAL CONSTRUCTIVIST CRITIQUE
OF PIAGET'S THEORY

Piaget's view on representation is stated clearly and concisely in a published statement in honor of the French psychologist Wallon (Piaget, 1975). We summarize in seven points Piaget's position, quoting him whenever possible:

P1. "The young child does not manifest any representation, in the sense of evoking objects or events not directly perceptible or not signalled by perceptual indices. His behaviour is exclusively sensorimotor, or sensori-tonic or emotive, etc." (Piaget, 1975, p. 169, translation, here and elsewhere, by JPL). "In contrast, during the second year, and in particular during its second half, takes place this event of capital importance for human thought, i.e., the birth of representation, which enables intelligence to become internalized into proper thought. How does it happen?" (Piaget, 1975, pp. 169–170).

P2. Representation is made possible by the developmental emergence of a symbolic / semiotic function (see first epigraph). Piaget understood by symbolic function a mode of cognitive (semiotic) processing characterized by "a differentiation of the signifiers and the significates" (Piaget, 1975, p. 170).

P3. Representation is made possible by complex mechanisms of structural learning, called "reflective abstraction"—a sort of learning often intended by current terms such as "representational redescription" (Karmiloff-Smith, 1992), *chunking,* and so forth. Reflective abstraction generates *mental* or conceptual (preoperational or operational) *schemes,* which are the main, but not the only, organismic cause of "re-presentations." The mechanism of reflective abstraction is innate "regulations" (endogenous organismic reorganizations). Because reflective abstraction is a recursive organismic function, mental schemes appear at different levels of reflective abstraction (there are schemes of schemes of schemes, etc.). And to each level of abstraction corresponds a different level of mental representation (representation, re-representation, etc.). In contrast, Piaget (Beth & Piaget, 1966) called "empirical abstraction" the sort of experiential learning of content that is possible without having/using reflective abstraction. Empirical abstraction is a sort of abstraction that babies exhibit in surprising ways. It serves to generate *sensorimotor schemes,* which produce both the subject's perceptual "presentations" and actions.

P4. In his effort to explain the ability of thought to represent change—transformations—as well as state descriptions, Piaget came to recognize a key dialectical pair of scheme modes: the *operative,* which for Piaget was primary, and the *figurative,* regarded by him as secondarily derived. Operative schemes were his alternative to the "responses" or "activities" of learning theoreticians, the neuroscientists' "efferent processes," and the "procedures/procedural processes" of cognitive science. Figurative schemes stood for the "stimuli" or "patterned cues" of learning theoreticians, the neuroscientists' "afferent processes," semioticians' "signs," and cognitive science's "perceptual," "representational," and "declarative" processes, and/or "mental models."

P5. Unlike cognitive science, which often conflates the dimensional category operative/figurative with the category experiential/conceptual, Piaget's theory tacitly maintains the distinction by claiming that at all levels of reflective abstraction, from experiential (sensorimotor) to conceptual processes, one finds the two kinds of representation: operative and figurative.

P6. Operative representations emerge, according to Piaget (1975), as a consequence of "coordinations among actions as such" (p. 178). Actions "as such" are concrete actions, that is, performance implementations of sets of compatible operative schemes from lower levels of abstraction. These coordinations serve to abstract the relations of coactivation and cofunctionality in praxis (i.e., in goal-directed activities) which, due to characteristics of either reality or the organism, obtain among schemes. Thus coordinations constitute "operative shells" or "macros" that reflectively abstract operative courses of action. In this manner, the courses of action become easier and eventually are internalized when the operative "shell" structure in question (explicated later as an L-structure) can be activated from within, by purely mental activation. Vygotsky and his school, despite terminological and substantive differences, have very similar notions of internalization (Pascual-Leone, 1996).

P7. "To the figurative aspect of knowing one can attribute perceptions, imitation in all its forms, and the many varieties of mental image: three grand categories that have in common the bearing exclusively on configurations (and the translating into figures or figural symbols all movements, and even transformations, that the subject attempts to perceive or reproduce)" (Piaget, 1975, p. 176). For Piaget these figurative schemes emerge from coordinations of a special sort, caused by a patterning (due to coactivations and cofunctionality) of the schemes that receptor-driven exploratory activities elicit. These perceptually driven coordinations of schemes are often more or less iconic (Piaget would say configural) in the sense that the patterning "imitates" in its structure the real form of spatiotemporal, or of part–whole object relations, found in the subject's environment. In this figurative structuring not only the resistances of reality play a role, but also the subject's own innate perceptual, sensori-tonic, and bodily postural coordinations, as well as his or her innate dispositions to imitate and to iconically explore the perceived environment, his or her emotions and affective goals that implicitly drive these explorations, and also his or her innate disposition to reflectively abstract these configural coordinations in the form of mental images. All these are factors that distinctly characterize figurative representations: "the figurative aspect of the representation depends on the sensori-tonic or postural system by the intermediate of imitation and the mental image" (Piaget, 1975, p. 178).

We do not review here the criticisms, often justified, that Piaget's theory of representation has received. A recent chapter by Mandler (1998) outlines criticisms from the perspective of current experimental information-processing theorizing. Instead, we give a set of seven alternative dialectical constructivist (DC) points, which correspond to and correct the seven Piaget (P) points just described.

DC1. Contrary to Piaget, and like the moderates among neo-nativist infancy researchers (e.g., Baillargeon et al., 1995; Karmiloff-Smith, 1992; Legerstee, 1992; Mandler, 1992; Wynn, 1992b), but for theoretically different reasons, we believe that simple representation can be found prior to the symbolic function that begins in the infant's second year. This is particularly so in facilitating situations (see later discussion). By simple or *content representations* we understand schemes (usually figurative), which are either innate or reductively abstracted from experience, and which act as signifiers (signals) for other schemes (figurative or operative) that in praxis are related to the content representations either indexically (i.e., via associative learning) or iconically (i.e., via a configural similarity relation produced by innate mechanisms or biases). *Reductive abstraction* (Pascual-Leone, 1984; Pascual-Leone & Irwin, 1994, 1998) is the distinguishing characteristic of content representation vis-à-vis direct perception; this is a form of reflective abstraction such that common features or relations, found across instances, are retained in the abstracted scheme, but differential or distinguishing features of each token experience are actively disregarded via active inhibition—what we call *interruption* (or *I*-operator). A possible instance of content representation is the distal-object schemes (or "image-schemas"—Mandler, 1992) that infants develop between 5 and 8 months (or even earlier) vis-à-vis physical objects in their environment, which they do by reductively abstracting a scheme—a content-structural "invariant"—that stands for and represents the manifold of perceptual manifestations that the physical object(s) in question produce(s) under exploratory praxis and perceptual analysis. These simple distal-object or distal-relation schemes were already seen by Piaget (e.g., his concept of incomplete object-permanence schemes—"permanence of objects without location"), but neo-nativist infancy researchers have appreciated more fully their theoretical importance.

Separate from content representation is *direct perception,* that is, enduring schemes (perceptual knowledge) that are not representational. Piaget (his "empirical abstraction") and, much more so, J. J. Gibson and his school, have emphasized the existence of direct perception. Direct perceptions and content representations are constructively different, although both are based on perceptual signals. Direct perception is based solely on direct collation of experiences (i.e., constructive abstraction without reduction of information) and is driven by ecological relations found *within* contexts. In contrast, content representation is based on reductive abstraction (i.e., reflective abstraction with reduction of information) and is *driven by ecological relations* (i.e., relations actually induced by the external infrastructure of experience) found *across* contexts. Content representations are either unconscious ("implicit") or potentially conscious (i.e., "explicit"). When content representations bear on purely operative processes, they are usually implicit; this is what Karmiloff-Smith (1992) might have in mind when she talked of representational level I (i.e., implicit). When content representations bear on complex figurative (or configural) patterning of the coordinations that operative processes and learning bring about, they function as early "conceptual" invariants that can be used in or out of context to categorize experience, as Spelke (Spelke, Breinlinger, Macomber, & Jacobson, 1992), Mandler (1992), Wynn (1992b), Baillargeon et al. (1995), and others have shown. We take the latter case to correspond to what Karmiloff-Smith called representations of level E1 (explicit-1).

DC2. After emergence of the symbolic function (an organismic function discussed later in terms of its mental-attentional demand) a new more complex form of representation appears, the only one that Piaget regarded as proper representation: the *executive* (or operational) *representation.* Executive representations use symbols (as defined later) and are based on reductive and causal abstraction (Pascual-Leone, 1984; Pascual-Leone & Irwin, 1994, 1998); they are *driven by executive/operational strategies or scripts;* and they monitor performance with reference to future or possible outcomes. These executive representations can be explicitly conscious or not. They can be verbal-conceptual (logological) or purely experiential (mereological—Johnson, 1991; Pascual-Leone, 1995;

Pascual-Leone & Irwin, 1994). These are the sorts of representation that Karmiloff-Smith (1992) classified, respectively, as levels E3 and E2. Note that executive representation turns into content representation with repeated practice and automatization.

DC3. Although reflective abstraction, under different names and formulations, has come to be recognized as referring to the causal processes of cognitive development, the Piagetian concept must be explicated (and deconstructed!) by positing a number of innate general-purpose mechanisms that in their dialectical interactions bring about, constructively, children's development and learning (Pascual-Leone, 1995). Most important, and yet missing not only in Piaget's but in other recent theories of representation, is the formulation of innate mechanisms for mental attention. Later, we summarize this model of attention.

DC4. The fundamental distinction between operative/efferent and figurative/afferent processes stems epistemologically from the need for biological organisms to adapt to their immediate environment (or context/world). The dynamic nature of these adaptive exchanges, and their urgency, create the need for codes that represent environmental (or organismic) contingencies; these are what Peirce (1955) called (external and/or internal) *signs* (i.e., Piaget's signifiers). The *figurative/afferent processes* are the brain's innate mechanisms for generating and processing signs. Dialectically complementing the figurative schemes, and developing concurrently with them, humans store blueprints for external and/or internal (mental) action, often conditional to signs, that are behavioral *interventions* on the environment and/or *processual transformations* of mental signs (i.e., Piaget's actions or transformations). These are the *operative/efferent processes* of the brains's machinery for producing interventions or transformations.

DC5. We believe that it is necessary to distinguish explicitly between two distinct but non-exclusive dimensions of variation, which together produce four different modes of representation. The first dimension is constituted by the dialectical pair operative/efferent schemes (processes) versus figurative/afferent schemes, which we have described previously. The second dimension is the dialectical pair conceptual/logological/generic schemes versus experiential/mereological/particular schemes (Johnson, 1991; Pascual-Leone, 1995; Pascual-Leone & Irwin, 1994). This second dimension of variation is the one that informed Piaget's conception of cognitive development. Stages of cognitive development, as conceived by Piaget and others, can be located along the structural continuum created by these polar attributes of information-bearing processes (i.e., schemes).

The second dimension can be clarified by explaining the labels we have used. Conceptual/logological corresponds to what Piaget called logical and cognitive scientists often call propositional/declarative networks. These are generic schemes because they stand for kinds rather than particulars, that is, types rather than token instances of experience; and because they are generic, we should see them as the processes of which concepts are made. Reductive abstraction, that is, the disregarding of unessential (noninvariant) aspects of experience, is the act of obtaining these generic representations that are concepts (in the broad sense of the word, used earlier). Experiential/mereological (*mereo* is Greek for "part," i.e., "part–whole relations") are the schemes that stand for particular objects of experience and their parts—the processes that encode real, nonreduced, pure and rich, experiences. That the two dimensions (i.e., operative/figurative vs. conceptual/experiential) are distinct is shown by the fact that their likely cortical projection in the brain is different (Pascual-Leone, 1987, 1995; Pascual-Leone & Johnson, 1991).

DC6. Piaget's idea that operative schemes literally derive from the coordination of actions can be regarded only as a suggestive analogy. Neural networks illustrate better construals, based on innate learning mechanisms that can increase the activation weights of neuronal connections as a result of experience and/or affect or mental attention (which is regulated, roughly speaking, in the prefrontal lobe).

DC7. For Piaget (and the French developmentalist Wallon) figurative schemes derive from internalized imitation, driven in part by innate sensoritonic and affective/social dispositions. This is, again, a suggestive analogy. It is more plausible to think (with Hebb, Luria, and many others) that both figurative and operative schemes are genetically prepared in humans by two distinct and dialectically complementary networks. The same principles of neural networks, suggested previously, when operating in the posterior cortical (i.e., figurative/afferent) nets, should produce figurative schemes. Imitation simply refers to operative processes that can help in the abstraction of configural afferent, that is, figurative, scheme coordinations.

A BRIEF ON OUR THEORY OF REPRESENTATION

Because the theory we propose has been discussed elsewhere (e.g., Johnson, Fabian, & Pascual-Leone, 1989; Pascual-Leone, 1984, 1987, 1989, 1995; Pascual-Leone & Goodman, 1979; Pascual-Leone & Johnson, 1991), we restrict discussion here to a few important aspects. The organism synthesizes performance dynamically—using all activated schemes in the subject's repertoire (or brain!)—at the moment when performance is produced. Thus performance is often truly novel (i.e., not solely determined by any single scheme stored in the brain's repertoire) and is always *overdetermined* by all compatible schemes currently activated. This principle of *schematic overdetermination of performance* (SOP principle) can be seen as a generalization of Piaget's principle of scheme assimilation or, neuropsychologically, as manifestation at the level of schemes—that is, cofunctional collections of neurons—of the spreading of activation in the brain's neural network. As happens in competitive neural networks (e.g., Hinton, Dayan, Frey, & Neal, 1995; Shultz, Schmidt, Buckingham, & Mareschal, 1995; Smolensky, 1988), schemes in the present theory compete for the codetermination of actual performance. One simple way of representing this codetermination is as follows: Schemes that are compatible in their application sum their activation levels/weights to form a dynamic cluster of compatible schemes, and the cluster of activated schemes that at any given moment applies to produce a part of the performance is the one that in this moment is dominant (i.e., has the highest total activation weight, irrespective of the source of this activation). Other incompatible clusters of schemes are (often momentarily) inhibited. Because this is a dynamic system, in which both activatory and inhibitory processes interact, and competition among schemes or clusters of schemes is common, one can usefully describe this theory as modeling a dialectical-constructivist organism.

In this theory there are four complementary sorts of dialectics, which together promote development: (a) a *natural external dialectics* between the individual and his or her life context—mediated by the releasing component or "cue" system of the schemes, which the features or "resistances" of the external context-situation can activate, (b) an *external intersubjective dialectics,* from each person to other persons, (c) an *internal dialectics* interrelating psychological processing components (schemes) within the individual, and (d) an *internal dialectics* interrelating, within the individual, schemes of action or representation with the resource capacities of the brain (e.g., attention's activatory or inhibitory mechanisms) via monitoring by executive scheme processes. These four sorts of dialectics together constitute situations as subjectively/objectively experienced. In this respect we mention the distinction between *facilitating situations* and *misleading situations* (Pascual-Leone, 1987); this distinction is not found in Piaget or in other theories of representation, but it is fundamental.

A situation is *facilitating* when all the schemes it activates are compatible with the task at hand. A situation is *misleading* when it elicits schemes that interfere with the task at hand. For instance, in Piaget's substance conservation task the situation elicits perceptual-global schemes of quantity that make the "sausage" appear to have more substance than the "ball" of clay. This is a misleading Gestaltist (S-R compatibility) "field effect" that supermarkets use very effectively in their packaging. Facilitating situations, because the schemes they elicit contribute to (or do not interfere with) the subject's task, are optimal for examining learning abilities, and have been traditionally so used by learning theoreticians, from behaviorist to Vygotskian to neo-nativist infancy researchers. When development is studied using facilitating situations, it appears as continuous, with a linear growth function being its characteristic curve.

Misleading situations, in contrast, are characteristic of problem-solving paradigms and have been used unwittingly by Piaget and others to investigate cognitive development. In these situations development often appears as discontinuous, in the sense of exhibiting a nonlinearly growing, at times stepwise, characteristic growth curve as a function of chronological age. This is found predominantly in cross-sectional studies, where there is no contamination with learning due to repeated testing (Johnson et al., 1989; Pascual-Leone, 1987).

From the perspective of the four sorts of dialectics mentioned previously, misleading situations (but not facilitating ones) are a source of internal conflicts —dialectical contradictions—between or among alternative processing strategies (not just overt motor responses or habits) elicited by the task, and these strategies usually draw on different processing resources (schemes or capacities) of the organism. Stages of development appear in misleading situations (and often not in facilitating ones), because learned habits (or innate automatisms), and their corresponding strategies, become obstacles to good performances. Thus in misleading situations subjects must use problem solving—that is, non-automatized methods (invention; creatively synthesized, truly novel performances)—to cope with task demands, and do so by way of *dynamic syntheses*. Dynamic syntheses are brought about by the tendency (this is Piaget's "assimilation") of dominant compatible schemes to apply together, and *overdetermine* (Freud—Rappaport, 1960; see also Pascual-Leone & Johnson, 1991; Pascual-Leone & Morra, 1991) representations and other mentations, or performances, of subjects. In these syntheses, task-relevant schemes not activated by the situation are internally activated by the subject's *mental attention* (Case, 1985; Houdé, 1992; Luria, 1973; Pascual-Leone, 1970, 1987; Pascual-Leone & Baillargeon, 1994).

Unlike orthodox Piagetians and many other theoreticians, we believe that organismic resources other than information-bearing units (schemes in our terminology) intervene in the emergence (i.e., generative construction) of novel representations, particularly in the context of misleading situations. Some of these innate but general-purpose organismic resources constitute in their dynamic interactions a function of mental attention, which is distinctly different from the informational units (schemes) on which it is normally applied to increase/decrease the level of activation.

Nonschematic Organismic Resources for Dynamic Representation

"Regulations" is Piaget's name for unexplicated (e.g., Garcia, 1980; Pascual-Leone, 1970, 1987, 1988) processes that overcome the limits of simple associative learning. Associative learning is a basic, "low-road" way of thinking and knowing (Pascual-Leone & Irwin, 1994, 1998) that is very powerful—as research on connectionist/neural networks has shown (e.g., McClelland, 1995; Shultz et al., 1995). But this "bottom-up" learning has its own severe limitations: Whenever the paradigm is a problem-solving one (i.e., a truly novel, misleading situation, particularly when subjects have had few exposures to the task), the powerful cue-driven bottom-up process of associative learning (whether in humans or in computers!) may become a hindrance, because it may activate schemes not relevant to the task. As a result, highly activated schemes, even if they are misleading, tend to dominate and determine performance. This is why purely associative organisms or machines are so limited in truly novel, creative problem solving. Associative learning models, not having "top-down" processing mechanisms, fall under the learning paradox (i.e., the paradox of not explaining where newly learned schemes come from—Bereiter, 1985; Jukes, 1991; Pascual-Leone, 1991a) and cannot solve Plato's problems (Pascual-Leone, 1987).

To solve these problems we need theories that have *more than one* learning mechanism *and* that can account for generation of dynamic syntheses (Pascual-Leone, 1987, 1991a, 1995; Pascual-Leone & Goodman, 1979). One of the learning mechanisms must deal with content/associative learning; we call this content or *C* learning. With repetition and automatization *C* learning produces an "effortless" but slow-to-acquire structural learning, which we call *LC* (i.e., Logical Content) learning. This is the sort of learning that behaviorists, perceptionists, Gibsonians, connectionist simulators, and so on, have emphasized. *LC* is a very efficient learning in facilitating situations, because it is then driven by salient "cues." What Vygotsky (1986; see also Kozulin, 1990) called "complexes" and "everyday" concepts (as distinct from proper or "scientific" concepts) are most likely products of *LC* learning in facilitating situations, created via human mediation—external intersubjective dialectics. In misleading situations, however, *LC* learning cannot be applied effectively by itself, because in that case salient cues can lead to error.

Another learning mechanism, which is driven by the executive processes of mental attention (Pascual-Leone, 1987; Pascual-Leone & Baillargeon, 1994) and leads to rapid Logical-structural learning is, therefore, needed; we call it *LM* learning. ("Logical" is used here in the sense of Piaget—functional structures—and does not refer to formal logic.) *LM* learning uses endogenous *mental (M) attention,* a content-free (noninformational, nonschematic) organismic resource or capacity that, monitored by executive (planning) schemes, can be used to hyperactivate ("with mental energy") task-relevant schemes—in particular, schemes that are not highly activated by the situation. This mental "energy" or *M*-capacity is a brain utility, controlled top-down by the prefrontal lobe (Pascual-Leone, 1989, 1995; Pascual-Leone & Johnson, 1991). *Mental attention* can also be used to centrally inhibit or "mentally interrupt" schemes that are task irrelevant (this is the *I*-interruption capacity, also controlled top-down by the prefrontal lobe). Schemes that are cofunctional (i.e., compatible in their function) and often coactivated (i.e., activated simultaneously or in immediate serial order) tend to become structured together—Piaget would say "coordinated"—into a common superordinate logical structure. The speed of this structural learning process is proportional to the activation level of the schemes involved.

From these learning assumptions three important consequences follow:

*LM*1. In *LM* learning, because *M*-capacity is hyperactivating task-relevant schemes while *I*-capacity is inhibiting task-irrelevant schemes, only schemes that are tagged as relevant by the dominant executive schemes will become part of the *LM* structure in question. Thus ordinary contextual schemes will be excluded and, so purified, the resulting *LM* scheme can function as a concept— a central conceptual structure (Case & Okamoto, 1996) or a Piagetian operational structure.

*LM*2. Because the growth of *M* is constrained by a maturational process that runs from the second month of life till adolescence (Johnson et al., 1989; Pascual-Leone, 1970, 1987; Pascual-Leone & Johnson, 1991), the level of complexity that the subject can generate in *LM* schemes will be, *within misleading situations,* bound by his or her (hidden) *M* capacity growth, a growth whose spurts (levels) correspond to Piagetian and neo-Piagetian (sub)stages. It follows that in misleading situations the processual complexity level, or *M* demand, of a given conceptual structure (*LM* scheme) cannot be greater than the subject's own *M*-capacity, if it is learned by a subject without the help of an external human mediator (who, *by creating a facilitating situation,* may lower the *M* demand). This is the reason why stages of development may become manifest only in misleading situations.

*LM*3. High cognitive functions, as well as Vygotsky's proper or "scientific" concepts (Kozulin, 1990; Vygotsky, 1986) emerge, from experience and historico-cultural interactions, by means of *LM* learning and often in misleading situations.

Because the processual complexity of the *LM* schemes available to a subject is a function of his or her mental capacity (i.e., *M*- and *I*-capacities), which increases with age and maturation, this model of *LM/LC* learning offers an explanation of one of Plato's problems—the one concerning distinctiveness and common origin of two modes of processing: properly "conceptual" (analytical—including what Mandler called perceptual analysis) versus experiential (automatized or global everyday notions). The key difference between these two modes of processing is the requirement for mental attentional capacity. In the top-down "conceptual" mode, that is, *LM,* the mental-attention demand is high, and so progress in this mode can easily be defeated by a limitation of mental attentional capacity (due, e.g., to young age of the subject). Thus developmental stages may be manifested in this mode. In the bottom-up experiential mode, that is, *LC,* the demand of mental attention is relatively low and developmental stages are usually not manifested within it. *LM* learning as processual mechanism corresponds to what cognitive science calls "effortful" or "controlled" processes, *LC* learning to what it calls "automatic" processes. Our theory contributes, to a cognitive science formulation, a developmental perspective and rational methods for estimating the attentional-effort demands of tasks. We also distinguish other kinds of learning such as "effortless" learning driven by affective schemes (*LA* learning—Pascual-Leone, 1991b).

Explanation of the "continuous representation" problem, and resolution of other representational problems (such as the learning paradox), necessitates, in addition to multiple types of learning, the acceptance of four other mechanisms, which neuroscience and connectionist/neuronal modeling have investigated under other names. I refer to the SOP principle, the Gestaltist internal "field" factor (S-R compatibility, minimum principle), the space structuration factor, and the time structuration factor.

The SOP principle was discussed earlier. It states that performance is synthesized by the dominant (most activated) *cluster of compatible schemes* available in the brain at the time of responding. The probability of this performance is proportional to the relative dominance of the cluster of schemes generating it (Pascual-Leone & Baillargeon, 1994; Pascual-Leone & Johnson, 1991; Pascual-Leone & Morra, 1991).

The "field" factor, which we call F operator, is an internal-field and performance closure mechanism akin to the neo-Gestaltist principles of "minimum" and "S-R compatibility" (Pascual-Leone, 1989; Pascual-Leone & Morra, 1991; Proctor & Reeve, 1990). *This F operator is a sort of minimax function* generated in the brain by neuronal "lateral inhibition" mechanisms in conjunction with the SOP principle. In process analytical terms this minimax function can be formulated as follows: The performance produced will tend to be such that it minimizes the number of schemes that directly apply to inform the performance (including perception or representation); and it does so while maximizing the set of distinct, salient features of experience (activated low-level schemes) that, directly or indirectly, inform this experience (Pascual-Leone, 1987, 1995; Pascual-Leone & Johnson, 1991). For example, errors in the Wechsler picture completion subtest, such as failing to see the missing doorknob in the picture of a door, are caused by this F minimax mechanism, which prevents the application of low-level (local-perceptual) schemes, like the simple doorknob scheme, because automatized higher order schemes, like the superscheme of a standard door with its own doorknob, can also be applied and incorporate the lower scheme's representation.

Because they are likely to be important in enabling or disabling easy representations, we also wish to mention the space and time structuration factors—the space (S) and time (T) operators of the brain. What we call the space operator includes the known (Farah, 1995; Maunsell & Ferrera, 1995) specific neural circuitry that carries space-relational information suitable to answer questions about the "where" of objects, but not about the "what" of objects. We speculate that this space operator helps to bring about some degree of dynamic, automatic but ephemeral, structuration of interobject relations given in actual experience, that is, objects as experientially coexistent and localized entities—a temporary "space" structuration that facilitates learning. This is, we think, an explication of Kant's (1929/1965) profound idea of a transcendental category of space.

Likewise, a "time operator" must exist in the organism to permit some degree of dynamic, automatic but temporary, structuring of evolving states or appearances. These states facilitate dynamic construction of new objects, and so the answer to questions about "what" they are. The time operator (Kant's transcendental time, i.e., the brain's general-purpose temporal-structuring processes) is crucial not only for the synthesis and construction of self (as Kant, Husserl, and other philosophers emphasized) and language acquisition (as Petitto's research, 1996, 1997, suggests), but also for the synthesis and construction of objects. The space and time operators are (together with learning) the "glue" that permits, via dynamic syntheses brought up by the SOP-F mechanism, the emergence of objects, scenes, sequences of events, and so on, out of the manifold of sensuous experience (Plato's world of appearances).

As a result of nonlinear dynamic interaction among all these mechanisms, a heuristic implicit "choice" and synthesis of performance (whether in action, perception, representation, or mentation) takes place, which is brought about by the F and SOP mechanisms. It is within such a nonlinear dynamics for constructing actual performance that the significance of mental attention, as major developmental mechanism, becomes fully clear. From this perspective endogenous attention appears (Pascual-Leone, 1987; Pascual-Leone & Baillargeon, 1994) as the organismic functional system (or modular "function" $< \ldots >$) constituted by three resource capacities and a special subrepertoire of schemes—the executive schemes of mental attention—in their interaction as *attentional operators*: $< E, M, I, F >$. The attention component E is the set of currently dominant attentional executives, usually called by the collective name "the executive"; the component M is mental "energy" or capacity; the component I is top-down (central) inhibition of task-irrelevant schemes; the component F is the neo-Gestaltist minimax field factor just mentioned. By boosting (with M operator) the activation of, and/or deactivating (I operator), schemes in the field of activation, mental attention (monitored by affects via the E operator) can effectively change the "choice" of performance that F and SOP will together synthesize in a given situation. These are the effortful top-down mental equilibration processes that generate Piagetian operations—whether these operations are described with Piagetian models or otherwise.

Language and conceptual thinking emerge in the organism in this manner: via both an external intersubjective dialectics and two internal dialectics, which in their interactions, serve to internalize historico-cultural processes used by and created within society. The historico-cultural processes become internalized in terms of executive schemes, general attentional executives, task executives, and executive controls for the capacity resources (M, I, F, LC, S, T, etc.) These various sorts of executives, acquired via human mediation, permit the learner to keep a mental distance from misleading factors in the situations, and thus enable freedom of will. This chain of transitions is illuminated by Vygotsky's "one-sentence" formula: "If *at the beginning* of development there stands the act, independent of the word, then at the end of it there stands the word which becomes the act, the word that makes man's action free" (Vygotsky & Luria, 1994, p. 170).

In the next section we illustrate applications of our theory to four tasks studied by other researchers. The tasks we discuss are all for young children, because data on such tasks can contribute most to the problems of representation, including Plato's problems. Given the wealth of new paradigms and tasks to choose from, our choice of tasks is somewhat arbitrary.

TASK ANALYSES OF REPRESENTATIONAL PERFORMANCE

Mental-Attentional Constraints in the Language Learning of Native Signers

Reilly and Bellugi's (1996) recent study of acquisition of American Sign Language (ASL) can serve to illustrate, when interpreted from our theoretical viewpoint, how mental attention intervenes in language acquisition, via the dialectics of sociocultural mediation that relate babies to mothers. We begin with a selective summary of the Reilly and Bellugi article. By the age of 7 months "infants can reliably discriminate between angry, happy and surprised faces" (Reilly & Bellugi, 1996, p. 221), and "by the end of their first year, both receptively and productively, infants consistently associate specific facial behaviours with affective states" (Reilly & Bellugi, 1996, p. 222). Note that the ability to make these discriminations is related to the child's capacity to process simultaneously the analytical perception of the other's face, and/or the child's own facial behavior, with the affective state for which the facial expression stands as a sign or symbol (e.g., Pascual-Leone, 1991b). Usually, in particular in misleading situations, this simultaneous processing is possible only with the help of mental attention.

Linguistic form patterns (figurative forms from all levels of grammar: phonology, morphology, and syntax) are often obtained in ASL by using co-occurring manual and facial features suitably structured in space and time. "[S]pecific facial behaviours . . . function as obligatory grammatical markers" in, for example, conditionals, relative clauses, and questions (Reilly & Bellugi, 1996, p. 219). It happens at times that obligatory facial expressions convey emotional states that are incongruous or conflicting with their morphological significance in ASL. This is the case for Wh-questions. The linguistic form pattern demands the manual signing of the appropriate Wh-sign (WHERE, WHY, WHO, etc.) accompanied by a nonmanual marker: "continuous eye contact with the addressee, furrowed brows, and a possible head tilt" (Reilly & Bellugi, 1996, p. 225), all produced in temporal coexistence with the manual signing.

This nonmanual marker closely resembles the affective expression of anger and puzzlement. Thus when the mother signs to the baby a Wh-sentence, the nonmanual component should constitute a misleading situation for the baby. This is because by itself the nonmanual component signals anger/puzzlement, although in conjunction with the signed Wh-sentence it marks the presence of a Wh-question.

Positive affective contact during communication with deaf infants, conveyed by means of positive facial expressions, is even more important than for hearing children (Reilly & Bellugi, 1996). Thus learning the nonmanual marker of Wh-questions should provoke a strong affective-cognitive meaning conflict (dialectical contradiction) among the baby's activated semantic schemes, a contradiction that can be resolved only if the baby can, using his or her mental attention, simultaneously interrelate the various manual and nonmanual cues that together constitute the Wh-question. Should the baby be unable to keep track simultaneously of all these (figurative) cue-schemes he or she will fail to reductively abstract into a linguistic scheme the semantic-pragmatic functional "invariant" that carries the meaning of the Wh-question. This is because by itself the nonmanual component of the Wh-question is interpreted by the child as a negative affective expression, which preempts the chances of positive communication.

Babies who cannot keep track simultaneously of both manual and facial information may end up feeling sad and crying when mother furrows her brows. This negative reaction should not occur, however, when the child perceives the mother's furrowed brows as an integral part of a different, cognitive rather than affective, scheme: the ASL sign. Because this is a misleading situation, babies must have enough power of mental attention to boost simultaneously with mental energy (this is the M-operator) all the sign constituents, thus bringing about their coordination, while at the same time actively inhibiting (this is the Interruption operator) the facial "anger" scheme. We can use our theory and method of task analysis (e.g., Alp, 1994; Benson & Pascual-Leone, 1997; Pascual-Leone & Johnson, 1991) to formulate a mental-attention dimensional complexity estimate for this coordination of the ASL Wh-question scheme. This model estimate appears in Formula 1.

$$COORD_3(COORD_2(face^*), COORD_1(hand_1^*, hand_2^*)) \quad (1)$$

Because ASL uses simultaneous motions with both hands (or else several sequential signs with one hand), to sign a sentence, the first coordination of information (schemes) needed is that of the motions produced by each hand. We symbolize these figurative schemes by $hand_1^*$ and $hand_2^*$. The semantic-pragmatic (experiential and linguistic) operative scheme that perceptually analyzes, assigns a meaning, and coordinates both hand motions we call $COORD_1$. When this operative applies upon (assimilates, Piaget would say) the two hand schemes, the result is a meaningful symbolic structure for the total configuration. We call "face*" the figurative scheme that stands for the patterned nonmanual gesture once it has been integrated as a perceptual totality, and we call

COORD$_2$ the semantic-pragmatic scheme that applying on "face*" produces its ASL meaning as a component. Finally, COORD$_3$ is the semantic-pragmatic operative that applying on both semantic components produces the meaning of the overall Wh-sentence form. A baby whose mental-attentional capacity permits the boosting with activation of each of these six schemes (and who at the same time can inhibit the misleading "anger" schemes) should be in a good position to represent, via LM learning, the meaning of the Wh-sentence that mother attempts to teach, and would thus easily learn the linguistic form. A child whose M capacity cannot handle simultaneously six schemes, however, would be prone to be distressed if the facial gesture corresponding to COORD$_2$(face*) accompanies the mother's manual sign, because this would cue in the child the negative affective scheme of "anger."

Our theory stipulates that M capacity grows throughout the sensorimotor period according to the schedule indicated in Table 9.1. Essentially, at the end of each Piagetian substage of the sensorimotor period there is an increment in mental capacity corresponding to one additional sensorimotor (or simple conceptual) scheme that can be boosted with mental capacity. Thus at about 1 month (the end of first Piagetian stage and beginning of second) the baby's mental attention can boost one scheme; at about 3 or 4 months (end of Stage 2 and beginning of 3) the baby can boost with mental attention up to two schemes, and so forth. Three experimental PhD theses from our laboratory

TABLE 9.1

The Sensorimotor Period (Six Substages)

1.	Me = 0	THE USE OF REFLEXES (0–1 mo.)
2.	Me = 1	ACQUIRED ADAPTATIONS & PRIMARY CIRCULAR REACTIONS (1–4 mos.)
3.	Me = 2	BEGINNING OF SECONDARY CIRCULAR REACTIONS & PROCEDURES FOR MAKING INTERESTING SIGHTS LAST (4–8 mos.)
4.	Me = 3	COORDINATION OF SECONDARY SCHEMES & APPLICATION OF SCHEMES TO NEW SITUATIONS (8–12 mos.)
5.	Me = 4	BEGINNING OF TERTIARY CIRCULAR REACTIONS & DISCOVERY OF NEW MEANS BY ACTIVE EXPERIMENTATION (12–18 mos.)
6.	Me = 5	INVENTION OF NEW MEANS THROUGH MENTAL COMBINATIONS (18–26 mos.). Executive performance representation is not possible until this stage. Five or four units are needed to spontaneously construct an executive.
7.	Me = 6	TRANSITION TO MENTAL PROCESSES (26–34 mos.)
8.	Me = 7	EARLY PREOPERATIONAL PERIOD (34–59 mos.). The child is able to mobilize an executive and relate one symbolic scheme to another. The child has an M-capacity of Me = 7, or M = e + 1.

Note. Me is the executive mental (M) capacity available during the sensorimotor period. The mental capacity added after this sensorimotor period we call Mk, and in many of our articles we have stated that the total M of an older child or adult is equal to e + k (i.e., the M-capacity that emerges during the sensorimotor period, later used in the processing of executives, plus the M-capacity that matures afterwards).

have upheld these mental capacity estimates originally proposed by Pascual-Leone on the basis of Piagetian data (Alp, 1994; Benson & Pascual-Leone, 1997; Holloway, Blake, Pascual-Leone, & Middaugh, 1987; Pascual-Leone & Johnson, 1991). As Table 9.1 shows, the baby cannot boost simultaneously, with mental attention, six schemes until after the second year (26 months). Our theory of representation would thus predict that difficulties in coping with a task such as that symbolized in Formula 1 will last until after the second year.

Reilly and Bellugi (1996) presented naturalistic data very clearly supportive of this prediction. Their data come from two studies, one cross-sectional and one longitudinal, of deaf mother–infant dyads. Their findings can be summarized in three points:

1. Deaf children at about 18 months can spontaneously sign their own Wh-questions, but they do so without using the facial grammatical components; that is, they sign showing neutral faces.

2. Prior to the baby's second year, deaf mothers do not use the facial grammatical component when signing Wh-questions to their babies. This unusual pattern of signing before the babies' second year is produced by mothers unconsciously, even though they exhibited it in both cross-sectional and longitudinal studies.

3. When the baby is beyond the second year of age, both deaf babies and mothers begin to sign Wh-sentences using the appropriate grammatical facial morphology.

Using the model just outlined to explain the performance of both deaf mothers and babies, and assuming the M-capacity maturational schedule given in Table 9.1, these data become clear. The distress of babies is caused, as Reilly and Bellugi (1996) intimated, by the facial anger scheme that they cannot control, and this distress shapes mothers' communicative praxis vis-à-vis babies, without mothers becoming aware. It induces mothers (operant conditioning?) to exclude from Wh-questions the grammatically obligatory facial component. This unconscious, linguistically abnormal pattern is abandoned as soon as babies have enough mental capacity to dynamically synthesize the full (manual and facial) grammatical configuration. Possibly mothers can recognize unconsciously when the baby may be ready to develop the mature adult representation of a signed Wh-question.

Our theory contributes to Reilly and Bellugi's (1996) work in that it predicts approximately at what age the baby should be ready to handle the adult, mature form of signed Wh-questions. The theory achieves this predictive power by way of a process analysis of the dynamic syntheses that in the organism produce representations. This example may serve to clarify the nontrivial sense of the last part of the Mandler epigraph: how attentive processing is used in perceptual analysis. The example also shows that innate general-purpose maturational factors such as the growth of M (working memory, if you will), interruption (i.e., active inhibition of task-irrelevant schemes), and the *SOP-F* mechanisms can bring about the learning of specific linguistic/grammatical patterns of representation—patterns that may not be acquired consciously.

Attentional Executive Controls and Infants' "Enumeration" of Actions

In a series of studies, Karen Wynn (1992a, 1992b, 1996) has demonstrated that infants can discriminate between small numerical differences within the context of facilitating situations. A recent study by Wynn (1996) implicitly illustrates a point we wish to make: The general-purpose innate attentional system constituted by executives (E operator) and the hidden ("silent") organismic hardware operators M, I, F (i.e., the complex substantive *function* of mental attention $< E$, M, I, $F >$) serves as an internal mediator permitting the subject to make specific, principled, and rule-governed discriminations, which are conceptual in the broad sense, even though they are learned as a result of experience.

In Wynn's (1996) task, 6 month-old infants were habituated to a puppet jumping either two or three times (in two different treatment conditions). Following habituation, six test trials were presented in which the puppet alternately jumped two and three times. The main finding from our perspective, replicated in a second control study, was that infants looked significantly longer on novel-number trials relative to old-number trials; and when the perceptual salience of these jumps was maximized by keeping the puppet still when it did not jump (so a more facilitating situation is created) the difference in looking time between novel- versus old-number trials was enhanced.

As Wynn (1996) indicated, there are two questions of particular theoretical interest in these results, questions that she did not answer:

1. What is the mechanism of "individuation" or segmentation into *units of the experience?* Because the discriminant stimulus is clearly the number of jumps, babies must be segregating every jump as a unit. How does this happen? In our theory this is done by means of *figurative schemes* synthesized via the space and time operators and the *SOP-F* mechanism described earlier. Each of these schemes stands for a jump.

2. What is the mechanism of "enumeration" whereby the *relative numerosity,* or relative perceptual quantity of "jump" experiences, is evaluated for each trial as a relational characteristic (a distal-relation scheme or dynamic feature) found in the puppet—the distal object in question? Wynn inferred that this mechanism is some form of primitive enumeration, because it is found in infants across all sorts of experiential units, whether objects or relations of many different kinds. This conclusion is premature, because one can explain the generality and rule-governed character of these content representations without having to appeal to the number concept in the proper sense. This is possible by making the following dialectical constructivist (DC) assumptions that one of us

has long held (Pascual-Leone, 1970, 1984; Pascual-Leone & Goodman, 1979; Pascual-Leone & Johnson, 1991).

(DC8) The attentional executives of the mechanism of mental attention can, in an innate manner, evaluate the amount of mental attentional energy that a certain cognitive act has consumed. This amount can be evaluated by an observer analyst, in terms of the number of separate schemes that mental attention has had to boost in order to generate the intended performance. One such intended performance might be, for instance, to perceive analytically the salient (or the task-relevant!) units of experience (schemes) available in the present situation. For instance, the experimenter produces three jumps of the puppet and the child attempts to analytically (i.e., discretely) perceive the three jumps. Each jump might be a new instantiation or concretization of the same distal-relation scheme, that is, a jump-scheme image. These various instantiations can simultaneously be perceived analytically (and thus can be subitized—i.e., perceived in their numerosity) with the help of mental attention and/or L-learning, as illustrated later.

(DC9) The maximum numerosity that this analytical perception can discriminate should be a function of the child's power of mental attention (M power), which in its "working memory" span of capacity ("slots" for schemes) has a naturally given and ready small-set measuring grid (or *psycho-set*) that can be used to appraise numerosity over sets of highly activated schemes in the internal field of activation, even if this set of schemes is arbitrarily chosen from any content domain. We talk of a psycho-set to emphasize this important idea (Pascual-Leone & Johnson, 1991). The largest set of schemes that a subject of a given age can boost simultaneously with mental attention serves as an innately given set-theoretical measure of complexity used in perceptual analysis. For instance, assume that a child can keep within mental attention only two sensorimotor schemes, that is, $Me = 2$. A model of how such a child could at first perceive analytically the sequences of jumps presented in Wynn's (1996) paradigm appears in Formulas 2 and 3, which represent respectively the child's experience in a two-jump trial and a three-jump trial.

$$\{M(\text{jump}_1{}^\star, \text{jump}_2{}^\star) \ldots\} \tag{2}$$

$$\{M(\text{jump}_1{}^\star, \text{jump}_2{}^\star) \text{jump}_3{}^\star \ldots\} \tag{3}$$

In these formulas we have represented symbolically the theoretical field of activated schemes in the child's brain (i.e., his or her *field of activation*) when he or she is in the critical moments of Wynn's (1996) task. The words found inside $\{\ldots\}$ stand for schemes in the field of activation; $M(\ )$ stands for the M-operator applying on the schemes found inside the parentheses, so as to boost maximally their activation level. Finally, the ellipsis mark indicates other schemes actually in the field of activation that we do not wish to represent explicitly. Among the schemes not explicitly represented are, for instance, affective/motivational schemes (Pascual-Leone, 1991b), such as curiosity vis-à-vis novel events (i.e., novel schemes appearing in the field of activation). Such affective schemes compel the baby to spend more time looking at the situation that contains (i.e., induces the activation of) novel schemes relative to situations that contain only old (habituated) schemes.[1]

Let us apply these models to explain the result of Wynn's (1996) experiment. Our theory proposes that 6-month-olds (the age of Wynn's subjects) can boost simultaneously with mental-attentional energy at most two simple schemes (see Table 9.1). In the treatment condition where infants are habituated to the two-jump trials, Formula 2 represents the analytical perception of the old stimulus: The puppet produces two jumps, and the respective jump-schemes become hyperactivated by mental attention (M-operator). In this treatment condition, Formula 3 represents, then, the analytical perception of the novel stimulus: Two jumps are hyperactivated but a third jump is also found, less activated, outside M but in the field of activation (outside M, because the infant has the capacity to boost with mental energy only two jump-schemes). Notice that in the other treatment condition, in which infants are habituated to three jumps, the reverse will apply: Formula 2 would then stand for the novel stimulus and Formula 3 for the old stimulus.

For the sake of simplicity, assume that the infants have been habituated to two-jump trials. Then due to the curiosity/novelty affect they should look significantly longer at the situation represented by Formula 3, but only if they can discriminate between the two fields of activation represented in Formulas 2 and 3. Wynn (1996) found that 6-month-olds could make this discrimination. What our theoretical analysis contributes is an explanation for why such results should be obtained at 6 months and never before 3 or 4 months (see Table 9.1).

Notice that our model makes unique testable (although as yet untested) predictions. Consider, for example, a model for a situation in which the number of puppet-jumps produced by the experimenter is either three or four. If the infant's mental attentional capacity is Me = 2 (which occurs within the stage between 3 or 4 months and 8 months—see Table 9.1), then the models in question will be as in Formulas 4 and 5:

$$\{M(jump_1{}^\star, jump_2{}^\star) jump_3{}^\star \ldots\} \tag{4}$$

$$\{M(jump_1{}^\star, jump_2{}^\star) jump_3{}^\star, jump_4{}^\star \ldots\} \tag{5}$$

Now theoretical predictions change, because in our theory the perceptual analysis that produces significantly longer looking to the novel stimulus is made possible by mental attention. Further fine discriminations, and thus content representation of the difference between the numerosities of old and novel stimuli, may not be possible or be very global when it bears on similar elements (e.g.,

---

[1] To show how Formula 1 and Formulas 2 and 3 in fact model the same mental-attentional mechanisms, we rewrite Formula 1 using the symbolic conventions used in the latter formulas:

$$\{M[COORD3(COORD2(face^\star), COORD1(hand1^\star, hand2^\star))] \ldots\} \tag{1a}$$

jumps*) that are found in the field of activation but *outside* mental attention. This is because gestaltist factors—*F*-operator—allow only simple processing of schemes placed outside attention. Because this is the case for the comparison depicted by Formulas 4 and 5, we would predict that the baby's tendency to look longer at the novel stimuli will be reduced, and so the difference in looking time may no longer be significant.

If the subjects chosen were older, however, so that they belonged to the next developmental stage (i.e., 8–12 months, *Me* = 3—see Table 9.1), the appropriate models for the three- and four-jump trials would be those represented in Formulas 4a and 5a. We predict that a child of 8–12 months would have the *M*-capacity to distinguish between the two situations and thus a statistically significant difference in looking times would again be expected.

$$\{M(\text{jump}_1{}^\star, \text{jump}_2{}^\star, \text{jump}_3{}^\star) \ldots\} \tag{4a}$$

$$\{M(\text{jump}_1{}^\star, \text{jump}_2{}^\star, \text{jump}_3{}^\star) \, \text{jump}_4{}^\star \ldots\} \tag{5a}$$

What Symbols and the Symbolic Function Add to Representations

Symbols and signals are *signs* (Johansson, 1993; Peirce, 1955). As such they have a triadic structure: (a) the token *sign* itself or signifier (Peirce's "representamen"), (b) the "object" that it represents, that is, its significate or *referent,* and (c) the *meaning* or signification that the token sign, as interpreted, attributes to the referent (Peirce's "interpretant"). One should talk of symbols when the mode of processing/learning is such that the token-sign appears *functionally detached* from its referent. This is possibly what Piaget (1975) meant by "differentiation of signifiers from significates" (see the first epigraph). We know that the token-sign is functionally detached from its referent when, for example, the meaning attributed to it changes with the context. For instance, when the infant first says "ma!" referring to his or her mother, the intended meaning is fixed for each child. In one child it might mean "(hug me!)," if it was learned in the context of playing-with-mother. In another child, however, it might mean "(give me more food)" if it was learned in the context of feeding. Children draw their own initial meaning from the context of learning, and for as long as this concrete meaning remains fixed, the scheme is only a signal. It becomes a symbol when the child can change the intended meaning of "ma!" to signify "(hug me!)" in the playing context, or "(feed me!)" in the context of feeding, and so on. Thus defined, symbolic schemes do not usually appear until after 12 months of age, and are not common until after 19 or 20 months. In contrast, adults who when hearing the word "fire!" stand up and begin to run out of the theater as if they were about to be burned, are functioning with the signalic mode. Signals indicate the here-and-now actuality of their referent, but symbols indicate only the actual *possibility* of their referent (e.g., "the theater may, but only may, be on fire").

Consider how the functional difference between signalic and symbolic processing could be incorporated into schemes. In signalic processing sign and meaning are functionally attached. Thus the sign-token function can be carried by the *releasing conditions* of the scheme (Pascual-Leone & Johnson, 1991), and these conditions become cues when the scheme assimilates the situation (i.e., applies to it). The meaning function of the signal can then be carried by the same scheme: the scheme's *effects* that become actions, images, or mentations when it applies. Because schemes are indivisible units (e.g., Pascual-Leone & Johnson, 1991), the meaning of a sign should indeed be fixed if the meaning is carried by the same scheme that carries the sign-token; this prescription fits well with the definition of a signal.

Using the same line of argument we conclude that the constituents of a proper symbol (i.e., token-sign, meaning, referent, context indicators) must be carried by different schemes, to allow the context-sensitive character of meaning—the functional detachment of meaning in symbols—to appear in mental processing. The consequence is that the learning of symbols, but not learning of signals, requires that a number of distinct schemes be activated simultaneously and coordinated into a functionally unitized new totality or structure—as our analysis of the Reilly and Bellugi (1996) data illustrated. Such learning necessitates mental attention and effort (Pascual-Leone, 1987; Pascual-Leone & Baillargeon, 1994; Pascual-Leone & Irwin, 1994)—what experimental psychologists often call controlled processes. We (e.g., Pascual-Leone & Goodman, 1979; Pascual-Leone & Irwin, 1994, 1998) refer to such learning as *LM* learning, because mental attentional capacity (*M* "energy") must be used to boost into hyperactivation the symbol's constituent schemes. The learning of signals, in contrast, does not need to be effortful. It can take place by simple conditioning or *LC* learning (learning of automatic, effortless, habitual schemes). The neuropsychological literature, which we cannot summarize here, suggests to us that *LM*/symbolic learning takes place in the left hemisphere for most people (e.g., right-handers), whereas *LC*/signalic learning occurs in the right hemisphere, a claim that has received empirical support (Pascual-Leone, 1987).

Figure 9.1 summarizes what we have just said about these two semiotic functions, symbolic and signalic (Cassirer, 1929/1957, 1944).[2] The diagram also illustrates, using an operator-logic notation, the types of schemes that a subject must coordinate to form symbolic versus signalic schemes. In this notation the Greek letter Ψ stands for an operative scheme—the type of schemes represented in Formulas 2 through 5 with words written in capitals; and the Greek letter Φ stands for figurative schemes (represented in Formulas 2–5 by words written in lowercase with a postfixed asterisk). The formula for a symbol (Fig. 9.1) indicates that it emerges from the coordination (dynamic synthesis) of figurative schemes that encode the context (Φ_{cx}), the sign token (Φ_{sg}), and the referent

---

[2]In his later years, Piaget changed to call semiotic function what we are here calling (with Cassirer and the early Piaget) symbolic function. This was an unhappy change, which we reject, because the signalic function is also semiotic.

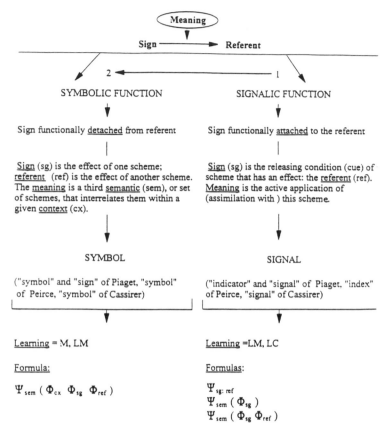

FIG 9.1.   Classification of signs.

(Φ_{ref}). This coordination is brought about by a semantic-pragmatic operative scheme (Ψ_{sem}) which represents the functional system or unit of praxis (intentional activity) within which the sign stands for the referent in the stipulated context. This operative scheme can be conceived as the system of semantic-pragmatic relations that exist, or are predicated, among the cognitive elements on which the operative in question applies.

When the baby uses the term "ma" as a holophrastic name for his or her mother, and this is a symbol, the component Ψ_{sem} of this symbol might be the operant/request "give me more food!", the Φ_{cx} might be the situation of "feeding time," and Φ_{sg} and Φ_{ref} would be, respectively, the utterance "ma" and the food being used. Notice that in the symbol, as opposed to a signal, the meaning of the operative scheme can change with the context, for a given sign and referent, and the alternative meanings represented by alternative schemes easily become misleading factors that could interfere with the intended meaning—

as happened with the facial anger scheme in the deaf infant's signing of Wh-sentences.

Thus the four schemes needed to generate the simplest symbol cannot be directly "chunked" (automatized) as happens with schemes in facilitating situations (which generate signals), but have to be coordinated using mental attention. Symbol-generating situations are typically misleading situations that demand representations that are context sensitive in their meaning, but otherwise detached from other schemes in the situation. The symbolic function (i.e., the active effortful coordination of the four semiotic schemes just mentioned) serves to make representations detached, and this situational detachment makes possible executive/operational representations as defined earlier.

Figure 9.1 also presents formulas for coordinations of schemes that generate signals. Because in a signal the meaning of the operative scheme is unconditional, the context (which with symbols serves as condition) need not be coordinated with the operative meaning scheme, the sign, or the referent: The most complex signal has at most to coordinate three semiotic schemes.

Figure 9.2 summarizes an observation made by Fogel (Reinecke & Fogel, 1994) on the emergence of an instance of symbolic play, as well as our analysis of the representational process underlying the child's plan (executive) for this behavior. In the days prior to the occasion summarized in Fig. 9.2, Hannah's mother had tried unsuccessfully to engage her in the pretend game of talking by telephone. Fogel described the first time that Hannah spontaneously enacted the game. According to our analysis, Hannah can acquire the general idea of the game—the plan or general executive of the task—in a single mental act of dynamic synthesis, given that she has sufficient mental attentional capacity. Figure 9.2 shows how this semantic synthesis maps onto the previously defined formula for a symbol. The resulting symbolic operative, an early executive scheme, is $\Psi_{\text{Pretend-talk-to-people}}$. Our claim is that when an infant's mental energy (Mc) is

At about 12 months [Me = 4] Hannah picks up the phone and offers it to mother. Mother takes the phone, puts it to her ear and says: "Hi, grandma!" Hannah smiles and reaches for the phone; she puts it to her ear (first time she does this) and says: "Ha-o!" Hannah looks and again offers the phone to mother for more pretend talk.

LEARNING THE SYMBOLIC TELEPHONE GAME

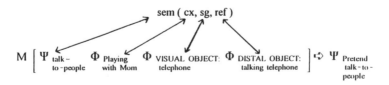

FIG 9.2.   Summary of observation by Fogel (Reinecke & Fogel, 1994) and task analysis of the emergence of the telephone game.

sufficient to boost simultaneously the activation of four different schemes—corresponding to semantic meaning (sem), context (cx), sign (sg), and referent (ref)—the executive representation will take place, if occasions / experiences socioculturally propitiate this learning. Thus the sociocultural operative "talk-to-people," is dynamically coordinated with the figurative of the situational context "playing with Mom," the figurative of the familiar visual object "telephone," and the figurative of the distal-intellective object (which she has seen Mom use) "telephone-for-talking." This coordination (symbolized by the arrow) brings about the emergence of the symbolic operative scheme (i.e., the executive) of pretending to talk to people by phone.

Hannah was about 12 months old at the time of Fogel's (Reinecke & Fogel, 1994) observation. According to our theory, this would give her a mental capacity of $Me = 4$, sufficient to boost simultaneously the requisite schemes. Note that what makes the situation just described misleading is the existence of a previously acquired LC-structure (i.e., habit) that would bias the child to interpret telephones as purely physical (not sociocultural) objects to be explored. This misleading habit makes difficult the access to symbolic play, unless (a) there is a human mediator who encourages symbolic play, and (b) the baby has an Me capacity of at least 4.

The Spatial-Mapping Representation Task

Judy DeLoache (e.g., 1987, 1995) discovered and has studied thoroughly a new paradigm in which executive-operational representation can be investigated in a complete yet simple form. In DeLoache's task the child is shown a miniature ("small scale") model of a room with all its furnishings, and then a separate full-size room of which the miniature is a model. The child is told that with the two rooms there are two toys: a very small "Little Snoopy" and a full-size "Big Snoopy." The two toys "like to do the same things in their rooms. Wherever Little Snoopy hides in his little room, Big Snoopy likes to hide in the same place in his big room" (DeLoache, 1995, p. 70). The child then observes the experimenter hide the miniature toy somewhere in the model, for example, behind the couch. Next, the experimenter tells the child that she is going to hide the big toy in the same place in the big room, and she does so without the child seeing. The experimenter then asks the child to find the big toy inside the big room, repeating that the two toys are hiding in the same place. At this point the child is brought to the big room to try to find the big toy. Only errorless retrievals are scored as correct. Finally, the child returns to the small room and is asked to retrieve the small toy; this serves as a memory and motivation check.

As DeLoache (1995) and other researchers (e.g., Halford, 1993) emphasized, to solve this problem a child must be able to coordinate, by way of a semantic–pragmatic mapping, his or her knowledge of the small-room model and small toy hidden in it, with his or her analytical perception of the full-size room and the big toy to-be-found in it. This is a misleading situation, because the great difference in scale between the two rooms makes mapping by simple perceptual generalization very difficult or impossible (unless facilitating circumstances, e.g., photographs [DeLoache, 1987, 1995] are introduced). Thus symbolic processing, as just described, becomes necessary and with it the need to use mental attention. The structure of this mapping and the amount of M capacity needed are clarified by our task analysis, which is symbolized in Formula 6.

$$MAP[(SEM = \text{hidden}, CX = \text{s-room}^*, SG = \text{s-couch}^*, REF = \text{s-toy}^{*L1})$$
$$(SEM = \text{find}^{L2}, CX = \text{b-room}^*\{REF = \text{b-toy}^*\}_{L1L2})] \rightarrow SG = \text{b-couch}^* \qquad (6)$$

In this process–analytical formula, there are two basic ideas: (1) The act of remembering where the small toy (s-toy) was hidden is encoded by means of a semantic operative (which embodies the functional "game" of hiding/finding an object), represented in this formula under two different instantiations: SEM = hidden and SEM = find. Then under this routine "game," and in the context of the small room (CX = s-room*—the asterisk indicates a figurative scheme), the object-screen (small couch) behind which the target-object is hidden and/or found becomes the symbolic sign (SG = s-couch*) of the hidden/found target-object, which functions as its referent (REF = s-toy*).

(2) We interpret the act of inference serving to mediate the distal transfer or cognitive transposition from small room to big room as a dynamic synthesis or coordination between the symbolic representations of the small-room task and the big-room task. This is our interpretation of what DeLoache (1995) and Halford (1993) very properly call a mapping—a semantic mapping from one task-situation to the other. Notice that in the symbolic representation of the big room, the sign is missing. This is the unknown of the problem to be found by analogy to the task situation of the small room; this analogy constitutes the mapping. Further, notice that the big-room task's referent (REF = b-toy*) is not being boosted by M-capacity but instead is being activated by the same L-structures (LC learning) that subtend the operative SEM = find and the figurative REF = s-toy*. The child's familiarity with this task ensures that b-toy* and s-toy* already are chunked into the same L-structure.

According to this model, the minimum number of separate sensorimotor schemes that must be boosted by M is 7, as Formula 6 indicates. As shown in Table 9.1, the power of M capacity does not reach the number 7 for sensorimotor schemes until 3 years of age. This developmental schedule explains the well-documented finding that children cannot solve this cognitive distal-transfer or mapping task until they have reached 3 years of age (DeLoache, 1987, 1995). Also supporting this mental-capacity interpretation of DeLoache's paradigm is Marzolf's (cited in DeLoache, 1995) finding that one can make the task too difficult for 3-year-olds by using as sign four identical white boxes, small and big, placed in a certain configuration; "so the child must encode which box contains the hidden toy. The only way to identify the relevant box is to encode its *relation*

[REL] to available landmarks in the model" (i.e., the small-room situation; De-Loache, 1995, p. 107). The modified Formula 6a represents this new task.

$$\text{MAP}[(\text{SEM} = \text{hidden}, \text{CX} = \text{s-room}^\star, \text{SG} = (\text{REL}(\text{s-boxes}^\star)), \text{REF} = \text{s-toy}^{\star L1})$$
$$(\text{SEM} = \text{find}^{L2}, \text{CX} = \text{b-room}^\star\{\text{REF} = \text{b-toy}^\star\}_{L1L2})] \rightarrow \text{SG} = \text{b-box}^\star \qquad (6a)$$

In this new formula the number of schemes that must be coordinated with the use of mental attention is 8—a number that according to our theory can only be integrated spontaneously at the approximate age of 5 (Johnson et al., 1989; Pascual-Leone, 1970; in these articles we talk about "e + 1," where "e" is equal to 6 sensorimotor schemes, and "2" is equal to 2 mental schemes).

GENERAL CONCLUSIONS

To evaluate the predictive power of our theoretical model, examples of representational tasks were chosen to cover a wide range of neo-Piagetian sensorimotor stages and a wide range of semantic contents. In each case—and we were able to discuss only four examples here—our theory-based task analyses accounted for developmental landmarks and showed habitual schemes or other factors that make these situations misleading for the child. Because they are misleading, mental attention (M capacity and active inhibition—I interruption) is needed to bring about the truly novel dynamic syntheses of performance that each task exhibits in the child when it is solved for the first time. This detailed demonstration of how mental attention participates in the genesis of representations is a contribution of our theory, for this aspect is usually ignored or glossed over by other theories. Mental attention alone is not sufficient, however. As the example from Reilly and Bellugi (1996) illustrates so well, representation and language are much enriched by sociocultural mediation, that is, by suitable mentors, who, via affective bonding and careful monitoring, guide the child's attention—thus making up for some of the baby's initial executive deficiency. Equally important, although not emphasized in our task analytical summaries, is the role of innate organismic factors—such as C, LC, LM, S, T, SOP, F, and so on—that effectively produce the dynamic synthesis (Piaget's equilibration) of a truly novel performance. In this synthesis, all activated compatible schemes summate their forces and tacitly collaborate to bring closure to a constructed performance that is simple and yet informed by all compatible schemes that are activated at the time when the performance is produced. The most decisive of these performance production mechanisms, often ignored in spite of the fact that modern connectionism has highlighted them, we have conceptualized as the principle of Schematic Overdetermination of Performance (SOP) and as the neo-Gestaltist field (i.e., F) factor. Although these important mechanisms were not emphasized in the analyses, the attentive reader may be able to see how they tacitly intervene in the analysis if he or she reviews the theory presented. More detailed discussions of these mechanisms in the context of task analyses have been offered elsewhere (e.g., deRibaupierre & Pascual-Leone, 1979; Johnson et al., 1989; Pascual-Leone, 1987, 1989; Pascual-Leone & Johnson, 1991; Pascual-Leone & Morra, 1991).

Notice that ours is a middle position relative to nativism and empiricist constructivism. Like modern neo-nativists we believe that human learning is not possible unless the child is born with a rich repertoire of mechanisms (such as innate schemes and powerful general-purpose "silent"—i.e., tacit—organismic "hardware operators"), which constitute mental attention, the space and time mechanisms, and various kinds of learning. These brain operators bring about the dynamic/dialectical syntheses that create truly novel performances. Yet as dialectical constructivists, we also wish to emphasize that innate factors in humans are likely to be general purpose vis-à-vis the content of experience, albeit processually very specific. This wide-content generality of our innate endowment, which promotes adaptability, is the mark of our species. Elman et al. (1996) adopt a similar stance.

We began the chapter with a formulation of Plato's problems. The first problem—the common origin (but irreducibility) of concepts/representations and experiences—we have been discussing all along in different terms. The same general-purpose hardware operators and partly different manifolds of schemes intervene in both, although the innate repertoire of schemes may already distinguish between "conceptual" and "experiential" kinds (this is currently a controversial issue). The second problem of Plato—to explain the genesis of *continuous* representations (i.e., the fact that humans never cease to perceive or represent something irrespective of the situation)—can be solved in principle by appealing to the mechanisms of dynamic synthesis, in particular, the *SOP* and the *F* operator, which together continuously resolve conflicts among schemes by tacitly or explicitly creating, again and again, new overdetermined configurations of life experience and/or conceptualization. Concept/representation and experience are both intertwined and distinct. As Ortega, the great philosopher of "vital reason" (i.e., life's rationality), said: "Never will the concept give us what we get from immediate experience, i.e., the flesh of things. But this is not a deficiency of the concept, because the concept does not aim to do this job. Never will immediate experience give us what we get from a concept, i.e., the form, the physical and the moral [i.e., practical—JPL] meaning of things" (Ortega y Gasset, 1914/1981, p. 63; translated from the original Spanish by JPL).

REFERENCES

Alp, I. (1994). Measuring the size of working memory in very young children: The imitation sorting task. *International Journal of Behavioural Development, 17*, 125–141.

Baillargeon, R., Kotovsky, L., & Needham, A. (1995). The acquisition of physical knowledge in infancy. In D. Sperber, D. Premack, & A. Premack (Eds.), *Causal cognition* (pp. 79–116). Oxford, England: Clarendon.

Bell, M. (1989). *Changes in frontal EEG in relation to cognitive and affective development between 7 and 12 months of age.* Paper presented at the meeting of the Society for Research in Child Development, Kansas City, MO.

Benson, N., & Pascual-Leone, J. (1997). *Mental capacity constraints on early symbolic processing.* Manuscript submitted for publication.

Bereiter, C. (1985). Toward a solution to the learning paradox. *Review of Educational Research, 55,* 201–226.

Beth, E., & Piaget, J. (1966). *Mathematical epistemology and psychology.* Dordrecht, The Netherlands: Reidel.

Case, R. (1985). *Intellectual development: Birth to adulthood.* New York: Academic Press.

Case, R. (Ed.). (1992). *The mind's staircase.* Hillsdale, NJ: Lawrence Erlbaum Associates.

Case, R., & Okamoto, Y. (with Griffin, S., McKeough, A., Bleiker, C., Henderson, B., & Stephenson, K.). (1996). The role of central conceptual structures in the development of children's thought. *Monographs of the Society for Research in Child Development, 61*(1–2, Serial No. 246).

Cassirer, E. (1944). *An essay on man.* New Haven, CT: Yale University Press.

Cassirer, E. (1957). *The philosophy of symbolic forms: Vol. 3. The phenomenology of knowledge* (R. Manheim, Trans.). New Haven, CT: Yale University Press. (Original work published 1929)

DeLoache, J. (1987). Rapid changes in the symbolic functioning of very young children. *Science, 238,* 1556–1557.

DeLoache, J. (1995). Early symbol understanding and use. *Psychology of Learning and Motivation, 33,* 65–114.

Demetriou, A., Efklides, A., & Platsidou, M. (1993). The architecture and dynamics of developing mind: Experiential structuralism as a frame for unifying cognitive developmental theories. *Monographs of the Society for Research in Child Development, 58*(5–6, Serial No. 234).

deRibaupierre, A., & Pascual-Leone, J. (1979). Formal operations and M-power: A neo-Piagetian investigation. In D. Kuhn (Ed.), *Intellectual development beyond childhood (new directions in child development)* (pp. 1–43). San Francisco: Jossey-Bass.

Diamond, A. (1988). Abilities and neural mechanisms underlying AB̄ performance. *Child Development, 59,* 523–527.

Elman, J., Bates, E., Johnson, M., Karmiloff-Smith, A., Parisi, D., & Plunkett, K. (1996). *Rethinking innateness: A connectionist perspective on development.* Cambridge, MA: MIT Press.

Farah, M. J. (1995) The neural basis of imagery. In M. S. Gazzaniga (Ed.), *The cognitive neurosciences* (pp. 963–975). Cambridge, MA: MIT Press.

Garcia, R. (1980). Postface: Dialectique, psychogenèse et histoire des sciences [Postscript: Dialectics, psychogenesis and the history of science]. In J. Piaget, *Les formes élémentaires de la dialectique* (pp. 229–249). Paris: Gallimard.

Halford, G. (1993). *Children's understanding: The development of mental models.* Hillsdale, NJ: Lawrence Erlbaum Associates.

Hinton, G., Dayan, P., Frey, B., & Neal, R. (1995). The wake-sleep algorithm for unsupervised neural networks. *Science, 268,* 1158–1161.

Holloway, R., Blake, J., Pascual-Leone, J., & Middaugh, L. (1987). *Are there common mental-capacity constraints in infant cognition, communication, and play abilities?* Paper presented at the meeting of the Society for Research in Child Development, Baltimore.

Houdé, O. (1992). *Catégorisation et développement cognitif* [Categorical classification and development]. Paris: Presses de Universitaires de France.

Jaspers, K. (1962). *Plato and Augustine* (H. Arendt, Ed.; R. Manheim, Trans.). New York: Harcourt Brace. (Original work published 1957)

Johansson, J. (1993). *Dialogic semiosis: An essay on signs and meaning.* Bloomington: Indiana University Press.

Johnson, J. (1991). Constructive processes in bilingualism and their cognitive growth effects. In E. Bialystok (Ed.), *Language processing in bilingual children* (pp. 193–221). New York: Cambridge University Press.

Johnson, J., Fabian, V., & Pascual-Leone, J. (1989). Quantitative hardware-stages that constrain language development. *Human Development, 32,* 245–271.

Jukes, T. (1991). Equilibration and the learning paradox. *Human Development, 32,* 245–271.

Kant, I. (1965). *Critique of pure reason.* New York: Saint Martin's Press. (Original work published 1929)

Karmiloff-Smith, A. (1992). *Beyond modularity.* Cambridge, MA: MIT Press.

Kozulin, A. (1990). *Vygotsky's psychology: A biography of ideas.* Cambridge, MA: Harvard University Press.

Legerstee, M. (1992). A review of the animate–inanimate distinction in infancy: Implications for models of social and cognitive knowing. *Early Development and Parenting, 1,* 59–67.

Luria, A. R. (1973). *The working brain.* New York: Penguin.

Mandler, J. (1992). How to build a better baby: II. Conceptual primitives. *Psychological Review, 99,* 587–604.

Mandler, J. (1998). Representation. In D. Kuhn & R. Siegler (Eds.), *Cognition, perception, and language* (pp. 255–308). New York: Wiley.

Maunsell, J. H. R., & Ferrera, V. P. (1995). Attentional mechanisms in visual cortex. In M. S. Gazzaniga (Ed.), *The cognitive neurosciences* (pp. 451–461). Cambridge, MA: MIT Press.

McClelland, J. (1995). A connectionist perspective on knowledge and development. In T. Simon & G. Halford (Eds.), *Developing cognitive competence: New approaches to process modeling* (pp. 157–204). Hillsdale, NJ: Lawrence Erlbaum Associates.

Ortega y Gasset, J. (1981). *Meditaciones del Quijote* [Meditations on Quixote]. Madrid: Alianza Editorial. (Original work published 1914; English translation published by W. W. Norton, New York, 1961)

Pascual-Leone, J. (1970). A mathematical model for the transition rule in Piaget's developmental stages. *Acta Psychologica, 32,* 301–345.

Pascual-Leone, J. (1984). Attention, dialectic, and mental effort: Toward an organismic theory of life stages. In M. Commons, F. Richards, & C. Armon (Eds.), *Beyond formal operations: Late adolescent and adult cognitive development* (pp. 182–215). New York: Praeger.

Pascual-Leone, J. (1987). Organismic processes for neo-Piagetian theories: A dialectical causal account of cognitive development. In A. Demetriou (Ed.), *The neo-Piagetian theories of cognitive development: Towards an integration* (pp. 531–569). Amsterdam: North-Holland.

Pascual-Leone, J. (1988). Affirmations and negations, disturbances and contradictions, in understanding Piaget: Is his later theory causal? *Contemporary Psychology, 33,* 420–421.

Pascual-Leone, J. (1989). An organismic process model of Witkin's field-dependence-independence. In T. Globerson & T. Zelniker (Eds.), *Cognitive development and cognitive style* (pp. 36–70). Norwood, NJ: Ablex.

Pascual-Leone, J. (1991a). A commentary on Boom and Jukes on the learning paradox. *Human Development, 34,* 288–293.

Pascual-Leone, J. (1991b). Emotions, development, and psychotherapy: A dialectical-constructivist perspective. In J. Safran & L. Greenberg (Eds.), *Emotion, psychotherapy, and change* (pp. 302–335). New York: Guilford.

Pascual-Leone, J. (1995). Learning and development as dialectical factors in cognitive growth. *Human Development, 38,* 338–348.

Pascual-Leone, J. (1996). Vygotsky, Piaget, and the problems of Plato. *Swiss Journal of Psychology, 55,* 84–92.

Pascual-Leone, J., & Baillargeon, R. (1994). Developmental measurement of mental attention. *International Journal of Behavioural Development, 17*(1), 161–200.

Pascual-Leone, J., & Goodman, D. (1979). Intelligence and experience: A neo-Piagetian approach. *Instructional Science, 8,* 301–367.

Pascual-Leone, J., & Irwin, R. (1994). Noncognitive factors in high-road/low-road learning: I. Modes of abstraction in adulthood. *Journal of Adult Development, 1,* 73–89.

Pascual-Leone, J., & Irwin, R. (1998). Abstraction, the will, the self, and modes of learning in adulthood. In M. C. Smith & T. Pourchot (Eds.), *Adult learning and development* (pp. 35–66). Mahwah, NJ: Lawrence Erlbaum Associates.

Pascual-Leone, J., & Johnson, J. (1991). The psychological unit and its role in task analysis: A reinterpretation of object permanence. In M. Chandler & M. Chapman (Eds.), *Criteria for competence: Controversies in assessment of children's abilities* (pp. 153–187). Hillsdale, NJ: Lawrence Erlbaum Associates.

Pascual-Leone, J., & Morra, S. (1991). Horizontality of water level: A neo-Piagetian developmental review. *Advances in Child Development and Behaviour, 23,* 231–276.

Peirce, C. (1955). Logic as semiotic: The theory of sign. In J. Buchler (Ed.), *Philosophical writings of Peirce* (pp. 98–119). New York: Dover.

Pettito, L. A. (1996). In the beginning: On the genetic and environmental factors that make early language acquisition possible. In M. Gopnik & S. Davis (Eds.) *The genetic basis of language* (pp. 46–71). Hillsdale, NJ: Lawrence Erlbaum Associates.

Petitto, L. A. (1997, January). *On the biological, environmental and neurogenetic factors determining early language acquisition.* Colloquium given at the University of Toronto, Toronto.

Piaget, J. (1975). Le role de l'imitation dans la formation de la représentation [Role of imitation in the emergence of representation]. In R. Zazzo, *Psychologie at Marxisme: La vie et l'oeuvre d'Henri Wallon* (pp. 169–181). Paris: Denoël/Gonthier.

Proctor, R., & Reeve, T. (1990). *Stimulus-response compatibility.* Amsterdam: North-Holland.

Rappaport, D. (1960). *The structure of psychoanalytical theory: A systematizing attempt.* New York: International Universities Press.

Reilly, J., & Bellugi, U. (1996). Competition on the face: Affect and language in ASL mothers. *Journal of Child Language, 23,* 219–239.

Reinecke, M., & Fogel, A. (1994). The development of referential offering in the first year. *Early Development and Parenting, 3,* 181–186.

Shultz, T. R., Schmidt, W. C., Buckingham, D., & Mareschal, D. (1995). Modeling cognitive development with a generative connectionist algorithm. In T. Simon & G. Halford (Eds.), *Developing cognitive competence: New approaches to process modeling* (pp. 205–261). Hillsdale, NJ: Lawrence Erlbaum Associates.

Smolensky, D. (1988). On the proper treatment of connectionism. *Behavioral and Brain Sciences, 11,* 1–74.

Spelke, E., Breinlinger, K., Macomber, J., & Jacobson, K. (1992). Origins of knowledge. *Psychological Review, 99,* 605–632.

Vygotsky, L. (1986). *Thought and language.* Cambridge, MA: MIT Press.

Vygotsky, L., & Luria, A. (1994). Tool and symbol in child development. In R. van der Veer & J. Valsiner (Eds.), *The Vygotsky reader* (pp. 99–174). Oxford, England: Blackwell.

Wynn, K. (1992a). Addition and subtraction by human infants. *Nature, 358,* 749–750.

Wynn, K. (1992b). Evidence against empiricist accounts of the origins of numerical knowledge. *Mind and Language, 7,* 316–332.

Wynn, K. (1996). Infants' individuation and enumeration of action. *Psychological Science, 7,* 164–169.

Representation Once Removed: Children's Developing Conceptions of Representational Life

MICHAEL J. CHANDLER
BRYAN W. SOKOL
The University of British Columbia

The first problem in studying matters of representation is knowing where to begin. Here are two sorts of possibilities: hearing Maria Callas sing (substitute a vocalist of your choice), or listening to a treatise on Callas' singing. Swimming hard against the current, this chapter makes for the far shore of the lecture by being, in this case, all about, not our own, but children's changing conceptions of the place of representation in the conduct of their own and others' mental lives.

Although hardly the same thing as beginning at the beginning, there are good reasons for using children's representations of representation as a preferred jumping-off place. One of these is the bewildering array of contradictory claims currently being put out about when it is that young persons actually first begin doing anything that might properly qualify as being representational at all. By certain accounts—what Bickhard (1992) called "encoding models of knowledge-as-representation"—simply behaving in ways that manifest a new adaptedness to one's surrounding is seen to necessarily imply access to some form of internal representation of outside events. Because remarkably simple organisms and children of every age are adaptive in this straightforward way, and because, on this account, representation is taken to be coextensive with any kind of informed way of behaving whatsoever (Furth, 1969), representational competence is automatically assumed, by advocates of such encoding models (e.g., Fodor, 1987; Macnamara, 1989), to be present at the very outset of mental life.

Alternatively, simply behaving knowledgeably is differently understood by others to involve no more than what Piaget (1936/1963) called "thoughts-in-action," a knowing process that is widely imagined to get underway quite nicely without the benefit of anything remotely resembling mental representations. To say anything else, it is argued, would be tantamount to saying that representation and computation are equivalent conditions. Such a position, in turn, would require us, as De Sousa (1991) pointed out, to ascribe some working representation of the laws of gravity, not only to those who inadvertently fall over, but also to rocks and other inanimate things that similarly manage to accelerate in free fall at the prescribed rate of 32 feet per second per second. In an effort to avoid making this kind of joke of the notion of representation, advocates of more constructivist models of the knowing process typically set as their own principled criterion for deciding who does or does not deserve to be credited with a capacity for representation the more hard-won ability to somehow "re-present" things in their absence. On this account, one may well know things they cannot represent, but not the reverse. Once excused from the responsibility of allowing for the possibility of any kind of knowledge whatsoever, bona fide representation, in the qualified sense proposed by Piaget (1936/1963), and other like-minded constructivists, is generally understood to be indexed by some newly found talent for remembering where things are kept, an ability that ordinarily puts in a first belated appearance somewhere toward the end of the infancy period.

Still others (e.g., Perner, 1991) hold out even longer, arguing that even children big enough to walk and talk ought not to be considered genuinely "representational," unless or until they also become capable of considering their representations *as* representations—a meta-representational competence widely assumed by so-called "theory-theorists" (Morton, 1980) to remain unavailable to young persons until they are, at a minimum, roughly 4 years of age. Finally, between the preschool accomplishment of such first and fledgling "theories-of-mind," and what Heelas (1981) called the "specialist psychologies" of those professional persons who actually work in the cognitive trade, there still remain to be detailed an unknown number of additional "commonsense" or "folk" accounts of representation. Some of these, like the failed astronomies of Stich's (1983) much maligned camel drivers, are perhaps actively misleading. Others, however, may well form the preconditions for any followable account of representational processes expressible in ordinary language (Smedslund, 1979), and so demand our careful attention.

Accompanying this confusing array of possibilities is an equally confusing list of common qualifiers upon the term "representation." Contributors to this literature regularly speak, not only of "encoding representations," but of "interactive representations," "tacit representations," "implicit representations," and "functional representations," as well as "symbolic representations," "reflective representations," "meta-representations," and "representations of representations," to name only a few. Further fueling this confusion are an additional number of disparate counting schemes that include talk of "zero-order representations," "first- and second-order representations," "level-one and level-two representation," "higher order representations," and so forth. Although taken individually, certain of these diverse naming and counting rituals are perhaps clarifying, the overall diet that they afford to the general consumer is at best bewildering and dyspeptic, and obviously not conducive to good digestion.

Given the word salad just documented, the concerned reader, eager to both get a better grip upon the available details of children's maturing representational competence, and choose among the shifting "specialist" theories meant to explain these data, is awkwardly confronted with an equation sporting, at the very least, two unknowns. As it is, two alternative solution strategies generally suggest themselves as possible escape routes out of this computational dilemma. One of these, actively promoted by so-called theory-theorists (Morton, 1980) from Churchland (1988) to Gopnik (1991; Gopnik & Wellman, 1992), takes as its "source model" for understanding whatever developmental changes actually do occur in children's shifting conceptions of mental life, all of those more revolutionary "paradigm shifts" that are often thought to mark the episodic course of scientific theory change (T. Kuhn, 1970). On this account, new paradigms (whether they belong to the course of intellectual history or the ordinary path of children's cognitive development) do not so much grow naturally out of ideas that have come before, as ride roughshod over them, or fly directly in their face. By contrast, Piaget (1965/1972), and many others of a related stripe, have tended to take children as a source model for science, rather than the reverse, by supposing that our best prospects for understanding and choosing among competing claims about scientific knowledge lie in first coming to some better understanding of such transformation in the course of ontogenetic development in general, and children's representations of mental representations in particular (Chapman, 1988; Garcia, 1987; Murray, 1979).

In our own more narrowly focused efforts to come to some informed choice between alternative specialist accounts of the representational process, we have elected to follow Piaget's lead by adopting a similar "bottom-up" search strategy. That is, we intend to use this chapter as an opportunity both to lay out something of what is currently known about children's own developing conceptions of the representational process, and to employ whatever insights are afforded by this genetic search strategy to help arbitrate the competing claims of other specialist theorists similarly bent upon taking the proper measure of representation.

As quickly becomes apparent, the primary obstacle that needs to be overcome in taking up this agenda of charting the developmental course by means of which young persons move toward an increasingly mature conception about their own and others' representational activities is that, despite the existence of a literal flood of recent research reports all aimed at explicating the emergence of what has come to be called a "representational theory of mind," the large bulk of this new work actually fails to properly qualify as developmental at all. That is, although most of the dozen new books and more than 200 journal articles that have appeared over the past decade on the topic of developing theories of mind are primarily about young children, and so perhaps qualify as a proper "child psychology," the large majority of these research efforts fail to satisfy even the minimal condition of supposing that development actually unfolds in real time. Instead, they champion what amounts to a singular, "one-miracle" view of change by paradigm revolution—that is, a "now-you-see-it, now-you-don't," one-off, salutary sort of accounting strategy that imagines the process of becoming representational as arriving without prefix, as having no sequel, and as effectively beginning and ending all in the same breath. On this account, children *younger* than approximately 4 are dismissed as incapable of telling us anything of interest about representational matters for the reason that they are all assumed to suffer from some across-the-board cognitive deficit that wholly blocks them from any possibility of representing their own representations. Similarly, everyone *older* than 4 is likewise dismissed as theoretically uninteresting for the reason that they are imagined to have already learned all of the real lessons that people are required to learn about mental representation.

As is no doubt made obvious by our intentionally dismissive tone, we do not ourselves subscribe to such a disjunctive one-miracle view. Instead, we mean to rail against it, and to damn its collective eyes, all as a way of warming to the task of framing our own hopefully better differentiated and arguably more developmentally true-to-life account of how growing children ordinarily do come to some increasingly mature representation of their own representations. In accomplishing this purpose we follow an agenda that unfolds in three parts. First, because not everyone who has read this far will have come equally well equipped with the required background knowledge concerning the recent flurry of writings on topic of children's developing theories of mind, the first major section is offered up as a kind of briefer course, meant to convey something of what is usually intended by talk about children's theory-like understanding of beliefs about beliefs or representations of representations. In particular, we mean to rehearse some of what is currently being said about how, without the apparent benefit of possible precursor forms, or the potential profit of consequent developmental change, young preschool children are imagined to come to the supposedly singular insight of "false belief understanding." Although there is no doubt a proper place for imagining such immaculate conceptions, and for supposing that certain of children's age-graded accomplishments actually do succeed in somehow standing outside of time, this, we argue, is not one of those places. Rather, as we mean to show, there already exists an impressively large and growing pile of empirical evidence sufficient to persuade anyone—at least anyone not otherwise caught in the grip of some eliminativist or modularized picture—that young persons actually do pursue a followable developmental course that gradually carries them toward some increasingly mature view of the role of representation in mental life. This developmental trajectory, we will argue, takes the form of a bumpy and discontinuous path that typically moves young persons from a starting position, according to which mental representations are understood to be mere copies of passively suffered experience, toward some later arriving and arguably more adequate view in which interprets mental representations are seen to be bona fide "interpretative" or constructive acts.

As a beginning step toward persuading you to join us in the oddly outlawed idea that there is a real developmental story to be told here, the second major section of what follows takes up the task of calling into question the preformist assertion, common to much of the theories of mind literature, that children younger than 4 necessarily suffer from some otherwise unspecified cognitive deficit that robs them of the possibility of still earlier insights into the representational character of their own and others' mental lives. Finally, in the third section, we work to show that mainstream theories-of-mind have somehow managed to awkwardly fall off both sides of the same log by mistakenly supposing that children older than the appointed witching age of 4 are also without any real agenda, and subsequently succeed in accomplishing nothing more than merely consolidating, or becoming more expert in the application of, their previous either–or insight regarding the possibility of false belief. Here our aim is to bring forward new lines of evidence demonstrating that, not withstanding their other real accomplishments, 4-year-olds are, nevertheless, still half a short lifetime away from first coming to even a beginning appreciation of the inherently interpretive nature of mental representation.

Although there is a serious shortage of research evidence of the sort that is necessary to effectively fill in the gap between the earliest glimmers of a truly "interpretive" theory of mind (which we show to be already evident in middle school children) and the fully fledged views of representation characteristic of the commonsense conceptions of most ordinary adults, we still end by arguing that the developmental data already in hand effectively make the case that any specialist theory of the representational process that is somehow less constructivistic than that already subscribed to by your typical 8- or 10-year-old would need to be seen as a serious case of professional backsliding.

CHILDREN'S DEVELOPING THEORIES OF MIND—A PRIMER

Before going on, in the second and third major sections, to find serious fault with the central tendency of the current theories of mind enterprise to reduce the whole of children's maturing conceptions of representation to some singular ability to entertain the possibility of false belief, it proves useful to first try to get really clear about what it is, in particular, that contributors to this literature have actually had to say about the emerging capacity to represent one's own representations. At the sacrifice of much of the detail contained in the 10,000 odd pages of published text that have been given over to this topic during the last decade, the real nuts and bolts that hold this literature together can, we argue, be reduced to the following four highly debatable talking points.

The first of these is that, in struggling to comprehend their own and others' actions, preschool children of approximately 4 years of age are commonly judged to join their elders in subscribing to a special sort of explanatory framework according to which certain classes of behavior are understood to be predicated on the particular beliefs (and desires) characteristic of those actions in question (Wellman, 1990). In doing so they are understood to become grist for the mill of so-called theory-theory, a view of change without precedent that, according to Russell (1992), is seen by its promoters as "so good that they had to name it twice."

The second in this short list of foundational assumptions is that the capacity to entertain any serious part of such an emerging theory of mind presupposes, and is uncontroversially marked by, the ability to entertain the possibility of false beliefs. In other words, it is argued that, because the whole point of open talk about beliefs and other forms of mental representation is to acknowledge that it is possible to somehow "misrepresent" reality (Davidson, 1984), and so behave with reference to a world that mistakenly exists only in one's own mind, anyone lacking the fundamental capacity to appreciate that beliefs can be, and often are, *false* is seen to be handicapped by a "reality bias" that wholly blocks them from any truly "theoretical" understanding of mental life.

Third, it is argued that, contrary to what are presumed to be the now discredited claims of earlier generations of investigators concerned with explicating the supposed decline of childhood egocentrism or the emergence of social role-taking competence, contemporary theory-theorists can legitimately count themselves as having successfully demonstrated, beyond any reasonable doubt, that 4-year-olds (but not still younger children) already appreciate the possibility of false beliefs, and so deserve being credited with a *fully* representational theory of mind.

Finally, on the strength of the good ability of 4-year-olds to regularly pass the so-called "litmus test" (Wellman, 1990) of false belief understanding, contemporary theorists of mind are generally quick to conclude that "by five years old, children . . . seem to understand that a person's beliefs about the world are not just recordings of objects or events stamped upon the mind, but are active interpreters or construers of them from a given perspective" (Meltzoff & Gopnik, 1993, p. 335). As such, it is regularly assumed that "around 4 years children begin to understand knowledge as representation with *all* of its essential characteristics" (Perner, 1991, p. 275).

The foregoing list of foundational assumptions, common to most contemporary theorists of mind, has not only served to shape the interpretation of available evidence, but has also given rise to a set of corollary expectations that, taken together, have guided the concrete research practices of the field. Two of these are particularly worthy of comment. The first is that, *if* 4-year-olds do in fact already subscribe to what amounts to their one and only theory of mind, and *if,* as a result of having unwisely relied upon other than "minimally complex" assessment tools, an earlier generation of social role-taking theorists somehow failed to properly process this fact; and *if,* as a result, almost all of the claims that Piaget and other like-minded investigators put forward about the child's conception of mental life have simply "turned out to be wrong" (Gopnik, 1993, p. 14); *then* history becomes worse than merely irrelevant and deserves to be consigned to the dustbin of things best forgotten. Evidence that this lesson has been taken seriously to heart is everywhere present in the theories of mind literature, most of which is written as though recorded history first began with the publication of Premack and Woodruff's seminal 1978 article, "Does the Chimpanzee have a theory of mind?". The index of Henry Wellman's synoptic 1990 volume, *The Child's Theory of Mind,* does not, for example, even contain the words *role* or *perspective taking,* whereas Josef Perner's 1991 companion volume, *Understanding the Representational Mind,* does so, but only for the purpose of unmasking what is said to be the hidden commitments of earlier role-taking theorists to a discredited form of Cartesian introspectionism.

A further practical consequence of theory-theory's simple and sovereign approach to the emergence of a representational theory of mind is that, not only has it left the resulting literature bereft of any real sense of history, but it has also effectively collapsed what one might have reasonably supposed would turn out to be a drawn out developmental affair onto a single moment of blinding insight, before and after which nothing else of real moment is imagined to occur. The contemporary theories of mind literature is not, then, only broadly ahistoric, but it is largely nondevelopmental as well.

This general tendency to do away with time has assumed two different forms. One of these, taken up in detail in the second major section of this chapter, involves the widely shared predilection of contributors to this literature to discount, as being about something else entirely, anything that might hold out the promise of counting as some antecedent form of the supposedly one-off miracle of false belief understanding. The second, which is considered in greater detail in the third major section, concerns an evident readiness to imagine that the representational view of mind available to 4- and 5-year-olds is already formally equivalent, in *all* of its important particulars, to the commonsense view of mental representation subscribed to by ordinary adults. Because of this readiness to redescribe anything and everything that might otherwise qualify as a *true* antecedent or consequence as merely another instance of what is entailed in grasping the possibility of counterfactual belief, there is little evident motivation for devoting much in the way of new research attention to anyone older or younger than the witching age of 4. As a result, something in excess of 90% of the thousands upon thousands of research subjects, whose responses form the empirical basis of contemporary claims about the development of a mature theory of mind, all fit in a common procrustean bed that lops off anyone awkwardly younger than 40, or older than 60, months of age.

A Quick Reprise of "Standard" Tests of False Belief

Having chosen to turn a collective blind eye to the past, having locked their sights on something smaller than even the 20th part of the usual developmental course, and having dismissed as lacking in the required methodological rigor any laboratory procedure that is not fully abristle with appropriate control questions, what is it exactly, you might well ask, that theorists-of-mind actually *do* as a way of backing their strong claims about previously unheard of cognitive deficits and heretofore unrecognized watersheds in the course of cognitive development? The answer is that they administer, in exquisite variation, a range of so-called "unexpected change" and "unexpected contents" tasks that are held out as "minimally complex" measures of false belief understanding. Because these assessment procedures are so elegantly simple, and because, like only a handful of other measures that have similarly captured the imagination of the professional public, they so reliably produce results that violate ordinary expectations, few will have failed to hear of them, or to need to be reminded of their results. Still, if only because we mean to set them up for a possible fall from grace, they deserve being recapped here, however briefly.

The paradigm case, you will recall, involves "Maxi" (a doll figure), his mother, a chocolate bar, and two containers A and B, which are described as kitchen cabinets, and into which the chocolate is variously put (Wimmer & Perner, 1983). Maxi and his mother are said to be returning from the store with a chocolate bar, which together they place in container A. On a pretext, Maxi is then moved to some remote location and, in his absence, his mother removes the chocolate, uses a bit of it for cooking, and then returns it, not to its original location in container A, but rather to previously empty container B. Maxi is then brought back and the young subjects, who have witnessed all of these comings and goings, are presented with the critical test question, intended to reveal their capacity for false belief understanding: "Where will Maxi look for his chocolate (or 'think' it to be)?" Interestingly, children younger (but not older) than 4 regularly confuse their own more up-to-date knowledge regarding the current whereabouts of the chocolate with what could only be Maxi's necessarily outdated belief by mistakenly pointing to, or naming, container B.

One could know a great deal about children and presumably still come away being surprised by this result. Some, who naturally stand in awe of just how clever most 2- and 3-year-olds tend to be, might well be taken aback by this uncharacteristic bit of evident stupidity. Others, and especially those whose knowledge of the reputed course of childhood egocentrism might lead them to anticipate "intellectual realism" at every preschool turn, could well err on the other side of caution by imagining that, not just 4-year-olds, but also children of 5 or 6 or even 7, would similarly fail to answer correctly. Altogether, then, almost every one's intuitions would likely lead them astray, leaving contemporary theory-theorists as the only ones not standing around in short pants. This is clearly the stuff out of which reputations and a long run on Broadway are predictably built.

Over and above their reputed surprise value, such measures of false belief understanding have other more procedural and conceptual things to be said in their favor as well. First, anyone in search of some ironclad way of establishing who does and who does not appreciate that mental representations are "about," but not "the same thing as" the reality to which they refer, could hardly do better than to fall upon such a seemingly straightforward test of false belief understanding. Four-year-olds who regularly pass such measures, by recognizing that Maxi would cling to and act upon beliefs that are objectively false, evidently grasp that it is this very possibility of error that, as the philosopher Donald Davidson (1984) put it, "gives belief its point" (p. 168). Second, such false belief measures also clearly succeed in side stepping a measurement problem that otherwise haunts more straight-ahead assessment strategies. What can scarcely be avoided when subjects are otherwise pressed for their understanding of beliefs that just happen to be true, but that tests of false belief provide a convenient methodological route around, is the fact that little or no measurable light typically separates actions that are driven by true beliefs from other mindless and contingently formed behaviors that are simply "run off" in the absence of thought one about belief. The "unexpected transfer" and "unexpected contents" tasks that currently dominate the theories of mind literature nicely avoid this measurement prospect, and so earn a procedural place front-and-center in the study of children's representation of representations.

Notwithstanding these and other good things that might be said in their favor, these now "standard" false belief measures still leave open two importantly different, but equally unanswered questions. One of these is whether such measures are, as advertised, really "minimally complex." The other is whether the realization that ignorance is bad for you, and can cause you to get things wrong (which, as far as we can see, is all that is actually measured by standard false belief tests), is in fact the same thing as understanding minds as "constructive" devices capable of differently interpreting one and the same stimulus event. That is, however relentlessly children younger than 4 can be shown to fail such measures, and however often it is demonstrated that 4-year-olds and adults respond to them in seemingly identical ways, nothing about these facts goes any real distance toward (a) reassuring us that, given access to other procedurally less encumbered measurement strategies, still younger subjects might not perform equally well, or (b) proving that, if pressed for more details, persons older than 4 might not reveal an understanding of representational diversity that goes well beyond the limited possibility that simple ignorance can lead one astray.

Rumbles of Protest

As it is, living on the margin of the theories of mind mainstream are two outlier groups of investigators that have made some part of a career out of taking up one or the other of these pieces of unfinished business. One of these groups has been hard about the business of demonstrating that, far from being the minimally complex measurement strategies they have been held up as being, standard measures of false belief understanding seriously underestimate young children's best abilities. The other has taken on the counterpart task of demonstrating that false belief understanding may be the first, but is certainly not the last step in a developmental course that only gradually carries young persons toward some grown-up conception of the representational process. Taken together, these two bodies of new work go some important distance toward demonstrating that the process by which children arrive at a mature appreciation of their own and others' mental lives actually needs to be reunderstood as both beginning *sooner* and lasting *longer* than is now widely supposed by those advocates of the one-miracle view that now dominates the current theories of mind literature.

Before going on to take up first one, and then the other, of these otherwise distinct lines of criticism, some last-minute attention is perhaps owed to the fact that both constitute reactive counterpunches, thrown in response to what amounts to the same provocation. That is, the job descriptions of those working to show that children entertain interestingly different thoughts about representation, whether in the years that *precede* or that *follow* the singular watershed of meta-cognitive development that is authorized by mainstream theorists of mind, are, in both cases, still carrying out a task set by the opposition.

An Alternative Vision

What clearly seems needed, but is not readily at hand, if research into children's developing theories of mind is to somehow get off of its present reactive footing, is some workable alternative to the either–or modularized theory that currently dominates the field; that is, some broader vision wide enough to make real room for the possibility that young persons might actually progress through a *series* of developmentally different way stations en route to some appropriately mature understanding of the place of representation in mental life. Because contemporary standards of scientific rigor so obviously favor precision over scope, there is scant hope of finding, at least among the living, anyone still foolhardy enough to risk fielding such a broad-ranging theory. Reaching back to those whom death has shielded from the necessity of seeing things only microscopically, theorists of the "grand design" (Merton, 1968), such as Piaget or J. M. Baldwin, come close, but not quite close enough to what we are looking far. After all, our hope is to find some new source model, not just start another fight.

Consider instead a 2,500-year-old Socrates trying to nudge his young colleague Theaetetus (Burnyeat, 1990) along a dialectical path toward some increasingly mature conception of the role of representation in the conduct of mental life. "From where," Socrates asked rhetorically, "does knowledge come?" Perhaps not unlike preschoolers of a certain tender age, Theaetetus was quick to answer, "knowledge is simply perception . . . we know what we see" (Burnyeat, 1990, p. 271). Although he feigns some initial approval of this simple "copy theory of knowledge" (Chandler & Boyes, 1982), pointing out that it interestingly likens the "soul" to "a block of wax [which records] our perceptions and thoughts in the way we take the imprint of signet rings" (Burnyeat, 1990, p. 325), Socrates was nevertheless quick to point out that any such essentially passive or reactive account of the knowing process leaves no real room for the fact that different persons often differently represent what is effectively the same reality. It is as if, he proposed, that "in some men, the wax in the soul is deep and abundant . . . and so the signs that are made in it are lasting, because they are clear and have sufficient depth. It is a different matter [he suggested, however,] when a man's heart is shaggy or when it is dirty and of impure wax; or when it is very soft or hard . . . for then the impressions have no depth" (Burnyeat, 1990, p. 329).

Too quickly impressed by the possibility that such individual differences in the wax department are sufficient to allow for certain idiosyncrasies of perception, without also enforcing any obligation to abandon the view that *active* experience is still the signet ring and knowledge the *passive* scars of such prior abuse, Theaetetus (not unlike your typical primary school student) was ready to reduce all of the representational differences that divide us to a series of alternative "misinterpretations." That is, at this interum juncture, Theaetetus took a view that simply allows for numerous ways of getting things wrong, and only offers one way of getting things right—by creating an essentially perfect "match" (von Glasersfeld, 1979) or "correspondence" between one's representations and reality.

Anticipating all of those critics who have always been quick to find fault with such simple correspondence theories of truth, Socrates remained characteristicly unsatisfied, pointing out that any account that continues to reduce the impact of experience to a form of passive victimization, leaves no real room for the evident fact that minds regularly and actively go about the business of composing thoughts in their own highly individualized ways. His and Theaetetus' first approximation of a model complex enough to allow for the possibility of a more interpretive or constructivistic way of knowing and representing involves supposing that the mind is in some way analogous to a sort of "aviary," and that the ideas that are housed there not unlike birds that, when "of a feather" actively flock together.

Finally, because it is recognized that although aviaries may be all aflutter with self-initiated mental activities, they still need some homunculus to go out and snare the birds, Socrates, and eventually Theaeteus, finally came to a conclusion (not unlike that subscribed to by certain adolescents and certain constructivist theorists of mind) that reasoning is propositional in character and active in form, and not otherwise unlike "a talk that the soul has with itself" (Burnyeat, 1990, p. 323).

Without wishing to see Socrates as somehow providing the answers to all of our contemporary questions, what makes this sometimes quaint Platonic dialogue worth repeating is that it not only identifies possible precursor forms to the version of the "copy theory of knowledge" that currently organizes most thinking about false belief understanding, but it also succeeds in bringing out the fact that, on pain of otherwise being simply mistaken, any satisfactorily complex and generally grown-up reading of one's own and others' minds must somehow allow for what John Searle (1983) described as both a "world-to-mind" and a "mind-to-world" direction of fit between mental and nonmental events. As Searle put it, minds need to be seen, not only as being changed by, and made to fit with, an independent reality, but must also be understood as being capable of altering experience in such a way as to make it fit more comfortably within the mind doing the knowing. By these lights, any even minimally complex account of one's own or other's mind must somehow allow for the operation of both endogenous and exogenous factors, must permit mental life to be portrayed as *assimilating* experiences to itself as well as *accommodating* to external realities, and must leave room for the possibility that mental contents can be actively constructed, as well as copied more or less directly, from the environment. That is, *if* children's movement toward a mature conception of the knowing process ordinarily takes place in at least *two* broad steps or stages, with notions of *accommodation,* or "mind-to-world" directions of fit, ordinarily preceding still later arriving notions of *assimilation,* or the fitting of "worlds-to-minds," *then* all those more monolithic theory-theories that keep collapsing these distinct accomplishments, by conflating them into a single vague and undistinguished *compromise view,* will end up by simultaneously falling off both sides of the same log. On the one side, adherents to such one-miracle views can hardly avoid doing young preschoolers the serious disservice of minimizing or trivializing their early grasp of the important possibility that false beliefs can and do arise out of simple ignorance. As a result, advocates of such monopolistic views naturally come to be seen as grudging and slow to grant such children any real understanding of the mind unless, or until, they can automatically acquit themselves on whatever obscure, usually alienating, and generally psychometrically inhospitable measurement procedure that happens to be thrown in their path. At the same time, advocates of these one-note theories also manage to regularly fall off the opposite side of this same log by mistakenly according those same young preschoolers an "interpretive" view of the mind, for no better reason than the fact that they already know that ignorance promotes mistaken beliefs. As we go on to demonstrate, the early insight that persons who are poorly informed often get things wrong is a far cry from the altogether more mature realization that two persons with precisely the *same* information nevertheless often manage to see the same situation differently.

In light of the foregoing analysis, at least two things need doing. The *first* of these is to show that the received view—that only 4-year-olds, but not still younger children, already understand the possibility of false belief—is in fact itself mistaken, and wrongly attributes to 2- and 3-year-olds a kind of "cognitive deficit" that, in point of fact, they do not have. The *second* is to provide evidence intended to convince you that simply acquiring the early arriving cognitive competencies that are necessary to allow for an understanding of false belief is in no way the same thing as acquiring those altogether different and later arriving abilities involved in appreciating that knowledge is *interpretively constructed*.

IS THERE META-REPRESENTATIONAL LIFE BEFORE "THE BIG 4.0"?

The question of whether children younger than 4 years of age can or cannot pass standard tests of false belief understanding is neither particularly open, nor especially interesting. Few findings in psychology are as trustworthy as is the mind-numbing regularity with which preschoolers of 2 or 3 take every occasion to insist that Maxi, the protagonist in Wimmer and Perner's (1983) now classic false belief measure, would, against all reason, end up knowing, as they legitimately know, where the missing chocolate bar finally ends up. Beyond this generally agreed upon fact, there is an important sense in which it would hardly matter if things were otherwise. That is, life as we know it would, in all likelihood, go on pretty much as it had before if the age of majority on this measure were to have been 6 or 5 (as Wimmer and Perner originally alleged that it was), or even if 3 year-olds had found this a particularly easy task to pass. Rather, what is at stake instead are the several matters of interpretation that are all seen to turn on the description of 4-year-olds as competent, and 3-year-olds incompetent, to judge their own and others representations *as* representations.

Among the group of sometimes strange bedfellows that have assembled to challenge this either–or, one-miracle claim, there are some—perhaps the least of the lot—whose objections seem only methodological. That is, among that crowd currently taking issue with the claim that 4-year-olds, but not still younger children, subscribe to a truly representative theory of mind, there are those who seem altogether comfortable with the enterprise of specifying the exact age at which true representation of representations become possible, and whose primary purpose seems to be to quibble over whether the true witching hour happens to be at 4 or some still earlier age. Although not, perhaps, the most toplofty of reasons for picking a quarrel, some of the methodological flaws uncovered in the pursuit of such modest purposes are still flaws, nevertheless, and so deserve being added to a growing list of the faults that plague standard false belief measures—a list that we mean to come to shortly. Others—those whom Olson (in press) called "intentional realists"—have reservations of a more transcendental sort, and would object just as vehemently to any line of evidence purporting to name any other age before which representational complexity was said to be at least tacitly present. The impossibility argument advanced by such neo-nativist theorists (e.g., Fodor, 1987; Leslie, 1987) is that nothing as "powerful" as a truly representational system could possibly arise out of an antecedent system of less complexity, and so representations of representation in some, perhaps modularized, form need to have existed from the outset. Still others (e.g., Dunn, 1991), spurred on by the recent discovery of so many previously unrecognized capabilities on the part of the very young, tend to be deeply suspicious of all categorical claims about what children cannot do, especially when such claims are based on an inability to pass some artfully arranged laboratory procedure. Finally, there are those (and here we mean to especially count ourselves) whose first commitment is to the working principle that nothing, or next to nothing, in the ontogenetic course ever really qualifies as a true one-trick pony, capable of arriving on the scene without antecedent, or departing without constantly changing consequences. By this way of reckoning, anything that is alleged to simply "pop up" at the age of 4, and that is subsequently imagined to go on being relentlessly itself through subsequent thick and thin, automatically falls under suspicion as probably being poorly thought out.

Whatever their motives, critics of mainstream claims that children acquire a first (and last) representational theory of mind at roughly 4 years of age have generally adopted one or the other of two strategies. One of these has typically involved trying to beat the opposition at its own game by finding some procedural fault with now standard assessment strategies. The obvious logic here is that, if it proves possible to work from within, by holding to the same demanding standards of proof otherwise being visited on the field, while still showing that minor procedural variation on standard tasks can result in a substantial lowering of the age at which subjects ordinarily pass such procedures, then the authority of these measures will come to be seen as less absolute, and the business of finding some new and more child-friendly index of the lower bound of the ability to represent representations will have been gotten profitably underway.

The second of these general approaches tends to be more broadly dismissive of the whole psychometric enterprise that has spawned the present theory of mind literature, and so tends to advocate in its place more "naturalistic" or observational approaches to the settling of any question about when it is that young children can be fairly said to first get "in the game" of treating their own and others' representations as representations.

Readers will not be surprised to learn that the long-standing debate between such champions of experimental rigor and the defenders of other more naturalistic or situated approaches to the assessment of children's abilities, have already drawn their familiar battle lines in the turf where the theory of mind wars are currently being waged. Accordingly, a new army of "boosters" (Hala, Chandler, & Fritz, 1991), committed to an "early-onset" view of representational competence, has already laid siege to a more entrenched force of "scoffers" whose "late-onset" views are rooted in a deep suspicion of any claims about representational matters that are not closely guarded by the canons of experimental science, or sanctified in the blood of those who have gone down fighting for still another control procedure. On this account, the scoffers' search for evidence of early representational competence in the responses of young persons to tightly orchestrated laboratory procedures (procedures that depend for their success on persuading preschoolers to submit themselves as patients to someone else's research agenda) is actually a fool's errand best left to those more committed to staving off possible criticisms than to getting things right. Operating in full recognition of the lurking possibility that their own commitments to greater ecology validity come equipped with some heightened risk of errors made on the side of leniency, such boosters, nevertheless, typically see methodological trade-offs that err on the side of the *in situ* as generally preferable to the more pristine process of holding out until the last possible false positive dog is dead.

Over the last decade, charter members of this booster group have collectively pointed to an impressively long list of early arising competencies, each of which, when taken piecemeal, pose some serious, if limited, challenge to the delayed-onset view, and, when combined, collectively constitute a rather impressive challenge to any would-be scoffer. Well up on any such list of possible challenges to the claim that only 4-year-olds have any real appreciation of the propositional character of their own and other's representations would need to be included the facts that, far in advance of any supposed 48-month watershed, still younger persons are already known to be uncommonly good at (a) taking active steps to disinform others by purposefully leading them into beliefs that are patently false (e.g., Chandler, Fritz, & Hala, 1989; Hala & Chandler, in press), (b) engaging in elaborate acts of social pretense that arguably require a working understanding of the distinction between things and their possible counterfactual representations (e.g., Dunn & Dale, 1984; Leslie, 1987), (c) salting their usual talk with mental state terms that attach to their own and others belief states (e.g., Bretherton, 1991), (d) behaving cooperatively and competently with others in ways that seem difficult to interpret without crediting them with knowledge of true belief states (e.g., Dunn, 1991; Reddy, 1990), (e) utilizing their caregiver's evident representations as social reference points in orchestrating their own approaches to unfamiliar persons and novel objects (e.g., Baldwin & Moses, 1994; Feinman, Roberts, Hsieh, Sawyer, & Swanson, 1992; Sorce, Emde, Campos, & Klinnert, 1985), (f) grasping the referential intent of adults interested to teach them the meaning of various words (e.g., Baldwin et al., in press; Tomasello & Barton, 1994), (g) declaratively pointing to interesting matters that lie outside another's perceptual field (e.g., Bates, Benigni, Bretherton,

Camaioni, & Volterra, 1979; Bretherton, 1991; Bretherton & Beeghly, 1982), and (h) distinguishing intentional from accidental actions (e.g., Tomasello & Barton, 1994). Although none of these claims is free of controversy, or somehow immune to a host of possible reductive interpretations, the combined weight of these several demonstrations, some of which present evidence of an ability to appreciate representation as representation in infant children hardly able to walk or talk, is enough to cause anyone not already blindly committed to a delayed-onset view to seriously rethink their position.

The second body of research meant to challenge the withholding view that only 4-year-olds deserve to be credited with a legitimately representational view of mental life is considerably more "in house," and has taken as its task the job of demonstrating that even relatively minor modifications to otherwise standard false belief measures are often enough to allow children of a much more tender age to successfully pass them with flying colors. Although various contributors to this literature each have had their own bone to pick with standard-issue unexpected transfer and unexpected contents tasks, the general thrust of these several efforts has been to show that there is something psychometrically inhospitable about procedures that oblige young preschoolers to sit through verbally saturated, third-party, "as-if" narratives concerning matters in which they have no personal stake, all as a prelude to answering a barrage of temporally ill-marked, hypothetical, and computationally complex questions that regularly pit children's known salience biases against their otherwise good intelligence. In response to these evident limitations, various investigators have worked to modify existing procedures in ways that are meant to retain their essential form, while somehow avoiding one or another of these procedural pitfalls.

By simply taking steps to further clarify or to better temporally mark the questions being posed (Freeman, Lewis, & Doherty, 1991; Siegal & Beattie, 1991), by better equating the salience of both false and true beliefs (Mitchell & Lacohee, 1991; Zaitchik, 1991), by working to reduce the memory load and other computational demands of the usual story narratives (Lewis, 1994), or by otherwise modifying these tasks in ways meant to more fully engage the interest of young subjects, or prompting them to exercise their own intentions or plans (Chandler et al., 1989; Hala & Chandler, in press; Hala et al., 1991; Moses, 1993; Wellman & Banerjee, 1991), essentially everyone involved in these rehabilitative efforts has ended up succeeding in moving back the apparent threshold of false belief understanding by 1 or more years—and eventually to an age before which still further attempts of formal testing tend to be impossible.

Again it will likely come as no surprise to learn that these and a long list of related studies have together prompted a second wave of fault finding and the casting of new doubts: "Maybe it's not a theory of mind, but a theory of behavior; maybe it's not deception but sabotage; maybe it's not a belief but a 'prelief;' maybe it's not verbal competence but a verbal tick; maybe someone put words into subjects' mouths; maybe reason is merely being read into what are actually random acts; maybe somebody greased the slide" (Chandler & Carpendale, in press)—all with the mischievous aim of creating an embarrassing incident. Although some of these post hoc excuses could very well have individual merit, the collective chorus they form threatens to approach a whine level that quickly becomes unseemly.

Summing, then, across all of those efforts to either repair the evident shortcoming of now standard tests of false belief understanding, or to entirely replace such measures with more psychometrically hospitable alternatives, the conclusion best afforded by a broad survey of the available evidence is that the now badly dated conclusion that only 4-year-olds deserve to be credited with a capacity to represent their own and others' representation is simply wrong and misleading. Rather, there now seems to be ample evidence to suggest that the task of coming to a first representational theory of mind involves a developmental process that reaches back all the way to a point in the developmental course where further attempts at formal testing become technically impossible. At the very least, then, the development of representational competence is not a process that can be fairly said to begin without precedent at something like 4 years of age. What this conclusion leaves still untouched, and what is unpacked in the next section, is what further development has in store concerning the subsequent achievement of any other even more grown-up representational theories of mind.

THE INTERPRETIVE TURN IN CHILDREN'S DEVELOPING REPRESENTATIONS OF REPRESENTATIONS

Looking Beyond False Belief Understanding

Having hopefully made the point that preschool children's beliefs about their own and others' representational activities are not without history, and so do not simply wink on at some unprecedented moment during the fourth or fifth year of life, we mean to go on now to take up the remaining question of whether or not 4-year-olds, who are broadly agreed to have at least a working understanding of the possibility of false belief, can also be fairly said to hold to a view of representation that is already equivalent, in *all* the important respects, to the commonsense viewpoint broadly subscribed to by ordinary adults. One's answer to this question will, obviously enough, depend very much on what this commonsense view, or even some absolute truth of the matter, is finally taken to be. One such conceivable answer—the "realist" answer that, according to Bickhard (1992), underpins the large bulk of contemporary writings on children's developing theories of mind—is that all representations, at least all those that are not somehow badly mistaken, amount to some proper "match" (von Glasersfeld, 1979) between one's own encodings and that particular chunk of objective reality being represented. By these lights, legitimate representations are seen to be passive by-products of unimpeded access to the full details of any matter, and ignorance ends up being the only conceivable intellectual crime. On this account, what passes for an "active" conception of mental life amounts to an appreciation of the fact that ignorance can be cumulative, with the result, that different persons, with different facts at their disposal, will "actively process" (Perner & Davies, 1991) any new fact in what amounts to idiosyncratic ways. Here, anything that might fairly count as a test of an individual's grasp of the "interpretive" character of the knowing process ends up reducing to what Ruffman, Olson, and Astington (1991) openly admitted is no more than "false belief tests at heart" (p. 90). On this account, any age-graded changes that might divide 4-year-olds from their elders is owed to no more than a simple tendency to grow more expert in keeping track of the cumulative differences in stored knowledge that increasingly separate us all. Although such a viewpoint does allow for a certain kind of talk about people as "active processors of information" (Perner & Davies, 1991), and so is "interpretive" after a fashion, the question raised and answered here is whether such an account is a fair rendition of what it is that growing children do, in fact, actually come to think about representational life. Our answer to this question, which we have already signaled in our earlier discussion of what Searle (1983) called the "world-to-mind" direction of fit between thinkers and things thought about, is a decided "No!"

In what follows, we mean to back our own sharply different reading of the developmental course that children follow in coming to a mature conception of mind in three different ways. First, at the risk of otherwise standing accused of having made the whole improbable thing up, we mean to better document our claim that serious contributors to the study of children's representations do in fact regularly subscribe to the view that holding to an interpretive theory of mind amounts to no more than a well-oiled talent for false belief understanding—a capacity that is widely understood to be well in place before the end of the preschool years. Second, we intend to more explicitly make the case that the commonsense folk psychology to which adults routinely subscribe is sharply different from, and in our view, definitely richer than the badly truncated one-miracle "specialist psychology" currently being put out by various contemporary theorists of mind. Finally, we plan to briefly summarize the results of a series of recent studies that will hopefully persuade you that coming to a first legitimately interpretive view of representation is not only different from, but is also altogether later arriving than, any still simpler ability to merely appreciate the possibility of false belief.

Do Contemporary Theorists of Mind Really Mean to Equate False Belief Understanding With a Genuinely Interpretive View of the Representational Process?

Because common sense is so quick to understand the possibility that different persons regularly find different meanings in what are effectively the same things, you could be forgiven for seriously doubting that there actually are specialists in the field of mental representation who are prepared to see false belief understanding as the same thing as an appreciation of the interpretive or constructive character of the representational process. As it is, however, just about anyone you might think to quote on this subject seems surprisingly willing to endorse exactly this improbable prospect. Wellman, for example, not only described preschool children, whose best performance to date includes no more than a first grip upon the possibility of false belief, as having already come to "an interpretive or constructive understanding of representation" (Wellman, 1990, p. 244), but further characterized them as having already acquired the view that the contents of mental life are actively constructed "on the basis of inference and subject biases, misrepresentations, and active interpretations" (Wellman & Hickling, 1994, p. 1578). In much the same fashion, Ruffman et al. (1991) also explicitly dismissed the possibility of *any*, let alone an interpretive, stage in children's understanding of representation beyond straightforward false belief understanding. Again, Meltzoff and Gopnik (1993) argued that 5-year-olds already understand that beliefs are "active interpretations or construals of them from a given perspective" (p. 335). More explicitly still, Perner (1991) argued that "around 4 years children begin to understand knowledge as representation with all its essential characteristics. One such characteristic is *interpretation*" (p. 275, italics in original). Although one could easily go on, this will perhaps suffice to make the point that contemporary theorists of mind, in large numbers, do soberly and self-consciously mean to equate false belief understanding with the achievement of an interpretive or constructive theory of representation, and consequently see little point in squandering a lot of resources actually testing school-age children who purportedly have little left to do beyond simply ensuring that practice makes perfect.

On the Distinction Between Being an "Active Information Processor" and a Singular Interpreter of Meaning

Although it is perhaps hazardous to speculate overmuch about why a group of colleagues that have so many otherwise admirable things to say might, in this case, end up—dare we say—"interpreting" matters so differently, here, at least, is a short list of candidate reasons. First, as already discussed, certain, perhaps closet, commitments to a realist epistemology easily contribute to a view that loosely equates being an "active information processor" (Perner & Davies, 1991) —by which is usually meant something like the fact that new information is counted differently by those who are more or less well informed—with being a person who imaginatively interprets or actively constructs meaning. Although there is no reason not to go along with the idea that one more candle of information will register differently in more or less well lit rooms, or even to doubt that 4-year-old children, who already appreciate that ignorance is bad for you, do not also appreciate that the same bit of new information has a different cash value to different people, none of this has anything evidently to do with the altogether different realization that there is an ineluctable mind-to-world direction of causality operating in the representational world that necessitates that meaning is always partially in the eye of the beholder.

Some further part of what divides our own, perhaps sunnier, constructivist view of representation, from what is evidently meant by talk of becoming an active processor of information is found in the fact that ordinary language usage naturally permits two fundamentally different ways of talking about the notion of interpretation. By one of these standard meanings, the term interpretation is understood to reference a form of *evaluation* that sometimes must be brought to bear upon unsettled or otherwise obscured matters of fact. "Understood in this 'world-to-mind' fashion, interpretation is a thing needing to be done in response to ambiguities brought on by a shortage of relevant information—a repair job required by recalcitrant or runaway facts. By these lights, children can be said to have an interpretive theory of mind as soon as they show some skill at determining when others are and are not in possession of sufficient information to work out the true nature of some potentially ambiguous situation" (Carpendale & Chandler, 1996, p. 1693).

The second of these standard meanings of the notion of interpretation has less to do with the fact that we are sometimes obliged to actively fill in the gaps left by facts, and has more to do, instead, with what Webster's dictionary has to say about the endemic mind-to-world necessity of always portraying what one knows from some situated perspective. "Here interpreting is not something we do in a pinch when full access to the facts is blocked, but rather a way of characterizing the routine process by which available inputs are taken up and constructively made our own" (Carpendale & Chandler, 1996, p. 1693). Seen from this vantage, what marks the onset of a genuinely interpretive representation of representation is not the simple realization that misinterpretation is possible, but rather some demonstration of an appreciation that different people can, and regularly do, find different meanings in one and the same event.

Finally, what must undoubtedly count as a candidate reason for the fact that many contributors to the theories of mind literature are so confident that what 4-year-olds know about false beliefs, plus a dollop of additional experience, adds up to an interpretive theory of mind is the fact that no one, or next to no one, has actually bothered to test still older children.

New Lines of Evidence Concerning the Acquisition of a First Interpretive Theory of Mind

Given all that has come before, there remains no real room for doubt that an unbridgeable impasse in understanding has been reached. Either the early recognition that persons are active processors of information is the same thing as holding to an interpretive or constructive understanding of representation, or it is not. Either 4-year-olds, who can routinely pass standard measures of false belief understanding, can also pass any fair-minded test of an interpretive view of mental life, or they cannot. Either the developmental pathway by which young persons come to approach a mature conception of representations *as* representations has fully run its course by the end of the preschool years, or it goes on leading young persons through still other interim solutions to the problem of how mental representations relate to their referents. We and our working colleagues (i.e., Carpendale, 1995; Carpendale & Chandler, 1996; Chandler & Lalonde, 1996; Hala, 1994; Hala & Chandler, in press; Lalonde, 1996) have convinced at least ourselves that none of these attempts to collapse the course of epistemic growth into a single developmental moment is conceptually sound, or, as we shortly attempt to demonstrate, empirically justified. Coming from an entirely different quarter, mainstream theorists of mind, who tend to equate interpretation with misinterpretation, who are persuaded that they are already in possession of a one-size-fits-all assessment procedure adequate to the task of measuring any manner of thoughts about thought, and who consequently excuse themselves from the necessity of actually testing preschool graduates, obviously disagree. Although clearly at loggerheads, these oppositional views fortunately do not reduce to yet another of those interminable paradigm debates that so often stalemate the field. Rather, what we seem to have here is one of those welcome, if rare, situations in which there really is some serious prospect of actually settling a strong difference of opinion with empirical evidence.

All that would seem to be required in order to put these disagreements to empirical test is to first find, or fashion, some assessment procedure that promises to measure commitments to the idea that representations are actually active constructions or interpretations of experience, and then to simply administer such a "test" to groups of young persons who have already incontrovertibly passed a standard measure of false belief understanding, but who might or might not already subscribe to the idea that there is an ineluctable world to mind direction of fit between things in the world and their mental instantiation. Assuming that it were possible to get even modest agreement that such an assessment procedure fairly accomplished what it set out to do, and was not simply harder for other incidental reasons, then any demonstration that success on tests of false belief is a necessary, but not otherwise sufficient, condition for the passing of tests of interpretation would need to be seen as counting seriously against the possibility that these two abilities are really one and the same thing. Instead, such a demonstration would be strongly in favor of the opposite conclusion that coming to a mature conception of representation is a later arriving and more developmentally drawn-out affair than it is currently imagined to be by practitioners of the widely popular one-miracle view.

Awkwardly, attempts to run this "critical experiment" have been seriously held up, due primarily to the fact that testing procedures capable of establishing who does and who does not subscribe to a bona fide interpretive theory of mind have not been ready at hand, and so have needed to be built from the ground up. To see what has been required in doing just this, imagine what it would take to convince you that a young child of a given age had already come on side by recognizing, along with her or his elders, that different persons can, and do, legitimately come to different interpretations about one and the same stimulus event.

Imagine this. Imagine that two couples, the Wimmers and the Perners, both go to a movie. At some disadvantageous moment in the plot line of the film, one of the Wimmers goes out for popcorn. Later they end up arguing over the meaning of what they saw. By contrast, the Perners remain glued to their seats throughout the film, but also exit in sharp disagreement about what they had both seen together from curtain to credits. The Wimmers, as we make plain, are in a situation not unlike that of Maxi and his mother who have access to differing amounts of information, and the basis of any disagreement (some might injudiciously say different interpretation) that they might have is easily laid at the door of the fact that going out for popcorn at the wrong moment often leads to false beliefs. By contrast, the Perners, who are also in disagreement, not about some nonepistemic matter such as whether they liked or disliked the film, but about the meaning of the actors' behaviors, closely approximate the kind of ideal test case we are looking for. They both have equivalent access to the "facts," they sharply disagree about the meaning of their common experience, and their disagreement has real epistemic content—that is, their disagreement is about what they hold out as matters of fact (rather than about some matter of taste or personal preference), and they are prepared to back their different claims by bringing out evidence in support of their interpretations.

As it is, nothing that looks very much like this proposed paradigm case currently exists in the theories of mind literature. What, perhaps, come closest is a set of research reports by Pillow and his colleagues (e.g., Pillow, 1991; Pillow & Weed, 1995) that describe efforts to establish the age at which young schoolage children first come to appreciate that people are quicker to read bad motives into the behavior of those that they actively dislike, or to *mis*interpret their actions. What is "wrong" with these otherwise promising efforts, or at least what prevents them from serving our own somewhat different purposes, is that they engineer matters in such a way that background knowledge on the part of various story protagonists always works to lead them astray, and so only to "misinterpret," as opposed to more simply "interpret," otherwise ambiguous matters.

Failing to find what we needed simply lying about, we and our research colleagues were obliged to home-build what we needed. In doing so, we were guided by a general blueprint that required our being able to present to young persons of 4 or 5 some common stimulus event ambiguous enough to support more than one "legitimate" (or at least defensible) interpretation regarding some fact of the matter, all with the aim of determining whether primary school children could respond in clear and succinct ways capable of signaling, without writing a book, their possible commitment to an interpretive theory of mind.

So far, two procedurally distinct lines of work have come out of this same general ground plan. One of these (Carpendale, 1995; Carpendale & Chandler, 1996) has focused attention on a small class of stimuli that, whether by nature or design, turn out to have the special feature of reliably prompting two—and only two—especially compelling and likely interpretations. Homophones are instances of this class for the definitional reason that they naturally support just two distinct interpretations, as are certain line drawings, such as Jastrow's (1900) "duck-rabbit" and Bugelski's (1960) "rat-man," which share the common property of being easily taken to be one or the other of two different things.

In this study sequence 5- to 8-year-olds (all of whom had been shown to easily succeed on a standard measure of false belief understanding) were given problems involving the two classes of stimuli just mentioned. In every case all that was required in order to "pass" these testing procedures was to variously acknowledge each of two puppet figures were understandably within their rights for offering up either one or the other of the two interpretations especially afforded by these stimuli. In the case of Jastrow's (1990) drawing, for example, one puppet figure was made to announce that it was a picture of a duck, whereas the other claimed that it was a rabbit. Despite the fact that all of these subjects were able to "see" for themselves both of the alternative meanings offered, only the 7- and 8-year-olds were able to regularly *acknowledge* and *explain* the legitimacy of the two different interpretations with which they were confronted, or recognize that there might be some legitimate grounds for uncertainty when asked to predict what some third puppet might offer up as an interpretation of these same stimuli. By contrast, 5-year-olds (and to a lesser extent children of 6), tended to be convinced that only one of the two interpretations offered could possibly be "correct," and typically found little in the way of grounds for uncertainty when asked to imagine what some additional puppet figure would likely take these ambiguous stimuli to be. This was true despite the fact that, young or old, these subjects found no difficulty in crediting different story characters with the right to exercise different likes and dislikes regarding matters of taste, and were more or less uniformly able to *explain* why one puppet figure thought that Maxi's chocolate was in container *A*, whereas another less well informed puppet wrongly supposed it to be in container *B*.

The second of these study sequences (Chandler & Lalonde, 1996; Lalonde, 1996) took the different tack of choosing as test items stimuli drawn from that general class of fundamentally amorphous stimuli that include Rorschach ink blots and clouds and puddles of spilled milk, all of which are sufficiently vague and nondescript that they easily afford an almost infinite variety of defensibly different interpretive possibilities. More particularly, the specific stimuli chosen for inclusion were part of a set of cryptic puzzle pictures originally popularized by cartoonist Roger Price (1953). Such drawings are perhaps better illustrated

FIG. 10.1   An example of Price's droodles: "A ship arriving too late to save a drowning witch."

than explained. Figure 10.1, for example, depicts a variation on a so-called "droodle" originally published by Price over the caption "A ship arriving too late to save a drowning witch." The humor in this and related drawings by Price uniformly turns on the fact that, given the restricted keyhole view offered, it would be farfetched to imagine that anyone could ever intuit the larger scene of which the droodle itself is only an ambiguous, fractional part. Once alerted by the captions, however, these otherwise nondescript fragments fall into place, and it becomes possible to imagine—even difficult not to imagine—that they are other than fractional parts of what is now understood to be a partially obscured larger drawing.

Several things especially recommend the use of these materials in the study of the development of children's emerging understanding of the interpretive character of mental life. One of these is that, when stripped of their captions, these drawings are sufficiently ambiguous that, at least for adults, it is not just "conceivable" that two different persons might interpret them differently, it has all of the marking of a felt necessity. Of perhaps equal importance is the fact that, with certain minor modifications, it is also possible to put these same drawings to work as straightforward (although perhaps not "minimally complex") measure of false belief understanding. Adopting a simplified version of a procedure originally published along with David Helm (Chandler & Helm, 1984), it is possible to proceed by first constructing a drawing (see Fig. 10.2) that depicts all of the details spelled out in one of Price's (1953) original droodle captions and then outfitting this larger picture with a windowed overlay that allows only the original "droodle" image to show through. Given these modifications it becomes possible to proceed in a way that allows subjects to first be made privy to the full-scale drawing, all before going on to press them for answers about what first one and then another person might imagine these now ambiguous drawings to be. When put to work in this fashion, such stimuli afford effectively all of the same particulars as are present in Wimmer and Perner's standard unexpected change measure. That is, subjects who are made privy to the completed drawings are analogous to subjects who witness all of the comings and goings of Maxi's chocolate bar. By contrast, anyone who is strategically left in the dark, by being allowed to see only the "droodle" portion of these larger drawings, is in a position roughly analogous to Maxi himself, who has some, but only some, of the information necessary to lead him to a correct judgment.

With these prospects in mind, a series of studies were mounted in which 5- to 7-year-olds were first assessed in terms of their understanding of the possibility of false beliefs (i.e., despite the fact that I know it is really a ship and a witch, what would Raggedy Ann think is depicted in the small window), and then, more crucially, invited to speculate about how a second puppet—Raggedy Andy— might "interpret" this same stimulus fragment.

In close agreement with the findings of the Carpendale (1995) and Carpendale and Chandler (1996) studies, a half-dozen experiments utilizing these droodle materials all point to the singular fact that 7-year-olds, but not still younger subjects, appreciate the possibility that two different doll figures might somehow be within their rights to find different meanings in one and the same ill-defined stimulus event. Younger 5- and most 6-year olds, by contrast, again showed themselves committed to the immature proposition that, no matter how vague the task, each and every ambiguous event still allows for one and only one warrantable interpretation.

Taken together these two study sets provide the necessary empirical support for our theory-driven expectation that false belief understanding is both different from, and a perhaps necessary, but in no sense sufficient condition, for the conceptually distinct ability to eventually appreciate that one and the same stimulus event can be open to more than one legitimate interpretation.

By focusing attention on stimuli that especially call out for one or the other of

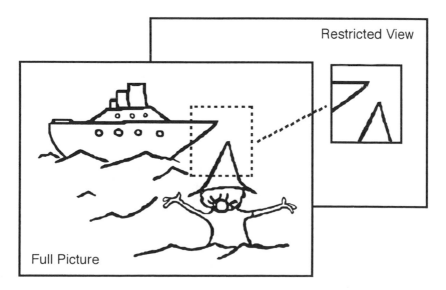

FIG. 10.2   Modified "Ship-Witch" droodle with windowed overlay.

two equally compelling interpretations, or that could easily afford almost any interpretation at all, the series of studies just summarized likely provide a lower bound estimate of children's earliest insights into the interpretive nature of knowing. Consequently, we do not mean to imply that this is the end of the story. Instead, there are good reasons to suppose that what 7- or 8-year-old children know about interpretation is only a first chapter in a continuing developmental course that, in all likelihood, extends at least through adolescence, and perhaps into early adulthood as well (e.g., Chandler, 1987; D. Kuhn, Amsel, & O'Loughlin, 1988; D. Kuhn, Pennington, & Leadbeater, 1983; Perry, 1970). Whatever the final answer might prove to be concerning precisely when in the course of their development young people first begin and finally end the process of coming to a mature conception of mental life, what now seems clear enough is that there are no correct conceptual or empirical reasons for supposing that all or even most of what is really interesting about this process just happens to fall within a province exclusively owned by 40- to 60-month-olds.

CONCLUSION

Counting back across the whole of this long chapter, we mean to have made what can perhaps be boiled down to the following four points.

First, we mean to have made the case that any complete account of the theoretical perspectives that might be brought to bear on the concept of representation needs to include the perspectives of developing children, whose ideas on the subject may well have lapped some of those who are meant to be studying them.

Second, by compiling a case in favor of the claim that children of 2 or 3, and perhaps younger still, already entertain serviceable beliefs about their own and others' representational life, we hope to have moved you well out of the orbit of influence of those contemporary theorists of mind who still insist, against a growing wall of counter evidence, that anyone younger than 4 is necessarily handicapped by a cognitive deficit that wholly blocks them from entertaining thought-one about the representational process.

Third, there now seems to be strong and growing support for the prospect that the insight, common to even very young preschool children, that ignorance can promote false beliefs, is by no means the last serious thought that growing children will have about the meaning of representation. Rather, there are now sound empirical reasons to imagine that, by 7 or 8, young persons have already begun to outgrow the limiting idea that all of representational diversity can be traced back to ignorance-based false beliefs, and are well on their way toward appreciating the possibility that, not only is the mind obliged to fit the world, but that there is also a world-to-mind direction of fit that operates to make knowledge a constructive or interpretive achievement.

Finally, if it is not too indelicate to say so, we mean to urge the possibility that some of the things that have come out of the mouths of the babes that have been our research subjects appear to be more praiseworthy than are certain of the one-miracle views of representation that are used to impugn their good names. Of course, the fact that even middle school children evidently subscribe to a view of mental life that already contains important elements of a more fully fledged interpretive or constructive view of representation is not the same thing as making it so. After all, common sense has promoted a great raft of ideas— phlogiston, the crystalline orbs, the philosophers' stone—that have had the lie put to them by modern science. Still, there is perhaps some room for collective embarrassment in the fact that the typical 8-year-old already sports organized thoughts about the nature of representation that are at least better textured and more nicely layered than are some of our more respected specialist theories.

ACKNOWLEDGMENTS

The preparation of this chapter was supported by a Natural Sciences and Engineering Research Council of Canada operating grant to the first author, and by a University of British Columbia Graduate Fellowship to the second author.

REFERENCES

Baldwin, D. A., Markman, E. M., Bill, B., Desjardins, R. N., Irwin, R. N., & Tidball, G. (in press). Infants' understanding that the speaker specifies the referent. *Child Development.*

Baldwin, D. A., & Moses, L. J. (1994). Early understanding of referential intent and attentional focus: Evidence from language and emotion. In C. Lewis & P. Mitchell (Eds.), *Children's early understanding of mind: Origins and development* (pp. 133–156). Hove, England: Lawrence Erlbaum Associates.

Bates, E., Benigni, L., Bretherton, I., Camaioni, L., & Volterra, V. (1979). Cognition and communication from 9–13 months: Correlational findings. In E. Bates (Ed.), *The emergence of symbols: Cognition and communication in infancy* (pp. 69–140). New York: Plenum.

Bickhard, M. H. (1992). Commentary. *Human Development, 35,* 182–192.

Bretherton, I. (1991). Intentional communication and the development of an understanding of mind. In D. Frye & C. Moore (Eds.), *Children's theories of mind: Mental states and social understanding* (pp. 49–75). Hillsdale, NJ: Lawrence Erlbaum Associates.

Bretherton, I., & Beeghly, M. (1982). Talking about internal states. The acquisition of an explicit theory of mind. *Developmental Psychology, 18,* 906–921.

Bugelski, B. R. (1960). *An introduction to the principles of psychology.* New York: Holt, Rinehart & Winston.

Burnyeat, M. (1990). *The Theaetetus of Plato* (M. J. Levett, Trans.). Indianapolis: Hackett.

Carpendale, J. I. M. (1995). *On the distinction between false belief understanding and the acquistion of an interpretive theory of mind.* Unpublished doctoral dissertation, The University of British Columbia, Vancouver, Canada.

Carpendale, J. I. M., & Chandler, M. J. (1996). On the distinction between false belief understanding and subscribing to an interpretive theory of mind. *Child Development, 67,* 1686–1706.

Chandler, M. J. (1987). The Othello effect: An essay on the emergence and eclipse of skeptical doubt. *Human Development, 30*(3), 137–159.

Chandler, M. J., & Boyes, M. (1982). Social cognitive development. In B. B. Wolman (Ed.), *Handbook of developmental psychology* (pp. 387–402). Englewood Cliffs, NJ: Prentice-Hall.

Chandler, M. J., & Carpendale, J. I. M. (in press). Inching toward a mature theory of mind. In M. Ferrari & R. Sternberg (Eds.), *Development of Self Awareness.*

Chandler, M. J., Fritz, A. S., & Hala, S. M. (1989). Small scale deceit: Deception as a marker of 2-, 3- and 4-year olds' early theories of mind. *Child Development, 60,* 1263–1277.

Chandler, M. J. & Helm, D. (1984). Developmental changes in the contribution of shared experience to social role-taking competence. *International Journal of Behavioural Development, 7,* 145–156.

Chandler, M. J., & Lalonde, C. (1996). Shifting to an interpretive theory of mind: 5- to 7-year-olds' changing conceptions of mental life. In A. Sameroff & M. Haith (Eds.), *Reason and responsibility: The passage through childhood* (pp. 111–139). Chicago: University of Chicago Press.

Chapman, M. (1988). *Constructive evolution: Origins and development of Piaget's thought.* New York: Cambridge University Press.

Churchland, P. M. (1988). *Matter and consciousness* (Rev. ed.). Cambridge, MA: Bradford Books/MIT Press.

Davidson, D. (1984). Thought and talk. In D. Davidson (Ed.), *Inquiries into truth and interpretation* (pp. 155–170). Oxford, England: Oxford University Press.

De Sousa, R. (1991). Does the eye know calculus? The threshold or representation in classical and connectionist models. *International Studies in the Philosohy of Science, 5*(2), 171–185.

Dunn, J. (1991). Understanding others: Evidence from naturalistic studies of children. In A. Whiten (Ed.), *Natural theories of mind. Evolution, development and simulation of everyday mindreading* (pp. 51–61). Oxford, England: Basil Blackwell.

Dunn, J., & Dale, N. (1984). I a daddy: 2-year-olds' collaboration in joint pretend with sibling and with mother. In I. Bretherton (Ed.), *Symbolic play* (pp. 131–158). New York: Academic Press.

Feinman, S., Roberts, D., Hsieh, K., Sawyer, D., & Swanson, D. (1992). A critical review of social referencing in infancy. In S. Feinman (Ed.), *Social referencing and the social construction of reality in infancy* (pp. 15–54). New York: Plenum.

Fodor, J. A. (1987). *Psychosemantics: The problem of meaning in the philosophy of mind.* Cambridge, MA: Bradford Books/MIT Press.

Freeman, N. H., Lewis, C., & Doherty, M. J. (1991). Preschoolers' grasp of a desire for knowledge in false-belief prediction: Practical intelligence and verbal report. *British Journal of Developmental Psychology, 9,* 139–157.

Furth, H. G. (1969). *Piaget and knowledge: Theoretical foundations.* Englewood Cliffs, NJ: Prentice-Hall.

Garcia, R. (1987). Sociology of science and sociogenesis of knowledge. In B. Inhelder, D. de Caprona, & A. Cornu-Wells (Eds.), *Piaget today* (pp. 127–140). Hove, England: Lawrence Erlbaum Associates.

Gopnik, A. (1991, April). *Is the child's theory of mind really a theory?* Paper presented at the biennial meeting of the Society for Research in Child Development, Seattle.

Gopnik, A. (1993). How we know our minds: The illusion of first-person knowledge of intentionality. *Behavioral and Brain Sciences, 16,* 1–14.

Gopnik, A., & Wellman, H. M. (1992). Why the child's theory of mind really is a theory. *Mind & Language, 7,* 145–171.

Hala, S. (1994). *The role of personal involvement in accessing false belief understanding.* Unpublished doctoral dissertation, The University of British Columbia, Vancouver, Canada.

Hala, S., & Chandler, M. J. (in press). The role of strategic planning in assessing false-belief understanding. *Child Development.*

Hala, S., Chandler, M. J., & Fritz, A. (1991). Fledgling theories of mind: Deception as a marker of 3-year-old's understanding of false belief. *Child Development, 62,* 83–97.

Heelas, P. (1981). Introduction: Indigenous psychologies. In P. Heelas & A. Lock (Eds.), *Indigenous psychologies: The anthropology of the self* (pp. 3–18). London: Academic Press.

Jastrow, J. (1990). *Fact and fable in psychology.* Boston: Houghton Mifflin.

Kuhn, D., Amsel, E., & O'Loughlin, M. (1988). *The development of scientific thinking skills.* San Diego: Academic Press.

Kuhn, D., Pennington, N., & Leadbeater, B. (1983). Adult thinking in developmental perspective. In P. Baltes & O. Brim, Jr. (Eds.), *Life-span development and behavior* (Vol. 5, pp. 157–195). New York: Academic Press.

Kuhn, T. (1970). *The structure of scientific revolutions* (2nd ed.) Chicago: University of Chicago Press.

Lalonde, C. E. (1996). *Children's understanding of the interpretive character of the mind.* Unpublished doctoral dissertation, The University of British Columbia, Vancouver, Canada.

Leslie, A. M. (1987). Pretense and representation: The origins of "theory of mind." *Psychological Review, 94,* 412–426.

Lewis, C. (1994). Episodes, events, and narratives in the child's understanding of mind. In C. Lewis & P. Mitchell (Eds.), *Children's early understanding of mind: Origins and development* (pp. 457–480) Hove, England: Lawrence Erlbaum Associates.

Macnamara, J. (1989). Children as common sense psychologists. *Canadian Journal of Behavioural Science, 21,* 426–429.

Meltzoff, A., & Gopnik, A. (1993). The role of imitation in understanding persons and developing a theory of mind. In S. Baron-Cohen, H. Tager-Flusberg, & D. J. Cohen (Eds.), *Understanding other minds: Perspectives from autism* (pp. 335–366). Oxford, England: Oxford University Press.

Merton, R. K. (1968). *Social theory and social structure.* New York: The Free Press

Mitchell, P., & Lacohee, H. (1991). Children's early understanding of false belief. *Cognition, 39,* 107–127.

Morton, A. (1980). *Frames of mind.* Oxford, England: Clarendon Press.

Moses, L. (1993). Young children's understanding of belief constraints on intention. *Cognitive Development, 8,* 1–25.

Murray, F. B. (1979). Preface. In F. B. Murray (Ed.), *The impact of Piagetian theory: On education, philosophy, psychiatry, and psychology* (pp. ix–xiii). Baltimore: University Park Press.

Olson, D. R. (in press). The development of representations: The origins of mental life. *Canadian Psychology.*

Perner, J. (1991). *Understanding the representational mind.* Cambridge, MA: MIT Press.

Perner, J., & Davies, G. (1991). Understanding the mind as an active information processor: Do young children have a "copy theory of mind"? *Cognition, 39,* 51–69.

Perry, W. G. (1970). *Forms of intellectual and ethical development in the college years.* New York: Holt, Rinehart & Winston.

Piaget, J. (1963). *The origins of intelligence in children.* New York: Norton. (Original work published 1936)

Piaget, J. (1972). *Insights and illusions of philosophy.* London: Routledge & Kegan Paul. (Original work published 1965)

Pillow, B. H. (1991). Children's understanding of biased social cognition. *Developmental Psychology, 27,* 539–551.

Pillow, B. H., & Weed, S. T. (1995). Children's understanding of biased interpretation: Generality and limitations. *British Journal of Developmental Psychology, 13,* 347–366.

Premack, D., & Woodruff, G. (1978). Does the chimpanzee have a theory of mind? *Behavioral and Brain Sciences, 1,* 515–526.

Price, R. (1953). *Droodles.* New York: Simon & Schuster.

Reddy, V. (1990). Playing with others' expectations: Teasing and mucking about in the first year. In A. Whiten (Ed.), *Natural theories of mind. Evolution, development and simulation of everyday mindreading* (pp. 143–158). Oxford, England: Basil Blackwell.

Ruffman, T., Olson, D. R., & Astington, J. W. (1991). Children's understanding of visual ambiguity. *British Journal of Developmental Psychology, 9,* 89–102.

Russell, J. (1992). The theory theory: So good they named it twice? *Cognitive Development, 7,* 485–519.

Searle, J. R. (1983). *Intentionality: An essay in the philosophy of mind.* Cambridge, England: Cambridge University Press.

Siegal, M., & Beattie, K. (1991). Where to look for children's knowledge of false beliefs. *Cognition, 38,* 1–12.

Smedslund, J. (1979). Between the analytic and the arbitrary: A case study of psychological research. *Scandanavian Journal of Psychology, 20,* 129–140.

Sorce, J., Emde, R. N., Campos, J. J., & Klinnert, M. (1985). Maternal emotional signalling: Its effect on the visual cliff behavior of one-year-olds. *Developmental Psychology, 21,* 195–200.

Stich, S. (1983). *From folk psychology to cognitive science.* Cambridge, MA: Bradford Books / MIT Press.

Tomasello, M., & Barton, M. (1994). Learning words in nonostensive contexts. *Developmetal Psychology, 30,* 639–650.

von Glasersfeld, E. (1979). Radical constructivism and Piaget's concept of knowledge. In F. B. Murray (Ed.), *The impact of Piagetian theory: On education, philosophy, psychiatry, and psychology* (pp. 109–122). Baltimore: University Park Press.

Wellman, H. M. (1990). *The child's theory of mind.* Cambridge, MA: MIT Press.

Wellman, H., & Banerjee, M. (1991). Mind and emotion: Children's understanding of the emotional consequences of beliefs and desires. *British Journal of Developmental Psychology, 9,* 191–214.

Wellman, H. M., & Hickling, A. K. (1994). The mind's "I": Children's conceptions of the mind as an active agent. *Child Development, 65,* 1564–1580.

Wimmer, H., & Perner, J. (1983). Beliefs about beliefs: Representation and constraining function of wrong beliefs in young children's understanding of deception. *Cognition, 13,* 103–128.

Zaitchik, D. (1991). Is only seeing really believing?: Sources of the true belief in the false belief task. *Cognitive Development, 6,* 91–103.

CHAPTER 11

The Development of Representation as the Coordination of Component Systems of Action

MICHAEL F. MASCOLO
Merrimack College

KURT W. FISCHER
Harvard University

Although there is considerable agreement about the importance of representation in human functioning, decades of psychological investigation and centuries of philosophical pondering indicate that there is little consensus regarding the nature and development of representation. To what do we refer when we speak of representation? How is representation constituted and how does representation develop? Different approaches in psychology frame the question of representation in terms of different aspects of human functioning (e.g., memory and retrieval, action, sociocultural processes, or the use of signs). In this chapter, we elaborate a dynamic skill approach to representation (Fischer 1980; Fischer & Granott, 1995; Fischer, Shaver & Carnochan, 1990) that proceeds from the assumption that a person cannot be broken into distinct components for memory, action, and sociocultural interaction. Instead, a person functions as a system in which all of these aspects work together. From this view, representation develops through the coordination of component actions within social and cultural contexts.

Some Prominent Conceptions of Representation

There are currently at least three prominent perspectives regarding the nature and development of representation in developmental psychology. A brief consideration of each perspective points to the lack of consensus that characterizes the concept of representation, and suggests the need for a model that describes how memory, action, and sociocultural activity work together in the creation of representation.

Information Processing. Within cognitive science, information-processing perspectives tend to define representation in terms of the ways in which information is internally preserved and transformed within and throughout the information-processing system (Kail & Bisanz, 1992). From this view, representation refers to the ways in which aspects of a stimulus or event are preserved and maintained by various types of internal codes throughout the course of information processing. Internal codes and representations can take on many forms, including semantic networks, episodic knowledge and procedural knowledge stored in long-term memory, verbal and imaginal codes that are acted upon in short-term memory, sensory and neural codes that occur in the process of perceiving, and so on. Developmental changes in representation occur through the invocation of *self-modification* processes. For example, Kail and Bisanz have discussed the role of *generalization* and *discrimination* as processes that account for changes in children's rule-based knowledge. In generalization, new rules are compared to existing rules and common elements are consolidated into more general rules; in discrimination, rules are refined and made more specific as a result of local conditions and constraints. From this view, change processes are internal to an individual's system rather than created by environmental circumstances. As such, generalization and discrimination reflect basic properties of internal cognitive architecture.

An important strength of the information-processing approach consists of its capacity to produce specific and testable models of changes in the representations and processes that occur when children perform various tasks (Siegler, 1983). Despite this strength, one might raise several questions about this approach. First, the information-processing view, which has origins in the computer metaphor, often suggests a mechanistic view in which representations exist as things—static and bounded internal entitites that can be stored or retrieved and that mediate between discrete stimuli and responses. Second, such views generally analyze representational development in terms of quantitative rather than qualitative changes. Third, information-processing psychologists have been more fruitful in their analysis of how representation changes than in the sources of representational development (but see Banks, 1987; Klahr, 1989; Siegler, 1989; Sternberg, 1984). Finally, many information-processing approaches embody the assumption that the environment is largely independent of representations and the processes by which they change. Piagetian and sociocultural views offer alternative ways of addressing these issues.

Piagetian/Constructivist Views. In contrast to information-processing theory, Piagetian views treat representation as a product of individual activity that assumes qualitatively different forms throughout ontogenesis. According to Piaget (1951), representation always involves a signifier through which people can recall objects that are not immediately present. Piaget defined two forms of representation: "In its broad sense, representation is identical with thought, i.e., with all intelligence which is based on a system of concepts or mental schemas and not merely on perceptions and actions. In its narrow sense, representation is restricted to the mental or memory image, i.e., the symbolic evocation of absent realities" (p. 67). Within Piaget's theory, symbolic representation begins at substage six of the sensorimotor period, with the construction of the image or sign as an instance of internalized, abbreviated imitative action (Piaget, 1951). Although genuine symbolic activity arises around this time, Piaget recognized that primitive forms of symbolization (i.e., "signals" and "indices") emerged even prior to the first birthday. It is important to note that from a Piagetian view, representation is the product of activity. In fact, Piaget spoke of *representative activity* rather than of representations per se. As an instance of activity, a representation is not something that can be stored or retrieved, but instead reflects the reconstitution of activity. As such, imaginal or verbal representations are reconstructed in action each time they are invoked. Thus to Piaget, representation involves making sense of the world in terms of internal or abbreviated actions that move functioning beyond concrete perception and sensorimotor action.

In general, representation undergoes developmental transformations toward increasingly differentiated and hierarchically integrated forms, through the processes of *equilibration* (Piaget, 1985). Piaget viewed the process of representational development in terms of the individual child's active adjustment of her own schemes to intrapsychological and interpsychological disequilibria. Such disequilibria can arise as a function of conflict from may sources, including inconsistency between assimilation and accommodation, conflicts between two cognitive subsystems, or disharmony between individual subsystems and the larger systems of which they are a part.

Critics of the Piagetian view have argued that symbolic representation and imagery emerge earlier in infancy than Piaget suggested, and that imitation need not be invoked to account for the origins of imagery and representation (Mandler, 1983). Others have suggested the need for greater specificity in mapping out pathways in representational development (Bidell & Fischer, 1992). Third, sociocultural psychologists have suggested that Piaget privileged children's own activity at the expense of social and cultural processes as determinants of representation and thinking, an issue to which we now turn.

Sociocultural Approaches.   Arguing that Piagetian approaches overlook social and cultural dimensions of meaning construction (but see Piaget, 1965/1995), sociocultural theorists view representation as knowledge that is socially and culturally constituted. Like Piaget, the unit of analysis of a sociocultural theory of mind is action. Sociocultural psychologists differ from Piaget in their focus on the *tool-mediated* character of higher forms of action, and the origins of mediated action in *social life* (Wertsch, 1991). From a sociocultural view, think-ing is viewed as a form of activity that is mediated through the use of cultural tools, most notably signs (Vygotsky, 1986). Thus, within the sociocultural per-spective, representation consists primarily of the mediation of meaning and knowledge through sign activity. This view is perhaps best understood in terms of Vygotsky's notion of thought as internalized speech. According to Vygotsky (1978), thinking has its origins in sign activity that emerges first between per-sons on the social plane of action. With the internalization of sign activity, chil-dren begin to use language to organize their own thinking and behavior. This occurs first in the form of private external speech, and later in the form of inner speech. Thus, representation is defined in terms of sign activity that represents shared meanings and ways of knowing. As such, representing has social origins.

Some sociocultural psychologists have attempted to articulate principles that portray the role of individuals in the sociocultural construction of knowledge and meaning. For example, Rogoff (1990, 1993) rejected internalization models of development that suggested that external cultural forms become internalized within children in the process of enculturation. According to Rogoff (1990), such a view implies that the cultural forms must be "brought across a barrier into the mind of the child" (p. 195). In contrast, Rogoff invoked the concept of "par-ticipatory appropriation" to refer to the processes by which children transform existing skills and understandings through active participation in joint activity.

Rogoff's (1993) notion of appropriation goes a long way toward eliminating the barrier between the child and other that is assumed by information-process-ing and other psychologists. Furthermore, it provides a useful elaboration of Piaget's individualist notion of equilibration by placing representational devel-opment within the sphere of social activity. However, several questions still re-main. Despite its value, it is insufficient simply to say that appropriation occurs. A set of conceptual and methodological tools are needed to describe specifically what is appropriated and how the appropriation is accomplished. What do chil-dren *do* when they appropriate from shared understandings, and how are the products of such activity represented in individual children (see Mascolo, Pol-lack, & Fischer, 1997)?

THE DEVELOPMENT OF REPRESENTATION AS THE
COORDINATION OF COMPONENT ACTION SYSTEMS

What should a theory of representation be a theory of? First, such a theory should articulate what it means to speak of representation both in its broad sense, as internalized or recalled meanings, and in its more narrow sense, as the use of one thing to stand for another. Such a theory should describe the processes by which representations are constructed within any given context. Second, it should explain the ways in which representation undergoes qualitative and quantitative change in development. Third, it should illuminate processes that prompt such transformations. In what follows, we describe a dynamic skill theory approach to the development of representation (Fischer, 1980; Fischer et al., 1990). Drawing upon systems metaphors, dynamic skill theory provides a framework that can help resolve contradictions between information-processing, Piagetian and sociocultural approaches.

According to dynamic skill theory, people construct representations in development through the hierarchical coordination of their actions within particular contexts. Thus, dynamic skill theory builds on Piagetian theory in its characterization of representations as instances of coordinative activity. However, it goes beyond Piaget's theory in its capacity to make precise assessments of the structure of actions and representations as they undergo developmental transformation. Like information-processing approaches, skill theory uses task analysis to break down tasks into their requisite components. However, skill theory analyzes tasks in terms of actions within contexts rather than in terms of structures and processes within the mind. Finally, like sociocultural approaches, skill theory embraces the idea that all representations are constructed within particular social and cultural contexts. However, unlike sociocultural models, skill theory provides tools for analyzing the specific ways in which children construct representations by coordinating component actions within sociocultural contexts.

Basic Assumptions of Dynamic Skill Theory

Dynamic skill theory provides a set of conceptual and empirical tools for understanding developmental changes in children's cognitive, affective, and behavioral skills (Fischer, 1980; Fischer & Bidell, in press; Fischer & Farrar, 1987; Fischer et al., 1990). The basic unit of analysis in skill theory is the *skill*. A skill refers to a child's capacity to control her behavior, thinking, and feeling within a specified context and within a particular task domain. As such, the concept of skill is founded upon three related notions: action, context, and control (Fischer, 1980). First, a skill refers to the individual's capacity to control or coordinate actions or various components of action, including cognitive, affective, or behavioral components. Second, a skill consists of a set of actions performed *on* something. A change in context or task will most often result in a direct change in a child's activity. As such, context must be seen as an actual part of skilled activity. As a result, a skill cannot be seen as a simple property of the individual; instead, it is best viewed as a property of the child-in-a-social-context. Third, the concept of skill is organized around the notion of control. Skills involve control in the sense that individuals actively attempt to coordinate elements of action in a given context. The notion that skills reflect the mutual contributions of child and context suggests that action is jointly controlled by the individual and other.

Any behavior can be understood in terms of its *control structure* (Fischer, 1980). A control structure refers to the capacity of the individual to coordinate or integrate specific behavioral elements within a given context. As such, development consists of transformations in the organization of action. Dynamic skill theory specifies a series of 13 levels of skill development spanning from birth through early and later adulthood. These levels are depicted in Table 11.1. Skills develop through four broad tiers of development, including the *reflexes* (0–4 months), *sensorimotor actions* (4–24 months), *representations* (2–10 years), and *abstractions* (10–11 years onward). Within each tier, skills develop through four levels (*sets, mappings, systems,* and *systems of systems*), with an indeterminate number of steps between each level. Within each tier, each higher order skill is the product of the hierarchical coordination of lower level skills, and the last level of each broad tier is equivalent to the first level of the next broad tier of development. For example, single reflexes refer to single-action components (e.g., looking at a ball in front of one's face) that emerge around 3–4 weeks of age. Reflex mappings, which emerge around 7–8 weeks of age, involve coordinations among two single reflexes (e.g., infant swipes arm toward seen ball). Reflex systems coordinate two reflex mappings (e.g., opening the hand while extending one's arm toward a seen ball). Around 4 months of age, infants gain the capacity to relate two reflex systems into a system of reflex systems, which is the same as a single flexible sensorimotor action (e.g., looking at a ball as it moves through a complex trajectory).

It is through use of the levels and steps postulated by skill theory that one can perform *task analyses* of the action components required to perform any given task or sociocultural activity. In conducting a task analysis, one provides specific descriptions of the particular coordinations of reflexes, sensorimotor actions, representations, or abstractions that must be performed in order to accomplish a given sociocultural activity within a given context. Using task analyses, one can document fine-grained developmental changes in an individual's capacity to perform any given task or sociocultural activity.

An important principle of skill theory is that individuals do not function at any single skill level at any particular point in development, but instead at a range of skill levels depending on context, task, emotional state, and a suite of other variables. For example, physical and social contexts exert a direct influence on the level of performance that an individual is able to achieve. In numerous studies, investigators have demonstrated that children perform at higher levels of development in the presence of contextual support than in the absence of support (Fischer, Bullock, Rotenberg, & Raya, 1993; Fischer & Kenny, 1986; Kitchener, Lynch, Fischer, & Wood, 1993; Rogoff, 1990; Vygotsky, 1978). In skill theory, contexts that provide high support enable children to perform at their *optimal levels,* that is, at the upper limits of an individual's skilled activity. Less supportive contexts prompt functioning at one's *functional level,* the level typically used in everyday contexts. The difference between an individual's functional and optimal levels constitutes the *developmental range* of the person's skill within a particular task domain (Fischer & Pipp, 1984). For example, when asked

TABLE 11.1
Levels of Skill Development

	Tier				
Level	Reflex	Sensorimotor	Representational	Abstract	Age[a]
Rf1: Single Reflexes	[A] or [B]				3–4 wks
Rf2: Reflex Mappings	[A —— B]				7–8
Rf3: Reflex Systems	$\left[A_F^E \longleftrightarrow B_F^E\right]$				10–11
Rf4/S1: Systems of Reflex Systems, Which Are Single Sensorimotor Actions	$\left[\begin{smallmatrix} A_F^E \longleftrightarrow B_F^E \\ C_H^G \longleftrightarrow D_H^G \end{smallmatrix}\right] \equiv \ [\mathbf{I}]$				15–17
S2: Sensorimotor Mappings		[**I** —— **J**]			7–8 mths
S3: Sensorimotor Systems		$\left[\mathbf{I}_N^M \longleftrightarrow \mathbf{J}_N^M\right]$			11–13
S4/Rp1: Systems of Sensorimotor Systems, Which Are Single Representations		$\left[\begin{smallmatrix} \mathbf{I}_N^M \longleftrightarrow \mathbf{J}_N^M \\ \mathbf{K}_P^O \longleftrightarrow \mathbf{L}_P^O \end{smallmatrix}\right] \equiv \ [Q]$			18–24
Rp2: Representational Mappings			[Q —— R]		3.5–4.5 yrs
Rp3: Representational Systems			$\left[Q_V^U \longleftrightarrow R_V^U\right]$		6–7
Rp4/Ab1: Systems of Representational Systems, Which Are Single Abstractions			$\left[\begin{smallmatrix} Q_V^U \longleftrightarrow R_V^U \\ S_X^W \longleftrightarrow T_X^W \end{smallmatrix}\right] \equiv \ [Y\,]$		10–12
Ab2: Abstract Mappings				[Y —— Z]	14–16
Ab3: Abstract Systems				$\left[Y_D^C \longleftrightarrow Z_D^C\right]$	19–20
Ab4: Systems of Abstract Systems, Which Are Principles				$\left[\begin{smallmatrix} Y_D^C \longleftrightarrow Z_D^C \\ A_D^C \longleftrightarrow B_D^C \end{smallmatrix}\right]$	24–25

Note. Plain letters designate reflex sets, bold letters sensorimotor sets, and italic letters representational sets, and script letters abstract sets. Multiple sub- and superscripts designate differentiated subsets. Long straight lines and arrows designate a relation between sets or systems. Brackets mark a single skill. Note also that structures from lower tiers continue at higher levels (reflexes in sensorimotor actions, etc.), but the formulas are omitted because they become so complex.

[a]Ages are modal for the emergence of optimal levels based on research with middle-class American and European children. They may differ across cultures or social groups.

to use dolls to act out a story about mean interactions in the absence of contextual support, a 4-year-old might construct a single representation by making one doll knock over another doll. However, when given the opportunity to imitate a model story in which one doll reciprocates one mean action for another, the same child might function at the level of representational mappings. Thus, individuals function at various points within a developmental range depending on task, social context, level of environmental support, and other variables.

The Nature and Emergence of Representation in Action

Figure 11.1 illustrates the ways in which representation builds upon sensorimotor activity through an analysis of a child's capacity to act on and represent a teddy bear from infancy through childhood. As indicated in Fig. 11.1, there are four levels of sensorimotor activity, each of which emerges through the coordination of lower levels of action of reflex components (see also Fischer & Hogan, 1989). Beginning around 4 months of age, an infant can begin to coordinate multiple reflex systems into a single, controlled *sensorimotor action*. At this level, an infant can control a single, flexible action on objects. As such, an infant can skillfully perform a single sensorimotor action on a teddy bear. As illustrated in Level S1 in Fig. 11.1, at this level an infant can skillfully use his hands to grasp a teddy bear lying on the bed beside him (without looking at it), or a baby can skillfully turn his head from side to side to actively look at a teddy bear sitting before him. At this step, although a child is capable of extending her hands toward a seen teddy bear and even making rudimentary adjustments in her hand movements to accommodate a moving teddy bear, she is incapable of fully coordinating looking with grasping. This skill is made possible with the onset of *sensorimotor mappings*, which begin to emerge around 7–8 months of age. Sensorimotor mappings result from the coordination of two sensorimotor actions. At this level, children can skillfully coordinate grasping and looking. For example, as indicated in Levels S2a and S2b in Fig. 11.1, an infant can grasp a doll in order to look at it, or look at a doll in order to grasp it. A child might look at a teddy bear in many different positions to guide how he reaches for it.

Sensorimotor systems emerge beginning around 12–13 months with the coordination of two sensorimotor mappings. Whereas a younger infant could coordinate looking and grasping into a sensorimotor mapping, many 13-month-olds can manipulate a teddy bear skillfully through multiple coordinated acts of grasping and looking. As illustrated in Level S3 in Fig. 11.1, using sensorimotor mappings, the younger infant can coordinate two sensorimotor actions into a single skill, for example, looking at a teddy bear in order to grasp it. Using sensorimotor systems, a 13-month-old can often control multiple coordinations between looking and grasping into a single skill. That is, she can coordinate different ways of grasping the teddy bear with different ways of looking at the teddy bear into a single skill. Such a child can thus experiment with different ways of

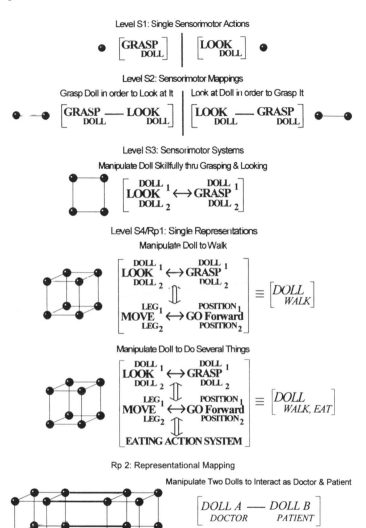

Level S1: Single Sensorimotor Actions

$\begin{bmatrix} GRASP \\ DOLL \end{bmatrix}$ | $\begin{bmatrix} LOOK \\ DOLL \end{bmatrix}$

Level S2: Sensorimotor Mappings

Grasp Doll in order to Look at It | Look at Doll in order to Grasp It

$\begin{bmatrix} GRASP — LOOK \\ DOLL \quad\quad DOLL \end{bmatrix}$ | $\begin{bmatrix} LOOK — GRASP \\ DOLL \quad\quad DOLL \end{bmatrix}$

Level S3: Sensorimotor Systems

Manipulate Doll Skillfully thru Grasping & Looking

$\begin{bmatrix} DOLL_1 \quad\quad DOLL_1 \\ LOOK \longleftrightarrow GRASP \\ DOLL_2 \quad\quad DOLL_2 \end{bmatrix}$

Level S4/Rp1: Single Representations

Manipulate Doll to Walk

$\begin{bmatrix} DOLL_1 \quad\quad DOLL_1 \\ LOOK \longleftrightarrow GRASP \\ DOLL_2 \quad\quad DOLL_2 \\ \Updownarrow \\ LEG_1 \quad\quad POSITION_1 \\ MOVE \longleftrightarrow GO\ Forward \\ LEG_2 \quad\quad POSITION_2 \end{bmatrix} \equiv \begin{bmatrix} DOLL \\ WALK \end{bmatrix}$

Manipulate Doll to Do Several Things

$\begin{bmatrix} DOLL_1 \quad\quad DOLL_1 \\ LOOK \longleftrightarrow GRASP \\ DOLL_2 \quad\quad DOLL_2 \\ \Updownarrow \\ LEG_1 \quad\quad POSITION_1 \\ MOVE \longleftrightarrow GO\ Forward \\ LEG_2 \quad\quad POSITION_2 \\ \Updownarrow \\ EATING\ ACTION\ SYSTEM \end{bmatrix} \equiv \begin{bmatrix} DOLL \\ WALK,\ EAT \end{bmatrix}$

Rp 2: Representational Mapping

Manipulate Two Dolls to Interact as Doctor & Patient

$\begin{bmatrix} DOLL\ A — DOLL\ B \\ DOCTOR \quad\quad PATIENT \end{bmatrix}$

FIG. 11.1. Levels of development of sensorimotor actions to form representations.

grasping and looking at the teddy bear. Using sensorimotor systems, infants are capable of performing acts involving primitive symbolization. For example, infants are capable of simple pretending using stereotyped actions, such as eating or drinking from an empty cup, sleeping by lying down on a pillow, washing hands and arms with a washcloth (Watson & Fischer, 1977). In addition, infants are capable of coordinating vocalizing with hearing combinations of sounds to producing their first words (Fischer & Corrigan, 1981; Piaget, 1951). Although such actions constitute rudimentary forms of symbolization, they are constrained in that they are limited to stereotypical action sequences that are tied to the local sensorimotor context. Genuine representation does not emerge until the next level in which children can use one sensorimotor system to stand for and evoke another such system in the absence of the represented event.

The definitive moment in the creation of representation begins around 18–24 months of age with the fourth level of sensorimotor development. At this level, infants can coordinate two sensorimotor systems into a system of sensorimotor systems, which constitutes a *single representation*. As such, the fourth level of the sensorimotor tier of development constitutes the first level of the representational tier of development. At this level, by coordinating two sensorimotor action systems, children can use one sensorimotor system to evoke or stand for an object, event, or person that is not actually present. This is reflected when children represent an absent event or characteristic in terms of a simple sentence, or when children perform simple acts involving pretend play. For example, at this level, a child can use a teddy bear to represent the action of walking. In so doing, he can coordinate one sensorimotor action system for skillfully manipulating the teddy bear through grasping and looking with another sensorimotor system for moving the legs and making the doll move forward. Thus, a child can use one sensorimotor system (skillfully manipulating a physically present teddy bear by looking and grasping) to evoke and represent properties beyond the information given in actions on the doll itself. For example, a child can move the doll in order to make the teddy bear walk. In so doing, a child does not simply push the teddy bear along as an object; instead, she makes the doll walk itself. As such, the child is using one representational system for looking and grasping to evoke and represent the activity of an agent walking. This skill structure is represented in step S4/Rp1 in Fig. 11.1.

Early language skills emerge from the same types of coordinations. The prototype for a single representation is a simple declarative sentence. When a child uses a sentence such as "Bear walk" in a representational way, she essentially uses a sensorimotor system for producing and hearing linguistic patterns to evoke or stand for a sensorimotor system for the movement of a teddy bear forward, as in walking. In this way, a child's production of a sentence like "Doll walk" is comparable to the capacity to make a teddy bear walk in pretend play. Both use one sensorimotor system to cognitively evoke or otherwise stand for another sensorimotor system.

Thus, representation can take many forms, including both symbolic play and sign activity. An additional example of the use of representation is using one action system to evoke or represent another action system in a problem-solving situation. One example of this process is Piaget's classic description of how his 16-month-old daughter Lucienne solved the problem of retrieving a chain placed in a matchbox. Being unaware of the opening and closing of the matchbox, Lucienne first attempted to retrieve the chain by turning the box over or sliding her fingers into the opening in the matchbox. After these actions failed, Lucienne paused. Piaget (1951) described his daughter's actions: "She looks at the slit with great attention; then, several times in succession, she opens and shuts her mouth, at first slightly, then wider and wider! . . . Lucienne unhesitatingly puts her finger in the slit, and instead of trying as before to reach the chain, she pulls so as to enlarge the opening. She succeeds and grasps the chain" (pp. 337–338). In this example, Lucienne used the opening and closing of her mouth as a signifier to represent the opening and closing of the matchbox. In so doing, she used one sensorimotor system to stand for and evoke another sensorimotor system, similar to the skill illustrated in Level S4/Rp1 in Fig. 11.1. Lucienne was able to construct a single representation by coordinating one sensorimotor system for moving and feeling her mouth open and close with another sensorimotor system for pulling and seeing the matchbox open and close. In so doing, Lucienne created a single representation for increasing the opening of the matchbox that mediated her attempt to retrieve the chain.

The capacity to construct representations continues to develop both within and beyond the level of single representations. Single representations are constructed from coordinations of at least two sensorimotor action systems. Within the level of single representations, children can construct more sophisticated representations through the coordination of multiple sensorimotor systems into a *compounded single representation*. For example, soon after the onset of single representations, a 2.5- or 3-year-old child can construct a compounded single representation of a teddy bear walking and eating. As depicted in Level Rp1/Compounded Representation in Fig. 11.1, this representational skill would emerge through the coordination of one sensorimotor action system for skillfully manipulating the bear through multiple looking and grasping actions with a second sensorimotor system for movement of the bears legs forward as if it were walking, with a third sensorimotor system for movement of the bear's head up and down as if it were eating from a bowl. In a compounded single representation, each action system is fully coordinated with each other to produce a single continuous representational skill. The child does not simply make the doll walk, and later on make the doll eat. Instead, the child can pretend that the doll can walk to a cup in order to eat. This new representational skill is constructed through the coordination of lower level action components. Using compounded representations, the child can construct similar representations of the agency in self or others, such as making a teddy bear eat a two- or three-course meal, making a doll enact a doctor role by making a doctor doll give another doll a pill and put on a pretend bandage, or making a doll named after the self act mean by knocking another doll over and saying "I don't like you!" (Fischer, Hand, Watson, Van Parys, & Tucker, 1984; Watson & Fischer, 1980).

The capacity to construct representations undergoes massive development beyond the level of single representations. Beginning around 3.5 to 4 years of age, in contexts that provide appropriate support, children gain the capacity to coordinate two single representations into a *representational mapping*. Using mappings, a child can represent the relationship between two or more representations. Representational mappings can be coordinated in terms of a variety of different concrete relations, including causality, temporal relations, part-whole, class-member, reciprocity, intention-action, similarity, just to name a few. A representative example of a representational mapping is the social role, which is defined in terms of the role expectations of one individual in relation to another individual. For example, in pretend play using dolls or in telling a story about a visit to the doctor, a child can coordinate the relationship between a representation of the doctor's role and a representation of the patient's role. As indicated in Level Rp2 in Fig. 11.1, the child can relate a patient's role in telling the doctor about a tummyache to the doctor's response in giving the patient medicine (Watson & Fischer, 1980). Research has documented a capacity to construct structurally similar representations around the age of 3.5 to 4 in a variety of social and cognitive domains, including nice and mean interactions (Fischer et al., 1990) and strategic representations in problem-solving tasks (Bidell & Fischer, 1994).

Representational development continues throughout ontogenesis. *Representational systems* begin to emerge around 6–7 years of age, which result from a child's coordination of two representational mappings within a given context. For example, a child may use representational systems to demonstrate role intersection, that is, how a single individual can perform two social roles at the same time (Watson & Fischer, 1980). *Single abstractions,* which begin to appear at around 10–11 years of age in high-support contexts, mark the culmination of the representational tier of development and the first level of the abstraction tier. Single abstractions emerge through the coordination of at least two representational systems. For example, using single abstractions, an adolescent would be able to explain the abstract concept of role intersection in terms of the generalized similarity between two specific examples of role intersection. Representational development continues throughout the tier of abstractions, as adolescents and young adults coordinate multiple abstractions into *abstract mappings* at around 14–16 years of age, *abstract systems* at around 19–20 years of age, and *abstract principles* at around 24–25 years.

THE SOCIAL DISTRIBUTION OF REPRESENTATIVE ACTIVITY

Up to this point, we have discussed representative activity as the product of the activity of individuals. Although the activity of individuals plays a central role in the construction of representations, representations do not develop or operate in a vacuum. Representations are not the product of solitary actors; individuals work together in the production of representative activity. Actions and representations are grounded in social activity and are usually shared. As such, research on the representations of isolated individuals is often misleading. What is needed is an approach that describes how people work together to construct representations out of their joint actions in real time. To address this issue, Granott (1993a, 1993b) examined the microdevelopment of problem-solving activity among pairs of individuals. Microdevelopment involves the construction of activity and representations over a relatively short time period, spanning from seconds or minutes to hours, days, weeks, or months (Fischer & Granott, 1995; Werner, 1957). The microdevelopment of action and in real time is an everyday process that occurs among both children and adults.

Granott (1993a) studied the microdevelopment of representations between pairs of adults who collaborated in solving problems about the properties of a series of Lego robots. Several different robots, which were called "wuggles," were built from Lego blocks, wheels, batteries, and electronic circuits. The wuggles were able to move around the floor on their own, changing direction as a function of sound, light, or touch. A group of eight adults were invited into a room containing the wuggles. The robots were placed around the room, and observers were asked to try and figure out how they worked. Observers were free to move about the room and to study the behavior of the wuggles in any way they wished. Observers spontaneously paired off into groups of two or more, which changed frequently as individuals inspected different wuggles with different partners.

Participants' communications naturally fell into episodes, called interchanges. Coders coded the organization and developmental level of each interchange using the complexity rules provided by dynamic skill theory (Fischer, 1980). For example, in one interchange Ann and Donald constructed a representational mapping when they indicated how the wuggle's capacity to move forward or backward occurred as a result of its sensor's capacity to respond to changes in light. As such, Ann and Donald coordinated two representations of the wuggle—that the wuggle moved in a specific way and that it reacted to light—into a causal mapping.

Figure 11.2 depicts microgenetic changes that occurred in Ann and Donald's capacity to represent the properties of the wuggle. There are several notable aspects of Ann and Donald's growth curve. First, as indicated in Fig. 11.2, Ann and Donald began their interchanges about the wuggle at a very low developmental level—that of single sensorimotor actions (Step 1)—a level that fell well below that expected of intelligent adults. At such levels, Ann and Donald's interchanges would involve references to singular actions produced by the wuggle, including statements and gestures alluding to a singular movement of the wuggle, or statements that the wuggle hit a side panel, and so on. Over time, the dyad noted relations between multiple actions produced by the wuggle, and coordinated these actions into sensorimotor mappings (Skill Level 2) and sensorimotor systems (Skill Level 3). At the level of single representations (Skill Level 4), which first emerged precipitously in this dyad after the 30th interchange, the

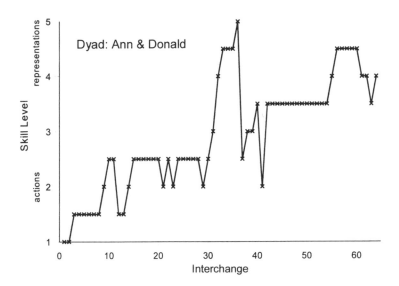

FIG. 11.2.   Microdevelopment of socially distributed representations.

dyad was able to represent single properties of the wuggle that were independent of any singular movements (e.g., that the wuggle moved in a specific way, that it moved in reaction to light, etc.). The highest skill level achieved by this dyad in the first 60 interchanges was representational mappings (Skill Level 5). At this level, the dyad was able to coordinate at least two representations into terms of some sort of relation. These results indicate problem-solving activity between adults exhibits microdevelopmental change. Adults begin problem solving through simple actions and observations of the wuggle. Over time, adults coordinate their actions into increasingly complex representations.

Second, although Ann and Donald's growth curve indicates general progressive change across their 60 interchanges, the curve is not linear. Instead the curve exhibits multiple oscillations showing many fits and starts (Granott, 1993a). Thus, although microdevelopment involves gradual development in the direction of greater complexity, it is characterized by local changes involving both progression and regression, abrupt and gradual movement, as well as qualitative and quantitative change. Such growth curves contradict commonly held assumptions that development shows linear or monotonic change.

It is important to note that the skill transformations represented in Fig. 11.2 reflect the results of collaboration between members of each dyad. No clear separation of the contributions of the members of a dyad within a given interchange was possible. As but one illustration of this point, Fischer and Granott (1995; Granott, 1993a) reported an analysis of Ann and Donald's leadership roles in each of the 65 interchanges. Results indicated that Ann and Donald shared leadership in dyadic exchanges, with both Ann and Donald leading almost half of the time, and with the two leading together on a smaller proportion of the interchanges. Further, the growth curves of each individual's leadership role within the dyad were virtually identical, showing that leadership was distributed evenly over microgenesis. Thus, the dyads examined seemed to collaborate as a unit in the microgenesis of action and representation in solving problems about the operation of the wuggle.

Overall, these analyses suggest that microdevelopment involves transformations similar to those that occur in ontogenesis. Like ontogenetic activity, the microgenesis of adult's representation of a new problem domain moved from sensorimotor actions through representations to abstractions. Moreover, like ontogenesis that occurs over months and years, the microdevelopment of new skills shows nonlinear development with fits and starts and progression and regression. Finally, these analyses also suggest that representations are not simply products of individuals; instead, representative activity can be distributed throughout a dyad or even a group of individuals, and thus is a product of co-constructive, socially distributed processes (see Fischer & Granott, 1995; Granott, 1993a)

CHANGE PROCESSES IN THE DEVELOPMENT OF REPRESENTATIVE ACTIVITY

Skill theory defines representation in terms of dynamic construction that builds upon sensorimotor activity. At the very least, within dynamic skill theory, representation is defined in terms of the coordination of two sensorimotor systems, where one sensorimotor system functions to evoke, stand for, or cognitively control the other independent of the presence of the represented object or event. With development, representative activity undergoes developmental transformations, showing nonlinear development both within and between individuals. Given this depiction of the nature of representative activity and its transformation in development and microdevelopment, what accounts for the processes by which representations change? What change processes promote representational development?

The Epigenesis of Representative Activity

Epigenesis refers to the idea that anatomical and psychological structures emerge in development as a result of inseparable coactions among multiple levels of the organism-environment system (Bidell & Fischer, 1996; Gottleib, 1991, 1992; Mascolo, Pollack, & Fischer, 1997). For our purposes, it is useful to distinguish broadly between *biogenetic, personal-agentive,* and *sociocultural* levels of the organism-environment system (Bidell & Fischer, 1996; Mascolo, Craig-Bray, & Neimeyer, 1997). Although each set of levels operates somewhat distinctly from each other set of levels, each level of functioning nevertheless interpenetrates each other level and are thus inseparable as causal factors in the production of any given behavior. Representational skills emerge and become transformed through coactions between the activity of biogenetic, personal-agentive, and sociocultural systems.

At the *biogenetic level,* behavior is supported by neural networks composed of massively interconnected components that are distributed throughout the brain and operate in parallel. With development, these neural networks grow in cycles, developing from an initial period of competition among neural systems to coordination of neural systems into a more complex structure. Fischer and Rose (1994) proposed that discontinuities in the emergence of each of the 13 levels of skill development specified in dynamic skill theory is supported by developmental discontinuities in brain growth and activity. For example, a spurt in brain development at 18–24 months would prompt neurological changes that would support the construction of single representations in the child, such as making a doll walk or talk in pretend play. Research on the development of changes in electroencephalogram (EEG), event-related potentials, and head size corroborate to suggest discontinuities in brain development at age ranges corresponding to the first 12 levels proposed by dynamic skill theory. Data are not currently available to assess the hypothesized relation between brain and skill development for the last level proposed by skill theory.

Brain growth and development may prompt transformations in neural networks that underlie changes in children's capacities to construct skills of various levels of complexity. As such, biogenetic changes constitute a major source of skill development. However, despite their importance, such changes are insufficient to explain the development of any new level of skill. In order to take advantage of the opportunities afforded by biogenetic changes, at the personal-agentive level of functioning, individuals must actively build the skills that biogenetic changes make possible. To the extent that new, higher order skills are created through the coordination of lower level component actions and representations, it follows that the creation of any new skill requires an *act of integration* (Bidell & Fischer, 1996; Mascolo, Pollack, & Fischer, 1997). This follows for skills at any level of development. For example, at the level of single representations, in pretending that a teddy bear is walking or talking, children must actively bring into correspondence two sensorimotor systems. At the very least, this would involve relating one sensorimotor system for holding and manipulating the teddy bear to a second sensorimotor system for making it walk or talk. Thus, at the personal-agentive level of functioning, a major function of the child-as-system is *the hierarchical coordination of component systems of action* within any given context (Bidell & Fischer, 1996; Mascolo, Craig-Bray, & Neimeyer, 1997). It is through effortful coordinative acts by the person-as-agentive system that new skills are constructed in development.

It is important to note that although the development of neurological structures supports the construction of any given level of skill, the causality between behavioral and biogenetic processes is not unidirectional. The neurological systems that support the creation of any given skill depend on skilled activity for their preservation and development. For example, Campos and his colleagues have reported that when controlling for age and thus maturation, the infant's own locomotor activity arises as the primary factor influencing the onset of a cluster of psychological and behavioral processes, including fear of heights, capacity to find hidden objects, and a series of other spatial skills at around 6–10 months of age (Campos & Bertenthal, 1987). Because of the abruptness of their onset, these skills were formerly attributed to neurological maturation. Such findings suggest the ways in which children's own coordinating activities channelize neurological and behavioral development.

Despite the importance of the personal-agentive activity of individuals, children do not coordinate skills in a vacuum. Consistent with a systems approach, the personal-agentive system coacts with sociocultural systems in the production of new levels of behavior. For example, at the cultural level, representative activity takes place in socioculturally defined contexts using cultural artifacts and tools, and is often mediated by signs and systems of shared meanings. For example, in pretend play with a teddy bear, the stuffed animal acts as a social artifact. Children act out a variety of social scripts in pretend play, such as shopping at a market, going to school, or even fighting with friends. Such scripts embody social and cultural meanings. In this way, cultural meanings and practices provide the frames within which children construct and enact their representations of the world.

Social interaction exerts a direct influence on an individual's personal-agentive functioning. As indicated earlier, children often function at much higher developmental levels when interacting with others, and particularly more accomplished others, than they do when working alone (Granott, 1993b; Rogoff, 1990, 1993; Vygotsky, 1978). This occurs because partners in dyadic interaction *mutually regulate* each other's representational activity through *continuous process communication* (Fogel, 1993). Unlike in discrete state communication (e.g., radio, mail, E-mail, fax, etc.) in which a fixed message must pass from sender to receiver before it can be transformed, in continuous process communication, information is continuously and simultaneously passed between individuals throughout the very process of communication. Partners continuously adjust their actions and reactions to the actual and anticipated actions of the other. For example, in joint play, when using dolls to act out a story about nice or mean interactions, a child must continuously adjust the actions of his doll to continuous changes in the actions of the mother's doll. As such, behavior and meaning in continuous process communication is *negotiated throughout the very process of communication*. As such, actions and meanings produced in joint interactions direct children toward more sophisticated, socially constituted ways of thinking and acting.

Thus, the activity of the personal-agentive system becomes transformed through its participation in sociocultural systems. As such, the higher level actions and representations produced in joint activity direct children's personal coordination of meaning and action. But how do jointly produced actions and representations on the interpersonal plane become translated into intrapersonal forms of acting and representing? How do children profit from their participation in social activity? We suggest that it is the self-organizing, coordinative activity of individuals that drives the appropriation and internalization of social and cultural patterns of activity (Bidell & Fischer, 1996; Mascolo & Fischer, 1995; Mascolo, Pollack, & Fischer, 1997). Although joint action raises children's performance, children profit from joint activity to the extent that they are able to coordinate for themselves representations that have a basis in actions coordinated between them and others in joint interaction. Although joint interaction provides the social matrix from which children create new skills, in order for development to occur, children must actively and effortfully bring together elements of jointly produced activity and representation.

An Illustration of Coactions Among Personal and Dyadic Systems in the Micro-development of Representation.   To illustrate the interparticipation of personal-agentive and social-dyadic systems in the construction of representations in children, consider a case study of question–answer sequences that occurred between a 5-year-old boy and his parents while reading a storybook on 6 different days (Raeff & Mascolo, 1996). This examination of question–answer sequences in storytelling proceeded as an attempt to illuminate the contributions of self and other in the joint creation of meaning. Raeff and Mascolo reasoned that as a participant in storytelling activity, children's questions would reflect their own active attempt to coordinate gaps in their knowledge with information from the storytelling, which itself proceeded as a joint, coactive activity.

The particular storybook was called *The Best Babysitter Ever,* by Richard Scarry, and is about Hilda who is babysitting for Pig Will, who is cooperative, and Pig Won't, who is not. At one point in the story, Pig Will and Hilda have been blowing soap bubbles in the kitchen, while Pig Won't is outside on his own. As Pig Won't goes back into the house, he pops one of the soap bubbles, and "the soap suds splash in his eye. It stings!" The child raised the topic of "stings" in four of the six storytelling sessions. In the first three such sessions, the child was able to represent "a stinging eye" at the level of single representations. By the last session, as a result of repeated queries about the cause of Pig Won't's stinging eye, the child's representation advances to the level of representational mappings.

In the second session, the following dialogue occurred:

Child: Why does it sting?
Parent: Well because when soap gets on your, in your eyes, it stings.

In this reading, the child's question reflects an attempt to represent the cause of stinging, and presumably to coordinate a presumed gap in his knowledge about stings with the content of the story. In asking a "why" question about stings, the child seemed to be attempting to elaborate an understanding of what it means to "sting" and to coordinate this meaning in terms of a mapping relation based on causality. The question of stings was next raised in the third reading session:

Child: Why does it sting?
Parent: Why DOES it sting?
Child: 'Cause it hurts.
Parent: Soap hurts your eyes.

In this sequence, we again see the child trying to represent the cause of the stinging. The parent probed the child in an apparent attempt to prompt the child to elaborate his own thinking. In so doing, we can see that the child was able to represent stings in terms of pain—"it hurts." Using the single representation "Soap hurts your eyes," the parent elaborated the child's understanding by linking the cause of the pain to the effect of the soap. The issue of stings was raised again in the fourth session:

Child: Why does it sting?
Parent: 'Cause soap. When soap gets in your eye it hurts.

This question–answer sequence recapitulates the dialogue that occurred in the second storytelling session. During the fifth reading session, there was no mention of the stinging event. However, the child reintroduced the topic of stings in the sixth storytelling session:

Child: That's sad.
Parent: Why is that sad?
Child: It's sad that Pig Won't has stings.
Parent: Yeah? Why? Why is it sad that it stings?
Child: Because when soap gets in your eyes it stings.
Parent: Right.
Child: When bumble bee stings, me. Does that stings?
Parent: When bumble bees sting do they sting? You betcha' it does.
Child: Why?
Parent: Well when bumble bees put their little stinger inside of you, it pierces the skin, and it stings.

In this interchange, the child provided evidence of coordination of knowledge that was produced jointly throughout the preceding storytelling sessions. In the first part of the exchange, the child elaborated his understanding of stings as something negative or sad. When queried on why stings were sad, the child responded by coordinating two previously independent *single representations* (of "stinging" and the "effects of soap") into a *representational mapping* based on a causal relation: "Because when soap gets in your eyes it stings." As such, drawing upon meanings that were *jointly created* in previous dyadic interchanges about stings, the child's representational development occurred as a result of an act of integration that coordinated previously independent knowledge elements into a coordinated whole. The child then elaborated further on his understanding of stinging, relating the concept of stinging produced by soap to stings produced by bees. The parent further elaborated on the child's understanding of bee stings, linking the stings of bees to the causal actions of their stingers.

This characterization of the social process that prompted these representational changes bears much in common with Sigel's (1991, 1994) distancing model of representational development. Distancing actions on the part of one individual prompt the other to separate his existing representation from the immediate present and to project himself onto some other plane (e.g., to the past or future, to meanings or relations that are not immediately apparent). The distancing model is based on the notion that all cognitive change has its origins in the registration of cognitive discrepancy by individuals. Distancing thus denotes a social process whereby others create a cognitive demand that prompts mental activity within the self aimed at reducing a discrepancy or gap in one's knowledge. The dialogue between the child and adult described earlier can be understood in terms of cognitive distancing. The socially communicated content of the story functions to register a discrepancy within the child, who thereupon asks a question indicating a gap in his knowledge. In responding to the child, the adult prompts the child to extend the sphere of his understanding beyond the present one. This is illustrated in the third reading session discussed previously. The child addressed the question of why Pig Won't's eye stings by saying "'Cause it hurts." The parent then drew the child's attention to the soap as the cause of Pig Won't's stinging eye. This act creates distance between the child's existing representation and the adult's causal explanation, presumably prompting cognitive effort within the child. By the sixth reading session, the child is able to extend his representation of the cause of stinging to include the action of the soap.

It is interesting to note the affective quality of the representations constructed by the child in the exchanges discussed previously. In these exchanges, the child focused his awareness on the issue of stings, which has obvious affective implications. The child himself made several explicit references to affect in connection to the question of stings (i.e., "'Cause it hurts," and "That's sad"). In many approaches to cognition, representation is defined as a cognitive product that is largely independent of affect (Gardner, 1985). We suggest, however, that affect plays an important role in the organization of representation and thinking. Although different ways of feeling are generated by different appraisals and interpretations of events, resulting feelings provides feedback that *selects,* from among the many inputs competing for conscious awareness, those events that have the most significance for the individual (Fischer et al., 1990; Kozak & Brown, 1998; Lewis & Douglas, 1998; Mascolo & Harkins, 1998). In the earlier exchanges about stings, it is likely that the affective dimension of stinging exerted an organizing effect on the child's representation of story content.

These exchanges provide a framework for examining the interplay among biogenetic, personal-agentive and sociocultural processes in the production of the child's developing representation of stings. At the *biogenetic level,* we assume that the 5-year-old's level of neurological development was sufficient to support the construction of meanings at the representational mapping level of development (Fischer, 1987; Fischer & Rose, 1994). At the *sociocultural level,* the dyadic interchanges discussed previously took place within the sociocultural activity of storytelling using cultural tools and artifacts (e.g., the storybook, language, culturally shared meanings, illustrations, etc.). Within this activity, however, the specific meanings produced about stings cannot be located either within the child, the parent, or the storybook. Instead, they were products of jointly produced question–answer sequences produced within the child–parent dyad. However, in order to profit from such jointly produced meanings, at the *personal-agentive level* of activity the child must perform acts of integration that *coordinate for himself* the meanings that were jointly created in the dyad. In the example discussed earlier, based on the child's existing knowledge and optimal level of skilled activity, the child was able to coordinate the representational mapping "when soap gets in your eyes it stings" from among the elements of meaning produced in dyadic interaction. Thus, *given a particular level of neurological functioning,* the development of children's representations in any given context is a product of meanings that are *jointly created by the dyad* but *individually coordinated* by the child.

The idea that children's representations are products of their active attempts to coordinate elements of action and meaning previously produced in joint activity relates to Rogoff's (1993) notion of *participatory appropriation.* Rogoff invoked the notion of appropriation to explain the processes by which individuals develop from their participation in sociocultural activity. The idea that children develop by coordinating component actions into higher order representations extends the concept of appropriation by specifying what children actually must do when they appropriate from joint activity. Skill theory also provides tools for specifying the structure of skills and understandings that are coordinated from participation in joint activity. As such, skill theory can provide a bridge between sociocultural and Piagetian approaches to representational development (Mascolo, Pollack, & Fischer, 1997).

DYNAMIC SKILL THEORY AS AN INTEGRATIVE FRAMEWORK FOR ANALYZING REPRESENTATIONAL ACTIVITY

Dynamic skill theory examines the representations as dynamic constructions and not fixed entities. Representations are constructed over time through the coordination of action systems, and are thus neither innate nor simply passed on through socialization or culture. Single representations begin to emerge around 18–24 months of age as infants gain the capacity to use one sensorimotor system to cognitively evoke or stand for another system of sensorimotor activity. After their emergence, the capacity to construct representations within specified domains and contexts undergoes massive development through a series of levels throughout ontogenesis. Using the 13 developmental levels and transformation rules proposed by skill theory, one can analyze the organization of actions and representations within any given task or sociocultural activity. Thus, building on systems metaphors, dynamic skill theory holds out the promise of synthesizing important insights from Piagetian, information-processing, and sociocultural perspectives on the nature and development of representation. As a neo-Piagetian perspective, dynamic skill theory builds upon Piaget's depiction of representation as founded in activity. Unlike Piagetian theory, skill theory rejects the assertion of broad, context-free stages of representational intelligence. Instead, skill theory provides a set of empirical tools for a much more fine-grained analysis of representational changes than was provided by Piaget. Further, skill theory provides a stronger role for social-dyadic processes in representational development than did Piaget.

Skill theory shares with information-processing psychology a concern with precision in the analysis of the representations that children and adults use in any given task. The analysis of tasks into their component actions and representations is central to skill theory analyses of any given representative activity. However, from the perspective of skill theory, representations are much more than internal codes that mediate between a stimulus and responses. Representations are products of activity, and of activity between individuals who engage in continuous process communication. As such, social context is an actual part of the processes that are involved in the construction or reconstruction of representation in any given context. Further, as dynamic reconstructions, representations are not entities that can be simply stored or retrieved. Instead, knowledge is represented in memory in the forms of neural networks that are activated and reactivated in the process of action. As such, knowledge is never stored in or retrieved from any particular place in memory or in the brain. Rather, knowledge elements are distributed in the connections among neural networks and among various memory and brain systems and are reconstructed each time they are invoked in action. It is in this way that biogenetic processes support the coordination of action at the personal-agentive and sociocultural levels of functioning.

Skill theory shares with sociocultural approaches to development a concern for the production of representations that occur as products of dyadic and group activity within sociocultural contexts. As indicated earlier, sociocultural psychologists have produced useful and insightful analyses of the processes by which representations arise through social and dyadic activity, especially co-constructive activity using cultural tools, such as language. However, sociocultural psychologists have been less concerned with analyzing the nature of the skills and representations that are produced within dyadic interaction. Unlike most sociocultural approaches, dynamic skill theory provides a framework for analyzing specific changes in the structure of individual and dyadic representations as they arise in joint interaction. Further, although acknowledging the role of social processes in the construction of knowledge, dynamic skill theory affirms an important role of the agentive child in the creation of representations.

Thus, the task analyses afforded by skill theory provide an alternative to flowchart descriptions of the microstructure of cognition, general stage analyses of representational development, and models that disavow individual representations in favor of dyadic and cultural processes. Instead, skill theory provides a framework for demonstrating the ways in which representational skills develop as children coordinate their actions into representations to meet the demands of specific tasks within social contexts. In this way, skill theory provides a framework for showing how memory, actions, and socially created meanings work together in the online construction of representations within particular social contexts.

ACKNOWLEDGMENTS

We wish to thank J. N. Buehler and Raymond Shaw for their contributions to the ideas expressed in this chapter. The research in this chapter was supported by a grant from Merrimack College to the first author, and from Mr. and Mrs. Frederick Rose and Harvard University to the second author.

REFERENCES

Banks, M. S. (1987). Mechanisms of visual development: An example of computational models. In J. Bisanz, C. Brainerd, & R. R. Kail (Eds.), *Formal methods in developmental psychology: Progress in cognitive development research* (pp. 339–371). New York: Spinger-Verlag.

Bidell, T., & Fischer, K. W. (1992). Beyond the stage debate: Action, structure, and variability in Piagetian theory and research. In R. Sternberg & C. Berg (Eds.), *Intellectual development* (pp. 100–140). New York: Cambridge University Press.

Bidell, T. R., & Fischer, K. W. (1994). Developmental transitions in children's early on-line planning. In M. M. Haith, J. B. Benson, R. J. Roberts, Jr., & B. F. Pennington (Eds.), *The development of future-oriented processes* (pp. 141–176). Chicago: University of Chicago Press.

Bidell, T. R., & Fischer, K. W. (1996). Between nature and nurture: The role of human agency in the epigenesis of intelligence. In R. Sternberg & E. Grigorenko (Eds.), *Intelligence: Heredity and environment.* New York: Cambridge University Press.

Campos, J. J., & Bertenthal, B. I. (1987). Locomotion and psychological development in infancy. In F. Morrison, K. Lord, & D. Keating (Eds.), *Advances in applied developmental psychology* (Vol. 2, pp. 11–42). New York: Academic Press.

Fischer, K. W. (1980). A theory of cognitive development: The control and construction of hierarchies of skills. *Psychological Review, 87,* 447–531.

Fischer, K. W. (1987). Relations between brain and cognitive development. *Child Development, 57,* 623–632.

Fischer, K. W., & Bidell, T. (1998). Dynamic development of psychological structures in action and thought. In W. Damon (Ed.), *Handbook of child psychology: Vol 1. Theory* (R. Lerner, Vol. Ed.). New York: Wiley.

Fischer, K. W., Bullock, D. H., Rotenberg, E. J., & Raya, P. (1993). The dynamics of competence: How context contributes directly to skill. In R. Wozniak & K. W. Fischer (Eds.), *Development in context: Acting and thinking in specific environments* (pp. 93–117). Hillsdale, NJ: Lawrence Erlbaum Associates.

Fischer, K. W., & Corrigan, R. (1981). A skill approach to language development. In R. Stark (Ed.), *Language behavior in infancy and early childhood* (pp. 245–273). Amsterdam: Elsevier.

Fischer, K. W., & Farrar, M. J. (1987). Generalizations about generalizations: How a theory of skill development explains both generality and specificity. *International Journal of Psychology, 22,* 643–677.

Fischer, K. W., & Granott, N. (1995). Beyond one-dimensional change: Parallel, concurrent, socially distributed processes in learning and development. *Human Development, 38,* 302–314.

Fischer, K. W., Hand, H. H., Watson, M. W., Van Parys, M., & Tucker, J. (1984). Putting the child into socialization: The development of social categories in preschool children. In L. Katz (Ed.), *Current topics in early childhood education* (Vol. 5, pp. 27–72). Norwood, NJ: Ablex.

Fischer, K. W., & Hogan, A. E. (1989). The big picture in infant development: Levels and variations. In J. Lockman & N. Hazan (Eds.), *Action in social context: Perspectives on early development* (pp. 279–305). New York: Plenum.

Fischer, K. W., & Kenny, S. L. (1986). The environmental conditions for discontinuities in the development of abstractions. In R. Mines & K. Kitchener (Eds.), *Adult cognitive development: Methods and models* (pp. 57–75). New York: Praeger.

Fischer, K. W., & Pipp, S. (1984). Processes of cognitive development: Optimal level and skill acquisition. In R. J. Sternberg (Ed.), *Mechanisms of cognitive development* (pp. 45–80). New York: Freeman.

Fischer, K. W., & Rose, S. P. (1994). Dynamic development of coordination of components in brain and behavior: A framework for theory and research. In G. Dawson & K. W. Fischer (Eds.), *Human behavior and the developing brain* (pp. 3–66). New York: Guilford.

Fischer, K. W., Shaver, P. R., & Carnochan, P. (1990). How emotions develop and how they organize development. *Cognition & Emotion, 4,* 81–128.

Fogel, A. (1993). *Development through relationships: Origins of communication, self and culture.* Chicago: University of Chicago Press.

Gardner, H. (1985). *The mind's new science.* New York: Basic Books.

Gottleib, G. (1991). Experiential canalization of behavioral development: Theory. *Developmental Psychology, 27,* 4–13.

Gottleib, G. (1992). *Individual development and evolution: The genesis of novel behavior.* New York: Oxford University Press.

Granott, N. (1993a). *Microdevelopment of co-construction of knowledge during problem-solving: Puzzled minds, weird creatures, and wuggles.* Unpublished doctoral dissertation, Massachusetts Institute of Technology, Cambridge, MA.

Granott, N. (1993b). Patterns of interaction in the co-construction of knowledge: Separate minds, joint effort and weird creatures. In R. H. Wozniak & K. W. Fischer (Eds.), *Development in context: Acting and thinking in specific environments* (pp. 183–207). Hillsdale, NJ: Lawrence Erlbaum Associates.

Kail, R., & Bisanz, J. (1992). The information-processing perspective on cognitive development in childhood and adolescence. In R. J. Sternberg & C. A. Berg (Eds.), *Intellectual development* (pp. 261–277). New York: Cambridge University Press.

Kitchener, K. S., Lynch, C. L., Fischer, K. W., & Wood, P. K. (1993). Developmental range of reflective judgment: The effect of contextual support and practice on developmental stage. *Developmental Psychology, 29,* 893–906.

Klahr, D. (1989). Information-processing perspectives. In R. Vasta (Ed.), *Annals of child development* (Vol. 6, pp. 133–185). Greenwich, CT: JAI.

Kozak, A., & Brown, T. (1998). Emotion and the possibility of psychologist's entering into heaven. In M. F. Mascolo & S. Griffin (Eds.), *What develops in emotional development?* (pp. 135–155). New York: Plenum.

Lewis, M. D., & Douglas, L. (1998). A dynamic systems approach to cognitive-emotion interactions in development. In M. F. Mascolo & S. Griffin (Eds.), *What develops in emotional development?* (pp. 159–188). New York: Plenum.

Mandler, G. (1983). Representation. In P. H. Mussen (Series Ed.) & J. H. Flavell & E. M. Markham (Vol. Eds.), *Handbook of child psychology: Vol. 3. Cognitive development* (4th ed., pp. 420–494). New York: Wiley.

Mascolo, M. F., Craig-Bray, L., & Neimeyer, R. (1997). The construction of meaning and action in development and psychotherapy: An epigenetic systems approach. In G. Neimeyer & R. Neimeyer (Eds.), *Advances in personal construct psychology* (Vol. 4). Greenwich, CT: JAI.

Mascolo, M. F., & Fischer, K. W. (1995). Developmental transformations in appraisals for pride, shame and guilt. In J. Tangney & K. W. Fischer (Eds.), *Self-conscious emotions: The psychology of shame, guilt, embarrassment and pride* (pp. 64–113). New York: Guilford.

Mascolo, M. F., & Harkins, D. (1998). Toward a component systems model of emotional development. In M. Mascolo & S. Griffin (Eds.), *What develops in emotional development?* (pp. 189–217). New York: Plenum.

Mascolo, M. F., Pollack, R., & Fischer, K. W. (1997). Keeping the constructor in development: An epigenetic systems approach. *Journal of Constructivist Psychology, 10,* 27–51.

Piaget, J. (1951). *Play, dreams and imitation.* Melbourne, Australia: Heinemann.

Piaget, J. (1995). *Sociological studies.* London: Routledge. (Original work published 1965)

Piaget, J. (1985). *The equilibration of cognitive structures* (T. Brown & K. J. Thampy, Trans.). Chicago: University of Chicago Press.

Raeff, C., & Mascolo, M. F. (1996, June). *Co-regulated coordination: Representational activities at the intersection of individual, social and cultural processes.* Paper presented at the 26th annual symposium of the Jean Piaget Society, Philadelphia.

Rogoff, B. (1990). *Apprenticeship in thinking.* New York: Oxford University Press.

Rogoff, B. (1993). Children's guided participation and participatory appropriation in sociocultural activity. In R. Wozniak & K. W. Fischer (Eds.), *Development in context: acting and thinking in specific learning environments* (pp. 121–154). Hillsdale, NJ: Lawrence Erlbaum Associates.

Siegler, R. S. (1983). Information processing approaches to development. In P. H. Mussen (Ed.), *Handbook of child psychology: Vol 1. History, theory and methods* (pp. 129–211). New York: Wiley.

Siegler, R. S. (1989). Mechanisms of cognitive development. *Annual Review of Psychology, 40,* 353–380.

Sigel, I. E. (1991). Representational competence: Another type? In M. Chandler & M. Chapman (Eds.), *Criteria for competence: Controversy in the assessment of children's abilities* (pp. 189–207). Hillsdale, NJ: Lawrence Erlbaum Associates.

Sigel, I. E. (1994). The centrality of a distancing model for the development of representational competence. In R. R. Cocking & K. A. Renninger (Eds.), *The development and meaning of psychological distance* (pp. 141–156). Hillsdale, NJ: Lawrence Erlbaum Associates.

Sternberg, R. J. (Ed.). (1984) *Mechanisms of cognitive development.* New York: Freeman.

Vygotsky, L. S. (1978). *Mind in society.* Cambridge, MA: Harvard University Press.

Vygotsky, L. S. (1986). *Thought and language.* Cambridge, MA: MIT Press.

Watson, M. W., & Fischer, K. W. (1977). A developmental sequence of agent use in late infancy. *Child Development, 48,* 828–836.

Watson, M. W., & Fischer, K. W. (1980). Development of social roles in elicited and spontaneous be-
   havior during the preschool years. *Developmental Psychology, 16,* 483–494.
Werner, H. (1957). The concept of development from a comparative and organismic point of view.
   In D. B. Harris (Ed.), *The concept of development* (pp. 125–148). Minneapolis: University of Min-
   nesota Press.
Wertsch, J. V. (1991). *Voices of the mind.* Cambridge, MA: Harvard University Press.

CHAPTER 12

A Bakhtinian View
of Egocentric Speech

BRUCE DORVAL
City University of New York

The approach to formulating a theory of representation that I will take is based on Michael Bakhtin, who is best known as a literary theorist though he saw his efforts as the basis for a general theory of linguistic representation. What is unique about his theory is its basic assumption that all language use is intersubjectively oriented and organized, reflecting in its composition the various voices that form the crosscurrents of its author's personal and/or professional worlds. Analyzes conducted from this perspective led Bakhtin to conclude that more complexly and evidently intersubjective compositions, more highly "dialogized" compositions, in his terms, result in more subtle and objective representations.

The implications of this conclusion for theories of linguistic representation are comparable to those of *Impressionism* for painting. Impressionism sought to overturn the assumptions of the reigning realist aesthetic. Underlying realism is what might be called a facsimile theory of representation, embodying the premise that the more accurately a painting seems to copy reality, the better representation it is. Considering such examples of this style of painting as Michaelangelo's frescoes, still-life studies by Dutch masters such as Van Dijk, and Wyeth's country scenes reveals that what is convincing is not accuracy, per se, but rather a persuasive way of seeing and rendering the subject. Impressionism sought to loosen the strictures of realism with the goal of giving freer and franker expression to the artist's way of seeing and rendering the subject. Examples of such experimentation include Van Gogh's self-portraits, Chagall's image of his boyhood village, and Monet's Waterlillies, as well as such Expressionist "off-shoots" as Picasso's portraits of his lovers. In each case, violations of realist cannons of representation were cultivated as a vehicle for expressing the author's perspective on the subject and, by that means, to represent something unique about the subject.

In a similar manner and toward a similar end, the openly dialogized representation that Bakhtin advocated contravenes realist assumptions about linguisitic representation. This study applies Bakhtin's approach to the problem of the socialization of linguistic representation. An impressionist image of egocentric speech is fashioned by placing Piaget's and Vygotsky's views into dialogue.

Recently, other researchers have taken up issues that intersect with those that will be opened this way. There has been a growing interest in Vygotsky's theory and its relations with Piagetian theory (e.g., *Human Development*, 1996; Lawrence & Valsiner, 1993; Tryphon & Voneche, 1996). As a result, there is a growing realization that there are important similarities between the theories, which is partly the consequence of a shared sociohistorical context (e.g., Harris, 1997; *Human Development*, 1997; Van der Veer & Valsiner, 1991).

BAKHTINIAN FRAMEWORK

Bakhtin viewed linguistic representation as something created by an author as a vehicle for communication. He argued that this is true for all verbalizations, from casual conversation to the most highly stylized works of literature and science. Thus, his basic unit of analysis is the *utterance*, defined roughly as a verbal representation created by an author in response to prior utterances and in anticipation of responses in turn.

Bakhtin worked out his ideas in greatest detail as a literary theory. Among other things, he executed in-depth studies of Dosteovsky (Bakhtin, 1984a), Rabelais (Bakhtin, 1984b) and the *bildungsroman* or novel of self-improvement that featured Goethe (Bakhtin, 1986). These projects were undertaken to forward a more general theoretical problem that Bakhtin had in view from the beginning (Bakhtin, 1990, 1993), which was to articulate a conception of human nature that would be deeply social and thoroughly individual at the same time. (For a similar characterization of Bakhtin as a "philosophical anthropologist," see Holquist's Introduction in Bakhtin, 1986.)

Of particular relevance for present purposes, Bakhtin believed that Dosteovsky's methods of representation could contribute much toward such a project because it was the most complexly dialogized that he encountered:

> Dosteovsky portrayed not the life of an idea in an isolated consciousness, and not the interrelationship of ideas, but the interaction of consciousnesses in the sphere of ideas (but not of ideas only). And since a consciousness in Dosteovsky's world is presented not on the path of its own evolution and growth . . . but rather *alongside* other consciousnesses, it can not concentrate on itself and its own idea, on the immanent and logical development of that idea; instead, it is pulled into interaction with other consciousnesses. In Dosteovsky, consciousness never gravitates toward itself but is always found in intense relationship with another consciousness. . . . It could be said that Dosteovsky offers, in artistic form, something like a

sociology of consciousnesses . . . Dostoevsky as an artist does arrive at an *objective* mode of visualizing the life of consciousnesses and the forms of their living co-existence. . . . (Bakhtin, 1984a, p. 32)

I emulated this model of overt dialogization in creating the following representation of Piaget's and Vygotsky's conceptions of egocentric speech. That they interacted with one another about that subject provided a solid basis for doing so by focalizing the question, "How did they respond to each other's conceptions of egocentric speech?"

Thus, what follows is an impressionistic representation of egocentric speech. It is an overtly dialogically structured representation; diffuse and fragmentary by realist standards, it suggests rather than explicitly depicts its subject. As such, it calls for a more actively integrative reading than a realistic account might. As an everyday equivalent, consider the impression of some unwitnessed incident that we derive from overhearing a discussion of it by those who did witness it.

VYGOTSKY ON PIAGET'S CONCEPTION
OF EGOCENTRIC SPEECH

The logical place to begin to answer the question of how Piaget and Vygotsky responded to each other was with Vygotsky, who was thoroughly in response to Piaget. While he was in dialogue with a wide range of researchers, Vygotsky's (1987) responsiveness to Piaget was the most extensive and intensive by far. Indeed, Vygotsky stated that his theory is based on Piaget's theory. Consistent with this, he wrote a lengthy chapter devoted to critiquing Piaget's conception of egocentric speech; and this forms the core of his own conception of not only language socialization but human development more generally.

Vygotsky's manner of responding was to submit Piaget to a dialectical interrogation, which culminated in a vigorous attack that invoked Lenin's critique of Hegel:

This attempt to derive the child's logical thinking and his development from a pure interaction of consciousnesses—an interaction that occurs in complete isolation from reality or any consideration of the child's social practice directed toward the mastery of reality—is the central element of Piaget's entire construction.

In his notes on Hegel's "Logic," Lenin discusses an analogous perspective, a perspective widely distributed in idealistic philosophy and psychology:
When Hegel strives to subordinate the unique activity of man to the category of logic—arguing that this activity is the "conclusion," that the subject (man) plays the role of a "component" of the logical "figure"—THIS IS NOT ONLY STRETCHING THE POINT, IT IS A GAME. THERE IS A PROFOUND POINT HERE, A PURELY MATERIALISTIC ONE. WE MUST REVERSE IT: MAN'S PRACTICAL ACTIVITY MUST BRING THE REPETITION OF VARIOUS LOGICAL FIGURES A BILLION TIMES OVER FOR THESE FIGURES TO BECOME AXIOMS . . .

And further: "Man's practice, repeated a billion times, anchors the figures of logic in his consciousness. These figures have the strength of prejudice, their axiomatic character, precisely (and only) because of this repetition." It is not surprising then that Piaget finds isolated verbal thought incomprehensible. Conversation without action is incomprehensible. (Vygotsky, 1987, p. 88)

Thus, Vygotsky engaged Piaget's conception of egocentric speech as an instance of idealism, which is to say an approach to understanding phenomena in terms of their abstract logical properties and apart from practical activity. Such an approach is delegitimized in Lenin's critique of Hegel by relocating the phenomenon in the context of practical activity, which is envisioned as "actual living reality." The quote from Lenin clinches Vygotsky's critique of Piaget, and it had served as his guide in performing it.

At the beginning of the chapter, Vygotsky (1987) noted that Piaget took a qualitative approach to understanding how children's thinking differs from that of adults rather than a merely quantitative one; and he congratulated him for having found, as a result, a phenomenon of great significance for understanding socialization. Then he introduced the problematic of the struggle between idealism and materialism in terms of what he called "the crisis in contemporary psychology."

> The crisis in psychology is primarily a methodological crisis. It is firmly rooted in history, with the struggle between the materialist and the idealist traditions lying at its core. . . . At almost every step, contemporary psychology demonstrates most pathetically how new and important discoveries . . . can become mired in pre-scientific concepts which shroud them in *ad hoc,* semi-metaphysical systems and theories. . . . In spite of his attempts, Piaget did not succeed in avoiding the fatal dualism to which the crisis in contemporary psychology has doomed even the best representatives of the science. Piaget attempted to hide behind a high wall of reliable fact. But the facts betrayed him. . . . They led him to theory, implicit and undeveloped theory to be sure . . . we must attempt to critique the theory and the methodological systems that provide the foundation for Piaget's studies. (pp. 56, 57)

Vygotsky proceeded by critiquing the idealistic basis of Piaget's conception of egocentric speech from a materialist perspective, which resulted in a materialist reformulation. He focused on three, interrelated aspects of Piaget's conception of egocentric speech: (1) its psychoanalytically derived assumption of an original autism or asociality, (2) emphasis on the similarity between autism and egocentric speech, and (3) characterization of the endpoint of development in terms of individual cognition seemingly separate from practical activity and concrete social participation. Also in keeping with a materialist perspective, he stated at one point and implied more generally that egocentric speech is not a kind of miscommunication but rather an effective form of communal speech.

Vygotsky's critique was interwoven with his own research results that provided empirical guideposts to flesh out an alternative conception of egocentric speech. For instance, he found that the proportion of egocentric speech increased when young children were faced with impediments to completing an activity, which suggested that egocentric speech functions as thinking out loud. He also found that it decreased sharply when there were barriers to communication, such as background music. This revealed that egocentric speech is intended to be overhead since it is suppressed when it can not serve that function.

After reporting on his own research, he returned to the general conceptual level that is anchored by the aforementioned quotation from Lenin. The quote served as the capstone of Vygotsky's argument, its general conclusion.

PIAGET'S REPLY TO HANFMANN AND VAKAR'S REVISION OF VYGOTSKY

Having characterized Vygotsky's response to Piaget as dialectical (see Van der Veer & Valsiner, 1991, for a similar view of his overall intellectual style), I sought to expand the representation of their dialogue by examining Piaget's response to that critique. Piaget (1962) wrote a commentary on Hanfmann and Vakar's revision of Vygotsky (1962), a revision designed to introduce Western psychologists to the then unknown Soviet scholar. (Although Piaget knew of Vygotsky since the 1920s and even apparently met him at a convention, he had not read his work.)

Piaget expressed gratitude to Vygotsky for his recognition that egocentric speech is a complex phenomenon that is at the heart of language socialization. He emphasized this by complaining that other researchers of child language, such as Dorothy McCarthy, did not demonstrate such a recognition. In doing so, Piaget was creating an alliance with Vygotsky against the prevailing empiricism, which tended to limit conceptions of phenomena to what could be readily measured and quantified about them. (See Wozniak, 1996, for further discussion of this point.)

In terms of the substance of Vygotsky's critique, Piaget granted his point that he had overemphasized the link between egocentric speech and autism, while explaining that he did so to demonstrate the limitations of egocentric speech *as an intersubjective phenomenon* in comparison to rational discourse. He also admitted that he took the psychoanalytic premise that the pleasure principle precedes the reality principle in development too literally. He stated that he now believes that both are continuously active throughout life and that they are manifested in the cognitive processes of assimilation and accommodation, respectively. Piaget also acknowledged that he did not emphasize the adaptive aspects of egocentric speech enough and accepted Vygotsky's thesis about egocentric speech *in terms of its practical value for the speaker.*

Piaget emphasized his continued disagreement with Vygotsky in terms of the intersubjective nature of egocentric speech. He criticized Vygotsky for failing to appreciate that egocentric speech constitutes an interference to intellectual co-operation, accusing him of being blinded by "excessive bio-social optimism," an oblique reference to the Communist view of human nature. Piaget acknowledged that the term *egocentric* was unfortunate because of its judgmental overtones. However, he also insisted on the concept's validity and that it remained focal in his view of socialization, a fundamental aspect of the human condition that is not extinguished through socialization but only ameliorated. As evidence, he reiterated the examples of adult egocentrism that he had presented in the summary to his work on egocentric speech (Piaget, 1926/1955): (a) an image of the beginning instructor whose lectures are comprehensible to himself or herself but not to students, and (b) the history of conceptions of the planetary universe.

In a related rebuttal to Vygotsky's critique of the psychoanalytically derived assumption of original autism, Piaget denied that he ever severed need from desire or, if he did so, that he quickly corrected the error. Piaget offered his later conception of the continuous interaction between assimilation and accommodation in the functioning of cognitive schemas as proof. Even if he was unfair in referring to a revision about which Vygotsky could not have known, Piaget was pointing to a crucial problem with Vygotsky's critique. Vygotsky did not attempt to decipher Piaget's view of reality; he applied a Marxist view of reality to Piaget. As such, his construction of the dialogical engagement between those two positions on the nature of reality was one-sided, "monological" in Bakhtin's terminology. By contrast, the depth and vibrance of Dostoevskian dialogue springs from ongoing conflicts among the characters that play out on the basis of divergent experiences and construals of reality.

Piaget's encounter with Vygotsky was similarly monological. He construed Vygotsky's reformulation in terms of his own view of reality, which was evident when Piaget replied to Vygotsky's criticism by citing a revision of his early theory to include assimilation and accomodation. That would only be an effective reply if Vygotsky held a similarly intrapsychic view of need and desire, which he did not. Further evidence that Piaget misconstrued Vygotsky's position in this way is that he stated later that the "motor of development" in Vygotsky's theory is generalization. With this move, Piaget obscured the fundamental difference in the relation between the subject and the social order that Vygotsky's theory entails. This constitutes a monologic tendency in Piaget's representation of the relation between himself and Vygotsky that is comparable to the monologic tendency in Vygotsky's representation of their relation. Each constructed the other in terms of his own view of the nature of reality.

REPLY TO HANFMANN AND VAKAR

This kind of monology is pervasive among psychological theories. For example, as complementary as he was in a preface to Flavell's (1963) introduction of his research to Anglo-American psychologists, Piaget also complained that its epistemological basis had been effaced and with it the actual view of reality that he had propounded. As well, Vygotsky's materialist solution for what he called "the crisis in psychology" is profoundly monological; materialism would provide the accurate view of reality necessary to integrate the welter of diverse theories and findings. Another example is Hanfmann and Vakar's characterization of Vygotsky's theory.

Before discussing it, I wish to point out that these instances of monology employ realist assumptions about representation, which is to say, the enforcement of the author's perspective by realistically rendering the subject in terms of his or her view of reality. Thereby, the actual view of reality expressed by the subject is altered and in a way that is unacknowledged.

With respect to Hanfmann and Vakar, they stated in the "Translators' Preface" that they edited as well as translated *Thought and Word,* pointing out that they removed "numerous polemical digressions" which necessitated reorganization of the chapter on Piaget that reduced its length by more than half. Because they expurgated the Marxist–Leninist position in this manner, their representation of Vygotsky's theory offers it as a conception that is not sharply divergent from Piaget's theory. That was apparently intentional because Hanfmann and Vakar stated in a footnote to the title of the chapter on Piaget, "Vygotsky's criticism . . . is hardly applicable to Piaget's later formulations" (Vygotsky, 1962, p. 9).

While Hanfmann and Vakar performed a valuable service in bridging Western and Soviet psychological discourses during the Cold War and for eliciting comment from Piaget, I disagreed strongly with their representation of Vygotsky. By means of both omissions and the rendering of key terms in translation, its meaning had been shifted markedly in comparison to the more literal translation. For instance, in place of the Leninist culmination just quoted:

> In light of these facts, Piaget's conclusions call for clarification concerning two important points. First, the peculiarities of child thought . . . such as syncretism, do not extend over quite so large an area as Piaget believes. We are inclined to think that the child thinks syncretically in matters of which he has no direct knowledge or experience. . . .

> The second point which calls for reappraisal and limitation is the applicability of Piaget's findings to children in general. His experiments led him to believe that the child was impervious to experience. Piaget draws an analogy that we find illuminating: Primitive man learns from experience only in a few, special limited instances of practical activity (agriculture and hunting). . . . We would not call agriculture and hunting negligible contacts with reality for primitive man; they are practically the whole of his existence. Piaget's view[s] are . . . not of universal significance. . . . They are not laws of nature but are socially and historically determined. (Vygotsky, 1962, pp. 23, 24)

The way these "clarifications" are presented suggests that Vygotsky accepted

Piaget's conception of egocentric speech as basically valid, if only in the context of bourgeois society. My take was that the thrust of Vygotsky's critique as presented in the more literal translation was to present an alternative that invalidated Piaget's conception.

Puzzling about this brought the realization that my image of the dialogical structure of Vygotsky's utterance was simplistic. Bakhtin's view of the nature of the relation between utterances as a dialogical interaction of positions came to mind. The following is from his essay "The Problem of the Text in Linguistics, Philology and the Human Sciences":

> One can not . . . understand dialogic relations simplistically and unilaterally, reducing them to contradiction, conflict, polemics, or disagreement. *Agreement* is very rich in varieties and shadings. Two utterances that are identical in all respects ("Beautiful weather!" — "Beautiful weather!"), if there are really *two* utterances belonging to *different* voices and not one, are linked by dialogic *relations of agreement*. This is a definite dialogic event in the interrelations of the two, and not an echo. (Bakhtin, 1986, p. 125)

So, my account of Vygotsky's relation to Piaget and Lenin was simplistic. It had equated Vygotsky and Lenin. Yet, Vygotsky's voice was distinct from Lenin's. Lenin shouted Hegel down, dismissing him as ridiculous and ripping the phenomenon out of his hands with a tersely worded alternative formulation. Vygotsky only spoke like this when he reported Lenin's speech. In Vygotsky's more specific comments on Piaget, the confrontation between idealism and materialism became less bombastic in tone and more specific in focus; and tracking the line of argument revealed that Vygotsky's stance toward Piaget is more openly ambivalent than Lenin's stance toward Hegel. (Interestingly, Wertsch, 1996, arrived at a similar evaluation of Vygotsky, which he characterized as an ambivalence about Enlightenment rationality.)

In consequence, Vygotsky's response to Piaget was neither fully consistent nor completely conclusive. It was not "finalized" in Bakhtin's terms, who used Dosteovsky to demonstrate this fundamental fact a about utterance construction. This was a good choice. Dostoevsky's late novels are so obviously unfinalized since they consist of complex and often fractious interactions among diverse characters. Unfinalizability is a feature of all utterances though less obviously so in utterances that are less overtly dialogized. For example, though Lenin demands the final word on reality, is his utterance actually finalized? Is it correct and complete, admitting no replies? Couldn't one ask of him, "What are the practical-activity impetuses and consequences of your own utterance?" or "Couldn't your argument be considered as an antithesis in an historically unfolding Hegelian dialectic?" Thus, Lenin's rhetoric might portray his utterance as finalized, but no utterance can actually fulfill such a promise.

In other words, a theory might entail this realist aspiration, but its actual execution as a representation will always fall short of that ideal. As long as the reader is led successfully to identify with the author's position as reflected in his or her main character—as I did in terms of Vygotsky's representation of Lenin, this limitation of realism will be obscured. Perhaps the most important consequence of the overt dialogization of positions is to make us more aware of such limitations by helping us to identify with the various characters that compose the author's utterance.

THE PIAGET THAT VYGOTSKY ENCOUNTERED

These findings about Vygotsky's response to Piaget created a context for examining the dialogical structure of the utterances of Piaget's to which Vygotsky responded, *The Language and Thought of the Child* (Piaget, 1955) and its companion, *Judgment and Reasoning in the Child* (Piaget, 1959). The outcome was to discover that Piaget too was ambivalent, and his representation correspondingly dialogized, though in a way that is somewhat different than Vygotsky.

In his critique of Piaget, Vygotsky focused on the first chapter of the first and the summary chapter of the second, which pertains to both volumes. Piaget stated in his reply to Vygotsky that the first chapter was meant as an introduction for the second chapter and expressed exasperation that Vygotsky as well as most other researchers had focused exclusively on the first chapter and, thus, missed the true scope of the phenomenon that he had unearthed.

Piaget did not dispute Vygotsky's detailed and strongly argued claim that his theory was based on psychoanalytic premises. In fact, he stated pointedly that, since Vygotsky was also a psychopathologist, he could hardly argue with the assertion that egocentrism is pervasive in adults as well as children. This statement calls for unpacking. Piaget is declaring himself as an adherent of psychoanalysis —in the broad sense of "adherent"—and "outing" Vygotsky as also an adherent. We now know that Vygotsky was a member of the Russian Psychoanalytic Association, as was Luria, during the 1920s (Van der Veer & Valsiner, 1991). As well, Piaget had some training in psychoanalysis that may have included a brief "training analysis" before going to Paris in 1919 where he maintained an interest in psychoanalysis (Gruber & Voneche, 1977; Harris, 1997). Piaget implies that, as such, both he and Vygotksy would know that egocentrism is pervasive, since it is so prominently displayed in psychopathological states that are an unavoidable part of human nature.

This retort also draws our attention to the fact that, like Vygotsky, Piaget modeled himself on an authority, which set the basic dialogical structure of his utterance. While Vygotsky modeled himself on Lenin's attack on idealism, Piaget represented an encounter between the psychoanalytically informed investigator and his child subject. (See Berthoud-Papandropoulos & Kilcher, 1996, for a discussion of the importance of the clinical method in Piaget's early period.) Like Vygotsky, Piaget employs the encounter to advance theory. In the latter's case, he strives to advance psychoanalytic theory, broadly considered:

Psycho-analysts have been led to distinguish two fundamentally different modes of thinking: *directed* or *intelligent thought* and *undirected* or, as Bleuler proposes to call it, *autistic thought*. Directed thought is conscious . . . adapted to reality and attempts to influence it. . . . It admits of being true or false, and can be communicate as such by language. Autistic thought is subconscious, which means that the aims it pursues and the problems it tries to solve are not present in consciousness; it is not adapted to reality but creates for itself a dream world of imagination...and it remains strictly individual and incommunicable as such by means of language. . . . (Piaget, 1926/1955, p. 63)

Piaget believed that his contribution was to discover that there are forms of thinking and speech that lie between autism and rationality that show how the former is transformed into the latter in socialization:

Now between autism and intelligence there are many degrees, varying in their capacity for being communicated. These intermediate varieties must therefore be subject to a special logic, intermediate too between the logic of autism and that of intelligence. The chief of those intermediate forms, . . . like that of our children [which] seeks to adapt itself to reality, but does not communicate itself as such, we propose to call *Ego-centric thought*. (Piaget, 1926/1955, p. 64)

Thus, the psychoanalytic distinction between conscious and unconscious mental processes provided the conceptual framework of Piaget's investigation and the clinical method his position as investigator. Furthermore, like the psychoanalysts of that time, he was focused on demonstrating the existence of unconscious and irrational mental processes in the face of the general turn-of-the-century assumption that thinking and speech are conscious and rational *by their very nature*. This helps us to understand why Piaget began his exposition of the topic as he did in chapter 1:

We have chosen this example from Pie (6½ years) because it is taken during the most sociable activity of which this child is capable. . . . It would therefore be natural . . . if the sole function of speech were to communicate thought. . . . [Yet] from the social point of view the significance of these sentences . . . is extremely varied. When Pie says [refers to 2 utterances of the directly prior example] . . . he is not speaking to anyone. He is thinking aloud over his drawing, just as people of the working classes mutter to themselves over their work. . . . (Piaget, 1955, p. 31)

Thus, Piaget focused on demonstrating the pervasive influence of unconscious mental processes in the speech of preschoolers; and his point of comparison was adult rationality as reflected in his own reactions to the preschoolers' talk:

Jac says to Ez: "Look, Ez, your pants are showing." Pie who is in another part of the room, immediately repeats: "Look, my pants are showing, and my shirt, too." Now there is not a word of truth in all this. It is simply the joy of repeating for its own sake that makes Pie talk in this way, i.e., the pleasure of using words not for the sake of adapting oneself to the conversation, but for the sake of playing with them. (Piaget, 1926/1955, p. 35)

As already noted, Piaget admitted that he was judgmental in these accounts of egocentric speech; but he also held to his basic conclusion that such speech is deficient from the perspective of achieving rational understanding, stating that it was the "only aspect of the problem" that interested him. This retort marked the limits of his engagement with Vygotsky as well as the children he observed. It reflects Piaget's insistence that others relate to him on his terms, which means relating to him in terms of his conception of adult rationality.

To refocus on Vygotsky momentarily, it is understandable that he would draw the conclusion that need and desire were divorced in Piaget's theory if he focused on the way Piaget characterized instances of egocentric speech in the first chapter. In that chapter, he built a case for it being essentially a manifestation of unconscious mental processes, the hallmark of which is the lack of rational communicative intent. Because he emphasized that, it is hard to see how egocentric speech could come to meet needs as well as express desires. However, if Vygotsky failed to carefully examine chapter 2, which appears to be the case, then he would have incorrectly concluded that Piaget did not offer a solution for this problem.

In chapter 2, Piaget focused on children's conversations rather than the remarks of target children; and he sketched a developmental sequence for the socialization of children's conversations. Along with this shift in focus to the intersubjective event, his commentary on examples in chapter 2 was less judgmental. This is the case because the representation of egocentric speech is no longer structured as an encounter between adult rationality and young children's irrationality. Now the representation is structured as an encounter among the children themselves that an adult observes but does not directly participate in. Furthermore, the adult authority is seeking to discover how young children's talk prepares for the developmental advance to an exchange of ideas:

> Pie (6;5): "Where could we make another tunnel? Ah, here Eun?"—Eun (4;11): "Look at my pretty frock." (The end) Cat (6;2): "Have you finished, Bur?"—Bur (4;11): "Now it goes that way, etc." Talk of this kind clearly anticipates future conversation. The speaker expects an answer from his hearer. If the two remarks together constitute only a collective monologue, it is because the hearer is not listening. . . . But conversation is there in embryo, because the several remarks are grouped into one bundle. (Piaget, 1926/1955, p. 76)

Thus, Piaget now represented egocentric speech as a step in the socialization of the norms of social participation that leads ultimately to rational discourse, which is contrary to Vygotsky's conclusion that Piaget views egocentric speech as fated simply for extinction.

The difference in the tone and substance of chapters 1 and 2 reflects Piaget's ambivalence in encountering the preschool child, who was alternately directly encountered and dismissed as irrational and observed in talk with peers and appreciated as enacting the basis for more advanced communication. Piaget appreciated and dismissed Vygotsky similarly, as we see from the preceding discussion. To characterize it, we might say that Piaget displays ambivalence about whether to engage the other. (By contrast, Vygotsky displays ambivalence over his allegiances to others.) Such ambivalence, as we see, is reflected in a dialogical structure characterized by oscillation between markedly divergent constructions of the subject that are not marked as such.

VYGOTSKY'S PSYCHODYNAMIC REFORMULATION OF HIS THEORY

This understanding of Piaget together with his retort to Vygotsky with respect to psychoanalysis threw a new light on the nature of Vygotsky's theory. Vygotsky rejected Piaget's appropriation of psychoanalytic theory, not psychodynamic theory itself as I had thought. His last theoretical project was to revise his own theory to give it the kind of affective–motivational basis that makes it, in effect, a psychodynamic theory (Vygotsky, 1987). He sketched this revision in the last chapter. It entailed three layers of meaning-making; to the layers of outer speech and inner speech that Vygotsky had previously described, he added an innermost plane of wordless thought, calling it the "affective/motivational core." The functioning of inner speech was revised accordingly. Vygotsky stated, "Inner speech is an internal plane of verbal thinking that mediates a dynamic relationship between thought and word" (Vygotsky, 1987, p. 279). Thus, inner speech is now a continually fluctuating process, a "fluorescence" that is governed by the forces of outer speech on one side and the affective–motivational core on the other side.

Marking the importance of this conceptual shift, Vygotsky now declared that understanding someone's speech requires understanding of its emotional and motivational basis. He worked this out by reconceptualizing the nature of language use. In a move that brought his view close to Bakhtin, he turned to the work of art for an image of the phenomenon. Specifically, he referred to such plays as those of Chekhov, invoking Stanislavsky's method of training actors as a guide. Stanislavsky argued that to play a part convincingly, the actor must somehow feel his or her way into the world of the character. In this way, he or she portrays the characters' words embedded in a paraverbal subtext that reflects the character's unspoken emotions and motivations. Thus, language use was now envisioned as the intertwined text and subtext of the utterance as it enacts plotted and socially embedded scenarios.

This realization about Vygotsky's theory shifted my understanding of his critique of Piaget as well as of the overall orientation of his own theory. His resonance with Piaget encompassed not only the cognitive aspect of his theory but its psychodynamic aspect as well. Unfortunately, Vygotsky did not live long enough to articulate the specifics of a psychodynamic reformulation of his theory.

This is quite different from typical characterizations of Vygotsky's theory, which are based on his earlier conceptualizations and, thus, emphasize the application of the zone of proximal development in the acquisition of cognitive skills from socialization agents (e.g., Rogoff, 1990; Wertsch, 1985). As useful as these responses to Vygotsky are, in his last writing, Vygotsky argued strongly for the need to broaden his theory to include affect and motivation, indeed to place it at the center of his theory.

As another indication that Vygotsky was still working out his theory in the last years of his life is that he was working on two different views to communication. (See Van der Veer & Valsiner's, 1991, for comments on inconsistencies and redundancies in Vygotsky's writing.) In his discussion of the phylogenesis of communication, Vygotsky (1987, chap. 4) drew a sharp distinction between verbal and nonverbal communication, emphasizing the limitations of the latter both motivationally and semantically. Yet when invoking Stanislavsky's method as the basis for a theory of communication, verbal and nonverbal communication are viewed as deeply integrated. The version that employs Stanislavsky attracted my attention. For one thing, it is surprisingly close to Bakhtin's view. For another, it suggests a parallelism in the structures of communication and of thought. Both domains are similarly layered and mutually constituting, which is similar in overall form to Piaget's conception.

DISCUSSION

The foregoing representation of egocentric speech is overtly dialogically structured, and it proceeds by a progressive deepening of the interrelation between Piaget's and Vygotsky's views that simultaneously deepens understanding of each and of the representation of the phenomenon of egocentric speech. The realistic assumptions of both Piaget's and Vygotsky's views were exposed and with it their internal ambivalence and lack of finalization. As such, the result is a more objective view of the nature of egocentric speech. Bakhtin drew attention to a comparable outcome of Dostoevsky's efforts to create deeper intersubjectivity–subjectivity among his characters by placing them in dialogue with one another and without overly identifying with one character or another. In emulating his style of representation, this study achieved a similar result.

This conclusion runs counter to the widespread assumption that the more objective representation would be more fully finalized and monological, that is, nonambivalently committed to and expressive of some "correct" view of reality. This is the sense in which a Bakhtinian view of representation has important implications for the philosophy of psychology. Its basic premise about objectivity is the diametrical opposite of the monological ideal of the empiricist perspective that is so widely accepted as the proper philosophical grounding of psychology.

In empiricism, facts are self-evident and theories are correspondingly monologized, the expression of a realist "philosophy of the fact" as Piaget might say.

Yet, some of his most famous discoveries were aimed at discrediting this view of reality by showing that what is perceived as factual is actually a construction. For example, young children do not realize that the volume of a fluid does not change with the shape of its container; and they do not automatically associate counting with numerosity. Conserving volume and number are cognitive achievements that crucially alter perception, though that is obscured because perceptual experience remains naively realistic. Thus, realism obscures the reality of the constructivism of perception.

Vygotsky made the same point in a different way. He argued against the tendency to aggregate empirically defined measurements of a phenomenon mechanically. Rather, he advocated beginning a study by finding a unit of analysis that clearly displays the relations among the elements of interest, in other words, imaging the phenomenon in such a way that these elements are intrinsic to it. Empirical indices are then fashioned to assess these elements together with methods that are capable of assessing relations among them that are perceived in individual instances of the phenomenon. Only in this way can the actual relations among the variable be accurately determined.

Thus, both Piaget and Vygotsky took issue with empiricism. Though they viewed egocentric speech somewhat differently, both viewed it as a complex phenomenon that integrates aspects of both psychic and interpsychic functioning. Their theories were designed as representations of that complex phenomenon, not as merely a collection of facts about it. However, they were both realistic in their modes of representing egocentric speech to the extent that they described it with respect to a particular perspective on reality that remained unquestioned.

As discussed, no matter how seemingly monologized a linguistic representation may seem, it contains within itself a condensed dialogical structure. It is perhaps the chief benefit of an overtly dialogized representation to draw out this structure. For example, in this study, both Piaget's and Vygotsky's theories were found to be strongly influenced by psychoanalysis; and the specificity of Vygotsky's responsiveness to Lenin was revealed. Furthermore, each author displays a characteristic ambivalence in the way he orchestrates dialogical positions. Thus, the monological ideal of a unitary and consistent conception of egocentric speech that is also value neutral was undermined.

The result is a more complex but also fragmented representation of egocentric speech. As with Impressionism, the reader must read differently. New aspects of the nature of egocentric speech were revealed in the violation of realist conventions, to which both Piaget and Vygotsky adhered. By destabilizing preconceptions of these authors and their representations of egocentric speech, the reader is invited to construct a new image of the phenomenon. Not only were Piaget's and Vygotksy's representations themselves found to be more complex than may have been apparent, a more complex and abstract image of the phenomenon is suggested that encompasses the interaction of both perspectives.

REFERENCES

Bakhtin, M. M. (1984a). *Dostoevsky's poetics*. Minneapolis: University of Minnesota Press.

Bakhtin, M. M. (1984b). *Rabelais and his world*. Bloomington: Indiana University Press.

Bakhtin, M. M. (1986). Introduction by M. Holquist. *Speech genres and other late essays*. Austin: University of Texas Press. (pp. iv–xxiii)

Bakhtin, M. M. (1990). *Art and answerability*. Austin: University of Texas Press.

Bakhtin, M. M. (1993). *Toward a philosophy of the act*. Austin: University of Texas Press.

Berthoud-Papandropoulos, I., & Kilcher, H. (1996). Relationships between clinical method and the zone of proximal development in a constructionist approach to language acquisision. In A. Tryphon & J. Voneche (Eds.), *Piaget-Vygotsky: The social genesis of thought* (pp. 171–188). East Sussex, England: The Psychology Press.

Flavell, J. H.(1963). Introduction by Piaget. *The developmental psychology of Jean Piaget*. Princeton, NJ: Van Nostrand.

Gruber, H. E., & Voneche, J. J. (1977). *The essential Piaget: An interpretive reference and guide*. New York: Basic Books.

Harris, P. (1997). Piaget in Paris: From 'Autism' to logic. *Human Development, 40*, 109–123.

Human Development (1996). Special issue on Piaget and Vygotsky, *39*(5)

Human Development (1997). Special issue, *40*(2).

Lawrence, J. A., & Valsiner, J. (1993). Conceptual roots of internalization: From transmission to transformation. *Human Development, 36*, 150–167.

Piaget, J. (1955). *The language and thought of the child*. New York: The World Publishing Company. (Original work published 1926)

Piaget, J. (1959). *Judgment and reasoning in the child*. Totowa, NJ: Littlefield, Adams and Company. (Original work published 1928)

Piaget, J. (1962). Comments. Attachment to L. S. Vygotsky, 1962, *Thought and language*. Cambridge, MA: MIT Press.

Rogoff, B. (1990). *Apprenticeship in thinking*. New York: Oxford University Press.

Tryphon, A., & Voneche, J. (1996). Editors, *Piaget-Vygotksy: The social genesis of thought*. Hove, England: The Psychology Press.

Van der Veer, R., & Valsiner, J. (1991). *Understanding Vygotsky: A quest for synthesis*. Oxford: Blackwell.

Vygotsky, L. S. (1962). *Thought and language*. Cambridge, MA: MIT Press.

Vygotsky, L. S. (1987). Thinking and speech. In R. W. Rieber & A. S. Carton (Eds.), *The collected works of L. S. Vygotsky* (Vol. 1). New York: Plenum Press.

Wertsch, J. V. (1985). *Vygotsky and the social formation of mind*. Cambridge, MA: Harvard University Press.

Wertsch, J. V. (1996). The role of abstract rationality in Vygotsky's image of mind. In A. Tryphon & J. Voneche (Eds.), *Piaget-Vygotsky: The social genesis of thought* (pp. 25–44). East Sussex, England: The Psychology Press.

Wozniak, R. H. (1996). Qu'est-ce que l'intellegence? Piaget, Vygotsky and the 1920s crisis in psychology. In A. Tryphon and J. Voneche (Eds.), *Piaget-Vygotsky: The social genesis of thought* (pp. 11–24). East Sussex, England: The Psychology Press.

CHAPTER 13

The Nature and Development of Representation: Forging a Synthesis of Competing Approaches

JAMES P. BYRNES
University of Maryland

Ever since the time of the ancient Greeks, scholars from a variety of fields have grappled with the idea of mental representation. Prior to the advent of behaviorism in the 1930s, most psychologists, philosophers, and linguists acknowledged the existence and important role of representation in the human mind but nevertheless argued about the nature, origin, and development of representational entities (Chomsky, 1980; Fodor, 1975). During the behaviorist period, these arguments were put on hold because the behaviorists maintained that (a) psychologists should only posit and employ constructs that help them predict or modify human behavior and (b) adding representational constructs (e.g., imagery, concepts, etc.) to a psychological theory does help a psychologist become more successful at predicting or modifying behavior (Skinner, 1974). Therefore, they argued that because representational constructs are fairly useless to the practice of psychological science (as they defined it), little time should be spent discussing the nature and origin of representations. During the 1950s, an increasing number of psychologists began to argue (or at least quietly acknowledge) that representations are useful explanatory constructs (Gholson & Barker, 1985). Then, after the Cognitive Revolution of the 1960s ushered in a plethora of cognitivist theories (e.g., Piaget, Vygotsky, schema theory, etc.), arguments about the nature and origin of mental representations reemerged.

A cursory reading of the literature on cognition and its development since the 1960s suggests that we have done little to resolve the epistemological arguments that have been with us since the time of the ancient Greeks. In particular, instead of having a "grand" theory that accounts for all of the cognitive phenomena that interest us, we have a variety of independent pockets of researchers who study individual, seemingly unrelated topics (e.g., theory of mind, the acquisition of verbs, deductive reasoning, etc.). Moreover, many of these researchers adhere to distinct epistemological stances (e.g., constructivism, nativism, or empiricism). This diversity in research topics and epistemologies seems to suggest that it would be impossible to find common ground among the various positions. However, I contend that the gaps among current positions are not as wide as they seem. It is only when one adopts an extreme position that the integration of the different stances becomes difficult or impossible. The primary goal of this chapter is to elucidate most of the contemporary stances on the nature of representation and describe how it is possible to effectively synthesize these perspectives into a coherent story.

The approach that I take is to examine the nature and development of representation by discussing a number of important distinctions. Various researchers originally proposed these distinctions after conducting logical or empirical analyses of a particular research topic. The first major part of this chapter is devoted to a discussion of each distinction and its significance. In the second major section, I summarize my integrative approach and draw conclusions.

EIGHT IMPORTANT DISTINCTIONS
RELATED TO REPRESENTATION

To lay the groundwork for a discussion of distinctions, it is useful first to provide my own working definition of representation: *A representation is a pattern of recurrent cortical activity that can be evoked or elicited by another pattern of cortical or subcortical activity. These patterns of activation, in turn, correspond to entities in the "real" world or are themselves components of an imagined world.* For example, when I see some object, certain cells in my retina become active and, by way of neuronal pathways, ultimately cause clusters of neurons in my occipital, temporal, and parietal lobes to become active (Kosslyn & Koenig, 1992). If I have seen the object that is causing this activity several times before, the pattern of activity that corresponds to seeing this object may become reflected in relatively permanent synaptic connections. Once formed, the existence of these synaptic connections may help me feel that I have seen the object before. We normally call this process "recognition" (Flavell, Miller, & Miller, 1993; Squire, 1987). As a second example, consider how some other cue (e.g., hearing the object's name) may cause me (through the cortical activity corresponding to the sound of the word) to reactivate the stored pattern of activity that corresponds to the object when it is in view, even when the object is not in view. We normally call the latter "recall" (Flavell et al., 1993; Squire, 1987). Through synaptic connections, then, we are able to retain our experiences in such a way that we recognize objects or events that recur, and can think about these objects or events even when we are not experiencing them now. In typical cognitive psychological terms (e.g., Anderson, 1995), we would say that we have "stored" a representation of the object in long-term memory and that we can "retrieve" this representation using certain "cues" (e.g., the object itself or its name). In my view, the cognitive psychological and cognitive neuropsychological descriptions are really referring to the same processes, but at different levels of explanation (Pylyshyn, 1984). As we see later, knowing something about both levels of explanation helps us to understand the distinctions described next.

Distinction 1: Knowledge Versus Thinking. The terms *knowledge* and *representation* are essentially coextensive. To say that someone knows a fact or skill is to say that he or she has created a representation for that fact or skill. The primary evidence that the person has specific knowledge is that the individual can evoke the relevant representation when cued in some way (e.g., asked a question). Of course, to say that someone has knowledge is not to say that he or she *uses* that knowledge to recognize something, make inferences, or solve problems (Bransford, Sherwood, Vye, & Rieser, 1986; Carey, 1985a). Knowledge is the grist for the thinking mill, but it is not the same as thinking. Similarly, we can sometimes engage in very elegant thinking but operate on the basis of flawed knowledge (Simon, 1986). In fact, much of the Piagetian research was conducted to show how young children certainly think, but often generate incorrect answers because their knowledge was not sufficiently developed (e.g., Inhelder & Piaget, 1964). For example, a young preoperational child might infer that a horse would bark because he or she has mentally grouped dogs and horses into the same category. This inference would not be made by an older child who has distinct categories for dog and horse, but note how both preoperational children and concrete operational children make inferences. Piaget (1962) called faulty categorical inferences "transductions." One could go so far as to say that if the preoperational child had the same knowledge as the concrete operational child, the former would make the same inferences as the latter.

The difference between Piagetians and "post-Piagetians" (i.e., scholars who challenged the Piagetian views after the 1960s) is that whereas Piagetians seem to think that a researcher could not find knowledge in a preoperational child that would support appropriate inference making, the post-Piagetians felt that a researcher could find such knowledge. The important point is this: The two groups are identical in their belief that inference making is a "functional invariant" (i.e., it is a mental process that is carried out in the same way at all age levels). Their beliefs about the possibility of finding underlying knowledge led the two groups to focus on different kinds of knowledge and tasks. Piaget, for example, examined deductive reasoning using task content related to bending rods, chemicals, and balances (Inhelder & Piaget, 1958). Such content is obviously biased toward older groups. The post-Piagetians, in contrast, examined deductive reasoning using fantasy characters (e.g., Dias & Harris, 1988; Hawkins, Pea, Glick, & Scribner, 1984). Piaget (1962) would agree, of course, that fantasy is within the grasp of preschoolers, but for some reason did not exploit this knowledge in studies of deductive reasoning. Similarly, whereas Piagetians would study the development of possibility by asking children to imagine a piece of paper that is cut up into smaller and smaller pieces (Piaget, 1987), post-Piagetians would employ content that is clearly within the grasp of preschoolers such as object permanence (e.g., Sophian & Somerville, 1988).

Together, these two research traditions reveal that the cognitive processes related to categorization, inference making, deductive reasoning, and so forth are functional invariants. The main source of developmental change seems to be changes in knowledge. As knowledge changes, the very same cognitive processes that are used to compute "wrong" answers are now computing "right" answers because the correct content is fed into the computational machinery. What seems to be lost in all of the arguments between Piagetians and post-Piagetians is that there are forms of knowledge that are within the grasp of preschoolers and *also* forms of knowledge that are not easily comprehended by preschoolers. In this sense, both groups are empirically correct but only half right. When one fails to keep the distinction between knowledge and thinking, one either assumes that preschoolers cannot think very well (as Piagetians suggest), or assumes that preschoolers can think really well about many or most things (as post-Piagetians seem to suggest). Both of these assumptions are incorrect in my view. Preschoolers can think very well when given a handful of topics that they have mastered. But when confronted with more difficult ideas (such as many of those presented in school), they perform more poorly (see Byrnes, 1996, for a review). The problem is not with their thinking ability per se, as much as inadequacies in their knowledge. By failing to see the other half of the argument, we have spent too little time charting real changes in knowledge growth that do occur.

Distinction 2: Declarative Versus Procedural Knowledge.   In fields as diverse as philosophy (Hintikka, 1975; Ryle, 1971), psychology (Anderson, 1983; Byrnes, 1988, 1992b; Inhelder & Piaget, 1980), and education (Garner, 1987; Hiebert, 1987), many individuals have advocated the distinction between declarative and procedural knowledge. One's declarative knowledge is the compilation of all of the facts one knows. An individual item of declarative knowledge can be prefaced with "I know that . . ." (e.g., "I know that Harrisburg is the capital of Pennsylvania"). One's procedural knowledge, in contrast, is the compilation of all of the skills, strategies, and algorithms one knows. An individual item of procedural knowledge can be prefaced with "I know how to . . ." (e.g., "I know how to tie my shoes"; "I know how to add fractions"; etc.). To see why so many scholars have advocated the distinction, consider how it is possible to know that shoes have shoelaces (declarative knowledge) but not know how to tie shoes (procedural knowledge). Similarly, it is possible to know that *carta* means letter in

Spanish (declarative knowledge) but not know how to string together a group of Spanish words such that a grammatically correct utterance can be produced (procedural knowledge).

I have recently suggested that there are actually three kinds of knowledge: declarative, conceptual, and procedural (e.g., Byrnes, 1992b). Conceptual knowledge involves comprehension of the meaning of facts and the outcomes of procedures (Inhelder & Piaget, 1980). Clearly, someone can know certain facts (e.g., the rights afforded by the 14th Amendment to the U.S. Constitution) and know the outcome of a procedure (e.g., my car will start when I turn the key) but not understand these facts and outcomes (e.g., why the "founding fathers" added the 14th Amendment and why the cars starts when I turn the key). Conceptual knowledge is relational and puts facts and procedures into the "big picture."

Although the declarative-procedural distinction has been widely advocated, it is not universally endorsed (nor is the declarative-procedural-conceptual trichotomy). Starting with a series of articles written in the 1970s and continuing up to today, a number of artificial intelligence scholars have shown how it is possible to create procedural-only systems that simulate human behavior as well as systems that contain both declarative and procedural subsystems (Newell, Rosenbloom, & Laird, 1989; Winograd, 1975). These empirical findings in conjunction with the prevailing scientific consensus that a more parsimonious explanation is better than a less parsimonious explanation have led many to question the reality of the declarative-procedural distinction. Instead of arguing explicitly against the distinction, some seem to question it in a more subtle way by first describing both forms of knowledge in earlier models and then emphasizing only procedural knowledge in later models (e.g., compare Anderson, 1983, to Anderson, 1995).

In my view, there are three reasons why the distinctions among declarative, procedural, and conceptual knowledge should be maintained. First, philosophers have shown in careful lines of argumentation that declarative knowledge cannot be reduced to procedural knowledge (Hintikka, 1975). Second, cognitive neuropsychologists have revealed the existence of "double dissociations" that tend to confirm separate declarative and procedural representational systems (Kosslyn & Koenig, 1992; Squire, 1987). For example, given certain brain injuries in a specific region of the brain, some individuals acquire impaired syntactic ability but retain their semantic ability; given other injuries located elsewhere in the brain, individuals show relatively impaired semantic ability but retain their synactic ability. Third, educational studies (e.g., Byrnes, 1992b) in which both conceptual and procedural knowledge have been assessed have shown that increased conceptual knowledge (e.g., knowing that -7 is a smaller amount than $+3$) serves as a foundation for procedural knowledge (e.g., knowing how to compute the answer to "$-7 + 3 = ?$"). That is, children with better conceptual understandings learn the procedures better than children with worse conceptual understandings (Geary, 1993).

Taken together, the evidence suggests that even though our minds *could* operate as procedural-only systems, they apparently do *not*. In addition to having implications for education (e.g., one should promote conceptual knowledge prior to introducing procedures), there is another important reason for keeping the distinction among types of knowledge that relates to issues of assessment. Theorists often attribute knowledge to children based on what they can do. For example, when children are asked to seriate a handful of sticks, older children use the strategy of holding the sticks upright on a table (such that all stick bottoms are touching the table top), and successively selecting the largest one left in the bunch (Byrnes, 1988; Piaget, 1965). Absence of this strategy (a form of procedural knowledge) is used to infer absence of knowledge that a stick can be both larger than one stick and smaller than another (conceptual knowledge). Similarly, absence of a search strategy on object permanence tasks is taken as evidence that children lack insight into object permanence (Harris, 1983). For Piagetians who ostensibly care more about concepts than strategies (given the term *concept* in nearly every title of Piaget's books), this overemphasis on strategies at the level of assessment is puzzling. For some post-Piagetians who study strategies exclusively and never really emphasize concepts (e.g., Pressley, Johnson, Symons, McGoldrick, & Kurita, 1989; Siegler, 1991), it is my view they have captured only half of development. Given the possibility that a individual child could have just one kind of knowledge (e.g., declarative but not conceptual or procedural), it is imperative that careful analysis be given to what kinds of knowledge are required on a given task. It is wrong for Piagetians to assume that comprehension of relative size is necessarily absent when the "table-holding" strategy is absent, but it is also wrong for post-Piagetians to assume that a full competence has been instilled in a child merely because he or she can be taught a strategy. Such a child may have no idea of what he or she is doing (at a conceptual level). When the distinctions among declarative, procedural, and conceptual knowledge are maintained, one recognizes that the data amassed by the Piagetians and post-Piagetians is not as contradictory as it seems. It actually is quite complementary.

Distinction 3: Implicit Versus Explicit Knowledge.   Some scholars treat the declarative-procedural distinction as if it were the same as the implicit–explicit distinction. Squire (1987), for example, suggested that being able to declare or say something about one's knowledge is what is meant by declarative knowledge. Procedural knowledge, in contrast, refers to computations or processes that are carried out in one's mind at an unconscious level (according to Squire). Examples include syntactic parsing and priming. Squire used his definition of the declarative-procedural distinction to explain deficits in individuals who acquire amnesia following damage to the hippocampus region in their temporal lobes. Whereas many of these amnesics show preserved procedural ability (e.g., they can still parse sentences and are likely to fill in the blank in "_at" with "b" after being primed with the word "bat"), they have great difficulty forming permanent encodings of new declarative information (e.g., the name of their new neurosurgeon). Given such findings, Squire has postulated that damage to the hippocampus primarily causes a permanent loss in the ability to store new declarative knowledge. That these amnesics can recall facts that they learned prior to their injury implies that the hippocampus is not a storage site and that storage sites are located elsewhere in the brain.

In my view, the implicit–explicit distinction is largely orthogonal to the declarative-procedural-conceptual distinction. Although it is difficult to conceive of someone who can be said to "know" a fact but not be able to consciously reflect on this fact and express it, it is possible for someone to have both implicit and explicit representations of conceptual and procedural knowledge. To illustrate implicit conceptual knowledge, consider the case of categorization. A child may implicitly abstract the physical properties that are relevant to distinguishing between one object and another (e.g., a dog vs. a horse), but be unaware of the properties that he or she uses to categorize these objects. For example, note how preverbal infants can form such perceptual categories (Mandler, 1992). In a similar way, a number of studies show that adults who view the credentials of applicants are often unaware of the characteristics that impress them when they place applicants into various categories (e.g., "admit" vs. "reject"; Nisbett & Wilson, 1977). Over time, implicit knowledge related to categorization and other conceptual enterprises can become available to conscious reflection; that is, implicit knowledge can become explicit knowledge (Karmiloff-Smith, 1992). A similar pattern of implicit use followed by explicit awareness has been found for procedures in domains as diverse as language and mathematics (e.g., Siegler & Jenkins, 1989).

As was the case for the first two distinctions described earlier, the primary implication of the implicit–explicit distinction pertains to the issue of assessment and what we can say about the real age trends in knowledge. Children and adults may not always be consciously aware of their knowledge or be able to express what they know. Implicit knowledge may have to be revealed through appropriate use of this knowledge, or through the detection of misuse of knowledge by others. For example, inference of grammatical rules or categories can be made on the basis of appropriate use (Pinker, 1989; Karmiloff-Smith, 1992) as can knowledge of principles in domains such as physics and math (Karmiloff-Smith, 1992; Gelman & Greeno, 1990). The possibility of implicit knowledge also calls into question the validity of the Piagetian clinical interview as well as the "think aloud" methodology that is common in the problem-solving literature (Ericsson & Simon, 1984). At minimum, one might infer absence of competence if the interviewee cannot articulate what he or she knows. At maximum, an individual's articulation may be at odds with what they know (Nisbett & Wilson, 1977; Siegler & Jenkins, 1989). That is, they may say they are doing one thing and really doing another.

It would seem that most scholars now acknowledge the existence of both implicit and explicit knowledge. And yet, acknowledging the existence of the distinction does not resolve all controversies related to it. For example, whereas some argue that young children have naive "theories" as long as they can use theory-related knowledge to make inferences and so forth (e.g., Carey, 1985b; Wellman, 1990), others suggest that a theory cannot be attributed to an individual until that individual has metacognitive access to his or her theory-related knowledge and can make a conscious distinction between a theory and the evidence that supports this theory (e.g., Kuhn, 1989). It strikes me that both positions can be accommodated if we adopt the convention of labeling the former competence an *implicit theory* and the latter an *explicit* (or *mature*) *theory*.

Distinction 4: Concrete Versus Abstract.   An assumption that is common to the approaches of Piaget, Vygotsky, and schema theorists is that knowledge can exist at different levels of abstraction (Byrnes, 1996). All of these scholars have argued that an experience can be encoded and stored in a format that is very "close" to the sensory impression of this experience (i.e., a veridical sensory trace of the experience, analogous to a photograph). However, they also argue that over time, the brain somehow abstracts what is common to related experiences and retains only this abstracted information; details and specific sensory-based representations are not retained. This common emphasis on abstraction, generalization processes, and partial decontextualization of knowledge makes these approaches different than a Thorndikean associationism or even some of the newer "situated cognition" approaches (e.g., Brown, Collins, & Duguid, 1989).

And yet, whereas the approaches of Piaget, Vygotsky, and schema theorists are similar in their emphasis on the difference between concrete knowledge (i.e., representations tied to immediate action or perception) and abstract knowledge (i.e., representations that reflect commonalities across concrete representations), these theorists nevertheless differ with respect to whether they describe a single type of abstract knowledge or multiple levels of abstract knowledge. For a Piagetian, for example, there is a difference between a mental image of a set of objects (e.g., an image of three apples), mathematical symbols corresponding to numbers (e.g., "3") and mathematical symbols corresponding to variables (e.g., "X" or "Y"). Each of these representations is abstract to a certain degree (e.g., even the image is a schema for all experiences with three apples), but they represent three distinct levels of abstraction (Byrnes, 1996). To my knowledge, neither Vygotskians nor schema theorists subdivide representations into multiple levels of abstraction in the same way.

Theorists in these three camps do not seem to have argued in print about whether there is one or more levels of abstraction, so it is possible that the difference in approaches has more to do with a difference in precision among the theories than an actual difference in beliefs. In my view, it is worthwhile to envision at least two levels of abstraction because the data suggest that different levels may exist. For example, whereas children seem to represent basic-level categories very early (e.g., categories for dog, cat, etc.), they do not seem to represent superordinate categories (e.g., animals) until much later (Callanan, 1991). Similarly, children have far less conceptual difficulty with whole numbers than they have with more abstract rational numbers (e.g., fractions, decimals) or variables (Byrnes, 1996).

Inasmuch as less abstract knowledge is acquired earlier in development than more abstract knowledge, it might be proposed (as Piaget did) that there are knowledge-based developmental constraints on what children can learn at different ages. The phenomenon of "talking over children's heads" is something that Piagetian or Vygotskian theory can account for, but not something that would be immediately predicted by schema theorists. Some would question the degree of "resistance" that is put up by current levels of knowledge and argue that the "concrete followed-by abstract" developmental trend is an artifact of what children are exposed to. For example, parents use basic-level terms before they use superordinate terms (Callanan, 1991). The implication seems to be that if parents were to use superordinate terms, children would acquire them as early and easily as they acquire basic-level terms. To my knowledge, this expectation has not been confirmed in experiments. In addition, few schools have deviated from the standard curriculum of presenting concrete ideas and then presenting abstract ideas later, so it is not clear what children could learn in earlier grades if abstract ideas were presented to them. My own view is that there are real constraints that would limit what a child could learn at a given age (e.g., a 4-year-old could not comprehend variables no matter how clever the presentation), but perhaps the window of successful assimilation presumed by Piagetians is too high. For example, Piagetians may believe that only 11-year-olds could comprehend variables but in fact 8-year-olds can. So, once again the post-Piagetians may be wrong in assuming that even 4-year-olds could understand third-level abstract ideas and Piagetians may be wrong in assuming that only 11-year-olds can. Empirical research is needed to document the actual windows of assimilation, but I think the studies will show that there are real constraints that reflect the fact that it takes time for the mind to create and comprehend second-order and third-order abstractions.

Distinction 5: Domain-Specific Versus Domain-General. In many ways, the distinction between domain-general and domain-specific knowledge overlaps with the second distinction that I described earlier. Declarative knowledge is inherently domain-specific because facts usually contribute to the core of a single domain. In psychology, for example, there are facts such as "most of the high scorers on the SAT-math (Scholastic Aptitude Test) are male" and "most of the top scorers on national assessments for writing are female." Of course, depending on the perceived boundaries of several related disciplines (e.g., sociology vs. psychology), a set of facts may be judged to be part of multiple disciplines (e.g., sociologists and psychologists are both interested in facts about gender differences). This does not make the shared facts domain-general, however. The notion of domain-general pertains to concepts, processes, or procedures that *can be applied* to content (including facts) from multiple domains (Byrnes, 1995). So, concepts such as "equality" can be applied to both mathematical and moral content. Similarly, processes such as inference making and attention are domain-general because we can make inferences about, and pay attention to, information from any domain. Finally, we can use the domain-general strategy of summarizing (a form of procedural knowledge) to help us comprehend and retain information from books about various topics (e.g., social studies, science, literature, etc.). Any given concept, process, or procedure may be (a) completely domain-general (i.e., it can be applied to any content), (b) only partially domain-general (i.e., it can be applied to several but not all types of content), or (c) domain-specific (e.g., parsing for language).

In sum, then, whereas declarative knowledge can be only domain-specific, cognitive processes, conceptual knowledge, and procedural knowledge can be both domain-specific and domain-general. There are a variety of implications of this analysis for the debate between Piagetians and post-Piagetians, and also for the debate between theorists who believe that intelligence is domain-specific (e.g., Ceci, 1990) and theorists who believe that intelligence is more domain-general (e.g., Jensen, 1987). In what follows, I describe some of these implications.

What does it mean to say that competencies such as concrete operations or intelligence are domain-general? Let's start with the evidence for domain-generality that is pertinent to Piaget's theory. It is empirically true that if one gives classic concrete operations tasks to children between the ages of 5 and 10, one finds the identical responses described by Piaget in his original books. For conservation tasks, for example, one finds that there is an age (e.g., age 5) in which most (75%) children say the amount of something has changed by an action that really does not change the quantity (e.g., flattening a clay ball), and another later age (e.g., age 7) in which most children say that the amount has not been changed. The problem for Piaget is not that the "same-followed-by-more" response sequence is not what he found; rather, the problem is that the ages at which the responses are found differ among formally similar conservation tasks. For Piaget, concrete operations is a domain-general competency because the consistent pattern of "more" followed by "same" is found for a number of different contents. For the post-Piagetians, thinking is not domain-general because the correct "same" response is not provided for all conservation tasks at the same age.

When viewed in this way, it is clear that there is a fundamental difference in how the two groups define the notion of domain-general. Whereas Piagetians focused on the way a child (or groups of children) conceptualized different contents at different times, post-Piagetians focused on how a single child conceptualized all of the contents at the same point in time. A theorist on one side of the debate (e.g., the Piagetian side) could try to resolve disagreements by attempting to convince others that his or her definition of domain-generality is better than the other definition, but such an approach would not really resolve the debate because there still would be a whole group of scholars who would remain unconvinced and prefer the opposite definition. In my view, a more profitable approach is to focus on the distinctions among facts, concepts, procedures, and processes. When one does, one finds that knowledge and processes are both domain-general and domain-specific. The emphasis shifts from questioning whether knowledge and processes are domain-general to considering questions such as (a) what experiences promote the transfer of concepts and skills across domains? (e.g., Singley & Anderson, 1989), (b) why is it that conservation of weight often occurs later than conservation of number? and (c) why is it that a collection of Piagetian tasks does not form a Guttman scale (i.e., the same order of acquisition for all children)? Piagetians and post-Piagetians who are not troubled by their own preferred definitions of domain-general would never try to answer these questions. That is, the post-Piagetians are content to use the finding that tasks are not acquired all at once as evidence against the domain-general view and leave it at that. The Piagetians, in contrast, do not see the lack of simultaneity (or the lack of an orderly sequence) as a threat to their definition of domain-general. As a result, neither group has tried to answer the previous three questions and we still have major gaps in our knowledge of cognitive development.

Turning next to the debate between the two camps of intelligence theorists, a different set of issues keep them apart. Intelligence tests such as the Wechsler Intelligence Scale for Children–Revised (WISC–R) and Stanford–Binet assess both cognitive processes (inference making, attention, problem solving, retrieval) and all three types of knowledge (declarative, procedural, and conceptual) in multiple domains. As a result, these tests tap into both domain-specific and domain-general processes and knowledge. One could not obtain an overall high IQ if one lacked knowledge, but one could do well on individual scales without substantial knowledge in multiple domains (e.g., coding or block design on the WISC–R). In contrast, tests such as the Raven's Progressive matrices rely far less on prior knowledge and more on cognitive processes (e.g., induction). Conceivably, the processes used on the Raven's could be used to reason about any content, so the test can be said to tap into domain-general aspects of intelligence.

Given this analysis, it is clear that both tests measure domain-general processes or domain-general knowledge. I cannot imagine how anyone could argue otherwise. Thus, as Sternberg (1989) noted, it is pointless to continue the debate about whether intelligence is domain-general or domain-specific. Some components of intelligence are domain-general (e.g., allocation of attention and speed of processing) and some are domain-specific (e.g., knowledge of the important concepts, procedures, and strategies of a single domain like math). Instead of asking whether both types of intelligence exist, I have argued that it is more useful to ask questions such as, Which type of intelligence is more important for explaining achievement in specific subject areas in school? My review of the literature shows that in 80% of published studies, domain-specific knowledge is far more important in explaining performance than domain-general intelligence (Byrnes, 1995). But note that both are equally important in the remaining 20% of studies and that even when domain-specific knowledge explains triple the variance in performance, domain-general intelligence often explains 10% of the variance.

Distinction 6: Ad Hoc (Short-Term) Versus Permanent. Consider the following question: Which city is farther east, Philadelphia or Baltimore? To answer this question, many people would probably consult their mental representation of the map of the United States and try to "read" off of this internal map. The correct answer is Philadelphia. If a researcher were to use this task as part of an experiment, he or she might give credit to subjects for "knowing" the correct answer when they reply "Philadelphia." But it is unlikely that subjects' represented knowledge of Philadelphia contains the fact "farther east than Baltimore." Creating or deriving a new fact online in response to a question is an example of what Barsalou (1991) called *ad hoc knowledge.* In cognitive psychological terms, we would say that derived facts are *working memory representations* that have no counterpart in long-term or permanent memory (Anderson, 1995). Ad hoc knowledge can be contrasted with permanent *records* in long-term memory that are embodied in a pattern of synaptic connections. An example would be "a large city in Pennsylvania" as part of one's nonderived factual knowledge of Philadelphia. When someone says "It's a large city in Pennsylvania" when told, "Tell me everything you know about Philadelphia," then the inference that the person knows this fact is a more appropriate attribution than when one assumes knowledge when it could be derived online.

The distinction between ad hoc and permanent knowledge has enormous implications for what we know about the cognitive competence of children, adolescents, and adults. Consider the case of categorical knowledge. One of the major claims of Piaget was that whereas knowledge in preschoolers is not hierarchically arranged (e.g., categories of dog and cat are not linked through a superordinate category of animal), knowledge in children older than 6 is usually organized into hierarchies (Inhelder & Piaget, 1964). When a child is given a shuffled deck of pictures of animals, food, and vehicles and asked to sort them (as Piagetians and many others have done), a child who groups dogs and cats together into the same pile might be credited with hierarchical knowledge. That is, placing dogs and cats together is used to infer that these categories really are linked together in the child's permanent memory. However, the action of sorting may actually prompt a child to form an ad hoc category online. The child sees the similarity only in the midst of being asked to do so and creates a category on the spot. Similarly, when asked questions such as "If all the animals in the world were to die, would there be any dogs left?" a child who does not have "is an animal" encoded in his or her knowledge of dogs may nevertheless be able to compute the correct answer via multiple inferences (e.g., "an animal is an alive thing that moves; a dog is alive and moves, so I guess it's an animal; . . . therefore it would die too"). Once again, older children who say "no" to this question might be credited with hierarchical knowledge when in fact their knowledge is not so arranged.

Most preschoolers do not sort objects in a manner suggestive of a hierarchy and many cannot provide the correct answer to questions like that just mentioned about animals dying. A number of post-Piagetians have questioned the validity of Piaget's claim that knowledge is nonhierarchical in preschoolers' minds because they felt that Piaget's tasks were unnecessarily difficult or insensitive. To reveal hierarchical knowledge in preschoolers, post-Piagetians have tried to create less difficult and more sensitive tasks. For example, they have used triads of pictures (e.g., a cat, a dog, and a truck) and asked "Which of these two (the dog or truck) is more like this one (the cat)?" (Rosch, Mervis, Gray, Johnson, & Boyes-Braem, 1976). Or, they have used the inductive projection technique of attributing a characteristic to an object (e.g., "People have spleens") and asking whether other objects have the same characteristic (e.g., "Do dogs have spleens too?") (e.g., Carey, 1985b). Objects that are attributed the same characteristics are then assumed to be mentally linked through a hierarchy. Contrary to Piaget's findings, research using the triads and inductive projection techiques have revealed responses suggestive of hierarchical knowledge in preschoolers.

But being able to note the similarity between cats and dogs when examining pictures does not mean that cats and dogs are mentally linked in permanent memory. The task itself could prompt the creation of an ad hoc category. To illustrate this notion in my own case, I recently was asked to discuss a paper by Hayne Reese that revealed a similarity between Skinnerian and Vygotskian theory (i.e., both are contextualists). I computed the similarity while I read the paper, but did not have these theorists linked in my mind before reading the paper. Similarly, a child's guesses about what objects should have a spleen if people do could also be computed following an online assessment of the similarity of people and other things like dogs. So, just as Piagetians may have attributed hierarchies to older children when hierarchies may not exist in older children's minds, post-Piagetians may have misattributed hierarchies to younger children.

What all of the categorization tasks may have revealed is the ability to note similarities in objects—not the actual constitution or organization of knowledge in permanent memory. To be sure, noting similarities requires having knowledge in memory, but seeking links between items is not the same as having these links represented in permanent memory.

I selected categorization as an example, but note that measures of any other form of knowledge may equally confuse the ability to compute answers online and having the right answers already in memory. As long as we are clear about what we are testing, the distinction is not an intractable problem. But when there is a debate about the existence of a particular form of knowledge in children's mind, it is crucial that we can show that knowledge has not been constructed online. Once again, the seeming chasm between the Piagetian and post-Piagetian claims may be smaller than once thought. If all of the categorization tasks really measure only similarity detection, then the post-Piagetians have used a technique that has worked for them multiple times before (as I noted in my discussion of other distinctions): Find a form of knowledge that even Piaget would agree is within children's competence and then reveal the ability. In the case of categorization, the skill in question is the ability to note perceptual similarities between objects. Piaget claimed that this is one of the hallmarks of pre-operational thought (Piaget, 1962) and even infants can note similarities (Piaget, 1980). But again, the larger issue is that the failure of most researchers to make the distinction between ad hoc and permanent representations means that we may still have a lot to learn about the reality of children's knowledge (e.g., when, if ever, do children have hierarchical knowledge in memory?).

In my own work, I became aware of ad hoc categories when I investigated children's comprehension of uncertainty. Most researchers who have studied uncertainty use tasks that require children to mentally group objects together online. For example, one task requires them to group a marble and a thin stick together in category that might be called "objects that could fit in a marble-sized hole." When told that one of these objects was placed into the hole (and they cannot see which one was placed), creation of this category allows them to comprehend that they do not know which object was placed (Byrnes & Beilin, 1991). Clearly, I do not think they have a permanent record of "objects that fit inside marble-sized holes," but success on these tasks requires the ability to form ad hoc categories.

Distinction 7: Can Versus Do.   The distinction between can and do relates to two sets of notions: (a) the Piagetian notion of graduated levels of performance, and (b) the Vygotskian notions of zone of proximal development and scaffolding. With respect to the notion of graduated levels of performance, one merely has to take any data-based book written by Piaget to see how he characterized children's responses in terms of six levels of performance (e.g., Level I-A, Level I-B, Level II-A, Level II-B, Level III-A, and Level III-B). With the exception of the totally correct response (Level III-B), each of the other five levels represents responses that are either a little (e.g., Level III-A) or a great deal off of the correct response (e.g., Level I-A). I suspect that when many researchers initially confront any of these analyses, they feel that Piaget was too strict in his scoring and should have given credit to responses near to the correct response (e.g., Levels II-B and III-A). For example, in some cases, children give the right response and can explain their answer, but when given a counterexample, they fall apart. Their failure to maintain the right response might get them a lower Level III-A scoring instead of a higher Level III-B scoring. Or, on a conservation task, children may have to count or measure to give the right response instead of knowing immediately that the quantities have been unchanged. Such near misses are also likely to be labeled Level III-A instead of Level III-B. Regardless, the feeling one gets from reading all of these books is that knowledge is not all-or-none. Rather, there is progressive insight into the phenomenon of interest. When one takes this apparent six-tiered continuum and creates a dichotomy (e.g, the first five levels = preoperational; the sixth = concrete operational), the notion of progressive insight seems to be lost.

In Vygotskian terms, Level III-B is what Vygotsky (1978) called the "independent mastery" level of performance. All (or several) of the prior levels could potentially provide the foundation for a higher level response if children are given appropriate hints and structure. In other words, a preoperational child could be helped to provide the concrete operational response with a little scaffolding. I am unaware of studies that have tested how much of a hint or scaffold is needed to produce the correct response in children, but it seems the Piagetian notion of levels could be synthesized to the Vygotskian notion of zone of proximal development. Moreover, it is reasonable to expect that whereas Level I-A children would need lots of hints and support to get the right answer, Level III-A children would need few hints and only a little structure.

My point is that children can often do a lot more with help than they can do without help or prodding (hence, the distinction between can and do). I view the majority of post-Piagetian studies as being very Vygotskian in the following sense: Researchers endeavored to create situations that either eliminated obstacles or provided scaffolds that would increase the likelihood that younger children would provide the correct response. Given what I have said so far, some of the scaffolds include (a) employing content that children are knowledgeable about (Distinction 1), (b) assessing children's implicit knowledge rather than their explicit knowledge (Distinction 3), and (c) employing concrete, imaginable content as opposed to abstract content (Distinction 4). But the fact that children *can* demonstrate competence at a particular age does not mean that they *do* demonstrate this competence on a regular basis on their own at home. I, for one, can be made to look quite competent in computer programming when I am given a great deal of scaffolding but am unable to solve hardware or software problems on my own at home. The point of cognitive developmental research is to reveal children's typical competencies so that we can say something about the natural history of cognition. If we scaffold too much in the lab, we may be painting an unrealistically optimistic portrait of children's competencies. I find it particularly striking how infants look so competent in math (e.g., Wynn, 1992) yet the same infant grows up to perform so poorly on Piagetian number tasks, national assessments of math, and the SAT.

Again, the answer to the debate between the Piagetians and the post-Piagetians is that they are both half-right and half-wrong. One should not interpret the numerous Piagetian findings as indicating that children who provide responses below Level III-B are completely incompetent. Similarly, one should not view the post-Piagetian research as indicating that infants and preschoolers can do everything that Piaget said they could not do. As long as 5-year-olds fail the Piagetian version of some task but pass the post-Piagetian version of the same task, the data suggest that researchers in both camps are empirically correct. One cannot deny the data, but one can attempt to explain why a child fails one task while passing the other. Moreover, it is important to explain why children need help at one point and do not need help at a later point. Something has changed in their minds to allow this progression, but neither the Piagetians nor post-Piagetians (including the Vygotskians) have provided sufficiently detailed explanations of this "something."

Distinction 8: Innate Versus Constructed Versus Learned. According to my definition of representation, to say that some aspect of knowledge (or a specific representation of something) is *innate* is to say that children come into the world with a pattern of synaptic connections that immediately helps them to identify or recognitize an object (e.g., their mother's face) or class of objects (e.g., the human face). That a newborn child looks at one object more than she looks at other objects does not mean that she has an innate representation of the preferred object. It may simply mean that she is innately predisposed to attend to certain types of stimulation (e.g., contrasts and movement) that are provided by the preferred object. After several exposures to the object, she may form a pattern of synaptic connections that corresponds to the object. When she does, she moves from being interested in stimulation to recognizing the object. Forming a pattern of synaptic connections that corresponds to specific environmental or internal stimulation is what is meant by *learning*.

The same stimulation that is provided to two different visual systems (e.g., that of a human vs. a fly) would presumably create two distinct representations of the object. In this sense, the representation is partly structured by the physical stimulation provided by the object (e.g., the frequencies of light rays) and partly structured by what the "hardware" of the visual system makes of the stimulation. So, even the "pure" empiricist would acknowledge the role of innately specified hardware in learning (Byrnes, 1992a). We do not see certain frequencies of light and do not hear certain frequencies of sound. Thus, we cannot form representations of experiences that contain these frequencies. In other words, we cannot learn from these experiences in the empiricist sense of the word *learn*. But if all that has been provided are innate constraints imposed by sensitivity to a range of stimulation, that is not what one means by innate knowledge. My computer can only "read" documents that are written in Word-Perfect. This constraint is not the same as having a chapter already written on the hard disk when I buy the machine. The latter would be analogous to innate knowledge.

Individuals who identify themselves as nativists (e.g., Chomsky, 1980) recognize that specific elements of knowledge (e.g., the grammatical rules of English) are not innate. What is innate has to be more abstract to be universally applied to various instantiations of the knowledge in question (e.g., English syntax vs. Russian syntax). So, what is common to multiple instances of a general class of representations is what is innately specified. That way, children can recognize an instance of something when they see it (e.g., a noun in either English or Russian; the number three in any group of three objects; etc.). If this account is correct, then ultimately it should be possible to verify it by inspecting the neuronal structure of young children. If we could figure out how specific patterns of neuronal connectivity correspond to a specific representation (e.g., how "noun" or "three" is represented by a group of neurons), then the nativist view could be validated by finding the pattern already configured at birth or showing how the pattern becomes configured over time in response to maturational factors (e.g., growth hormone), not experiential factors (e.g., stimulation promotes synaptogenesis; Squire, 1987).

I am not saying that neuropsychology is likely to provide the only way to resolve the debates among the nativists, constructivists, and empiricists; instead, I am saying that it is a very promising way. Until we know what knowledge "looks like" at the neuronal level and know more about what happens to neurons when we form a representation of something, we cannot really say whether a specific aspect of knowledge is innate, constructed, or simply learned. Once we learn more about the links between neurology and knowledge, we will be able say (a) when knowledge has emerged via maturation (supporting the nativists), (b) when a conceptual link has been imposed by a child and does not seem to have emerged due to maturation or direct instruction (supporting the constructivists), and (c) when an unelaborated, sensation-based representation for an object has formed (supporting the empiricists).

Elsewhere I have noted that there is evidence that seems to support the viability of all three epistemologies (Byrnes, 1992a). That is, one can find examples of knowledge that support each epistemology. In my view, nativism, constructivism, and empiricism work like special divining rods that point a theorist toward specific kinds of knowledge. For example, one does not find a nativist trying to explain how children learn the names of the 50 states (as an empiricist would). Similarly, Piaget intentionally focused on topics that were not taught in school and showed that children's reasoning was often at odds with what they could observe in adults (e.g., My 2-year-old recently bumped his head and said, "I hurt my haircut"). Piaget did not focus on topics that may be innate (e.g., aspects of language) nor did he focus on factual knowledge that could be learned by rote. Thus, it is possible that all three epistemologies are correct for certain subsets of knowledge. Thousands of years of philosophical argumentation has not resolved the debates among adherents to the three epistemologies and I do not believe argumentation ever could resolve these debates. I also believe, however, that traditional experiments will not resolve them either, because it is usually possible to construct an account that is consistent with any of the three epistemologies. That is why I have argued that a new approach is needed (e.g., cognitive neuropsychology or some other approach).

In the meantime, part of the way around the debates is to ask questions such as, What is innate and what is constructed (e.g., Karmiloff-Smith, 1992)? If specific representations are not innate, then what might be (abstract universals like "noun" or more basic tendencies like similarity seeking?)? That is, instead of asking whether all knowledge is innate, constructed, or learned, one assumes that some knowledge is innate, some is constructed, and some is learned. The task for cognitive developmentalists is to determine which is which.

CONCLUSION

One of the nicest things about being a scientist (as opposed to a philosopher) is the focus on data and possible explanations of it. If Piaget merely advocated constructivism at a philosophical level and the post-Piagetians simply supplied elegant counterarguments, there would be little hope that the debates among these two groups would be ever resolved. As I have repeatedly shown in this chapter, there are data in support of both perspectives and it is not possible to explain away the existence of one or the other set of findings. The task for contemporary scholars is to figure out how *both* of these traditions could be right in a nontrivial way. I have begun to develop a nontrivial synthesis by examining eight distinctions that relate to the nature of representation.

When viewed as a set, the eight distinctions demonstrate the complexity of representation in the human mind. I realize that acknowledging the reality of the distinctions goes against conventions of parsimony, but if the data suggest that a more parsimonious model is insufficient, we have to accept the less parsimonious model. Note that any given representation or cognitive process may be a specific combination of the elements of the eight distinctions. For example, a single representation may exemplify implicit, domain-general, procedural knowledge. If the elements of each distinction develop in a particular pattern (e.g., implicit before explicit, domain-specific before domain-general, etc.), then certain combinations would be expected to be acquired later in development than others (e.g., explicit-domain-general acquired much later than implicit-domain-specific). If so, then when two researchers find different age trends for seemingly the "same" competence, it could easily be due to the fact that one focused on a given combination of distinction elements (e.g., implicit, domain-specific) and the other focused on a different combination (e.g., explicit, domain-general). Thus, the findings really do not contradict each other. In fact, when one views the Piagetian and post-Piagetian findings within the perspective of the eight distinctions, the findings make perfect sense and cohere together nicely.

In sum, instead of viewing the last 30 years of research as evidence that the field of developmental psychology is disintegrating, I view the debate between the Piagetians and post-Piagetians to be quite useful and illuminating. If the two groups did not find different age trends, I would not have asked myself, How could they both be right? If we remained content with the Piagetian account, we would have never emphasized the importance of, say, implicit or domain-specific knowledge. Similarly, had the post-Piagetians not used Piagetian findings against Piaget (e.g., using object permanence in preschoolers to reveal insight into uncertainty), the important distinction between knowledge and thinking would not have been made so salient. What seems very clear to me after I have conducted this analysis is that representational (i.e., knowledge) change lies at the heart of cognitive development. It is time we stopped showing that good thinking is possible in infants and preschoolers and begun to study *why and how representations change.*

The other important implication of the present analysis is that many researchers may have been too imprecise in how they assessed children's knowledge. That is, they may not have carefully considered whether their tasks require implicit or explicit knowledge, ad hoc or permanent knowledge, and so on. Thus, the view of cognitive development that is presented in standard textbooks could easily change if researchers were to take the eight dimensions seriously and apply them when conducting their own research and evaluating the research of others (e.g., as when we act as journal reviewers). When we say that children do or do not demonstrate an ability (e.g., deductive reasoning), what exactly do we mean? According to the present analysis, we have to qualify our claims with respect to the distinctions. To argue that a competence is totally lacking, we have to show that children would not do better if the content were changed, or scaffolds were provided, or if they could detect errors in others, and so on. Conversely, to claim that a competence is present in young children (e.g., in infants or preschoolers), we have to be careful to recognize that a higher order version of the same competence may not be available until later (e.g., when it can be applied to more abstract content in an explicit way).

REFERENCES

Anderson, J. R. (1983). *The architecture of cognition.* Cambridge, MA: Harvard University Press.
Anderson, J. R. (1995). *Learning and memory: An integrated approach.* New York: Wiley.
Barsalou, L. W. (1991). Deriving categories to achieve goals. *Psychology of Learning and Motivation— Advances in Research and Theory, 27,* 1–64.
Bransford, J., Sherwood, R., Vye, N., & Rieser, J. (1986). Teaching thinking and problem solving. *American Psychologist, 41,* 1078–1089.

Brown, J. S., Collins, A., & Duguid, P. (1989). Situated cognition and the culture of learning. *Educational Researcher, 18*, 32–42.

Byrnes, J. P. (1988). Formal operations: A systematic reformulation. *Developmental Review, 8*, 1–22.

Byrnes, J. P. (1992a). Categorizing and combining theories of cognitive development and learning. *Educational Psychology Review, 4*, 309–343.

Byrnes, J. P. (1992b). The conceptual basis of procedural learning. *Cognitive Development, 7*, 235–257.

Byrnes, J. P. (1995). Domain-specificity and the logic of using general ability as an independent variable or covariate. *Merrill–Palmer Quarterly, 41*, 1–24.

Byrnes, J. P. (1996). *Cognitive development and learning in instructional contexts*. Boston: Allyn & Bacon.

Byrnes, J. P., & Beilin, H. (1991). The cognitive basis of uncertainty. *Human Development, 34*, 189–203.

Callanan, M. A. (1991). Parent–child collaboration in young children's understanding of category hierarchies. In S. A. Gelman & J. P. Byrnes (Eds.), *Perspectives on language and thought: Interrelations in development* (pp. 440–484). Cambridge, England: Cambridge University Press.

Carey, S. (1985a). Are children fundamentally different thinkers and learners from adults? In S. F. Chipman, J. W. Segal, & R. Glaser (Eds.), *Thinking and learning skills* (Vol. 2, pp. 485–517). Hillsdale, NJ: Lawrence Erlbaum Associates.

Carey, S. (1985b). *Conceptual change in childhood*. Cambridge, MA: MIT Press.

Ceci, S. J. (1990). *On intelligence . . . more or less: A bio-ecological treatise on intellectual development*. Englewood Cliffs, NJ: Prentice-Hall.

Chomsky, N. (1980). *Rules and representations*. New York: Columbia University Press.

Dias, M. G., & Harris, P. L. (1988). The effect of make-believe play on deductive reasoning. *British Journal of Developmental Psychology, 6*, 207–221.

Ericsson, K. A., & Simon, H. A. (1984). *Protocol analysis: Verbal reports as data*. Cambridge, MA: MIT Press.

Flavell, J. A., Miller, P. A., & Miller, S. A. (1993). *Cognitive development* (3rd ed.). Englewood Cliffs, NJ: Prentice-Hall.

Fodor, J. A. (1975). *The language of thought*. Cambridge, MA: Harvard University Press.

Garner, R. (1987). Strategies for reading and studying expository text. *Educational Psychologist, 22*, 299–312.

Geary, D. C. (1993). Mathematical disabilities: Cognitive, neuropsychological, and genetic components. *Psychological Bulletin, 114*, 345–362.

Gelman, R., & Greeno, J. G. (1989). On the nature of competence: Principles for understanding in a domain. In L. B. Resnick (Ed.), *Knowing, learning, and instruction: Essays in honor of Robert Glaser* (pp. 125–186). Hillsdale, NJ: Lawrence Erlbaum Associates.

Gholson, B., & Barker, P. (1985). Kuhn, Lakatos, and Laudan—Applications in the history of physics and psychology. *American Psychologist, 40*, 755–769.

Harris, P. L. (1983). Infant cognition. In M. M. Haith & J. J. Campos (Eds.), *Handbook of child psychology: Vol 2. Infancy and developmental psychobiology* (pp. 689–782). New York: Wiley.

Hawkins, J., Pea, R. D., Glick, J., & Scribner, S. (1984). "Merds that laugh don't like mushrooms": Evidence for deductive reasoning by preschoolers. *Developmental Psychology, 20*, 584–594.

Hiebert, J. (1987). *Conceptual and procedural knowledge: The case of mathematics*. Hillsdale, NJ: Lawrence Erlbaum Associates.

Hintikka, J. K. J. (1975). *The intentions of intentionality and other new models for modality*. Boston: Reidel.

Inhelder, B., & Piaget, J. (1958). *The growth of logical thinking from childhood to adolescence*. New York: Basic Books.

Inhelder, B., & Piaget, J. (1964). *The early growth of logic in the child*. New York: Basic Books.

Inhelder, B., & Piaget, J. (1980). Procedures and structures. In D. R. Olson (Ed.), *The social foundations of language and thought* (pp. 19–27). New York: Norton.

Jensen, A. R. (1987). The *g* factor beyond factor analysis. In R. R. Ronning, J. A. Glover, J. A. Conoley, & J. C. Witt (Eds.), *The influence of cognitive psychology on testing* (pp. 87–142). Hillsdale, NJ: Lawrence Erlbaum Associates.

Karmiloff-Smith, A. (1992). *Beyond modularity: A developmental perspective on cognitive science.* Cambridge, MA: MIT Press.

Kosslyn, S. M., & Koenig, O. (1992). *Wet mind: The new cognitive neuroscience.* New York: The Free Press.

Kuhn, D. (1989). Children and adults as intuitive scientists. *Psychological Review, 96,* 674–689.

Mandler, J. M. (1992). How to build a baby II: Conceptual primitives. *Psychological Review, 99,* 587–604.

Newell, A., Rosenbloom, P. S., & Laird, J. E. (1989). Symbolic architectures for cognition. In M. I. Posner (Ed.), *Foundations of cognitive science* (pp. 93–131). Cambridge, MA: MIT Press.

Nisbett, R. E., & Wilson, D. T. (1977). Telling more than we can know: Verbal reports on mental processes. *Psychological Review, 84,* 231–259.

Piaget, J. (1962). *Play, dreams, and imitation.* New York: Norton.

Piaget, J. (1965). *The child's conception of number.* New York: Norton.

Piaget, J. (1980). *Recherches in sur les correspondances* [Research on correspondences]. Paris: Universitaires de France.

Piaget, J. (1987). *Possibility and necessity: Vol. 1. The role of possibility in cognitive development.* Minneapolis: University of Minnesota Press.

Pinker, S. (1989). Language acquisition. In M. I. Posner (Ed.), *Foundations of cognitive science* (pp. 359–400). Cambridge, MA: MIT Press.

Pressley, M., Johnson, C. J., Symons, S., McGoldrick, J A., & Kurita, J. A. (1989). Strategies that improve children's memory and comprehension of text. *The Elementary School Journal, 90,* 3–32.

Pylyshyn, Z. W. (1984). *Computation and cognition.* Cambridge, MA: MIT Press.

Rosch, E., Mervis, C. B., Gray, W. D., Johnson, D. M., & Boyes-Braem, P. (1976). Basic objects in natural categories. *Cognitive Psychology, 8,* 382–439.

Ryle, G. (1971). Knowing how and knowing that. In G. Ryle (Ed.), *Collected papers* (Vol. 2, pp. 212–225). New York: Barnes & Noble.

Siegler, R. S. (1991). Strategy choice and strategy discovery. *Learning and Instruction, 1,* 89–102.

Siegler, R. S., & Jenkins, E. (1989). *How children discover new strategies.* Hillsdale, NJ: Lawrence Erlbaum Associates.

Simon, H. A. (1986). Alternative visions of rationality. In H. Arkes & K. Hammond (eds.), *Judgment and decision-making* (pp. 97–113). Cambridge, England: Cambridge University Press.

Singley, M. K., & Anderson, J. R. (1989). *The transfer of cognitive skill.* Cambridge, MA: Harvard University Press.

Skinner, B. F. (1974). *About behaviorism.* New York: Knopf.

Sophian, C., & Somerville, S. C. (1988). Early developments in logical reasoning: Considering alternative possibilities. *Cognitive Development, 3,* 183–222.

Squire, L. R. (1987). *Memory and brain.* Oxford, England: Oxford University Press.

Sternberg, R. J (1989). Domain-generality versus domain-specificity: The life and impending death of a false dichotomy. *Merrill–Palmer Quarterly, 35,* 115–130.

Vygotsky, L. S. (1978). *Mind and society.* Cambridge, MA: Harvard University Press.

Wellman, H. M. (1990). *The child's theory of mind.* Cambridge, MA: MIT Press.

Winograd, T. (1975). Frame representations and the declarative/procedural controversy. In D. G. Bobrow & A. Collins (Eds.), *Representation and understanding: Studies in cognitive science* (pp. 185–210). New York: Academic Press.

Wynn, K. (1992). Addition and subtraction by human infants. *Nature, 358,* 749–750.

PART II

Application of Representation in Practice

CHAPTER 14

Developing an Understanding
of External Spatial Representations

LYNN S. LIBEN
The Pennsylvania State University

The contributors to this volume have been invited to discuss their uses of the construct of "representation" (see Sigel, chap. 1, this volume). My own work has focused on spatial representation, and here I consider children's developing understanding of a subset of external spatial representations. I first consider their defining features, and then discuss what it means to say that someone has "understood" them. I next propose a six-level developmental sequence that begins with the child's ability to respond to the depicted referential content, and ends with the sophisticated ability to reflect upon how various kinds of representations may be created and used. In my closing comments, I speculate about mechanisms and experiences that facilitate progress through the proposed developmental sequence.

WHAT ARE SPATIAL REPRESENTATIONS?

Space is arguably one of the basic categories of human thought, as evidenced by the attention it receives in the disciplines of philosophy, physics, mathematics, and, of course, psychology (e.g., see Eliot, 1987; Jammer, 1954; Liben, 1981). Space is clearly fundamental to human life at a practical level as well. We—like other species—live in and move about space. Furthermore, we rely upon *representations* of that space for a myriad of reasons. We draw sketch maps to give directions to our home, use diagrams to show how to assemble a piece of furniture, employ satellite images of Earth to study land use and plan irrigation systems, produce architectural renderings to decide about the structure and placement of buildings, create paintings to convey a sense of the beauty of a landscape or even a bowl of fruit. We rely upon cognitive maps to make decisions about which route or which vacation to take, and mentally rotate internal spatial images to make judgments about how to pack suitcases in the trunk of a car or to rearrange the furniture in our living room. In short, representations of space are pervasive and important in human thought, action, and communication.

Within the examples just given are some that fall within the category of what I have elsewhere referred to as *spatial products* (Liben, 1981). These are the external entities that represent space, and may be in any medium, including three-dimensional, concrete objects (as in scale models), two-dimensional graphic representations (as in photographs, paintings, or drawings), verbal language (as in prose descriptions of a landscape), or numerical notations (as in latitude and longitude).

Although all spatial products provide information about space, my discussion here is limited to representations in which at least some information about a spatial referent is carried via the spatial arrangement of the elements of the representation itself, referred to here as "external spatial representations." Prototypical exemplars include maps and drawings in which there is a systematic mapping between the arrangement of the elements of the referent and the arrangement of the elements of the representation. These contrast to representations of space that are in a nonspatial format (such as language) in which the spatial arrangement of the representational components conveys nothing about the spatial arrangement of the referent. For example, the sentences: "The dog is in front of the cat" and "The cat is behind the dog" convey the same information about the spatial referent irrespective of where the animals' names appear within the sentences (see also Liben & Downs, 1992).

With respect to content, representations may stand for spatial or nonspatial referents. Spatial referents are any that have spatial properties, and thus include large geographic places (such as cities) as well as objects (such as a bowl of fruit) that have spatial properties such as shape and size. In contrast, nonspatial referents are referents that have neither extension nor location. The referents "liberty" and "poison" are illustrations. Only abstract concepts fall into the category of nonspatial referents because the moment that a referent has any form or location in space, that form or location is spatial. One might, of course, *spatialize* some aspect of inherently nonspatial concepts, as, for example, creating thematic maps that depict the distribution of democracies or poisonous landfills over the Earth. But now the spatial form of the representation depicts a spatial referent of the spatial distribution of liberty and poisons. It is not that the referents "liberty" and "poison" have themselves become inherently spatial.

Despite the seemingly simple set of defining qualities just discussed, it is not always a simple matter to decide if a particular entity is or is not an external spatial representation of some referent. My own position is that an external spatial representation must not only have spatial features that carry meaning, but, in addition, (a) must *be* something other than the original (referent) thing itself,

(b) must be *interpreted as* something other than the referent itself, and (c) must be *used as* something that stands for the referent. With these three simple rules, I have implicitly taken the position that determining whether or not a particular entity is a true external spatial representation rests on an analysis not only of the features of the concrete external entity itself, but also on the way in which an individual sees, understands, or uses it. As such, my analysis is rooted squarely within in a constructivist theoretical orientation.

A failure to meet the first criterion occurs in cases of *identity* (see Table 14.1). The concept of something serving as a representation of itself is an absurdity. This case is illustrated by a passage from Lewis Carroll's *Sylvie and Bruno Concluded* in which a map scale is changed gradually from 6 inches to the mile, to 6 yards to the mile, to 100 yards to the mile, to a scale of a mile to a mile. At last the farmers complain that "it would cover the whole country and shut out the sunlight! So now we use the country itself, as its own map, and I assure you it does nearly as well" (Carroll, 1893, p.169).

The concept of using a thing to represent itself is clearly outside the realm of what anyone would accept as an external spatial representation. However, there may be other slightly less fanciful circumstances under which a viewer might interpret one entity as if it were the original object itself, even though to an out-

TABLE 14.1
Things *Are* Sometimes What They Seem:
The Case of Nonrepresentation

Definition: *Nonrepresentational cases* are those in which phenomenologically the object under analysis functions as an original object itself. That is, irrespective of what the object is, it is *experienced* as the object itself. Nonrepresentational cases occur under conditions of:

- *Identity.* The object under analysis *is* the original object itself (e.g., a country as its own map as in Lewis Carroll quotation in text).
- *Replication.* The object under analysis is a duplicate of the original object itself, indistinguishable by the viewer from the original object. A failure to distinguish may be traced to the precision of the replication in interaction with perceptual or analytic skills of the viewer (e.g., chemical analysis of paint or high expertise may reveal that an artistic forgery is not an original even though it appears so to the untutored or unaided eye).
- *Perceptual equivalence.* The perceptual experience mimics the perceptual experience that would have been experienced by this particular viewer at this particular station point if the depicted object had actually been present. Here the experience is equivalent *not* because the object under analysis replicates the referent object, but rather because the perceptual information mimics that of the original object (e.g., *trompe l'oeil* art). The phrase "by this particular viewer" acknowledges that different viewers (e.g., of different species, maturational levels, or experiential histories) may be differentially sensitive to information in the optic array.
- *Cognitive trickery.* The viewer is tricked into believing that the object in question is the original object. Here (in contrast to *replication* and *perceptual equivalence*) the viewer perceives the object in question as perceptually different from the original object, but tricked into interpreting it as the original despite the fact that it looks different (e.g., the shrunken room of DeLoache described in text).

side observer, it is in actuality distinct from the original (referent) object. According to the criteria offered earlier, I would argue that if the viewer does not interpret the entity as separate from the original, then that entity cannot function as a representation for the original. Next I consider three conditions under which a viewer might fail to distinguish a second entity from the first: replication, perceptual equivalence, and cognitive trickery (see Table 14.1).

The case of *replication* is that in which the original is reproduced in every detail. In actuality, a perfect replication is impossible. Even if the same types of materials as found in the original are used to create a second, the particular set of materials is necessarily different. Perhaps we might disassemble the original and then reassemble the pieces elsewhere, as one might do, say, in creating a "reconstructed Colonial village." But the reconstructed object is still different from the original insofar as its geographic location and thus also its surrounding context are different. (This would be true for biological clones as well.) What if we now move it back to its original location? Can we claim to have a replica if the original no longer exists? In essence, the "replica" has *become* the original.

Although these kinds of questions hold great philosophical interest (see Goodman, 1976), it is perhaps less fanciful and psychologically more useful to focus on less extreme cases in which the viewer cannot distinguish the replica from the original, even though some other more privileged observer knows that the replica is not the original. Consider, for example, the case of an identical twin who might be mistaken for his or her sibling, or an artistic forgery that might be mistaken for an original. In these cases, although there is a differentiation between the original and the replica in the physical world, there is no psychological differentiation by the viewer. Rather, the replica is interpreted *as* the original. Note that erroneously interpreting a replica as the original stems from characteristics of the objects (i.e., the similarity of the original and replica) as well as characteristics of the viewer (i.e., the viewer's perceptual and cognitive skills and knowledge). For example, a viewer who is ignorant of a twinship would be more likely to think mistakenly that the replica was the original than would someone who knew of the existence of identical twins. Similarly, an artistic novice would be more likely to mistake a forgery for an original painting than would an expert, particularly one with access to analytic aids that augment human perceptual capacities (e.g., X rays or chemical analyses of paint). Or, a young child who had not yet developed an understanding of classes might have difficulty in individuating members of a class, mistakenly thinking each (in fact new) instance is the original. For example, Piaget (1951) reported that at about 2.5 years, Jacqueline used the term *the slug* for the slugs they saw every morning during their walk along a particular road. "At 2;7 (2) she cried: '*There it is!*' on seeing one, and when we saw another ten yards further on she said: '*There's the slug again*'" (p. 225). This is a case in which the child has interpreted a replica as the original, and thus cannot be credited with having understood the second slug as separate from the first.

However, it need not be only cases in which the original and copy are physically alike in substance and structure that one may fail to differentiate a representation from the original. There are also perceptual conditions that lead the viewer to *perceive* a representation as if it were an original object, even though the physical qualities of the two are very different (*perceptual equivalence,* see Table 14.1). The best example of perceptual equivalence is *trompe l'oeil* art. As the English translation—"fool the eye"—implies, this art form fools the viewer into thinking that the referential subject of the painting (such as a hat hanging on a hook) is actually physically present. Here the mistaken interpretation is only momentary, however, because as soon as the viewer moves, the perceptual information differs from what would have been available if the real objects had been present (see J. J. Gibson, 1979; Hagen, 1986). Movement thus enables viewers to realize that they have been fooled. At the moment of this realization, the painting begins to function as a representation.

Perceptual equivalence may be achieved through newer media such as holograms, three-dimensional computer displays, and virtual realities (see Liben, 1997; Wilson, 1997). Although with these media, viewers are undoubtedly aware that they are looking at a representation, now and then they respond as they would to the object itself (e.g., by reaching out to touch an apparent object and being surprised that they cannot feel it; by flinching at a looming image). At these moments, the "representational" entities are functioning as real or original objects rather than as representations of referents.

The cases discussed so far are rooted in physical similarity or perceptual mimicry, but the viewer might also be fooled by some higher level *cognitive trickery* (see Table 14.1). A clever demonstration of this case is found in the work of DeLoache. In her initial work, DeLoache (1987) showed that very young preschoolers (2.5 years) have difficulty finding analogous locations across two rooms that are alike except for size. In her paradigm, a big toy dog is hidden under the big couch in the big room and the child is asked to then find a small toy dog hidden in the same place in a scale model of the room. Young children were unable to do so, apparently unable to use one room as a representation for the other. When she later fooled preschoolers into thinking that the big room (again containing the dog under the couch) had been reduced in size by a "shrinking machine," children were able to find the small toy dog without difficulty (DeLoache, 1995). As in *trompe l'oeil,* albeit for different reasons, what we (as outside observers) know is a representation is interpreted by the viewer as the thing itself.

In summary, I take the position that we have not tested viewers' understanding of external spatial representations under conditions in which viewers have a phenomenological experience that is psychologically undifferentiated from that experienced when they encounter the referential object itself, that is, under any of the cases summarized in Table 14.1.

It is not sufficient, however, to recognize that one object is distinct from another object to qualify as representation. In addition, the viewer must *use* all or part of the object in a "stand-for" or symbolic relation to the original object. That is, following the third criterion offered earlier, it is necessary for the viewer to appreciate that things are not only what they seem (that they are entities in and of themselves), but also that they have a *second* existence as representations of something else (that they are symbolic). This quality has been referred to as the "dual nature of symbols" or "duality" by both philosophers and psychologists (e.g., DeLoache, 1989; Langer, 1942; Liben & Downs, 1992; Potter, 1979; Sigel, 1978). Unless this "stand-for" condition is met, the viewer interprets the second object as distinct from, but not informative about, the first.

The recognition of the existence of a second object provides the *potential* for its representational use. Thus, although replicas do not *necessarily* serve a representational function, they *can* do so once they are recognized as separate from the original. For example, engineers and astronauts on Earth used a replica of the space capsule during the Apollo 13 mission to devise and test solutions to deal with damage to the spaceship. In this case, the replica served as a representation because it was used to stand for the original.

Replicas thus can serve a representational function, but these anchor one end of an important continuum of physical similarity between the referent and representation, as depicted in Fig. 14.1. Representations that bear high similarity to their referent primarily serve what might be called a "re-presentation"

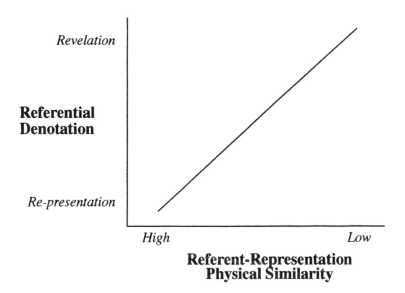

FIG 14.1.   Kinds of referential information conveyed in relation to physical similarity between representation and referent.

function. That is, they re-present information about the referent that is much like the original. The extreme case, of course, is a reproduction or replica (within the limitations discussed earlier) that can be a useful re-presentation because it is convenient (as in the Apollo 13 example). A slightly less extreme case, still highly similar to the original, is a working scale model such as one that might be used by engineers to test equipment more quickly or cheaply than would be possible if they had to build a full-scale prototype. But representations of these kinds are useful primarily because they enable the viewer to construct knowledge about the referent that is like the knowledge that could have been gained by interacting with the referent itself, and are thus primarily re-presentational.

As the representation moves further away from providing an experience that mimics what would already have been accessible from direct interaction with the original referent, the representation provides increasing potential for achieving new insights or revelations about the referent. If the referent is large enough, scale reduction alone may allow revelation because the representation can permit the viewer to see relationships that would be otherwise unobservable. For example, a scale model of a city would allow the viewer to see spatial relationships among areas of the city that might otherwise go unnoticed.

But representations may also communicate some new insight or vision by presenting highly processed and transformed information about the referent. This revelation function of representations is generally recognized in painting and drawing, but is often overlooked for other art forms such as sculpture and photography. The latter are often naively assumed to show the world "as it is" (see Goodman, 1976), a misconception also found in people's naive beliefs about maps (e.g., see Downs, 1981; Downs & Liben, 1988; Liben & Downs, 1989, 1992). The general point holds for any medium: Representations do not merely reproduce the world as it is, but rather are artifacts that communicate or construct new visions or insights that would have been difficult and often impossible to achieve from direct interaction with the real, physical world. In some cases, the insight may precede the creation of the external representation, so that the process is primarily one of creating an external spatial representation to record or communicate that insight; in other cases the insight may be revealed in the act of producing or viewing the external representation as when a computer-generated map, graph, or model allows the viewer to "see" a relation among variables that had not been previously understood. But in either case, the external spatial representations are more than denotations of the external world that simply re-present that world in another form. Given this interpretation of external spatial representations, the task of understanding them is naturally more complex than simply identifying their denoted referents. In the next section, I discuss this richer view of what it means to understand external spatial representations.

UNDERSTANDING WHAT WE MEAN BY "UNDERSTANDING" EXTERNAL SPATIAL REPRESENTATIONS

In this section I discuss what it might mean to say that someone has used and understood external spatial representations. One possible interpretation, that might be called a "transparency" view of understanding (see Downs & Liben, 1988), is depicted in Figure 14.2. Here the viewer sees through an external spatial representation directly to the referent (here necessarily depicted by yet another external spatial representation). The disembodied eye is used to imply that information is extracted from the representation via perceptual processes much like those used in picking up information from the three-dimensional world itself. Under this model, it is assumed that the translation from the three-dimensional world to the two-dimensional representation is a relatively straightforward one, made possible through perceptual skills already available from infancy.

Because the transparency view suggests a phenomenological experience much like that which would be achieved by interacting with the referential world itself, I believe that it is more re-presentational than representational. Not surprisingly, then, I argue for a more complex view of what it means to understand external spatial representations—the "embedded" view that is depicted in Fig. 14.3. Here the understanding of external spatial representations is embedded within the context of understanding the referent itself, as well as within the context of understanding representational strategies (the means by which representations can be created). Note that the prior two sentences (and the graphics of Fig. 14.3) present a strong stand that "understanding external spatial representations" is *not* limited to "identifying the referent for which the representation stands." In the discussion that follows I highlight some of the major

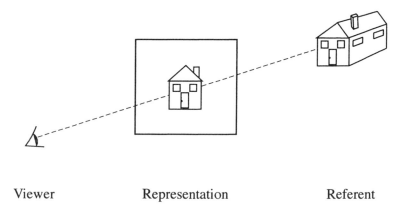

Viewer   Representation   Referent

FIG 14.2.   A depiction of the "transparency" interpretation of understanding external spatial representations.

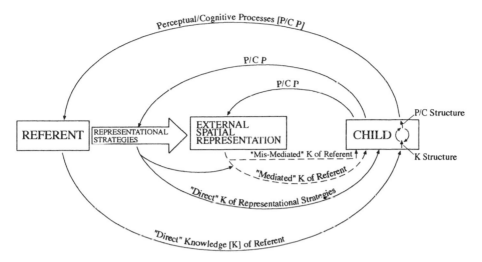

FIG 14.3. A depiction of the "embedded" interpretation of understanding external spatial representations.

components of this model which I am in the process of developing in more detail (Liben, 1998).

It is useful to begin by pointing out two major contrasts between the model shown in Fig. 14.3 and the earlier Fig. 14.2. First, the "eye" has been replaced by the construct "child." This substitution reflects my constructive theoretical orientation noted earlier. We are not simply sensation-recording devices, but instead we are active explorers and creators of our own knowledge. We proactively reach out with our "perceptual/cognitive processes" to interact with the world (outward arrows from the child in the top half of Fig. 14.3). The products of these interactions in turn lead to various kinds of knowledge (incoming arrows to the child in the bottom half of Fig. 14.3). The child is a biologically prepared, self-regulating system that at any moment is the consequence of prior constructive history, and is prepared to reach out for new and developmentally progressive experiences.

The second major contrast between the models shown in Figs. 14.2 and 14.3 is that there are now three major external constructs with which the child is concerned. In addition to the constructs of the referent and the representation (instantiated in Fig. 14.2 as the depiction of the referent house and the depiction of the representation or drawing of the house), there is also now the construct labeled "representational strategies." The idea is that strategies or techniques for producing external spatial representations are also a kind of content that must be explored for a full understanding of representations. Thus, the embedded model posits that perceptual-cognitive processes are addressed to the strategies or techniques for producing external spatial representations as well as to the products that result from applying those techniques.

The purpose of including external representational strategies in the model is to depict the role of understanding the multiple (indeed, infinite) ways that a referent can be represented. When—as here—we are concerned with *spatial* representations, these strategies include the spatial or geometric systems by which representations can be created. In cartography, for example, any given representation is at a specific scale, uses a particular projection (e.g., Mercator), and has a particular orientation. Likewise, representational art may use alternative geometries. As Hagen (1986) reminded us, the projective geometry used in Western art allows the artist to convey different information than that conveyed by, say, the affine geometry of Asian art.

Strategies also include media-specific processes. Understanding at least some components of these processes may be essential in understanding the referential meaning of particular representations. An extremely dark photographic image might indicate something about the light in the referent room, but it might indicate something about the size of the lens aperture or the exposure length. Or a blurred image might indicate something about the referent (e.g., movement of a person in the photograph), but it might instead indicate something about the photographer (e.g., camera shake). Knowing something about the photographic process can allow one to distinguish between which is the case in a given photograph. Without understanding these strategies, the viewer runs the risk of inappropriately assigning *referential* meaning to a *representational* quality.

Empirical illustrations of overextending representational qualities to referential qualities come from earlier work on children's understanding of representations of place (Liben & Downs, 1989) in which we interviewed preschool children to explore their understanding of road maps and aerial photographs. Although preschoolers typically had no difficulty in understanding that the maps and photos stood for places, they often gave responses suggesting they sometimes misunderstood the relation between specific qualities of the representation and the referent. In some cases, they inappropriately overextended an attribute of the representation to an attribute of the referent. For example, a red line on the map was thought to indicate a red road in the real world, and yellow areas (standing for built-up areas) were thought to indicate "eggs" and "firecrackers." Relatedly, they often had difficulty accepting something as a representation of a referent if its attributes did not match the attributes of a potential referent. For example, one preschooler rejected a line as showing a road because "it's not fat enough for two cars to go on," and rejected a rectangular shape on an aerial photograph as his father's office building because "his building is *huge!* It's as big as this whole map!" Others said they were unable to find grass on a black-and-white aerial photograph because "grass is green." These examples illustrate the kinds of misconceptions that can occur if the child does not appreciate the strategies by which one creates representations of referents. This point is made in Fig. 14.3 by showing that in the absence of knowledge of representational strategies, the knowledge derived from representations will be *"mis-mediated"* knowledge of the referent.

Having taken the position that the understanding of external spatial representations goes beyond identifying the denoted referent, it is not surprising that I take the position that the mastery of this understanding is a protracted and multifaceted developmental process. In the next section, I suggest a sequence of accomplishments in this process.

CHARACTERIZING THE DEVELOPMENT OF REPRESENTATIONAL UNDERSTANDING

As implied by the arguments made in the prior sections, any developmental account of the course of understanding external spatial representations is heavily dependent on what is meant by *understanding*. If we mean simply that the viewer can recognize qualities of the spatial referent by examining the depiction—even a depiction that shares high physical similarity with the referent—then understanding may be said to occur very early. If, however, we mean that the viewer can interpret even abstract representations and can appreciate the variety and power of representations and use them for new insights, then understanding may be said to occur considerably later. In this section I suggest six levels of understanding that are anchored by these two extremes (see Table 14.2). Given the arguments made earlier, I prefer to take a conservative position, and credit children with true understanding only once they have acquired "representational insight" (DeLoache, 1995; see Table 14.2). Others, however, may well prefer to be more inclusive, and consider all six of these levels as demonstrations of representational understanding. Indeed, it is likely that disagreements about where to place the boundary of "understanding" underlie past controversies about when children can understand aerial photographs and maps (see Blaut, 1997a, 1997b; Downs & Liben, 1997; Liben & Downs, 1997). Irrespective of where one places definitional boundaries, however, the levels can be used to describe a sequence that characterizes ontogenetic development. (This sequence may also characterize changes that occur in the course of skill acquisition as individuals move from novice to expert performance within particular domains, although I have not made any attempt to evaluate this possibility here.)

Before asking whether the viewer can use information from a spatial representation to reveal information about a spatial referent, it is relevant to ask whether the viewer can appreciate spatial information in the actual physical world itself. How early this appreciation is accomplished is itself controversial. Piaget (1954) argued that the infant's understanding that objects—as well as self—are located in a three-dimensional world (or even exist permanently at all) is a very gradual accomplishment that takes place over the course of infancy as a consequence of complex interactions with the physical environment. Others

TABLE 14.2
Progressive Competencies in Understanding External Spatial Representations

I. **Referential Content.** The viewer begins to identify the referential meaning of the representation, with varying ease depending on the physical similarity of representation and referent. Thus, the viewer "understands" the representation in the sense of identifying the denoted referent, but appears to confuse them (as in trying to pick up a depicted object).

II. **Global Differentiation.** The viewer identifies the denotative meaning of the representation, distinguishes the representation and referent, and responds to them differentially. The viewer does not, however, reflect upon the correspondence between the two. The "stand for" relation is implicit in identification, but not generally subject to intentional manipulation.

III. **Representational Insight.** The viewer distinguishes between representation and referent, and intentionally interprets or assigns "stand for" meaning to the representation. Representational insight occurs first for objects that are inherently representational (as a photograph) and only later for objects that do not normally function as representations, but rather are most salient as objects in their own right (as a scale model).

IV. **Attribute Differentiation.** The viewer comes to appreciate that some, but not all attributes of the representation are motivated by attributes of the referent, and that some, but not all attributes of the referent motivate graphic attributes of the representation. Until doing so, the viewer inappropriately expects that attributes of the representation necessarily mimic attributes of the referent (as in inferring that a red line means a red road) and that attributes of the referent will necessarily be mimicked by attributes of the representation (as in expecting that a large building will appear large in the representation).

V. **Correspondence Mastery.** The viewer extends the prior understanding of attribute differentiation to develop understanding of the formal representational and geometric correspondences between representation and referent. The former allows the viewer to understand the referential content of symbols; the latter allows the viewer to understand the referential meaning of graphic space.

VI. **Meta-representation.** The viewer is able to reflect upon the mechanisms by which, and the purposes for which, graphic representations are created, including understanding that different correspondence rules and conventions are used in different media (as in maps vs. graphs), different traditions (as in Western vs. Asian art), and different renditions (as in a world map in a Mercator vs. a Peters projection). As a result, the viewer is able to understand representations not simply as convenient substitutions for referents, but rather as cognitive tools that enrich understanding of the referent, and to select among them appropriately for particular purposes.

hold that human infants are prewired to pick up information about space far earlier, perhaps even in the first month of life (e.g., see E. J. Gibson, 1987; Spelke, 1991).

In either case, it appears fairly clear that sensitivity to spatial information in the dynamic three-dimensional physical world occurs before sensitivity to spatial information in the static two-dimensional representational world (e.g., Adolph, Eppler, & E. J. Gibson, 1993). This is not to suggest that there is necessarily a terribly long lag before babies appear to respond to spatial information in static representations. For example, habituation studies have shown that by about 5 months, infants recognize objects pictured in photographs (e.g., DeLoache, Strauss, & Maynard, 1979; Dirks & E. J. Gibson, 1977), and are sensitive to depth information in pictures by about 5 to 7 months (e.g., see Yonas, Arterberry, & Granrud, 1987). Even monkeys and other nonhuman species show considerable ability to respond to photographs (e.g., see review in Beilin & Pearlman, 1991) and to pictorial depth (e.g., Gunderson, Yonas, Sargent, & Grant-Webster, 1993). Thus, the first level of competence—extracting *referential content*—appears to occur early, at least with some kinds of representations.

What is less clear is whether babies who are able to extract meaning from representations are also able to *distinguish* between the representation and the referent. Some investigators have reported that differential responding to photographs versus objects occurs within days of birth, whereas others have placed this accomplishment later (e.g., DiFranco, Muir, & Dodwell, 1978; Rose, 1977). Even after babies seem to be able to pick up cues that distinguish two-dimensional representations from three-dimensional objects in the real world, they appear to confuse representations and referents. There are informal accounts of young infants trying to pick up patterns drawn on fabric or paper (Liben & Downs, 1992; Ninio & Bruner, 1978) or other kinds of flat images such as light patterns on the floor (Church, 1961). More formal research has also revealed instances in which infants appear to be acting upon two-dimensional representations as if they were the three-dimensional objects they depict. DeLoache, Pierroutsakos, Uttal, Rosengren, and Gottlieb (1998), for example, found that 9-month-old infants grabbed at objects shown in photographs, even adjusting their hand shape appropriately to the depicted object, and persisting when they were unable to lift the object the first time. Of course, it is difficult (or perhaps impossible) to know whether the repeated attempts to grab depicted objects imply that the infant "believes" that the object is truly there, or whether instead these behaviors are efforts at testing qualities of the representation itself (i.e., that indeed it is flat and cannot be grasped in the same way that three-dimensional objects can be grasped). Thus, at this point in development, it appears that either there is some confusion of representation and referent, or at the very least, there is a struggle to confirm and test the boundaries between representation and referent. But in either case, it seems reasonable to conclude that the developmental task during this level of development is coming to master the differentiation between the representation and referent at some general level (i.e., that there are, in fact, two different kinds of entities).

Probably by toddlerhood, and certainly by preschool, children can recognize and name representations of a wide variety of objects in a wide variety of representational media (e.g., Potter, 1979), without giving signs that they are confusing the representation with the depicted object at the global level. That is, young children do not really try to eat pictures of food, or play with depicted toys, or put on represented pieces of clothing (although they may pretend to do so in play). At this point, then, children are making a *global differentiation* between the representation and the referent (see Table 14.2).

There are, however, still some indications that surface features of the representation may inadvertently intrude into the conceptualization of the depicted object. Sigel (1971), for example, reported that at least some groups of preschool children categorized real objects differently than they categorized photographs of those same objects. More recently, Melendez, Bales, and Pick (1995) reported that 4-year-olds sorted toys by function more often when they were sorting the real toys than when they were sorting drawings of the identical toys, and further, sorted line drawings by color or size more often than by function. Similarly, Deák and Bauer (1995) found that preschoolers categorized three-dimensional objects differently than they categorized line drawings. These data suggest that representations are not yet understood completely in a stand-for relation to the referent such that their role as representations (rather than as things in and of themselves) has not yet been fully understood.

It is not until the child achieves *representational insight* (see Table 14.2) that the child is able to *assign* referential meaning. As described earlier, DeLoache (1989, 1995) has shown that representational insight appears at about the age of 3 years, such that information provided by one object (the representation) may be used to provide specific information about the other (the referent).

Interestingly, the child's ability to employ a particular representation symbolically is affected by the extent to which the qualities of the representation make it salient as a thing in its own right. Representations that are more "thinglike" and thus useable in and of themselves are *less* likely to support representational insight than are representations that have little nonrepresentational use (see DeLoache, 1995). For example, representational insight that a location shown in a representational room can stand for a location in the referent room is more difficult when the representation is a scale model of the room than when the representation is a photograph of the room. The representational role of the scale model is more obscure because the primary use of a miniature room is as a toy for dollhouse play. In contrast, the representational value of the photograph is more salient because the primary use of a photograph is *as* a representation. Children are usually asked or told what photographs are "of" (as when looking through the family photo album), and are discouraged from using them as nonrepresentational objects. For example, children are cautioned to treat photographs carefully, not to draw on them, fold them, rip them, and so on, all of which diminish the salience of the photograph as a piece of paper, and increase its salience as a representation. In short, children initially show representational insight with objects that they already think of as representations, and only later extend this insight to objects that are not already viewed as inherently representational.

Even after achieving representational insight, the child has not yet fully mastered the details of the relation between the representation and referent. Children must also develop an appreciation of the boundaries between the two or what I call *attribute differentiation* (see Table 14.2). That is, children must come to understand that only some of the many attributes of the representation carry meaning about the referent and some do not, and similarly, that some of the many attributes of the referent are reflected by attributes of the representation, and some are not.

There is evidence that children are confused about the boundaries between qualities of representations and the qualities of referents in a variety of domains. Piaget, for example, reported spontaneous comments by young children that suggested confusion in differentiating the representational world from the referential world, as when at 2;8 (14), Laurent said spontaneously: "It's very heavy [a picture book] because there's a little girl in it," (Piaget, 1951, p. 225). Vygotsky (1962) noted that preschoolers appeared to believe that qualities of referents cling to their labels as evidenced by their explaining the assignment of names by appealing to the referents' attributes. For example, he reported that one preschooler reasoned that: "an animal is called 'cow' because it has horns, 'calf' because its horns are still small, 'dog' because it is small and has no horns" (p. 129). Preschoolers likewise rejected the possibility of interchanging names, refusing to "call a cow 'ink,' and ink 'cow' . . . because ink is used for writing, and the cow gives milk" (p. 129). And, when asked to use the word *dog* for *cow*, the child then insisted that the animal, so named, *must* have horns: ". . . if it is a cow, if it's called cow, it has horns. That kind of dog has got to have little horns" (p. 129).

Confusions about attribute boundaries are also evident in research on children's understanding of external spatial representations. In research on children's understanding of photographs, for example, Beilin and Pearlman (1991) found that young preschoolers showed evidence of what they termed "iconic realism" (see also Beilin, 1991). In particular, they found that preschoolers (especially 3-year-olds and less often 5-year-olds) confused physical properties of photographs and referents. For example, when asked: "If you shook this picture would you hear the rattle?" 3-year-olds not infrequently answered in the affirmative, or when asked "If you touched this picture [of an ice cream cone] here, how would the picture feel?" they not infrequently answered "cold." Although young preschoolers also sometimes gave iconic realism responses to questions that asked about function (e.g., "Can you eat this picture of an ice cream cone?"), they never maintained these iconic responses in the face of counter-iconic challenges (e.g., inviting the child to actually eat the cone). In contrast, many of the younger children *did* maintain iconic responses to questions about the physical properties, even after testing them (e.g., asserting that when they felt the photograph, the ice cream did, indeed, feel cold). The data reported by Beilin and Pearlman (1991) are thus consistent with the conclusion that even after children are able to differentiate between representations and referents, they may still confuse their attributes.

As noted earlier in this chapter (and described in more detail elsewhere, see Liben & Downs, 1989, 1991, 1992), similar kinds of boundary confusions have been found in research on young children's understanding of graphic representations of place. Preschool children often assume, first, that a quality of a referent should be seen in a quality of the representation (as in rejecting a small rectangle on an aerial photograph as a large building because the rectangle is too small, or rejecting a line as a road because it is too narrow for two cars), and second, that a quality of the representation must be extended to a quality of the referent (as in reasoning that a red line indicates that the referent road is red as well).

Once having understood the general concept that there is not a perfect match between the attributes of the representation and the attributes of the referent, the child must still come to understand the systematic correspondences between the representation and referent, or what I call *correspondence mastery*. That is, the next developmental challenge is to understand the formal or informal rules by which some attributes of referent and representation come to be shared and others do not. Thus, for example, children must learn that on maps, color choices are arbitrary (as in using red lines for two-lane highways), whereas depiction of size is not (once one has selected a particular scale and projection). Or, to put it differently, the challenge of the prior level of attribute differentiation is for the child to recognize that there is not a one-to-one correspondence between attributes of the representation and attributes of the referent; the challenge of the current level of correspondence mastery is for the child to come to understand how the correspondences between referent and representation work for various types of representational media (e.g., maps, photographs) and for various instances within each (e.g., this particular map or this particular photograph). More specifically, two kinds of correspondences between the referent and representation must be understood—representational and geometric (see Liben & Downs, 1989).

Representational correspondences refer to the links between the "things" in the actual in the referent world, and the symbolized entities included in the representation. Even representations such as photographs that have high referent-representation similarity (see Fig. 14.1), cannot re-present all information about all referents available in any particular referent world. They must, for example, be taken from a particular viewing angle (thereby necessarily obscuring some parts of the referent objects), with a particular film (thereby recording some but not all light), with a particular lens and focal length (thereby recording sharply only objects at a particular distance), printed in a particular way (thereby affecting color and contrast), and so on. And of course graphic representations that share even less physical similarity with the referent involve even more selectivity and abstraction. On a map, for example, only some information is represented (e.g., all population regions greater than some size), at a particular level of categorization and generalization (e.g., grouping populations into, say, five groups), using particular symbols (e.g., different-sized circles corresponding to different populations).

Geometric correspondences refer to the links between the space of the actual referent world and the symbolized space in the representation (see Downs, 1981, 1985). The same referent space may be represented by a virtually infinite array of representations that vary along geometric qualities of viewing angle (e.g., an elevation vs. a nadir view), scale, and viewing azimuth (e.g., looking north vs. west). In maps (see MacEachren, 1995; Muehrcke, 1986), as in paintings (see Hagen, 1986; Kubovy, 1986), different geometries are used to represent the three-dimensional world on the two-dimensional surface, and these result in strikingly different representations.

The correspondences between referent and representation are differentially systematic in different representational genre. Some representational forms allow the viewer to recover precise spatial information about the referent on the basis of the representation as, for example, in an architect's blueprint or a surveyor's map. Others are far less precise, as in a painter's still life that might preserve the general arrangement, but not the sizes of different pieces of fruit. The process of mastering an understanding spatial correspondences thus includes learning the conventions of the genre, and when appropriate, understanding the precise meaning of representational space (as in "reading" distances on a scaled map). Empirical work suggests that the mastery of these precise geometric correspondences is particularly challenging, presumably because the specific spatial concepts on which they draw are developing over a relatively long period during childhood (e.g., see Liben & Downs, 1993; Liben & Yekel, 1996).

The accomplishments of the correspondence mastery just discussed are medium-specific. It is not until the next level, which we have termed *meta-representation* (Liben & Downs, 1992), that the focus is on the coordination of understanding the variations among, as well as within, different representational media. With meta-representation, the individual comes to appreciate how different correspondence rules and systems provide different means of communicating different visions to others, or of supporting different kinds of revelations or realizations for self. It is by recognizing that different goals require different kinds of representations and that new representations can lead to new insights that the full power of external spatial representations can be appreciated.

To summarize, understanding external spatial representations develops gradually, and proceeds through the six-level sequence of competencies defined in Table 14.2. The developmental pattern of emergence is depicted in Fig. 14.4. It should be clear from Fig. 14.4 that although I have suggested an age-related progression, I am not suggesting that there are abrupt, discrete phases through which individuals pass in some chronologically precise manner. For example, even adults may fail to show global differentiation under some circumstances, and children who fail to differentiate in one setting, may nevertheless do so in another. But I would argue that in general the infant is not aware of the dual nature of representations whereas in general adults are, and when cognitively normal adults are lulled or fooled into equating a representation with its referent (as in *trompe l'oeil*), they quickly and easily recognize the foolishness of their initial response. In general, the very young preschooler is likely to confuse representational and referential attributes, whereas the adult does so only occasionally (as

AGE GROUP	COMPETENCY					
	Referential Content	Global Differentiation	Representational Insight	Attribute Differentiation	Correspondence Mastery	Meta-Representation
Infants	[shaded]	○				
Toddlers	•	[shaded]	○			
Preschoolers	•	○	[shaded]	○		
Young Children	•	•	○	[shaded]	○	
Older Children	•	•	•	○	[shaded]	○
Adolescents +	•	•	•	•	○	[shaded]

FIG 14.4.   Developmental progression in understanding external spatial representations. Shaded cells indicate the focal competency under development. Cells marked with a large open circle indicate that considerable development in that competency is continuing or beginning. Cells marked with a small closed circle indicate that the basic competence has been achieved, although further minor development may still be occurring. Blank cells indicate that little development is yet under way. Definitions of competencies are given in Table 14.2.

in the "Greenland effect" in which adults often believe that Greenland is larger than Brazil because it appears to be so on the Mercator projection).

If it is not age, or age alone, that controls progression in understanding, what mechanisms are responsible for progress in understanding? It is this topic that I consider in the concluding section of this chapter.

FACILITATING REPRESENTATIONAL DEVELOPMENT

Factors that facilitate development through the six levels summarized in Table 14.2 may be organized into three major groups: (a) general perceptual and cognitive achievements, (b) factors that enhance knowledge of referents, and (c) factors that enhance understanding of external spatial representations per se.

The first means by which representational understanding develops is through the general cognitive structures or strategies that develop over the life course. Although theorists may disagree about the specific characterization of these developmental changes, all would agree that there are age-linked advances in the knowledge and reasoning skills that may be brought to bear on any particular cognitive task. Clearly it is impossible to review these developmental changes here—they comprise the entire corpus of work on cognitive development. But by way of illustration, I note that children's developing spatial skills (e.g., see Eliot, 1987) should be relevant for children's understanding of geometric correspondences, that children's developing analogical reasoning skills (e.g., Gentner, 1988) should be relevant for developing representational insight, and that children's growing understanding of appearance–reality distinctions (e.g., Flavell, 1986), should be relevant to understanding attribute differentiation.

The second category concerns understanding the referent itself. As discussed earlier, understanding that there are objects in a three-dimensional world occurs sometime during infancy (earlier or later depending on one's theoretical perspective). However, many other kinds of knowledge of the referential world develop later and are relevant for understanding representations. To illustrate, consider what happens when viewers are shown an external spatial representation of a cat (e.g., a drawing). To interpret the cat-drawing as showing a cat, they must have some concept of the referential cat to which the representation may be linked, a concept that may have been formed slowly on the basis of experience with real cats, or built by other kinds of experiences such as verbal descriptions, perhaps paired with earlier images. (The latter route is important for representations of imaginary referents such as unicorns, as discussed at length by Goodman, 1976.) They must, for example, perceive cats as coherent objects moving as a whole; come to recognize cats as distinct from, say, dogs; recognize cats from the side, back, and front; appreciate that cats may appear in many different colors and patterns; and so on. As long as the child has knowledge of the referent cat, asking the child to interpret a cat-representation challenges the child's *representational* skills. But the referential knowledge base is not necessarily well developed for all referents. Consider, instead, asking the child to interpret an aerial photograph of a city. If the child has difficulty interpreting a pattern that shows a clover-leaf intersection of an interstate highway, the child's difficulty may reflect ignorance about clover-leaf intersections or about how they look from overhead even in the physical world (as from an airplane), rather than necessarily reflecting inadequate understanding of how to interpret the representation. One implication of this observation is to acknowledge that much prior research (including my own) has not differentiated clearly between the two sources of difficulty. A second implication is to recognize that developmental progress in understanding spatial representations may be based on an expanding knowledge and understanding of the referent world itself, quite apart from expanding knowledge and understanding of representations.

The third category concerns factors directly tied to representations per se. Interestingly, although as a discipline we have conducted extensive research on everyday experiences that foster children's comprehension and production of language (e.g., the role of motherese, the impact of hearing stories read aloud, exposure to early reading-related curriculum such as letter-recognition drills on "Sesame Street"), with few exceptions (e.g., Sigel, 1978) we have done relatively little to study the everyday experiences that might foster children's understanding of spatial or graphic representations. Most extant research has been addressed to understanding unusually skilled performance in individuals (such as artistic prodigies; see Winner, 1996) or in cultures (as in China, where instruction in drawing begins very early; see Gardner, 1989). Given the scarcity of research, there is little empirical work on which to formulate and test hypotheses. Thus, the suggestions that follow about what may enhance development are necessarily presented as "speculations."

First, I would speculate that competencies in understanding external spatial representations should be enhanced by exposure to many different kinds of external spatial representations (e.g., drawings, paintings, photographs, models, maps, graphs). Consistent with this conjecture is work by Sigel (1971) suggesting that early limitations in preschoolers' experience with representational materials are linked to difficulty in using conceptual criteria to categorize pictures even when these criteria can be used successfully to categorize actual objects.

Second, and relatedly, I would speculate that competencies should be enhanced by exposure to many different examples within any one particular medium, particularly those providing alternative representations of the identical referent. For example, as argued elsewhere (e.g., Downs & Liben, 1988), one likely reason that many people—even adults—often seem to hold rigid, naive (and incorrect) beliefs about the "proper" form of maps is that they have been repeatedly exposed to very limited exemplars in which north is always at the top, water is always shown in blue, the projection is invariably Mercator, and so on. Given these restricted experiences, it is perhaps not surprising that even adults find it difficult to believe (for example) that red shows vegetation (as in false-color GOES satellite images), or become confused when using maps in which north is not at the top of the page (as in strip maps produced by the Automobile Association of America), or have trouble interpreting a map when water is not in blue (as when a New York City subway map had to be recalled because users were confused by the use of brown to symbolize the Hudson River). Seeing that the same referent can be depicted in different forms should help people decouple referents from particular representational instantiations.

Third, I would speculate that understanding should be enhanced by experiences in which the child's attention is drawn explicitly to representational strategies in the context of referential meaning. As an example, consider the opening page of *The Travels of Babar* (De Brunhoff, 1934), in which Babar and Celeste are first shown drifting away in a hot-air balloon. One parent might focus the child's attention exclusively on the story line of the departure of Babar and Celeste, but another might direct the child's attention to the graphic representation of distance by the tiny size of the balloon, perhaps also using this as an opportunity to point out that things only appear smaller from a distance. Or, consider a parent and child examining a family photo album. One parent might comment exclusively on the referential content, but another might also draw attention to the photographic process (e.g., "Look at how blurred the baseball bat looks in this picture—you must have been swinging at the ball really quickly!"). In short, just as we have decades of evidence showing that richer linguistic environments are associated with children's more advanced language skills, so too, we may find that richer "graphic representational environments" are likewise associated with children's enhanced understanding of external spatial representations.

Fourth, I would speculate that understanding external spatial representations should be enhanced by explicit practice in creating and interpreting alternative external spatial representations. Thus, for example, understanding should be better in individuals who learn to produce representations as an end in themselves (e.g., painters or photographers), who routinely produce representations in the service of some other goal (e.g., engineers or architects), or who frequently manipulate external spatial representations in their work (e.g., geologists who use scientific visualization tools to display seismic data in new ways). To the extent that children are taught how to produce and manipulate representations, their understanding should be facilitated as well.

Finally (and most speculatively of all), I would suggest that understanding may be affected by familiarity with a class of representations that I label *ego-deictic*. The term is meant to denote representations that point to (hence "deixis") themselves (hence "ego"). These are representations that in some way make their status *as* representations salient to the viewer. In other words, ego-deictic representations are those in which surface features are intentionally brought to center stage. There may be any one of a number of ways in which ego-deixis may be accomplished, presumably each having somewhat different psychological consequences.

One of the most direct means of drawing attention to the representational nature of the representation is by including a representation of the creator of the representation within the representation. Examples include Escher's *Drawing Hands* (see Escher, 1992), or the *Purple Crayon* series in which the crayon draws objects that then become "real" (Johnson, 1956).

A second means of effecting ego-deixis is by layering representational world inside representational world, or by playfully shifting the referential meaning of the representation. The former is illustrated when Mary Poppins enters the Match-Man's chalk drawing to spend a day in the park (Travers, 1934). The latter is illustrated by the books *Zoom* and *Re-Zoom* (Banyai, 1995a, 1995b) in which viewers are led to interpret a pictorial representation in one way, only to turn the page to discover that the prior interpretation was wrong (e.g., we first see a farm yard from overhead, only to discover that it is really a toy farm set being played with by a child, only to discover that it is really a picture on the cover of a toy catalogue, and so on).

In the cases of ego-deixis just described, the reinterpretations are sequential, with a reevaluation of referential meaning occurring because the viewer is given an alternative context. One can instead begin with graphics that are referentially opaque as in droodles (e.g., see Price, 1953) and are made meaningful by providing information external to the original representation (by word or graphics). In still other cases, ego-deixis may be achieved by representations that simultaneously support more than one referential interpretation. Well-known examples include ambiguous figures such as the face/vase drawings (e.g., see Block & Yucker, 1989), upside-down drawings that take on entirely different meanings depending on which direction they are held (e.g., a drawing that shows a bird in one direction, but an island, fish, and boat when the drawing is turned upside down; see Ernst, 1986); and, of course, the group of spatially impossible draw-ings in which components of the representation can support two conflicting meanings simultaneously (e.g., the ascending and descending ramps and stair-cases found, respectively, in Escher's *Waterfall* and *Ascending and Descending,* see Escher, 1992; or in the impossible representations created by Shepard, 1990).

Another way in which representations may be made ego-deictic is by juxta-posing the presentation of information through symbolic and nonsymbolic means. An illustration is provided by the classic children's book, *Pat the Bunny* (Kunhardt, 1940). The story line is given representationally with words and pic-tures, but interspersed throughout the book are objects that convey meaning through their actual, rather than their representational, properties. For exam-ple, "Daddy's beard" is described as rough. But rather than simply depicting the roughness by graphic techniques (such as stippling), it is conveyed physically by including a piece of sandpaper for the child to feel. Of course, the sandpaper is still a metaphorical representation of the roughness of Daddy's face, but there is nevertheless an interesting interplay of representational and actual physical qualities. In the realm of spatial relationships, a similar interplay between repre-sentational and actual space may be found in "Pop-Up" books, as, for example, when a pop-up dog is physically located behind a pop-up house. In such cases, at least some of the spatial relations defined by station point can be experienced di-rectly, and may support the child's ability to understand the spatial relations shown representationally on another page.

To my knowledge, there has been no systematic empirical work on children's understanding of these kinds of representations, or on how exposure to ego-deictic representations may affect children's representational competencies. One might hypothesize that exposure to ego-deictic representations may promote children's understanding of the boundaries between representations and reality because these boundaries are made salient. An equally plausible possibility is that exposure to ego-deictic representations may confuse children by reinforc-ing the notion that representations and referents share qualities. It is also possi-ble that either outcome may occur, depending on the contexts in which ego-deictic representations are encountered (e.g., whether an adult draws explicit at-tention to the representational devices).

In closing, I observe that whereas earlier sections of this chapter demonstrate that we already know a considerable amount about children's developing under-standing of external spatial representations, the final section makes it clear that many important questions remain virtually unexplored. This observation leads me to end with the more general point that as a society (and as a discipline) we often view instruction (and research) on external spatial representations as an expendable luxury, aimed "merely" at developing aesthetic appreciation (or as an interesting extension of research on language). I hope that the arguments presented here are convincing in demonstrating that external spatial representa-tions are a major part of our human symbolic lives, and as such, should take a central place in our educational curricula and in our scholarly pursuits on the development of representational thought. It is not only children to whom the title of this chapter applies.

ACKNOWLEDGMENTS

I am grateful to Richard Carlson, Roger Downs, and Irving Sigel for providing extremely thoughtful comments on an earlier draft of this chapter, and to Holleen Krogh, for turning my sketches into finished figures. Partial support for the preparation of this chapter was provided by the National Science Foundation (NSF) Grant #RED-9554504, although opinions, findings, conclusions, and recommendations expressed here do not necessarily reflect the position or policies of the NSF.

REFERENCES

Adolph, K. E., Eppler, M. A., & Gibson, E. J. (1993). Development of perception of affordances. *Advances in Infancy Research, 8*, 51–98.

Banyai, I. (1995a). *Zoom*. New York: Viking.

Banyai, I. (1995b). *ReZoom*. New York: Viking.

Beilin, H. (1991). Developmental aesthetics and the psychology of photography. In R. M. Downs, L. S. Liben, & D. S. Palermo (Eds.), *Visions of aesthetics, the environment, and development: The legacy of Joachim F. Wohlwill* (pp. 45–86). Hillsdale, NJ: Lawrence Erlbaum Associates.

Beilin, J., & Pearlman, E. G. (1991). Children's iconic realism: Object versus property realism. In H. W. Reese (Ed.), *Advances in child development and behavior* (Vol. 23, pp. 73–111). New York: Academic Press.

Blaut, J. M. (1997a). Children can. *Annals of the Association of American Geographers, 87*, 152–158.

Blaut, J. M. (1997b). Piagetian pessimism and the mapping abilities of young children: A rejoinder to Liben and Downs. *Annals of the Association of American Geographers, 87*, 168–177.

Block, J. R., & Yucker, H. E. (1989). *Can you believe your eyes?* New York: Gardner.

Carroll, L. (1893). *Sylvie and Bruno concluded*. London: Macmillan Co. [In Dodgson, C. (1939). *The complete works of Lewis Carroll*. London: Nonesuch Press.]

Church, J. (1961). *Language and the discovery of reality*. New York: Random House.

Deák, G., & Bauer, P. J. (1995). The effects of task comprehension on preschoolers' and adults' categorization choices. *Journal of Experimental Child Psychology, 60*, 393–427.

De Brunhoff, J. (1934). *The travels of Babar*. New York: Random House.

DeLoache, J. S. (1987). Rapid change in the symbolic functioning of very young children. *Science, 238*, 1556–1557.

DeLoache, J. S. (1989). The development of representation in young children. In H. W. Reese (Ed.), *Advances in child development and behavior* (Vol. 22, pp. 1–39). New York: Academic Press.

DeLoache, J. S. (1995). Early symbol understanding and use. *The Psychology of Learning and Motivation, 33*, 65–114.

DeLoache, J. S., Pierroutsakos, S., Uttal, D. H., Rosengren, K. S., & Gottlieb, A. (1998). Grasping the nature of pictures. *Psychological Science, 9*, 205–210.

DeLoache, J. S., Strauss, M. S., & Maynard, J. (1979). Picture perception in infancy. *Infant Behavior and Development, 2*, 77–89.

DiFranco, D., Muir, D., & Dodwell, P. (1978). Reaching in very young infants. *Perception, 7,* 385–392.

Dirks, J., & Gibson, E. J. (1977). Infants' perception of similarity between live people and their photographs. *Child Development, 48,* 124–130.

Downs, R. M. (1981). Maps and mappings as metaphors for spatial representation. In L. S. Liben, A. H. Patterson, & N. Newcombe (Eds.), *Spatial representation and behavior across the life span: Theory and application* (pp. 143–166). New York: Academic Press.

Downs, R. M. (1985). The representation of space: Its development in children and in cartography. In R. Cohen (Ed.), *The development of spatial cognition* (pp. 323–345). Hillsdale, NJ: Lawrence Erlbaum Associates.

Downs, R. M., & Liben, L. S. (1988). Through a map darkly: Understanding maps as representations. *Genetic Epistemologist, 16,* 11–18.

Downs, R. M., & Liben, L. S. (1997). The final summation: The defense rests. *Annals of the Association of American Geographers, 87,* 178–180.

Eliot, J. (1987). *Models of psychological space, psychometric, developmental, and experimental approaches.* New York: Springer-Verlag.

Ernst, B. (1986). *The eye beguiled: Optical illusions.* Germany: Benedikt Taschen.

Escher, M. C. (1992). *The graphic work.* Germany: Benedikt Taschen.

Flavell, J. H. (1986). The development of children's knowledge about the appearance–reality distinction. *American Psychologist, 41,* 418–425.

Gardner, H. (1989). *To open minds.* New York: Basic Books.

Gentner, D. (1988). Metaphor as structure mapping: The relational shift. *Child Development, 59,* 47–59.

Gibson, E. J. (1987). What does infant perception tell us about theories of perception? *Journal of Experimental Psychology: Human Perception and Performance, 13,* 515–523.

Gibson, J. J. (1979). *The ecological approach to visual perception.* Hillsdale, NJ: Lawrence Erlbaum Associates.

Goodman, N. (1976). *Languages of art: An approach to a theory of symbols.* Indianapolis: Hackett.

Gunderson, V. M., Yonas, A., Sargent, P. L., & Grant-Webster, K. S. (1993). Infant macaque monkeys respond to pictorial depth. *Psychological Science, 4,* 93–98.

Hagen, M. A. (1986). *Varieties of realism: Geometries of representational art.* Cambridge, England: Cambridge University Press.

Jammer, M. (1954). *Concepts of space.* Cambridge, MA: Harvard University Press.

Johnson, C. (1956). *Harold's fairy tale.* New York: HarperCollins.

Kubovy, M. (1986). *The psychology of perspective and Renaissance art.* Cambridge, England: Cambridge University Press.

Kunhardt, D. (1940). *Pat the bunny.* Racine, WI: Western.

Langer, S. K. (1942). *Philosophy in a new key.* Cambridge, MA: Harvard University Press.

Liben, L. S. (1981). Spatial representation and behavior: Multiple perspectives. In L. S. Liben, A. H. Patterson, & N. Newcombe (Eds.), *Spatial representation and behavior across the life span: Theory and application* (pp. 3–36). New York: Academic Press.

Liben, L. S. (1997). Children's understanding of spatial representations of place: Mapping the methodological landscape. In N. Foreman & R. Gillett (Eds.), *Handbook of spatial research paradigms and methodologies* (pp. 41–83). East Sussex, England: Psychology Press, Taylor & Francis Group.

Liben, L. S. (1998). *Children's understanding of graphic representations.* Manuscript in preparation.

Liben, L. S., & Downs, R. M. (1989). Understanding maps as symbols: The development of map concepts in children. In H. W. Reese (Ed.), *Advances in child development and behavior* (Vol. 22, pp. 145–201). New York: Academic Press.

Liben, L. S., & Downs, R. M. (1991). The role of graphic representations in understanding the world. In R. M. Downs, L. S. Liben, & D. S. Palermo (Eds.), *Visions of aesthetics, the environment, and development: The legacy of Joachim Wohlwill* (pp. 139–180). Hillsdale, NJ: Lawrence Erlbaum Associates.

Liben, L. S., & Downs, R. M. (1992). Developing an understanding of graphic representations in children and adults: The case of GEO-graphics. *Cognitive Development, 7*, 331–349.

Liben, L. S., & Downs, R. M. (1993). Understanding person-space-map relations: Cartographic and developmental perspectives. *Developmental Psychology, 29*, 739–752.

Liben, L. S., & Downs, R. M. (1997). Can-ism and can'tianism: A straw child. *Annals of the Association of American Geographers, 87*, 159–167.

Liben, L. S., & Yekel, C. A. (1996). Preschoolers' understanding of plan and oblique maps: The role of geometric and representational correspondence. *Child Development, 67*, 2780 - 2796.

MacEachren, A. M. (1995). *How maps work*. New York: Guilford.

Melendez, P., Bales, D., & Pick, A. (1995, April). *Direct and indirect perception: Four-year-olds' grouping of toys*. Paper presented at the biennial meetings of the Society for Research in Child Development, Indianapolis.

Muehrcke, P. C. (1986). *Map use: Reading, analysis and interpretation* (2nd ed.). Madison, WI: JP Publications.

Ninio, A., & Bruner, J. (1978). The achievements and antecedents of labeling. *Journal of Child Language, 5*, 1–15.

Piaget, J. (1951). *Play, dreams and imitation in childhood*. New York: Norton.

Piaget, J. (1954). *The construction of reality in the child*. New York: Ballantine.

Potter, M. C. (1979). Mundane symbolism: The relations among objects, names, and ideas. In N. R. Smith & M. B. Franklin (Eds.), *Symbolic functioning in childhood* (pp. 41–65). Hillsdale, NJ: Lawrence Erlbaum Associates.

Price, R. (1953). *Droodles*. New York: Simon & Schuster.

Rose, S. A. (1977). Infant's transfer of responses between two dimensional and three dimensional stimuli. *Child Development, 48*, 1086–1091.

Shepard, R. N. (1990). *Mind sights*. New York: Freeman.

Sigel, I. E. (1971). The development of classificatory skills in young children: A training program. *Young Children, 26*, 170–184.

Sigel, I. E. (1978). The development of pictorial comprehension. In B. S. Randhawa & W. E. Coffman (Eds.), *Visual learning, thinking, and communication* (pp. 93–111). New York: Academic Press.

Spelke, E. (1991). Physical knowledge in infancy: Reflections on Piaget's theory. In S. Carey & R. Gelman (Eds.), *The epigenesis of mind* (pp. 133–169). Hillsdale, NJ: Lawrence Erlbaum Associates.

Travers, P. L. (1934). *Mary Poppins*. New York: Revnal & Hitchcock.

Vygotsky, L. S. (1962). *Thought and language*. Cambridge, MA: MIT Press.

Wilson, P. N. (1997). Use of virtual reality computing in spatial learning research. In N. Foreman & R. Gillett (Eds.), *Handbook of spatial research paradigms and methodologies* (pp. 181–206). East Sussex, England: Psychology Press, Taylor & Francis Group.

Winner, E. (1996). *Gifted children: Myths and realities*. New York: Basic Books.

Yonas, A., Arterberry, M. E., & Granrud, C. E. (1987). Space perception in infancy. *Annals of Child Development, 4*, 1–34.

CHAPTER 15

The Development of
Representational Abilities
in Middle School Mathematics

RICHARD LESH
Purdue University

This chapter describes a variety of ways that theoretical perspectives borrowed from developmental psychology have been productive in mathematics education, even within 60-minute problem solving episodes that we refer to as *construct-eliciting activities*. Also, because theory-borrowing has evolved into significant forms of theory-building, the chapter suggests some ways that mathematics educators currently may be in a position to repay some of their conceptual debts, especially in areas related to children's uses of representations in problem solving.[1]

MATHEMATICS IS ABOUT *SEEING* AT LEAST AS MUCH
AS IT IS ABOUT *DOING*

Piaget and his followers have been perhaps the foremost sources of developmental perspectives in mathematics education. Why was the appeal of Piaget so strong? One reason is that Piaget was interested in the development of ideas at least as much as the development of the children in which these ideas developed.[1] But, a more fundamental reason is that children's mathematical judgments are

---

[1] It might seem strange to speak about the development of ideas apart from the individuals in which these ideas are evolving. But, individuals are not the only problem-solving entities that develop mathematical constructs. For example, groups, or whole classrooms of students, develop constructs.

based on conceptual systems (cognitive *structures*) that students themselves gradually develop and refine; and, above all, *mathematics* is the study of structure.

Contrary to conclusions that many people have formed based on school experiences, mathematics is *not* simply about doing what you're told, and mathematical knowledge is *not* simply a checklist of machine-like, condition-action rules (definitions, facts, or skills) that need to be programmed in students' heads and executed flawlessly. Mathematics is about relationships among quantities at least as much as it is about operations with numbers; and, it is about *seeing* at least as much as it is about *doing*. Or, alternatively, one could say that *doing* mathematics involves more than simply manipulating mathematical symbols. It involves *interpreting* situations mathematically; it involves *mathematizing* (e.g., quantifying, visualizing, or coordinatizing) structurally interesting systems; and, it involves using specialized language, symbols, graphs, graphics, concrete models, or other representational systems to develop mathematical descriptions, or explanations, or constructions that enable useful predictions to be made about such systems.

All of the preceding activities make obvious heavy demands on representational capabilities. But, whereas mathematizing involves making symbolic descriptions of meaningful situations, the kind of word problems that are in traditional textbooks and tests emphasize almost exactly the opposite kind of processes. That is, beyond the factual and computational difficulties associated with traditional textbook exercises, what is problematic about them is that students need to make meaning out of symbolic descriptions (Lamon, 1995; Greer, 1992). Results that students are expected to produce seldom include descriptions, explanations, or justifications that reveal how students are interpreting the problem-solving situations. Therefore, when researchers investigate roles that representations play in the solution of such problems, many processes have been neglected that highlight the development of mathematical interpretations (see Fig. 15.1).

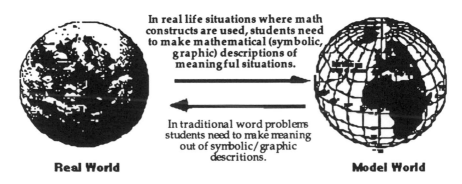

In real life situations where math constructs are used, students need to make mathematical (symbolic, graphic) descriptions of meaningful situations.

In traditional word problems students need to make meaning out of symbolic/graphic descritions.

Real World   **Model World**

FIG 15.1. Mathematizing versus deciphering.

DISTINCTIONS BETWEEN MATHEMATIZING
AND CALCULATING

To emphasize the distinction between mathematizing and calculating, one tactic that mathematics educators have used is to investigate the many varieties of appropriate interpretations that students use to make sense of stereotypic word problems such as: *Tom ran 3 miles in 24 minutes. How long did it take him to run 5 miles?* (Thompson, 1994).

Even though school texts tend to offer only a single canonical way of thinking about the relationships among quantities in such problems, a variety of alternative exist using graphs, diagrams, tables, or other representational devices. For example, even if attention is restricted to interpretations that emphasize descriptions using written algebraic symbols, Thompson identified seven distinct ways that students commonly use to make sense of the preceding problem. Student 1 may compare the speeds (miles-per-minute) for each of the two runs. Student 2 may compare the rate that time is accumulating (minutes-per-mile) for each of the two runs. Student 3 may think of the relationship between distance and time as a fixed ratio (distance-to-time or time-to-distance) without thinking of this ratio as an intensive quantity (or rate: miles-per-minute or minutes-per-mile). Student 4 may compare the first distance to the second distance, and the first time to the second time, and may then consider these two relationships to be equal. Notice that, for all four of the preceding cases, two separate situations are described using proportional reasoning of the form: *A is to B as C is to D*. But, instead of thinking in terms of two separate situations that involve similar relationships among the relevant quantities, it also is possible to think of the first run as if it were included in the second race. For example, students may think of the longer race as several of the smaller races following one another. Or, for readers to recognize other legitimate possibilities, the problem can be modified slightly to a form such as: (a) *Tom ran 3 miles in 24 minutes. How long did it take him to run a 26 mile marathon?* or (b) *Tom ran 1 mile in 4 minutes. How long did it take him to run 5 miles?* In either of the preceding cases, simple proportional reasoning $(A / B = C / D)$ is not sensible because a pace that a runner can maintain for a short distance is not likely to be extended to a significantly longer distance. More appropriate ways to think about the situation may involve graphs or equations designed to emphasize trends or changes in relationships over time. Or, if students' responses are given using pictures, graphs, or experience-based metaphors, rather than simply written symbols and spoken language, then these descriptions may vary considerably in detail or elaborateness depending on (for example) whether what's needed is a 5-second answer, a 5-minute answer, or a 5-hour answer. So, a single interpetation can lead to many levels and types of solutions; and, the factors that influence quality depends on needs for accuracy, precision, timeliness, or simplicity.

MATHEMATIZING INVOLVES MODELS AND MODELING

To further illustrate the distinction between mathematizing and calculating, it is useful to consider problems that are less like stereotypical word problem. For example, in our research, we've used the following *test scores problem* (Fig. 15.2) to help elementary school teachers understand what it means to use arithmetic operations as models to describe "real life" situations (Lesh, Hoover & Kelly, 1993).

When teachers work on the test scores problem, they often disagree about

Read the newspaper article below. Then, write a letter to the committee that was appointed by the Superintendent. Describe an procedure that you recommend for them to use to solve their problem. Use the data below to demonstrate how your procedure can be used to rank students; and, explain why your procedure is better than other suggestions that might be made.

NAME	QUALITY	QUANTITY
Ann	8	8
Bob	8	9
Carl	8	10
Dave	9	8
Emma	9	9
Fran	9	10
Gail	10	8
Herb	10	9
Ida	10	10

School Board Debates Fair Way To Combine Test Scores!

Last night, at the town's monthly school board meeting, an argument broke out about how to rank the quality of students' work in art.

The art department doesn't use short-answer tests to assess students. Instead, each student completes 10 complex projects during the year. Then, two scores are given for the entire group of projects.

Fred Wright, the chairman of the art department explained the system ... The QUANTITY score focuses on "product objectives." We count how many projects each student completes satisfactorily. The QUALITY score focuses on "process objectives." We count of how many different tools and techniques each student uses.

Arguments started when the administration tied to rank every student on a single scale from lowest to highest ... so special awards can be given to the top students, and so unproductive students can be held back.

The problem was that participants at the meeting couldn't agree about how the two scores should be combined. Five different procedures were suggested; and, when different procedures were used, different students appeared to be ranked high and low.

QUALITY+QUANTITY: The original plan was to simply add the two scores: "That's what people usually do with two scores!" - - -

QUALITY-QUANTITY: Then, the tennis coach said that "When the score in tennis is ADD OUT, we don't care how many points were scored to arrive at this point. She suggested that it might make sense to find the difference between the two scores. She said, "Quality is what we should care about most. So, we should subtract to factor out the quantity rating."

QUALITYx QUANTITY: Next, a local business leader pointed out the two scores could be multiplied to produce a score that means "total quality." But, a physics teacher said that it also makes sense to divide the scores to produce a score of quality-per-unit-quantity [QUALITY+QUANTITY].

√(QUALITY^2+QUANTITY^2): Finally, a math teacher argued that QUALITY and QUANTITY represent two completely different dimensions. So, the Pythagorean Theorem should be used to calculate the length of the vector sum .

The school district's testing specialist mumbled "Who cares how we combine the scores as long as the results are significant at the .05 level."

To close the meeting in a productive way, the Superintendent formed a committee to make a recommendation about how to rank the students using the scores that were available.

FIG 15.2. The test scores problem.

whether it is best to solve the problem by adding, subtracting, multiplying, or dividing (or by taking vector sums, or by using some other student-generated procedure, such as weighted averages). For example, if multiplication is used to combine test scores, then the resulting rank order is: Ann, Barb, Dave, Carl, Greg, Emma, Fran, Herb, Ivan (from lowest to highest). But, if division is used, the rank order becomes: Carl, Barb, Fran, Ann, Emma, Ivan, Herb, Dave, Greg. Consequently, it is clear that, when students decide which operation(s) to use, they are also automatically making decisions that treat completely different pairs of scores as if they were equivalent.

To emphasize how different operations are linked to different equivalence relationships, the following activity (Fig 15.3) is a useful follow-up to the test scores problem.

If professional statisticians were asked to work on the test scores problem, the equations (or computational formulas) that they'd produce might be referred to as mathematical models of the situation. The term *models* is used because the equations are based on different descriptive systems (or models) that involve different kinds of quantities and different assumptions about the underlying relationships among these quantities. For example, the diagram titled "Equivalence Classes for Basic Arithmetic Operations" shows how a Student S might be considered to be equivalent to: (a) Student D if division is used to combine scores, (b) Student M if multiplication is used to combine scores, (c) Student A if addition is used to combine scores, (d) Student V if vector sums are used to combine scores, or (e) other students if other types of equivalence classes were formed (that might not be based on results of an operation with numbers). Yet, Students D, M, A, and V range in performance from poor to good regardless which of these four operations is used (see Figs. 15.4 & 15.5).

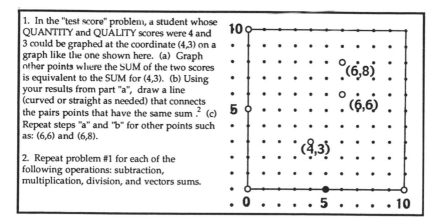

1. In the "test score" problem, a student whose QUANTITY and QUALITY scores were 4 and 3 could be graphed at the coordinate (4,3) on a graph like the one shown here. (a) Graph other points where the SUM of the two scores is equivalent to the SUM for (4,3). (b) Using your results from part "a", draw a line (curved or straight as needed) that connects the pairs points that have the same sum.[2] (c) Repeat steps "a" and "b" for other points such as: (6,6) and (6,8).

2. Repeat problem #1 for each of the following operations: subtraction, multiplication, division, and vectors sums.

FIG 15.3. The equivalence class activity (to be completed after the text scores problem).

[2]Possible answers include (3,4), (2,5), (8,3), (1,6), and (0,7) or any other points that lie on the diagonal line through these points.

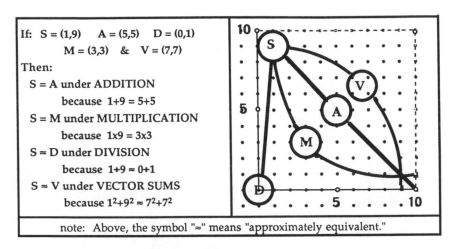

FIG 15.4. Equivalence depends on operations.

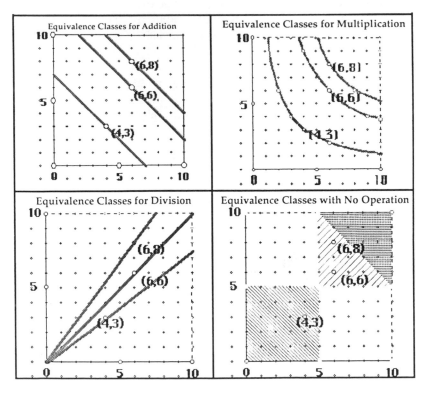

FIG 15.5. Equivalence classes for basic arithmetic operations.

328

When teachers work on the *test score problem* followed by the *equivalence class activity*, the graphs they construct make it clear that, when the problem solvers choose to combine test scores using some computational operation (addition, subtraction, multiplication, division): (a) they are not simply choosing a procedure for processing data, they are also adopting qualitatively different systems for describing the situation; (b) these descriptive systems include assumptions about relationships and equivalence classes as well as assumptions about appropriate procedures for operating on data; and (c) these assumptions, usually tacit, have enormously important consequences for the decisions that are to be made about ranking.

In addition to clarifying the preceding facts, the graphs in the equivalence class activity also introduce another type of representation system that can have enormous power in elementary mathematics: Cartesian Coordinate Systems (Nemirovsky, 1992). *Cartesian Coordinate Systems* enable students to use numbers to describe geometric shapes, or to use geometric shapes to describe number relationships; and, in other ways, they provide powerful "conceptual amplifiers" that help students to get more power out of the conceptual systems that they develop (Lesh, 1987).

Although it is not difficult to guide average ability middle-school students to develop significant proficiency in the use of Cartesian Coordinate Systems, it took the genius of Rene Descartes to create this system in the first place. So, if middle schoolers from today could be sent back in time before the birth of Descartes, and if they could be equipped with a powerful collection of such tools, then they would appear to be geniuses in this pre-Cartesian world. Conversely, today, without such tools, there are many things that students cannot think about effectively. Therefore, helping students develop these sorts of powerful conceptual tools should be among the most important goals of mathematics instruction (Confrey, 1994; Lehrer, Horvath, & Schauble, 1996).

MODELING INVOLVES MAKING SYMBOLIC STATEMENTS ABOUT MEANINGFUL SITUATIONS

It is easy to generate a variety of problems for children that are similar to *the Test Scores Problem* that was described for use with teachers. For example, in our research, one such problem involves a contest for paper airplanes. Teachers bring to class a collection of 20 paper airplanes (Bringhurst, 1994), and students test these planes for characteristics such as "best hang time," "best long distance landing accuracy," "best fancy flying," or "most durable." Scores for such characteristics can be based on measurements involving quantities such as the distance that each plane flies, or the amount of time that it is able to remain in the air, or how close it comes to the designated target; and, it also may involve quantifying qualitative information, perhaps by assigning "weights" to various factors. But, a single raw score usually is not enough to provide a useful "operational definition" of constructs such as *hang time*. In general, combinations of several counts or measurements are needed; and, the kind of issues that need to be considered are similar to those that teachers consider in the *test score problem*. For different constructs, different arithmetic operations are appropriate.

For constructs such as *hang time,* the process of producing sensible operational definitions is similar to the process that teachers use to generate scoring rubrics to assess students' work; and, it also is similar to scoring procedures that are used by business people to quantify constructs such as *productivity* or *cost-effectiveness* or *best buys.* In fact, one of the most common ways that ordinary people use mathematics is when they invent useful ways to think about constructs such as *effectiveness* or *costliness* in fields that range from sports, to weather, to politics, to business. These constructs often involve combinations of several quantities that can be counted or measured directly (e.g., time, distance, money); and, in general, different number operations yield different results, with different advantages and disadvantages.

For the *paper airplane problem,* quantification is involved at several levels. First, when students decide how to measure characteristics such as fancy flying, hang time, accuracy, durability, the quantification of qualitative information is a factor that is often heavily involved. Second, even after a consensus has been reached about how to measure the preceding characteristics, combinations of these measures tend to be needed to define higher order constructs such as *best overall* or *most versatile.* Third, when pairs of quantities are involved, high scores may be "good" for one of the quantities, but low scores may be "good" for the other quantity. Therefore, students may need to deal with signed quantities ($+/-$) or directed quantities. Or, if the quantities are not considered to be equally important, then some form of weighted sums or weighted averages may be needed.

In problems like the paper airplane problem, where students mathematize meaningful situations, a variety of representational abilities tend to be emphasized that are commonly overlooked in stereotypical textbook word problems. For example, students frequently use a rich array of interacting representations, many of which tend to involve idiosyncratic diagrams and notation systems that are introduced by students themselves. Consequently, students who are able to invent powerful constructs often include many who have been labeled *below average in ability* based on their performance in situations involving traditional tests, textbooks, and teaching, where only a narrow and shallow range of mathematical abilities tend to be emphasized (Lesh, Hoover & Kelly, 1993).

Another point that the paper airplane problem helps to emphasize is that, to make sense of a wide range of everyday experiences, the kind of quantities, relationships, and operations that are needed include much more than the simple counts, measures, and shapes. Yet, in the United States, by the time most students complete the K–12 mathematics curriculum, few students (even those who are most successful) are encouraged to develop more than an impoverished collection of models and representations for making sense of systems in which the "objects" include: rankings, coordinates, directed quantities, signed quantities, quantified qualitative information, accumulating quantities, continuously changing quantities, transformations, patterns or quantities referring to characteristics of *sets* of data (rather than isolated *pieces* of data).

REPRESENTATION: SIMPLIFYING EXTERNAL SYSTEMS OR EXTERNALIZING INTERNAL SYSTEMS

In the preceding sections, the kind of mathematical representations that were mentioned included: written symbols, diagrams, graphs, graphics, and stories (or experience-based prototypes); and, later in this chapter, other examples will be given that involve spoken language, concrete materials, or other types of structural metaphors. But, so far, the representations were described as though they were functioning primarily as externalizations of internal systems of thought. Yet, when students use representations to mathematize problem-solving situations, the mathematical representations that they use tend to function as simplifications of *external* systems at least as much as they function as externalizations of *internal* systems.[3] The *summer jobs problem,* given in this section, is an example where this later function is emphasized (see Fig. 15.6).

A similarity between the summer jobs problem and the paper airplane problem is that both are *construct-eliciting activities.* That is, for each, the student's goal is to produce an operational definition that specifies how to the student believes construct (such as "productivity" at summer jobs, or "hovering ability" for paper airplanes) should be measured. Therefore, descriptions, explanations, and justifications are not simply accompaniments to useful responses, they are the heart of the responses that are needed.

To focus on students' representational abilities, another important characteristic of the summer jobs problem is that it is intended to be addressed by three-person teams of average ability middle school students. Therefore, the task tends to make heavy demands on students' communication capabilities. Representational fluency is needed for purposes such as: (a) analyzing problems, and planning solutions involving multiple steps and multiple resources and constraints; (b) justifying and explaining suggested actions, and predicting their consequences; (c) monitoring and assessing progress; and (d) integrating and communicating results in forms that are useful to others. In other words, the purpose of representations is not simply for students to communicate with one another, it is also for students to communicate with themselves and to externalize their own ways of thinking so they can be examined and improved.

---

[3]Just as a model airplane is a simplified version of a real plane, mathematical models always lack some characteristics of the modeled system, and always include some characteristics not possessed by the modeled system.

Last summer Maya started a concession business at Wild Days Amusement Park. Her vendors carry popcorn and drinks around the park, selling wherever they can find customers. Maya needs your help deciding which workers to rehire next summer.

Last year Maya had nine vendors. This summer, she can have only six – three full-time and three half-time. She wants to rehire the vendors who will make the most money for her. But she doesn't know how to compare them because they worked different numbers of hours. Also, when they worked makes a big difference. After all, it is easier to sell more on a crowded Friday night than on a rainy afternoon.

Maya reviewed her records from last year. For each vendor, she totaled the number of hours worked and the money collected – when business in the park was busy (high attendance), steady, and slow(low attendance). (See the table.) Please evaluate how well the different vendors did last year for the business and decide which three she should rehire full-time and which three she should rehire half-time.

Write a letter to Maya giving your results. In your letter describe how you evaluated the vendors. Give details so Maya can check your work, and give a clear explanation so she can decide whether your method is a good one for her to use.

HOURS WORKED LAST SUMMER

	JUNE			JULY			AUGUST		
	Busy	Steady	Slow	Busy	Steady	Slow	Busy	Steady	Slow
MARIA	12.5	15	9	10	14	17.5	12.5	33.5	35
KIM	5.5	22	15.5	53.5	40	15.5	50	14	23.5
TERRY	12	17	14.5	20	25	21.5	19.5	20.5	24.5
JOSE	19.5	30.5	34	20	31	14	22	19.5	36
CHAD	19.5	26	0	36	15.5	27	30	24	4.5
CHERI	13	4.5	12	33.5	37.5	6.5	16	24	16.5
ROBIN	26.5	43.5	27	67	26	3	41.5	58	5.5
TONY	7.5	16	25	16	45.5	51	7.5	42	84
WILLY	0	3	4.5	38	17.5	39	37	22	12

MONEY COLLECTED LAST SUMMER (IN DOLLARS)

	JUNE			JULY			AUGUST		
	Busy	Steady	Slow	Busy	Steady	Slow	Busy	Steady	Slow
MARIA	690	780	452	699	758	835	788	1732	1462
KIM	474	874	406	4612	2032	477	4500	834	712
TERRY	1047	667	284	1389	804	450	1062	806	491
JOSE	1263	1188	765	1584	1668	449	1822	1276	1358
CHAD	1264	1172	0	2477	681	548	1923	1130	89
CHERI	1115	278	574	2972	2399	231	1322	1594	577
ROBIN	2253	1702	610	4470	993	75	2754	2327	87
TONY	550	903	928	1296	2360	2610	615	2184	2518
WILLY	0	125	64	3073	767	768	3005	1253	253

Figures are given for times when park attendance was high (busy), medium (steady), and low (slow).

FIG 15.6.   The summer jobs problem.

Solutions tend to require at least one or two full class periods to complete (assuming that suitable warm-up questions have been given, and assuming that relevant tools are available such as calculators, and graph paper). This is because construct development is what solutions to such problems is all about, and because the development and refinement of these constructs tends to involve a series of modeling cycles (in which progressively more sophisticated representations and ways of thinking are introduced, tested, and refined). Therefore, the meanings and functions of representations that students use are not static, they are continually evolving; and, the same is true for the underlying constructs that these representations embody, as well as for the external systems that they describe. For example:

• *Some Characteristics of Students' Early Interpretations.* Early interpretations often consist of a hodgepodge of several disorganized and sometimes inconsistent ways of thinking about givens, goals, and possible solution steps. For example, if three people are working in a group, they often fail to recognize that each is: (a) thinking about the situation in somewhat different ways, (b) focusing on different information and relationships, (c) aiming at somewhat different goals, and (d) envisioning different procedures for achieving these goals. In fact, even for a single individual, the student may fail to maintain a consistent interpretation, and will switch unconsciously from one way of thinking to another without noticing that a change has been made. Also, because problems such as the summer jobs problem frequently involve both too much and not enough information, students' first representations and ways of thinking often focus on only a subset of the information, and students often tend to be preoccupied with finding ways to simplify or aggregate (sum, average) all of the available information. For example, in their early interpretations of the summer jobs problem, students often focus on earnings while ignoring work schedules; or, they focus on fast sales periods while ignoring slow and steady periods; or, they focus on only 1 month and ignore the other 2 months. Yet, at the same time that students are preoccupied with finding ways to simplify or reduce information, they also may express concerns about not knowing additional information that they believe is relevant. For example, for the summer jobs problem, such information may include facts about the needs, flexibility, or friendliness of potential employees, or their willingness to work. Yet, even though this information is not available, it tends to be clear that the client in the problem would not find it useful if students refused to respond to her request for help simply because some relevant information was not available. Therefore, even at early stages of thinking about the problem, students generally recognize that, to solve the problem, a simplified description (or model) needs to be developed that focuses on significant relationships, patterns, and trends, and that simplifies the information and puts it into a useful form, while avoiding distractions related to surface-level details or gaps in the data. Consequently, these purposes tend to be reflected in the representations that they produce.

• *Some Characteristics of Students' Intermediate Interpretations.* Later, more sophisticated ways of thinking tend to go beyond organizing and processing isolated *pieces* of data to focus on *relationships,* or *patterns,* or *trends* in the data. For example, whereas early responses to the summer jobs problem tend to involve quantities that can be read directly from the statement of the problem, later responses tend to emphasis ratios, rates (e.g., dollars-per-hour), or other quantities that are based on comparisons involving other directly provided quantities, such as time and money. Also, in intermediate responses, students generally begin to sort out the following kinds of options. (a) Students may begin by calculating rates within each category (slow, steady, fast; June, July, August). Then, they may find ways to aggregate these rates; (b) Students may begin by calculating sums or averages across categories (slow, steady, fast; June, July, August). Then, they may calculate rates based on these aggregates. Whereas, earlier, students may have failed to differentiate between (a) calculating an average of several rates, and (b) calculating single rate that is based on average earnings and times.

• *Some Characteristics of Students' Final Interpretations.* The displayed example shows a solution that was generated by one group of inner city minority students who were considered to be *below average* in activities emphasized in traditional tests, textbooks, and teaching. This example is typical in the sense that the final results that students produce often go beyond "static" solutions to also involve conditional statements, which include a variety of options or mechanisms for taking into account additional information. For example, the solution may enable the clients to assign different "weights" to reflect the client's views about the relative importance of information about different months or different periods of work; it may enable the client to adjust suggested weights to suit their own preferences; it may use supplementary procedures, such as interviews, to take into account additional information; or, it may consider new hiring possibilities that were not considered when the problem was posed (such as hiring more or fewer full-time or part-time employees). Also, rather than using only a single rule, which is applied uniformly across all of the possible employees, the procedure that students use may involve a series of telescoping procedures. For example, students may use one approach to select employees that are in a *must hire* category; then, they may use a different procedure to select employees among the possibilities that remain. Or, to simplify the information that is given, students may use graphs like the ones shown (Fig 15.7) to focus on trends rather than relying exclusively on sums or averages.

During the solutions of construct-eliciting activities similar to the summer jobs problem, the general processes that students go through tend to be straightforward. When an initial description is produced, it may involve a combination of spoken words, written symbols, pictures or diagrams, or references to concrete models or real life experiences. But, in any case, the representation organizes and simplifies the situation so that additional information can be noticed, or so that attention can be directed toward underlying patterns and regularities which may, in turn, force changes in conceptions. Then, this new information often creates the need for a more refined or more elaborate description; and, this new description makes it possible for another round of additional

Dear Maya,

We think you should hire Kim and Cheri and Jose for full time, and we think you should hire Willy and Chad, and Tony for part time. Look at this graph to see why these people are best.

The graph is only about busy times and steady times. You don't make much money during slow times, and you won't hire people for slow times.

Some workers got better at the end of the summer. But, some didn't get better. So, August is most important, and July is also important. July is when you make the most money.

Alan, Barb, and Carla

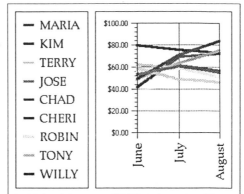

FIG 15.7. An example solution to the summer jobs problem.

information to be noticed. So, internal conceptual systems and external representational systems both tend to be unstable, interacting, and continually evolving; and, the general cycle of development repeats until the match between the model and the modeled is experienced as being sufficiently close and powerful to produce the desired results without any further adaptations.

The preceding observations lead to a number of corollaries about the forms and functions of representations in mathematics learning and problem solving. For example, when one person perceives a system that another person has constructed, the perceived system is not necessarily identical to the constructed system. In fact, even when individuals observe systems that they themselves have constructed, the perceived system is not necessarily identical to the constructed system. For instance, when a student draws a diagram of a complex situation, or when the situation is described using spoken language or written symbols, the person who constructed the description often reads out more information or different information than they read in. Perhaps, before the representation was generated, attention was focused on details; but, after the representation became available, new patterns or regularities often become apparent. Students early conceptualizations may fail to recognize the proverbial forest because of the trees, or vice versa; or, when they focus on one type of detail, other details may be conceptually neglected. But, in these and other ways, the meanings of both constructs and representational systems tend to be unstable; and, this lack of stability, together with adaptations that are made which are aimed at increasing stability, are some of the most important driving forces behind construct development. For conceptual systems, just as for other types of complex self-organizing systems, "survival of the stable" tends to the be the most relevant modern counterpart of Darwin's law of "survival of the fittest" (Minsky, 1986).

The language, symbols, graphs, and organizational schemes that students introduce are partly descriptions (simplifications) of external systems. Yet, because these descriptions focus on hypothesized relationships, patterns, and regularities that are *attributed to* external systems, rather than being *derived from* them, the representations are also externalizations of internal systems. Consequently, solutions to such problems involve interactions among three types of systems: (a) (internal) conceptual systems that can be thought of as residing in students' minds; (b) (external) systems that are given in nature, or that were constructed by humans; and (c) (external) models or representational systems that function both as externalizations of internal conceptual systems and as internalizations of external systems.

CONSTRUCT-ELICITING ACTIVITIES ARE
LOCAL CONCEPTUAL DEVELOPMENT SESSIONS

When the product that is needed to solve a problem involves explicitly developing a mathematical construction, description, or explanation, we refer to such activities as *construct-eliciting*. This is because the goal is not simply to produce brief answers to someone else's questions. Instead, the goals involve developing interpretations that explicitly reveal how the situations are interpreted (Lesh, Hoover & Kelly, 1993)

On other occasions, we have referred to the preceding kinds of problem-solving episodes as *local conceptual development sessions*. This is because, when students develop solutions to such problems, the construct-development cycles that they go through often are strikingly similar to the unfolding stages that developmental psychologists have observed for the conceptual systems that underlie the relevant constructs: for example, ratios, rates, fractions, or proportional reasoning (Lesh & Kaput, 1988). That is, the modeling cycles that students go through during 60-minute problem-solving sessions often appear to be local or situated versions of the stages that developmental psychologists have observed over time periods of several years. Furthermore, the processes and mechanisms that contribute to the development of these constructs tend to be the same as those that contribute to large scale conceptual development. In particular, cognitive conflict, or the need to develop increased conceptual stability, is a primary factor that creates the need for conceptual adaptation; and, representation systems facilitate the progressive differentiation and integration of relevant conceptual systems.

For construct-eliciting activities, where solutions typically involve a series of interpretation cycles, two of the most important phenomena that need to be explained are: How is it that students perceive the need to develop beyond their first primitive conceptualizations of a problem situation, and how is it that they are able to develop toward interpretations that are less barren and distorted? To answer the preceding question, theories generated by developmental psychologists have proven to be relevant because, when construct-eliciting activities are interpreted as local conceptual development (LCD) *activities:* (a) mechanisms that contribute to general conceptual development can be used to help explain students' problem solving processes (Lesh & Zawojewski, 1987), and (b) mechanisms that are important in local conceptual development sessions can be used to help explain the situated development of students' general reasoning capabilities (Lesh & Kaput, 1988). Also, it is possible to observe these mechanisms directly because, during construct-eliciting activities, the relevant constructs often are modified (extended, refined, revised) significantly during relatively brief periods of time. Therefore, as relevant constructs are extended, refined, differentiated, integrated, or adapted in other ways, it is possible for researchers to go beyond descriptions of successive states of knowledge to observe the mechanisms that promote development from one state to another. Furthermore, because it is possible to create conditions that optimize the chances that development will occur, without dictating the directions that this development must take, mathematics education researchers have been able to go beyond investigating *typical* development in *natural* environments to also focus on *induced* development within *carefully controlled* and *mathematically enriched* environments.

The application of developmental perspectives to problem solving is a relatively new phenomenon in mathematics education research where, traditionally: (a) problem solving has been defined as *getting from givens to goals when the path is not immediately obvious or it is blocked;* and (b) heuristics have been conceived to be answers to the question: *What can you do when you are stuck?* When attention focuses on construct-eliciting activities, the essence of problem solving involves finding ways to interpret these situations mathematically. Therefore, in general, it is more important for students to find ways to adapt, modify, and refine ideas that they *do have,* rather than to try to find ways to be more effective when they are stuck (i.e., when they have no relevant ideas or when no substantive constructs appear relevant, as often happens in puzzles and games). Consequently, to develop useful responses to construct-eliciting activities, the kinds of heuristics and strategies that are most useful tend to be quite different than those that have been emphasized in traditional problems where the solutions involve only a single interpretation cycle, and where fewer demands are made on students abilities to introduce, modify and adapt useful representations.

To focus on other representation-relevant mechanisms that contribute to the interacting development of constructs and representations, the next two sections will emphasize three themes. First, humans continually project constructs into the world. That is, the constructs that humans develop to make sense of their experiences are also used to mold and shape that world in which these experiences occur. Second, for a variety of reasons, it often is useful to demystify the nature of both mathematical constructs and representations by thinking of them as "smart tools" (or conceptual technologies). Third, the meaning of mathematical constructs tends to be distributed across several interacting representation systems; and, each of these representation systems

emphasizes and de-emphasizes somewhat different characteristics of the underlying constructs.

HUMANS CONTINUALLY PROJECT CONSTRUCTS
INTO THE WORLD

When we speak of systems that exist in a real world, some philosophers might
claim that the only patterns that students perceive in these systems are those
that they themselves construct (von Glasersfeld, 1990); and, there is some validity underlying this point of view. But, it is also overly simplistic and misleading.
For example:

• One of the most important characteristics of an *age of information* is that
the constructs or conceptual systems that are in human minds today may be
used to create systems that function as concrete objects in the world tomorrow; and, systems that are created for their own sake today may be used in
symbolic ways to make sense of other systems tomorrow. For example, when
a business manager uses a graphing calculator (or a graphics-linked spread-
sheet) to make predictions about maximizing cost-benefit trends, these tools
enable the manager to create completely new types of business systems that
did not exist before the tools were available, and they also amplify the manager's conceptual and procedural capabilities when dealing with these newly
introduced external systems. Consequently, among the mathematical "objects"
that impact everyday lives, many of the most important are *systems*—complex,
dynamic, interacting systems—which range in size from large-scale communication and economic systems, to small-scale systems for scheduling, organizing, and accounting in everyday activities.

• Another important characteristics of a technology based society is that
humans know how to create systems that they themselves do not know how
to describe, explain, predict, or control. This is why some of the most important goals of mathematics instruction consist of helping students develop
powerful constructs or "conceptual technologies" for making sense of these
systems. Sometimes these conceptual technologies involve only primitive representational props; but, in other cases, they involve spreadsheets, graphs,
graphics, software, or other representational systems that are embedded in
calculators, computers, or other technological gadgets; or, they may involve
"smart tools" based on Cartesian coordinates, matrices, and vector spaces,
complex diagrams, or other symbol systems involving spoken language, written symbol, or other representational media (Bransford, in press).

In any of the preceding cases, humans continually project their constructs into
the world in the form of artifacts that are not used for representational pur-

poses, as well as in the form of representation systems and other conceptual technologies.

REPRESENTATIONS CAN BE THOUGHT OF AS CONCEPTUAL TECHNOLOGIES ("SMART TOOLS")

Thinking of representation systems as "smart tools" has a number of useful implications. For example:

1. Even though there is a sense in which it is natural to speak of mathematical constructs as though they were pure systems disembodied from any tools, representations, or external artifacts, in practice beyond trivial situations, these conceptual systems seldom function without the support of powerful tools in which they are (partly) embedded.

2. When smart tools involve computers, calculators, or other conceptual amplifiers, it is clear that their users' conceptual systems do not reside solely within the boundaries of their minds. Their intelligence, their conceptualizing powers, and their processing powers, are distributed across a variety of levels and types of tools and representations.

3. Some tools clearly are more powerful than others; and, different tools tend to be most useful for different purposes. For example, many years ago, Bruner (1973) emphasized important roles that representation systems play to help humans go beyond the information that is given in particular learning or problem solving situations. Yet, if students are never asked to develop reusable tools, or sharable tools, or tools that can be easily modified for use in other situations, then we should not be surprised if their constructs lack generalizability, transportability, or modifiability.

4. To build a general tool does not guarantee that a the builder will be able to generalize. On the other hand, it is well known that when a person has a hammer in their hand, lots of things tend to look like nails. So, with tools, the key learning problem is not necessarily acquiring the ability to generalize. Often, the key problem is for students to become more discerning about identifying situations where the tool is appropriate.

THE MEANING OF CONSTRUCTS IS DISTRIBUTED ACROSS MULTIPLE REPRESENTATIONS

To emphasize several remaining roles that representations play in mathematics learning and problem solving, it is useful to reconsider several "realistic" versions of the kind of textbook word problems that were described in the earliest sections of this chapter. To generate such problems, one early method that we used was to begin by simply reviewing problems in textbooks and tests, and by sorting them into piles from "nonsense" to "reasonable" using criteria such as: (a) Could we envision this question ever arising in a realistic situation? (b) Would the answer that the test or textbook counted as correct really be the one that would be most sensible to give in this realistic situation? Then, for problems that were in the "reasonable" pile, we staged situations that were similar to the old television series, "Candid Camera." That is, in lumber yards, in pizza shops, and in other everyday situations that are familiar to students and their families, we set up problem situations similar to those that were described in textbooks (Lesh, Landau, & Hamilton 1983).

Example 1

In textbooks and tests, it is easy to find problems that refer to real objects or events. Boats go up and down streams; trains pass one another going in the same or opposite directions; swimming pools fill with water; ladders slide down walls; and, students are asked questions about how long, how fast, when, or where. But, very few of such situations really would be likely to occur in the everyday lives of students, or their friends or families; or, the answers that the authors consider to be "correct" often would not be sensible in real situations. For example, the multiple-choice exercise on the left (Fig. 15.8) was one that we found in a famous test produced by a famous test maker. Clearly, answer choice *b* is the one that the authors considered to be correct; but, in a real situation, it is equally clear that none of the answer choices is very reasonable. Choices *c, d,* and *e* imply that the whole board is shorter than the sum of its parts, a practical impossibility. But, answer *b* (the intended "correct" answer) is also impossible, because saw blades are not infinitely thin; so, some material must be lost during sawing, and the amount of loss depends on the factors such as the type of wood being cut (hardwood versus soft pine), the type of cut (ripping versus crosscutting), and the type and width of the saw blade. Answer *a* is the only feasible solution; yet, it implies a huge loss in sawing, perhaps by a very wide, dull saw blade, followed by vigorous sanding. The result is that, if a real woodworker confronted such a problem in a real situation, the only way they could given the "correct" school answer would be to turn off their real heads, thus engaging only their "school reasoning" (where nonsense is often rewarded).

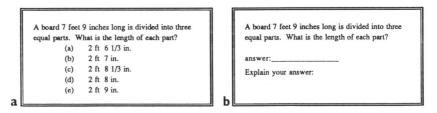

FIG 15.8.   (a) A typical multiple-choice question; (b) An attempt by teachers to improve the task.

To make several points that are most pertinent to this section, it is instructive to look at common attempts by teachers to improve the preceding exercise, by making it more realistic. For example, the problem in Fig. 15.8b shows the results from one such attempt that was based mainly on the current widespread aversion to multiple choice (pre-answered) items. The original multiple choice format was replaced by a politically correct "constructed response" format. Imagine what would happen if we asked a professional woodworker this revised question. What kind of response would we expect? Is it possible that 7 feet 9 inches might be an acceptable answer to the revised question? (a rip cut) Should the cuts preserve the thickness and width, but divide the length; should it preserve the width and length, but divide the thickness; or, should it preserve the length and thickness, but divide the width? How quickly is the answer needed? Is overestimating preferable to underestimating? How important is accuracy, precision, or lack of waste; what assumptions are reasonable to make about the effects of sanding and finishing the parts; and so on. Among other things, to answer such questions, a real woodworker would need to know the purpose of cutting the wood; and, if an explanation is needed, the woodworker would need to know who needs the explanation, and why. Without such information, there is no basis for deciding (for example) whether a 30-second or a 30-minute explanation is preferable.

What does the preceding example suggest about representations? One answer is that, when the problems are formulated in such a way that students need to construct purposeful descriptions, explanations, and justifications, they tend to introduce a much wider range of representations into their solutions and solution processes. Furthermore, when the purpose of a description is clear, students tend to deal with representation-related issues about appropriate levels of precision, accuracy, timeliness, and so on. Therefore, when an initial description is given, it nearly always needs to be extended, refined, or revised in order to be sufficiently useful. So, solutions involve a series of representation refinement cycles.

Example 2

When researchers such as Saxe (1990), Lave (1988), and Carraher, Carraher, & Schliemann (1985) observed people "doing mathematics" in supermarkets, lumber yards, or other everyday settings, one consistent observation has been that the ideas and procedures that people use in real situations are often quite different than those that they use in comparable school situations. For example, in real life situations, the ways most people calculate 15% tips tend to be quite different than the way they solve comparable word problems in textbooks or tests. Furthermore, whereas their performance may be nearly flawless in real situations, their performance is often poor for comparable school problems.

To investigate differences between "school answers" and "real answers," another tactic is to search newspapers, television advertisements, and other situations in which people use mathematics. Some relevant observations from these investigations include the following:

• Whereas textbook problems tend to involve only a few (often two) numbers that the student must combine using a simple rule (adding, subtracting, multiplying, dividing), real problems often involve whole collections of data, the data include quantities as well as numbers, it is often necessary to quantify qualitative information, and the relevant information often comes in the form of graphs, diagrams, or a combination of other representation systems.

• The relevant mathematical information goes far beyond simple counts and measures to also involve rankings, signed quantities, vector-valued quantities, coordinates, ratios and other relationships, continually changing quantities, accumulating quantities, or other types of quantities in which interesting representational issues tend to arise.

• Relevant "smart tools" tend to be available (such as calculators, spreadsheets, or graphics software). Therefore: (a) *problem interpretation* often is problematic because it is necessary to convert the situation to a form that facilitates tool use, and (b) *response interpretation* is problematic because the results that the tools produce may not be in a form that is immediately useful. For example, decimals may need to be converted to fractions, or graphic information may be converted to numeric information.

• The mathematical abilities that are highlighted often emphasize communication, planning, monitoring, and other types of higher order thinking that emphasize representational abilities. That is, students go beyond thinking *with* mathematical representations to also think *about* the relative strengths and weaknesses of alternative representations.

Example 3

In places like The Spot pizza shop in Evanston, Illinois, we staged "real life" versions of textbook word problems like the one below. One of the first children who came into the restaurant was a sixth grader named Jimmy Wyatt, a child we recognized from earlier research in Jimmy's school. The brief transcript that follows shows Jimmy's response.

Pat ate ¼ of a pizza, and Jan ate ⅓ of a pizza. How much pizza did they eat altogether?

Researcher: *Hi Jimmy. How about sitting down with me for a few minutes. I've got a couple of questions I want to ask you.*

Assistant: A research assistant, dressed like a waiter, put a plate on the table with ¼ of a pepperoni pizza. *Is this how much pizza you wanted Mr. _____?*

Researcher: *How much pizza is this, Jimmy?*

Jimmy: *About a fourth of a pizza.*

Assistant: Next, the waiter pushed the pepperoni pizza aside and put another plate on the table with ⅓ of a sausage pizza.

Researcher: (pointing to the sausage pizza) *Now, how much is this, Jimmy?*

Jimmy: *About a third of a pizza?*

Researcher: (pointing to both pizzas together) *So, if I ate this much pizza, how much pizza would I eat altogether?*

Jimmy: *That much! A little more than half.* (Jimmy was looking at the researcher quizzically, as if to say, "What a foolish question?")

The researcher tried several times to get Jimmy to give the "correct" school answer (¼ + ⅓ = ⁷⁄₁₂), but Jimmy clearly considered his answer to be appropriate, and he clearly *did not* consider it to be an appropriate to do a calculation (in spite of the fact that follow-up questioning confirmed that Jimmy was quite able to do the appropriate calculation correctly.)

What is the difficulty here? Why didn't Jimmy consider a calculation to be appropriate? If we (the researchers) were sitting right in front of some pizza, then in what sense is the textbook notion of "correctness" (⁷⁄₁₂ of a pizza) better than Jimmy's answer ("That much!")? How could we change the situation so that the kind of response that we were trying to elicit would be the one that would really make sense? In follow-up investigations, we discovered that pizza at The Spot usually was cut into sixths or eighths; but, unless some strange person (such as a mathematics education researcher) made a specific request, they never divided their pizzas into twelfths. Furthermore, even when we specifically asked for a pizza to be sliced into twelfths, the pieces varied in size so that referring to them as "twelfths" was not terribly accurate.

In what way could we modify the preceding task so that, when students gave the most sensible response, they would produce the kind of quantitative answer we were seeking? One solution is shown. (Note: We didn't want to reduce the problem to a commandment: "Do this calculation whether it makes sense or not.")

Put ¼ of a real pepperoni pizza on the table, and ask the child to notice how much pizza is in the box. Then, close the box and ask, "If I ate this much pizza, how much did I eat?" [If children need to see the pizza again, allow them to do so; but, once they have given an answer, close the lid and write this answer (¼) on the lid.] Next, put ⅓ of a real sausage pizza on the table, and ask the child, "If I eat this much pizza, how much will I eat?" Finally, with the sausage pizza box open and the pepperoni box closed, point to both boxes together and ask, "If I ate this much pizza, how much did I eat altogether?"

When the second version of the problem was used, students began to produce much more interesting, thoughtful, and representationally rich responses. One reason was because the children understood the need for the answers that they were being asked to produce. For example, it was no longer possible to simply point to the answer, by pointing to real pizzas that were in front of their noses). Therefore, children understood why some type of symbolic description was needed. Furthermore, the problem explicitly required students to combine two quantities that involved two different modes of representation (a symbol and a pizza). That is, the two quantities that were to be added did not simply involve two symbols (¼ and ⅓), or two words (one-fourth and one-third), or two objects (two pieces of pizza to be combined).

In our attempts to present textbook word problems in ways that make sense in everyday life, we noticed that, when two quantities occur, they are often expressed using different representation systems. That is, in realistic settings, the problem setting itself often inherently involves multiple modes of representation. One quantity may be represented using written symbols, and the other quantity may represented by real objects, such as a pizza. Therefore, one of the child's problems is to translate the given quantities into a single model of representation.

Example 4

Another way to focus on translations among representations, as well as to investigate differences between "school answers" and "real answers," is to begin with calculation tasks that commonly cause difficulties for children, and to ask teachers (or children) to use alternative representations to explain *why* their computational procedures work (Post, Behr, Lesh & Harel, 1991). For example, for the computation ¼ + ⅓ = ___, the brief descriptions that follow (see Fig. 15.9) show idealized abstracts of several different kinds of successful explanations that teachers have given using: (a) pictures or diagrams, (b) concrete manipulatives, (c) real life experiences, (d) language, or (e) symbols. Each of these explanations depends on ideas of equivalence and transformation. Yet, depending on which representation is used, somewhat different notions of equivalence tend to be emphasized. Some highlight part-whole relationships, whereas others emphasize part-part relationships. Some involve parts that cannot be subdivided, whereas others involve parts that are partitionable into smaller pieces. Some involve units that are "whole" objects, while others involve units that are simply aggregates of objects.

The preceding descriptions are referred to as idealized abstracts because the actual explanations that teachers gave usually were more complex and less internally consistent than those suggested here. For example, they often involve using more than a single mode of representation. One step might have emphasized written symbols; the next step might have involved spoken language; and, the following step might have involved references to a picture or to experiences with concrete materials. This is because different representation systems have different strengths and weaknesses. One may be ideally suited for describing states, whereas others may be better suited for describing actions. So, if they are challenged to explain why their computational procedures work, both students

Models Using Pictures or Diagrams
ADDING FRACTIONS USING RECTANGLES

Rectangles emphasize that FOURTHS and THIRDS are not the same size. So, to add, the following steps can be used to convert to the same kind of units.	1 FOURTH + 1 THIRD
1. Recut each pie using the same kind of cuts as in the other pie. The result is: 3 TWELFTHS + 4 TWELFTHS	
2. Rearrange the pieces so that it's easy to see what their sum will be.	
3. Find the sum by putting all of the parts into a single "whole" to get: 7 TWELFTHS	

Models Using Concrete Manipulatives
ADDING FRACTIONS USING COUNTERS

Counters emphasize part-part relationships. But, the "wholes" are not the same size. So, the following steps must be used to convert to the same kind of units.	1 FOURTH	◎ ○ ○ ○
	1 THIRD	◎ ○ ○
1. Add more counters, but keep the same ratios.	2 EIGHTHS	◎ ○ ○ ○ ◎ ○ ○ ○
	2 SIXTHS	◎ ○ ○ ◎ ○ ○
2. Add more counters, but keep the same ratios.	3 TWELFTHS	◎ ○ ○ ○ ◎ ○ ○ ○ ◎ ○ ○ ○
	3 NINTHS	◎ ○ ○ ◎ ○ ○ ◎ ○ ○
3. Find the sum by adding more counters until the "wholes" are the same.	3 TWELFTHS	◎ ○ ○ ○ ◎ ○ ○ ○ ◎ ○ ○ ○
	4 TWELFTHS	◎ ○ ○ ◎ ○ ○ ◎ ○ ○ ◎ ○ ○
	============	
The result is:	7 TWELFTHS	◎ ◎ ○ ◎ ◎ ○ ◎ ◎ ○ ◎ ○ ○

FIG 15.9. Teachers' explanations.

and teachers tend to switch back and forth among a variety of a modes of representation. It is only at quite advanced levels of development that they are able to restrict all of their work and/or explanations to a single mode of representation.

Example 5

Regardless whether students confront traditional word problems, computations, or real life situations, one of the most effective ways to improve understanding and competence has proven to be: (a) to focus on the kinds of transformations

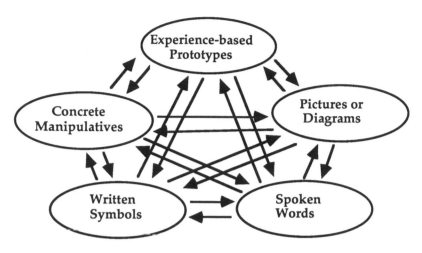

FIG 15.10.   Translation diagram.

and equivalence relationships that were emphasized in the preceding examples, and (b) to focus on translations within and among the kinds of representation systems depicted in the "translation diagram" (Lesh, Behr & Post, 1987).

In Fig 15.10, the arrows correspond to: (a) *symbol-to-picture translations:* for example, Given the symbol ⅓, draw an appropriate picture using a *pie diagram,* (b) *materials-to-words translations:* for example, Given an array of counters in which *one-third* are blue, generate an appropriate description using written or spoken language, (c) *pictures-to-materials translations:* for example, Given a picture showing a pie diagram in which *one-third* is shaded, use colored counters to construct an array in which *one-third* of the counters are blue, and so on. These translations were first emphasized in research with students who were identified as having "learning disabilities" (Lesh, 1979). But, we soon extended this research to average students and their teachers. The results showed that: (a) many students have difficulty with the preceding kinds of translations (Lesh, Landau, & Hamilton, 1983), (b) improving representational fluency is often a highly effective way to improve both problem solving ability and computational ability (Post, Behr, Lesh & Harel, 1992), (c) teachers generally find the *translation model* to be easy to use to convert traditional textbook problems into interesting and productive activities for instruction or assessment (Lesh & Zawojewski, 1987).

DIRECTIONS FOR THE FUTURE: REPRESENTATIONS MAY BE LINKED AND DYNAMIC

An overall purpose of this chapter has been to give examples that might help to forge new links between research in mathematics education and in developmental psychology. Special attention has been given to interactions among: (a) children's developing mathematics constructs, (b) representations that amplify the power and effectiveness of the preceding constructs, and (c) problem solving situations in which the preceding constructs and representations are useful.

In the future, changes can be expected to occur in the kind of constructs, representations, and problem solving situations that will need to be considered. For example, as technology based tools are used on a daily basis in fields ranging from the sciences to the arts and the humanities, and in professions ranging from agriculture to business and engineering, and in employment positions ranging from entry-level to the highest levels of leadership, these tools will increasingly expand: (a) the kinds of problem-solving and decision-making situations that need to be emphasized in instruction and assessment, and (b) the kinds of knowledge and abilities that are considered to be basic for success in a technology based society. To live and work in a technology based society, preparation for success will need to include much more than simply: *geometry* from the time of Euclid, *algebra* from the time of Descartes, *shopkeeper arithmetic* from the pre-industrial age, elementary *logical reasoning* from the time of Aristotle, and a few science topics from the time of Newton. Students will need to mathematize systems that involve more than simple counts, and simple measures. They will need to develop representational fluency for dealing with mathematical entities such as signed quantities (e.g., positive or negative), directed quantities (e.g., simple or intuitive uses of vectors [arrows]), ratios of quantities, rates (i.e., per quantities, or intensive quantities), coordinates, accumulating quantities, continuously changing quantities, quantified qualitative information, derived measures (e.g., based on a formula), student-invented constructs (e.g., based on a formula), measures associated with frequencies of events (probabilities), measures associated with sets of data (statistics), patterns (trends, sequences, series, etc.), logical statements (e.g., simple directions, programming commands, calculator commands, Boolean statements), and so on.

In the future, the nature of relevant representations also must change because, as human conceptualizing and processing capabilities are increasingly embedded within powerful technology based gadgets (such as computers and calculators), the kind of representation systems that are most useful tend to be both dynamically functioning and functionally linked (Kaput & Roschelle, 1996). So, the kind of representational fluency that was described in this chapter must be extended to include computer generated animations, graphs, tables, and notation systems; and, at the same time that new types of dynamic representations are used to make sense of real life situations (Pea, 1993; Kaput & Nemirovsky, 1995), real life activities also will be used as prototypes for thinking about computer based systems and real world artifacts that they are used to construct (Schank, 1990; Strom & Lehrer, in press).

REFERENCES

Bransford, J. D. (in press). *Enhancing thinking and learning.* San Francisco, CA: Freeman & Co.

Bringhurst, J. (1994). *Planes, jets & helicopters: Great paper airplanes.* Summit, PA: McGraw-Hill.

Bruner, J. (1973). *Beyond the information given.* New York, NY: Norton & Co.

Carraher, T., Carraher, D., & Schliemann, A. D. (1985). Mathematics in the streets and the schools. *British Journal of Developmental Psychology, 3,* 21–29.

Confrey, J. (1994). Splitting, similarity, and rate of change: A new approach to multiplication and exponential functions. In G. Harel & J. Confrey (Eds.), *The development of multiplicative reasoning,* (pp. 293–332). Albany, NY: State University of New York Press.

Greer, B. (1992). Multiplication and division a models of situations. In D. A. Grouws (Ed.), *Handbook of research on mathematics teaching and learning* (pp. 276–295). New York: Macmillan.

Kaput, J., & Nemirovsky, R. (1995). Moving to the next level: A mathematics of change theme throughout the K-16 curriculum. *UME Trends, 6*(6), 20–21.

Kaput, J., & Roschelle, J. (1996). SimCalc: Simulations for calculus learning (Computer Program). UMass Dartmouth, Mathematics Dept. 285 Old Westport Rd., No. Dartmouth, MA 02747–2300. Available via web site: http://www.simcalc.umassd.edu.

Lamon, S. J. (1995, July). Mathematical modeling and the way the mind works. Plenary lecture, 7th International Conference on the Teaching of Modeling and Applications (ICTMA7), University of Ulster. Jordanstown, Northern Ireland.

Lave, J. (1988). *Cognition in practice: Mind, mathematics and culture in everyday life.* New York: Cambridge University Press.

Lehrer, R., Horvath, J., & Schauble, L. (1996). Developing model-based reasoning. Manuscript submitted for publication.

Lesh, R. (1979). Mathematical learning disabilities: Considerations for identification, diagnosis, remediation. In R. Lesh, D. Mierkiewicz, & M. Kantowski (Eds.), *Applied mathematical problem solving* (pp. 111–180). Columbus, OH: ERIC.

Lesh, R. (1987). The evolution of problem representations in the presence of powerful conceptual amplifiers. In C. Janvier (Ed.), *Problems of representation in teaching and learning mathematics.* Hillsdale, NJ: Lawrence Erlbaum Associates.

Lesh, R., Behr, M., & Post, T. (1987). Rational number relations and proportions. In C. Janvier (Ed.), *Problems of representation in teaching and learning mathematics.* Hillsdale, NJ: Lawrence Erlbaum Associates.

Lesh, R., Hoover, M., & Kelly, A. (1993). Equity, technology, and teacher development. In I. Wirszup & R. Streit (Eds.), *Developments in school mathematics education around the world: Volume 3.* Reston, VA: National Council of Teachers of Mathematics.

Lesh, R., & Kaput, J. (1988). Interpreting modeling as local conceptual development. In J. DeLange & M. Doorman (Eds.), *Senior secondary mathematics education.* Utrecht, the Netherlands: OW&OC.

Lesh, R., Landau, M., & Hamilton, E. (1983). Conceptual models in applied mathematical problem solving research. In R. Lesh & M. Landau (Eds.), *Acquisition of mathematics concepts & processes* (pp. 263–343). New York: Academic Press.

Lesh, R., & Zawojewski, J. (1987). Problem solving. In T. Post (Ed.), *Teaching mathematics in grades K-8: Research-based methods.* Boston: Allyn & Bacon.

Minsky, M. (1986). *The society of mind.* New York: Simon & Schuster.

Nemirovsky, R. (1992). *Students' graphical representations of motion: A basic vocabulary of shapes* (TERC Technical Report). Cambridge, MA: TERC.

Pea, R. D. (1993). Practices of distributed intelligence and designs for education. In G. Salamon (Ed.), *Distributed cognition* (pp. 47–87). New York: Cambridge University Press.

Post, T., Behr, M., Lesh, R. & Harel, G. (1991). Intermediate teachers' knowledge of rational number concepts. In E. Fennema, T. Carpenter, & S. Lamon (Eds.), *Integrating research on teaching and learning mathematics.* Albany, NY: SUNY Press.

Post, T., Behr, M., Lesh, R. & Harel, G. (1992). Learning and teaching ratio and proportion: Research implications. In D. Owens (Ed.), *Mathematics education research in the middle.* New York: Macmillan.

Saxe, G. (1990). The interplay between children's learning in formal and informal social contexts. In M. Gardner, J. Greeno, F. Reif, & A. Schoenfeld (Eds.), *Toward a scientific practice of science education.* Hillsdale, NJ: Lawrence Erlbaum Associates.

Schank, R. (1990). *Tell me a story: A new look at real and artificial memory.* New York: Scribner.

Strom, D., & Lehrer, R. (in press). Springboards to algebra. In J. Kaput (Ed.), *Employing children's natural powers to build algebraic reasoning in the content of elementary mathematics.* Manuscript in preparation.

Thompson, P. W. (1994). The development of the concept of speed and its relationship to concepts of rate. In G. Harel & J. Confrey (Eds.), *The development of mulitplicative reasoning in the learning of mathematics* (pp. 179–234). Albany, NY: State University of New York Press.

von Glasersfeld, E. (1990). Environment and communication. In L. P. Steffe & T. Wood (Eds.), *Transforming children's mathematics education: International perspectives* (pp. 30–38). Hillsdale, NJ: Lawrence Erlbaum Associates.

CHAPTER 16

Representational Issues in Assessment Design

DREW H. GITOMER
LINDA S. STEINBERG
Educational Testing Service

Assessment, and its associated representations, have a dominant presence in education. As but one example, imagine the annual reporting of standardized test scores to parents and communities each spring. Children bring home score reports, while schools, districts, and states provide information about student performance at group levels. Each of these reports is a communication that relies on powerful representational forms that are designed to serve one or more specific purposes—to indicate an individual student's, school's, or state's relative standing, or to identify specific areas of weakness for an individual or group.

The communication of assessment results is but one aspect of assessment that depends on and is affected by representational form. Within the assessment community, as well as among the general public, a great deal of attention has been given to the response format of the assessment itself—whether students are asked to choose between available options (i.e., multiple choice) or whether they engage in more open-ended tasks (e.g., essays), for example.

Issues of assessment format and reporting of results, though most salient, are but a subset of representational issues that determine the character and quality of an assessment. In this chapter, we attempt to make two points. First, we introduce the design of educational assessment as a much larger set of representational challenges that need to be addressed in consideration of the purpose of an assessment. We argue that attention to response format alone, independent of the nature and purpose of an assessment, is counterproductive. In fact, a preoccupation with form, especially with increasing use of technology, as in the burgeoning preference for multimedia instruments and authentic performances, threatens to overwhelm considerations of the essential purpose and value of an assessment.

An assessment is a tool to convey and capture meaning through a set of forms and structures. Although assessments are often categorized on the basis of task response demands (e.g., multiple choice vs. essay), or on presentation medium (e.g., paper or via computer) (e.g., Bennett, 1993), an assessment is defined by far more than the superficial appearance of a task and its response demands. Forms and structures are the tools used to solicit and collect evidence from students, to make inferences about the students and their performances, and to provide feedback (Mislevy, 1994). Forms and structures are not inherently good or bad—their adequacy can be considered only in terms of their ability to satisfy the purpose(s) of a given assessment.

Second, we attempt to clarify how the choice of physical representations in assessment design support students' interpretations and responses to an assessment. We describe how representational choices have a significant effect on how individuals respond to the assessment, whether as individuals who take assessments[1] or as individuals who are consumers of information produced by the assessments (e.g., policymakers).

Representational choices must be made in light of two principles that govern the design of any assessment. A first principle is that assessment claims made about individuals and groups, and corresponding feedback provided, are determined by the purpose of the assessment. So, for example, if the purpose of an assessment is to identify third-grade mathematics achievement, claims about student knowledge of matrix algebra are irrelevant. If, on the other hand, the students were advanced high school mathematics students, then claims about matrix algebra are much more germane. Second, claims about student performance must be supported by defensible inferences grounded in relevant evidence. Simply put, is there a legitimate basis from which to claim that a student knows or can do something? Additionally, there must be some assurance that inferences based on an individual's performance are due to his or her own ability and not because the assessment task is unclear or irrelevant to the ability being measured.

Given these principles, the assessment task presented (what the student sees) is only one aspect of the assessment design, and is the consequence of a complex set of choices made during design. Throughout this chapter, when we refer to representation, we make no claim that the external representation system used in the assessment has the same properties as any internal mental representations, only that there are "informational equivalencies" between the two (see Goel, 1995).

---

[1] For purposes of this chapter, we use the umbrella term *students* as a shorthand for those individuals who take assessments used within educational institutions, although certain assessments in education are developed for other groups of individuals (e.g., teachers).

Though assessments are ubiquitous in education, these assessments have different purposes, different appearances, and occur in widely varying circumstances: college entrance selection using a standardized test booklet in an auditorium with many other students; remedial tutoring using a computer adaptive test in the cubicle of a learning center; guidance for a teacher's instructional decisions using Socratic dialogue, writing tasks, or laboratory experiments in a classroom; professional development using an intelligent tutoring system in a job location. In all these contexts, students have the common experience of being part of an interchange that requires them to attend to prompts, figure out what is wanted, and respond. Assessments play a role in this interchange to the degree that they are responsive to the student, provide support to encourage and shape student responses, interpret responses, and provide some form of feedback with, for example, another question, a score, or a comment. Whether delivered by human, paper-and-pencil, or machine, all aspects of an assessment give shape to the student's experience. We posit that the design features contribute to a kind of discourse, *the discourse of assessment,* which is made up of the interactions and interpretations shaped by the student and the assessment itself. In order for any discourse to be effective, it must be guided by certain pragmatic building blocks (Grice, 1975), such as a shared understanding of goals by participants, use of commonly accepted general and specific ground rules, and the holding of common knowledge by those who are engaged (Edwards & Mercer, 1987). Just as there are principles for carrying out an effective discourse generally, we propose a set of guiding principles for effective discourse within assessment contexts.

Throughout this chapter, we refer to the assessment as an active participant in the discourse. We do not intend to anthropomorphize assessment. Instead, we take the position that an assessment reflects the intentions of its designers. The properties of the assessment (e.g., how a task performance is scored) represent prescribed and often automated methods for communicating to the student the intent of the designers.[2] In some cases, such as the scoring of portfolios, the inferences may indeed be made by human beings, whereas in other cases the scoring will be carried out through automated rules programmed into a computerized scoring system.

Much has been written about the role that discourse plays in describing and defining social relationships (e.g., Foucault, 1980; Gee, 1990; Hicks, 1995; Lemke, 1995; Luke, 1995). Analyses of discourse have helped us understand how meaning is developed, represented, and communicated in classrooms (e.g., Cazden, 1988; Edwards & Mercer, 1987; Lemke, 1990; Rosebery, Warren, & Conant, 1992). In a parallel way, we propose a framework to analyze the discourse of as-

---

[2]Note that the stance of treating an artifact as an active participant in a discourse is a hallmark of a number of theories of literary analysis (e.g., Rosenblatt, 1978). Similarly, computer programs are often referred to in anthropomorphic terms, not because we believe them to be human, but because the information they present are representations conceived and implemented by human designers.

sessment that we hope will contribute to an understanding of assessment by assessment designers as well as consumers of assessment information.

The framework addresses representational challenges at four interacting levels—the *purpose* of the assessment, the *domain* of the assessment, the assessment *task,* and assessment *feedback.* At each level, we describe how representational challenges can be addressed to design effective assessments. Effective assessments are those that allow for meaningful inferences relevant to the purpose of the assessment and that do so by supporting a productive discourse in which there is a shared goal of conveying and communicating meaning on the part of student, assessment, and consumer of assessment information. That is, the purpose and structure of the assessment is clear to students, students respond to the best of their ability in ways that can be adequately interpreted by the assessment, inferences about student performance are grounded in clear evidence, and feedback is soundly based and clear to students and other consumers of assessment information.

When the discourse is not completely effective and when representational choices do not support the assessment purpose, the outcome of the assessment is less successful. We point out common assessment practices that do not fully take into account these representational challenges, with resulting weaknesses in the assessment.

PURPOSE AND ITS ROLE IN SHAPING ASSESSMENTS

Claiming that assessments need to be designed and used with their purposes in mind might seem obvious, but oftentimes assessments are put to use for purposes never intended or justified. Clarity of purpose enables the specification of the entire assessment design by providing significant constraint and guidance on the types of inferences drawn, evidence elicited from the student in the form of responses, and feedback given to the individual taking the assessment as well as to other interested parties. When we speak of clarity of purpose, it is with the understanding that assessment instruments are commonly expected, rightly or wrongly, to fulfill more than a single purpose. By clarifying *all* purposes, it becomes possible to place them in order of priority and discover whether there are inherent conflicts of purpose and decide whether multiple purposes can be accommodated within a single instrument.

An effective assessment discourse is one in which the participants share an understanding of the assessment's rationale—its purpose and consequences, decisions that will be made, and actions that will be taken. The prerequisite for a productive discourse requires that the student and the assessment design begin with the same fundamental questions:

- What is the reason for this assessment?
- How are the results of this assessment going to be used?

There are many different reasons why an assessment is designed. An assessment might be used to determine *achievement:* Does a student demonstrate mastery of core competencies necessary for high school graduation? Other assessments will attempt *prediction:* Does a job candidate evidence a set of aptitudes associated with a strong likelihood of employment success. Still other assessments have the primary purpose of being *diagnostic:* Are there specific areas of weakness that can be identified for remediation? Understanding the purpose of an assessment is of special importance because the consequences of inappropriate test use should be strenuously avoided (Messick, 1989). Inappropriate test use can result when misunderstandings of the assessment's purpose exist on the part of any of those engaged with an assessment—the designers, the student, or those who use assessment results for information or guidance. In other words, the discourse is not coherent—there is not shared meaning among participants.

Representational forms such as speech or writing support meaningful discourse precisely because they are familiar and accepted ways of communicating. However, assessment discourse is often incoherent, particularly to students, because of the confounding of purpose and representation. From many quarters, there have been criticisms of assessment practice (e.g., Resnick & Resnick, 1985; Schwartz & Viator, 1990; Stiggins, 1991; Wiggins, 1993). We believe these criticisms to have two primary sources. First, there have been fundamental disagreements, misunderstandings, and mismatches involving the purpose of given assessments. When some parties hold that the purpose of an assessment is to improve student learning, and others believe that the primary purpose ought to be to provide a relative rank of individuals, any resultant discourse is likely to be disjointed.

The second source of dissatisfaction has been a mismatch between the representational forms and formats of assessment and the given purpose of an assessment. If, for example, the purpose of an assessment is to probe deeply a student's understanding in order make very specific instructional decisions, then assessment representations that summarize performance into a single score are most likely inadequate.

For any and all intended purposes, representations are needed that support valid inferences about a student. Messick (1980, 1989) has made the point that there is nothing inherently "valid" about an assessment. Validity can be considered only in terms of whether the inferences and actions taken on the basis of an assessment are justified and appropriate given the purposes of the assessment. Using an assessment for selection based on a prediction of future performance is very different from using an assessment for instructional diagnosis. For example, when considering a selection instrument, the discourse, and corresponding representations are focused on an underlying construct described by a single number, such as mathematical or verbal ability. Conversely, in order for an assessment to be useful instructionally, specific learning goals and indices of performance with respect to those goals must be explicitly articulated in sufficient detail to support instructional feedback. Nevertheless, there are myriad examples of invalid use of assessments that are valid for other purposes. The use of Scholastic Aptitude Test (SAT) scores as a measure of educational quality across states (e.g., Bell, 1984), rather than as a predictor of first-year college success, is but one example. Such scores say more about the demographics of a state than they do about educational quality per se.

Invalid use of assessments are invariably linked to a mismatch between the content of the assessment with its associated representations, and the intended purpose of an assessment. If an assessment has the purpose of illuminating a student's reasoning processes, then asking students to represent their understanding by selecting one of several available options is probably insufficient. If the purpose of the assessment is to rank individuals with respect to some criterion, individualized descriptions of the strengths and weaknesses of a given individual will be insufficient representations to justify all but the most general rankings.

For effective design, all of the features of the assessment must be consistent with its purpose. Of utmost importance are considerations of the domain of the assessment itself: What niche of human performance does it address and how are knowledge and skills represented?

THE DOMAIN AS THE FOCUS OF ASSESSMENT

The domain of an assessment refers to both the *nature and scope* of the subject matter being assessed as well as the *representational forms* in which the subject matter is expressed. If purpose is the *why* of the assessment discourse, then domain considerations define the *what* of the discourse. The choice of representation conveys meaning about the essential nature of a domain that includes not only the declarative content of a domain, but also the ways in which the content is structured, represented, and reasoned about in the course of problem solving. In arithmetic, for example, we can verbally articulate that *two plus three equals five*. However, mathematics uses alternative representations such as $2 + 3 = 5$, and in order to say that someone can "do arithmetic," the expectation is that an individual can work with mathematical representations. Further, arithmetic ability is not simply knowledge of a set of number facts, or even the ability to apply an algorithm. Arithmetic skill also requires conceptual understandings of order, magnitude, and place value.

Thus, in building an assessment for arithmetic, or for any other domain, we must be explicit about the nature of the subject matter and what part of the domain is to be assessed. Equally important, we need to be explicit about the forms and structures used to express domain content and ensure that they are considered in assessment design. Certainly, we would be surprised if a mathematics assessment contained only words, but no numbers. A strong impetus behind the push for authentic assessments is the recognition that academic assessments have not always employed representational forms consistent with the nature of the domain. For example, assessments of writing ability frequently neglected to ask students to write!

Scope of Content Representation

Obviously, a mathematics assessment will have different content from a history assessment. However, subject matter alone does not determine the content of an assessment. The purpose of the assessment also will shape how the domain is represented in terms of the scope of the domain that is assessed. For example, if the purpose of an assessment is to determine whether a student has attained a sufficient level of mathematical understanding to graduate from high school, the domain representation only need include content that characterizes high-school-level knowledge of mathematics. Contrast this, though, with an assessment that has as its purpose the diagnosis of mathematical skill in order to make instructional decisions. In this case, the domain content needs to include features of the domain that address the development of understanding and skilled performance within the domain. In the former case, the domain representation does not need to include content that describes how one acquires skill—the only concern is whether an individual has a skill at the moment of testing. In the latter case, diagnosis and remediation can occur only if there is a more detailed understanding of why an individual could not solve a problem that is likely to include knowledge of what kinds of problems the individual is able to solve successfully.

For assessments with other purposes, what gets represented in the domain may be substantially different. For example, in developing an assessment that is used for selection purposes, the most salient aspects of domain knowledge will be those that yield individual differences on which selection can be based—possibly the more complex aspects of the domain. Here the goal is to distinguish people, not to diagnose with specificity what an individual knows or does not know. Hence, for an assessment in a highly competitive situation (e.g., fighter pilot, prestigious university), most students may have impressive capabilities. The purpose of the assessment is not to identify the competencies people have in common, but to focus on those competencies that will distinguish a subset of individuals from the rest of the pack.

Nature of Content Representation

The nature of content representation is an important epistemological question that is the subject of significant philosophical inquiry across disciplines. Any assessment needs to confront the question, *"What does it mean to know"* as well.

Perhaps the most common issue in the nature of content representation concerns the relationship between the declarative knowledge of the domain and the processes that are needed to reason about that knowledge. Declarative knowledge refers to *knowing that* understanding, knowledge that can be demonstrated by verbal retrieval—"*I know that the first president of the United States was George Washington.*" Reasoning processes can range from very general inductive and deductive strategies to specific reasoning strategies developed in the context of learning a domain, for example, structuring a mathematical proof.

For both heuristic and substantive reasons, domain representations often separate declarative knowledge from reasoning processes (e.g., Doran, 1990; Sternberg, 1985). With such bifurcated modes of representations, assessments typically focus on knowledge of either content or process in the absence of content. In science, for instance, a process question might focus on experimental design using a variable as a control, whereas a declarative question might focus on facts about meiosis. However, such representations are not conducive to assessments of how, for example, one sets up a controlled experiment to study meiosis.

The tendency to represent process and content as distinct entities runs counter to what is known about the nature of skilled performance across almost all domains. Proficiency or expertise in virtually all domains of educational import requires the integration of conceptual structures, reasoning strategies, and specific skills and abilities that are necessary to engage in reasoning within the domain (Glaser et al., 1985). Hodson (1992) made the argument that it is fallacious to think about reasoning processes as being independent of content. In fact, with regard to science, Hodson argued that even processes such as "observation" are affected by the understanding and theoretical underpinnings that the observer brings to the situation. As just one example, both the marine biologist and fly fisherman may be keen observers of bodies of water, yet what they choose to focus on in their observations, and even when they choose to make their observations, is determined by the problems they are trying to solve and the relevance of certain features to the task at hand.

For assessment design, the nature of representation is not simply a philosophical problem. Decisions about representation determine the character of the assessment and the kind of evidence collected to measure performance. Many tests of achievement tests, whether standardized or developed by teachers for classroom use, represent the domain as declarative knowledge only. Often, knowledge is represented as a set of discrete concepts ("facts") as well, rather than as interrelated conceptual structures. With such representations of the domain, a set of multiple-choice items, each focused on a single concept, is a natural and efficient assessment design solution.

If reasoning processes in a domain are represented apart from content, this has an important consequence for design as well. In science, for example, questions may be developed that focus on experimental design, but in contexts for which the content issues are intended to be irrelevant, or at least the content is so simple that it is assumed to be known by all students. For example, a question might ask students to design the following experiment: Given an inclined plane and two small vehicles with wheels made of different material, how could you design an experiment that could tell you which was a better wheel material for faster cars? A student would need to produce a response that showed an understanding of controlled experimentation (e.g., rolling both vehicles off the same plane at the same place), recording measurements, and so on. However, what would not be expected in this kind of item is an explanation of physical forces that underlie the findings.

When the domain is represented as having interrelated content and reasoning processes, assessment tasks tend to take on a different quality. In order to capture evidence about these complex interrelationships, assessment tasks will share much more with tasks that are undertaken as part of negotiating the domain outside of the assessment context. The gulf between domain tasks and assessment tasks is narrowed. In science, for example, the assessment task might have students design a study to explore a particular issue in science, or provide an explanation given a set of data, tasks that share much more with practices engaged in by scientists than do assessment tasks that ask for the recall of factual information.

In the vernacular of assessment, tasks that are more consistent with practices of the domains themselves are considered to be "authentic." However, it is important to note that what makes the assessment authentic is that the evidence collected addresses the student's understanding of content and reasoning simultaneously. Simply designing an assessment task that shares certain task characteristics, but does not attend to the relationship of content and process does not reflect an interrelated domain structure. So, for example, if a student is asked to design an experiment, but only methodological procedures are assessed whereas conceptual issues are ignored, then the assessment task does not accurately reflect the domain representation

Forms of Content Representation

As important as the scope and nature of the domain are the actual forms used to represent domain concepts. These representations have significant impact on how information is communicated to students in an assessment and how students are able to respond. More than that though, representational forms provide a "language"—a particular grammar and lexicon for communication about the domain, specifically within an assessment. An effective assessment must use representational forms that are consistent with the nature of the domain and allow for inferences about a student's knowledge about the domain.

The language, which may be expressed in one or many forms, comprises the legitimate representations (e.g., verbal, mathematical, graphical, etc.) that can be used to elicit and express knowledge. One can image the very different representational forms necessary according to the domain and/or domain tasks. Imagine a student asked to engage in different kinds of written communication tasks in different domains. Asked to describe a summer vacation, the student is apt to use prose, and may even include pictures and/or photographs. For giving written travel directions to visitors from a foreign, non-English-speaking country, the student may best represent information with a map. Writing about mathematics is likely to best be communicated in the language of mathematics, using mathematical expressions and graphs. A student writing about scientific processes may use diagrams to convey understanding.

Availability and choice of representational forms serve to clarify the nature and scope of the domain as well. A mathematics assessment that did not present, or solicit mathematical expressions in student responses would most likely be thought of as an inadequate assessment of the mathematics domain. In mathematics, the forms are not only useful for communication within the assessment, but provide a language that students of mathematics use to reason about mathematics. Thus, if the assessment does not support mathematical expressions as representations, then it is likely that important aspects of mathematical reasons will be assessed inadequately.

In assessment design, the attention to both purpose and domain cannot be underestimated. Only with clarity on these two fronts can a coherent, well-designed assessment be constructed. In the next section, we discuss design considerations of the assessment task (or set of tasks) itself. The assessment task is the vehicle through which an understanding of student ability or achievement is constructed.

CONSTRUCTING MEANING
THROUGH THE ASSESSMENT TASK

When we refer to assessment task design, we mean far more than simply the question or prompt asked of the student. In addition to the prompt itself, we include specifications of the claims to be made about a student's knowledge, the evidence that will be considered from a student's response and how it will be collected, and the inferential processes for using evidence to make valid claims about a student's knowledge state.

We adopt a framework that considers assessment as a process that includes the collection and synthesis of evidence together with judgment and other inferential processes that operate on the evidence in order to make claims about a student or students (Mislevy, 1994). A well-designed assessment is one in which good evidence of student understanding is collected and sound judgments of that evidence are made. Specifically, four distinct but interdependent elements must be considered:

1. *Inferential goals.* Based on student performance in the assessment, these are the claims, explanations, or predictions made about the student (e.g., how well the student understands concept X). Not only must these goals be defined, but they must also be communicated clearly to students and others involved in the assessment process.

2. *Evidence.* This is the information arising from student performance in the assessment that supports the claims we would like made about the student. Mislevy (1994) has clarified the distinction between data and evidence for assessment purposes. Data become evidence when they are relevant to a given hypothesis (e.g., the work shown contributes to a demonstration of student understanding of concept X; the age of the student, for example, though valid data, does not constitute evidence for such a claim). Defining evidence requires an explication of assumptions that articulates the relationship between states of knowledge that cannot be observed directly but wish to make claims about (our hypotheses) and those things that can be observed (the evidence).

3. *Inferential processes.* This is the reasoned use or integration of one or more types and items of evidence to support claims, explanations, or predictions. Inferential processes require principled assumptions about how evidence can be aggregated to reflect beliefs about the way knowledge is structured in the domain.

4. *Management of uncertainty.* In assessment, the mapping of evidence to claims is never absolute. Did the person make a lucky guess? For what claims does the evidence not provide information? Although an assessment system can never eliminate uncertainty, it can make more credible claims if uncertainty is recognized explicitly and incorporated into the inference and communication components of the assessment.

Defining and Communicating Inferential Goals. An effective assessment and assessment discourse requires that the inferential goals, the assessment evidence, inferential processes, and management of uncertainty are all consistent and congruent with the defined purpose and domain of the assessment. Further, the student must understand what is being asked, lest the response be evidence of something other than what is intended by the designers of the assessment.

Inferential goals arise, in part, from clarity about domain representation in the context of an assessment's purpose. However, with respect to task design, further specificity is needed. A sound assessment communicates very clearly to the student what claims will be made based on the assessment. These typically are communicated, with differing levels of effectiveness, in test bulletins, test directions, and scoring rubrics, but can also be communicated within the assessment itself. Effective communication can help the students prepare for the assessment. Guidance about what is sought can change the way students study or prepare materials for submission in a context such as an essay or portfolio assessment. Absent such guidance, it becomes problematic to draw inferences about a student's performance. If a student is attempting to provide evidence about an aspect of understanding deemed irrelevant or less important from the perspective of the assessment designer, then it is difficult to disentangle whether the inference is about student understanding of the domain or student understanding of what kind of evidence the assessment designers are seeking. Good assessment should not involve gamesmanship about figuring out what "they" want, whether the "they" be the teacher or the test developer for a large-scale standardized assessment.

To the extent that a student misunderstands the kinds of evidence sought to support specific inferences to be made, there is a risk that the evidence provided in a performance will not yield valid interpretations of what a student knows about a domain. Though desired inferences ought to be related directly to purpose and domain, there are often inconsistencies in the discourse between the assessment and the student that lead to dissatisfaction with the assessments. When students or teachers raise complaints that an assessment does not really tap important understandings, then it may be that the assessment has not adequately represented its inferential goals and associated requirements for evidence. Failure to understand such goals (*"Oh, you mean you wanted to know how I figured this problem out, not just if I knew the answer? That means I should have shown my work"*) can lead to assessment performances that are not valid indicators of student understanding.

Eliciting and Interpreting Data for Evidence. An effective assessment is one in which assessment tasks elicit data with two essential characteristics. First, the data must be relevant to the targets of inference. Second, the data must be interpretable in that they are understandable as evidence of inferential claims. Data can be relevant, yet the assessment may not have sufficient interpretive capacity to recognize the data as evidence. Regardless of the vastness of data collected, there is no useful assessment information unless the data can be adequately interpreted and classified or categorized as supporting some inference. In fact, one of the challenges to performance assessment is the difficulty in creating rubrics that provide scorers with clear and consistent frameworks for structuring evidence out of the often complex and ambiguous data that are presented in student work samples.

The implication for task design is that there must be consideration of both relevance and interpretability. If interpretation is problematic, then the nature of data elicited and/or the interpretive structures must be modified. The goals of relevance and interpretability should be considered iteratively, for these two aspects of assessment design cannot be isolated from each other.

What evidence is being sought must be clear to the student. In highly constrained assessments (e.g., multiple choice), the student typically has a good idea of response requirements (e.g., selecting the best choice among available options). For less constrained response forms, such as essays, forms of guidance need to be communicated to students to enhance the likelihood of their providing data that can become reliable evidence of their understanding. In a performance assessment, such guidance can be communicated through clear task instructions, expectations, examples, prompts, and cues. For example, if a writing task has three subsections, page limits for the length of each subsection communicate to the student the relative import of each subsection, guiding students in the allocation of time and resources to different portions of the response. The assessment task directions can also state that evidence of such things as student reasoning and not only final solutions is sought, again helping the student to provide evidence from which valid interpretations can be rendered.

The task should also communicate the forms of representation that are admissible as data. Must all responses be written verbally, or does the student have the potential (or mandate) to use graphical, mathematical, and/or oral representations for their work? Decisions about admissible representational forms involves two classes of considerations, both of which must be considered as trade-offs that need to be weighed against the kinds of representational forms that are inherent to the nature of the domain:

1. *Operational constraints.* Constraints of time, cost, and technology constrain the kinds of representations a student will be able to use. If the time available for an assessment is only 1 hour, for example, then representations that are time consuming would not be appropriate. The cost of scoring may make certain representations, particularly those that require significant human capital, prohibitively expensive. Available technological tools will also impose limits on available representational forms.

2. *Usability by the student.* A second consideration is the extent to which the assessment can facilitate, or block, the student's use of different representations. Some support issues are related to conceptual guidance. For example, if a student is asked to provide a diagram, is it clear to the student what expectations are to be met through the use of the diagram? Are verbal annotations allowable? Is it clear to the student what qualities of performance are being evaluated during an oral presentation?

Other support issues are often technical, and relate to how the assessment captures student performance. In constructing a diagram, for example, one could envision a student inventing a representation on paper with very few constraints or, on the other hand, constructing a diagram with a limited set of operators and options provided within a computer system. Although the latter approach constrains the potential responses, it has the virtue of providing evidence that is more easily interpreted by the scoring apparatus. To the extent that constraints on the response are reduced, additional demands are placed on the interpretive capacity of either a human or automated scorer. For assessments with complex and open-ended response requirements, only repeated experience by both students and assessors will lead to clear understanding of what is expected as evidence of quality performance.

Giving Meaning to Evidence.   Once students have provided representations in their responses, inferences about student understanding are possible. Whether scorers are humans or computers, there need to be reasoning structures that connect students' representations to inferences and claims about student understanding.

Try as we may, we can never directly observe what a student knows. The best we can do is collect evidence about what a student does. In some few instances, such as an Olympic race, what the "students" do *is* all we care about. We do not care who is generally "faster," who is more likely to win a race next week, or who would make a better football player or coach. All we care about is who won on that day in that race. For almost all educational assessments however, this is not the case, for it is the constructs underlying the performance that are the real target of interest. The assessments are designed to tell us about more general levels of accomplishment that go beyond the specific prompts, or to predict academic or career success in other settings, for instance.

In order to make these kinds of inferences, a *theory of performance* must exist as the framework within which evaluation of evidence takes place. Theories of performance are embodied in the task(s) selected to generate assessment evidence, the assumption being that examining the performance of those tasks can yield legitimate inferences about what a student knows. The theory allows for claims such as *Given (high, low) understanding of Concept X, it is (more, less) certain that the student should produce Evidence Y when performing Task Z.* A theory of performance characterizes domain understanding, evidence, and tasks in terms of performance expectations and certainty.

The value and meaning of the same evidence elicited from the same task is heavily influenced by performance expectations. For example, the interpretation of a given response will be considered differently in mathematics depending on whether it is produced by a 4th-grader or a 10th-grader. With the linkage of explicit assumptions about what a student knows with explicit expectations about what a student should be able to do, claims about student performance can be made.

It is possible that task evidence can relate to a single domain construct, or to multiple constructs. The inferential challenge is to determine how different pieces of evidence change the beliefs and claims about student understanding. One challenge is how to aggregate evidence across different tasks to make coherent and defensible claims about a student. For traditional assessment approaches, that aggregation is, more or less, a summary of the number of correct items (Lord, 1980). More modern psychometric models also account for the difficulty of items in considering an aggregated score (Lord, 1980; Wainer, 1990). For many of these assessments, the inferential machinery is a mathematical summary of individual response accuracy, which may or may not be weighted, and is represented by a single score along with some metric for describing the certainty of the inference (e.g., a standard error of measurement).

Aggregation into a single score, however, is insufficient for assessments that have instructional diagnosis as their primary purpose. For these kinds of assessments, aggregations are needed that are based on, and locate, patterns of performance associated with multiple discrete and instructionally addressable issues within the domain representation (Haertel & Wiley, 1993).

In order to provide more detailed claims about student understanding, the assessment design must have certain characteristics. First, the relationship between each task and all relevant aspects of the domain must be clearly articulated in order to understand the commonality and uniqueness between and among assessment tasks. Articulation permits evidentiary links to be forged between task performances and specific aspects of the domain structure. In addition, the process of articulating these links can, given the evidence provided by existing tasks, reveal ambiguities about what inferences can legitimately be made about particular domain constructs. Such ambiguities can suggest elaborations of the domain representation, creation of new tasks, or both. It is also a way of beginning to identify and manage problems related to redundant, missing, and hearsay (second hand) evidence (Schum, 1987).

Second, a substantial understanding of the relationship between different aspects of the domain is needed. Are certain understandings prerequisite to others? Do deficits in some aspects of understanding make it likely that there are other deficits? The articulation of these relationships with assessment tasks is especially valuable in that it allows evidence to be seen as bearing directly or indirectly on given aspects of the domain. For example, in assessing mathematics understanding, if a student does well with calculus problems, one can assume an understanding of algebra, though the converse is not true. However, the further the inferences drawn are removed from direct sources of evidence, the more problematic and less informative they become, even when they are statistically correlated. For example, although a vocabulary test is related empirically to other measures of reading and writing skill, one would not use a vocabulary test as a direct assessment of writing accomplishment, nor as the basis for making instructional recommendations about a student's writing.

Third, there must be processes and structures for aggregating diverse, and potentially contradictory, forms of evidence. For some assessments, this aggregation is the product of human judgment, disciplined by scorer-training processes (e.g., LeMahieu, Gitomer, & Eresh, 1995). For other assessments, the aggregation is statistical, but also grounded in an understanding and articulation of conceptual links between aspects of the domain and assessment tasks. With these approaches, claims about student understanding of different aspects of the domain are updated as new task performance evidence is integrated (e.g., Gitomer, Steinberg, & Mislevy, 1995; Mislevy & Gitomer, 1995). Taken together, these likelihoods represent belief about a student's coordinated domain understanding.

Thus, effective task design must address the structure of knowledge and its relationship to performance, the value and meaning of discrete pieces and aggregations of evidence, the explicit assumptions underlying a theory of performance, and uncertainty. Given this design, the likelihood of being able to make valid and defensible claims about student understanding is enhanced. Such design also facilitates the design of effective feedback to students and others about assessment results.

THE PLACE OF FEEDBACK IN ASSESSMENT

Though different types of communication and representations within the assessment have been described to this point, much is tacit and embedded within the assessment design. The most explicit communication in the discourse of assessment involves feedback that the student receives from the assessment. Explicit feedback can be given during an assessment as well as upon completion. During the assessment, effective feedback supports desired actions and makes clear what kinds of student responses to the feedback are admissible. Effective feedback upon the completion of the assessment will be relevant, informative, and support desired actions by the student.

Undoubtedly, the most recognizable form of feedback is the single test score, together with any decision resulting from the test score (e.g., *"I passed the course"*). However, feedback can serve other purposes, such as evaluating, motivating, correcting, and directing the student. Feedback is also likely to have unintended consequences (Messick, 1989), but we limit this discussion to intended aspects of feedback design. Relevant and useful feedback is not simply a matter of content. The context, timing, clarity, and tone of feedback all contribute to whether or not the feedback is effective. Poor design decisions in any regard can lead to dismissal, confusion, or rejection of the content of the feedback.

The purpose of an assessment influences the level of detail contained in the feedback. For certain assessments, no particular actions are expected from the student following the assessment. In these cases, a simple score report may be appropriate. For other assessments, the feedback is intended as instructional advice, so needs to have sufficient detail to provide concrete suggestions that provide sufficient information to the student on which to act.

As the role of feedback changes, so too do the assessment inferences and representations needed to support feedback. In assessment for which feedback is a final score report, the operative assumption is that feedback during the assessment has no impact on a student's performance. This may not be true, of course, for students may have a very clear idea of how they are performing (another aspect of feedback)—especially with the advent of computer adaptive testing, where students can tell if they have responded incorrectly to an item because the next one given them is obviously easier or probes further. This type of inadvertent feedback certainly has consequences for student motivation on subsequent tasks.

For other assessments, in which more explicit feedback is provided during the assessment, there is an even clearer relationship between feedback from the system and subsequent performance. In fact, in a diagnostic instructional situation, the definitive goal is to improve student understanding via participation in the assessment. Thus, the nature of the inferencing must acknowledge and address potential learning that occurs during the assessment process. In fact, if a student did not improve over the course of the assessment, then not only the relevance of the feedback, but the effectiveness of the entire process would be brought into question.

Feedback upon completion of the assessment can be far more than a score or set of scores. Representations can be verbal descriptors, graphs and tables, and item or section breakdowns. Students may even be provided exemplars of performances that represent differing levels of success.

Typically, feedback not only is provided to students, but serves other audiences as well. Depending on the purpose, feedback provided to students may go to other users of the information (e.g., college admissions officers). In other cases, summary feedback may be provided to information users (e.g., school reports of student achievement by grade level). In all cases, effective assessment design will result in feedback that is relevant and useful to those that are provided such information.

CONCLUSIONS

The design and associated representational issues discussed in this chapter are germane to the design of any effective assessment, regardless of its purpose or how it is delivered (e.g., computer or paper-and-pencil). A systematic focus on assessment design is particularly important at a time when the explosion of technology has presented assessment designers and developers with new opportunities and simultaneous challenges that heighten the import of complex design decisions.

For all assessment design, the primary need in supporting a disciplined, integrated, and comprehensive process of assessment design is a tool-based methodology that begins with capturing essential features of domain content and performance expectations in representations that can be understood by those who must use them—representations that are useful "mediators" in acquiring knowledge and cognitive understanding of the domain (Boose, 1992).

The dominant tradition in assessment has been psychometric measurement, with its associated set of representations. As assessments address a more diverse and ambitious set of purposes, there comes an increasing need for inferencing that can address complex task performance and instructionally useful information. Thus, the focus is shifting to evidence—what the standards of evidence are for given domains and what the representational possibilities are for achieving those standards. Evidence is the fulcrum balancing student knowledge and task performance.

Hopefully, with this changing assessment focus will come more powerful tools, technical and cognitive, to help analyze these relationships. Evidentiary frameworks are key to task design tools for generating useful data. Already powerful measurement technologies must evolve further to meet the challenges of using increasingly complex evidence to ground the inferences necessary to useful and relevant feedback. Tools to support human judgment processes are also needed for tracking evidence and hypotheses and building arguments about the state of a student's knowledge.

One key contribution of technology is the ability to provide rich representations, as well as the heightened awareness technology brings to representational issues in assessment design in general. Awareness of and attention to representational issues, when considered in light of the purpose and domain of an assessment, remain the key considerations for effective assessment design and productive assessment discourse in all its guises.

REFERENCES

Bell, T. (1984). *State education statistics.* Washington, DC: U.S. Department of Education.

Bennett, R. E. (1993). On the meanings of constructed response. In R. E. Bennett & W. C. Ward (Eds.), *Construction versus choice in cognitive measurement* (pp. 1–27). Hillsdale, NJ: Lawrence Erlbaum Associates.

Boose, J. H. (1992). Knowledge acquisition. In *Encyclopedia of artificial intelligence* (2nd ed., pp. 719–742). New York: Wiley.

Cazden, C. (1988). *Classroom discourse.* Portsmouth, NH: Heineman.

Doran, J. (1990, November). *Portfolios for professional development: An administrator's story.* Paper presented at the annual meeting of the National Council of Teachers of English, Atlanta.

Edwards, D., & Mercer, N. (1987). *Common knowledge: The development of understanding in the classroom.* New York: Routledge.

Foucault, M. (1980). *Power/knowledge* (C. Gordon, Ed.; C. Gordon, L. Marshall, J. Mepham, & K. Soper, Trans.). New York: Pantheon.

Gee, J. P. (1990). *Social linguistics and literacies.* London: Falmer.

Gitomer, D. H., Steinberg, L. S., & Mislevy, R. J. (1995). Diagnostic assessment of troubleshooting skill in an intelligent tutoring system. In P. Nichols, S. Chipman, & S. Brennan (Eds.), *Cognitively diagnostic assessment* (pp. 73–101). Hillsdale, NJ: Lawrence Erlbaum Associates.

Glaser, R., Lesgold, A., Lajoie, S., Eastman, R., Greenberg, L., Logan, D., Magone, M., Weiner, A., Wolf, R., & Yengo, L. (1985). *Cognitive task analysis to enhance technical skills training and assessment* (Final report to the U.S. Air Force Human Resources Laboratory on Contract F41689-83-C-0029). Pittsburgh: University of Pittsburgh, Learning Research and Development Center.

Goel, V. (1995). *Sketches of thought.* Cambridge, MA: MIT Press.

Grice, H. P. (1975). Logic and conversation. In P. Cole & J. Morgan (Eds.), *Syntax and semantics: vol. 3. Speech acts* (pp. 41–58). New York: Academic Press.

Haertel, E. H., & Wiley, D. E. (1993). Representations of ability structures. In N. Frederiksen, R. J. Mislevy, & I. I. Bejar (Eds.), *Test theory for a new generation of tests* (pp. 359–384). Hillsdale, NJ: Lawrence Erlbaum Associates.

Hicks, D. (1995). Discourse, learning, and teaching. *Review of Research in Education, 21, 49–95.*

Hodson, D. (1992). Assessment of practical work: Some considerations in philosophy of science. *Science & Education, 1,* 115–144.

LeMahieu, P. G., Gitomer, D. H., & Eresh, J. T. (1995). Portfolios in large scale assessment: Difficult but not impossible. *Educational Measurement: Issues and Practices, 14*(3), 11–28.

Lemke, J. L. (1990). *Talking science: Language, learning, and values.* Norwood, NJ: Ablex.

Lemke, J. L. (1995). *Textual politics.* London: Taylor & Francis.

Lord, F. M. (1980). *Applications of item response theory to practical testing problems.* Hillsdale, NJ: Lawrence Erlbaum Associates.

Luke, A. (1995). Text and discourse in education: An introduction to critical discourse analysis. In *Review of Research in Education, 21,* 3–48.

Messick, S. (1980). Test validity and the ethics of assessment. *American Psychologist, 35,* 1012–1027.

Messick, S. (1989). Validity. In R. L. Linn (Ed.), *Educational measurement* (3rd ed., pp. 13–104). New York: American Council on Education and Macmillan.

Mislevy, R. J. (1994). Evidence and inference in educational assessment. *Psychometrika, 59,* 439–483.

Mislevy, R. J., & Gitomer, D. H. (1995). The role of probability-based inference in an intelligent tutoring system. *User Modeling and User-Adapted Interaction, 5,* 253–282.

Resnick, D. P., & Resnick, L. B. (1985). Standards, curriculum, and performance: A historical and comparative perspective. *Educational Researcher, 14,* 5–21.

Roseberry, A., Warren, B., & Conant, F. (1992). Appropriating scientific discourse: Findings from monority classrooms. *Journal of the Learning Sciences, 2,* 61–94.

Rosenblatt, L. M. (1978). *The reader, the text, the poem: The transactional theory of the literary work.* Carbondale: Southern Illinois Press.

Schum, D. A. (1987). *Evidence and inference for the intelligence analyst.* New York: University Press of America.

Schwartz, J. L., & Viator, K. A. (Eds.). (1990). *The prices of secrecy: The social, intellectual, and psychological costs of testing in America* (A report to the Ford Foundation). Cambridge, MA: Educational Technology Center, Harvard Graduate School of Education.

Sternberg, R. J. (1985). *Beyond IQ: A triarchic theory of human intelligence.* New York: Cambridge University Press.

Stiggins, R. (1991). Assessment literacy. *Phi Delta Kappan, 72,* 534–539.

Wainer, H. (1990). *Computerized adaptive testing: A primer.* Hillsdale, NJ: Lawrence Erlbaum Associates.

Wiggins, G. (1993). *Assessing student performance.* San Francisco: Jossey-Bass.

CHAPTER 17

Representational Competence

URI SHAFRIR

Ontario Institute for Studies in Education, University of Toronto

The ability to represent experience has been viewed by psychologists as generic to the child and a prerequisite for development (Bruner, 1966; Piaget, 1962; Sigel, 1970; Vygotsky, 1978; Werner, 1957). These theoreticians also believe that changes in the nature of mental representations lie at the core of the developing child's increase in cognitive abilities. Although definitions of representation are usually designed to capture the specific theoretical biases underpinning different theories and perspectives of development, most share a common view of representation as the ability to create and to maintain an internal trace—a representation—of experience. The age at which the newborn infant unequivocally demonstrates the ability to represent experience has been revised downward continuously as this issue has been increasingly examined. For example, a recent study reported that infants as young as 6 weeks old can generate actions on the basis of stored representations (e.g., Meltzoff & Moore, 1994).

The concept of representation also plays a fundamental role in disciplines other than psychology that are concerned with development, such as neurobiology and artificial intelligence. Dudai (1989), working within a neurobiological developmental perspective, defined internal representation as "neuronally encoded structured versions of the world which could potentially guide behaviour" (p. 5); Dudai also defined learning as experience-driven generation of new —or lasting changes to existing—internal representations. Artificial intelligence theorists who use computer models to simulate development are divided on the role of representation in development and learning. Connectionists view development as synonymous with nonrepresentational learning through parallel distributed processing (PDP), that is, parallel interactions of weighted excitatory and inhibitory connections among large numbers of neurons (e.g., McLelland, 1995). According to this view development is an implicit, experience-driven process, that builds gradually on existing knowledge (e.g., patterns of activation weights), and does not lend itself to easy mapping on explicit representations and propositional knowledge. In contrast, some philosophers and other theorists view representation as the basic unit of analysis underlying development and learning (e.g., Dennett, 1987; Dretske, 1983; Fodor, 1975; Lloyd, 1989). Lloyd claimed that an operational definition of representation should be informed by metatheoretically derived constraints; following this rationale Lloyd created simulations of simple organism-environment interactions by constructing simple models of organisms capable of reacting to external stimuli by sensing, processing, storing, retrieving, and responding to information. Lloyd claimed that this "bottom-up" approach captures an emergent quality of these interactions that he labeled representation: an internally encoded, content-laden, external event that can be analyzed in terms of nonrepresentational components or capacities.

Children's knowledge about representations is initially acquired at an early age; young children come to realize that culturally defined signs (e.g., names, numbers, pictures, maps) have "dual lives": In addition to being objects in their own right, they also represent—stand for—other objects, events, or ideas (DeLoache, 1993). Children also learn early that other ordinary and familiar items may also have dual lives: A hat and a scarf may be familiar playthings on their own; however, when the young infant is being dressed in these objects they represent—create an expectation of—an impending stroll outdoors; an engraving may be a familiar object on its own, but at age 3 years a child recognizes it as the image of his grandfather "whom he had not seen for exactly six months, instantly recognized him and mentioned a whole string of events which had occurred whilst visiting him, and which had certainly never been mentioned in the interval" (Darwin, 1877, p. 291). As children develop they become more knowledgeable about the relationships between signs and referents, signifying and signified (Piaget, 1962). They come to realize that the mapping of signs on referents is not a simple, one-to-one relationship, and that a specific sign stands not only for a specific object, but for a category of objects. For example, the utterance "dog" may initially refer only to the family dog; however, later exposure to other dogs will eventually convert "dog" into a category label. As children develop they also come to realize that a referent may be signified by different signs within a sign system (e.g., "daddy" is equivalent to "father," who also has a proper name); and that a referent may be signified by signs belonging to different sign systems (e.g., a color photograph, a video clip, and the utterance "dog" all refer to the same beloved family pet).

What are the mediators of the development of children's knowledge about the relationships between signs and referents? Studies conducted by Sigel and his collaborators (e.g., Sigel, Anderson, & Shapiro, 1966; Sigel & McBane, 1967; Sigel & Olmstead, 1970a, 1970b) showed that low socioeconomic status (SES) children, in contrast to middle-class children, had difficulties in classifying certain two-dimensional representations—pictures—but not three-dimensional models of the same objects. Sigel and his collaborators hypothesized that the ability to master and to operate effectively on this many-to-many correspondences between signs and referents lies at the core of development, and defined it as the conservation of meaning, or representational competence. Following these initial findings, Sigel and his collaborators have, over the past 30 years, conducted programmatic research on the development of representational competence in children of different ages, as well as different SES and parenting styles (Sigel, 1970, 1986: Sigel & Cocking, 1977). They concluded that the acquisition of representational competence is intimately related to distancing acts, which they defined as behaviors of parents, caregivers, and teachers that help the child to separate perceptually accessible features of the here-and-now from their distal, intellective representations, thus facilitating the development of representational competence.

Our goal in this chapter is to examine different aspects of the developmental construct representational competence. We begin by examining some aspects of the relationship between the ability to use sign systems and development; proceed by formulating a definition of representational competence that lends itself to empirical refutation; and, finally, describe and analyze experimental data from two different studies that test practical aspects of representational competence as a mediator of development.

MEANING EQUIVALENCE

Comparative studies of representational systems and, specifically, the equivalence of meaning between two representations, are the objects of inquiry of semiotics, the science of sign systems within a shared language collective. For Morris (1938) the relations between S (a sign vehicle), D (the designatum or the signified), and I (the interpretation of the interpreter) are: "S is a sign of D for I to the degree that I takes account of D in virtue of the presence of S. Thus in semiosis something takes account of something else mediately, i.e., by means of a third something" (p. 82). Following Morris, Eco (1976) defined a sign as "everything that, on the grounds of a previously established social convention, can be taken as *something standing for something else*" (italics in original; p. 16). A sign system is a collection of one or more types of signs, together with a set of rules that specify how to combine signs in order to create semiotic text that can convey meaning adequately.

Two constructs that lie at the core of semiotic theories are of great interest to developmental psychologists. The first is the view that the basic function of every sign system as a model of the world may be regarded as a program that controls the behavior of the individual and the collective. The Soviet semiotician Ivanov (1965/1977) claimed that there is a direct link between the use of different sign systems and human development: "In evaluating a collective, as in evaluating an individual, it is important to look for possession of a maximum number of [sign] systems on different levels, from the simplest to the most complex" (pp. 31–32).

An example of a simple sign system that acts as an early model of the world, and which exercises early control over the behavior of the infant, contains only two signs: the bipolar opposites "yes/no" (e.g., "good/bad"; "correct/incorrect"; "I like it/I dislike it"). The ability to receive and to signal differential-valence feedback is an important prerequisite for the initial construction, by the infant, of an internal representational system. In this nonverbal, prelinguistic stage, feedback reception and signaling plays the role of a metalanguage that provides the means of differentially reinforcing communication patterns and their outcomes, as well as associations between signs and meanings. The initial learning of verbal labels of objects and events critically depends on the infant's ability to encode and decode the correct affective valence (positive or negative) of the feedback embedded in the communication flow. The association between affect and verbal concepts is ontogenetically related to the transition from the initial nonverbal subjective-affective mode of communication to the later use of a conventional symbol system to convey meaning (Izard & Malatesta, 1987; Sroufe, 1979; Stern, 1985). The infant learns verbal concepts as an additional, alternative mode of expression of an affective state, then uses these verbal concepts to share inner meanings with others.

The young infant's ability to express and receive signs that encode valence is also intimately related to affective attunement development. Early competence in encoding and decoding valence in gestures, facial expressions, and verbal utterances has been documented in studies of social referencing; children as young as 1 year, when exposed to ambiguous situations, were reported to make referential looking at their parents, then to use the information to regulate their own behavior (e.g., Feinman, 1992; Walden & Baxter, 1989; Walden & Ogan, 1988). Emde (1994) described this as "emotional communication occurring in the context of uncertainty" (p. 723). Fogel (1993) viewed communication competence as a necessary element in the coregulation of communicative sequences that play a critical role in his theory of infant development through relationships, which culminates in the emergence of the self, viewed by Fogel as "the individual's participatory and imaginative cognition of co-regulated relationships" (p. 146).

A recent study of early communicative development (Fenson et al., 1994) reported that the bipolar opposites "yes/no" were among the earliest nonperceptual concepts to be acquired: Infants were reported by their parents to understand the words yes and no at age 12 and 8 months, respectively; and to gesture "yes" (by nodding) and "no" (by shaking head) at age 14 and 12 months, respectively; finally, infants were reported by their parents to produce the words yes and no at age 19 and 15 months, respectively. In particular, it appears that competence in receiving and signaling negative feedback is acquired consistently and at an earlier age compared to positive feedback.

The simple metalanguage that contains only the bipolar opposites "yes/no" continues to play an important role in development beyond infancy. For example, there is growing evidence that children's acquisition of language is feedback facilitated, and therefore inferential in nature (e.g., Bohannon & Stanowitz, 1988; Sokolov, in press). This claim is supported by results of intervention studies that showed that differential parental feedback in response to children's erroneous utterances facilitates language learning (e.g., Baker & Nelson, 1984; Nelson, 1977; Nelson, Carskaddon, & Bonvillian, 1973; Nelson, Denninger, Bonvillian, Kaplan, & Baker, 1984; Sokolov, in press; see review by Sokolov & Snow, 1994). This evidence supports the constructivist view of development and stands in contrast to the nativist claim that language learnability depends exclusively on exposure to positive instances (e.g., Chomsky, 1965; Pinker, 1984). Gold (1967) examined various hypothetical language-learning scenarios, and provided a mathematical proof that only finite-state languages are learnable from positive data alone (e.g., positive feedback and reinforcements), whereas the acquisition of natural languages, which are context dependent and are not finite-state automata, depends on the availability of negative feedback. We view this as important support for the constructivist position that the bipolar opposites "yes/no" constitutes an initial sign system that continues to play a pivotal role throughout development. Differential-valence feedback lies at the core of learning from experience and makes it possible for the developing child not only to acquire new knowledge, but also to develop new mental structures—to literally "make up her mind"—as she matures. We discuss this issue in the context of the rationale for defining the combination of both pre- and postfailure reflective behavior as Level 2 representational competence (Experiment 2).

The second semiotic construct of particular interest to developmental psychologists is that the analysis of a sign system can only be accomplished by a formal description through a sign system—a metalanguage—that may or may not be identical to the system under analysis. A natural language is a sign system that may be analyzed by using it as a metalanguage; however, not every sign system may be used as a metalanguage for the description and analysis of itself or of other sign systems. For example, English is habitually used to describe and analyze musical codes, but a musical code cannot be used to describe and analyze English text (e.g., Simon & Sumner, 1968). From a developmental perspective the crucial point is that in order to establish equivalence of meaning between two representations, one has to use a sign system that can act as a metalanguage with respect to both.

The Soviet semiotician Lotman who, together with Ivanov, organized and led the Moscow-Tartu school of semiotics between the early 1960s and the mid-1980s, pointed out the evolutionary nature of sign systems and the dynamic nature of their interactions across historical epochs as well as at any given historical moment (Lotman, 1990). In parallel to the evolutionary concept of an ever-changing biosphere, Lotman proposed the concept of a "semiosphere" as the total symbolic environment of the individual and the collective. For Lotman the static definition of text as a semiotic corpus that conveys meaning does not capture its essentially dynamic nature: "A Text is a semiotic space in which languages interact, interfere, and organize themselves hierarchically" (Lotman, 1981/1988, p. 37). Lotman described the semiotic text as serving three separate functions: (a) univocality—the transmission of meaning; (b) dialogic—the creation of new meaning: "the text is a generator of meaning, a thinking device, which requires an interlocutor to be activated" (p. 40); and (c) memory—encoding the past within the semiotic text. This multifunctional view of the semiotic text has rather profound implications for development. For example, Wertch and Bivens (1993) claimed that the tendency to pay attention mostly to the univocal function of text—the transmission of meaning—at the expense of the dialogic function—the generation of meaning—obstructs an important aspect of the text as catalyser of internalization of socially mediated procedures and the transition from intermental to intramental functioning of the developing child.

The semiosphere is the symbolic environment into which the child grows and that defines the types of representations to be encoded in the developing child's mind. The semiosphere is dynamic and multifunctional; it also includes a class of meaning-preserving transformations; these are symbolic transformations that generate multiple representations with equivalent meaning, and inevitably result in the overdetermination of meaning within the semiosphere. A corollary of this aspect of the semiosphere is that the developing child is continuously and simultaneously exposed to multiple models of the world; the child may therefore interact, at any specific time, with any given aspect of the world through multiple representations (signifiers) that, nevertheless, preserve equivalent meanings. The ability of the developing child to represent experience—to model the world—in a multitude of ways, lies at the core of the developmental construct representational competence.

DEFINITION OF REPRESENTATIONAL COMPETENCE

The conceptual definition of representational competence has undergone considerable change since it was first formulated by Sigel (1954) in response to Osgood's (1952) claim that "meanings are quite independent of the stimulus characteristics of the signs themselves" (p. 206). Sigel proposed that "meaning of an object is not only independent of the stimulus characteristics of the object itself, but is also apparently dominant as a basis of organization of the objects. Meaning dominance is the term we suggest to apply to this phenomenon" (p. 207). Later Sigel and his collaborators (Sigel, 1970; Sigel & Cocking, 1977) defined representational competence as the ability to conserve meaning across different specific representations; in a recent chapter Sigel (1993) introduced a metacognitive aspect into the definition of representational competence: "Representational competence refers to the individual's awareness and understanding that an instance can be represented in various forms and still retain its essential meaning" (p. 142).

Following Sigel's (1954), Ivanov's (1965/1977), and Lotman's (1990) insights, we offer the following definition of representational competence. Our definition consists of two hierarchical levels: In Level 1 representational competence is conceptualized as the ability to convey and receive equivalent meaning through multiple representations within and/or across different sign systems; in Level 2 representational competence is defined as the ability to re-represent equivalent meaning by incorporating higher order relations within and/or across different sign systems.

The first level requires that an individual is able to express and to recover equivalent meanings embedded in at least two different representations in one or more sign systems. The semiotician Sebeok's (1994) comments on the relationship between multiple representations of equivalent meaning and depth of comprehension are worth quoting here: "There is no doubt that an intralingual synonym or paraphrase of, or extended discourse on, any sign will enrich comprehension of the object it represents, as will also its interlingual translations and intersemiotic transmutations" (p. 13). The linguist Jacobson (1959/1990) also emphasized the critical importance that paraphrasing—what he called "equational propositions"—plays in language learning: "The interpretation of concepts through equivalent expressions, is precisely what linguists understand by 'meaning' . . ." (p. 329). Thus, an individual who possesses a good Level 1 representational competence may be able to represent equivalent meanings in natural language, as well as through other sign systems (e.g., arithmetic, musical notation, charts, spatial projections, Morse code).

The second—and higher—level of representational competence requires that the individual is able to re-represent an equivalent meaning by encoding sub/superordinate relations; for example, by using linguistic descriptions of higher order concepts, or by incorporating additional aspects or relations that were not encoded into the initial representation. Another way of thinking about Level 2 representational competence is in terms of Werner and Kaplan's (1963) distancing theory of symbol formation; unlike Sigel's use of the term, where *distancing* refers to the mediator's acts (e.g., a parent's or a teacher's distancing strategies), Werner and Kaplan's distancing refers to the individual's own mental acts: the ability to distance oneself from the symbolic vehicle on one hand, and to distance the symbolic vehicle from the referential object on the other hand. Such mental distancing is a prerequisite for re-representation of equivalent meaning in terms of higher order relations.

The rationale for our definition of representational competence rests on two main arguments that may be briefly summarized as follows: First, the overdetermination of meaning in the semiosphere—the great number of possible different representations for conveying a specific meaning—suggests that the ability to model reality in multiple ways is an important prerequisite for development and learning; stated differently, multiple representations may capture multiple aspects of the phenomena being represented and therefore facilitate comprehension. The second argument stems from the difficulty of making a judgment about the nature of a representation in another person's mind. Because representation is a mental construction that can not be directly observed, it seems that judgments by an external observer regarding the nature of an internal representation in another person's mind can be rendered only on the basis of some overt behavior of that person that is assumed to reflect (to signify), in the opinion of the observer, the existence of that representation. Such judgments—mappings of behaviors on hypothesized inner representations—are notoriously difficult to make (e.g., Siegler's work on the development of numerical representations in children; Siegler & Robinson, 1982). By introducing the concept of meaning equivalence, we provide the observer with a strategy—making relative rather than absolute judgments—that is expected to facilitate the task of evaluating the nature of internal representations.

Finally, we note that our definition of representational competence is applicable across ages and, in particular, is not limited to development during childhood. Whereas Sigel and his collaborators investigated the development of representational competence in children, we present evidence on representational competence of adolescents and adults.

The following experiments were designed to explore different operational derivatives of this conceptual definition. In Experiment 1 we investigated the ability of university students to recognize meaning equivalence in printed text (Level 1). In Experiment 2 we studied the ability of 9- to 12-year-olds to spontaneously shift from an initial representation of an inference task to a superordinate re-representation of the same task that includes differential-valence feedback (Level 2).

EXPERIMENT 1:
REPRESENTATIONAL COMPETENCE OF PRINTED TEXT

Experiment 1 was designed to evaluate representational competence of printed text by asking university students to recognize meaning equivalence among several sentences (Shafrir, Sigel, & Kingsland, 1995). In this study we examined the relationship between the representational competence of text and both low-level reading skills (e.g., single-word decoding) and high-level reading skills (e.g., reading comprehension) in two groups of university students: reading disabled (RD) and normal readers (NR). We were particularly interested in the ability of these students to distinguish between the two levels of representation involved in text comprehension, namely, the surface level (e.g., the morphological appearance of a sentence), and the deeper level of the meaning conveyed by the text. This is a specific application, in the domain of reading, of our definition of representational competence—Level 1. Here we operationalized representational competence of text as the ability to recognize meaning equivalence in text samples that varied syntactically or grammatically.

Procedures

The 40 subjects were students at a university in Ontario, Canada. Twelve of these students reported that they were having problems with the reading of course material and that they experienced reading problems in elementary school; they also scored below the 50th percentile on the Woodcock Word Attack test. These students formed the RD group in this study (six men, six women; mean age 25.4 years, $SD = 4.5$). A nonselected control group of 28 university students who were NR (13 men and 15 women; mean age 24.3 years, $SD = 3.1$) volunteered to participate in this study.

The main task was a 10-item pencil-and-paper test of representational competence of text (RCT). Each item contained five sentences. The subject was told that at least two of the five sentences mean the same thing, but that possibly more than two sentences may mean the same thing, and was asked to mark all the same-meaning sentences among the group of five sentences for each item. In addition to the main task and the Woodcock Word Attack, each subject was administered the following tests: WAIS–R (Wechsler Adult Intelligence Scale–Revised); WRAT–R (Wide Range Achievement Test–Revised; reading); GORT–R (Gray Oral Reading Tests–Revised); and the Nelson–Denny Test (reading comprehension). The procedure for administering the Nelson–Denny was as follows: After the normed time of 20 minutes, the answer sheet was marked and the subject was told that he or she may continue for as long as they need in order to complete the test. This procedure yielded the following measures: Score (in percentile) at 20 minutes; score (in percentile) at own time; and own time (minutes).

Results and Discussion

In addition to the two ability groups, we divided the population into two groups by the level of RCT; the low group scored 3 or below ($n = 14$) and included 8 RD and 6 NR; and the high group scored 4 or above on the RCT ($n = 26$) and included 4 RD and 22 NR ($\chi^2 = 7.56$, $p < .006$). A three-way analysis of variance (ANOVA), ability group (RD and NR), level of RCT (low and high), and score on Nelson–Denny (at 20 minutes and at own time), with a repeated measure on the scores on Nelson–Denny, showed a main effect for time ($F(1,39) = 27.43$, $p < .0001$); and for RCT ($F(1,38) = 4.1$, $p < .05$ (all results reported for Type III SS); but not for ability group; there were no interactions. A two-way ANOVA, ability group (RD and NR) by level of RCT (low and high) for GORT–R (reading quotient) showed a main effect for ability group ($F = 5.73$, $p < .02$), but not for RCT. No interaction was found.

Because we conceptualized representational competence as the ability to represent experience in alternative ways and operationalized it, in this study, as the ability to recognize meaning-equivalence in printed text, it can be argued that our measure of RCT is (a) just another test of reading comprehension; or, alternatively, (b) a new type of general ability, a sort of surrogate-IQ measure. In order to test the difference between RCT and general intellectual functioning on the one hand, and reading skills on the other hand, we carried out three commonality analyses with the three measures of reading comprehension (e.g., GORT–R, Nelson–Denny at 20 minutes, and Nelson–Denny at own time) as dependent variables; the independent measures were IQ (full scale), RCT, WRAT–R, and Woodcock Word Attack. The total variances accounted for were: $R^2 = 0.54$; $R^2 = 0.58$ and $R^2 = 0.31$ for GORT–R; Nelson Denny (at 20 minutes); and Nelson–Denny (own time), respectively. In this analysis, each R^2, the squared zero-order correlations between the dependent variable and each independent variable, was partialed into two components: unique variance of each independent variable, and common variance shared between the particular independent variable and one or more of the other independent variables (Kerlinger & Pedhazur, 1973).

The commonality analysis shows that RCT accounted for a significant amount of unique variance only for Nelson–Denny (own time) but not for GORT–R (where IQ accounted for a large portion of unique variance) or for Nelson–Denny at 20 minutes (where single-word decoding accounted for a large portion of unique variance). Of the three tests of reading comprehension, only the Nelson–Denny (own time) captured the maximal level of performance. Our interpretation of this analysis is that RCT is not just another measure of reading comprehension or a correlate of IQ, but that it is a measure of the ability to recognize equivalence in meaning among text samples that may vary along syntactic and grammatical dimensions. This corresponds to representational competence—Level 1. This interpretation is further supported by the results of the ANOVAs. It is also supported by recent studies by Royer and his collaborators (Royer, Greene, & Sinatra, 1987; Royer & Sinatra, 1994), who administered a procedure based on equivalence of meaning, known as the sentence verification technique (SVT) for assessing reading comprehension, to children and adolescents in the age range third grade to college. They found that the test is a good measure of paragraph comprehension, has high reliability, and has good construct validity. The studies of SVT by Royer and his collaborators showed that paraphrasing offers a good method to establish meaning equivalence between two sentences.

Our exploratory study showed that RCT is an important measure that captures a fundamental aspect of development that is differentiated from the general level of intellectual functioning on one hand, and from domain-specific expertise in reading on the other.

EXPERIMENT 2:
REPRESENTATIONAL COMPETENCE IN AN INFERENCE TASK

The nature of inductive inference has long been a source of disagreements among philosophers, logicians, psychologists, and—recently—information-processing and artificial intelligence theorists. However, most have recognized the centrality of inductive inference as a process that provides clues for action in unfamiliar circumstances, that may test the adequacy of rules in the stored knowledge base, and that allows knowledge to be transformed and modified through its use (e.g., Holland, Holyoak, Nisbett, & Thagard, 1986).

An inference task may be defined as a learning task where response is followed by feedback, which is the main source of learning. An important potential source of information in an inference task is the valence of the feedback. Whereas positive feedback simply confirms the adequacy of the response, negative feedback signals the presence of flaws in the mental procedures that guided the subject's response. Therefore, paying attention to negative feedback may be expected to play an important role in improving performance on inferential tasks.

Paying attention to errors, signaled by negative feedback on an inference task, was operationalized recently by the measure of postfailure reflectivity (Shafrir & Pascual-Leone, 1990). Postfailure reflective children spend long periods of time following the production of incorrect response, compared to the time they spend following the production of correct response. Shafrir and Pascual-Leone conceptualized postfailure reflectivity as an exploratory mental executive, a spontaneously activated "debugging" procedure that helps children reexamine and correct faulty internal plans.

Researchers reported that children who spent a lot of time contemplating errors (postfailure reflective children) scored higher than postfailure impulsive children on an inference task, as well as on other measures of intellectual functioning and academic achievement (Shafrir & Pascual-Leone, 1990), that postfailure reflectivity generalized across tasks and across domains, and that postfailure reflective children were intentional learners and good planners (Shafrir, Ogilvie & Bryson, 1990, Experiment 2). In other studies, children with a reading disability were found to be significantly less postfailure reflective than normal controls (Shafrir, Ogilvie, & Bryson, 1990, Experiment 1; Shafrir, Siegel, & Chee, 1990). Shafrir, Ogilvie and Bryson claimed that paying attention to errors plays an important role in learning.

In Experiment 2 (Shafrir, 1996) we attempted to shed light on representational competence—Level 2—by reanalyzing Shafrir and Pascual-Leone's (1990) data. We reasoned that because task instructions in the studies by Shafrir and his collaborators did not mention feedback, and, specifically, did not mention the need to pay attention to negative feedback, children who did pay attention to such feedback did so spontaneously by re-representing the task; they moved from an initial task representation based on the need to respond to the immediate features of the stimulus in a given trial, to a re-representation of the task that included, in addition to the stimulus, also the response, and the valence of the feedback to the response in the current trial. According to our definition, children who spontaneously change their task representation to include *both potential and actual negative feedback* on an inference task, demonstrate Level 2 of representational competence.

The two specific hypotheses tested in this study were: (a) 12-year-olds spontaneously produce re-representations that include the valence of the immediate feedback; and score higher on an inference task as well as on other intellectual and academic tasks, than younger children; (b) within each of the four age groups tested (9, 10, 11, and 12 years old), children who spontaneously produce task re-representations that include *both potential and actual negative feedback* on an inference task, score higher than children who do not produce such re-representations, as well as on other intellectual and academic tasks.

Procedures

Subjects were students in grades 4 through 7 in public schools in Israel. We tested an unselected sample of 377 subjects, aged 9 ($n = 109$), 10 ($n = 114$), 11 ($n = 85$), and 12 ($n = 69$).

Scores for the Israeli version of an IQ test ($M = 106.1$, $SD = 11.5$), and for Raven's (1960) standard progressive matrices (SPM; $M = 32.5$, $SD = 8.6$), were obtained when children entered third grade. Scores for computer-based drill and practice in arithmetic, and for teachers' evaluations of the student's general level of intellectual functioning (*not* level of academic achievement) in percentiles, were available at the time of this study. The Figural Intersection Test (FIT) for mental attentional (M) capacity (Pascual-Leone & Ijaz, 1989) was group administered. The PAR (Pattern Recognition) task was administered individually. PAR is a computer-based inference task, with 80 stimuli of repeated designs shown through bars of different colors, heights, colors + heights, and colors + heights + sounds of varying pitch, where intertrial intervals are subject controlled. Subjects were asked to decide whether the stimulus was a repeating design; if the subject's answer was "no," he or she was asked to point to the location of the "mistake" in the design with a blinking light on the computer screen; response was immediately followed by a yes/no feedback; the subject had to strike a key in order to see the next stimulus.

The response latency was classified into two mutually exclusive classes, that is, *presuccess* and *prefailure;* similarly, the postresponse latency was classified as *postsuccess* and *postfailure.* Prefailure and postfailure reflectivities were calculated from Equations 1 and 2, as follows:

$$\text{Prefailure reflectivity} \ = \ \frac{\text{Mean prefailure latency}}{\text{Mean response latency}} \qquad (1)$$

$$\text{Postfailure reflectivity} \ = \ \frac{\text{Mean postfailure latency}}{\text{Mean postresponse latency}} \qquad (2)$$

Children in each age group were divided by a double median split on prefailure reflectivity and on postfailure reflectivity, into four quadrants: children who were *both pre- and postfailure reflective* were assumed to have spontaneously produced a re-representation of the inference task that includes potential and actual negative feedback; these children were conceptualized as having high Level 2 representational competence. Children who were *both pre and postfailure impulsive* were conceptualized as not having developed such a re-representation and therefore as having low Level 2 representational competence; finally, there were two groups of *mixed* conditions.

Results and Discussion

Results of two-way ANOVAs, age (four levels: 9, 10, 11, and 12 years old) by Level 2 representational competence (four levels: high, low, and two mixed conditions) showed that 12-year-olds scored significantly higher on the FIT task for attentional capacity, showed higher Level 2 representational competence (were more prefailure *as well as* more postfailure reflective) than children in the 9 to 11 years age range; the 12-year-olds also scored higher on PAR. Within each age group, children with high Level 2 representational competence performed better on the PAR task, scored significantly higher on a variety of tasks of intellectual functioning, on teacher's evaluations of intellectual functioning, and on arithmetic drill and practice, than children with low Level 2 representational competence; the two groups of mixed conditions scored in the intermediate range. The younger children in the 9 and 10 years old age groups with high Level 2 representational competence scored as high as the 12-year-olds on a measure attentional capacity (a score of 5 on the FIT task); these younger children scored significantly higher than the children in the 12 years old age group who had low Level 2 representational competence, on the various tasks.

Finally, we performed a commonality analysis of the variance of the score on PAR as the dependent variable, and age, FIT, IQ, SPM, math, and pre- and postfailure reflectivities as the independent variables (teachers' evaluations were available for only 252 children and were not included in this analysis). The unique contribution of the Level 2 representational competence (pre- and postfailure reflectivities) to the variance of the score on the PAR inference task was higher (about 15%) than the unique contributions of all of the other independent variables combined: age (2.3%), M-capacity (0.8%), IQ (2.7%), SPM (0.6%), and arithmetic drill and practice (0.0%).

These results lend support to the two hypotheses. The significant increase in Level 2 representational competence at age 12 corresponds to an increase of attentional capacity from four to five units as predicted by Pascual-Leone (1987), and to the onset of the stage of formal operations (Piaget, 1950), vectorial operations (Case, 1985), and abstract sets (Fischer, 1980). The newly acquired ability of 12-year-old children to operate on operations, and not only on concrete entities, facilitates the development of Level 2 representational competence—to spontaneously produce a re-representation that includes, in addition to the task itself, the differential-valence feedback, and possibly also concomitant internal procedures that "debug" and improve currently operating action plans. This ability also incorporates an important affective component; attending to one's own errors requires the retracing of mental steps and a reexamination of one's plans that turned sour—contained faulty elements. In other words, postfailure reflective behavior is predicated on the ability to concentrate and draw conclusions from environmentally driven negative feedback under conditions of affective adversity. It is interesting to recall, in this context, the findings of the study of early communicative development (Fenson et al., 1994) that showed that competence in receiving and signaling negative feedback is acquired consistently and at an earlier age compared to positive feedback. The adaptive advantage derived from such early competence may be reflected later during development in acquiring the ability to incorporate negative feedback into representations of inference tasks.

The longer periods of time that 12-year-olds spent both *prior to,* as well as *following* the production of incorrect response, compared to the time they spent prior to as well as following the production of correct response, appear to signal the emergence of this higher level of representational competence that incorporates differential-valence feedback, and that results in an emphasis on *optimizing* performance. However, these results also show large individual differences within age groups, suggesting that the ability to re-represent a task by incorporating super/subordinate relations is an important measure of intellectual development that is not explicitly captured by Piagetian and neo-Piagetian theories of development.

GENERAL DISCUSSION AND CONCLUSIONS

We believe that the overdetermination of meaning in the semiosphere plays a central role in development; it stems from the concurrent availability, to the child, of a multitude of ways to represent experience by constructing different representations within a sign system, as well as across different sign systems. Representational competence is the ability to model important features of the world in different ways while maintaining equivalence of meaning. This means that a child with a high degree of representational competence decodes and encodes experience differently, and in more ways, than a child with a low degree of representational competence. The richer mode of interaction with environmental inputs can be expected to result in differential rates of learning and development. This is a strong—and speculative—argument. We provide support for this claim by summarizing the results of our two studies presented earlier.

Results of Experiment 1 showed that the ability to recognize equivalence of meaning of printed text contributed unique variance only to a test of reading comprehension that was designed to elicit maximal results (e.g., Nelson–Denny, own time), but not to two other tests that put various constraints on the demonstration of reading comprehension (e.g., Nelson–Denny at 20 minutes, and GORT–R). The pattern of contribution of unique variance to three different tests of reading comprehension was different than the patterns of contribution of unique variance of two other independent variables, namely, single-word decoding and IQ. University students who reported having reading problems beginning at an early age, and who showed deficits in nonword decoding that are often associated with a core phonological deficit (Stanovich & Siegel, 1994), did not score uniformly low on representational competence of text; similarly, an unselected group of university students who did not report having reading problems did not score uniformly high on representational competence of text. Representational competence of printed text seems to reflect a dimension of reading that is different from reading ability (e.g., single-word decoding) on one hand, and from IQ on the other. These results support our view that representational competence is an important mediator of learning.

Results of Experiment 2 showed that the ability to spontaneously re-represent an inference task, where the "new" representation incorporates the superordinate relations of differential-valence feedback as well as debugging routines, is associated with higher intellectual functioning and higher academic achievement; this finding held across the four age groups (e.g., 9 to 12 years old), but was more pronounced for the 12-year-olds.

The relationship between Level 2 representational competence and development may be illuminated by examining it vis-à-vis three other measures administered in Experiment 2. High ability to spontaneously re-represent an inference task while incorporating higher order relations *successfully postdicted*—for all four age groups—high scores on IQ and RPM, the two main measures of intellectual functioning, that were obtained between 1 and 4 years prior to the time of Experiment 2. This high ability on Level 2 representational competence was also associated with higher scores on a short-term memory test of M-capacity (FIT) that was administered—together with the PAR inference test and other measures—at the time of this study. M-capacity assessment with FIT is viewed by some neo-Piagetian theorists as a culture-free measure of developmental intelligence and a robust measure of developmental stages (Pascual-Leone, 1987;

Pascual-Leone & Ijaz, 1989); therefore, children in all four age groups who showed high ability to spontaneously re-represent an inference task while incorporating higher order relations, were more advanced developmentally than those who showed low ability to achieve such a re-representation of the inference task. These results support the view that representational competence is an important mediator of development, and are inconsistent with some neo-Piagetian theories of development.

We would like to close this chapter with a comment on a possible relationship between representational competence and individual differences. The claim that children with a high degree of representational competence develop a richer repertoire of representations of experience than children with a low degree of representational competence has, potentially, important implications for the development of individual differences, because it posits representational competence as a candidate mechanism for cognitive growth. An initial disposition to construct multiple representations of experience at an early age may develop into a positive-feedback-driven, self-sustaining process that feeds on itself: A richer mode of interaction with environmental inputs will result in an ever richer, diverse repertoire of the products of such interactions—representations—that can be expected to result in differential rates of learning and development. Ceci's (1990) bio-ecological theory of intellectual development implies the existence of such a mechanism, and posits it as the core of the observed increased differentiation of abilities as children develop and mature. A similar— but domain-specific—mechanism, labeled *Matthew effect*, based on reciprocal relations between print exposure (e.g., reading volume), vocabulary knowledge, and reading comprehension growth was described by Stanovich (1986).

If the claim that representational competence is a self-sustaining mechanism that propels development and learning has merit, then it deserves careful consideration and further empirical exploration. For example, it would be interesting to establish the age range, or, alternatively, critical periods, during which intervention is most effective. Can training in constructing multiple representations of equivalent meaning be effective during adolescence or even adulthood? The developmental implications of such questions are evident and compelling.

REFERENCES

Baker, N. D., & Nelson, K. E. (1984). Recasting and related conversational techniques for triggering syntactic advances by young children. *First Language, 5,* 3–22.

Bohannon, N. J., & Stanowitz, L. (1988). The issue of negative evidence: Adult responses to children's language errors. *Developmental Psychology, 24,* 684–689.

Bruner, J. S. (1966). *Toward a theory of instruction.* Cambridge, MA: Harvard University Press.

Case, R. (1985). *Intellectual development: Birth to adulthood.* New York: Academic Press.

Ceci, S. J. (1990). *On intelligence . . . More or less: A bio-ecological treatise on intellectual development.* Englewood Cliffs, NJ: Prentice-Hall.

Chomsky, N. (1965). *Aspects of the theory of syntax*. Cambridge, MA: MIT Press.

Darwin, C. (1877). A biographical sketch of an infant. *Mind, 7*, 285–294.

DeLoache, J. S. (1993). Distancing and dual representation. In R. R. Cocking & K. A. Renninger (Eds.), *The development and meaning of psychological distance* (pp. 91–107) Hillsdale, NJ: Lawrence Erlbaum Associates.

Dennett, D. C. (1987). *The intentional stance*. Cambridge, MA: MIT Press.

Dretske, F. I. (1983). Why information? *Behavioral and Brain Sciences, 6*, 82–90.

Dudai, Y. (1989). *The neurobiology of memory: Concepts, findings, trends*. Oxford, England: Oxford University Press.

Eco, U. (1976). *A theory of semiotics*. Bloomington: Indiana University Press.

Emde, R. N. (1994). Individuality, context, and the search for meaning. *Child Development, 65*(3), 719–737.

Feinman, S. (1992). *Social referencing and the social construction of reality in infancy*. New York: Plenum.

Fenson, L., Dale, P. S., Reznick, J. S., Bates, E., Thal, D. J., & Pethick, S. J. (1994). Variability in early communicative development. *Monographs of the Society for Research in Child Development, 59*(5, Serial No. 242).

Fischer, K. (1980). A theory of cognitive development: The control and construction of hierarchies of skills. *Psychological Review, 87*(6), 477–453.

Fodor, J. A. (1975). *The language of thought*. New York: Crowell.

Fogel, A. (1993). *Developing through relationships: Origins of communication, self, and culture*. Chicago: University of Chicago Press.

Gold, E. M. (1967). Language identification in the limit. *Information and Control, 10*, 447–474.

Holland, J. H., Holyoak, K. J., Nisbett, R. E., & Thagard, P. R. (1986). *Induction: Processes of inference, learning, and discovery*. Cambridge, MA: MIT Press.

Ivanov, V. V. (1977). The role of semiotics in the cybernetic study of man and collective. In D. P. Lucid (Ed.), *Soviet semiotics* (pp. 27–38). Baltimore: Johns Hopkins University Press. (Original work published 1965)

Izard, C. E., & Malatesta, C. Z. (1987). Perspectives on emotional development: 1. Differential emotion theory of early emotional development. In J. D. Osofsky (Ed.), *Handbook of infant development* (2nd ed., pp. 494–554). New York: Wiley.

Jacobson, R. (1990). Boas' view of grammatical meaning. In L. R. Waugh & M. Monville-Burston (Eds.), *On language*, (pp. 324–331). Cambridge, MA: Harvard University Press. (Original work published 1959)

Kerlinger, F. N., & Pedhazur, E. J. (1973). *Multiple regression in behavioral research*. New York: Holt, Rinehart & Winston.

Lloyd, D. (1989). *Simple minds*. Cambridge, MA: MIT Press.

Lotman, Y. M. (1988). Text within a text. *Soviet Psychology, 26*, 32–51. (Original work published 1981)

Lotman, Y. M. (1990). *Universe of the mind: A semiotic theory of culture*. Bloomington: Indiana University Press.

McLelland, J. L. (1995). A connectionist perspective on knowledge and development. In T. J. Simon & G. S. Hallford (Eds.), *Developing cognitive competence: New approaches to process modelling* (pp. 157–204). Hillsdale, NJ: Lawrence Erlbaum Associates.

Meltzoff, A. N., & Moore, M. K. (1994). Imitation, memory, and the representation of persons. *Infant Behavior and Development, 17*, 83–99.

Morris, C. W. (1938). Foundations of the theory of signs. In O. Neurath, R. Carnap, & C. W. Morris (Eds.), *International encyclopædia of unified science* (Vol. 1, Part 1, pp. 77–137). Chicago: University of Chicago Press.

Nelson, K. E. (1977). Facilitating children's syntax acquisition. *Developmental Psychology, 13*(2), 101–107.

Nelson, K. E., Carskaddon, G., & Bonvillian, J. D. (1973). Syntax acquisition: Impact of experimental variation in adult verbal interaction with the child. *Child Development, 44*, 497–504.

Nelson, K. E., Denninger, M. S., Bonvillian, J. D., Kaplan, B. J., & Baker, N. D. (1984). Maternal input adjustments and non-adjustments as related to children's linguistic advances and to language acquisition theories. In A. D. Pellegrini & T. D. Yawkey (Eds.), *The development of oral and written language in social contexts* (pp. 31–56). Norwood, NJ: Ablex.

Osgood, C. E. (1952). The nature and measurement of meaning. *Psychological Bulletin, 49,* 197–237.

Pascual-Leone, J. (1987). Organismic processes for neoPiagetian theories: A dialectical, causal account of cognitive development. In A. Demetriou (Ed.), *The neoPiagetian theories of cognitive development: Toward an integration* (pp. 25–64). Amsterdam: North-Holland.

Pascual-Leone, J., & Ijaz, H. (1989). Mental capacity testing as a form of intellectual developmental assessment. In R. Samuda, S. Kong, J. Cummings, J. Pascual-Leone, & J. Lewis (Eds.), *Assessment and placement of minority students: A review for educators* (pp. 143–171). Toronto: Hogrefe.

Piaget, J. (1950). *The psychology of intelligence.* London: Routledge & Kegan.

Piaget, J. (1962). *Play, dreams and immitation in childhood.* New York: Norton.

Pinker, S. (1984). *Language learnability and language development.* Cambridge, MA: Harvard University Press.

Raven, J. C. (1960). *Guide to the standard progressive matrices.* London: Lewis.

Royer, J. M., Greene, B. A., & Sinatra, G. M. (1987). The sentence verification technique: A practical procedure teachers can use to develop their own reading and listening comprehension tests. *Journal of Reading, 30,* 414–423.

Royer, J. M., & Sinatra, G. M. (1994). A cognitive developmental approach to reading diagnostics. *Educational Psychology Review, 6*(2), 81–113.

Sebeok, T. A. (1994). *Signs: An introduction to semiotics.* Toronto: University of Toronto Press.

Shafrir, U. (1996, June). *Representational competence.* Paper presented at the Twenty-Sixth Annual Symposium of the Jean Piaget Society, Philadelphia.

Shafrir, U., Ogilvie, M., & Bryson, M. (1990). Attention to errors and learning: Across-task and across-domain analysis of the post-failure reflectivity measure. *Cognitive Development, 5,* 405–425.

Shafrir, U., & Pascual-Leone, J. (1990). Postfailure reflectivity/impulsivity and spontaneous attention to errors. *Journal of Educational Psychology, 82*(2), 378–387.

Shafrir, U., Siegel, L. S., & Chee, M. (1990). Learning disability, inferential skills and post-failure reflectivity. *Journal of Learning Disabilities, 23,* 506–517.

Shafrir, U., Sigel, I. E., & Kingsland, L. (1995, June). *Representational competence of text in university students.* Paper presented at the Twenty-Fifth Annual Symposium of the Jean Piaget Society, Berkeley, CA.

Siegler, R. S., & M. Robinson (1982). The development of numerical understandings. In H. W. Reese & L. P. Lipsitt (Eds.), *Advances in child behavior and behavior* (Vol. 16, pp. 242–308). New York: Academic Press.

Sigel, I. E. (1954). The dominance of meaning. *The Journal of Genetic Psychology, 85,* 201–207.

Sigel, I. E. (1970). The distancing hypothesis: A causal hypothesis for the acquisition of representational thought. In M. R. Jones (Ed.), *Miami symposium on the prediction of behavior, 1968: Effect of early experiences* (pp. 99–118). Coral Gables, FL: University of Miami Press.

Sigel, I. E. (1986). Early social experience and the development of representational competence. In W. Fowler (Ed.), *Early experience and the development of competence* (pp. 49–65). San Francisco: Jossey-Bass.

Sigel, I. E. (1993). The centrality of a distancing model for the development of representational competence. In R. R. Cocking & K. A. Renninger (Eds.), *The development and meaning of psychological distance* (pp. 141–158). Hillsdale, NJ: Lawrence Erlbaum Associates.

Sigel, I. E., Anderson, L. M., & Shapiro, H. (1966). Categorization behavior of lower and middle class Negro preschool children: Differences in dealing with representation of familiar objects. *Journal of Negro Education, 35,* 218–229.

Sigel, I. E., & Cocking, R. R. (1977). Cognition and communication: A dialectic paradigm for development. In M. Lewis & L. A. Rosenblum (Eds.), *The origins of behavior: Vol. 5. Indexation, conversation, and the development of language* (pp. 207–226). New York: Wiley.

Sigel, I. E., & McBane, B. (1967). Cognitive competence and level of symbolization among five-year-old children. In J. Hellmuth (Ed.), *The disadvantaged child* (Vol. I, pp. 433–453). Seattle: Special Child Publications of the Seattle Sequin School.

Sigel, I. E., & Olmstead, P. (1970a). The development of classification and representational competence. In A. J. Biemiller (Ed.), *Problems in the teaching of young children* (pp. 49–67). Toronto: OISE Press.

Sigel, I. E., & Olmstead, P. (1970b). Modification of cognitive skills among lower-class Black children. In J. Hellmuth (Ed.), *The disadvantaged child* (Vol. 3, pp. 300–338). New York: Brunner-Mazel.

Simon, H. A., & Sumner, R. K. (1968). Pattern in music. In B. Kleinmuntz (Ed.), *Formal representation of human judgement* (pp. 219–250). New York: Wiley.

Sokolov, J. L. (in press). Parental imitations and implicit negative evidence in a multiple factors framework. *Journal of Child Language.*

Sokolov, J. L., & Snow, C. E. (1994). The changing role of negative evidence in theories of language development. In C. Gallaway & R. J. Richards (Eds.), *Input and interaction in language acquisition* (pp. 38–55). Cambridge, England: Cambridge University Press.

Sroufe, L. A. (1979). Socioemotional development. In J. D. Osofsky (Ed.), *Handbook of infant development* (pp. 462–516). New York: Wiley.

Stanovich, K. E. (1986). Matthew effects in reading: Some consequences of individual differences in the acquisition of literacy. *Reading Research Quarterly, XXI/4*, 360–407.

Stanovich, K. E., & Siegel, L. S. (1994). Phenotypic performance profile of children with reading disabilities: A regression-based test of the phonological-core variable-difference model. *Journal of Educational Psychology, 86*(1), 24–53.

Stern, D. N. (1985). *The interpersonal world of the infant.* New York: Basic Books.

Vygotsky, L. S. (1978). *Mind in society: The development of higher psychological processes.* Cambridge, MA: Harvard University Press.

Walden, T. A., & Baxter, A. (1989). The effect of context and age on social referencing. *Child Development, 60*, 1511–1588.

Walden, T. A., & Ogan, T. A. (1988). The development of social referencing. *Child Development, 59*, 1230–1240.

Werner, H. (1957). *Comparative psychology of mental development.* New York: International Universities Press.

Werner, H., & Kaplan, B. (1963). *Symbol formation: An organismic-developmental approach to language and the expression of thought.* New York: Wiley.

Wertsch, J. V., & Bivens, J. A. (1993). The social origins of intellectual mental functioning: Alternatives and perspectives. In R. R. Cocking & K. A. Renninger (Eds.), *The development and meaning of psychological distance* (pp. 203–218). Hillsdale, NJ: Lawrence Erlbaum Associates.

CHAPTER 18

Representational Thought in Ego Identity, Psychotherapy, and Psychosocial Developmental Theory

JAMES E. MARCIA
Simon Fraser University

> *According to . . . Euripides, Helen was a phantom. According to Homer, Helen was the phantom . . . The phantom, or image is precisely [an] act of representation . . . for Greeks and Trojans alike Helen had posed the danger of the phantom, the image. Living with the phantom is ruinous, but neither of the two sides had wanted to live without.*
>
> —Calasso (1993, pp. 363–365)

> *You got to have a dream. / If you don't have a dream, How you gonna have a dream come true?*
>
> —Hammerstein (1949, *South Pacific*)

When I was child, I went to a summer camp based, as so many in the North American Midwest are, on an Indian (Native American, First Nations, etc.) motif. Living in cabins with names like Mandan, Massasoit, and Tecumseh, and divided into competitive athletic groups with names like Shawnee, Sioux, and Iroquois, we approached the final campfire at the end of the camping period at least half-Indian in our imaginations. Wrapped in blankets, carrying flashlights, circling the "council fire," we repeated every year a particular ritual: the story of Mowana, acted out in the ring around the council fire. Three sons of the dying chief and his starving tribe departed for a distant mountain as a trial for leadership. Each returned bearing his treasure from the mountain. The first two, carrying silver and gold, respectively, were told that they had gone only partway up the mountain, and, hence, "not for them was the council's honor." After a long pause, one heard footfalls coming from the dark forest outside of the fire-lighted ring of the council circle—it was the long-awaited Mowana. When he trudged around the circle and stood before the chief, he slowly opened his hands and revealed—nothing. They were empty. Instead, he said that from where he stood on top of the mountain, he had seen a vision of a fair land, across the great river, where his tribe might live for many years in peace and prosperity. To this brave was given the council's honor and the chiefship of the tribe.

READER'S GUIDE

The preceding quotations and story all involve aspects of representational thought beyond its initial development in childhood. It is with such cognitively advanced applications of the concept that I deal in this chapter in discussing identity formation, psychotherapy, and Erikson's psychosocial developmental theory. Jean Mandler (1983) described two senses of the use of the term *representation:* as symbolic (the use of symbolic productions to stand for some aspect of the world), and as the organization of knowledge about the world (one's model of the world). Because I am writing about representation on such a broad and developmentally advanced scale, I use both of these definitions. In a sense, this chapter concerns my representation of representation.

I employ the Piagetian terms of *disquilibration, assimilation,* and *accommodation* in a general social cognitive sense rather than more formally as responses to experiences of problems presented by the physical world. Disquilibration, here, refers to the actual or potential experience of a disconfirmation of one's existing schemes representing relationships between the self and other persons. Negative assimilation refers to a tendency to not experience, or to retreat from, the disquilibration of a familiar representative scheme even when that scheme is inadequate. The disquilibratory input may not be perceived, may be distorted in perception, or may be absorbed into the already existing, but not quite sufficient structures. This differs from positive assimilation in which the existing schema is adequate to account for undistorted experience. Accommodation refers to the accurate perception of disquilibratory evidence and the subsequent modification of representative structures.

I begin this chapter with identity development because that is the area within which I and my students and colleagues have done the most research relevant to representational thought. A discussion of psychotherapy and transference-countertransference follows this because I see therapeutic change and identity formation as involving similar processes and similar aspects of representational thought. Next, Eriksonian psychosocial developmental theory is discussed as an example of representation writ large: a portrayal of the human life cycle. Finally, representational thought is described, paradoxically, as a process that can lead us to isolation from our direct experience of the world and from each other, as well as furnishing us a way out of the consequences of this distantiation dilemma, and enriching our experience of the world by endowing it with meaning.

EGO IDENTITY FORMATION[1]

The envisioning of an alternative future is involved in both identity formation and structurally oriented psychotherapy. Some would say the construction of alternate pasts as well. Ego identity, in the Eriksonian developmental sense, is, at its optimum, the outcome of an integrative, constructive process undergone by late adolescents (Erikson, 1980; Marcia, Waterman, Matteson, Archer, & Orlofsky, 1993). Integrated are the fragments of childhood part-identifications, current needs and abilities, into one's imagination of one's place in a viable future. What is constructed by means of this integration and imaginative envisioning is a self-schema or self-theory that will serve to give both meaning to experience and direction to behavior. This identity structure is more than a collection of roles and beliefs. It is an integration of these into a more or less smoothly functioning unity. At this fundamental level, one does not possess multiple selves or multiple identities; although an observer, or the individual-as-observer, might witness different aspects of the person in different situations. Even though one may feel, behave, or believe differently in differing contexts, there remains an agentic one, an "I," across contexts. When such an inner core or sense of unity is missing, we speak of "identity diffusion"; and such an individual does have multiple selves, which are unintegrated or partially integrated. This person, even sometimes adaptively, responds primarily to the demands of the moment, rather than from any coherent core.

Fundamental to the identity formation process is the imagination[2] of oneself into probable futures. The social demand, in some cultures, to do this is especially acute at late adolescence when one must leave the "cared-for" position of childhood and early adolescence and adopt the "caring-for" position of young adulthood. Once initiated, the identity construction process does not end at late adolescence. Rather, given a suitable cultural context, this initial identity furnishes only the embarkation point for a lifelong journey of identity reconstruction. Like cognitive schemas, like scientific theories, an identity, once formulated, is subject to disquilibration and subsequent accommodative change. The "present" that an adult of 40 experiences is not likely to be construed accurately

---

[1] Identity *formation* can take place in two ways: conferral or construction. A conferred identity (foreclosure) is one that is given to an individual by a family or tribe based on familial or cultural prescription. The person becomes aware of a conferred identity, but does not participate significantly in determining its content. A constructed identity (identity achievement) begins where a conferred identity ends. The individual, having become aware of familial or cultural prescriptions, explores the fit among these, their own abilities and needs, and viable societal niches. Following this exploratry process, the person makes commitments to certain beliefs and occupational directions. The resulting inner integration and sense of self constitute the constructed ego identity.

[2] I am using *imagination* here to refer to one's representation of future possibilities. It does not connote the "anything goes" imagination of the toddler, but the creative construction of a future, together with some imagined realistic constraints.

by a late adolescent; and the future imagined by the 40-year-old is even less accessible to that late adolescent. The initial identity of the 19-year-old, if it is a constructed one, is unlikely to be serviceable at 40; and the 40-year-old constructed identity is unlikely to be useful at age 65.

The foregoing suggests that most people in our society change or reconstruct their identities to meet changing life circumstances and changing times. That is less frequently the case than most of us in North America would believe. There are probably more people, globally, who do not construct their identities than those who do. Not everyone goes through an identity *construction* process. In fact, looking at the issue worldwide, rather than from just a Western perspective, only a minority of persons live in sufficiently wealthy cultures that permit the luxury (and, sometimes, pain) of identity construction (Marcia, in press). Across the earth, most persons have identities conferred upon them. The world imagined by the late adolescent whose identity is conferred is the world of their forebears; thus, it is not the adolescent's imagination at work, but his or her parents', and likely the parents' parents, too. In discussing those, usually traditional, cultures that confer identities, one might speak of the "intergenerational transmission of identity." It would be interesting from a cognitive developmental perspective to study those persons in identity-conferring cultures who go on to construct identities even though they are not encouraged, and sometimes discouraged, from doing so. What allows them to experience disequilibration? Whence comes the courage to decide their own direction?[3]

Even in our society, one can bypass the process of identity construction by adopting an identity conferred by one's family or childhood authority figures. And one can retain this identity, unreconstructed throughout the life span, either by limiting life contexts to those similar to the one in which the initial identity was formed, or by limiting one's experience of disequilibratory information by means of ego defenses. Hence, through a kind of psychological surgery, the ablation of experience, a 19-year-old identity can be made to be serviceable at 40.

Do such self-limiting persons, whom we have called *foreclosures* in the identity status research paradigm, lack imagination? It would seem so when it comes to construing alternative futures for themselves. They are who they have been told to be, and will be who they are supposed to have been. In some ways, it is not easy to live a life free from major disequilibratory experiences. There certainly exist in anyone's life cycle sufficient major disconfirmatory events to any belief system, to any life plan, to necessitate identity reconstruction. But, of course, this disconfirmatory data must be *experienced* in order to be effective, and foreclosed persons have learned that the exploration attendant on identity disconfirmation arouses experiences of anxiety and/or guilt. Perhaps the origins of

---

[3] I am indebted to a former graduate student, Dr. Frances Newman, now an analyst in Toronto, for this suggestion.

this learning lie in insecure attachment and the resultant inhibition of early exploratory behavior or subsequent exploratory activity that was met with parental punishment. In any case, by adolescence, the individual is more intent on fulfilling a plan laid down in childhood than on exploring alternative routes for a future life. Still, this foreclosed identity, in which only one future is imagined—for life, is preferable to the identity-less state of diffusion, in which so many futures are imagined that none is likely to realized.

When, as developmental researchers, we investigate late-adolescent identity formation, we use a structured interview in which respondents are asked to describe how they arrived at their occupational choices, ideological stances, and interpersonal values. They are also asked how committed they are to the alternatives they have articulated. Regarded in terms of the theme of this book, we are asking our research participants for their representations of their past experiences and their projections of their represented selves into their yet-to-be experienced futures. From this perspective, the identity status interview might be described as an "exercise in representation" for the respondents.[4] It is a similar exercise for the researcher who then "re-presents" her or his experience of the interview in the form of an identity status rating comprising the dimensions of *identity achievement* (has explored, is committed), *foreclosure* (has not explored, is committed), *moratorium* (is exploring, is trying to make commitments), and *identity diffusion* (has wandered more than explored, and is not committed).

These four identity statuses have become something like a psychological map for many researchers studying the identity formation process. To locate and label a person as displaying predominant characteristics of one or another of the identity statuses suggests immediately a number of psychological attributes or coordinates that have been determined in the span of 30 years of research (Marcia et al., 1993). So that if an identity researcher says that a recent interview respondent is, say, "a moratorium," there is an adjectival picture that immediately comes to mind: struggling, both engaging and exhausting to listen to, morally sensitive, cognitively complex, perhaps creative but not dependable, ambivalent, rebellious, and so on. Consider how complex an exercise in representation this whole procedure is. We are not dealing with the process of going from an actual apple to a pictured apple to the squiggly lines "apple," and learning to treat all of these as equivalents, a development almost miraculous in itself. At least apples exist, or so I assume, and they are out there constituting a cognitive demand. Ex-

---

[4]Thus far, some version of the identity status interview has been used across social class in North America, Western and Eastern Europe, Mexico, Kuwait, Taiwan, Nigeria, South Africa, Japan, and India. The level of sophistication and verbal experession necessary for participants to understand and respond to the interview is not great, and the interview itself can be modified to be extremely basic. Nor are high levels of representational sophistication necessary for either conferred or constructed identity formation, although cognitive complexity is positively related to identity achievement (Marcia et al., 1993). However, representational sophistication, verbal flexibility, and interpersonal sensitivity are necessary in the *researcher* who assesses identity status.

cept in the mind of the investigator, there is no such "thing" as a "moratorium." But, on a more concrete level, there remains the problem of the explicability of our experience of individuals at a certain age—a problem that the construct, "moratorium," was invented to resolve. "Ever since she went away to college, she seems like a stranger!" Represent to the anguished parent this grown-child-turned-alien as "a moratorium" (with all of the construct's accompanying meaning) and a sense of relief can ensue—maybe not as transformative as the emergence of a partial experience of an apple from a bunch of squiggly lines, but a potentially emotionally significant accommodation, nevertheless.

I have hedged deliberately in the preceding paragraph: "relief *can* ensue"; "*potentially* emotionally significant accommodation." If the distressed parent cannot hear, because of personal threat, the psychological implications of "moratorium," then that information—probably together with the informant and psychologists in general—rather than being constructively disequilibratory, is negatively assimilated back into the preexisting scheme of the "angel-child corrupted by the diabolical university." Compared to issues such as this, the negative emotional consequences of disequilibration when dealing with the world of apples and elementary physics problems are minimal. In fact, it is usually delightful to achieve a previously obscured solution to a primarily cognitive problem. However, in the realm of events with emotional significance, "adequate" solutions can be resisted—often *because* of their accuracy. The issue of dealing with persons instead of things casts the Piagetian cognitive developmental process of assimilation-disequilibration-accommodation, as well as the concept of representation, in a different light.

I think that the central issue in the construction versus the conferral of identity lies in the openness to disequilibration. We discuss later the emotional aspects of disequilibration with reference to psychotherapy, but, here, in terms of identity formation, we are speaking of the initiation of the moratorium process. It is only by undergoing the exploratory moratorium period that an identity is constructed; otherwise, most persons adopt a conferred identity. What, then, are the necessary and sufficient conditions for exploring identity possibilities different from those given by one's childhood? Put another way, what accounts for one person's multiple representations of alternative futures and alternative beliefs and another's single-mindedness? Clearly, when we speak of representation on this level, we are some distance from the development of representational thought in children (Mandler, 1983; Sigel, 1991). We are speaking of the *use* to which representational thought can be put in psychological development, and of levels of representation, in which reality is not just represented, but alternative realities are created.

We had thought that necessary conditions for the initiation of the identity exploratory period (moratorium) were the cognitive, social, and physiological changes accompanying puberty. But because all adults have gone through this, and only a small number have constructed their own identities, these early adolescent changes are only contributory, not necessary, conditions. Another important condition that has emerged, based more on long-term observation than on experimental research, is not an individual-psychological state, but a social-economic circumstance: a fairly high level of cultural wealth and/or technological advancement. Some societies can permit their adolescents the luxury of identity exploration and some cannot. If there are roles that must be filled in order for a society or tribe or group to survive, then the young have to be funneled into those roles, and survival precludes the luxury of an extended identity moratorium period. Australian aborigine "walk-abouts," during which an adolescent is to find a future direction by contacting ancestor spirits, last no longer than 2 weeks, a far cry from that exploratory period of about 10 years (12–22) that we grant our young people. And the aborigine's identity "solution" will be construed within fairly circumscribed tribal bounds.

Still, not everyone within the eligible society undergoes the identity exploration and construction process. In fact, only about one third do. The remaining two thirds consist of those who maintain their childhood identities intact into adulthood and those whose identity is diffuse, with the former outnumbering the latter about two to one. Why, then, in a society such as North America, which provides the opportunity for identity exploration, does such a sizable minority not use the psychological launching pad provided by puberty to imagine and explore alternative futures for themselves? I think that there are two additional crucial ingredients for identity exploration and subsequent identity construction: secure attachment (the interpersonal aspect of Eriksonian basic trust) and a certain level of cognitive sophistication.

In several studies now, identity researchers have established relationships of the higher identity statuses of identity achievement and moratorium with secure emotional attachment, whether determined by attachment status measures or by more general object relational assessments (Marcia, 1994a). It seems that some adolescents, as Blos (1979) observed a number of years ago, do go through another separation-individuation period similar to that of the 2-year-old. But a precondition for them doing this appears to be a securely internalized relational base, whether this is called positive introjects, Basic Trust, or secure attachment. Of course, external support is also helpful but the presence of a solid sense of self derived from internalized interactions with empathic caregivers (Bacal & Newman, 1990) seems to be one of two conditions sufficient to intitiate identity.

The second sufficient condition appears to be a certain level of cognitive sophistication. In fact, for some persons, it appears that this can override or compensate for deficits in the secure relational base. Initially, we had thought that formal operational thought would be necessary for identity construction. It appears that we had been too narrow in our requirements, and that it is a fairly high level of cognitive complexity and sophistication (Slugoski, Marcia, & Koopman, 1984) that is important, especially when these are available to the individual in the interpersonal sphere. Within limits, it seems that advanced reasoning about relationship issues can even override the deleterious effects of insecure attachment to produce identity achievement. In a recent study (MacKinnon & Marcia, 1996), we found that young mothers who were in the identity achievement or moratorium statuses were characterized by sophisticated reasoning about childrearing, whether or not they were securely attached. Thus, whereas most research has found secure attachment to be highly related to identity development, cognitive sophistication is at least, and apparently in some cases, even more important (Marcia, 1994a).

To summarize, our observations to date suggest that two important general conditions for identity exploration leading to identity construction are pubertal changes occuring within a society that can tolerate an apparently "nonproductive" or relatively "noncontributive" period during adolescence (Erikson's "psychosocial moratorium"), likely made possible by a certain level of societal wealth/technology. The sufficient conditions seem to be secure attachment and/or cognitive sophistication.

IDENTITY AND DISTANCING

I think that the level at which these two sufficient conditions are related is childrearing practices. The conditions necessary, for most children, to enhance cognitive development are similar to those that foster secure attachment. Following are Sigel, Stinson, and Flaugher's (1991) descriptions of "representational competence" and the "distancing strategy" shown to enhance this essential cognitive skill: "Representational competence refers to the child's ability to understand that experience can be transformed into some symbolic mode. Furthermore, it refers to the ability to manipulate symbols mentally, and in so doing, perform mental operations that organize, reorganize, integrate, and elaborate physical and social events into internal representations" (p. 125). Later on, we find that in identity development it is this same representational competence that underlies adolescents' and adults' ability to construe alternative futures for themselves. "Distancing refers to placing a cognitive demand on the child to separate the self mentally from the ongoing present. . . . Distancing strategies create a cognitive environment in which the child is stimulated to reconstruct past events, anticipate the future, or assume alternative perspectives on the present . . ." (p. 126). The careful reader will be struck, I think, by the correspondence of the foregoing to the description of the identity construction process described previously.

I would propose that the kind of parenting necessary to create the conditions for distancing and subsequent representational competence are the same as those underlying the sufficient conditions for identity development: secure attachment and cognitive sophistication. The latter is self-evident. Concerning the former, it is interesting to look at those parental behaviors that promote distancing. It appears that parents who use didactic-controlling techniques, reflecting a basically authoritarian orientation, do not provide optimal conditions for the development of representational competence or for psychological autonomy (Sigel et al., 1991). By contrast, parents who encourage children to learn by thinking and reasoning, considering options, drawing inferences, and so forth, promote children's academic achievement and general intellectual functioning. These parents would have to be fairly well attuned to their children, at least along the cognitive dimension. One might assume that such close attention would also extend to their children's emotional lives, thus establishing conditions for autonomy, one aspect of which is secure attachment.

Cast in identity developmental terms, the issue comes down to parental permission and encouragement for their children to explore alternatives. The same parents who ask questions, rather than always furnishing answers, would be expected to be more tolerant and supportive of their children's general exploration. At adolescence, there are a number of findings for the identity statuses that bear on this issue. Of all the statuses, foreclosures (who have engaged in little exploration) are, consistently, the most subscribing to authoritarian beliefs, and they have difficulty being critical of their parents. They are the most stereotyped in terms of gender roles and seem to be the most cognitively rigid. Diffusions feel estranged from their parents, whom they also see as nonemulatable and perform the poorest among the statuses on cognitive tasks. One can imagine two childrearing scenarios for these two identity statuses. Foreclosures are attended to by parents, generally in a loving way, but with a great deal of emphasis on doing things the right way, getting the right answers, and never questioning too strongly parental dictates. Diffusions are relatively unattended to, or inconsistently attended to by parents whose stake in them rises and falls with the narcissistic significance of the child's performance for the parent's self-esteem.

In order to do what is necessary to promote a distancing strategy, the parent must have enough attention free from their own concerns to attend closely to the child's reasoning. It is considerably easier to toss off an answer to a child's question than it is to respond to the question with a question that pushes the child's cognitive limits a bit, and then to stay there, attentively, while the child explores alternative solutions. All of the adult's anxieties about their own necessities to achieve "right" answers are engaged as well as their narcissistic stake in their child being "right." In short, to be effective teachers of the distancing strategy, parents, and other psychological socializers, have to be sufficiently psychologically (and probably economically!) unencumbered to be able to be attentive and caring to the ongoing process of the child's reasoning through a problem. I think that the parent who can promote distancing is the same parent who can foster secure attachment through accurate attunement to the child's needs and emotions. And the child growing up in this context who emerges into adolescence will be more likely to construct an identity than to latch onto a conferred one. Again, a key idea is parental encouragement of children's exploration and tolerance for disquilibration, which might then become adolescents' and, ultimately, adults' self-encouragement and tolerance for their own uncertainities and searches.

The support for exploration is not so great in these times as one might think, even in academia. Several years ago, I was asked by the then-president of our university to give a talk to the parents of the incoming first-year students. I prepared a short speech based on the identity research, the importance of exploration, and the university's role in fostering that. It could have been entitled: "In praise of the university as a disquilibrating experience." I had wanted to gently prepare parents for the changes their children might be going through in the next 4 years. I looked out at the composition of the audience and realized that many of them were likely to have come from fairly traditional backgrounds. Nevertheless, I proceeded with the talk; their faces remained fairly impassive, but the president's descended from distress to dejection. I think that he could see dollars winging their way out of the room as I was, as nonthreateningly as possible, suggesting that these parents support their children in questioning the values and career directions with which they had been brought up. I finished to brief, polite applause. Not surprisingly, I have not been asked back.

STRUCTURALLY ORIENTED PSYCHOTHERAPY

The conceptual distance between the identity development process and the change process underlying structurally-oriented psychotherapy is not great. As Kuhn (1970) made clear, paradigm shifts on a large scale are not acccomplished easily or without conflict. Neither are they on the scale of individual lives. Most of us make the best representation of ourselves and the world that we can at a particular point in time. When patients come in for psychotherapy, they are not there because they are stupid or stubborn (even though some schools of symptom-oriented treatment tend to treat them as if they were). They have done the best they can to make sense of their lives and they almost always have a valid reason for being stuck just where they are. I think that what most structurally oriented psychotherapies do, regardless of the theoretical language in which their techniques are cast, is to enable the client to construct a new representation of themselves-in-relationship and of themselves-in-the-world. Structurally oriented psychotherapy, as contrasted with behavioral or counseling approaches, aim at fundamental realignments in personality. This may involve new dynamic balances among processes mediating sanctions, competencies, and impulse expression and/or a revised view of "who one is." Some examples of this are the realization, integration, and non-self-destructive expression of a "dark side" in a monochromatically sunny personality; the acknowledgment and integration of segments of personal and familial history that have been ignored or treated dismissively; the recapture of the initiative to construct one's own life, realizing that one has been living out a script written by others.

Seldom do persons come into psychotherapy wanting to change. Usually they want to feel better in as short a time and with as little pain as possible. There is certainly nothing wrong with that, and there are therapeutic approaches that aim to effect just such cosmetic changes via symptom reduction. Sometimes this basically assimilative strategy is effective and is all that either a patient requires or a therapist is capable of. Understandably, most of us would like to resolve the life difficulties we are facing with the strategies we already have in place, rather than venture into unknown accommodations. Prozac and Zoloft (these will likely be replaced by other magic compounds before this chapter sees publication) are among the first choices for the assimilative solution, followed closely by six- to eight-session problem-solving "MacTherapies" mandated by some managed health plans. However, when the quick fix fails and individuals enter psychotherapy that aims at some sort of structural change, sometimes they are in for an unpleasant surprise. They will be undergoing even more disequilibration than that occasioned by the circumstances that brought them in, and, hence, more discomfort than they have already been experiencing—although it is both true and important that they now do not have to face it alone. The distress of major disequilibration may occur when clients learn that it is not just an "adjustment" problem that they are dealing with, but a life theory. That is, they have been living with a set of assumptions about their lives, a particular representation of themselves and of life, that has come to the end of its usefulness, and is now creating more problems than it is resolving—not unlike the phlogiston theory of combustion in the realm of science. Such representations serve well enough until their inadequacies are recognized because the "goodness-of-fit" becomes disequilibrated. Thus, not only must the presenting problem be dealt with, but also the theory of life that led to the current dead end.

Solving a specific problem with new techniques is one thing; reorienting one's life with a new theory of oneself is another. Changing self-theories is painful, both because of the wish to remain consistent, dependable to oneself and others, and because one must relinquish a familiar and often highly valued view of oneself. People can die for a cherished identity, and they can feel as if they are dying when an identity is, even gently, challenged. In a sense, there *is* a self that is dying as a new one is emerging. There is a period of time between the dis-integration of one identity, or life story, and the formation and integration of a new one. That space between a fundamental disequilibration and the subsequent accommodation is probably the most crucial and uncomfortable period in a course of life changes and of psychotherapy. During the encounter groups of the 1960s and 1970s, we found numerous techniques for initiating disequilibration; but the mistake that many of us made was to stop at disintegration and assume that reintegration would take place as a result of some kind of naturally occuring Rogerian organismic growth tendency. Unfortunately, this resulted in too many well-disequilibrated but nonaccommodated persons. It is just as important to accompany a client through the often lengthy accommodative period, during which a new self-perspective is being constructed, as it is to judiciously disquilibrate an existing self-theory.

It is at the level of structural change that psychodynamic theory and cognitive developmental theory meet. The former furnishes an emphasis more on content, the latter more on process. Ingredients for a structurally oriented, psychodynamic therapeutic approach are fairly few in number and easily described. There must be a safe "holding" environment created where the patient can feel understood, accepted, and respected. Within this context, similar to that promoting secure attachment, exploration can occur—exploration of the past, of the present, of the therapeutic relationship (or transference), of the future. As a new identity, or self-theory, or self-narrative is constructed, different aspects of it can be tried out in the world outside of therapy. Moving through the different phases of psychotherapy, the role of the therapist changes from a receptive, nonjudgmental, calming/soothing nurturer/mother, to a gently probing, logically analytic, sometimes judiciously skeptical detective, to an encouraging, logically synthetic, reality-oriented coach. I don't think that therapists from a stucture-modification orientation consciously take these positions; however, there is a quality to the process of this deeper kind of psychotherapy that evokes these roles. These therapeutic positions, or roles, do not always occur in sequence, or in the particular sequence just outlined. More often, some aspect of each role is present simultaneously. However, most therapy aimed at structural change involves *at least* these roles in approximately the sequence described.

It may be clear to the reader that the description of structurally oriented psychotherapy, based on disequilibration and accommodation is similar to the late adolescent (and subsequent adult) developmental process of identity formation, based on exploration and commitment. And the contextual requirements for optimal identity development are similar to those roles that the therapist takes in facilitating less specific kinds of structural changes. In the case of the initial identity construction, the family serves the holding, mothering function; the adolescent, him or herself, does the detective work; and the society, at its best, via its institutions (schools, guidance counselors, vocational training programs) provides coachlike directions, suggestions, and, optimally, a variety of occupational and ideological niches.

Lest it seem that the "accommodative shift" described earlier can be accomplished quickly or easily, consider the usually significant amount of cognitive and emotional work most psychotherapy patients have *already* put into their self-theories. Most persons who enter psychotherapy are neither crazy nor fools. As noted previously, most have a quite valid reason for being exactly in their current uncomfortable position. For most, their current operating theory of self has been thoughtfully constructed to deal with the world as they have represented it to themselves. But, now, the emotional cost of maintaining that view of themselves has become greater than the emotional distress and confusion it moderates or absorbs. The expectation that a major shift in this hard-won position is going to be accomplished promptly or painlessly is both disrespectful of the patient and an underestimation of a sometimes discouragingly recalcitrant reality. Most patients "get the idea" fairly early on in treatment. It is the internalization of this idea, the exploration of its ramifications in the world, and the often wholesale shift in one's experience of oneself that takes its toll in time and tears. The old analytic phrase, "working through," used to refer to what happens *after* insight, was singularly aptly stated. Accommodative answers to physics problems, once arrived at, can open up a new exciting world of answers to further problems. Accommodative solutions to psychological problems are usually initially emotionally resisted and subsequently realized in the world only uncertainly, clumsily, and with varying degrees of distress.

TRANSFERENCE AND COUNTERTRANSFERENCE

Representational thought is central to a number of different schools of psychotherapy. The Gestalt approach considers all parts of a dream to represent psychological aspects of the dreamer. These are actively re-represented in therapy sessions, so that the client "becomes" the representations rather than experiencing them as split-off, disowned parts. Jungian psychotherapy searches out the mythic representations in patients' lives as presented in their dreams, their creative products, and their life patterns in order to enable persons to access their spiritual core. Psychodynamic psychotherapy has made representation a central aspect of treatment in the form of the transference analysis. Transference is the imposition of childhood wishes and personages, still alive in the patient, onto the therapist. Its presence in therapy provides a kind of window onto the patient's childhood as well as onto their current interpersonal functioning in the world. Countertransference refers to the resulting wishes and personages aroused in and expressed by the therapist. It was once thought that the analyst could be a nonemotionally responsive "blank screen" onto which the patient's transference impulses and images could be projected. Unfortunately, things are not so clear-cut, and it became evident that the "screen" was anything but static and blank. What had been considered *only* as transference projections, interpretable by the putatively interpersonally invisible analyst, gave way to a more interactional view: In Sullivan's terms, the observer (psychotherapist) was also a participant.

Acknowledgment of the real presence of the personality of the therapist does not obviate the existence or usefulness of transference and countertransference. Sitting with a patient who becomes progressively more laudatory, submissive, dependent, and grateful (or derogatory, contemptuous, rebellious, and dismissing), therapists, of whatever orientation, become increasingly uncomfortable. "This isn't me," they feel; "it's someone else who is being responded to." Patients finding themselves expected to be the grateful recipient of a therapist's overly parental care, concern, affection, and pride (or neglect, boredom, indignation, censure) likewise experience discomfort. They may become wary as they see the therapist becoming increasingly affected by them or they may become hopeful or fearful of extratherapeutic involvement. It can be very confusing for patients who find themselves confronted not only with their own problems but responding to their therapist's feelings as well. Hopefully, it is less often the client who spots the countertransference, than the sufficiently perspicacious therapist, who, upon observing his or her reactions to the client, finds that these are inconsistent with his or her own self-representations: "I don't understand why I keep feeling this way, why I feel impelled to act when I know that's not appropriate or helpful."

What is occuring with both transference and countertransference is the imposition of a representation by either the therapist or client onto the other that ignores or distorts important features of those persons' representations of themselves. Who the therapist really is and who the patient really is, is irrelevant and, anyway, unknowable. What is important is who each of them *thinks* she or he is (i.e., represents themself to themself as), and the degree to which the other's responses, based on the other's representations, correspond to this self-representation. So if a therapist thinks she's God, and the patient responds to her in this way, the therapist is not going to call it transference, nor will she see her attempts to arrange successfully (in her terms) her client's life as countertransference.

Analysis of the transference is one of the major disequilibrating events in psychodynamic psychotherapy. Although it is usually cast, operationally, in terms of a question ("Who else have you felt this way about?"), from a representational perspective, what is really being said is, "Your view of, and reaction to, me is inconsistent with my view of myself, and my view of what your view of me should be. So let's see where the origins of that (mis)representation lie." This "analysis of the transference" has at least two effects. It challenges the client's current representation of the therapist and thereby induces some disequilibratory anxiety. Furthermore, it sets the stage for an accommodative change to the client's theory about the therapist, and, of course, ultimately, for a change in the client's theory of himself. The therapist and the client are engaged in the mutual task of theory revision (Marcia, 1994b).

I would submit that the best therapy is that which does not aim to revise the client's theory to fit the therapist's. Freudian patients should not necessarily become Freudians, nor Jungian patients, Jungian. It was a valid criticism of early psychoanalysis that everything, in Procrustean fashion, had to be reduced to sex or aggression, oedipal or preoedipal strivings. All stories had the same basic plot; all melodies were variations on a single theme. It is just as valid to criticize some forms of cognitive behaviorist theory for their *processual* (as contrasted with content-based) rigidity in reducing the complex narratives of patients' lives to the grammatical elements of symptom clusters. One theory does not fit all. I think that the best therapy involves a kind of negotiation of meaning. Hopefully, the therapist has at her disposal a variety of representational systems among which she is willing to alternate, and any one of which she is able to modify, in order to achieve a "fit" with a particular patient. Hopefully, what occurs as the patient's story begins to be re-represented by the therapist's story (i.e., the therapist begins to retell the client's story with the therapist's story about the client's story) is that the client makes an accommodative shift in his self-theory that allows him to see (or construct) new alternatives for action in his world, to have new feelings about himself, and to achieve greater freedom of response in relationships.

ERIKSON'S THEORY OF PSYCHOSOCIAL DEVELOPMENT

In the chapter thus far, I have been offering you my representation or construction of the identity formation process and of psychotherapy. Both of these occur within a larger developmental-theoretical context that has served to represent, for me, a largely adequate and satisfying picture of human psychological growth. I am referring here to Erik Erikson's theory of psychosocial development (Erikson, 1980, 1982). Most readers will be familiar with Erikson's theory so I limit myself to a discussion of those aspects of the theory that lead me to describe it as "adequate" and "satisfying."

As I represent to myself the human life cycle, I see both the familiar Eriksonian 64-square chart as well as the same cells arranged on a three-dimensional spiral. The advantage of the spiral is that it better illustrates the cyclic nature of the repetition of all eight previous life cycle periods in the current period. Hence, the resolution of each psychosocial issue is preceded by contributory resolutions of that issue before the issue's ascendancy at a particular age; and each issue recurs at subsequent stages after its ascendancy and major resolution. For example, trust is resolved for the first time in infancy, but recurs as an issue at every succeeding life cycle stage, colored by the dominant issue of that stage. The initial identity resolution does not occur until late adolescence, but there have been Identity issues as part of the preceding four psychosocial stages. This "preparatory" aspect of the theory allows for precocious resolution of a stage forced by life circumstances (e.g., the teenage parent facing issues of identity, intimacy, and generativity simultaneously). The "repetitive" aspect permits the possibility of remediation. Even though the optimal period for the resolution of a period-specific issue has passed, there are opportunities for its solution at later ages; for example, the late adolescent in psychotherapy struggling with identity issues that may have, at their core, problems in autonomy.

I think that the adequacy of Erikson's theory stems from its breadth of perspective. It attempts to account for somatic, psychological, and social aspects of personality development. Hence, its basis is in the body and the demands made at different ages by different physiological configurations. In this way, it is similar to classical psychoanalytic theory—so far as the latter goes. Fashioning a theory that saw most major personality development as having occurred by age 7, Freud did not say much about psychological development during that portion of the life cycle when brilliant old men find their bodies betraying them and work steadily through the pain of cancer of the jaw. Thanatos does not quite capture the issue. It is difficult to derive developmentally the quiet heroics involved in maintaining psychological integrity, when physical integrity is endangered, from considering only the soma of a growing child or adolescent.

Erikson has been less specific about the social aspects of psychosocial development than he has been about the psychological. Although he has outlined some of the aspects of social institutions necessary to promote ego development, I do not think it is either his specificity, or lack of it, here that is important. Rather, it is his insistence, pioneering at the time within classical analytic theory, that we consider the impact that one's social-economic-cultural-historical position has on the development of personality structure. Classical psychoanalytic theory promoted a kind of imperialism of the interior. Erikson helped to balance this picture by portraying the social context as more than the source of civilized humankind's discontent, and considering it the necessary, although not always optimally, nurturing context in which human development *must* take place. It is the consideration of the importance of both the individual's adaptation to the environment, as well as the environment's adaptation, over generations, to individuals, that Erikson, together with his fellow ego analytic colleagues, emphasized and made a vital part of most current psychodynamic thinking.

Still, Erikson has been most comprehensive and eloquent in the realm of the psychological, as compared with the somatic and social. He has outlined eight ego qualities, presented in dialectical form, each having a crucial chronological period for their initial resolution. As discussed previously in this chapter, the ego strength developed during the life cycle era of adolescence is ego identity-identity diffusion. The dialectical aspect of these age-related developmental issues is absolutely essential to the theory's depth and richness, especially as it applies to age periods from adolescence on. The resolution of the late adolescent period is not just "ego identity"; it is the individual's unique synthesis of both identity (integrative) processes and diffusion (dis-integrative) processes. It is the individual's own way of being both integrated *and* diffuse, of incorporating aspects of continuity *and* inevitable change into an operating theory of self. Similarly, the resolution of the last stage, integrity-despair, is not *only* an optimistic sense of wholeness and completeness. There are also necessary elements of regret, remorse, futility, and frustration. It is the admixture of elements that rescues this theory from being merely, as Erikson once warned, an achievement scale of psychosocial development. It is the darker antitheses that give the positively toned resolutional syntheses their fully existential human quality. A tragic view of life is not lost in Erikson's theory; but neither is the lot of humankind seen as the replacement of misery by mere unhappiness.

What Erikson offers in the way of a vision of development is what might be called the "heroics of everyday life" (Marcia, 1994b). The stage-specific positive poles of trust, autonomy, initiative, industry, identity, intimacy, generativity, and integrity are part of being human. We all begin as dependent on the regular nurturing care of others, are required to relinquish some of our willfulness for social concerns of safety and hygiene, learn to hone our growing intellectual and interpersonal skills within our family, acquire the tools necessary for survival and contribution to our culture, construct or adopt a view of ourselves vis-à-vis our society, select or have selected for us a mate, care for our own and/or others' offspring (biological or otherwise), and face the imminence of nonbeing. Birth, self-control, becoming competent, self-definition, mating, childrearing, and death are essentials of the human condition. The question of whether or not Erikson's theory is "cross-culturally valid" can apply only to details of timing or varieties of outcome; it cannot be a meaningful question if we are speaking of the fundamental elements of being human.

The task at which one labors in the striving for the heroics of the everyday is the negotiation of one's life cycle. Consider the monumentalness of the project: preserving trust and hope in the face of inevitable abandonment, disappointment, betrayal; maintaining a sense of the validity of one's will while acknowledging the shamefulness of one's littleness and ever-present doubts about the consequences of self-exposure; being able to continue striking out on one's own, knowing that being the initiator always risks being the guilty wounder; working diligently with the awareness that one's best efforts will always be surpassed by another; forging and maintaining an identity that, in our current world, is liable to be threatened regularly by disconfirmation from within and without; risking that identity in a vulnerable loving relationship while maintaining the capacity for solitude; spending oneself in care for the next generation(s) while preserving one's own right to be, also, one's own cared-for child; and, finally, maintaining some sense of meaning and wholeness in the light of the ultimate futility of sometimes the most precious of one's life's projects. What makes the story of Sisyphus "heroic" is its illustration of the human capacity for the imposition, and then the affirmation, of meaning onto ultimately meaningless projects.

What I find "adequate and satisfying" about this view of human personality development through the life span is its breadth of scope and its possibility of attainment. We are not speaking here of "transcendence" or "self-actualization" or "salvation"—just the meat and potatoes of a well- and fully lived life. I do not mean that it is easy and that our societies are necessarily benevolent and geared to our comfortable and optimum psychological survival. To the contrary, it seems to me that societies, institutions, and social groups are entities in themselves, with lives of their own, geared to their *own* survival. But even in that pursuit, they must account to some extent for the needs and abilities of their constituent members. They must not ask too much and must give back enough or their individual constituents will forsake them and they will die. So, at some level, a balance must be struck between individual needs and abilities and societal rewards and demands. And it is from the interplay of these individual somatic and psychological attributes, more or less synchronized with socially provided developmental contexts, that the stage-specific resolutions described by Erikson emerge.

The realm of psychological theory is, by definition, representational, although the possibility of treating it nonrepresentationally exists. Some theories are aesthetically more pleasing in their configurations than others, either because of their elegant simplicity or because of their complexity; yet, they all aim at some level of representation. There are forms of thought and expression, however, that are primarily nonrepresentational, and these are described briefly next.

REPRESENTATION AND EVOCATION

What is thought that is not representational? One example comes to mind. Bruno Walter and Gustav Mahler were walking together in the Austrian Alps. Walter wanted to stop a moment to take in the view. Mahler commented, "Don't bother. I've written all of that already" (Walter, 1947). Now, probably few people hearing the music Mahler was referring to would see a picture postcard Alpine view. But many, hearing the passages Mahler had in mind, would experience a feeling or a sense evoked in common by both the mountains and the music. Following from this example, I think that *evocation* is either distinguishable from representation or a fair distance from it along a continuum of denotative specificity. There is a general disparagement among musical cognescenti of "programmatic music," such as Tchaikowsky's "1812 Overture," that is frankly representative of, or signifies, a particular event or scene. The more clearly representative, the more dismissed. Bach, by contrast, is almost universally esteemed. Although there are also formal, structural rationales for this, one reason is that it is the evocative quality of music that is valued over the representational. Perhaps this is because representational or programmatic music has a "right answer"; there is a scene or idea that one is *supposed* to experience. Hence, programmatic music is more experience binding, whereas nonprogrammatic allows for a multitude of individual representations, or none at all, and is more experience expanding. Much poetry aims less at representation than it does at evocation. The words are not intended to stand for experiences, but to evoke them. Prose books, written in poetic style, can be incomprehensible if they are taken as representative rather than evocative. Probably anything written *can* be responded to evocatively rather than representationally, even articles written in American Psychological Association style, although one wouldn't want to attend, evocatively, to the experience too long.[5] In a great deal of poetry and music, then, there is a quality to the rhythm and flow of words and images, or tone and timbre, that demands the consideration of the work as an event in itself, as a piece of the world that calls forth a response, not as a representation of something else.

A CRITICAL VIEW OF REPRESENTATIONAL THOUGHT

Thus far, I have considered the employment of mature representational thought as a positive process that underlies both identity development and structurally based psychotherapy. In fact, representational thought, especially formal operations and dialectical reasoning, might be considered the hallmark of cognitive adulthood. However, the very problem with representational thought *is* its power and its inherent nature of distancing us, emotionally and sensually, from the represented, the sensate present. Recalling the first of this chapter's opening quotations, it is conceivable that the flower of Acheaen and Trojan youth perished for a mere phantom, an idea, a representation. It is also conceivable that the slaughters of our own century were driven by ideological issues as well as economic ones. Certainly the "patriotism" fueling the prewar enthusiasm of the contending populaces was more ideologically than materially based. It is not the experienced everyday reality of the Croats, Muslims, and Serbs in the former Yugoslavia that necessitated their "cleansing," but the historical representation of each group by the others. The scriptural point that "men shall not live by bread alone" is clearly a double-edged sword: Representations, endowed with emotional power, can transcend in importance the physical sustenance necessary for mere existence. Suicides are less frequently driven by physical exigencies than they are by ideals unfulfilled or unobtained.

Once we become able to re-create "the" world in our heads, we begin to create "a" world in our heads, and then to project it onto the world that, in the beginning, we were only re-presenting to ourselves. This would not be problematical if the reality of the world were easily recoverable. However, once we have re-presented it to ourselves, and then subsequently re-created it, the original becomes lost or severely blurred, and we can lose touch with all but our own ideas. We become lost in "a very heaven" (and hell!) of our own constructions. People rarely come into psychotherapy because tragedy has befallen them. I doubt that much psychotherapy occurred in the concentration camps of World War II. But the children of the survivors of the Holocaust, largely because of their con-

---

[5]For a related discussion see Madigan, Johnson, and Linton (1995) and Josselson and Lieblich (1996).

struction, and their parents' constructions, of what that tragedy *meant* and *means* are frequent participants in therapy.

The loss of the real world and our subsequent efforts to recover it may be one of the reasons we engage in "unnecessary" strenuous activities, activities that focus us unwaveringly on our bodies, or on a ball, or on a rocky and torturous mountain path. It is refreshing to escape from the worlds of our own construction, from our representations into contact with the "represented," that which is immediate for us in the world. In so doing, we seek to make the represented *present* in experience. In the quest for the "unrepresented," meditational techniques are considered by some to be one of the most efficient daily means. Psychedelic, not psychotropic, drugs can create a strong feeling of having contacted the prerepresentational world, but to assert that the reality thus experienced is ultimate rather than alternative is overselling the product. What is important is the hunger for the nonrepresentational. D. H. Lawrence (1972), in one of his most passionately philosophical poems, "A New Heaven and Earth," described a struggle to escape from a world experienced only through the medium of his own constructions:

> I was so weary of the world,
> I was so sick of it,
> Everything was tainted with myself, . . .
> I shall never forget the maniacal horror of it all in the end
> when everything was me, I knew it all already, I anticipated it all in my soul
> because I was the God and the creation at once; . . . (p. 257)

Dying, finally, to the world of constructions, he exclaims with delight:

> I put out my hand in the night, one night, and my hand
> touched that which was verily not me,
> verily, it was not me.
> Where I had been was a sudden blaze,
> a sudden flaring blaze!
> So I put my hand out further, a little further
> and I felt that which was not I,
> it verily was not I,
> it was the unknown. (p. 259)

The foregoing is not meant to be a case for the "noble cognitive savage." But it is intended to indicate that there are limits to the benefits of representational thought. The fact is that we have no choice but to develop this capacity to its fullest in our current informationally oriented world in order to ensure a level of comfortable survival. In Canada's Maritime provinces, cod fishermen (fast becoming *former* cod fishermen) are learning this quickly and the hard way. They are confronted with a similar difficult lesson that small farmers in the United States have had to learn over the past 40 years: become, not just representationally competent, but representationally expert, or you will be economically redundant. And, as all scholars (I did not say academics) know, the play of the mind can be one of the highest pleasures. Just because ideals can lead to the slaughters of war, and unfullfilled ideals can beget suicide, that is no rationale for not representing alternative futures and goals for oneself and others. Perhaps the poison is also the antidote: Meta-representational thought, by which the limits of representation can be understood, can produce suggestions of alternative experiences to counteract the dangers of living too much in the mind.

IDEALS, DREAMS, AND IDEAS: THE BALANCING ACT

Ideals become problematical when they furnish the basis for zealous idealism that often obscures the concern for individuals that gave rise to the ideals in the first place. It is not ideals, but idealism that leads to mindless killing; and idealism is living in the world of representations without the necessary salutary contact with the nonrepresented. "No, you are not, and never will be, the best (tennis player, research psychologist, psychotherapist, writer, etc.) in the world, but doesn't that apple taste good!" The problem with living primarily in the world of representations is that the representations of experience can come to obliterate any experience except the experience of the representations, especially when these are representations of ideals. The solid "thunk" of a well-hit ball, a risky, but theoretically important hypothesis confirmed, a well-timed interpretation and the resulting appearance of the client's insightful illumination, an elegant and pithy sentence—the experience of all of these can become lost in their subordination to a representational ideal of what *could* be or what *ought* to be. The danger is that the representation of apples can acquire so much importance that the ability to experience the actuality of the apple is diminished. On the other hand, the more representationally capable one becomes, the more access to apples one can have. Whereas one can live in maps that become substitutes for the experiences of territories they encode, venturing mapless into unknown territory is unlikely to produce much expansion of experience, unless one has never before been lost. Furthermore, in the world of representation as symbolism, "apple" can take on an enriched meaning as temptation, or knowledge, or poison. That is, because of advanced representational capacity, "apple" can achieve a metaphoric significance far beyond its connotative function. In this symbolic sense, representation works two ways: It points "backward" to a concrete object, and "forward" to symbolic, even mythic, portents.

"You got to have a dream. If you don't have a dream, how you gonna make a dream come true?" An interesting switch of cart and horse, if one pays attention to the lyrics. We all say that we want our (day) dreams to come true. "Dreams coming true" is so powerful for us that that outcome can constitute the reason for dreaming in the first place, regardless of content. But, of course, they never do, at least not experientially. By the time a dream is realized, our dreams—our representations of possible futures—have moved beyond the present fulfill-ment of a past dream. The dream came true, but we have already awakened to the possibility of a new future; and the successful present realization of a past future, although it may be pleasurably acknowledged, certainly does not fill us with the joy that the realization of the current dream would, if only *it* were to be fulfilled.

But one must have a dream. That's what the Mowana story was about—not the actualities of gold and silver, but the dream of a bountiful future. The wisest in the tribe likely know that after they have crossed the river and set up the new village, the same petty bickerings and competitiveness will begin again, and per-haps even the crops and hunting again become sparse—not to mention the un-foreseen White Man. But to those boy campers trudging back to their cabins in the dark, with heads full of smoky memories, a message had been imprinted in-delibly: Climb high and dream the dream of your future. True, the emotional impact diminishes somewhat when one speaks of the importance in psycho-structural, nonmythic terms of construing alternative futures, but it comes down to the same thing: the identity construction and reconstruction process as the replacement of a worn-out dream by a new one. Similarly, structurally based psychotherapy, by encouraging the accommodative rather than the assimilative process, enables a participant to become less a victim of her or his history, less one who could only be a past, and more one who can envisage and begin to act upon a possible future.

The scope of representation of self and other increases almost exponentially as one moves through the Eriksonian psychosocial periods. One begins as al-most wholly dependent on predictably nurturant others; learns to bend his will to that of his beloved caretakers; tries out different strategies to "have" them all to herself; relinquishes this (usually) impossible task and becomes a student and classmate and friend in whatever context the technology of the culture is taught; begins to define himself no longer as a given-to child, but as an imminent worker, citizen, mate, and parent; establishes an emotionally deep and mutual relationship with at least one other person, sharing the identity achieved during the previous stage; assumes generative care for the life cycles of others and her "children" (biological, tutorial, creative); and, finally, comes to include the whole of humankind in her concern, realizing on a grand scale, through time and across the world, that we are, in H. S. Sullivan's words, "all more alike than different." What began as the ability to equate squiggly lines on paper with a ripe, red apple, ends with the capacity to envision a better world "across the river" for our children, our children's children, and all children of the world. But the path to that vision leads through the anguish of numerous disquilibrations. At our best, we can be sources of encouragement to each other as we undertake these. Only by not disequilibrating and by not accommodating do we betray our destinies.

ACKNOWLEDGMENTS

I would like to thank Dr. Janet Strayer who read an initial draft of this chapter and contributed significantly to its content. In addition, I appreciate the clarifying comments of Dr. Irving Sigel. I would like to acknowledge the helpful suggestions of Dr. Harke Bosma and also those of the developmental discussion group at Simon Fraser University. Finally, thanks to Jamie Afifi who collected and sent me reprints while I was on study leave.

REFERENCES

Bacal, H. A., & Newman, K. M. (1990). *Theories of object relations: Bridges to self psychology.* New York: Columbia University Press.

Blos, P. (1979). *The adolescent passage: Developmental issues.* New York: International Universities Press.

Calasso, R. (1993). *The Marriage of Cadmus and Harmony* (Tim Parks, Trans.). New York: Knopf.

Erikson, E. H. (1980). *Identity and the life cycle: A re-issue.* New York: Norton.

Erikson, E. H. (1982). *The life cycle completed: A review.* New York: Norton.

Hammerstein, O., II. (1949). Lyrics from *South Pacific.* New York: Williamson Music Inc.

Josselson, R., & Lieblich, A. (1996). Fettering the mind in the name of "Science". *American Psychologist, 51,* 651–652.

Kuhn, T. S. (1970). *The structure of scientific revolutions* (2nd ed. enlarged, Vol. 2, No. 2, *The International Encyclopedia of Unified Science*). Chicago: University of Chicago Press.

Lawrence, D. H. (1972). New heaven and earth. In *The complete poems of D. H. Lawrence* (Collected and edited by V. de Sola Pinto & W. Roberts, pp. 257–261). New York: Penguin.

MacKinnon, J., & Marcia, J. E. (1996). *Patterns in women's development: Interrelationships among attachment styles, identity status, and cognitive sophistication.* Unpublished manuscript, Department of Psychology, Simon Fraser University, Burnaby, B.C., Canada.

Madigan, R., Johnson, S., & Linton, P. (1995). The language of psychology: APA style as epistemology. *American Psychologist, 50,* 428–436.

Mandler, J. (1983). Representation. In P. H. Mussen (Ed.), *Handbook of child psychology* (4th ed., pp. 420–494). New York: Wiley.

Marcia, J. E. (1994a). Ego identity and object relations. In J. M. Masling & R. F. Bornstein (Eds.), *Empirical perspectives on object relations theory* (pp. 59–103). Washington, DC: American Psychological Association.

Marcia, J. E. (1994b). Identity and psychotherapy. In S. L. Archer (Ed.), *Interventions for identity* (pp. 89–104). Newbury Park, CA: Sage.

Marcia, J. E. (in press). The importance of conflict for development in adolescence. In L. Verhoefstadt-Deneuve & C. Braet (Eds.), *Conflict and development in adolescence.* London: Routledge.

Marcia, J. E., Waterman, A. S., Matteson, D. R., Archer, S. L., & Orlofsky, J. L. (1993). *Ego identity: A handbook for psychosocial research.* New York: Springer-Verlag.

Sigel, I. (1991). Representational competence: Another type? In M. Chandler & M. Chapman (Eds.), *Criteria for competence: Controversies in the conceptualization and assessment of children's abilities* (pp. 118–132). Hillsdale, NJ: Lawrence Erlbaum Associates.

Sigel, I., Stinson, E. T., & Flaugher, J. (1991). Socialization of representational competence in the family: The distancing paradigm. In J. Okagaki & R. J. Steinberg (Eds.), *Directors of development: Influences on the development of children's thinking.* Hillsdale, NJ: Lawrence Erlbaum Associates.

Slugoski, B. R., Marcia, J. E., & Koopman, R. F. (1984). Cognitive and social interactional characteristics of ego identity statuses in college males. *Journal of Personality and Social Psychology, 47,* 646–661.

Walter, B. (1947). *Theme and variations.* New York: Knopf.

CHAPTER 19

The Use of Cultural Tools:
Mastery and Appropriation

LESLIE RUPERT HERRENKOHL
University of Washington

JAMES V. WERTSCH
Washington University

The issue of representation is one that has intrigued, as well as vexed psychologists and other scholars in the human sciences for decades. There are perhaps as many representations of representation as there are those who are doing the representing. Our purpose in discussing this topic is not to review various perspectives and the similarities and differences among them. Instead, we limit ourselves to focusing on a particular issue that arises within a particular theoretical tradition. Namely, we are concerned with some aspects of representation as it has been understood from a sociocultural perspective deriving from the writings of L. S. Vygotsky (1978, 1981, 1987) and his followers.

From the perspective of the sociocultural approach we employ, the issue of representation arises in connection with the *mediational means,* or *cultural tools* (terms we use interchangeably) employed in human action. Cultural tools involve representation in some sense, but we approach this representation from the perspective of the functions it has in human action. In this respect our view is similar to the approach Dewey (1938) took toward the hypotheses and symbols in the practice of logic. He viewed symbols as instruments in the process of inquiry. As Hickman (1990) has noted, Dewey "thought it unproductive and misleading to talk about the 'essences' of tools, suggesting instead that they should be considered in instrumental terms" (p. 22). In proceeding from the sociocultural approach we employ, we are taking an analogous stance toward representations: Our focus is on the instrumental role they play in action rather than on representations removed from an action context.

Following in this tradition, we employ the theoretical constructs we introduce to examine a set of concrete phenomena. The phenomena we have in mind concern the development of critical thinking in school settings. In our process of inquiry we are concerned not only with how children can develop the requisite skills to carry out critical thinking, but also with how they can be encouraged to develop a disposition to use these skills.

DISPOSITIONS FOR CRITICAL THINKING

The terms *critical thinking* and *higher order thinking* have recently come to be widely used in psychological and educational research. Researchers suggest that skills such as relating evidence to claims (Kuhn, 1992) and being able to analyze and guide one's own cognition (Resnick, 1987) are important indicators of "good" thinking. As a result, programs in schools have been instituted to increase student proficiency and use of these strategies (Lipman, 1995; Yelland, 1995).

Even though these general thinking processes have received much attention, there are some scholars who argue that a focus on skills alone is not the answer to reforming school-based practices to encourage student involvement, self-reflection, and thoughtfulness. These researchers suggest that it is necessary to consider affective and motivational dimensions of thinking such as the desire to engage in thoughtful behavior and the proclivity to do so when given the opportunity. In this regard, there has been a growing interest in examining the "dispositions" (Barell, 1995; Perkins, Jay, & Tishman, 1993), "critical spirit" (Siegel, 1988), and "character traits" (Schrag, 1988) associated with thoughtfulness.

Investigators interested in thoughtfulness share a common perspective that calls for viewing thinking as more than a set of cognitive skills. For example, Onosko and Newmann (1994) argued that dispositions, as well as knowledge and skills are necessary for a successful higher order thinking program. They suggested that although the dispositions component of this combination is not frequently addressed, "without dispositions of thoughtfulness, neither knowledge nor the skills for applying knowledge are likely to be used intelligently" (p. 30). Dispositions involve a number of traits including a desire for claims to be well supported by evidence, a tendency to define and reflect on problems for oneself, an inquisitiveness about novel problems, a willingness to weigh multiple perspectives on one issue, a level of patience and perseverance in the face of difficulty, and an ability to monitor one's thinking processes (Onosko & Newmann, 1994; Perkins et al., 1993). Siegel (1988) defined the totality of these traits as the "critical spirit" (p. 39) that is necessary for a life of reason. He suggested that one needs a certain amount of "rational passion" (p. 40) that combines values, attitudes, and virtues with requisite skills.

Given that such dispositions are necessary to foster and guide thinking, the question arises as to how one would go about developing them in oneself or facilitating their development in others, especially in educational settings. Schrag (1988) suggested that the answers to such questions are to be found in the environments in which dispositions are fostered. In his view, "an educator whose prime interest lies in the development of character (i.e., dispositions) needs to be sensitive to the total physical and, more importantly, the social environment in which any specific training takes place" (p. 10). In addition to considering environments that are conducive to developing a critical spirit, we suggest that it is necessary to articulate a sound theoretical explanation of the relationship between social environments and the development of what appear to be individual character traits and attitudes. Although much of the literature discusses dispositions as properties of individuals, we argue that they are generated in social contexts and are a product of social roles and the concomitant rights and responsibilities associated with them.

A SOCIOCULTURAL VIEW OF DISPOSITIONS

In an attempt to differentiate and clarify some of the issues that fall under the broad notion of dispositions, we approach this notion from a sociocultural perspective (Wertsch, 1991, 1995). Such a perspective starts with the assumption that its task is to explicate the relationships between human action, including mental action, on the one hand, and the cultural, institutional, and historical settings in which such action occurs, on the other. The specific kind of action involved in this account is "mediated action." This means that humans are viewed as tool-using actors, and the cultural tools involved provide the link between sociocultural setting and individuals. To develop in this view means to develop skills and dispositions for using various mediational means.

As the basic unit of analysis, mediated action is viewed as involving two "elements" (Burke, 1969) that exist in an irreducible tension: agents and mediational means, or cultural tools. It is possible, indeed useful, to make an analytic distinction between these two elements, but we would argue that it is important not to lose sight of the fact that they are moments of mediated action rather than freestanding objects that could somehow exist independently of one another. Neither of these elements, taken in isolation, provides an adequate foundation for interpreting mediated action. Agents without cultural tools are incapable of acting, on the one hand, and cultural tools do not mechanistically determine agents' actions, on the other.

One of the major problems we see in this respect is that the powerful role that mediational means play in shaping mediated action is often overlooked, and the result is that we give too much credit to the agents employing them when trying to account for how action is carried out. The implication is that we live in a kind of "copyright age" (Wertsch, 1995) in which action is viewed as being the product solely of the individual creativity of the agents involved, a view that loses sight of the inherent role of mediational means in shaping what we say, think, and otherwise do. Instead of searching for some simple, core notion of agency, we believe it is essential to recognize a notion of "agent-acting-with-mediational-means" (Wertsch, Tulviste, & Hagstrom, 1993).

The cultural tool that we focus on is language, in particular language as it is used to carry out strategic reasoning processes. From this perspective language is not viewed simply as a reflection of preexisting strategic reasoning processes in the individual. Instead, it is viewed as an element of the agent-acting-with-mediational-means that is responsible for carrying out these processes. Furthermore, when we speak of language in this context, we are not referring to the general grammatical and semantic system of, say, English. Instead, we are concerned with specific patterns of speaking, or "speech genres" (Bakhtin, 1986) that typically first appear in social interaction, or on the "intermental plane" (Vygotsky, 1987; Wertsch, 1985) and then are taken over by the individual to form "intramental" functioning.

As is the case for other cultural tools, the relationship between language in this sense and agents can be quite varied and dynamic. When trying to understand the nature of these dynamics, it is useful to invoke a distinction between what we term *mastery* and *appropriation*. This is a distinction that has several precursors in the research literature, but it is often included under the heading of internalization or a more general version of appropriation. It is a distinction that is often difficult to maintain because mastery and appropriation are in fact so thoroughly intertwined in many empirical examples.

The mastery of a cultural tool, or mediational means, concerns the skill to use it effectively. For example, we may speak of having mastered the skill to ride a bicycle, to use a computer program, or to use a speech genre effectively (e.g., to introduce evidence in a convincing way in rational argumentation). Mastery is a measure of the kinds of skills that fall under what Ryle (1949) called "knowing how," as opposed to "knowing that," and is discussed in contemporary cognitive science (Bechtel & Abrahamsen, 1991) under headings such as the distinction between experts and novices. In general, the point we wish to make about mastery is that it is concerned with cognitive skills, defined in a fairly narrow way, involved in using cultural tools.

In contrast, appropriation as used here focuses on the agent's tendency or disposition to use a cultural tool, a disposition that is in some cases distinct from the level of mastery involved. The meaning of *appropriation* we are using derives largely from the writings in Russian of Bakhtin (1981) and, to some degree, Leont'ev (1981). The Russian term at issue, *usvoenie*, and the verb *usvoit'* are related to the possessive adjective *svoi*, which means "one's own." *Usvoit'* means to take something over and make it one's own, and the noun *usvoenie* means something like "the process of making something one's own." Actual dictionary definitions of *usvoit'* include, "to adopt, acquire (a habit, etc.); to imitate; usvoit' chuchoi vygovor: to pick up someone else's accent" (Wheeler, 1972, p. 847).

The form of appropriation involved in producing utterances, or speaking, is one in which speakers take the words of others and make them, at least in part, their own. Holquist (1981) has formulated this general point in terms of how we "rent" others' words when we speak. From a Bakhtinian perspective, there is no way to speak *without* renting, or invoking the words of others. As outlined by Holquist, such a view of appropriation contrasts with one in which we can "own" meaning, on the one hand, and with a view in which no one owns meaning, on the other.

With regard to critical thinking and higher order thinking, creating instructional contexts in which skills in these areas are both mastered *and* appropriated is a major goal. The fact that appropriation does not always occur alongside mastery has been borne out in studies such as that by Tulviste and Wertsch (1994). The findings from this study were not formulated in terms of appropriation as outlined here, but they can be interpreted as indicating that it is quite possible for individuals to master a cultural tool (in the form of "official history" narrative text in this case) but not to appropriate it. Indeed, this study examined a case in which individuals who had mastered a cultural tool resisted using it, or even rejected it outright. Similar arguments have been made with regard to appropriating language or language variants (Gilyard, 1991).

From the perspective of a sociocultural approach concerned with mediated action, the notion of appropriation makes it possible to provide a more grounded and motivated account of issues such as character traits and disposition for rational passion and a critical spirit. From this perspective, students should not only be acquainted with tools and strategies that represent their cultural legacy but they should also appropriate these tools, often modifying them in the process and thereby further contributing to their own as well as their culture's development.

In our view, one of the most effective ways to foster the appropriation, and not just the mastery of cultural tools is to coordinate these cultural tools with sociocognitive roles. These sociocognitive roles can be understood in terms of rights and responsibilities. It is often the case that the term *right* is invoked to support individualistic ends such as one's freedom to speak one's opinions. As Bellah, Madsen, Sullivan, Swidler, and Tipton (1985) pointed out, contemporary American culture places a good deal of emphasis on one's individual rights, and one's individual fulfillment often becomes the motive for action in social context. This, however, is not the only way that the issue of rights can be conceptualized. It is possible to see rights as being inherently tied to responsibilities such that people exercise their rights as a way of being responsible to their community. For example, if a building inspector exercises her right to stop construction on a building because the contractor is suspected of using materials of an unacceptable quality, she is exercising a right in the context of her responsibility to protect public safety. Very simply, she is performing her job. Promoting such an idea of "doing one's job" by emphasizing the responsibilities to one's community and the set of rights that come along with these responsibilities is the way we are proposing to encourage students to become more engaged in thinking and discussion within their classrooms. By situating students in certain sociocognitive roles that make them responsible for thinking in the classroom, it is possible to provide them with opportunities and the encouragement to practice these skills and begin to master and appropriate them.

In carrying out these roles students are often put in a position of demonstrating "performance before competence" to use the felicitous phrase coined by Cazden (1988). In the terms we are using, this means that a child uses a cultural tool in a way that he may not fully understand, but it is precisely through this practice that students come to master and appropriate the cultural tool. Therefore, although it is a common practice to have the teacher institute and discuss social norms and expectations for dispositions in classrooms (i.e., students have the right to ask for help and the duty to give help when asked), we are arguing that if students are to truly take on such dispositions they need extensive opportunities to "try them on" or "act them out" in the classroom. In so doing, students might act as if they had important dispositions toward learning before they actually do. We are not advocating that discussions of classroom norms and dispositions be discontinued. Instead, we are pointing to the importance of students' coming to view them as crucial through their own interactions within classroom settings rather than through the use of a posted set of classroom guidelines alone.

THE MASTERY AND APPROPRIATION OF CULTURAL TOOLS FOR SCHOOL-BASED SCIENTIFIC REASONING: SOME ILLUSTRATIONS

In order to exemplify the points we have made, we draw on an intervention study completed in a large urban elementary school in New England. This study examined student engagement in the context of two fourth-grade science classrooms (Class 1 and Class 2). Both classes had the same instructor. Twelve students were assigned to each class using a matched pairs procedure. As a result, the classes did not differ with respect to teacher involved, nor did they differ significantly with regard to gender, race, or standardized test scores. The same set of 12 balance and building lessons was used in each group. The objective was to involve students in substantial discussions regarding their explanations about phenomena related to the balance and building activities. Examining the function of cultural tools as well as sociocognitive roles in promoting student engagement and sustained discourse among classroom members were of primary interest.

The lessons in both classes were organized into three parts: Whole-class introductory comments, small-group activities, and whole-class reporting sessions (i.e., students reported about their small-group activities to the whole class) occurred every day. Students worked in groups of four to complete their small-group activities. Two students in each small group were assigned the role of "reporter" whereas the other two students acted as "scribes." The reporters were responsible for presenting their group's activity orally to the whole class whereas the scribes were responsible for using large chart paper or other mate rials to organize relevant information that could be used by the reporters during the reporting session. These roles rotated so that all small-group members had a chance to be reporters and scribes. Reporters and scribes were considered a primary set of sociocognitive roles that were used in Class 1 and Class 2.

At the beginning of the intervention, students in both classes were introduced to three strategic steps to guide them in producing explanations of scientific phenomena. These steps included (a) predicting and theorizing, (b) summarizing findings, and (c) coordinating predictions and theories with existing evidence (i.e., findings). From the perspective of mediated action, these steps constitute cultural tools, or mediational means in the form of patterns of speaking. The goal was to encourage these patterns of speaking in social interaction in the classroom and eventually to master and appropriate them on the intramental plane as well. These cultural tools provided the framework for discussion in both classes throughout all three segments of each lesson.

Class 2 differed from Class 1 in that during the whole-class reporting segment students in Class 2 were each assigned an "audience role" that corresponded to one of the three steps. Thus, there were some audience members who were responsible for checking the group reports for predictions and theories, others who were responsible for the summary of findings, and still others who were responsible for determining if the reporters discussed the relationship between their group's prediction, theory and findings. In Class 1 no special roles were given to the audience members. Because all students were familiar with reporting sessions in their regular science classrooms, it was assumed that, without specific role assignments, students in Class 1 would behave in a manner that was consistent with their prior experience in this setting (see Herrenkohl & Guerra, 1998 for further discussion of methods). These audience roles comprised another set of sociocognitive roles, but a set that was in use only in Class 2.

Analyses of transcribed classroom discussions during the whole-class reporting time revealed significant differences between Class 1 and Class 2. Students in Class 2, who were instructed in the three strategic steps, the use of the reporter and scribe roles, and the use of audience roles related to the strategies, were much more engaged in discussion and in building scientific explanations. Students in this group were more likely to ask questions of other students, to monitor their own comprehension of the ideas presented by others, to share responsibility for negotiating, defining, and distributing the cognitive work among classroom members, to coordinate theories and evidence, and to challenge one another's explanations (Herrenkohl & Guerra, 1998). Three findings from this study are used to illustrate the importance of offering students certain socio-cognitive roles with concomitant rights and responsibilities in order to foster the appropriation as well as the mastery of mediational means.

The first illustration is a case example of a Class 2 student, who, at the beginning of the study did not like to take on the role of the reporter for her group. This example chronicles the student's acceptance of this sociocognitive role, highlighting her appropriation of important ways of speaking within the context of a supportive classroom environment. The second example is an excerpt of transcript from Class 2 that demonstrates the connection between the audience roles and the development of important dispositions toward learning. The third finding presents a general perspective on the importance of audience role taking in fostering the activity of students posing questions to reporters.

Taking on the Role of Reporter in Class 2: Christie's Case Example

In an effort to provide a specific example of student engagement and appropriation of cultural tools, the following case example is offered. It chronicles the experience of one student, Christie, over the course of the study as she changed her mind about taking on the sociocognitive role of reporter for her group. It also examines the crucial support that she received from the teacher and other students in this process. Christie, a 10-year-old Euro-American girl, tended to be quiet and a bit withdrawn, but she was also capable of causing trouble on occasion by refusing to cooperate with her group. Early on in the study Christie told Mrs. Glenda, the teacher, that she did not like to be the reporter for her group. In addition, she mentioned this during an interview after Day 4 of the study.

> INTERVIEWER: Is there anything you don't like about it [the science program]?
> CHRISTIE: To report.
> INTERVIEWER: You don't like to report, and why don't you like to report?
> CHRISTIE: Cuz I don't like talkin' that much and plus sometimes I don't understand some of the questions the kids ask.

Christie's response suggests that she did not like to report for some very good reasons. If talking in front of a group is not enjoyable for someone, then reporting would be a difficult sociocognitive role for them to take on. Furthermore, it was often difficult for Christie to decipher the questions that other students asked. In many cases this was more difficult for her than trying to understand what the teacher asked. The interviewer and Christie proceeded to talk about what she might do if she did not understand a question in the future. They decided that it might be useful for Christie to ask the student to repeat the question using different words or ask someone else for help. This is an important strategy that is discussed further in the context of a report that Christie made. Throughout the remainder of her interview she discussed her interest in drawing and how it related to being in the sociocognitive role of the "scribe," which allowed her to make diagrams and pictures to illustrate what her group did while the group reporters prepared to present the group's activity orally to the class.

In order to understand the context of Christie's report on Day 7, the report that is the focus of this example, it is important to understand how the teacher, Mrs. Glenda, described the oral reporting sessions to the students in Class 2 on the first day of the study. After assigning students their first audience role, Mrs. Glenda completed a full description of what students assigned to each role must be looking for in the reports. At the end of this lengthy description, Mrs. Glenda said: "Remember one thing, this is the first time, yes this is hard, the hardest job is not the reporter's job, the hardest job is all of our jobs here [someone laughs] so that we can get a good explanation. We're gonna construct an explanation all together, ok?"

In this summary Mrs. Glenda emphasized that all of the students had hard jobs and that they were all going to work together in order to construct an explanation. This relieved some of the pressure typically placed on the reporter and directed some responsibility for the explanation onto the students in the audience. Mrs. Glenda used inclusive pronouns to talk about this shift. She referred to *"our"* jobs, including herself as well as all of the students in the class. In addition she emphasized that *"We're* gonna construct an explanation *all* together" indicating that the whole group, rather than only the reporter standing in front of the class, was responsible for the explanation. This formulation of the procedure introduced the students to the science program as one that was collaborative and required everyone to participate.

When Christie's group came before the class to report on Day 7, they were having some problems. Dai was a reporter for this group, but the other reporter was absent. This group worked on an activity that required them to build a balance scale out of soda straws and try to use paper clips as weights in order to get the scale to balance. Mrs. Glenda had closely watched this group during their small-group work time and had noticed that Christie had been working hard to think about the activity and write things down pertaining to the three strategic steps. Mrs. Glenda suggested that Christie should come up to help Dai with the report because the other reporter was absent. After Dai explained what had been involved in their activity, he encountered problems because he and his partner were not able to completely finish their soda straw balance.[1] At this point Mrs. Glenda offered him the opportunity to let Christie talk because she finished the activity and wrote some things down.

It is important to remember that Christie had already told Mrs. Glenda that she did not like reporting. Also, this was not a day on which Christie had been

---

[1] It is not a common practice for the children to split up in their small groups and work in pairs to complete their activities, but on this day the students in this group decided to do this.

scheduled to take on the sociocognitive role of reporter. Therefore, Mrs. Glenda was suggesting that Christie do something that she did not really like to do when she had not been scheduled to do it:

DAI: We had to build a straw balance so and we had to make it balance, and, um, I didn't make it balance because um there's not enough time for me to make it so, um.

TEACHER: [whispers to Dai] So do you want Christie to talk?

DAI: But I don't know what Christie [did].

TEACHER: OK, Christie has her thing that she did, she can do it, go ahead.

CHRISTIE: [reads from her notebook] My prediction was that I thought that it would not balance because when I first when I first had the straws, they were not even.

TEACHER: [whispers] OK then you've got [inaudible speech].

CHRISTIE: [again continues reading from her notebook] . . . because the distance the weight was from the end was different, I was right and it did not balance the farther out side went down [pause] they have questions for us [meaning the audience].

There are two interesting points to note about Mrs. Glenda's support for Christie to take on the role of the reporter. Mrs. Glenda overtly stated that "she can do it." She gave Christie an introduction that supported her effort to take on a role that was particularly difficult for her. Also, as Christie began her report, Mrs. Glenda whispered a prompt to encourage her to keep going (Mrs. Glenda was speaking so softly that part of her turn was inaudible). The overall message that Mrs. Glenda was sending to Christie was that she was able to report and that what she had to say was important.

Christie responded to Mrs. Glenda's support by continuing to engage her classmates in an effort to outline her perspective more clearly. The next segment of her report that we discuss demonstrates how Christie responded to being placed in the role of reporter and how she engaged with other students in an effort to understand their questions. The following interaction is an example of how Christie monitored her own comprehension and asked for clarification of the question asked by Tammy and Olivia:

TAMMY: How did you know it [the prediction] was correct?

OLIVIA: How did you know it was correct?

CHRISTIE: What does she mean?

TEACHER: She means, she means how did you know . . .

OLIVIA: How did you know, how did you know this was all of you . . .

DAI: Correct, how did you know you did it right?

TEACHER: Wait a sec, it's great to ask questions but let the girl answer.

CHRISTIE: Because I guessed it would go down and it did.

In this stretch of transcript, Christie indicated that she was not exactly sure what Tammy and Olivia were asking her. She appealed to other classmates and the teacher to explain to her what they meant. Through initiating this kind of episode, Christie was indexing her engagement with the questions of her fellow students. She employed one of the strategies that she and the interviewer discussed during their interview after Day 4. She indicated that she did not fully understand what the girls were asking and that she could draw upon other resources in the classroom context to help her. Mrs. Glenda in conjunction with Olivia and Dai helped clarify the question for Christie.

Each of the turns by these classroom members finished a previous one. This series of speaking turns is often referred to as co-construction or proposition across utterances and speakers (Cazden, 1988; Ochs, Schieffelin, & Platt, 1979). It highlights the collaborative nature of reporting and explaining in Class 2.

After Mrs. Glenda, Olivia, and Dai clarified what the question meant, Mrs. Glenda offered Christie a chance to respond. She indicated that she now understood the question by answering it. Thus, in this segment we do not see Christie as incapable of taking on the role of reporter nor do we see her as being particularly uncomfortable in this role. She engaged her fellow students and Mrs. Glenda in an effort to answer a question en route to building a coherent scientific explanation.

The next segment of transcript illustrates the role of audience members in engaging with and understanding the reporter's ideas. Rosie, a student in charge of examining the report for a prediction and a theory, asked Christie to identify which theory she used from the chart of theories that they have accumulated over the course of the study. It was a common practice for Mrs. Glenda to write new theories onto chart paper during the oral reporting time so that all the students could have a chance to see the different theories that had been generated by the groups.[2] This piece of chart paper was displayed during the oral reporting time every day and additions were made to it as the group deemed necessary. Rosie's question regarding which theory Christie was using indexed her engagement with the theories that have been presented over the course of 6 days. Her question indicates that she was monitoring her own comprehension of Christie's theory in reference to other theories that had been previously discussed. In addition to engaging with these theories herself, her question focuses the whole class on the theories on the chart in comparison to the theory that Christie was presenting. As a result, an interesting discussion ensued:

ROSIE: Which theory did you use, Theory 1, Theory 2, Theory 3, or Theory 4?
[referring to the theory chart]
RAUL: Did you use anything or did you just get the theory outta your head?
QING: Or did you use some theory here? [referring to the theory chart]
DAI: I think she was usin' Theory 1.
OLIVIA: No, Theory 1 is double the distance to double the weight, and this one too.

---

[2] This practice of recording theories was used in both Class 1 and Class 2. Each class had a separate chart that accumulated new theories as they were presented. These charts were displayed every day in both classes.

TEACHER: Christie, [whispers] we don't even have your theory up there!

A few points about this segment deserve highlighting. First, five students in addition to the teacher participated in this discussion. Thus, it is not possible to say that only Rosie was engaging with the theory presented by Christie. Second, as a result of Rosie's question, it was determined that Christie's theory was not represented on the chart and would need to be added. In the segment of transcript that followed this interaction, Mrs. Glenda supported Christie in outlining her theory to be added to the chart. After they finished outlining her theory, it was time for the students to get ready to leave and Mrs. Glenda began to bring the session to a close:

TEACHER: You know what, can I say something before you guys leave?
STEVEN: Yeah.
TEACHER: Um Christie really hates to do reports, but I think she really did an excellent job at her explanation today. [the students spontaneously start clapping]
STUDENT[3]: She did.
STUDENT: Yeah.

Again, Mrs. Glenda overtly supported Christie's efforts. Her public praise of Christie's report was met with an equally enthusiastic response on the part of her fellow classmates. This response recognized Christie's engagement as well as the engagement of classmates who helped support her to outline her perspective more clearly. The overwhelming message to Christie appears to have been that she was a capable reporter who had important things to say.

In an interview conducted with Christie 1 day after this reporting session, she had some interesting comments with regard to her perspective on reporting:

INTERVIEWER: Can you tell me anything you like about doing science with Mrs. Glenda?
CHRISTIE: Building things and drawing.
INTERVIEWER: Building things and drawing.
CHRISTIE: Reporting.
INTERVIEWER: Reporting. So you like reporting? Do you like reporting now? This is new isn't it? Is this something that you're just [pause] . . .
CHRISTIE: Startin' to like.
INTERVIEWER: Ye, yeah.
CHRISTIE: Yeah.
INTERVIEWER: You're just starting to like it huh?
CHRISTIE: Yeah.
INTERVIEWER: Well, that's really neat, that's really interesting. Can you tell me a little bit more about that? Why do you think you're starting to like it?
CHRISTIE: Because I'm getting used to being in a science group.

---

[3]In cases where it was not possible to discern which student was speaking, the designation STUDENT is used.

From this interview collected after Day 8 of the study, it is possible to see that Christie had changed her mind about reporting. Although she was not able to pinpoint what helped change her mind, she had a general idea that part of it was related to "getting used to being in a science *group*." Christie's use of *group* marked her recognition of reporting as part of a larger group event. The important point here is that Christie stated clearly in an interview on Day 4 that she did not like reporting. After participating in a successful report where she was engaging with classmates and the teacher who supported her to articulate her perspective, Christie changed her mind.

Through examining the transcript and the interviews it is possible to see Christie, other Class 2 students, and Mrs. Glenda as highly engaged in the process of discussing science problems. In addition, this case points to the relationship between the level of student action and a transformation in attitudes toward taking on important and valued roles such as reporter. In this case, Christie's interview responses indicate that she had a change in her disposition toward engaging in science discourse. She was able to add to her repertoire of drawing and charting by taking on the role of reporter with the support of the other children and the teacher. She indicated her new appreciation for this role in the interview after Day 8 of the study. Further interview data from Day 8 suggest that such a shift in her attitude toward reporting also involved a recognition of the importance of the three strategic steps in connection with the audience roles. During her interview on Day 4, Christie did not mention anything about the three strategic steps, even when asked, "Is there anything that's different in the science that you do with Mrs. Glenda when compared to the science with Mrs. Smith [her regular classroom teacher]?" On Day 8, this is her response to the same question:

> INTERVIEWER: Is there anything that's different in the science that you do with Mrs. Glenda when compared to the science with Mrs. Smith?
>
> CHRISTIE: The teacher don't pick the groups and we don't have theories.
>
> INTERVIEWER: And you don't have theories. OK, can you tell me a little bit more about what you mean by that? The teacher doesn't pick the groups and you don't have theories?
>
> CHRISTIE: She don't pick the people that like the theory or the predicting person.
>
> INTERVIEWER: Oh, OK, so basically like Mrs. Glenda tells you guys your job today is like predicting and theorizing, your job today is summarizing results, those kinds of things?
>
> CHRISTIE: Yeah.
>
> INTERVIEWER: Do you like the jobs?
>
> CHRISTIE: Yeah.
>
> INTERVIEWER: Do you think they help you explain in science?
>
> CHRISTIE: Yeah.
>
> INTERVIEWER: Can you tell me a little bit more about that?
>
> CHRISTIE: Because they're fun.

It is difficult to draw any definitive conclusions from this interview segment, as Christie was not able to articulate her perspective very clearly. Although her perspective was not complete, it still suggests that Christie was not coming to understand the three strategic steps in isolation as skills per se. Instead, she seems to have been coming to understand them in conjunction with the audience roles that are assigned to her and her classmates. These audience roles may not have been clear to her on Day 4 because she had not had as much experience with them and therefore was not able to mention anything about the three strategies. It is also possible that her "successful" performance in the role of reporter helped her to understand the importance of the audience roles. Her comments about "startin' to like" the role of reporter and seeing the steps as connected with the roles marks a progression in Christie's mastery and appropriation of the patterns of speaking Mrs. Glenda was encouraging in the classroom.

The Connection Between Audience Roles and the Development of Important Dispositions

In the next excerpt of transcript we examine, important dispositions toward learning are demonstrated by Denise, a student who was assigned the role of checking a report for predictions and theories. Rosie and Rich were presenting their report for their group:

 1 ROSIE: Oh, yeah, Emma.
 2 EMMA: Um did anyone else in the group have a theory?
 3 RICH: No.
 4 DENISE: Rosie was gonna say one and then Rich was gonna say one. Rosie,
 5   what was your theory?
 6 RICH: We already said it, I said it.
 7 DENISE: They were both gonna say a theory.
 8 TEACHER: Do you think they had the same theory or different theories?
 9 DENISE: Different.
10 TEACHER: Excuse me, time out, there's an excellent point being made here, Denise
11   thinks that there's two theories over here.
12 DENISE: Because you were gonna say one and Raul was gonna say one.
13 RICH: My name's . . .
14 STUDENT: Rich.
15 RICH: Not Raul.
16 STUDENT: Rich.
17 RICH: I already said it.
18 DENISE: What were you gonna say, Rosie? What were you gonna say?
19 RICH: Everybody knows what I said, right?
20 STUDENT: No.
21 STUDENT: Shhh.
22 STUDENT: Not me, not me.
23 ROSIE: Well, I don't know which one because [pause] . . .

24 DENISE: Why did you think that was gonna happen?
25 RICH: Because we didn't even start yet when we predicted.
26 DENISE: You made your theory; I want to hear Rosie's.

In this segment of transcript, Emma asked a question (Line 2), and Denise responded in a way indicating that she thought Rosie and Rich each had their own theory. In Lines 4 and 5, Denise asked Rosie to tell the class her theory. In Line 6, Rich responded to Denise's question by stating that they already told the class their theory. He further emphasized his role by noting "I said it." In Line 7, Denise again indicated that she thought that Rich and Rosie both had theories and that they were both going to say them. At this point, Mrs. Glenda stopped the conversation and emphasized Denise's "excellent point" to the class. In Line 12, Denise again resumed her quest by addressing her comment directly to Rosie saying, "you were gonna say one and Raul was gonna say one."

After correcting Denise for calling him Raul instead of Rich, Rich answered Denise's question again by noting that, "I already said it" (Line 17). In Line 18, appearing to ignore Rich's comment, Denise again turned to Rosie and said, "What were you gonna say, Rosie? What were you gonna say?" For the third time, in Line 19, Rich asserted that he had already spoken for his group by saying, "everybody knows what I said, right?" After a few other students in the class speak in response to Rich, Rosie began to take a turn for the first time in this segment of transcript (Line 23). She seems to have had a hard time articulating her perspective and when she paused for a few seconds, Denise offered another prompt for her in Line 24, "Why did you think that was gonna happen?" Then, in Line 25, Rich answered again for his group for the fourth time. In Line 26, Denise turned to Rich and stated, "You made your theory; I want to hear Rosie's."

Throughout this interaction, Denise pursued Rosie's theory even in the face of continued resistance from Rich. It was Denise's job to check predictions and theories and to feel satisfied with her understanding of them. In this case, she detected what she thought were two different theories, one advocated by Rich and another offered by Rosie. Because she was not clear about Rosie's theory and she took her job seriously, she continued to ask questions so that she could understand Rosie's perspective. Finally, after Rich repeatedly interjected his thoughts, Denise explicitly told him that he had had his chance to talk about his theory and that she wanted to hear Rosie's as well.

In this case Denise displayed a number of dispositions toward learning, including the need to hear and weigh multiple alternatives and persistence in pursuing her goal. In addition, Rosie, who was frequently dismissed by her peers, had a chance to have someone explicitly request and value her ideas. It might appear that Denise may have asked Rosie for her theory simply as part of a personal attempt to be sensitive to Rosie's feelings, but other evidence suggests that additional factors were at work. For example, there were many other instances in which Denise did not seem to consider others' feelings when acting in the role of reporter and audience member. She was frequently ready to dispute someone's perspective or insist that she be allowed to report what she considered to be the most interesting part of her group's explanations of their science activities.

For these reasons, we view Denise's questioning of Rosie as being largely a function of the sociocognitive role she was occupying. Because this occurs on Day 11 of the study, it is reasonable to assume that Denise had already understood the need to consider multiple theories (remember Rosie's question to Christie in the previous example, asking her to compare her theory to others presented on previous days). It is through the role taking that Denise was put in a position where she was encouraged to master and appropriate the kinds of speech patterns that constitute critical scientific discourse. It is also in, and arguably *because* of this context that Rosie was encouraged to engage in a discussion about her theory—a crucial step to be mastered and appropriated in order to participate effectively in scientific discourse. From a sociocultural perspective concerned with mediated action, these are processes that result in the dispositions or "habits of mind" (Rutherford & Ahlgren, 1990) that are viewed by others as being crucial to successful speaking and thinking in science.

Questioning Activity in Class 1 and Class 2

One of the most striking differences between Class 1 and Class 2 is that students in Class 2 asked many more questions than students in Class 1. Table 19.1 presents the number of questions that Class 1 and Class 2 students directed to re-

TABLE 19.1
Number of Questions Directed to the Reporters
by Students in Class 1 and Class 2

Class 1 Students	Questions	Class 2 Students	Questions
Zeree	0	Rosie	29
Salvador	0	Tammy	16
Jeanie	0	Olivia	24
Susan	1	Denise	19
Peter	1	Emma	3
James	0	Steven	22
Kathy	0	Raul	39
Carrie	0	Carson	2
Billy	0	Dai	11
Nam	0	Rich	15
Julie	1	Qing	41
Carl	0	Christie	5
Teacher	368	Teacher	117
Total	371	Total	343

Table 19.1 reprinted from Herrenkohl (1996) with permission.

porters over the course of the study. Again, reporters were students who were assigned the role of reporting about their small-group activities to the whole class at the end of each day's session. Different children took on this sociocognitive role on different days in Class 1 and Class 2. Class 2 students who were audience members also took on the responsibility for checking reports for predicting and theorizing, summarizing findings, and coordinating predictions and theories with evidence.

As Table 19.1 shows, virtually all the questions directed to reporters in Class 1 were from the teacher. In contrast, Class 2 students, rather than the teacher, were responsible for a large majority of the questions. Although some students in Class 2 asked many more questions than others, every one of the students in Class 2 asked more questions than any student in Class 1.

Although Table 19.1 provides general information on questioning, it does not address how the quantity and quality of questioning may have changed over time. Not surprisingly, there was a wide range of forms of participation by Class 2 students. Some students immediately took on their roles and began asking questions, whereas others took several days to become accustomed to this practice. For example, Emma rarely spoke before Day 8 of the study. All three of her questions were asked after that point.

The patterns of questioning in Class 1 are far more straightforward because only three students asked one question each throughout the study. Students in Class 1 were never told by the teacher, researcher, or anyone else that they could *not* ask questions, but they virtually never did so. The absence of questions on the part of Class 1 students is especially striking given their familiarity with the three strategic steps that guided the oral reporting sessions. It suggests that there is a "social gravity" (Gee, 1991) that operates against substantial student involvement in the whole-class reporting sessions characteristic of Class 2. The absence of students' questions in Class 1 might reflect, at least in part, a general need to maintain order and discipline in classroom settings (Schrag, 1988). By the time students reach fourth grade, they are well aware of this standard "rule" of teacher control and responsibility within the classroom. It appears that without specific procedures for encouraging them to participate (i.e., assigning them to audience roles for checking each report for the three strategic steps), students simply allow the teacher to adopt the role of questioner. As a result, being a reporter in Class 1 gave students access to questions directed to them by the teacher. Such individual attention from the teacher to reporters was not as characteristic of Class 2. In contrast, audience members in Class 2 were encouraged, or even required to be more engaged and responsible for their own and others' understandings.

Thus, the major form of participation and engagement was different for the two groups. In Class 1 it involved group reporters interacting with the teacher while in Class 2 it involved students as well as the teacher interacting with the reporters. Hence, the audience roles given to Class 2 students encouraged them to appropriate an important cultural tool, posing questions to others in a public forum. These sociocognitive roles would seem to be effective in encouraging further appropriation, as well as mastery of cultural tools associated with effective scientific reasoning in schools.

CONCLUSION

In this chapter we have examined claims about dispositions, critical spirit, and character traits that are associated with critical thinking. Instead of viewing these as traits or essential properties of individuals, however, we have reinterpreted them from the perspective of mediated action. From this perspective, dispositions and other such issues are viewed in terms of a relationship between agents and mediational means. An essential aspect of this relationship has to do with agents' mastery of mediational means, and this has often been examined under the heading of internalization. We have sought to differentiate two phenomena that usually are conflated under the heading of internalization—mastery and appropriation—and we have focused primarily on the latter.

It is difficult to use the term *appropriation* in English without hearing connotations of individual volition and free choice. Somehow it suggests that the process is one of an individual's standing back and considering alternatives and then making a decision. The empirical illustrations we have reviewed, however, suggest that appropriation is a function of the socialization contexts in which one has participated, and in this sense it need not be so closely associated with conscious reflection and individual choice. This is not to say that we participate in such contexts mindlessly, but it is to suggest that appropriation may not be adequately interpreted from a perspective of "methodological individualism" (Lukes, 1977). Instead, it appears to be something that can be encouraged or discouraged by the social setting in which one participates. The illustrations we have provided contrast two different, systematically organized "participant structures" (Phillips, 1972). In these two settings children occupied different sorts of sociocognitive roles and engaged in quite different patterns of discourse—patterns that are generally viewed as being relevant for the development of critical thinking in science.

Several specific points are worth noting in this respect. Class 2 provided a setting in which children took over much of the responsibility for asking questions that the teacher carried almost exclusively in Class 1. This striking difference between Class 1 and Class 2 did not emerge easily and immediately at the outset of the study. Some of the excerpts of interaction we examined suggest that various forms of encouragement and support were necessary for the children to go through this transition. This suggests that the preexisting set of sociocognitive roles (probably reflecting something like Mehan's, 1979, "IRE" sequence) is not easily dropped or transformed.

Through examining Table 19.1, however, it is obvious that children in Class 2 did indeed come to engage in interaction on the basis of a quite different set of sociocognitive roles than those found in Class 1. The large difference found in Table 19.1 between Class 1 and Class 2 does not derive from instances in which individual children were responding to directives by the teacher to ask questions. Instead, it reflects differences in how children more or less spontaneously posed questions. We take this to be evidence that children in Class 2 came to appropriate the audience roles provided in the setting, at least on the intermental plane. Our evidence does not allow us to make strong claims about mastery in this setting or about mastery or appropriation in other settings when children operate in groups or individually. However, studies of "reciprocal teaching" (Palincsar & Brown, 1984) and other such procedures strongly suggest that questions such as the ones that characterized discourse in Class 2 are likely to be mastered and appropriated on an intramental, as well as the intermental plane.

In many respects, the issues we have raised here are old ones. Figures such as Dewey (1915 / 1966) have been concerned with them for decades. By differentiating the notions of mastery and appropriation, however, and by examining the influence of patterns of sociocognitive roles on how appropriation seems to occur, we hope to have opened up a set of questions that have not been thoroughly examined. These are questions about cognition as well as emotion, and they are questions about social as well as individual mental functioning. In our view the issues we have raised must be addressed in any account of representation that hopes to provide insight into human action. We by no means claim to have provided final answers, but as Dewey (1938) noted over a half century ago, "inquiry is a *continuing* process in every field with which it is engaged" (p. 8).

ACKNOWLEDGMENTS

The writing of this chapter was assisted by a McDonnell Postdoctoral Fellowship awarded to the first author and a grant from the Spencer Foundation to the second author. The statements made and the views expressed are solely the responsibility of the authors.

REFERENCES

Bakhtin, M. M. (1981). *The dialogic imagination: Four essays by M. M. Bakhtin* (C. Emerson, Trans.). Austin: University of Texas Press.

Bakhtin, M. M. (1986). *Speech genres and other late essays* (V. W. McGee, Trans.). Austin: University of Texas Press.

Barell, J. (1995). *Teaching for thoughtfulness: Classroom strategies to enhance intellectual development* (2nd ed.). White Plains, NY: Longman.

Bechtel, W., & Abrahamsen, A. (1991) *Connectionism and the mind: An introduction to parallel processing in networks.* Oxford, England: Blackwell.

Bellah, R. N., Madsen, R., Sullivan, W. M., Swidler, A., & Tipton, S. M. (1985). *Habits of the heart: Individualism and commitment in American life.* New York: Harper & Row.

Burke, K. (1969). *A grammar of motives.* Berkeley: University of California Press.

Cazden, C. (1988). *Classroom discourse: The language of teaching and learning.* Portsmouth, NH: Heinemann.

Dewey, J. (1938). *Logic: The theory of inquiry.* New York: Holt, Rinehart & Winston.

Dewey, J. (1966). *Democracy and education.* New York: The Free Press. (Original work published 1915)

Gee, J. P. (1991, April). *Social gravity.* Paper presented at the meeting of the American Educational Research Association, Chicago, IL.

Gilyard, K. (1991). *Voices of the self: A study of language competence.* Detroit: Wayne State University Press.

Herrenkohl, L. R. (1996). Enhancing student engagement in the context of school science. (Doctoral dissertation, Clark University, 1995). *Dissertation Abstrats International, 56,* 7063.

Herrenkohl, L. R., & Guerra, M. R. (1998). Participant structures, scientific discourse, and student engagement in fourth grade. *Cognition and Instruction.*

Hickman, L. A. (1990). *John Dewey's pragmatic technology.* Bloomington: Indiana University Press.

Holquist, M. (1981). The politics of representation. In S. Greenblatt (Ed.), *Allegory in representation: Selected papers from the English Institute* (pp. 163–183). Baltimore: Johns Hopkins University Press.

Kuhn, D. (1992). Thinking as argument. *Harvard Educational Review, 62,* 155–178.

Leont'ev, A. N. (1981). The problem of activity in psychology. In J. V. Wertsch (Ed.), *The concept of activity in Soviet psychology* (pp. 37–71). Armonk, NY: Sharpe.

Lipman, M. (1995). Moral education, higher-order thinking and philosophy for children. *Early Child Development and Care, 107,* 61–70.

Lukes, S. (1977). Methodological individualism reconsidered. In S. Lukes (Ed.), *Essays in social theory* (pp. 177–186). New York: Columbia University Press.

Mehan, H. (1979). *Learning lessons.* Cambridge, MA: Harvard University Press.

Ochs, E., Schieffelin, B. B., & Platt, M. (1979). Propositions across utterances and speakers. In E. Ochs & B. B. Schieffelin (Eds.), *Developmental pragmatics* (pp. 251–268). New York: Academic Press.

Onosko, J. J., & Newmann, F. M. (1994). Creating more thoughtful learning environments. In J. N. Mangieri & C. C. Block (Eds.), *Creating powerful thinking in teachers and students: Diverse perspectives* (pp. 27–50). Fort Worth, TX: Harcourt Brace College Publishers.

Palincsar, A. S., & Brown, A. L. (1984). Reciprocal teaching of comprehension-fostering and comprehension-monitoring activities. *Cognition and Instruction, 1,* 117–175.

Perkins, D. N., Jay, E., & Tishman, S. (1993). Beyond abilities: A dispositional theory of thinking. *Merrill–Palmer Quarterly, 39*(1), 1–21.

Phillips, S. (1972). Participant structures and communicative competence: Warm Springs children in community and classroom. In C. B. Cazden, V. P. John, & D. Hymes (Eds.), *Functions of language in the classroom* (pp. 370–394). New York: Teachers College Press.

Resnick, L. (1987). *Education and learning to think.* Washington, DC: National Academy Press.

Rutherford, J., & Ahlgren, A. (1990). *Science for all Americans.* New York: Oxford University Press.

Ryle, G. (1949). *The concept of mind.* New York: Barnes & Noble.

Schrag, F. (1988). *Thinking in school and society.* New York: Routledge.

Siegel, H. (1988). *Educating reason: Rationality, critical thinking and education.* New York: Routledge.

Tulviste, P., & Wertsch, J. V. (1994). Official and unofficial histories: The case of Estonia. *Journal of Narrative and Life History, 4*(4), 311–329.

Vygotsky, L. S. (1978). *Mind in society: The development of higher psychological processes.* Cambridge, MA: Harvard University Press.

Vygotsky, L. S. (1981). The genesis of higher mental functions. In J. V. Wertsch (Ed.), *The concept of activity in Soviet psychology* (pp. 144–188). New York: Sharpe.

Vygtosky, L. S. (1987). *The collected works of L.S. Vygotsky* (Vol. 1, N. Minick, Trans.). New York: Plenum.

Wertsch, J. V. (1985). *Vygotsky and the social formation of mind*. Cambridge, MA: Harvard University Press.

Wertsch, J. V. (1991). *Voices of the mind*. Cambridge, MA: Harvard University Press.

Wertsch, J. V. (1995). Sociocultural research in the copyright age. *Culture and Psychology, 1*(1), 81–102.

Wertsch, J. V., Tulviste, P., & Hagstrom, F. (1993). A sociocultural approach to agency. In E. Forman, N. Minick, & C. A. Stone (Eds.), *Contexts for learning: Sociocultural dynamics in children's development* (pp. 336–356). New York: Oxford University Press.

Wheeler, M. (1972). *The Oxford Russian–American dictionary*. Oxford, England: Clarendon.

Yelland, N. J. (1995). Encouraging young children's thinking skills with logo. *Childhood Education, 71*(3), 152–155.

CHAPTER 20

A Representational System
for Peer Crowds

JEFFREY A. MCLELLAN
JAMES YOUNISS
The Catholic University of America

The aim of this chapter is to offer an analysis of the role of representation in adolescents' functioning within peer crowds. In every high school studied by social scientists, students have been found to differentiate one another and are differentiated by their membership in crowds. Crowds are conceptually organized in a categorical system in which, for instance, serious students are distinguished from adolescents who do not care for school, or, adolescents who smoke marijuana and attend rock concerts differ from students who do voluntary community service. The stable patterning of crowds within schools can be understood to have several important functions. It helps students cognitively order the array of peers within a school according to a shared symbolic system and allows individuals to use that system to present themselves clearly to the rest of their peers (Goffman, 1967).

Crowds also stand for more abstract orientations to society in that they provide practice with behaviors and thinking that are associated with various stances that adults take toward society. Thus, crowds signal adolescents' current stances toward society and are potentially connected to stances adults have. In this last regard, crowds also enable or restrict access to the number and kinds of adults with whom adolescents might interact. Consequently, crowds may ultimately determine the degree to which adolescents form ideas in common with adults and acquire the "social capital" that facilitates taking on adult citizenship (Coleman & Hoffer, 1987).

Although the literature on peer crowds implies that a representational system is needed to function effectively within the peer domain, an appropriate theory has not yet been articulated for this purpose. One aim of the present chapter is to offer a preliminary outline of such a theory. We believe this effort is important for two reasons. It should help to clarify the importance of cognition for functioning within crowds. In complement, a focus on representation in terms of crowds may generate ideas that advance theories of representation in general. This is because the topic of crowds introduces new issues that are not ordinarily brought into the discussion of representation. In particular, the phenomenon of crowds forces recognition of the importance of collective symbols and shared representational understandings that are neglected in most developmental accounts, which tend to be focused on the individual symbol user's veridical conceptualization of objective events.

We begin by offering a list of six issues that the topic of crowds brings to the study of representation. We then describe the general function of crowds in terms of adolescents' involvement in establishing identity. Next, we focus on a scheme that describes two functions of representation and two levels at which it operates. Finally, we illustrate the usefulness of this scheme with examples from recent studies of crowds in high school students.

WHY IS REPRESENTATION IMPORTANT?

There are at least six important issues that implicate representation in the study of crowds:

1. It is generally agreed that crowds are reputationally based social categories (Brown, 1990). Crowds are not material things nor are they easily captured by single behaviors. They are complexly composed and have existence only at a conceptual level. They are real only at this level and, thus, identification of a crowd and differentiation among crowds require a representational system.

2. Students in high schools typically know which crowds exist, what each crowd stands for, and how any crowd differs from other crowds. It follows that conceptions of crowds are shared by peers and are part of the peer culture (Corsaro & Eder, 1990). Shared understanding, by definition, necessitates the presence of a representational system.

3. If individual students are to negotiate effectively within the peer domain, they must have knowledge of the system by which crowds are categorized. This fact suggests that adolescents know how to interpret the symbols that define and differentiate crowds within schools (Lesko, 1988).

4. Individual students are not simply observers, but are also members of crowds. It follows that adolescents know how to symbolize or present themselves, in Goffman's (1967) sense, so that others will know the crowds to which they belong. This shows that individual and collective aspects of representation are intertwined.

5. Knowledge of crowds is not contained or bounded by the peer domain. Crowds have significance for society beyond the high school. In this regard, the representational system is abstract and does not map directly onto adult roles and statuses, even though crowds are unambiguously associated with these roles and statuses (Hollingshcad, 1949).

6. Adult society, in terms of roles and statuses, is recapitulated within crowds by affecting intercrowd dynamics and adolescents' choices of crowd membership. Thus, participation in crowds, knowingly or implicitly, prepares adolescents for adult roles and statuses. In this respect, observers of crowds are able to understand the symbolic connections between crowds and adult society (Eckert, 1989).

7. From a developmental perspective, the representational system by which crowds are known serves a broader function as adolescents proceed through the identity process. They utilize this system to obtain feedback about directions they are taking and the places various trajectories might lead. This imagined relation between present behavior within the peer domain and adult life to come in the future obviously requires a symbolic system that connects real to hypothetical possibilities.

This last point merits emphasis. Because the identity process involves constructing a historically legitimate orientation to society (Erikson, 1968), crowds should not be treated in isolation from society outside the school. Whereas crowds provide an immediate context for practicing styles of interpersonal relationships with peers, they simultaneously represent orientations to society beyond the school and prepare adolescents differentially for the positions they might eventually take toward society. Accordingly, crowds are not happenstance collections of peers. They are chosen in the service of the identity process that is salient to adolescents and, as signals of identity choices, they facilitate peers' collective construction of identity (Youniss & Yates, 1997).

IDENTITY DEVELOPMENT: A TWO-LEVEL PROCESS

We have proposed previously that Erikson's writings on identity have tended to be interpreted in a too narrow and individualistic manner (Yates & Youniss, 1996). Commentators have typically focused on an inward search for authenticity characterized by a lonely struggle within individuals to make sense of others' responses to them. Erikson (e.g., 1968) can be read differently, however, to stress a more social process and outcome. Adolescents seek a place in history that entails joining others in a particular orientation toward society. Data for this task come from the immediate world of peers and from the social-historical world known as adult society and that students, themselves, will soon enter as adults.

Erikson (1968) depicted the process of identity in terms of individuals' entering history by adopting particular orientations to society. Rather than limiting the process to a person's biographical experiences, Erikson consciously extended it to the collective sphere of interpersonal interaction where adolescents form relationships with one another. Individuals need to go outside themselves to find meaning that has transcendent lastingness. This is why adolescents assess their fit with, for example, religious, political, ethnic, or interest groups, which signify various collective understandings of human experience. Transcendence inheres in the collective and historical nature of these positions, because each had an existence that predated the individual, is constituted solely by the assent of other persons, and has the potential for future existence that should, in principle, outlive the individual adolescent.

In summary, this view on the identity process places focus on establishing a relationship to society, in the social-historical sense. Individuals seek, with some degree of consciousness, to become part of a transcendent and collective outlook that has a known past and likely future. For example, they may choose to identify with the "working class" (Willis, 1977), some religious group (Litchfield & Thomas, 1997), or an ethnic-political nationality (Barber, 1997). This task cannot be completed through an inward focus on the self with its limited experiences and fluctuating subjective base. To find stability, individuals must go outside themselves to join positions that have historical legitimacy, provide transcendent meaning for current behavior, and promise hope for the future.

PEER CROWDS

Brown (1990) has defined groupings of students, or crowds, as reputationally based social categories. In any school, students are sorted into crowds that are known by the places they hang around, the clothes they wear, the dialect they speak, their attitudes toward school, preferred musical tastes, and other dimensions salient to youth. For example, Arnett (1996) has reported that *metalheads*, whose chief feature is preference for "heavy metal" music, tend to hang around outside the school, wear jeans and black T-shirts with the logos of heavy metal bands, and dislike school. In contrast, adolescents in "popular" crowds are more likely to be found in the school cafeteria, wear "preppy" clothing, enjoy school, and listen to "top-40" music (Lesko, 1988).

The literature on adolescent peer crowds shows that they are a stable phenomenon within high schools. All researchers who have looked have found that adolescents can reliably assign their classmates to their proper crowds. Although specific crowd names and stylistic accoutrements may differ from school to school, the social categories represented by crowds are invariably found within each school. Several investigators have reported that the variation includes recurring prototypical groups with agreed-on reputations (e.g., Brown, Mory, & Kinney, 1994; Eckert, 1989; Youniss, McLellan, & Strouse, 1994).

Crowds carry meanings that go beyond the immediate persons and relationships involved in members' social interactions. Brown et al. (1994) noted that crowds resemble social categories in Tajfel's (1981) sense, because they allow a large array of social data to be systematically ordered in a shared way. As such, crowds are cognitive entities that are ways of making sense of, or representing, salient conceptual distinctions within the social world of the high school. This sharing of representations provides adolescents with a common outlook that enables them to operate effectively with peers and jointly to negotiate this categorical ordering more carefully.

Crowds differ from cliques, which are social groups that have no existence outside the particular persons immediately involved (Dunphy, 1963). For example, "Sally's clique" may be a salient category for students who are acquainted with Sally and her friends; however, it does not carry any representational capacity to other students who are not so acquainted. In contrast, the term *popular crowd* carries a collective meaning such that a student need not be acquainted with the persons involved to be able to describe its characteristics in some detail. For instance, members of popular crowds probably like school, play sports, wear the latest styles, are snobbish, and gossip about students in other crowds (Eder, 1985).

In support of this viewpoint, Brown, Lohr, and Trujillo (1990) have proposed that certain crowd categories are more-or-less universally recognized by U.S. high school and college students. They immediately recognize the meaning of crowd names such as *nerds, druggies, jocks, populars, loners, rejects,* and the like. It follows that crowds may be useful in providing adolescents with a range of "prescriptive identities" (Brown et al., 1994) from which to choose and by which to differentiate one another. Given our view on identity, crowds serve to help situate individuals in relationship to types of other persons and the sociohistorical ideologies they represent.

TWO FUNCTIONS OF REPRESENTATION

Within the typical high school milieu, crowds make up a highly differentiated representational system with salience to students, and also to teachers, administrators, and parents. This system provides ready-made slots for establishing an orientation to the social world and signifies to others the orientation that one has taken. We now look at these functions of representation in more detail.

We start with the notion that identity entails choice. There are, in our society, any number of plausible ideological positions individuals can take, for example, in ethical or political terms. Indeed, for two centuries, the United States has been a proving ground for this hypothesis as immigrants have had to reestablish themselves under new circumstances where old ready-made identities might not have been adaptive. Similarly, during the same period, there was abundant opportunity for socioeconomic mobility so that the status into which one was born may not have been the status that was achieved in adulthood.

Citing Allport and reporting new data, Tajfel (1981) noted that children are apt to accept the social category in which they live, if only because it seems obvious, natural, and immutable. Because children tend to identify with the dominant adults in their lives, they are not apt to question the social slots they share with them. From a cognitive perspective, one could say also that children may even be unable to question these categories until they are capable of imagining hypothetical and possible realities in a systematic manner (Inhelder & Piaget, 1958).

Note that our conceptualization proposes that crowds are social cognitive representations that have a consensual basis. We emphasize this social cognitive basis of crowds because it provides adolescents and others with meaningful categories for thought and discussion that are abstracted from knowledge of individual persons. Using the term *group* rather than *crowds,* Lesko (1988) proposed that through groups, "personal and social identities are wrestled with and visualized . . . [as] the articulated differences between groups [symbolize] alternative images of persons and of society" (p. 74).

As was observed, most school settings provide students with an array of crowds that vary in reputation and representational signification. These arrays represent a range of possibilities to individual students. For example, when asked to describe the crowd he was in, a student said: "I play hockey like the jocks, but I don't drink like they do, and I enjoy school like the brains." This student is defining portions of his current identity in crowd category terms, using shared understandings about reputation to represent aspects of the self. Eckert's (1989) ethnography of a suburban high school also illustrates this point well. She showed how students used two major crowd categories of school-oriented *jocks* and non-school-oriented *burnouts* to represent oppositional facets of their identity.

For whom is this representational system designed? We propose that has two basic directions. On the one hand, it helps adolescents individually and collectively, to make sense of the possibilities available for identification. Insofar as the jocks versus burnouts scheme represents opposing orientations to the academic curriculum, the system provides students with a basis for selecting the crowd affiliation that is anchored in the definite referent of the school. On the other hand, by taking on membership in crowds, adolescents also signal to others the reputation they desire and orientation by which they want to be known (Stone & Brown, in press).

Neither function could operate apart from a shared representational system. The fact is that students spend considerable time thinking and talking about the crowds in their schools, for example, being critical or negotiating changes from one to another crowd (Lesko, 1988). This talk continually reestablishes the system with which students then operate. At the same time, membership in crowds would not carry signaling capacity unless students shared the same representational system. For example, popular cheerleaders and other girls who want to be their friends, understand the limits on their relationship, even though the former belong to the desired group and the latter have never been and probably will not become members of this group (Eder, 1985).

TWO LEVELS OF SOCIETY

Crowds provide adolescents with a menu of options for representing social possibilities to the self and symbolizing the self to others. At a relatively superficial level, clothing style, extracurricular activities, musical tastes, and other visible characteristics distinguish one crowd from another. But, we propose that crowds represent more about identity than is apparent from these surface differences in that there is more significance to apparently trivial stylistic differences than meets the eye. The main function of these differentiating features is to symbolize the position the self has taken within the world of peers and to communicate it to other students using their shared representational system.

There is a tendency among persons a few years beyond their teens to think of adolescents who appear "unusual" or "faddish" in appearance or behavior as simply displaying adolescent rebellion or some sort of generic antinomian or hedonistic orientation. In fact, such characteristics as taste in music should not be treated lightly. They are close to being signals in the classic sense that smoke signifies fire, leaving little room for ambiguity. Adolescent groups that appear similar to outsiders, may, in fact, be highly differentiated from the perspective of peers. Arnett's (1996) work on metalheads is instructive in this regard. Adolescents know that peers who listen to recordings by Metallica are "real" metalheads in contrast to peers who listen to the superficially similar music of Bon Jovi and are judged as mere poseurs by true metalheads.

The material features that go into the differentiation of crowds are means for communicating identity choices within the peer milieu. We would now add a second level to this analysis. Identity involves moving beyond the peer domain to society itself. Although crowds are understood according to the representational system we have just described, they also symbolize orientations to society beyond the high school domain. For example, Eckert's (1989) work demonstrates that crowd affiliation has clear societal implications. Jocks like school and spend much of their time in activities that are endorsed by the school and approved of by parents. Being a jock, then, signifies an orientation within the high school and also implies a positive evaluative orientation to normative society. Similarly, burnouts, who dislike school and regularly partake of deviant behaviors, clearly differentiate themselves by signaling an oppositional stance toward normative society, or at least middle-class normative society.

This second-level aspect of crowd membership has also been described well by Rigsby and McDill (1975), who showed that students' orientations within the peer world were correlated with the same students' orientations toward adult society. Rigsby and McDill assessed the degree to which students participated in school-based activities or peer-based fun-oriented activities. They found that students in the former category were likely to achieve high grades and aspire to college, whereas students in the latter category were likely to get low grades and not aspire to college.

In a more recent study, Youniss, Yates, and Su (in press) extended this finding with data from a national sample of high school seniors. Students described their participation in various kinds of daily activities that included partaking in school government, playing team sports, reading alone, going to rock concerts, and so on. Four major groupings resulted, with some students being school oriented, others being fun oriented, still others being both school and fun oriented, and others being disengaged in showing no clear orientation. The group that was both school and fun oriented was also the most involved in doing community service; roughly four times as many of these students as disengaged students said they did service on a regular basis. In distinction, students with a fun orientation were much more likely to have used marijuana than students with a school orientation.

IDENTITY AND REPRESENTATION

Table 20.1 offers a scheme that illustrates the representational functions of crowd categories. It characterizes identity development in adolescence as taking place at two levels. Level 1 pertains to identity within adolescents' immediate

TABLE 20.1
Representational Functions of Crowd Categories

	Represent the Social World to the Adolescent	Represent the Adolescent to the Social World
Level 1 Identity in the Adolescent's Immediate World (school, youth culture)	1.1 e.g., Help the adolescent make sense of social complexity: "'Brains' get along better with teachers than they do with other kids."	2.1 e.g., Demonstrate that the adolescent is not to be taken lightly: "They know that if they start a fight with us we'll finish it."
Level 2 Identity in the Social-Historical World (ideology, politics, morality, ethnicity)	1.2 e.g., Exemplify societal inequality: "It is not fair that kids whose parents can't afford to buy the latest clothes are excluded."	2.2 e.g., Make a political statement: "We believe that the government should do more to protect the environment."

world of school and youth culture. Level 2 refers to identity in the social-historical world of adults that involves ideology, politics, morality, and ethnicity. We see crowd categories as serving two general representational functions at each level. One function is to represent and make sense of the social world to the adolescent and the second is to represent the adolescent to other persons by showing them the choices that one has made about identity. Both of these functions imply that there is a known representational system and that it is shared by peers, and sometimes by adults, to whom these symbols are addressed and who understand these symbols.

For the remainder of this chapter, we exemplify the four cells of the table with results from studies of crowds.

Making Sense of the Peer World. Cell 1.1 illustrates one way in which crowds are categories that help adolescents make sense of their immediate social world of the school. In this illustration, knowledge of characteristics of members of the "brain" crowd provides adolescents with an explanation as to why some students have better relationships with teachers than others. Brown et al. (1994) have spelled out the usefulness of crowd categories for adolescents who "find that the crowd system gives them a language by which to understand and express the complicated and sometimes confusing patterns of social relations with peers" (p. 162). Lesko's (1988) work on differences between the *rich and populars* and *burnouts* in the school she studied, showed how talk about peer groups and their characteristics provided students with a forum for considering issues of "belonging and treating others decently, making something of oneself, and defining a good member, or citizen of the school" (p. 96).

Fordham (1996) has shown further how African-American students in an urban high school use the term *brainiacs* to identify students who do well in school and, thereby, differentiate themselves from their peers by "acting White." The term brainiacs, therefore, is a sign of respect, but is coupled with resentment at students who are trying to "act different."

Making Sense of Society. The example in Cell 1.2 shows how adolescents can have the social world outside of the high school represented and recapitulated within the crowd context. In this example, a student reflects on the injustice of social stratification as she encounters it within these peer groups. Eckert's (1989) characterization of how American socioeconomic divisions are reflected in the peer group divisions of the high school she studied is an empirical example: "Even those Burnouts who can afford to dress on a Jock scale tend not to, as an expression of solidarity with those who cannot. Lack of means is in itself a positive value, and Burnouts criticize Jocks for what they see as unnecessarily expensive and competitive dressing" (p. 63).

Representing Group Meaning to Peers. Cell 2.1 is an example of the usefulness of peer crowds in asserting an identity of being a formidable opponent. In this sense, students can use affiliation with the group to make a collective representation of a position within the school. Kinney's (1993) longitudinal study describes how the formerly dominant "trendy" group from middle school ran into opposition from other crowds as a cohort of students began attending high school: "Some of the trendies ostracized members of the headbangers and punk rockers, which seemed to reduce the amount of negative attention they directed at the nerds. Members of the subcultures, especially the headbangers, criticized the trendies and competed with them for schoolwide popularity" (p. 29).

Representing Group Meaning to Society.   The function of crowd categories in representing the group to persons and entities beyond the school is illustrated in Cell 2.2. In this case, the group is representing a political belief regarding the proper role of government. A variety of studies have shown the utility of peer groups in "making a statement" to authorities or to the broader community. Willis' (1977) work on the solidarity of working-class youth in the face of middle-class expectations is one example.

A more alarming example is the presence in some schools of "skinhead" crowds connected with White supremacist racist organizations outside the school. Accounts in both the popular press (e.g., Henrichs, 1996) and the research literature (e.g., Hamm, 1993; Moore, 1993) indicate that explicit links exist between "White power" organizations such as the White Aryan Resistance and groups of high school youth who embrace the skinhead style. Hamm's summary of this connection is instructive: "These skinhead groups have emerged under various social, economic, and political conditions. Hence, they do not share a common street corner or neighborhood culture. But they do share a common ideology. According to every published account filed to date, this ideology is *neo-Nazism* supported and sustained by specific *outward appearance* of shaved heads, Nazi regalia, Doc Martens' boots, and racial/ethnic violence; and white power rock music" (p. 65). Political convictions that are similarly strong but more benign are held be some members of "enviro" or "granola" crowds in some schools who have a great degree of commitment to the environmental movement.

CROWD CATEGORIES, SOCIETY, AND
FUTURE PROSPECTS FOR ADOLESCENTS

Our purpose in writing this chapter was to examine the identity-engendering functions of high school crowds from the perspective of representation. To this end, we have depicted identity development as taking place both at the level of adolescents' immediate world and at the level of the social-historical world. At the same time, we have distinguished between how crowds represent the social world to the adolescent and how they permit the adolescent to represent the self to the world.

Crowds provide a two-way link between adolescents and the broader society beyond the school. This is possible because of the differentiated nature of the stances represented by crowds through their different characteristics. Some crowd characteristics, such as illegal drug use or liking school, are obvious in the way they represent a stance toward normative society (Rigsby & McDill, 1975; Youniss et al., 1997). Members of groups involved in illegal drug use are, by definition, defying civil authority, and risking arrest, criminal charges, and other sanctions. In contrast, members of crowds that favor school and participate in extracurricular activities have higher grades and more frequently intend to go to college (McLellan, 1992). Obviously, crowd affiliation is not to be construed as mere child's play, but is relevant to the future prospects of adolescents.

Characteristics that distinguish one crowd from another are consequential both within the peer social world and outside of it. One barrier to an appreciation of the importance of crowd phenomena is the lumping of adolescents together as a bloc that adheres to a single belief or ideology. Such an approach was intimated in the early work of Coleman (1961) on the frivolous and anti-academic "adolescent society." The sharpening of this image by youth demonstrations in the 1960s led commentators such as Aldridge (1969) to call for a defense of civilized values against the "current armies of self-righteous puberty" (p. xiii). Although it is true that crowds afford adolescents a means of collectively representing a perspective on society, this does not mean that they are representing a single perspective. All recent work in the area has emphasized the existence of a multiplicity of adolescent peer groups with a corresponding multiplicity of stances toward the world beyond the school.

Another barrier to an appreciation of the importance of crowd categories is that they are irrelevant to society or to the future prospects of adolescents. It would be wrong to view "stylistic" crowd differences in dress or musical tastes as merely trivial fads with no long-term consequences. Though we do not claim that every passing fashion in dress is necessarily significant, we do maintain that stylistic differences among crowds are frequently emblematic of differing perspectives toward normative society. The shaved heads of the skinhead groups discussed earlier are an extreme example. However, it is also true that the conservative style of dress known as preppy among adolescents goes together with a lifestyle that conforms well with normative adult expectations (McLellan, 1992), whereas the black T-shirt and jeans of the metalhead are part of a lifestyle that likely signals reckless behavior, illegal drug use, and other lawbreaking acts (Arnett, 1996).

In short, the domain of peer crowds is significant at several levels, most pointedly in the identity process. We have tried to show that a complex system of representation is involved and to outline some of its functions. We hope this work is sufficiently clear to encourage others to pursue this important, but neglected area of study.

REFERENCES

Aldridge, J. W. (1969). *In the country of the young.* New York: Harper's Magazine Press.

Arnett, J. (1996). *Metalheads: Heavy metal music and adolescent alienation.* Boulder, CO: Westview.

Barber, B. (1997). Palestinian youth and the Intifada movement. In M. Yates & J. Youniss (Eds.), *International perspectives on community service and political engagement.* Manuscript under review.

Brown, B. B. (1990). Peer groups and peer cultures. In S. S. Feldman & G. R. Elliott (Eds.), *At the threshold: The developing adolescent* (pp. 171–196). Cambridge, MA: Harvard University Press.

Brown, B. B., Lohr, M. J., & Trujillo, C. (1990). Multiple crowds, multiple life styles: Adolescents' perceptions of peer-group stereotypes. In R. E. Muus (Ed.), *Adolescent behavior and society: A book of readings* (pp. 30–36). New York: Random House.

Brown, B. B., Mory, M., & Kinney, D. (1994). Casting adolescent crowds in a relational perspective: Caricature, channel, and context. In G. Montemayor, G. Adams, & T. Gullotta (Eds.), *Personal relationships during adolescence* (pp. 123–167). Thousand Oaks, CA: Sage.

Coleman, J. S. (1961). *The adolescent society.* New York: The Free Press.

Coleman, J. S., & Hoffer, T. B. (1987). *Public and private schools: The impact of communities.* New York: Basic Books.

Corsaro, W. A., & Eder, D. (1990). Children's peer cultures. *Annual Review of Sociology, 16,* 197–220.

Dunphy, D. (1963). The social structure of urban adolescent peer groups. *Sociometry, 26,* 230.

Eckert, P. (1989). *Jocks and burnouts: Social categories and identity in the high school.* New York: Teachers College Press.

Eder, D. (1985). The cycle of popularity: Interpersonal relations among female adolescents. *Sociology of Education, 58,* 154–165.

Erikson, E. (1968). *Identity: Youth and crisis,* New York: Norton.

Fordham, S. (1996). *Blacked out.* Chicago: University of Chicago Press.

Goffman, E. (1967). *Interaction ritual: Essays in face-to-face behavior.* Garden City, NY: Doubleday.

Hamm, M. (1993). *American skinheads: The criminology and control of hate crime.* London: Praeger.

Henrichs, E. (1996). I was a Nazi girl. *YM, 44,* 56–59.

Hollingshead, A. (1949). *Elmtown's youth.* New York: Wiley.

Inhelder, B., & Piaget, J. (1958). *The growth of logical thinking from childhood to adolescence.* New York: Basic Books.

Kinney, D. (1993). From "nerds" to "normals": Adolescent identity recovery within a changing social system. *Sociology of Education, 66,* 21–40.

Lesko, N. (1988). *Symbolizing society: Stories, rites and structure in a Catholic high school.* New York: Falmer.

Litchfield, A. W., Thomas, D. L., & Li, B. D. (1997). Dimensions of religiosity as mediators of the relations between parenting and adolescent deviant behavior. *Journal of Adolescent Research, 12,* 199–226.

McLellan, J. (1992). *Characteristics of members of different high school "crowds."* Unpublished doctoral dissertation, The Catholic University of America, Washington, DC.

Moore, J. B. (1993). *Skinheads shaved for battle: A cultural history of American skinheads.* Bowling Green, OH: Bowling Green State University Popular Press.

Rigsby, L. C., & McDill, E. L. (1975). Value orientations of high school students. In H. R. Stub (Ed.), *The sociology of education* (pp. 53–75). Homewood, IL: Dorsey.

Stone, M., & Brown, B. B. (in press). Identity claims and projections: Descriptions of self and crowds in secondary school. In J. A. McLellan & M. J. Pugh (Eds.), *Stability and change in adolescent peer group participation: New directions for child development.* San Francisco: Jossey Bass.

Tajfel, H. (1981). *Human groups and social categories.* London: Cambridge University Press.

Willis, P. (1977). *Learning to labour.* London: Columbia University Press.

Yates, M., & Youniss, J. (1996). Community service and political-moral identity in adolescents. *Journal of Research on Adolescents, 6,* 271–284.

Youniss, J., McLellan, J., & Strouse, D. (1994). "We're popular, but we're not snobs": Adolescents describe their "crowds." In G. Montemayor, G. Adams, & T. Gullotta (Eds.), *Personal relationships during adolescence* (pp. 101–122). Thousand Oaks, CA: Sage.

Youniss, J., & Yates, M. (1997). *Community service and social responsibility in youth: Theory and policy.* Chicago: University of Chicago Press.

Youniss, J., Yates, M., & Su, Y. (1997). Social integration into peer and adult society: Community service and marijuana use in high school seniors. *Journal of Adolescent Research.*

PART III

Visual Representation as Pictorial

CHAPTER 21

The Form of Thought

Sandra L. Calvert
Georgetown University

Two 10-year-old boys watch a television cartoon together. They look at the television set; they look at each other; they read comic books. They laugh at a joke and a funny picture from the program. They talk about the story. Although the boys engage in the sorts of activities that they do when they watch television in their homes, they are not at home. They are at school.

As they view, two experimenters sit behind a one-way mirror. We videotape and score each boy's visual attention to the television program. After viewing, I interview one boy while the other experimenter interviews the other boy. First, I ask him to sequence a set of pictures photographed from that television program. He does so perfectly. I then ask him to tell me the story as he looks at the pictures. He provides a coherent verbal text to his visual sequence. Next, I ask him to answer multiple-choice questions about the *central* (essential) and the *in-cidental* (nonessential) story events. He selects a response for each item. We finish before the other two, so we chat about the program further. I asked him how he remembered the order of the pictures. He told me that he watched the program again in his head (Calvert, 1992).

The way that children like this boy think, particularly in relation to media stories, is the focus of my inquiries. More specifically, I examine children's use of the visual action and the verbal linguistic forms of television and computer presentations as modes to represent the content. This issue of how children use iconic and symbolic media codes as representational devices is explored in this chapter.

CHILDREN'S REPRESENTATIONS OF TELEVISION CONTENT

Each day children spend 3 to 4 hours watching television programs (Condry, 1989), a medium in which content is presented in combined audio and visual representational forms. What sense do children make of the depictions that so rapidly pass by them? Televised stories are truncated, the pictures are often discontinuous, and reality never uses sound overs or musical tracks. How, then, do children create representations of these stories?

To answer these questions, I look at the interface between how the information is presented via formal features, the symbol system of television, and how children subsequently remember that content. Formal features are audiovisual production features that structure, mark, and represent content; these features include the amount of action on the screen, how rapidly the scenes change, visual camera techniques, and auditory techniques such as sound effects and dialogue (Wright & Huston, 1983). This audiovisual symbol system, which presents television content, must be understood for children to extract story messages (Huston & Wright, 1983).

The content of television includes material that is either central or incidental to the program plot (Collins, 1970). Attention to the central, plot-relevant information, representation of those events, and memory of that material are all linked together as children make sense of the stream of audiovisual images represented on the screen via these formal features. Children's representations of these events are one facet of the dynamic process of story comprehension.

To tap into children's story construction, I question children about their memories of program events. The boy in my scenario, for instance, understood how he was able to accomplish the visual sequencing task; that is, he knew how he knew, demonstrating metacognitive competence (Flavell, 1985). Second, his description highlights the importance of matching the visual images he saw from television (i.e., input devices) with an independent assessment task, in this case a picture-sequencing task (i.e., output devices). The link between how the content is originally displayed (e.g., visual) and how it is eventually remembered (e.g., iconic form) is central to my study of representation. Most important was the form of his thought: As he performed the picture-sequencing task, he could rewatch the visual content of the program in his head. Visual, iconic ways of expressing information have long been established as a mode of representational thought (Bruner, Olver, & Greenfield, 1968; Piaget, 1951). Implicit in this boy's description, however, was a dynamic quality inherent in those visual images; his images *moved*. Moving visual images, particularly in relation to verbal forms of thought, have been a focal point in my study of representation. This kinetic quality is what makes media research unique in the scientific study of representation and representational thinking.

THE FORM OF TELEVISION PROGRAMS

For children to understand any televised message, they must be able to decode and use the audio and visual symbol systems of the television content (Calvert,

1999). These audiovisual forms, the grammar of television content, are referred to as *formal features.* Through form, content is transmitted. What does form contribute to representational thinking? This is the central representational question in my research.

As seen in Table 21.1, formal features include macro- and microtechniques. *Action,* the amount of physical movement, and *pace,* the rate of scene and character change, are macrofeatures. Visual and auditory microfeatures are also used to present content. The visual microfeatures include camera techniques such as *fades* to black, rapid *cuts* from one picture to the next, dreamy *dissolves* that often mark major time transitions such as flashbacks, *zooms* to focus in on the details of a scene, and *pans* of entire scenes as the camera sweeps across a visual depiction. These visual techniques parallel the way that children can use their eyes, as when they turn their head to take in an entire scene (pan) or move an object close to their eyes so they can see it more precisely (zoom). Thus, story-

TABLE 21.1
Formal Features of Children's Television Programs

Category	Definition
Macrolevel	
Action	Gross motor movement through space, including locomotion activities such as walking, running, or riding in vehicles.
Pace	Change of scenes, sets, or characters (unfamiliar or previously shown).
Microlevel—Visual	
Cuts	Instantaneous shifts between cameras.
Pans & trucks	Vertical or horizontal movement of camera.
Zooms	Camera moves continuously in (toward) or out (away from) a scene or object in the scene.
Fades	Picture/scene to black, followed by a different picture/scene.
Dissolves	One picture superimposed on top of another as the visual image changes.
Visual special effects	Visual camera techniques such as freeze frames, special lenses, distorting prisms, slow motion, fast motion, superimposition, trick photography, instant appearances or disapperances.
Microlevel—Audio	
Dialogue	Adult, child, or nonhuman (e.g., animals or robots) speaking to one another.
Narration	Speech from an off-screen person.
Vocalizations	Noises that are not speech.
Music	Prominent foreground music versus background music overlaid with speech.
Laugh track	Sound of laughter from unseen audience.
Singing	Music and language in combination.
Sound effects	Prominent noises.

tellers use the camera to represent content selectively just as viewers use their eyes to take in information. Both television production people *and* viewers, therefore, employ selective attention to create representations of content.

Auditory techniques complement the visual message, for visual features alone do not present a story that approximates reality. Auditory techniques are employed in two ways: verbal techniques and nonverbal techniques. Verbal features include *dialogue* and *narration*. Dialogue is comprised of *adult dialogue, child dialogue,* and *nonhuman dialogue* (animal dialogue, e.g., is often found in children's programs). Much of the content that advances the plot is carried via verbal forms. Nonverbal auditory techniques include *sound effects* of unusual noises, character *vocalizations,* loud *foreground music,* and less prominent *background music* that occurs in conjunction with speech. *Singing* is unique in that it combines both nonverbal music and verbal language in a form that is thought to be comprehensible to children (although the convention is often more for production quality than to convey any particular story content).

Media-literate adults barely notice formal features, for the features are commonly practiced conventions that are accepted automatically. Yet children must be able to decode this representational system in order to extract messages portrayed on television. For instance, televised events are not portrayed as they happen in real time (Calvert, 1988). Instead, time is condensed and represented with various features such as dreamy dissolves, fades to black, or rapid cuts to other scenes. When do children come to understand the meaning of these features? Do formal features assist them in understanding television messages, or do certain features interfere with accurate understanding of the story messages?

CHILDREN'S PROCESSING OF TELEVISION CONTENT

To understand a television story, children select the important content for processing, organize it into a story scheme, and draw inferences about important, but hidden, program content (Collins, Wellman, Keniston, & Westby, 1978). Formal features assist children in all phases of this information-processing task, particularly when children are young (Calvert, 1999).

Formal Features and Children's Selective Attention to Content

Attention is the first step in the complex process of story comprehension, for children must have the right content available to create an accurate representation of televised events (Calvert, 1999). But because television is a casual activity in America, children rarely view it with sustained visual attention. Children typically view to be entertained. Because of this motivation, children often participate in multiple activities, such as playing with toys during television viewing. Visual attention, even in simulated lab settings, is often less than 50% when alternate activities are available for children to do (Calvert, Huston, Watkins, & Wright, 1982; Lorch, Anderson, & Levin, 1979). If children see only about half of a television program, then how do they understand televised stories?

The answer involves *selective attention:* Children's visual attention can be elicited to the television story when the central, plot-relevant content is being presented. One way that their attention can be elicited is by selectively using formal features, such as a crescendo in music or a sound effect, to tell them *when* to look. In this way, involuntary attentional orienting mechanisms can be used to draw visual attention to the most important story content. Formal features that are perceptually salient play a significant role in this selection process.

Perceptual salience involves a set of collative variables in our environment that are likely to elicit attention and promote processing because they embody movement, contrast, incongruity, surprise, and novelty (Berlyne, 1960). These perceptually salient features have been applied to the symbolic world presented via television formal features, yielding a classification system of perceptually salient and nonsalient features (Huston & Wright, 1983). For instance, action involves movement; sound effects and visual special effects involve surprise, novelty, and incongruity; pace involves novelty and incongruity. Dialogue and narration, by contrast, are not perceptually salient, yet they carry the most informative aspects of a television program.

In an initial study in this area (Calvert et al., 1982), we examined two ways that perceptually salient formal features might influence attention: (a) as elicitors of attention via involuntary attentional orienting mechanisms, and (b) as learned markers of important program content. These were called the *salience* and *marker* functions of features, respectively. Children were expected to attend to perceptually salient features, particularly at young ages when they rely more on involuntary mechanisms to guide attention.

To examine these hypotheses, we scored the formal features of a children's cartoon called "Fat Albert and the Cosby Kids." Next, we showed this cartoon to children in a setting that approximated their viewing at home, just like the one that I described in the opening scenario. As pairs of kindergartners or third- and fourth-graders viewed the program, we scored their visual attention. Visual attention was later correlated with the presence or absence of specific formal features, yielding an index of selective attention.

As expected, children attended more to the perceptually salient than to the nonsalient formal features. Children were particularly attentive when content was presented with rapid character action, moderate character action, vocalizations, sound effects, camera pans, and visual special effects. Perceptually salient auditory features were more effective than salient visual features as a way to recruit children's attention to specific content. Obviously, the visual medium of television cannot get a nonlooking child to attend. Using attention-getting auditory forms, however, pulls children back to the program content, thereby increasing the odds that the content will be represented in memory. Sound effects and character vocalizations, such as the "hey, hey, hey" of Fat Albert, were particularly important features for eliciting visual attention to the program. Whether children attended to perceptually salient auditory forms because of their salience or because of their ability to mark important content could not be evaluated. We did find that children of both age groups attended to these salient auditory features, suggesting the potency of these techniques in children's programs.

Formal Features for Children's Memory of Content

Attention is necessary, but insufficient, for children to remember stories. Therefore, our second area of inquiry involved how formal features impact children's memory of content.[1] We expected children's memory of program content to improve because: (a) the content that followed the salient feature was likely to be processed and represented in memory, and (b) the features per se provided visual and verbal modes that children can use to represent content. We called these effects *contiguous presentation* and *modes to represent content,* respectively. Once again, younger children were expected to benefit from perceptual salience more than older children, primarily because young children often think in a visual mode of thought (Bruner et al., 1968; Piaget, 1951).

After children had viewed the Fat Albert cartoon, we asked them questions about the story content. These measures involved a visual, picture-sequencing task, much like the visual depictions that one sees in a newspaper cartoon, and a multiple-choice questionnaire that assessed children's memory of the *central,* plot-relevant versus the *incidental,* irrelevant program content. The program content had also been classified as being presented with *perceptually salient* or *nonsalient* formal features. The features that were perceptually salient included the moving visual actions of characters and auditory techniques like sound effects and character vocalizations. Nonsalient features included character dialogue or narration portrayed without moderate or rapid action.

As expected, contiguous presentation of perceptually salient forms with the important central content led to better processing of this televised story. Auditory features that marked significant program content were associated with improved memory of central story content, particularly for the youngest children. Young children's selective attention to character vocalizations predicted their memory of both the central and incidental program content; selective attention to sound effects predicted their memory of incidental program events. Moreover, the youngest children who did not attend to the nonsalient narration of

---

[1]Historically, children's online comprehension of television content was inferred from their subsequent memory of story events after they had completely viewed a program (Calvert, 1995). Because memory is technically the correct term, I use the term *memory* to describe the earlier "comprehension" as well as the current "memory" literature in the television area.

Bill Cosby understood the incidental story content better than those who attended when he was speaking. For the older children, selective attention to vocalizations was also associated with memory of central program material; however, selective attention to sound effects and vocalizations had no impact on their memory of incidental program material. The results suggest that older children use salient features to gather information that advances the story plot, whereas younger children remember any content that is highlighted by salient features and fail to remember content presented in nonsalient forms.

A second way that visual and verbal formal features can improve memory of central story content is by providing modes that children can use to represent the content. Visual features, in the form of action, provide an iconic way to represent content. Verbal features, in the form of dialogue and narration, provide a symbolic way to represent content. When paired together, action and dialogue provide dual modes that children can use to represent content. Central content presented with perceptually salient features, such as action, was well understood by both age groups. By contrast, central content presented only in language was poorly understood, particularly by the youngest children. Incidental content that was presented with salient character actions was not remembered well, perhaps because language was seldom paired with incidental visual program events. Thus, younger children relied on visual action sequences to make language comprehensible to them. These findings suggest that the combination of action and language is an effective way of presenting television story content to children through middle childhood. Moreover, verbal modes without moving visual referents are incomprehensible to the youngest viewers. This is an interesting and perplexing outcome for an age group who are most likely to read bedtime stories, but remember that those stories are accompanied by visual images to emphasize the story content.

Auditory Features as Markers of Significant Story Content

The initial link between visual attention to sound effects and improved memory of program material was only for incidental program content. What if the central program material was selectively marked with sound effects? Would young viewers' memory of the central material improve? My next step was to establish a causal link between attention to perceptually salient auditory features and children's memory of the important central, plot-relevant content.

An episode of "Spanky and Our Gang," which depicted a dream sequence, was shown to kindergarten and to third- and fourth-grade children (Calvert & Gersh, 1987). In the experimental condition, three sound effects were inserted at important scene transitions surrounding the dream. The control condition had no sound markers. Children watched this program individually with a variety of toys and comic books available for play. As they viewed, their attention to the program was videotaped. After viewing, children were asked to sequence pictures from the program in the order that they had occurred in the story. Then children answered multiple-choice questions about the central, plot-relevant content (explicitly presented), the incidental, irrelevant content (explicitly presented), and the inferential, plot-relevant content (implicitly presented).

From the videotapes, we scored children's selective attention to the three program transitions immediately before and after the spot where the sound effect was inserted. Not surprisingly, children who heard sound effects looked at these three transitions more than children who had not heard sound effects.

What was surprising was children's memory of the inferential program content. Kindergartners who heard sound effects understood the inferential, implicit program content better than the kindergartners who did not hear sound effects. The inferential content was comprised of material about character motivations, character feelings, and links among program events over time. Thus, it involved the most difficult, yet the most important, program information. Whereas the youngest children's comprehension clearly benefited from these markers, the older children did not need them. Sound markers can draw attention selectively to program material, thereby increasing the chances that young children will link program content over time.

In a second marker study (Calvert & Scott, 1989), we inserted five sound effects immediately before important visual program events. Two programs were used, one that was rapidly paced (the rate of scene and characters changed quickly, placing high demands on children's temporal integration skills) and one that was slowly paced (the rate of scene and characters changed slowly, placing low demands on children's temporal integration skills). A control group did not have sound effects to mark important program events. Two age groups were compared: kindergartners versus third- and fourth-graders. Children who heard the sound effects selectively attended to the visual program events more than those who did not hear sound effects, but only for the rapidly paced television program. Visual attention, in turn, predicted children's temporal sequencing for both the marked and an unmarked set of pictures. The results suggest that perceptually salient sound cues can highlight important visual program material, thereby bringing that content to children's attention for processing, storage in memory, and eventual retrieval from memory.

In a third marker study (Calvert, 1988), I used sound effects to mark the transitions of a flashback sequence in a children's cartoon, "Tarzan: Lord of the Jungle." The sound effects preceded one of two visual features: dreamy camera dissolves (the typical media technique for representing a flashback) or camera cuts (an avant-garde camera technique, rarely used to represent major time changes in children's programs). Kindergarteners and first-graders were compared with fourth- and fifth-graders. As before, children were videotaped as they viewed the episode. After viewing, children were asked if they had seen anything that had happened in the past. Contrary to previous findings, sound effects had little impact on children's visual attention, primarily because all children tended to look at the program transitions. This happened, I believe, because mysterious music marked the flashback in all conditions, thereby eliciting attention from all viewers. Visual features, by contrast, did impact children's memory of story material. As expected, children who saw dreamy dissolves were more likely to remember that past events had been portrayed than were those that saw camera cuts. As seen in Table 21. 2, the *dreamy dissolve,* the conventional media representation of major time changes, was mastered by many children by Grade 1, and by most children by Grades 4 and 5. Visual markers are symbolic codes used by the television and film industries to represent events, such as a flashback in time. There is no inherent reason that dissolves mean a change in time, for there is no analogous way of thought inherent to humans. Media symbols are often an arbitrary representational code that are learned by children, just like the letters of the alphabet. Thus, children become media literate as they master the meaning of the symbolic codes of television.

Taken together, these studies suggest that sound effects can improve children's attention to, representation of, and memory of significant story content. Initially, the perceptually salient qualities of sound effects are an effective form for eliciting children's attention to specific television content. Selective attention, in turn, increases the probability that children will represent and later remember the sequence of visual program events as well as understand the implicit, verbal content. Media conventions like visual camera dissolves are also understood by the early grade school years, increasing the odds that children will understand the jumps in time and place that are typical of television programs. This mastery of media codes has to take place if children are to make sense of the dynamic flow linking television story events. It would be interesting for the industry to learn some of the representational features children use, rather than always the other way around. Video game makers are beginning to do just that (Kafai, 1996).

TABLE 21.2

Frequencies of Children's Flashback Comprehension Responses
as a Function of Visual Formal Features and Grade

	Kindergarten and First Grades		Fourth and Fifth Grades	
	Incorrect	Correct	Incorrect	Correct
Cut	14	2	6	10
Dissolve	8	8	4	12
Both Conditions	22	10	10	22

Note. N = 64. From Calvert, S. L. (1988). Television production feature effects on children's comprehension of time. *Journal of Applied Developmental Psychology, 9,* 263–273. Copyright © 1988 by Ablex Publishing Corporation. Reprinted by permission.

Features as Modes to Represent Content

The second line of research that evolved from the early Fat Albert study involved the use of formal features as modes to represent content. Specifically, visual action and verbal language are similar in form to the iconic and symbolic ways that children represent information. In the case of television depictions, we had demonstrated that action and language together provide dual modes that children can use to represent content (Calvert et al., 1982).

The Visual Superiority Hypothesis. A controversy arose about the role of visual presentation for children's memory of verbal content. In a seminal television study, Hayes and Birnbaum (1980) argued that visual presentation interferes with children's memory of auditory material. In this study, preschoolers were shown television programs in which the visual track was sometimes in conflict with the auditory track. For example, the audio track from a cartoon named "Fang Face" was paired with the visual track of "Scooby Doo." In these situations, young children remembered the visually presented information better than the verbally presented information. Dubbed the visual superiority hypothesis, Hayes and Birnbaum argued that young children process the visual track at the expense of the auditory track. Indeed, mismatching visual and auditory tracks does lead to superior recall of the visual material over the verbal material (Pezdek & Hartman, 1983; Pezdek & Stevens, 1984).

Nevertheless, a number of caveats emerged from these modality studies that mismatched visual and audio tracks. First, visual and verbal materials typically support each other rather than interfere with each other. We did not evolve in a world in which visual material contradicts verbal material. It is the match between visual and verbal messages that make so much of our world comprehensible. Early-reading books, for example, match a word with a picture of the associated object. The visual emphasis, I believed, supported the superiority of visual material to assist children's information-processing activities. Verbal tracks alone were insufficient for effective recall because young children are less likely to think in a solely verbal mode. Second, I believed that visual superiority was actually action superiority. Action, comprised of dynamic visual moving images, was the form that aids information-processing activities, not the visual images per se. In both television and computer studies, I began to unravel the role of action as a way to assist children's memory of content.

The Action Superiority Hypothesis. After the initial Fat Albert study, we manipulated visual and verbal inserts in another episode of the Fat Albert series. This episode was about Flora, a girl whose parents were divorced.

Within this episode, we created audiovisual inserts called *preplays*, which were designed to show and to tell children what would happen next in the story (Calvert, Huston, & Wright, 1987). A fortune teller looked into her crystal ball to see upcoming program events. In *visual preplays,* children were shown cartoon actions in a bubble that summarized the upcoming story plot. In *nonvisual preplays,* children saw only the narrator as she summarized the information. The narrator used two types of verbal summaries comprised of *concrete* or *inferential* language. In concrete summaries, she spoke about events in very specific terms. In inferential summaries, she spoke about the motives, feelings, and reasons for characters' actions. For instance, a concrete summary was "Flora cried," whereas an inferential summary for that same event was "Flora cried because she was upset that her parents were divorced."

Children from ages 6 through 10 viewed the program in one of the four conditions: visual concrete language, visual inferential language, nonvisual concrete language, and nonvisual inferential language. Children's visual attention to the program was scored. After viewing, children answered visual picture-sequencing and verbal multiple-choice questions.

As seen in Table 21.3, children attended more to visual preplays than to nonvisual preplays. Children who saw the visual preplays sequenced pictures of the program events better than children who saw nonvisual preplays. Visual attention to the visual preplays also predicted picture-sequencing scores. By contrast, children who heard inferential summaries remembered the abstract, implicit program information better than those who heard concrete narration. Boys did particularly poorly after seeing nonvisual, inferential preplays. The results of this study support the idea of modality-specific processing: That is, visually presented information is represented in a visual mode whereas verbally presented information is represented in a verbal mode. No interference effects of action were found. Similar findings are reported in radio and television comparisons

TABLE 21.3
Percentage of Visual Attention and Mean Comprehension Scores
for Significant Treatment Effects

	Visual Treatment		Verbal Narration	
	Visual	Nonvisual	Concrete	Inferential
Attention to Preplays	60%	43%		
Segment Sequencing	15.32	14.37		
Whole Program Sequencing				
Girls	17.53	17.94	17.44	18.03
Boys	17.69	15.53	17.38	15.85
Implicit Content			10.92	11.50

Note. All effects are based on 64 pairs of subjects. From Calvert, S. L., Huston, A. C., & Wright, J. C. (1987). The effects of television preplay formats on children's attention and story comprehension. *Journal of Applied Developmental Psychology, 8,* 329–342. Copyright © 1987 by Ablex Publishing Corporation. Reprinted by permission.

(Beagles-Roos & Gat, 1983) and in storybook and television comparisons (Meringoff, 1980). Thus, visual and auditory content may be processed in separate channels.

ACTION SUPERIORITY FOR CHILDREN'S MEMORY OF COMPUTER CONTENT

If action is the form that is represented by children, then moving images should be more memorable to children than static visual ones. I began to address this question in computer research where tighter control of movement could be controlled via programming.

In a series of studies, my colleagues and I examined the role that action plays in children's preferential selection of content, in their spontaneous use of memory strategies, and in their memory of linguistic material. To do so, we created a microworld called "Park World" in which a park scene served as the backdrop. Objects such as a car, train, dog, or cat could appear in the park by keying in the words. Some of these visual objects moved; other visual objects were presented in still frame.

In the first study (Calvert, Watson, Brinkley, & Bordeaux, 1989), preschoolers heard a story about the characters in Park World for 4 successive days. After hearing the story each day, children were asked to select objects that they wanted in their park. Children *preferentially selected* moving objects over stationary objects. On the last day, children were asked to tell the experimenter all the objects that they could remember from Park World. Preschoolers *recalled* moving objects better than stationary objects, thereby supporting the thesis that visual superiority is really action superiority.

In a second study (Calvert, Watson, Brinkley, & Penny, 1990), "Park World" became "Talk World." A voice synthesizer made it possible for objects to be named. So when the train appeared in Talk World, it might say "train." Some words were labeled (label condition) and others were not (no-label condition); some objects moved and some appeared in still frame. Teachers classified kindergartners and second-graders as good or poor readers. Children then came individually to a room in their school where they heard the story as the objects appeared in Talk World. After hearing the story, the objects were hidden. Children were then asked to tell us all the objects from Talk World that they could remember. Effects occurred only for second-graders. Specifically, we found that second-graders who read poorly could recall just as many objects as second-graders who read well if the objects were presented in action. By contrast, second-graders who read poorly recalled fewer objects than those who read well when the visual objects were presented in still frame. The results suggest that action assists children's learning of verbal material, particularly those who are developmentally behind their peers in reading skills.

TABLE 21.4
Mean Number of Words Recalled
as a Function of Grade, Verbal Labels, and Action

		Preschoolers		Kindergartners	
		Verbal Labels		Verbal Labels	
		Absent	Present	Absent	Present
Action	Absent	1.20^d	2.30^{bc}	2.10^{bc}	2.60^b
	Present	1.80^c	2.30^{bc}	2.00^{bc}	3.35^a

Note. Means with different letter superscripts are significantly different at $p < .05$. Cell means are based on 20 subjects. From Calvert, S. L. (1991). Presentational features for young children's production and recall of information. *Journal of Applied Developmental Psychology, 12,* 367–378. Copyright © 1991 by Ablex Publishing Corporation. Reprinted by permission.

In a third study (Calvert, 1991), I examined the role of action by comparing the computer presentation with a comparable felt board presentation. The felt board depicted the same park scene, and felt objects were created that were the same size as those in Talk World. As the experimenter read the story to the preschool and kindergarten subjects, she did not say some of the target objects (no-label condition), but did say others (label condition). As before, objects moved or did not move. Both age groups *recalled* more objects that had been presented with both action and verbal labels than with neither feature. As seen in Table 21.4, kindergartners recalled objects particularly well when both features were present, whereas preschoolers had difficulty recalling objects when neither feature was present. This suggests that action and language are integrated in memory at about age 5. Naming objects, an early rehearsal strategy, also emerged in this study. Specifically, both age groups produced the names of objects more often when verbal labels were absent rather than present, but they were particularly likely to do so when action was also present. Interestingly, presenting the information on a computer or on a felt board made no difference whatsoever. Thus, action prompts early rehearsal activities and improves recall regardless of the medium, suggesting general facilitative memory properties of this form.

SUMMARY OF ACTION EFFECTS

Taken together, the results of the television and computer studies suggest that: (a) visual superiority exists vis-à-vis other modalities, but that action superiority supersedes even the visual; (b) visual presentation, particularly in the form of action, supports initial intake of information, as indexed by both preferential selection and visual attention measures; (c) visual presentation, particularly in the form of action, increases children's memory of visual content, and in many instances, their memory of verbal content; (d) action presentations promote early rehearsal activities, such as naming objects; (e) action assists children's memory of important information from early childhood through middle childhood, particularly for those who are youngest or who are developmentally behind their peers; and (f) these effects are general across a range of different media, including television, computer, storybook, and storyboard presentations. The implication is that action is a potent vehicle of thought that deserves more attention from memory researchers.

IMMERSION IN SYMBOLIC VIRTUAL REALITIES

The newest frontier of symbolic media captures the kinetic aspect of representational thought. This is the newly emerging area of virtual reality. Virtual reality simulations involve computer immersions in representational depictions of symbolic realities. These range from cartoonlike fantasies to surgical simulations of heart catherizations.

In virtual reality, a symbolic scenario is created complete with visual and auditory sensory stimulation. A computer program is used to construct different visual scenes. By wearing headgear to deliver visual and auditory images, the person can enter this symbolic experience. The goggles are much like a television/computer screen, but they are directly in front of one's eyes and respond to one's every movement, thereby yielding scenes that are continuous rather than boxed into a screen. The perceptual result is that the person feels embodied, looking out of their own eyes into this imaginary world. They can move through a virtual space and act on imaginary representational objects.

Entering virtual reality simulations adds new dimensions for representational experiences. The person is not only a part of the representation, but a creator of it. Experiences are felt personally because you are the character in this scenario (Calvert, 1999). You see the objects in three dimensions, not as two-dimensional television or computer monitor depictions. In addition to the visual iconic and verbal symbolic representations of television (Calvert et al., 1982, 1987) and video game experiences (Greenfield, 1993; Greenfield et al., 1996), people also experience enactive ones. They can move, for instance, by walking on a treadmill.

In my first virtual reality study (Calvert & Tan, 1996), we had adolescent college students play, observe, or simulate game movements from "Dactyl Nightmare." Dactyl Nighmare involves two players who shoot at one another as they move in a three-dimensional virtual reality world. You pull a trigger to shoot your opponent, an enactive representation of that event.

Students attended a fair on a college campus where the game was available for play. One group of students played the game; a second observer group watched them play; a third control group simulated game movements except for pulling the trigger of the gun. After playing, observing, or simulating the game movements, subjects were asked to report their *thoughts*. We also took their pulses immediately before and after they played, observed, or simulated the game movements in order to assess *arousal* effects. Effects were far stronger for players than for observers or game simulators. Specifically, arousal increased and aggressive thoughts were more prevalent for game players than for the other groups. The results suggest that immersive technologies are a powerful way to personalize symbolic experiences for participants.

Being part of the representation is an unparalled experience for those who choose to participate in them. What kinds of exciting new representational research about kinetic/dynamic representation is being opened by this new technology? What theoretical implications emerge as we move from observational to interactive media interfaces? Clearly, the interactive nature of the virtual reality experience may expand social cognitive theory because the person participates in, rather than observes, actions. Enactive encoding may become a more prevalent mode of thought, making behaviors, including aggression, more accessible to participants. These actions, in turn, may blur the lines between learning a behavior and performing it, a classic distinction in social cognitive theory. With immersion, the lines between reality and fantasy may also become indistinguishable, particularly for children.

CONCLUSION

In my research activities, I use representation as an intermediary step between children's intake of information, assessed via selective attention and preferential selection of content, and their eventual output of information, via memory assessments. Without representational thought, my research line could not exist, for children must store information in memory or they can never remember or even comprehend a coherent, televised story. The dynamic actions and audible sounds, unique to video presentations, contribute to my understanding of how children use form to represent story content. These audiovisual forms of the medium are central in understanding whether children will attend to the information, will have it available for representation, will rehearse the information in some manner, and will ultimately remember it.

In the television area, perceptually salient formal features play key roles in getting children to attend selectively to content by serving as markers of significant story content. Once attention is gained, children are more likely to process and represent the content that follows that salient sound. Perceptually salient forms, particularly action, can also serve as a mode that children can use to represent the content. Children can either use the same form in their own representations (e.g., action presentation and action representation), transform the representation to another modality (e.g., action to language), or combine forms (e.g., audiovisual presentation and audiovisual representation) (Sigel, 1993). To date, the literature suggests that children represent television content in visual, particularly moving visual forms, or that they combine action and language in their representations of television story content. There is little evidence to suggest that the dynamic, moving images of television programs are transformed and represented solely in verbal modes. But, as I have pointed out, precious little research has been conducted on the action aspects of the media.

Formal features now represent the content of our new computer technologies. The impact of computer features yields similar findings to the television research. Young children are likely to select and to name moving over stationary objects. Moreover, action has emerged as a powerful moving iconic form that children use to represent computer content, thereby improving their memory of that material.

Virtual reality simulations extend these representational frontiers into increasingly personalized and interactive interfaces, allowing enactive as well as iconic and symbolic encoding of content. As the transition to this three-dimensional representational world takes place, realistic interfaces may increasingly blur the distinction between realistic representations of life with actual experiences.

In the 21st century, most cultures will increasingly rely on information technologies to transmit content, thereby expanding the role that formal features play in representational thought. Theoretical models of representation must increasingly incorporate advances in the presentation of symbolic, yet realistic, depictions of reality. The shift from a predominantly written to a multimodal representational interface will allow children to use visual, auditory, and kinetic modes of representation readily, perhaps altering the very way they will think in the future. The children who master these media codes, who learn to move fluently across the information highway, are the children who will control the future.

ACKNOWLEDGMENTS

I would like to thank Dr. Rodney R. Cocking and Dr. Irving Sigel for helpful comments in the preparation of this manuscript.

REFERENCES

Beagles-Roos, J., & Gat, I. (1983). Specific impact of radio and television on children's story comprehension. *Journal of Educational Psychology, 75,* 128–137.
Berlyne, D. E. (1960). *Conflict, arousal, and curiosity.* New York: McGraw-Hill.

Bruner, J. S., Olver, R. R., & Greenfield, P. M. (1968). *Studies in cognitive growth.* New York: Wiley.

Calvert, S. L. (1988). Television production feature effects on children's comprehension of time. *Journal of Applied Developmental Psychology, 9,* 263–273.

Calvert, S. L. (1991). Presentational features for young children's production and recall of information. *Journal of Applied Developmental Psychology, 12,* 367–378.

Calvert, S. L. (1992). Pictorial prompts for discursive analyses: Developmental considerations and methodological innovations. *American Behavioral Scientist, 36,* 39–51.

Calvert, S. L. (1995). Pictorial discourse. In R. Harre & P. Stearns (Eds.), *Rethinking psychology: Vol. 3. Discursive psychology in practice* (pp. 194–204). Newbury Park, CA: Sage.

Calvert, S. L. (1999). *Children's journeys through the information age.* New York: McGraw-Hill.

Calvert, S. L., & Gersh, T. L. (1987). The selective use of sound effects and visual inserts for children's television story comprehension. *Journal of Applied Developmental Psychology, 8,* 363–375.

Calvert, S. L., Huston, A. C., Watkins, B. A., & Wright, J. C. (1982). The relation between selective attention to television forms and children's comprehension of content. *Child Development, 53,* 601–610.

Calvert, S. L., Huston, A. C., & Wright, J. C. (1987). The effects of television preplay formats on children's attention and story comprehension. *Journal of Applied Developmental Psychology, 8,* 329–342.

Calvert, S. L., & Scott, M. C. (1989). Sound effects for children's temporal integration of fast-paced television content. *Journal of Broadcasting and Electronic Media, 33,* 233–246.

Calvert, S. L., & Tan, S. L. (1996). Impact of virtual reality on young adults' physiological arousal and aggressive thoughts: Interaction versus observation. In R. R. Cocking & P. M. Greenfield (Eds.), *Interacting with video: Cultural causes and psychological consequences* (pp. 67–81). Oakland, NJ: Ablex.

Calvert, S. L., Watson, J. A., Brinkley, V., & Bordeaux, B. (1989). Computer presentational features for young children's preferential selection and recall of information. *Journal of Educational Computing Research, 5,* 35–49.

Calvert, S. L., Watson, J. A., Brinkley, V., & Penny, J. (1990). Computer presentational features for poor readers' recall of information. *Journal of Educational Computing Research, 6,* 287–298.

Collins, W. A. (1970). Learning of media content: A developmental study. *Child Development, 41,* 1133–1142.

Collins, W. A., Wellman, H., Keniston, A. H., & Westby, S. D. (1978). Age-related aspects of comprehension and inference from a televised dramatic narrative. *Child Development, 49,* 389–399.

Condry, J. (1989). *The psychology of television.* Hillsdale, NJ: Lawrence Erlbaum Associates.

Flavell, J. (1985). *Cognitive development* (2nd ed.). Englewood Cliffs, NJ: Prentice-Hall.

Greenfield, P. M. (1993). Representational competence in shared symbol systems: Electronic media from radio to video games. In R. R. Cocking & K. A. Renninger (Eds.), *The development and meaning of psychological distance* (pp. 161–183). Hillsdale, NJ: Lawrence Erlbaum Associates.

Greenfield, P. M., Camaioni, L., Ercolani, P., Weiss, L., Lauber, B. A., & Perucchini, P. (1996). Cognitive socialization by computer games in two cultures: Inductive discovery versus mastery of an iconic code? In R. R. Cocking & P. M. Greenfield (Eds.), *Interacting with video: Cultural causes and psychological consequences* (pp. 141–167). Oakland, NJ: Ablex.

Hayes, D. S., & Birnbaum, D. (1980). Preschoolers' retention of televised events: Is a picture worth a thousand words? *Developmental Psychology, 17,* 230–232.

Huston, A. C., & Wright, J. C. (1983). Children's processing of television: The informative functions of formal features. In J. Bryant & D. R. Anderson (Eds.), *Children's understanding of television: Research on attention and comprehension* (pp. 35–68). New York: Academic Press.

Kafai, Y. (1996). Gender differences in constructions of video games. In R. R. Cocking & P. M. Greenfield (Eds.), *Interacting with video: Cultural causes and psychological consequences* (pp. 39–66). Oakland, NJ: Ablex.

Lorch, E. P., Anderson, D. R., & Levin, S. R. (1979). The relationship of visual attention to children's comprehension of television. *Child Development, 50,* 722–727.

Meringoff, L. (1980). Influence of the medium on children's story apprehension. *Journal of Educational Psychology, 72,* 240–249.

Pezdek, K., & Hartman, E. (1983). Children's television viewing: Attention and comprehension of auditory and visual information. *Child Development, 54,* 1015–1023.

Pezdek, K., & Stevens, E. (1984). Children's memory for auditory and visual information on television. *Developmental Psychology, 20,* 212–218.

Piaget, J. (1951). *Play, dreams, and imitation.* New York: Norton.

Sigel, I. E. (1993). The centrality of a distancing model for the development of representational competence. In R. R. Cocking & K. A. Renninger (Eds.), *The development and meaning of psychological distance* (pp. 141–158). Hillsdale, NJ: Lawrence Erlbaum Associates.

Wright, J. C., & Huston, A. C. (1983). A matter of form: Potential of television for young viewers. *American Psychologist, 38,* 835–843.

Author Index

A

Abbott, L. F., 48, 49, *58*
Abdi, H., 89, 90, *107*
Abrahamsen, A., 418, *433*
Acredolo, L., 70, *84*
Adolph, K. E., 308, *319*
Ahlgren, A., 430, *434*
Ahn, W.-K., 89, *107*
Albert, G., 79, 80, *85*
Aldrige, J. W., 447, *448*
Allman, J. M., 47, *56*
Alp, I., 184, 186, *197*
Aman, C., 79, 80, *85*
American Psychiatric Association, 44, *55*
Amsel, E., 226, *229*
Andersen, R. A., 48, 50, 55, *59, 60*
Anderson, D. R., 457, *469*
Anderson, J. R., 148, *166*, 275, 276, 277, 283, 284, *291, 293*
Anderson, K. N., 65, 70, 71, 76, *84*
Anderson, L. M., 72, *85*, 372, 373, *388*
Andrews, G., 162, *166*
Archer, S. L., 393, 395, *413*
Arezzo, J. C., 51, *59*
Arievitch, I., 134n, *143*
Armstrong, S. L., 125, *126*
Arnett, J., 440, 443, 447, *448*
Arterberry, M. E., 309, *321*
Asanuma, A. C., 48, *55*
Aslin, R. N., 35, 36, *55*
Astington, J. W., 140, *144*, 218, 219, *229*
Atran, S., 92, 96, 97, 98, *107*
Auld, P. A., 53, *58*

B

Bacal, H. A., 397, *413*
Backscheider, A. B., 101, 104, *107*
Baddeley, A. D., 16, *29*, 152, *166*
Baillargeon, R., 100, *110*, 156, 163, *166*, 170, 173, 174, 178, 179, 181, 182, 191, *197, 199*

Bain, J. D., 149, 154, 164, *167*
Baizer, J. S., 48, *55*
Baker, N. D., 375, *386, 388*
Bakhtin, M. M., 258, 259, 264, *271*, 418, *433*
Baldwin, D. A., 94, 99, *107*, 215, *227*
Bales, D., 310, *321*
Banerjee, M., 216, *230*
Banks, M. S., 232, *253*
Banyai, I., 317, *319*
Barber, B., 440, *448*
Barell, J., 416, *433*
Barker, P., 273, *292*
Baron, J., 26, *29*
Barrett, S. E., 89, 90, *107*
Barsalou, L. W., 87, 92, 93, 94, 96, 104, 105, *107, 110*, 284, *291*
Bartlett, F. C., 22, *29*
Barton, M., 215, 216, *230*
Bates, E., 197, *198*, 215, *227*, 374, 384, *387*
Bauer, P. J., 105, *108*, 310, *319*
Baumrind, D., 141, *143*
Baxter, A., 374, *389*
Beagles-Roos, J., 464, *468*
Beattie, K., 216, *230*
Bechtel, W., 418, *433*
Beckwith, L., 37, *59*
Bedi, G., 54, *59*
Beeghly, M., 216, *227*
Behr, M., 344, 346, *348, 349*
Beilin, H., 286, *292*, 309, 311, *319*
Beitel, R., 34, *60*
Bejar, I. I., 39, *55*
Bell, M., 171, *198*
Bell, T., 356, *368*
Bellah, R. N., 419, *434*
Belliveau, J. W., 47, *59*
Bellugi, U., 183, 184, 186, 191, 196, *200*
Belsky, J., 78, *84*
Bem, S., 96, *107*
Benasich, A. A., 34, 35, 36, 39, 40, 42, 44, 52, *55, 56, 59*
Benigni, L., 215, *227*
Bennett, R. E., 352, *368*
Benson, N., 184, 186, *198*

Bereiter, C., 179, *198*
Berk, L. E., 135, *144*
Berlyne, D. E., 457, *468*
Berman, N., 49, *59*
Berridge, D., 140, *144*
Bertenthal, B. I., 247, *253*
Berthoud-Papandropoulos, I., 265, *271*
Best, C. T., 35, *55*
Best, J. B., 158, *166*
Beth, E., 172, *198*
Beuhring, R., 125, *127*
Bever, T. G., 4, 9, *12*
Bickhard, M. H., 130, 138, *143*, 201, 217, *227*
Bidell, T. R., 233, 235, 242, 245, 246, 248, *253*,
        254
Biemiller, A., 25, *30*
Bierwisch, M., 92, *107*
Bill, B., 215, *227*
Binns, K. E., 34, *60*
Birnbaum, D., 462, *469*
Bisanz, J., 232, *254*
Bishop, D. V. M., 36, *56*
Bivens, J. A., 376, *389*
Blades, M., 66, *84*
Blake, J., *198*
Blaut, J. M., 307, *319*
Bleiker, C., *198*
Block, J. R., 317, *319*
Blos, P., 397, *413*
Boat, B. W., 78, *84*
Bobrow, D. G., 6, *12*
Bohannon, N. J., 375, *386*
Bonham, B. H., 51, *59*
Bonvillian, J. D., 375, *387, 388*
Boose, J. H., 367, *368*
Bordeaux, B., 464, *469*
Bornstein, M. H., 37, 39, 52, *56, 60*
Boster, J., 101, *109*
Bower, G. H., 16, *29*
Bowerman, M., 104, *108*
Bowlby, M., 35, *59*
Bowman, L. L., 90, *110*
Boyes, M., 139, *143*, 211, *228*
Boyes-Braem, P., 116, *128*, 285, *293*
Brady, T. J., 47, *59*
Braig, B., 97, 104, *111*
Braine, M. D. S., 119, *127*, 132, *143*
Braisby, N., 87, *107*
Bransford, J. D., 275, *291*, 338, *348*
Breinlinger, K., 174, *200*
Bretherton, I., 215, 216, *227*
Brinkley, V., 464, *469*
Brown, A. L., 75, *84*, 433, *434*
Brown, B. B., 438, 440, 441, 442, 445, *448*
Brown, C. P., 45, *56*
Brown, I., 36, *60*
Brown, J. S., 26, *29*, 141, *144*, 154, *168*, 280, *292*

Brown, T., 250, *255*
Bruck, M., 79, 80, *84*
Bruner, J. S., 105, *108, 309, 321,* 339, *348,* 371,
        386, 454, 458, *469*
Bryson, M., 381, *388*
Buchsbaum, M., 36, *57, 60*
Buckingham, D., 165, *168,* 177, 178, *200*
Bugelski, B. R., 223, *227*
Bukatko, D., 72, *84*
Bullock, D. H., 236, *254*
Burch, S., 67, *84*
Burke, K., 417, *434*
Burns, N. M., 71, 72, *84*
Burnyeat, M., 211, 212, *227*
Butler, J., 46, *56*
Byma, G., 54, *59*
Byrne, R. M. J., 119, 120, *127*
Byrnes, J. P., 276, 277, 278, 280, 281, 282, 284,
        286, 288, 289, *292*

C

Cairns, R. P., 3, *12*
Calasso, R., *413*
Callanan, M. A., 103, *110,* 281, *292*
Calvert, S. L., 453, 454, 456, 457, 458n, 459,
        460, 462, 464, 465, 466, *469*
Camaioni, L., 216, *227,* 466, *469*
Campbell, H., 46, *57*
Campos, J. J., 215, *230,* 247, *253*
Caramazza, A., 106, *108*
Carey, S., 98, 100, 101, 102, 104, 105, 106, *108,*
        111, 118, 123, *127,* 275, 280, 285,
        292
Carnochan, P., 231, 235, 242, 250, *254*
Caron, A. J., 46, *56*
Caron, R. F., 46, *56*
Carpendale, J. I. M., 130, 131, 132, 133, 134,
        138, 139, 142, *143, 144,* 216, 220,
        221, 223, 225, *227, 228*
Carpenter, P., 152, *166*
Carraher, D., 341, *348*
Carraher, T., 341, *348*
Carriger, M. S., 34, 37, *58*
Carroll, L., 299, *319*
Carskaddon, G., 375, *387*
Case, R., 170, 171, 178, 180, *198,* 384, *386*
Cassirer, E., 170, 191, *198*
Cattell, R. B., 21, *29*
Cazden, C., 353, *368,* 420, 425, *434*
Ceci, S. J., 79, 80, *84,* 282, *292,* 386, *386*
Chandler, M. J., 139, 141, 142, *143, 144,* 211,
        215, 216, 220, 221, 223, 224, 225,
        226, *227, 228*
Chapman, M., 129, 130, 131, 132, 133, 134,
        141, 142, *143, 144,* 203, 216, *228*

Chee, M., 381, *388*
Cheng, P. W., 120, 121, 122, *127*
Chi, M., 105, *108*
Choi, S., 104, *108*
Chomsky, N., 273, 289, *292*, 375, *387*
Chugani, H. T., 34, 50, *56*
Church, J., 309, *319*
Churchland, P. M., 203, *228*
Clark, A., 147, *166*
Clark, E. V., 91, *108*, *109*
Clausner, T., 101, *109*
Clement, J., 23, *29*
Clements, W. A., 141, *144*
Cocking, R. R., 373, 376, *388*
Codd, E. F., 153, *166*
Cohen, L. B., 37, 46, 56, 116, *127*
Cohen, P., *58*
Cohen, R., 15, *30*
Cohen, S. E., *59*
Colbourn, C. J., 121, *127*
Colby, C. L., 48, *56*
Coleman, J. S., 437, 447, *448*
Coley, J. D., 87, 90, 92, 97, 101, 105, *107*, *108*, 117, 118, 122, 124, 125, *127*
Collins, A., 6, *12*, 18, 26, *29*, *30*, 97, *111*, 280, *292*
Collins, W. A., 454, 456, *469*
Collman, P., 105, *108*
Colombo, J., 46, *56*
Conant, F., 353, *369*
Condry, J., 453, *469*
Confrey, J., 329, *348*
Conte, J. R., 78, *84*
Corrigan, R., 78, *84*, 239, *254*
Corsaro, W. A., 438, *448*
Cosmides, L., 120, 121, 122, *127*
Craig-Bray, L., 245, 246, *255*
Craik, K., 26, *29*
Crenshaw, M. C., 79, 80, *85*
Croft, W., 101, *109*
Crowley, K., 135, *145*
Csikszentmihalyi, M., 25, *29*
Curtiss, S., 36, *60*
Cynader, M., 49, *59*

D

Daehler, M., 72, *84*
Dale, A. M., 47, *59*
Dale, N., 215, *228*
Dale, P. S., 374, 384, *387*
Dalenoort, G. J., 13, *29*
Damon, W., 4, *12*, 140, *145*, *146*
Daneman, N., 152, *166*
Daniel, V., 96, *108*
Darwin, C., 372, *387*

Davidson, D., 206, 209, *228*
Davidson, N. S., 90, 99, *108*, 125, *127*
Davidson, P. M., 130, 140, *144*
Davies, G., 218, 219, *229*
Dayan, P., 177, *198*
Deák, G., 105, *108*, 310, *319*
De Brunhoff, J., 316, *319*
DeLoache, J. S., 62, 64, 65, 66, 67, 70, 71, 72, 73, 75, 76, 77, 78, 79, *84*, *85*, *86*, 194, 195, *198*, 301, 302, 307, 308, 309, 310, *319*, 372, *387*
Demetriou, A., 171, *198*
Denis, M., 13, 14, 16, 17, *29*
Dennett, D. C., 372, *387*
Denniger, M. S., 375, *388*
deRibaupierre, A., 197, *198*
Desimone, R., 48, *55*
Desjardins, R. N., 215, *227*
De Sousa, R., 202, *228*
De Valois, R. L., 46, 47, *60*
Dewey, J., 415, 433, *434*
Diamond, A., 46, 49, 50, *56*, 171, *198*
Dias, M. G., 275, *292*
Diaz, R. M., 135, *144*
DiCarlo, J. J., 159, *168*
Dickson, J. C., 154, 164, *167*
Diesendruck, G., 90, 91, 98, *108*
DiFranco, D., 309, *320*
Dirks, J., 308, *320*
Dodwell, P., 309, *320*
Doherty, M. J., 141, *144*, 216, *228*
Donlan, C., 36, *56*
Doran, J., 358, *368*
Douglas, L., 250, *255*
Dow, G. A., 65, *84*
Downs, R. M., 298, 302, 303, 304, 306, 307, 309, 311, 312, 313, 316, *320*, *321*
Dretske, F. I., 372, *387*
Drislane, F. W., 36, 45, *58*
Dudai, Y., 371, *387*
Duguid, P., 26, *29*, 280, *292*
Duhamel, J. R., 48, *56*
Dunn, J., 141, *144*, 214, 215, *228*
Dunphy, D., 441, *448*
Dupré, J., 91, 96, *108*

E

Eastman, R., 358, *368*
Ebeling, K. S., 102, *109*
Eckert, P., 439, 440, 442, 443, 445, *448*
Eco, U., 373, *387*
Eden, G. F., 45, *56*
Eder, D., 438, 441, 443, *448*
Edwards, D., 353, *368*
Efklides, A., 171, *198*

Eggermont, J. J., 51, *56*
Eilers, R. E., 36, *56*
Eimas, P. D., 94, *108*
Eliot, J., 297, 314, *320*
Elman, J., 197, *198*
Emde, R. N., 215, *230*, 374, *387*
English, L. D., 153, *166*
Eppler, M. A., 308, *319*
Ercolani, P., 466, *469*
Eresh, J. T., 365, *369*
Ericsson, K. A., 279, *292*
Erikson, E., 439, 440, *448*
Erikson, E. H., 393, 405, *413*
Ernst, B., 318, *320*
Escher, M. C., 317, 318, *320*
Essick, G. K., 48, *55*
Estin, P., 97, *107*
Evans, J. St. B. T., 120, 125, *127*
Everson, M. D., 78, *84*
Eyster, C., 79, *85*

F

Fabian, V., 176, 178, 180, 196, 197, *199*
Fagan, J. F., 37, *60*
Falkenhainer, B., 153, *166*
Falmagne, R. J., 123, *127*
Farah, M. J., 181, *198*
Farmer, M. E., 36, *56*
Farrar, M. J., 235, *254*
Feinman, S., 215, *228*, 374, *387*
Feldman, J. F., 37, *58*
Fenson, L., 78, *85*, 374, 384, *387*
Ferrera, V. P., 181, *199*
Fersen, L. von, 162, *168*
Fischer, K. W., 78, *86*, 231, 233, 234, 235, 236,
          238, 239, 241, 242, 243, 244, 245,
          246, 248, 250, 251, *253*, *254*, *255*,
          256, 384, *387*
Fitch, R. H., 45, *56*, *57*
Flaugher, J., 398, 399, *413*
Flavell, J. A., 274, *292*, 454, *469*
Flavell, J. H., *12*, 27, *29*, 262, *271*, 314, *320*
Flax, J., 34, 36, 44, *55*, *59*
Flowers, L., 36, *57*, *60*
Fodor, J. A., 113, *127*, 201, 214, *228*, 273, *292*,
          372, *387*
Fogarty, L., 78, *84*
Fogel, A., 193, 194, *200*, 247, *254*, 374, *387*
Follmer, A., 79, 80, *85*
Forbus, K. D., 153, *166*
Ford, M., 15, *29*
Fordham, S., 445, *448*
Foucault, M., 353, *368*
Fox, P. T., 47, *56*
Franks, B., 87, *107*

Freeman, N. H., 140, 141, *144*, *145*, 216, *228*
Frey, B., 177, *198*
Friedman, M., 78, *85*
Fritz, A. S., 215, 216, *228*
Frye, D., 67, 69, 83, *86*
Fu, P., 101, *109*
Fulker, D. W., 37, *60*
Furth, H. G., 134, *144*, 201, *228*

G

Galaburda, A. M., 36, 45, 53, *56*, *57*, *58*
Gallagher, J. M., 89, 90, *107*
Gallistel, C. R., 76, *85*
Garcia, R., 123, *128*, 178, *198*, 203, *228*
Gardner, H., 21, 23, 24, 28, 29, *29*, 250, *254*, 315,
          320
Garner, R., 276, *292*
Gat, I., 464, *468*
Gavin, W. J., 36, *56*
Gayler, R. W., 152, 153, 159, *167*
Geary, D. C., 277, *292*
Gee, J. P., 353, *368*, 431, *434*
Gell-Mann, M., 22, *30*
Gelman, R., 76, *85*, 96, 106, *108*, *110*, 153, 154,
          167, 279, *292*
Gelman, S. A., 87, 89, 90, 91, 92, 93, 98, 99, 101,
          102, 103, 104, 105, 106, *107*, *108*,
          109, *110*, *111*, 117, 118, 122, 124,
          125, *127*
Gentner, D., 18, *30*, 94, 99, 103, *109*, 123, *127*,
          153, 154, *166*, *167*, 314, *320*
Gentner, D. R., 18, *30*
Gersh, T. L., 459, *469*
Gholson, B., 273, *292*
Gibson, E. J., 301, 308, *319*, *320*
Gibson, J. J., 71, *85*, 174, *320*
Gillett, G., 131, *144*
Gilyard, K., 419, *434*
Girotto, V., 121, *127*
Gitomer, D. H., 365, *368*, *369*
Glaser, R., 18, *30*, 358, *368*
Gleitman, H., 125, *126*
Gleitman, L.R., 125, *126*
Glick, J., 276, *292*
Glucksberg, S., 92, *110*
Godfrey, J. J., 35, *57*
Goel, V., 352, *368*
Goffman, E., 437, 438, *448*
Gold, E. M., 375, *387*
Goldberg, M. E., 34, 48, *56*, *60*
Goldberg, S., 46, *57*
Goldman-Rakic, P. S., 34, 46, 48, 49, 50, *57*
Golinkoff, R. M., 103, *109*
Goodale, M. A., 48, *57*
Goodman, D., 176, 179, 188, 191, *199*
Goodman, G. S., 79, 80, *85*

Goodman, N., 22, 28, *30*, 88, *109*, 300, 303, 315, *320*
Goodwyn, S., 70, *84*
Gopnik, A., *12*, 104, *108*, 138, *144*, 203, 206, 207, 219, *228, 229*
Gordon, B. N., 79, 80, *85*
Gottfried, G. M., 87, 92, 98, 101, 105, *108, 109*, 117, *127*
Gottleib, G., 245, *254*
Gottlieb, A., 64, *84*, 309, *319*
Goulandris, N., 35, *59*
Granott, N., 231, 243, 244, 245, 247, *254*
Granrud, C. E., 309, *321*
Grant, P., 152, *167*
Grant-Webser, K. S., 309, *320*
Gray, W. D., 116, *128*, 285, *293*
Graziano, M. S. A., 48, 49, *57*
Greenberg, L., 358, *368*
Greene, B. A., 380, *388*
Greenfield, P. M., 454, 458, 466, *469*
Greeno, J. G., 18, *30*, 154, *167*, 279, *292*
Greer, B., 324, *348*
Gregory, R. L., 71, *85*
Grice, H. P., 137, 142, *144*, 353, *369*
Griffin, S., *198*
Gross, C. G., 48, 49, *57*
Gross, L., 21, *30*
Gruber, H. E., 265, *271*
Guerra, M. R., 421, 422, *434*
Guilford, J. P., 21, *30*
Gunderson, V. M., 309, *320*
Guo, J., 152, 153, 159, *167*
Gzesh, S. M., 152, *168*

H

Habermas, J., 140, 142, *144*
Haertel, E. H., 365, *369*
Hagen, M. A., 301, 306, 313, *320*
Hagman, J., 36, *57*
Hagstrom, F., 418, *435*
Hala, S., 138, 141, *143, 144*, 215, 216, 221, *228*
Halford, G. S., 148, 149, 150, 152, 153, 154, 159, 161, 162, 163, 164, *166, 167, 168*, 170, 171, 194, 195, *198*
Hamilton, E., 340, 346, *348*
Hamilton, J., 79, *85*
Hamm, M., 446, *448*
Hammerstein, O., *413*
Hampton, J. A., 87, 92, *107, 109*
Hand, H. H., 241, *254*
Harel, G., 344, 346, *348, 349*
Harkins, D., 250, *255*
Harris, P. L., 258, 265, *271*, 275, 278, *292*
Hartman, E., 462, *470*
Hawkins, J., 275, 276, *292*
Hayes, D. S., 462, *469*

Hebb, D. O., 45, *57*
Heelas, P., 202, *229*
Heise, D., 87, 94, 100, 105, *111*
Heit, E., 89, *109*
Helm, D., 224, *228*
Henderson, B., *198*
Henrichs, E., 446, *448*
Herman, A., 45, *57*
Herrenkohl, L. R., 421, 422, *434*
Hesselink, J. R., 36, 53, *57*
Hickling, A. K., 101, *109*, 219, *230*
Hickman, L. A., 415, *434*
Hicks, D., 353, *369*
Hiebert, J., 276, *292*
Hillis, A., 106, *108*
Hintikka, J. K. L., 276, 277, *292*
Hinton, G., 177, *198*
Hirschfeld, L A., 96, 106, *109*
Hodson, D., 358, *369*
Hoffer, T. B., 437, *448*
Hogan, A. E., 238, *254*
Holland, J. H., 149, 154, *167*, 381, *387*
Hollingshead, A., 439, *448*
Holloway, R., 186, *198*
Holquist, M., 419, *434*
Holyoak, K. J., 120, 121, 122, *127*, 149, 153, 154, 163, *167*, 381, *387*
Hoover, M., 326, 330, 336, *348*
Horvath, J., 329, *348*
Houdé, O., 170, 171, 178, *198*
Howell, P., 35, *59*
Hsieh, K., 215, *228*
Human Development, 258, *271*
Humphrey, G., 150, 156, *167*
Humphreys, M. S., 161, *167*
Humphreys, P., *57*
Huston, A. C., 454, 457, 462, 466, *469, 470*
Hutchinson, J. E., 105, *108, 110*

I

Ijaz, H., 382, 386, *388*
Imai, M., 94, 99, 103, *109*
Inhelder, B., *30*, 115, 118, 119, *127*, 275, 276, 277, 284, *292*, 442, *448*
Irwin, R., 171, 173, 174, 175, 178, 191, *200*, 215, *227*
Ivanov, V. V., 373, 377, *387*
Izard, C. E., 374, *387*

J

Jackendoff, R., 104, *109*
Jacobson, K., 174, *200*
Jacobson, R., 377, *387*
Jammer, M., 297, *320*

Jaspers, K., 169, *198*
Jastrow, J., 223, *229*
Jay, E., 416, *434*
Jay, M. F., 34, *57*
Jenkins, E., 279, *293*
Jenkins, J. M., 140, *144*
Jenkins, W. M., 45, 54, *58*, *59*
Jensen, A. R., 282, *292*
Jernigan, T., 36, 53, *57*, *59*
Johansson, J., 190, *198*
Johnson, C., *293*, 317, *320*
Johnson, C. J.,
Johnson, D. M., 116, *128*, 278, 285, *293*
Johnson, J., 171, 174, 175, 176, 178, 179, 180,
        181, 184, 186, 188, 191, 196, 197,
        199, 200
Johnson, K. E., 99, 101, *109, 110*
Johnson, M. H., 46, 50, *57*, 197, *198*
Johnson, S., 409n, *413*
Johnson-Laird, P. N., 13, 17, 18, 21, 29, *30*,
        109, 119, 120, 123, *127*, 133, *144*,
        148, *167*
Johnston, P., *58*
Jones, S. S., 87, 93, 94, 99, 100, 104, 105, *109*,
        110, 111
Josselson, R., 409n, *413*
Jukes, T., 179, *199*
Jusczyk, P. W., 35, 36, *55*, *57*

K

Kafai, Y., 461, *469*
Kagan, J., 46, *58*
Kahneman, D., 148, *167*
Kail, R., 232, *254*
Kalish, C., 89, 98, *107, 109*
Kant, I., 181, *199*
Kao, C. Q., 49, *57*
Kaplan, B., 375, 377, *388, 389*
Kaput, J., 336, 337, 347, *348*
Karmiloff-Smith, A., 118, *127*, 147, *166, 167*,
        171, 173, 174, 175, 197, *198, 199*,
        279, 290, *293*
Katz, W., 36, *57, 60*
Kaufmann, W. E., *57*
Keating, M. J., 34, *60*
Kee, D. W., 125, *127*
Keil, F. C., 5, 6, *12*, 89, 96, 97, 98, 100, 105, *109*,
        111, 117, 118, 121, 122, 123, 124,
        127, 128
Kelly, A., 326, 330, *348*
Kelly, M. E., 154, 164, *167*
Kendall-Tackett, K. A., 78, *85*
Keniston, A. H., 456, *469*
Kenny, P. A., 44, *60*
Kenny, S. L., 236, *254*

Kerlinger, F. N., 380, *387*
Kilcher, H., 265, *271*
King, W. M., 37, *60*
Kingsland, L., 378, *388*
Kinney, D., 440, 441, 445, 446, *448*
Kirzhner, M., 103, *109*
Kitchener, K. S., 236, *254*
Klahr, D., 232, *255*
Klein, R., 36, *56*
Klinnert, M., 215, *230*
Knox, C. M., 35, *57*
Knudsen, E. I., 49, *57*
Koenig, O., 274, 277, *293*
Kolstad, D. V., 65, 70, 71, 76, *84*
Kolstad, V., 100, *110*
Koopman, R. F., 397, *414*
Kossylyn, S. M., 16, 17, 18, *30*, 51, *57*, 274, 277,
        293
Kotovsky, L., 170, 173, 174, *197*
Kozak, A., 250, *255*
Kozulin, A., 179, 180, *199*
Krebs, D. L., 142, *143*
Kubovy, M., 313, *320*
Kuhl, P. K., 35, 51, 52, *57*
Kuhn, D., *4*, *12*, 226, *229*, 280, *293*, 416, *434*
Kuhn, T. S., 203, *229*, 400, *413*
Kunhardt, D., 318, *320*
Kurita, J. A., 278, *293*
Kwong, K. K., 47, *59*
Kyriakidou, C., 140, *144*

L

Lacerda, F., 35, *57*
Lacohee, H., 216, *229*
Laird, J. E., 277, *293*
Lajoie, S., 18, *30*, 358, *368*
Lakoff, G., 131, *144*
Lalonde, C. E., 221, 223, *228, 229*
Lamberts, K., 105, *110*
Lamon, S. J., 324, *348*
Landau, B., 93, 94, 99, 100, *109, 110, 111*
Landau, M., 340, 346, *348*
Lang, E., 92, *107*
Langer, S. K., 302, *320*
Larkin, J. H., 15, *30*
Lashley, K. S., 156, *167*
Lassaline, M. E., 89, *107*
Lauber, B. A., 466, *469*
Lave, J., 341, *348*
Lawrence, D. H., 410, *413*
Lawrence, J. A., 134n, *144*, 258, *271*
Leadbeater, B., 226, *229*
Lebowitz, K., 90, 91, 98, *108*
Lee, D. N., 49, *60*
Leek, E. C., 106, *108*
Leekam, S. R., 139, *145*

Legerstee, M., 173, *199*
Lehrer, R., 329, 347, *348, 349*
LeMahieu, P. G., 365, *369*
Lemke, J. L., 353, *369*
Leonard, C. M., 37, *60*
Leont'ev, A. N., 418, *434*
Lesgold, A., 18, *30,* 358, *368*
Lesh, R., 326, 329, 330, 336, 337, 340, 344, 346, *348, 349*
Lesko, N., 438, 440, 442, 445, *448*
Leslie, A. M., 71, *85,* 214, 215, *229*
Leventhal, J. M., 79, *85*
Levin, S. R., 457, *469*
Levitt, H., *57*
Lewis, C., 138, 140, 141, *144, 145,* 216, 228, *229*
Lewis, M., 46, *57*
Lewis, M. D., 250, *255*
Li, B. D., *448*
Liben, L. S., 297, 298, 301, 302, 303, 304, 305, 306, 307, 309, 311, 313, 316, *320, 321*
Lieblich, A., 409n, *413*
Light, P., 121, *127*
Lillard, A. S., 66, 71, *85*
Lindblom, B., 35, *57*
Lindenberger, U., 132, 133, *144*
Linton, P., 409n, *413*
Lipman, M., 416, *434*
Litchfield, A. W., 440, *448*
Livingstone, M. S., 36, 45, 53, *56, 58*
Llinás, R., 45, *58*
Lloyd, D., 372, *387*
Locke, J., 91, *110*
Loftus, E. F., *30*
Logan, D., 358, *368*
Lohr, M. J., 441, *448*
Lombardino, L. J., 36, *60*
Lonardo, R., 72, *84*
Lopez, A., 118, *128*
Lorch, E. P., 457, *469*
Lord, F. M., 364, *369*
Lotman, Y. M., 375, 377, *387*
Lourenço, O., 131, *145*
Luka, B. J., 92, 93, *107*
Luke, A., 353, *369*
Lukes, S., 432, *434*
Luria, A. R., 178, 183, *199, 200*
Lynch, C. L., 236, *254*

M

Maccoby, E. E., 105, *108*
MacEachren, A. M., 313, *321*
Machado, A., 131, *145*
MacKinnon, J., 398, *413*
Macnamara, J., 201, *229*

Macomber, J., 174, *200*
Madigan, R., 409n, *413*
Madsen, R., 419, *434*
Magone, M., 358, *368*
Maisog, J. M., 45, *56*
Malatesta, C. Z., 374, *387*
Maloney, L. T., 92, *110*
Malt, B. C., 87, 96, 98, *110*
Mandler, G., 233, *255*
Mandler, J., 5, *12,* 14, 17, 21, 22, *30,* 100, 106, *110,* 170, 171, 173, 174, *199,* 279, 293, 392, 396, *413*
Manktelow, K. I., 122, 124, 125, *128*
Marcia, J. E., 393, 394, 395, 397, 398, 404, 407, *413, 414*
Mareschal, D., 165, *168,* 177, 178, *200*
Marey, E. J., *85*
Maridaki-Kassotaki, K., 140, *144*
Markman, E. M., 90, 98, 99, 103, 104, 105, *109, 110,* 215, *227*
Markow, D. B., 99, *111*
Marshall, S. P., 18, 19, 22, 26, 27, *30*
Marzolf, D. P., 65, 70, 71, 72, 76, 79, *84, 85*
Mascolo, M. F., 234, 245, 246, 248, 250, 251, *255*
Massey, C., 101, 105, *110*
Matteson, D. R., 393, 395, *413*
Maunsell, J. H. R., 48, *60,* 181, *199*
Maybery, M. T., 149, 152, 154, 164, *167*
Maynard, J., 308, *319*
Mayr, E., 91, 96, *110*
Mazziotta, J. C., 34, *56*
Mazzoni, P., 50, *59*
McBane, B., 372, 373, *389*
McBride, M., 132, 133, 134, 142, *143, 144*
McCall, R. B., 34, 37, 46, *58*
McCarton, C., *58*
McClelland, J., 178, *199*
McCloskey, M. E., 92, *110*
McDill, E. L., 444, 447, *448*
McDonald, M., 148, *167*
McDonough, L., 100, *110*
McGoldrick, J. A., 278, *293*
McHaffie, J. G., 49, *57*
McKeough, A., *198*
McLellan, J., 440, 447, *448, 449*
McLelland, J. L., 371, *387*
McNamara, T. P., 13, 16, 17, *30*
Medin, D. L., 87, 88, 89, 91, 92, 93, 95, 96, 97, 98, 104, *107, 109, 110, 111,* 114, 117, 124, *128*
Mehan, H., 432, *434*
Meichenbaum, D., 25, *30*
Melendez, P., 310, *321*
Mellits, D., 35, 36, *59*
Meltzoff, A. N., *12,* 206, 219, *229,* 371, *387*
Menard, M. T., 45, *57*

Mercer, N., 353, *368*
Meredith, M. A., 34, 49, 50, *57, 58, 59*
Meringoff, L., 464, *470*
Merriman, W. E., 90, *110*
Merton, R. K., 210, *229*
Mervis, C. B., 99, 101, *109, 110,* 116, *128,* 285, 293
Merzenich, M. M., 34, 37, 45, 50, 54, *58, 59, 60*
Messick, S., 355, 366, *369*
Meyers, R. S., 46, *56*
Middaugh, L., 186, *198*
Miezin, F. M., 47, *56*
Millay, K. K., 35, *57*
Miller, G. A., 19, *30*
Miller, K. F., 73, *84*
Miller, P. A., 274, *292*
Miller, S. A., *59,* 274, *292*
Miller, S. L., *58*
Millis, K. K., 15, *30*
Milner, A. D., 48, *57*
Minsky, M., 335, *348*
Miozzo, M., 106, *108*
Mislevy, R. J., 352, 360, 361, 365, *368, 369*
Mitchell, D. W., 46, *56*
Mitchell, P., 138, *145,* 216, *229*
Mix, K. S., 92, 93, *107*
Moore, J. B., 446, *448*
Moore, M. K., 371, *387*
Morra, S., 171, 181, 197, *200*
Morris, C. W., 373, *387*
Morrongiello, B. A., 39, *58*
Morse, P. A., 36, *56*
Morton, A., 202, 203, *229*
Mory, M., 440, 441, 445, *448*
Moses, L. J., 215, 216, *227, 229*
Most, R. K., 78, *84*
Motter, B. C., 48, *58*
Mountcastle, V. B., 48, *58*
Muehrcke, P. C., 313, *321*
Muir, D., 309, *320*
Müller, U., 130, *145*
Murphy, C., 36, *57*
Murphy, G. L., 89, 90, 92, *107, 110*
Murray, F. B., 203, *229*

N

Nagarajan, S. S., 54, *59*
Nass, R., 53, *58*
Neal, R., *177, 198*
Needham, A., 170, 173, 174, *197*
Neimark, E. D., 123, *128*
Neimeyer, R., 245, 246, *255*
Nelson, K. E., 375, *386, 387, 388*
Nemirovsky, R., 329, 347, *348*
Newell, A., 277, *293*
Newman, K. M., 397, *413*

Newmann, F. M., 416, *434*
Nickerson, R. S., 26, *30*
Nida, R. E., 79, 80, *85*
Ninio, A., 309, *321*
Nisbett, R. E., 121, *127,* 149, 154, *167,* 279, *293,* 381, *387*
North, T., 36, *56*

O

Ochs, E., 425, *434*
Ogan, T. A., 374, *389*
Ogilvie, M., 381, *388*
O'Hare, A. W., 152, *167*
Okamoto, Y., 170, 180, *198*
Olguin, R., 103, *109*
Oliver, L. M., 121, *127*
Oller, D. K., 36, *56*
Olmstead, P., 372, 373, *389*
O'Loughlin, M., 226, *229*
Olseth, K. L., 92, 93, 94, *107, 110*
Olson, D. R., 214, 218, 219, *228, 229*
Olver, R. R., 454, 458, *469*
Onosko, J. J., 416, *434*
Orlofsky, J. L., 393, 395, *413*
Ornstein, P. A., 79, 80, *85*
Ortega y Gasset, J., *199*
Ortony, A., 95, *110*
Osgood, C. E., 376, *388*
Osherson, D., 118, *128*
Over, D., 122, 124, 125, *128*
Overton, W. F., 130, 131, *145*

P

Pacha, P., 76, *85*
Paivio, A., 16, *30*
Palincsar, A. S., 433, *434*
Palmer, S. E., 149, *168*
Parisi, D., 197, *198*
Pascual-Leone, J., 170, 171, 172, 173, 174, 175, 176, 177, 178, 179, 180, 181, 182, 183, 184, 186, 188, 191, 196, 197, *198, 199, 200,* 381, 382, 384, 385, 386, *388*
Pea, R. D., 276, *292,* 347, *348*
Pedhazur, E. J., 380, *387*
Peirce, C., 175, 190, *200*
Pennington, N., 226, *229*
Penny, J., 464, *469*
Pepper, S. C., *12*
Perkins, D. N., 22, 24, *30,* 416, *434*
Perlman, E. G., 309, 311, *319*
Perner, J., 66, 68, *85,* 138, 139, 141, *144, 145, 146,* 202, 206, 207, 208, 213, 218, 219, *229, 230*

Perry, W. G., 226, *229*
Perucchini, P., 466, *469*
Pethick, S. J., 374, 384, *387*
Pettito, L. A., 182, *200*
Pezdek, K., 462, *470*
Phelps, E., 141, *145*
Phelps, M. E., 34, 50, *56*
Phillips, S., 148, 150, 152, 153, 161, 163, *167,*
     168, 432, *434*
Piaget, J., 6, 7, *12, 30,* 115, 118, 119, 123, *127,*
     128, 130, 140, 142, *145,* 147, 148,
     153, *168,* 171, 173, 190, *198, 200,*
     202, 203, *229,* 233, 239, 240, 241,
     255, 261, 262, 265, 266, *271,* 275,
     276, 277, 278, 284, 286, *292, 293,*
     300, 307, 311, *321,* 371, 372, 384,
     388, 442, *448,* 454, 458, *470*
Pick, A., 310, *321*
Pick, H. L., 65, *84*
Piercy, M., 35, 39, *59*
Pierroutsakos, S., 64, *84,* 309, *319*
Pillow, B. H., 222, *229*
Pinker, S., 279, *293,* 375, *388*
Pipp, S., 236, *254*
Pisoni, D. B., 35, *55*
Platsidou, M., 171, *198*
Platt, M., 425, *434*
Plunkett, K., 197, *198*
Pollack, R., 234, 245, 248, 251, *255*
Posner, M. I., *12*
Post, T., 344, 346, *348, 349*
Potter, M. C., 71, *85,* 302, 309, *321*
Pouget, A., 48, *58*
Premack, D., 163, *168,* 207, *229*
Pressley, M., 278, *293*
Price, R., 223, *229,* 317, *321*
Proctor, R., 181, *200*
Puranik, C. S., 37, *60*
Putnam, H., 8, *12,* 130, 131, *145*
Pylyshyn, Z. W., 17, *30,* 51, *58,* 275, *293*

Q

Quine, W. V. O., 89, *110*

R

Raeff, C., 248, *255*
Raichle, M. E., 47, *56*
Ramsay, D. S., 78, *85*
Rappaport, D., *200*
Ratterman, M. J., 123, *127*
Raven, J. C., 382, *388*
Raya P., 236, *254*

Read, H. L., 48, *58*
Recanzone, G. H., 54, *58*
Reddy, V., 215, *229*
Reed, M. A., 35, *58*
Reed, S. K., 19, *30*
Reeve, T., 181, *200*
Reilly, J., 183, 184, 186, 191, 196, *200*
Reinecke, M., 193, 194, *200*
Rekedal, S., 79, *85*
Reppas, J. B., 47, *59*
Resnick, D. P., 355, *369*
Resnick, L. B., 18, *30,* 355, *369,* 416, *434*
Reznick, J. S., 374, 384, *387*
Richmond-Welty, E. D., 76, *85*
Rieser, J., 275, *291*
Rigsby, L. C., 444, 447, *448*
Riley, C. A., 148, 154, *168*
Riley, M. S., *167*
Rips, L. J., 89, 97, 105, *111*
Roberts, D., 215, *228*
Robin, A., 105, *108*
Robinson, M. E., 34, *60,* 378, *388*
Robinson, R. J., 36, *58*
Robison, G., 126, *128*
Rogoff, B., 234, 236, 247, 251, *255,* 269, *271*
Rosa, J., 78, *84*
Rosch, E., 88, *111,* 116, *128,* 131, *145,* 148, *168,*
     285, *293*
Roschelle, J., 347, *348*
Rose, S. A., 37, *58,* 309, *321*
Rose, S. P., 246, 251, *254*
Roseberry A., 353, *369*
Rosen, B. R., 36, 47, *59*
Rosen, G. D., 45, *56,* 57, *58*
Rosenblatt, L. M., 353n, *369*
Rosenbloom, P. S., 277, *293*
Rosengren, K., 64, 73, *84,* 309, *319*
Ross, G., 36, 53, *58*
Rotenberg, E. J., 236, *254*
Rothbart, M. K., *12*
Rovee-Collier, C., 46, *56*
Royer, J. M., 380, *388*
Ruan, W., 103, *109*
Rubinstein, J., 89, *109*
Rudy, J. W., 156, 163, *168*
Ruffman, T., 139, *145,* 218, 219, *229*
Rumain, B., 119, *127*
Rumsey, J., 45, *56*
Russell, J., 133, *145,* 206, *230*
Rutherford, J., 430, *434*
Ryle, G., 276, *293,* 418, *434*

S

Salinas, E., 48, 49, *58*
Sargent, P. L., 309, *320*

Sawyer, D., 215, *228*
Saxe, G., 341, *349*
Schaeken, W., 119, *127*
Schank, R., 347, *349*
Schauble, L., 329, *348*
Schieffelin, B. B., 425, *434*
Schiller, P. H., 49, *59*
Schliemann, A. D., 341, *348*
Schmajuk, N. A., 159, *168*
Schmid-Schönbein, C., 135, *145*
Schmidt, W. C., 165, *168*, 177, 178, *200*
Schneps, M. H., 23, *30*
Scholnick, E. K., 114, 116, 125, 126, *128*
Schorin, M. Z., 141, *145*
Schrag, F., 416, 417, 431, *434*
Schrager, J., 125, *128*
Schreiber, J. C., 75, *86*
Schreiner, C. E., 34, 45, 50, 51, 54, *58, 59, 60*
Schultz, T. R., 165, *168*
Schum, D.A., 365, *369*
Schwartz, J. L., 355, *369*
Schwartz, S. P., 91, *111*
Scott, M. C., 460, *469*
Scott, P., 99, *110*
Scribner, S., 276, *292*
Scudder, K. V., 78, *86*
Searle, J. R., 212, 218, *230*
Sebeok, T. A., 377, *388*
Sejnowski, T. J., 48, *58*
Selman, R. L., 141, *145*
Sereno, M. I., 47, *59*
Shafir, E., 118, *128*
Shafrir, U., 378, 381, 382, *388*
Shapiro, H., 72, *85*, 372, 373, *388*
Shatz, M., 101, *107*
Shaver, P. R., 231, 235, 242, 250, *254*
Shepard, R. N., 318, *321*
Sherwood, R., 275, *291*
Shipley, C., 147, *168*
Shoben, E. J., 89, *110*
Shuff-Bailey, M., 103, *109*
Shultz, T. R., 177, 178, *200*
Siegal, M., 216, *230*
Siegel, H., 416, *434*
Siegel, L. S., 381, 385, *388, 389*
Siegel, R. M., 48, *55, 58*
Siegler, R. S., 4, *12*, 125, *128*, 135, *145*, 147, *168*, 232, *255*, 278, 279, *293*, 378, *388*
Sigel, I. E., 5, *12*, 27, 28, *30*, 71, 72, 73, *85*, 147, *168*, 250, *255*, 302, 310, 315, 316, *321*, 371, 372, 373, 376, 377, 378, *388, 389*, 396, 398, 399, *413*, 468, *470*
Sigman, M. D., 37, *56, 59*
Silverman, M. S., 46, 47, *60*
Silverstein, M., 105, *111*

Simon, H. A., 15, 24, *30*, 275, 279, *292, 293*, 375, *389*
Simons, D. J., 105, *111*
Sinatra, G. M., 380, *388*
Singley, M. K., 283, *293*
Skinner, B. F., 273, *293*
Slomkowski, C., 141, *144*
Slugoski, B. R., 397, *414*
Smedslund, J., 202, *230*
Smith, C. M., 67, 79, *84, 85*
Smith, E. E., 88, *111*, 117, 118, 124, *128*
Smith, L. B., 5, *12*, 36, *57*, 87, 93, 94, 99, 100, 104, 105, *109, 110, 111*, 131, *145*, *168*
Smith, S. B., 149, 154, 164, *167*
Smolensky, D., 177, *200*
Snow, C. E., 375, *389*
Snowling, M., 35, *59*
Sober, E., 91, 96, *111*
Soja, N. N., 100, 101, 102, 104, *111*
Sokol, B., 130, *145*
Sokolov, E. N., 45, *59*
Sokolov, J. L., 375, *389*
Somerville, S. C., 276, *293*
Sophian, C., 276, *293*
Sorce, J., 215, *230*
Sorenson, E., 78, *84*
Sowell, E. J., 36, 53, *57*, 78, *85*
Sparks, D. L., 34, *57*
Spearman, C. E., 154, *168*
Spelke, E. S., 100, 101, 102, 104, *111*, 118, *127*, 174, *200*, 308, *321*
Spencer, C., 66, *84*
Spitz, R. V., 34, 35, 36, 42, 44, *55, 59*
Squire, L. R., 274, 277, 278, 289, *293*
Sroufe, L. A., 374, *389*
Staddon, J. E. R., 162, *168*
Stanovich, K. E., 385, 386, *389*
Stanowitz, L., 375, *386*
Stark, R., 35, 36, *59*
Stein, B. E., 34, 49, 50, *57, 58, 59*
Steinberg, L. S., 365, *368*
Steinschneider, M., 51, *59*
Stephenson, K., *198*
Stern, D. N., 374, *389*
Sternberg, R. J., 148, *168*, 232, *255*, 283, *293*, 358, *369*
Stevens, E., 462, *470*
Stevens, K. N., 35, *57*
Stewart, J. E. M., 152, 153, 154, 159, 164, *167*
Stich, S. P., 113, *128*, 202, *230*
Stiggins, R., 355, *369*
Stinson, E. T., 398, 399, *413*
Stone, C. R., 141, *145*
Stone, M., 442, *448*
Strauss, M. S., 46, *59*, 308, *319*
Stricanne, B., 50, *59*

Strom, D., 347, *349*
Strouse, D., 440, *449*
Stryker, M., 49, *59*
Su, Y., 444, 447, *449*
Sullivan, W. M., 419, *434*
Sumner, R. K., 375, *389*
Suppes, P., 149, *168*
Surber, C. F., 152, *168*
Swanson, D., 215, *228*
Swidler, A., 419, *434*
Switkes, E., 46, 47, *60*
Symons, S., 278, *293*
Syrdal-Lasky, A.K., 35, *57*

T

Tajfel, H., 441, 442, *448*
Tallal, P., 34, 35, 36, 39, 40, 42, 44, 45, 53, 54, *55, 56, 57, 58, 59, 60*
Tallal, R. R., 36, *59*
Tamis-LeMonda, C. S., 37, *60*
Tan, S. L., 466, *469*
Tanaka, A. K., 51, *60*
Tardif, T., 104, *111*
Taylor, C., 130, 142, *145*
Taylor, M. G., 105, *111*
Tebano-Micci, A., 79, *85*
Tees, R. C., 35, *60*
Terr, L., 78, *86*
Tesla, C., 141, *144*
Tesman, J., 53, *58*
Thagard, P. R., 13, *31*, 149, 153, 154, 163, *167*, 381, *387*
Thal, D. J., 374, 384, 387, *387*
Thelen, E., 5, *12*
Thomas, D. L., 440, *448*
Thompson, E., 131, *145*
Thompson, L. A., 37, *60*
Thompson, P. W., 235, 325, *349*
Thorndyke, P. W., 19, *31*
Thurstone, L. L., 21, *31*
Tidball, G., 215, *227*
Tincoff, R., 76, *85*
Tipton, S. M., 419, *434*
Tishman, S., 416, *434*
Tomasello, M., 215, 216, *230*
Tootell, R. B. H., 46, 47, *59, 60*
Townsend, J., 36, *60*
Trabasso, T., 148, *168*
Trauner, D., 53, *59*
Travers, P. L., 317, *321*
Treiman, R., 76, *85*
Troseth, G. L., 67, 71, *84, 85*
Trujillo, C., 441, *448*
Tryphon, A., 258, *271*
Tucker, J., 241, *254*

Tufte, E. R., 62, *86*
Tulving, E., 21, *31*
Tulviste, P., 418, 419, *434, 435*
Turkewitz, G., 44, *60*
Tversky, A., 148, *167*

U

Uchida, N., 94, 99, 103, *109*
Ungerleider, L. G., 48, *55*
Uttal, D. H., 64, 75, 78, *84, 86*, 309, *319*

V

Valsiner, J., 3, 6, *12*, 134n, *144*, 258, 261, 269, 271
van der Meer, A. L. H., 49, *60*
Van der Veer, R., 134n, *143*, 258, 261, 269, *271*
van der Weel, F. R., 49, *60*
Van Essen, D. C., 47, 48, *56, 60*
VanLehn, K., 154, *168*
VanMeter, J. W., 45, *56*
Van Parys, M., 241, *254*
Varela, F. J., 131, *145*
Vaughan, H. G., 51, *59*
Viator, K. A., 355, *369*
Volterra, V., 216, *227*
Voneche, J., 258, 265, *271*
von Glasersfeld, E., 7, *12*, 130, 131, *144*, 211, 217, *230*, 338, *349*
Vye, N., 275, *291*
Vygotsky, L. S., 61, *86*, 132, 142, *145*, 180, 182, 183, *200*, 234, 236, 247, *255*, 259, 260, 261, 263, 268, *271*, 287, *293*, 311, *321*, 371, *389*, 415, 418, *434*

W

Wainer, H., 364, *369*
Walden, T. A., 374, *389*
Wallace, I. F., 37, *58*
Walter, B., 408, *414*
Wang, X., 34, 45, 54, *58, 59, 60*
Ward, T. B., 105, *111*
Warren, B., 353, *369*
Wason, P. C., *109*
Waterman, A. S., 393, 395, *413*
Watkins, B. A., 457, 462, 466, *469*
Watson, J. A., 464, *469*
Watson, M. W., 78, *85, 86*, 239, 241, 242, *254, 255, 256*
Waxman, S. R., 97, 99, 104, 105, *111*
Weed, S. T., 222, *229*
Weiner, A., 358, *368*
Weiss, L., 466, *469*

Wellman, H., 456, *469*
Wellman, H. M., 89, 106, *109, 111,* 121, *128,* 138, *144,* 203, 206, 207, 216, 219, *228, 230,* 280, *293*
Werker, J. F., 35, *60*
Werner, H., 165, *168,* 243, *256,* 371, 377, *389*
Wertsch, J. V., 142, *145, 146,* 234, *256,* 264, 269, *271,* 376, *389,* 417, 418, 419, *434, 435*
Westby, S. D., 456, *469*
Wheeler, M., 419, *435*
White, P. A., 89, *111*
Wiggins, G., 355, *369*
Wilcox, S. A., 91, *109*
Wiles, J., 152, 153, 159, 161, *167*
Wiley, D. E., 365, *369*
Wilkie, O., 118, *128*
Williams, K. A., 35, *57*
Willis, P., 440, 446, *448*
Wilson, D. T., 279, *293*
Wilson, P. N., 301, *321*
Wilson, W. H., 148, 149, 150, 152, 153, 159, 161, 163, *167, 168*
Wimmer, H., 138, *145, 146,* 208, 213, *230*
Winer, G. A., 116, *128*
Wing, C. S., 125, *128*
Winner, E., 315, *321*
Winograd, T., 277, *293*
Wisniewski, E. J., 89, *111*
Withington-Wray, D. J., 34, *60*
Wittgenstein, L., 130, *145, 146*
Wolf, R., 358, *368*
Wong, S., 51, *59*
Wood, F., 36, *57, 60*
Wood, P. K., 236, *254*
Woodruff, G., 207, *228, 229*

Wozniak, R. H., 261, *271*
Wright, B. A., 37, *60*
Wright, J. C., 454, 457, 462, 466, *469, 470*
Wu, L.-.L., 92, 93, *107*
Wulfeck, B., 36, *60*
Wurtz, R. H., 34, *60*
Wynn, K., 173, 174, 187, *200,* 287, *293*
Wynne, C. D. L., 162, *168*

Y

Yap, G. S., 48, *57*
Yates, A., 78, *86*
Yates, M., 439, 444, 447, *449*
Yeh, W., 92, 93, *107*
Yekel, C. A., 313, *321*
Yelland, N. J., 416, *435*
Yengo, L., 358, *368*
Yonas, A., 309, *320, 321*
Youngblade, L., 141, *144*
Younger, B. A., 116, *127*
Youniss, J., 140, *144, 145, 146,* 439, 440, 444, 447, *449*
Yucker, H. E., 317, *319*

Z

Zaitchik, D., 216, *230*
Zawojewsk, J., 337, 346, *348*
Zeffiro, T. A., 45, *56*
Zelazo, P. D., 67, 69, 83, *86*
Zinnes, J. L., 149, *168*
Zipser, D., 48, *60*

Subject Index

Note. Page references in *italics* refer to figures; those in **boldface** refer to tables.

A

Abstraction levels, in dynamic skill theory, *237*, 242
Abstracts, idealized, 344
Achievement, identity, 395
Action superiority hypothesis, 462–464
Active information processor view, 219–220
Affect, 25, 250
Age, and false belief tests, 213–217
Amodal representations, 17
Analogical knowledge, 16–19
Analogy, in relational knowledge, 153–154
Appropriation
 of cultural tools, 418–419, 422–432
 Rogoff's notion of, 234, 251
Argumentation, 152
Artificial intelligence theorists, 371
Assessment, educational
 criticisms of, 355
 discourse of, 353–354
 domain of, 356–360
 feedback in, 366–367
 inferences from, 364–366
 purpose of, 354–356, 357
 task design in, 360–366
Association, concept of, 154–156
Associative cortex, 48, 50–51
Associative learning, 150, 162–163, 178–179
ATP, *see* Auditory temporal processing
Attention
 mental, 179–180, 182, 183–187, 191
 selective, 456–458
Attribute differentiation, 311–312
Auditory temporal processing (ATP), 34–37, 39–44, *40, 41, 42, 43*

B

Bakhtinian theory of linguistic representation, 258–259
Binary relations, 157, *160*
Biogenetic process, 245–251

C

Cartesian coordinate systems, 329
Categorization
 and cognitive development, 115
 and concepts, 88–92, 93, 97–99
 defined, 114
 developmental stages of, 122–123
 faulty inferences in, 275
 multiple representation strategies in, 124–125
 Piaget's theory of, 115, 116–117
 role of shape in, 99–104
 Rosch's theory of, 115–117
 syntactic theory of, 114–118
 theory-based, 117–118, 124
Category domain, 98
Category levels, 98, 103
Change processes, in representational development, 245–251
Chunking, conceptual, 161–162
Class inclusion, 133–134, 149
Co-construction, across utterances and speakers, 425
Cognitive conflict, 336
Cognitive development, *see also specific theories of*
 and categorization, 115
 differentiation of neural nets in, 164–165
 effect on representational development, 314
 history of, 6, 147–148
 and identity status, 397–398
 relational concepts in, 148–150
 and representational competence, 213–217
 and sensory processing, 37–39, *38*
Cognitive functioning, levels of, 154–158, *155*
Cognitive science, 6
Cognitive trickery, 301
Collaboration, in representation, 243–245
Colliculus, superior, 48–49
Communication
 continuous process, 247
 Vygotskian view of, 269
Comparator model, 46

Competence, representational, 27
Concepts
    context sensitivity of, 92–95
    dialectical constructivist view of, 182
    and domain specificity, 97–99
    essentialist, 91–92, 95–97
    role of shape in, 99–104
    stability in, 104–106
    symbols as core of, 93–94
    theory-based, 88–92
    variability of, 92–95
Conceptual development sessions, local, 336
Conceptual schemes, 175–176
Conceptual technologies, 338–339, 347
Conditional discriminations, 156
Conditional thought
    defined, 114
    developmental stages of, 123–124
    domain specificity in, 120–121
    inferential strategies in, 125–126
    logical approach to, 118–119
    schema-based approach to, 121–124
    semantic approach to, 119–120
Configural associations, 156
Connectionists, 371–372
Constraints
    in educational assessments, 363
    relationships of, 140–141
Construct-eliciting activities
    defined, 336
    as local conceptual development sessions,
        336–337
    paper airplane problem, 330–331
    representation processes in, 334–335
    summer jobs problem, 331–334, 332, 335
Constructivism
    as base of Piagetian theory, 131–132
    caveat of, 142
    correction of Piagetian theory, 173–176
    described, 130–131, 232–233
    dialectical view of representation, 176–182
    vs. active information processor view,
        219–220
    vs. nativism and empiricism, 288–290
    vs. other knowing process models,
        201–202
Constructs
    and multiple representations, 339–346
    projection of, 338–339
Content-independence of thought, 147
Content representation, 173–174, 357–360
Context sensitivity, of concepts, 92–95
Controlled processes, 191
Control structure, in dynamic skill theory,
        235–236
Cooperation, relationships of, 140–141
Copy theory of knowledge, 211, 212

Correspondence mastery, 312–313
Correspondence theory, 66–67, 130, 149,
        211–212
Countertransference, 403–405
Criteria, Wittgenstein's concept of, 132
Critical spirit, 416–417
Critical thinking, 416–417
Crowds, peer
    barriers to importance of, 447
    and identity development, 439–441
    implications for representation, 438–439
    representational functions of, 441–446, 444
    social cognitive basis of, 442
Cultural tools
    mastery and appropriation of, 422–432
    and mediated action, 417–420

D

Decomposability, 153
Depictive representation, 51–52
Developmental range, in dynamic skill the-
        ory, 236–238
Differentiation, 164
Diffusion, identity, 395, 399
Dimensionality of relations, 152–153
Direct perception, 174
Discrimination, 232
Dispositions
    for critical thinking, 416–417
    sociocultural view of, 417–420
Distancing, 72, 147, 373, 377, 398–400
Doll interviews, and symbol use, 78–82
Domain specificity
    of categories, 117–118
    of concepts, 97–99
    of conditional relations, 120–121
    of knowledge, vs. domain generality,
        281–284
Dostoevsky, Bakhtin on, 258–259
Duality, 71–75, 302
Dynamic skill theory
    basic assumptions of, 235–238
    representation development in, 241–242
    skill development levels in, 237, 238–242
Dynamic syntheses, 178
Dyslexia, 44–45
Dysphasia, developmental, see Language im-
        pairment

E

Education, and flexibility in representation,
        22–25
Egocentric speech

Piaget's response to Vygotsky, 261–262, 265–268
Vygotsky's critique of Piaget, 259–261, 263–265, 267
Vygotsky's theory of, 262–265, 268–269
Ego-deictic representation, 317–318
Empirical abstraction, 172
Empiricism
    vs. constructivism and nativism, 131, 288–290
    vs. Piaget and Vygotsky, 270
Encoding, 44–45, 52–53, 201
Epigenesis, 245
Epistemic triangle
    in Chapman's view of knowledge, 132
    and children's theories of mind, 138–141
    defined, 129
Equilibration process, 233
Equivalence class activity, 327–329, *327, 328*
Essentialism, psychological, 91–92, 95–99
Evidence, in educational assessments, 361–366
Evocation, 408–409
Executive control, 27, 174, 187–190, 194
Experience, symbolic, 76–77
Experiential schemes, 175–176

F

Facilitating situations, 177–178
False belief understanding
    age conclusions of, 213–217
    compared to interpretive theory
        as different from, 220–226
        equated with, 218–219
    criticism of, 209–210
    as tenant in theory of mind, 206
    tests of, 138–141, 208–209
Feedback, in educational assessment, 366–367
Field factor, neo-Gestaltist, 181
Figurative/afferent schemes, 172–173, 175, 176, 187
Flexibility
    in cognitive development, 147
    of representation, 21–25
Flow, Csikszentmihalyi model, 25
Foreclosure, identity, 395, 399
Formal features, in television research
    described, 455–456, **455**
    and selective attention, 456–458
    and visual memory, 458–459, **461**, 462, **463**
Fragile knowledge syndrome, 22, 24

G

Generalization, 232

Global differentiation, 309–310
Goals
    inferential, in educational assessments, 361–362
    pursuit of, and representations, 25–26
Go/No Go Operant (G/N-G) Head-Turn procedure, 42–44

H

Habituation paradigm, 37–39, *38*
Higher order relations, 150–151

I

Identity
    formation of
        and crowd affiliation, 439–441
        and distancing, 398–400
        process of, 393–398
        and representational competence, 398
        and representational functions of crowds, 441–446, **444**
    in spatial representation, 299
    statuses of, 395
Imagery, and mental models, 18
Image/verbal dichotomy, 15–17, *16*
Individual differences, 386
Infant information processing
    measuring, 37–44, *38, 40, 41, 42, 43*
    neurological models of, 45–46
    and sensory map alignment, 46–49, *47*
    temporal deficits in, 35–37
    time and modality dependence of, 44–45
Information processing theory, 232
INRC group, 119
Intellectual development, bio-ecological theory of, 386
Intelligence theorists, 283
Internalization process
    and mastery and appropriation, 418
    in operational semantic theory, 134
    Piagetian theory of, 172
    Rogoff's rejection of, 234
    role of language in, 134–138
IQ, and sensory processing, 37

J

Justification, role in internalization, 134–138

K

Knowledge
    ad hoc vs. permanent, 284–286

concrete vs. abstract, 280–281
constructed character of, 21–22
declarative
    vs. procedural vs. conceptual, 276–278
    vs. reasoning processes, 358–359
domain-specific vs. domain-general,
    281–284
hierarchical, 285
implicit vs. explicit, 278–280
innate vs. constructed vs. learned, 288–290
theories of, 130–132
vs. thinking, 275–276

L

Labeling, and concepts, 90–91, 93, 99
Language
    as cultural tool, 418
    role in internalization process, 134–138
Language impairment (LI)
    defined, 34
    family history influence on, 41
Learning mechanisms, and Plato's problems,
    179–180
Learning paradox, 179
LI, *see* Language impairment
Linguistic development
    and auditory temporal processing, 34–37,
        39–44, *40, 41, 42, 43*
    dialectical constructivist view of, 182
    and habituation and recognition memory,
        37–39
    and mental attention, 183–187
    in Piagetian theory, 131–132
    role of shape in, 99–104
    and sensorimotor development, 240
    sign systems in, 374–375
Linguistic expression, 98–99
Linguistic representation, Bakhtin's theory
    of, 258–259, *see also* Egocentric
    speech
LM learning, 179–180, 191
Logical Content learning, 179–180

M

Manipulatives, and symbol use, 78
Mapping
    abstract, 242
    DeLoache studies in, 64–71, *73, 74, 75, 77,*
        82, 194–196
    in educational assessment, 361
    representational, 242
    sensorimotor, 238

Mastery, vs. appropriation, 418
Mathematics, *see also* Construct-eliciting ac-
        tivities
    instruction goals of, 338
    nature of, 324
    real life problems in, 339–346
    textbook exercises in, 324, *324,* 339–346,
        340, 345
Mathematizing
    defined, 324
    externalizing internal systems in, 331–334
    increasing need for, 347
    models and modeling in, 326–331
    vs. calculating, 325–329
Matthew effect, 386
Meaning equivalence
    concept of, 377–378
    experiment in, 378–381, 385
Mediated action, 417–420
Mediational means, *see* Cultural tools
Memory
    auditory, 459–461
    episodic, 21
    kinetic, 462–465
    recognition, 37–39, *38*
    representational, 49–53
    and selective attention, 456–458
    visual, 458–459, **461,** 462, **463**
Mental models, 17–18, *20,* 133
Meta-representation, 313
Microdevelopment, 243–245
Microgenetic method, defined, 135
Mind, theories of, *see also* False belief under-
        standing
    alternative vision of, 210–212
        empirical evidence for, 220–226
    criticisms of, 204, 207–208, 210
    foundational assumptions of, 206–207
Misconceptions, 22–25
Misleading situations, 177–178
Models and modeling, in mathematizing,
    326–331
Monology, 262–263
Moratorium status, identity, 395
Motivation, 25
Mutual exclusivity, 90–91

N

Nativism, vs. constructivism and empiricism,
    288–290
Neo-nativism, 173, 214
Neural nets, 158–161, 164–165
Neurological models, infancy, 45–46
Nonrepresentation, **299**

O

Omni-directional access, 151
One-miracle view
  described, 204
  vs. commonsense view, 217–218
Operant conditioning paradigms, 39–44
Operations on relations, 153
Operations theory
  Piagetian, 131, 132
  semantic, 132–134
Operative/efferent schemes, 172, 175, 176

P

Paper airplane problem, 330–331
Perceptual equivalence, 301
Perceptual features
  and concepts, 99–104
  and essentialism, 97, 99
Perceptual salience, 457
Performance
  graduated levels of, 286–288
  theories of, for educational assessment,
    364
Personal-agentive process, 245–251
Piagetian theory
  constructivist correction of, 173–176
  of egocentric speech
    reply to Vygotsky, 261–262, 265–268
    Vygotsky's critique of, 259–261,
      263–265, 267
  graduated levels of performance, 286–288
  of knowledge, 131–132
  of levels of abstraction, 280–281
  of reasoning, 132–133
  of relationships, 140–141
  of representation, 170–173, 232–233
  vs. post-piagetians, 275–276, 278, 282–283,
    285, 286, 288
Planning, in relational knowledge, 153–154
Plato's problems
  described, 170
  solving, 179–180
Postfailure reflectivity, 381–384
Predication, 150
Prefrontal cortex, 49–50
Problem solving
  in construct-eliciting activities, 330–334,
    332, 335
  in mathematics education research, 337
  representation in, 15, 240–241, 243–245
Process studies, defined, 135
Proposition, across utterances and speakers,
  425
Propositional knowledge, 16–19

Propositional representation, 51–52
Psychology, crisis in contemporary, 260, 263
Psychosocial development, Erikson's theory
  of, 405–408
Psychotherapy
  structurally-oriented, 400–403
  transference and countertransference in,
    403–405

Q

Quaternary relations, 157–158
Quinary relations, 158

R

Ranks, of cognitive functioning
  in children, 163–164
  described, 154–158, 155, 162
  in neural nets, 158–161
  species differences in, 163
Realism, intentional, 214
Reasoning
  mental models theory of, 133
  operational semantic theory of, 132–134
  Piagetian theory of, 132–133
  role of justification in, 134–138
Recognition memory paradigm, 37–39, 38
Reductive abstraction, 170–171, 173
Referential content, 309
Referent-representation similarity, 302
Reflective abstraction, 171–172, 173, 175
Regulations (Piagetian), 178
Relational knowledge
  processing load of, 161–162
  properties of, 150–154
  transition to, 161–162
Relational systematicity, 151
Replication, in spatial representation, 300
Representation, see also specific theories
  conceptual development of, 4–6, 372
  conceptual diversity in, 5–9, 201–202,
    231–234, 371–372
  criticism of, 490–410
  forms of, 19–21, 20
  meanings of, 4, 7, 13–15, 14, 34, 202–203,
    274–275
Representational competence
  conceptual definition of, 376–378
  experiments in
    inference task, 381–386
    printed text, 385, 378–381
  history of research in, 373
  and identify formation, 398
Representational insight, 310

Representational memory
   model for in infants, 50–53
   neural substrates for, 49–50
Retinotopic maps, 46–47, 47
Roles, sociocognitive
   case studies in, 422–432
   and cultural tools, 419–420

S

Schemas
definitions of, 18–21, 20, 22, 26
pragmatic, 121–124
Schema theorists, and levels of abstraction,
   280–281
Schematic overdetermination of perfor-
   mance, see SOP principle
Secure attachment, 397–398
Segmentation, 161
Self-theories, changing, 401–402
Semiosphere concept, 375–376
Semiotics
   constructs of, 373–377
   defined, 373
Sensorimotor activity levels, in dynamic skill
   theory, 238–240, 239
Sensorimotor period, 185
Sensory maps, 46–49, 47
Sensory processing, see also Auditory tempo-
   ral processing
   and cognitive development, 37–39, 38
   development of, 44
   and IQ, 37
Sentence verification technique (SVT), 380
Shape-bias theory, 99–104
Signals, task study of, 190–194
Sign systems
   defined, 373
   in semiotic theory, 373–377
Skeletal structures, 96–97, 106
Skill, in dynamic skill theory, 235
Smart tools, see Conceptual technologies
Sociocultural process, 245–251
Sociocultural theory, 233–234
SOP principle, 176–177, 181, 187
Space structuration factor, 181
Spatial products, 298
Spatial representation, external
   defining features of, 297–303, 299, 302
   development of, 307–314, 308, 314
   embedded view of, 304–307, 305
   facilitating, 314–318
   transparency view of, 304, 304
Summer jobs problem, 331–334, 332, 335
Symbols
   and concepts, 93–94

defined, 61–62
dual representation in, 71–75
effect of experience with, 76–77
-referent relationship, 62–64, 63
and sensorimotor development, 239–240
task study of, 190–194
understanding and use of
   development, 83
   doll interviews, 78–82
   manipulatives, 78
   in problem solving, 243–245
   studies in, 64–71, 73, 74, 75, 77, 82
Synaptogenesis, 50

T

Tallal Repetition Test, 39
Task analysis, through dynamic skill theory,
   236
Taxonomization, see Categorization; Cate-
   gory levels
Television research
   auditory memory in, 459–461
   formal features in, 455–458, 455
   kinetic memory in, 462–465
   selective attention in, 456–458
   visual memory in, 458–459, 461, 462, 463
Temporal processing deficits, and linguistic
   development, 35–37, 53
Ternary relations, 157
Test scores problem, 326–329, 326
Theory-theory, 138–139, 202, 203, 206
Thinking, vs. knowledge, 275–276
Thoughtfulness, 416–417
Time structuration factor, 182
Topographic representation, 46–47
Transference, 403–405
Transfer studies, in symbol use, 76–77
Transitive inference, 148–149, 164
Translations, of representations, 346, 346–346
Two-Alternative Forced-Choice Head-Turn
   task (2-AFC), 39–42

U

Unary relations, 157
Uncertainty, 26–27

V

Virtual reality, 466–467
Visual cortex, 46–47
Visual superiority hypothesis, 462
Vygotskian theory

of egocentric speech, 262–265, 268–269
of levels of abstraction, 280–281
zones of proximal development, 287

Z

Zones of proximal development, 287